D1208672

# COLLECTED WORKS OF ERASMUS

## VOLUME 76

Erasmus
Portrait medal by Quinten Metsys (1519)
Historisches Museum Basel

# COLLECTED WORKS OF
# ERASMUS

CONTROVERSIES

DE LIBERO ARBITRIO ΔΙΑΤΡΙΒΗ SIVE COLLATIC

HYPERASPISTES 1

edited by Charles Trinkaus

translated by Peter Macardle and Clarence H. Miller

annotated by Peter Macardle, Clarence H. Miller,
and Charles Trinkaus

University of Toronto Press

Toronto / Buffalo / London

The research and publication costs of the
Collected Works of Erasmus are supported by
University of Toronto Press.

© University of Toronto Press 1999
Toronto / Buffalo / London
Printed in Canada

ISBN 0-8020-4317-8

Printed on acid-free paper

**Canadian Cataloguing in Publication Data**

Erasmus, Desiderius, d. 1536
[Works]
Collected works of Erasmus

Partial contents: v. 76. Controversies: De libero arbitrio.
Hyperaspistes 1 / edited by Charles Trinkaus.
Includes index.
Includes bibliographical references.
ISBN 0-8020-4317-8 (v. 76)

1. Erasmus, Desiderius, d. 1536. I. Title

PA8500 1974     876'.04     C74-006326-X rev

University of Toronto Press acknowledges the financial assistance to its
publishing program of the Canada Council and the Ontario Arts Council.

# Collected Works of Erasmus

The aim of the Collected Works of Erasmus
is to make available an accurate, readable English text
of Erasmus' correspondence and his
other principal writings. The edition is planned
and directed by an Editorial Board, an Executive Committee,
and an Advisory Committee.

# Contents

# Illustrations

# Introduction

*But it is possible that the spirit of Christ may not have revealed the whole truth to the church all at once. And while the church cannot make Christ's decrees of no effect, she can none the less interpret them as may best tend to the salvation of men, relaxing here and drawing tighter there, as time and circumstance may require.*

Erasmus' letter of 11 August 1519 to Jacob of Hoogstraten,
inquisitor of Cologne (Ep 1006:201–5)

## I
## ERASMUS' HUMANIST THEOLOGY

The events of early sixteenth-century Europe included the first explorations and conquests by Europeans of the Americas, the spreading conquests of the Ottoman Turks in the Mediterranean and southeast Europe, the invasions of Italy by the major monarchies of western Europe and the wars between them. To these military and territorial incursions may be added the subversion of political idealism in the writings of Francesco Guicciardini and Niccolò Machiavelli, the vision of a more just human society among the Utopians of Thomas More's imagination, and the reaffirmation of political idealism in the educational writings of Desiderius Erasmus. It was in keeping with these visionary social and political ideals that Erasmus constructed his humanist exegetical theology. This theology was based on

\* \* \* \* \*

Works cited frequently are referred to in the notes in abbreviated form; a list of abbreviations and full bibliographical information is given at 324–7 below. References to Erasmus' correspondence are to the English translation of the letters in CWE, where these have already been published, or to the Latin edition of Allen.

and completed the moderate intra-ecclesial theological reforms projected by certain of the Italian humanists of the previous century and a half. More compatible with the new political realism and the emergence of political and military power, but also socially critical in its implications, was Martin Luther's movement of ecclesiological and doctrinal reformation culminating in a total break away from the Roman Catholic church.[1]

Both Erasmus and Luther viewed the Christian faith as attenuated and distracted by the perilous condition of the affairs of the world. Erasmus' projected theological reforms and Luther's actual reformation, however, represented rival and very different approaches to the problem of the renewal of the Christian faith. Hence it was not at all unlikely, if not inevitable, that Erasmus and Luther would drift into confrontation, and that this would be a clash of religious and political visions that was one of the more astonishing happenings of this astonishingly disorderly but order-seeking epoch. The immediate effect of the debate between Erasmus and Luther on the great process of Christian renewal embodied in the various Protestant reformations and in the Catholic reformation was slight. But it has continued to exercise a paradigmatic influence on the perennial conflict within western civilization over the relations of God and mankind and the consequential relations among humankind itself.

The major texts of Erasmus' presentation of his vision of mankind within Christianity vis-à-vis that of Luther and his lengthy but resourceful reply to Luther's response are presented in a complete English translation in these two volumes. Each of these texts has its own history and its place in the spiritual biography and reforming program of its author. To identify such contexts it is important to outline some of the pertinent features of Erasmus' spiritual journey. Luther's journey will be dealt with only to the extent that is necessary in order to provide the context of these writings of Erasmus.

In 1487 Erasmus became an Augustinian canon regular in their convent at Steyn. Later in life, though remaining bound by his vows, he obtained a dispensation from the pope permitting him to live away from his

* * * * *

1 Out of the vast literature on the Reformation a reader may find two recent books especially useful. Spitz *Reformation* is a distillation of a lifetime of immersion in this subject beginning with what remains the most judicious and informative study of German humanists and the Reformation, his *The Religious Renaissance of the German Humanists* (Cambridge, Mass 1963). Oberman *Luther* places Luther within the mentality of the early sixteenth century and the background of late medieval scholastic theology.

community as a secular priest.[2] While he was in Paris (1495–1500) he attended some lectures on Scotus at the Franciscan *studium*. In the course of these early years he came to seek a way of life that would combine piety and spiritual freedom with a mode of theologizing that would relate the evangelical truths of the Gospels to the spirituality of the individual Christian. Although he never totally rejected monasticism or scholastic theology, he became permanently critical of their inadequacies for what he considered to be a truly Christian existence. In place of these two basic institutions of the medieval church Erasmus set forth a humanistic version of the pious Christian life and a new humanistic mode of theologizing. These became the decisive features of his spiritual journey.

Erasmus' essay *On Disdaining the World* (*De contemptu mundi*) was written in the late 1480s.[3] In its last chapter Erasmus points out the many faults of the monasticism of his day.[4] In early days 'to be a monk meant nothing more than to be a true Christian ... Now most monasteries are in the midst of worldly affairs and so entangled in them that they are no more parted from the world than are kidneys from a living body. So far are their institutions from preserving religious discipline that they are mere breeding places of impiety in which it is hardly possible to remain pure and innocent.' Hence he advises his friend's young nephew to 'leave the world in another sense: associate with men of integrity and consider yourself in a monastery whenever you are in the company of those who love truth, chastity, sobriety, and modesty ... You need no Carmelite or Dominican cowl if you have kept unsullied the white gown given you at your baptism. Let it not disturb your mind that you are not one of [a monastic] community, if only you are truly a member of the Christian community.'[5] Indeed this is Erasmus' ideal, expressed more than once: to realize the Christian life in human society at large, secular as well as religious, lay as well as ordained.

Erasmus expresses the same thoughts in a well-known passage at the end of his *Enchiridion*, first published in 1503.[6] For the July 1518 Froben

* * * * *

2 See James K. McConica's introductions to Epp 446 and 447 for explanations of Erasmus' clerical status.
3 CWE 66 137–75
4 Though it may have been written as late as 1521, Rummel shows its many similarities of outlook and tone to earlier writings; see her introductory note (CWE 66 131–3).
5 CWE 66 173–5; in the second sentence of the quotation 'less' has been corrected to 'more.'
6 CWE 66 127

edition Erasmus added a dedicatory letter to Paul Volz.[7] This famous and much-discussed letter may well be Erasmus' most explicit description of his vision of the Christian community. This vision was not theological in a formal sense, though it may have been closely related to his *Way of Arriving at a True Theology*, (*Ratio ... perveniendi ad veram theologiam*) revised and republished in this same year.[8] In this letter to Volz he again speaks of a universal community of all Christians as a replacement of the monastery:

> Once, as I said, the monastic life was a refuge from the world. Now men are called monks who spend all their time in the very heart of worldly business and exercise a kind of despotism in human affairs. And yet because of their dress, or because of some name they bear, they claim so much sanctity for themselves that compared with them they think other people hardly Christians. Why do we so closely confine the professed service of Christ, which he wished to be as wide open as possible? If we are moved by splendid names, what else, I ask you, is a city than a great monastery?[9]

Erasmus was following the path of a number of Italian humanists who found lay Christianity to be as valid if not more truly 'religious' than that of the professed.[10] Petrarch debated in his writings whether an ascetic Christian such as a member of a monastic order was leading a more truly Christian life than a poet and orator such as himself.[11] Salutati, wavering over the same question, became an eminent example of the humanist lay moralist and counsellor.[12] Lorenzo Valla denied that he was any less meritorious when spontaneously moved by an impulse of charity than was a person who had bound himself by vows of poverty, chastity, and obedience.[13]

For Erasmus, too, the way of the humanist, the way of the poet and orator, the way of the biblical philologist, the way of the preacher and the priest was the better way of finding Christ and of leading his fellows to

* * * * *

7  Ep 858 and CWE 66 8–23
8  Holborn 175–305. The *Ratio* is a revised and expanded version of his *Methodus* of 1516 (Holborn xiv–xv).
9  Ep 858:586–94 / CWE 66 22
10 See 'Humanist Treatises on the Status of the Religious' in Trinkaus *Image and Likeness* 651–82. See also Salvatore Camporeale's review article on Lorenzo Valla's *De professione religiosorum* ed Mariarosa Cortesi (Padua 1986), 'Lorenzo Valla: etica umanistica e prassi cristiana. Il *De professione religiosorum*' *Memorie Domenicane* n s 22 (1991) 335–80.
11 See Trinkaus *Image and Likeness* 654–62.
12 Trinkaus *Image and Likeness* 662–74
13 Trinkaus *Image and Likeness* 674–82; Camporeale 'Lorenzo Valla ...' (n10 above)

their own discoveries of Christ. The monastic life, even at its ideal best, such
as he had encountered it in the Franciscan Jean Vitrier, was no longer the
most suitable way to be a Christian.[14] His own age needed religious leaders to inculcate an active moral life in all mankind. This meant not only the
conversion of infidels such as the Turks but also the reform of the Christian world.[15] Erasmus' vision of lay piety was not confined exclusively to
socially desirable behaviour, though concord, tolerance, and mutual support were certainly part of it. More important was the inspiration of the
example and teachings of Christ that might induce faith in salvation and a
tranquillity that might well engender truly neighbourly and charitable behaviour. Erasmus' theology was thus founded upon his vision of lay piety,
and it should be counted a genuine theology because it was centred on
the deity and the knowledge and understanding of God's nature and desires. It was focused on acquiring a precise knowledge of God's revelation
in the Scriptures through the sayings of Christ and through the prophets,
evangelists, and apostles, all divine and divinely inspired. Erasmus' theology was therefore an exegetical and transformative hermeneutic of sacral
history and divine mysteries.[16]

* * * * *

14 See Erasmus' famous description of Jean Vitrier in Ep 1211 of 13 June 1521.
   However, it was Vitrier's pastoral activities as a priest that he admired, not
   his affiliation with the Franciscans: 'The regular way of life into which he had
   slipped or had been drawn in the ignorance of youth by no means appealed
   to him. He used to say in my hearing that it was a life for idiots rather than
   religious men to sleep and wake and sleep again, to speak and be silent, to
   go and to return, to eat and stop eating, all at the sound of a bell, and in a
   word to be governed in everything by human regulations rather than the law
   of Christ' (Ep 1211:34–9).
15 See his further comment on Jean Vitrier: 'He was absorbed by a kind of in-
   credible passion for bringing men to the true philosophy of Christ, and from
   labours of this sort he hoped to win the glory of martyrdom. And so, as I have
   heard from his most intimate friends, he had long ago obtained permission
   from his superiors to voyage to countries in which Christ is either unknown
   or worshipped falsely, thinking he would be fortunate if in this service he
   could win a martyr's crown. But he was recalled in mid-course, hearing as
   it were a voice from heaven, "Return, Jean; you will not fail of martyrdom
   among your own people"' (Ep 1211:77–84).
16 This and the ensuing paragraphs on Erasmus' projection of a new humanistic
   theology rest on broad historical observations as well as specific items from
   Erasmus' oeuvre. Many studies have contributed to a growing consensus concerning the religious thought of Erasmus and his own sense of his particular
   vocation. See, for example: McConica 'Consent'; Georges Chantraine 'Mystère'
   and his 'L'Apologia ad Latomum: deux conceptions de la théologie' in Scrinium II
   51–75; John B. Payne Sacraments and his 'Toward the Hermeneutics of Erasmus'

Erasmus repudiated scholastic theology in so far as it failed to assist in the striving for his theological goals. To Erasmus' mind scholastic theology was for the most part disdainful of the crucial aesthetic and affective qualities of Scripture. To the humanist eyes and ears of Erasmus, Scripture, the discourse of God, recorded and transmitted by inspired humans, was the most beautiful and moving writing in existence. Accordingly, he attacked the scholastics who stubbornly relied upon erroneously and insensitively translated versions of the Greek and Hebrew originals, or who were oblivious to or tolerant of the errors, distortions, and misunderstandings that had inevitably infiltrated the texts. Finally, most scholastic theologians were seemingly indifferent to the forms in which Scripture was available to ordinary Christians, how it was received and understood by them. Scripture had become a code rather than a message, an invocation, a spiritual guide for the laity.

It is this call for a revival of the role of Scripture in Christian life that is the message of Erasmus' letter to Volz:

> I am therefore unmoved by the jeers of some men I could name who despise this small book as unlearned and the kind of thing that any schoolmaster could write, because it handles no Scotistic problems ... It need not equip men for the wrestling-schools of the Sorbonne if it equips them for the tranquillity proper to a Christian. It need not contribute to theological discussion provided it contributes to the life that befits a theologian ... Who can carry the *Secunda secundae* of Aquinas round with him? And yet the good life is everybody's business, and Christ wished the way of it to be accessible to all men, not beset with impenetrable labyrinths of argument but open to sincere faith, to love unfeigned, and their companion, the hope that is not put to shame.[17]

The thought process of Erasmus' new theology, and its conceptual reality, rested on a dramatic model of the historical interplay between God and

\* \* \* \* \*

in *Scrinium* II 13–49; Boyle *Language*; John W. O'Malley's introduction to CWE 66; Hoffman. It should be noted that the one-time notion of a northern Christian humanism, of which Erasmus was the centerpiece, in contrast to a secular or even pagan Italian humanism, is no longer tenable. Rather Christian humanism should be seen as a single movement, starting in Italy and spreading to the north, in which Erasmus was the culmination of what had begun with Petrarch and developed further with other Italian predecessors – above all, Lorenzo Valla.

17 Ep 858:35–8, 39–42, 67–71 / CWE 66 8–9. The *Secunda secundae* is the second part of the second part of Thomas Aquinas' *Summa theologiae*; it deals mainly with questions of morality.

mankind, divine actions and addresses stimulating human response. The script for the grand drama of God's creation and direction of this earthly realm was the Bible itself and the tale it unfolds in all its complexity, depth, tragedy, suffering, betrayal, reconciliation, despair, and triumph.[18] The theologian needs to comprehend this drama and transmit it with its redemptive power to the rest of mankind. For this he needs the instruments of rhetoric, of literary understanding, and of historical insight.

The physical cosmos is the stage upon which the action is played out. It does not constitute the ingredients or compose the determining elements of this sacred drama, except as God may choose to use a deluge or a rainbow, an earthquake or conflagration, the starry night, the beauties of the day, the darkening of storm clouds as warnings or promises in his great discourse with mankind. Hence the science of the Greeks, especially that of Aristotle, is essentially irrelevant to the true understanding of God and his purposes and works. The auxiliary sciences of Erasmus' theology cannot be dialectics or physics, useful as they might be for man in his dealings with nature.

The distinction between Erasmus' theology and scholastic theology does not consist only in that between spirit and flesh as he, himself, seems to say in the *Enchiridion*.[19] It is one between a theology that is dramatic

* * * * *

18 Chantraine has analysed Erasmus' conception of the 'drama of Christ' (*Christi fabula*), basing his discussion on Erasmus' *Ratio* (Holborn 209:1–4): 'It will confer no meagre aid in these matters if, carefully perusing the books of both testaments, we attentively give heed to that cycle and harmony of the entire drama of Christ, as I thus call it, which, having been made man, he acted out for our benefit.' Chantraine reviews Erasmus' usage of drama and follows out its theological bearings ('*Mystère*' 274–95; he cites the above passage at 274). It should be noted as well that this is the context the art of rhetoric assumes for its roles.

19 Cornelis Augustijn in his important study (now translated into English) *Erasmus, His Life, Works, and Influence* (Toronto 1991) 47–8 regards this distinction as central in Erasmus, yet at the same time he sees it as tempered and controlled. Augustijn quotes from the *Enchiridion*: 'But why should we refer to one passage or another? Paul's whole purpose is simply this: that the flesh be despised as it is a source of contention, and that he establish us in the spirit, the source of charity and liberty' (CWE 66 78). Augustijn adds: 'There is thus no absolute separation between the world of the spirit and that of the flesh. Man has a share in both and is a pilgrim in the visible world. Not only does his path lead to the invisible world, but ... the path in many ways already belongs to the heavenly world. Such a train of thought can easily lead to a complete rejection of earthly things, but Erasmus shrinks from this last step. He is not, so he says, attacking externals as such, and certainly not those that have been approved by the church.'

and historical and one that is logical and scientific. In both humanist and scholastic theology the divine is related to an underlying conceptual reality by analogy: in the Erasmian by analogy to human history and literary culture, in the scholastic by analogy to the physical universe.

To be sure there is much overlapping between the two types of theologizing. Scripture plays an enormous and crucial role in scholastic theology, but its interpretive and ratiocinative categories and modes of discussion and analysis come from Greek science. Logic and natural science (or more exactly, Aristotelian metaphysics) are interpretive devices often used to formulate, defend, or refute statements of doctrine.[20] Much of the doctrine promulgated by scholastics was shared by Erasmus and his humanist predecessors, but its verity was established by literary and historical interpretive methods. When Erasmus is criticizing scholasticism, he is not necessarily criticizing doctrinal positions of various theologians or theological schools. He sometimes agrees and sometimes disagrees with particular positions. He accepts dogma as officially established by the church both through the decrees of popes and those of general councils. He accepts in a more ultimate sense what has for long been the consensus of the community of believers, as James K. McConica[21] and others have shown. Theological truth is derived both from critical analysis of authentic biblical texts and from venerable established traditions within the church. Such

* * * * *

20 Charles H. Lohr argues that study of Aristotles' *Metaphysics* gave rise to a 'science of God': 'Aristotle's ideas provided an ontological foundation for traditional theological concepts, such as "essence," "nature," "person," and "subsistence" in trinitarian theory, and "substance" and "accident" in the theory of grace and transubstantiation. His fixed essences and static conception of reality matched, moreover, [the scholastics'] own hierarchical view of the world. Most importantly, his conception of metaphysics as the science of being enabled them to maintain the necessity of revelation for knowledge of God's nature'; see *The Cambridge History of Renaissance Philosophy* (Cambridge 1988) 587. It is sometimes argued that Erasmus' and other humanist theologies represented a return to twelfth-century, pre-scholastic theology where, as Lohr puts it, 'the task of the theologians had been the presentation of the teaching of the Bible and the Church Fathers' (586). In this respect humanist theology was conservative whereas scholasticism was novatory.
21 'Consent' 97: 'At the very source of Erasmus' whole outlook on theology and the Church there was a tenacious adherence to the tradition and unity of the community, an adherence which it is possible to label "conservative."' (He also holds it to be 'revolutionary'). Also see Payne's detailed analysis of Erasmus' relation to the sources of doctrinal authority and ecclesiastical traditions in *Sacraments* 15–33.

traditions are, however, subject to change over long periods of time both because of historical changes in human circumstances and the deepening of the revelation from the Holy Spirit.

In recent decades there has been a growing recognition of the centrality of Erasmus' religious thought and of his conception of it as a new theology. Different scholars have attempted to attribute Erasmus' theology, whether recognized as new or not, to a number of different figures, influences, or schools of earlier Christian thought or theology. Noteworthy among such figures and movements are Origen, Jerome, Augustine, twelfth-century pre-scholastic thinkers such as Abelard, Bernard, and monastic scholars, as well as Thomas Aquinas, the Scotistic or the Ockhamistic currents of the *via moderna*, and of course the *devotio moderna*.[22] Although some of these attributions are less likely than others, it is true that all of the figures and movements mentioned above were used or referred to by Erasmus. In part this is because they were all significant sources for the formation of the late fifteenth- and sixteenth-century European Christian culture in which Erasmus lived and wrote.

\* \* \* \* \*

22 For example, the following scholars, though they are for the most part not rigid in their attributions, do find some features or facets of Erasmus' religious thought drawing upon a model: André Godin *Erasme lecteur d'Origène* (Geneva 1983); Eugene F. Rice Jr *Saint Jerome in the Renaissance* (Baltimore 1985) chapter 5, 'Hieronymus redivivus: Erasmus and Saint Jerome' 116–36; Charles Béné *Erasme et saint Augustin ou l'influence de saint Augustin sur l'humanisme d'Erasme* (Geneva 1969); Ernst-Wilhelm Kohls 'La position théologique d'Erasme et la tradition dans le "De libero arbitrio"' in *Colloquium Erasmianum* (Mons 1968) 69–87, especially 83–6, where he argues for the influence of St Thomas Aquinas; Jean-Pierre Massaut 'Erasme et Saint Thomas' *Colloquia Erasmiana Turonensia* (Paris 1972) 581–611; Payne *Sacraments* 228–9 concludes his book: 'We have noticed that, far from repudiating scholasticism, however much he may have detested the subtleties of scholastic argument, Erasmus had considerable knowledge of and appreciation for some of the scholastics, especially the late medieval nominalistic tradition. He enlists the support especially of Gerson and Durandus, but also of Biel, for his views on [the sacraments]. On the subjects of faith and reason, Scripture and tradition, justification and predestination, the relation of sign and the thing signified in the sacraments, Eucharist as memorial, and penance, we have shown that Erasmus' thought bears many resemblances to the nominalistic tradition.' As *A Discussion of Free Will* and *Hyperaspistes* reveal, Erasmus was hesitant about the positions of the *via moderna* on free will, but he also reveals some inclination to endorse them. On the *devotio moderna* see Albert Hyma *The Christian Renaissance: A History of the Devotio Moderna* (Grand Rapids 1924) and R.R. Post *The Modern Devotion* (Leiden 1968).

What the above list does not include is the humanistic rhetorical theology that was still in a state of formation as Erasmus was engaged in mastering the literature of the classical world as well as that of the patristic and the medieval Christian traditions. The question that inevitably occurred to him was how these two traditions, one of which was the creation of pagans, could be reconciled. Erasmus seems clearly to have repudiated the more recent scholastic version of Christian study at the time he became acquainted with Scotism during his years at the university in Paris. His resolution of the problem of how to be both a classicist and a Christian found early expression in his *Antibarbari*, but there is no doubt that it continued to challenge him for the rest of his life.

Erasmus clearly was not without predecessors on this basic issue, which was central to the Renaissance. The question of what should and should not be absorbed into contemporary moral and religious reform from ancient letters and philosophy led Petrarch to the discovery of the moral power of rhetoric as a replacement of dialectic in the pursuit of a truly Christian life. Other figures, both northern and Italian, and especially Lorenzo Valla, contributed to Erasmus' realization of his literary/religious vocation in the 1490s and 1500s.[23] The emergence of the Renaissance humanist move-

\* \* \* \* \*

23 Erasmus' discovery in 1504 and publication (Paris 1504) of a manuscript of Lorenzo Valla's *Adnotationes in Novum Testamentum* (called in its first version, not known to Erasmus, *Collatio Novi Testamenti*) is well known. Petrarch's *De otio religioso* may or may not have been known to him, but he would have responded to Petrarch's report of the joy he took in his discovery of sacred letters and of their beauty, which exceeded what he had previously loved in the pagan classics. Erasmus had probably read Valla's *Repastinatio dialectice et philosophie*, since he requested it from Robert Gaguin in January 1498 (Ep 67:5–6), and Gaguin replied that he was sending it (Ep 68:3–4). A version of it was published by Josse Bade at Paris in 1509. He would have found in it a systematic critique of scholastic theology, ethics, natural philosophy, and dialectic. Such influential Italian humanists as Petrarch and Valla also shared Erasmus' desire to restore a personal, spiritual relationship to religion. On Valla see Salvatore Camporeale *Lorenzo Valla, umanesimo e teologia* (Florence 1972) and his *Lorenzo Valla: tra medioevo e rinascimento, Encomium sancti Thomae* (Pistoia 1977) originally published in *Memorie Domenicane* n s 8 (1976) 1–190. For the *Collatio* see the edition of Alessandro Perosa (Florence 1970). On Petrarch see Marjorie O'Rourke Boyle, *Petrarch's Genius: Pentimento and Prophecy* (Berkeley and Los Angeles 1991). The *De otio religioso* has been edited by Giuseppe Rotondi, Studi e Testi 195 (Vatican City 1958). On the religious orientation of leading Italian humanists see Trinkaus *Image and Likeness* part 1: 'Human Existence and Divine Providence in Early Humanist Moral Theology.' It is important to point out that Erasmus, though he was authentically a humanist

ment was a response to professional, juridical, and political needs of the late medieval world, but it was also a reaction to the moral disorientation and religious anxiety and confusion of this world. These maladies derived at least in part from the over-technicalization and isolation of scholastic theology from the lives of ordinary Christians. What Erasmus set out to do was historically called for and mediated to him through his own experience. But his achievement was also the culmination and full articulation of a movement that had its beginnings in fourteenth-century Avignon, Padua, Milan, Florence, and Rome, among other places.

Thus it was that Erasmus, when Luther came upon the scene, had clearly established his historical identity, both in his own mind and in that of his many friends, patrons, and collaborators, as the leader of a reform movement within the church. It was a movement that aimed at no institutional changes but sought a spiritualization and purification of the entire community of believers from the pope on down, through the ranks of the clergy and among the simplest of lay Christians. 'I would that even the lowliest women read the Gospels and the Pauline Epistles ... Would that, as a result, the farmer sing some portion of them at the plough, the weaver hum some parts of them to the movement of his shuttle, the traveler lighten the weariness of the journey with stories of this kind!' So reads the *Paraclesis*, Erasmus' preface to his corrected Latin translation and his Greek edition of the New Testament.[24] The method of his reform movement was, indeed, his purification of the scriptural texts, based on his humanistic philological collation of the Greek manuscripts and the early Latin versions culminating in the Vulgate. The content of his new mode of theology is displayed in his interpretive readings of the New Testament manifested in his *Paraphrases* on the books of the New Testament. Erasmus' reform movement intended to rely on the gradual transformation of the spirits, attitudes, and behaviour of his Christian readers, stimulated by the quiet voice of his writings and the preachings and works of his collaborators, high and low. Erasmus was not a Savonarola. Neither was he a Luther.

\* \* \* \* \*

himself, discriminated among varieties of humanists; among 'humanists,' for example, he attacked the classical purists in his *Ciceronianus*. For the important dissidence between religiously oriented and purely philological humanism see Charles Trinkaus, 'Humanistic Dissidence: Florence versus Milan, or Poggio versus Valla' in *Florence and Milan: Comparisons and Relations* (Florence 1989) 17–40. Erasmus spoke of this quarrel in the prefatory letter to his edition of Valla's *Adnotationes* (Ep 182:98–111).
24 Trans John Olin in *Christian Humanism and the Reformation* (New York 1965) 97

Perhaps it was inevitable that Erasmus would find himself in an equivocal position. There is little evidence that he ever had considered leaving the
Roman Catholic church. Yet his criticisms of abuses and of the misdirection
of institutions were severe. Christendom required a head, the pope, but
individual popes (such as Julius II) departed drastically from their proper
roles, becoming secular rulers and engaging in warfare rather than leading
the way to peace.[25] Members of religious orders indulged in blatant sen-
suality instead of living as the purest and truest Christians of all. Scholastic theologians took part in constant controversies over questions that did
not seem even remotely connected with a life of Christian charity. Erasmus
was not the only critic of these practices, but his voice was the most powerful and persuasive. Many conservative ecclesiastics feared that the entire
system of church governance and guidance so elaborately and accumula-
tively developed over the previous five centuries might disintegrate. For
them the danger lay in the combination of humanist, textually-based theology and the pastoral, transformative vision of the priestly role that Erasmus
was so effectively promoting. The issue had been thus drawn both in his
controversies with Maarten van Dorp in 1515 and with Jacobus Latomus
in 1519.[26] Erasmus said in his *Apologia* against Latomus: 'I have admonished in a certain place that we should deal most thoroughly with those
matters in the Scriptures which transform us into Christ rather than end-
lessly quarrelling over questions of this kind,' namely whether true theology is not the same as the interpretation of the Scriptures. Latomus had
gone so far as to claim that knowledge of divine matters brought about
through grace and the use of logic, the substance of scholastic theology,
could dispense with scriptural exegesis, which was a separate and different
discipline from theology.[27]

Erasmus' theology would not dispense entirely with logic and dialectic, the disciplines at the heart of the scholastic method of distinguishing divine substances and their qualities, causes, effects, necessities,
contingencies, means, and ends. But it was mainly concerned with determining the concrete circumstances within which divinity manifested itself
in the Scriptures and human experience, authenticated in both cases by the
critically established oral and written sources.

\* \* \* \* \*

25 Cf James K. McConica 'Erasmus and the "Julius": A Humanist Reflects on the
Church' in *The Pursuit of Holiness* ed Charles Trinkaus with Heiko A. Oberman
(Leiden 1974) 444–71.
26 Rummel *Catholic Critics* I 1–13 and 63–93
27 See Georges Chantraine 'L'*Apologia ad Latomum*' in *Scrinium* II 63–5 and 72.

Erasmus' mode of theologizing was sensitive to the ways in which revelation was accommodated to particular events, personalities, and conditions in the same manner in which Christ himself spoke in the Gospels, or in which Paul adapted his message to his audience. Reciprocity between divine love reaching towards man and man's search for God and holiness within the Scriptures and by means of the Scriptures was also a major focus of his theology. Historical contextuality, too, was a central consideration, for mankind at various points in its history would be sensitive in differing ways to the divine message, which would be accommodated accordingly. Mediation between God and man through Christ was fundamental. It could not be assumed that revelation had occurred once and for all and was now over; it continues to unfold itself in the history of postlapsarian man.[28]

Erasmus thought mankind was brought closer to the living world of scriptural revelation through the drama of history than by the abstract philosophical determination of eternal immutable states and processes. If God was dynamic, purposeful, seeking to make himself available to human insight and human salvation, so man was viewed either as actively searching both to comprehend divinity and to respond to the possibility of salvation proffered by God or as ignoring that possibility so as to fall into evil ways. Knowledge of God through Scripture went hand in hand with piety, which was itself the quality of responsiveness to Christ. This was Erasmus' scenario of salvation, his *fabula Christi*. Within it man could not be other than possessed of free will and moved by the affections of love and hate.

## II
## ERASMUS' PREOCCUPATION WITH LUTHER:
### 1516–27

*The antagonists and their positions: 1516–19*
Martin Luther (10 November 1483–18 February 1546) is the antagonist of our story.[29] Erasmus attacked him first in the supposedly even-handed *Dis-*

* * * * *

28 This paragraph formulates the basic qualities of Erasmus' theology in humanistic terms. His theology is accommodative, reciprocal, contextual, mediatory, transformative. Or one may apply to it adverbial nouns which, as Lorenzo Valla argued, are not true nouns but reifications of qualities; see his *Repastinatio* ed Gianni Zippel (Padua 1982) book 1 chapter 4 (30–6), entitled 'Nulla nomina in "itas" descendere a substantivis sed ab adiectivis, nec his omnibus.'

29 See n1 above for references to works of Lewis W. Spitz and Heiko A. Oberman

*cussion of Free Will* of early September 1524. But Luther's response, *The En-slaved Will* of late fall 1525, followed the classical tactic of 'the best defence is an offence'; it was an onslaught weighing no alternatives and conceding no middle ground. Erasmus, he thought, may have provided him with the opportunity of making one of the strongest and clearest statements of his own theology. But that is for later.

Luther was the child of a comfortable, middle-class Saxon family. In 1505 at the age of twenty-two he received his master of arts degree from the University of Erfurt and matriculated at its law school. At this point he had either long felt or was suddenly made to feel that his life was directly controlled by God. Nearly struck by lightning on 2 July in that same year, he prayed in fear and pledged to become a monk. Two weeks later he sought admission to the house of the Augustinian Hermits in Erfurt. In view of the importance of St Paul's Epistle to the Romans in his later theology, it is not surprising that this incident later seemed to Luther to have been his 'road to Damascus.'

Subsequently he came under the tutelage of two professors of theology among the Erfurt Augustinians: Jodocus Trutfetter and Bartholomaeus Arnoldi of Usingen, both well known proponents of the *via moderna*.[30] Luther's early theology was nominalist; he boasted that he was of the school of Ockham. He was ordained to the priesthood in 1507 and taught at Erfurt until he was transferred to the chapter of the Augustinian Hermits at Wittenberg in 1511. In 1512 he received his doctorate in theology and was appointed to the chair of biblical theology at the recently founded University of Wittenberg. Though it is notable that he taught 'biblical,' not dialectical, theology, it appears that he remained highly capable of the dialectical argumentation commonly employed by Ockhamist theologians.

But by 1515/16 Luther had broken with the theology of the *via moderna* and had begun to develop his own reformationist theology. Some Luther scholars believe that he underwent a sudden conversion through a so-called 'tower experience.' The 'tower experience' was a recollection of the old

\* \* \* \* \*

on Luther. Also see Oberman's *Werden und Wertung der Reformation* (Tübingen 1977); English translation entitled *Masters of the Reformation* (Cambridge 1981); Leif Grane *Contra Gabrielem: Luthers Auseinandersetzung mit Gabriel Biel in der Disputatio Contra Scholasticam Theologiam 1517* (Gyldendal 1962) and his *Modus Loquendi Theologicus: Luthers Kampf um die Erneuerung der Theologie (1515–1518)* (Leiden 1975); McSorley. An excellent and extensive bibliography of Luther and the Reformation period is in Spitz *Reformation* 385–429.

30 See Oberman *Luther* 117–21.

Luther in 1545 that the insight of salvation by faith alone came to him in the tower room and library of the monastery while reading Paul's Epistle to the Romans. It meant that his previous pursuit of salvation by strenuous moral endeavour (which was sanctioned by nominalist teaching that God will not withhold his grace from him who does his very best) was wrong and that salvation came from utter trust in Christ's atoning love as expressed by Paul. Other scholars maintain that through his readings of St Augustine and his lectures on the Psalms in 1513–15 and on Romans in 1515–16, he gradually formed his new vision of salvation through faith alone.[31] Whatever its genesis, Luther's new soteriology was evident in his marginal comments of 1515/16 on Gabriel Biel's *Collectorium* on Peter Lombard's *Sentences* and Biel's *Sacred Canon of the Mass*. In February 1517 he wrote to Johannes Lang to inform his old professors Trutfetter and Arnoldi that their teaching had been a complete waste of time and to warn them that he was about to publish an attack on Aristotle and Biel.[32] If Luther actually wrote the commentary on Aristotle mentioned in his letter to Lang, it has not survived, but we do have his attack on Biel and other nominalists, his *Disputation against Scholastic Theology* of September 1517.[33]

The *Disputation against Scholastic Theology* is an attack upon a long list of formulations taken from the teaching of William of Ockham, Pierre d'Ailly, and Gabriel Biel. These formulations posit that prior to receiving grace a person can will and perform good deeds such as will grant him 'congruous merit' (*meritum de congruo*), that is, a fitting merit that can lead on to a more worthy merit, which with the aid of grace will confer justification or salvation.

Among these formulations there were some that Erasmus also endorsed, or seemed to Luther to endorse, including 'congruous merit,' but they also contained one point that had appeared in *The Disputation* as theses 82 and 83 and that Luther had already criticized in Erasmus. As Luther puts it, 'Not only are the religious ceremonials not the good law and [not only are they] the precepts under which one does not live (in opposition

\* \* \* \* \*

31 McSorley holds that vestiges of Ockhamism are still present in Luther's *Dictata super Psalterium* of 1513–15, but with signs of new insights (221–4). Luther had clearly changed his views of grace, free will, and justification in his notes to Gabriel Biel's *Collectorium* of 1515 and in his *Lectures on the Epistle to the Romans* of 1515 to September 1516 (McSorley 224–38). The exact date of the 'tower experience,' if there was one, is indeterminable. Oberman's account is more complex and nuanced (*Luther* 151–74).

32 WA *Briefwechsel* 1 88–9 no 34 / LW 48 36–8 no 12

33 WA 1 221–8 / LW 31 9–16

to many teachers); but even the Decalogue itself and all that can be taught and prescribed inwardly and outwardly is not good law either.'[34] Many of these formulations will also appear again in the debate with Erasmus. Erasmus' own position on 'congruous merit' will be equivocal in the debate, but some of his statements suggest that he was inclined to agree with it. Some scholars argue plausibly that Erasmus was basically in agreement with these doctrinal positions of the *via moderna*, though he emphatically rejected theologies that employed dialectic as their instrument of proof rather than textual analysis, historical contextualization, and literary interpretation of Scripture.[35] The argument made by the scholastics of the *via moderna* and rejected by Luther affirmed that the works of the Law Paul declared to be sin in Romans 3:20 were the Jewish ceremonies, not the good deeds of the commandments.

It is not clear whether Erasmus knew of Luther's *Disputation against Scholastic Theology* before 1520, when it was published in a collection of disputations. What is clear, however, is that Luther knew Erasmus' *Annotations on the New Testament*, published in the spring of 1516, a year and a half before his own *Disputation*. For Luther criticized Erasmus, as he was to criticize the scholastics, for identifying the 'law of works' in Paul as ceremonial. Luther also criticized Erasmus for doubting in his *Annotations* that a passage in Romans supported the doctrine of original sin and for favouring the scriptural interpretations of Jerome over those of Augustine. He made these charges in a letter to Georgius Spalatinus of 19 October 1516 almost a year before his *Disputation*.[36] In a letter to Erasmus of 11 December 1516, Spalatinus quoted this letter almost word for word as coming from

\* \* \* \* \*

34 *Disputatio contra scholasticam theologiam* WA 1 228 / LW 31 15; for Luther's earlier criticism of Erasmus see n36 below.

35 Statements referring to this position, including some that indicate at least tentative approval on Erasmus' part, are noted in the commentaries to *A Discussion of Free Will* and *Hyperaspistes*. Erasmus, however, professedly supports the position of Augustine in his later anti-Pelagian writings: it is 'more probable' that special grace is needed for the first meritorious movement of the will towards justification. Oberman sees Erasmus as favouring the medieval position, which would be that of Biel, whereas Luther returns to Augustine: 'The outstanding Bible scholar was more scholastic than ever before.' Yet he was more modern in favouring the long view (*Luther* 216). McSorley (288–93) stresses the extent to which Erasmus favours a semi-Pelagian position despite his formal endorsement of Augustine's stricter view. Payne *Sacraments* (228–9) concludes that Erasmus favoured the position of Biel. For a reconciliatory interpretation, see the final pages of this introduction.

36 WA *Briefwechsel* 1 69–72 no 27 / LW 48 23–6 no 9

an Augustinian priest.[37] These were the issues about which Erasmus and Luther eight and ten years later would debate. E.W. Kohls, an important interpreter of Erasmus' theology, quoted Luther's letter and commented: 'Luther already attacks the foundation of Erasmian theology, the summit of which is the comprehension of free will. The real public quarrel between Erasmus and Luther and the confrontation between the two systems was no more than a question of time.'[38]

Another scholar, this time a student of Luther, Leif Grane, also comments on Luther's early criticism of Erasmus. After discussing Luther's letter to Spalatinus of 19 October 1516, Grane refers to a letter of Luther to Johann Lang of 1 March 1517.[39] From day to day Luther thinks less of Erasmus: 'The human prevails more than the divine in him.' He does not wish to attack him publicly so that he will not seem to join the enviers of Erasmus. Jerome, who read five languages, was not the equal of Augustine, who knew one. Correct Christian understanding does not come because someone knows Greek and Hebrew. 'The judgment of the man who grants something to human free will is one thing, of the one who knows nothing but grace is another.' He does not want to injure Erasmus and help their

\* \* \* \* \*

37 Ep 501:50–76
38 'La position théologique d'Erasme' in *Colloquium Erasmianum* (Mons 1968) 73. In the letter of Luther to Spalatinus cited in n36, his reference to the 'law of works' in Paul and to the doctrine of original sin is based on Erasmus' *Annotations* on Paul's Epistle to the Romans 9:31–2 (LB VI 616F / CWE 56 274), 10:3 (LB VI 617E / CWE 56 277), and 5:12 (LB VI 585B–590B / CWE 56 139–62). This last is the famous annotation for which Erasmus was attacked by scholastic theologians as well as by Luther; in his 1516 version he changed Vulgate 'in quo omnes peccaverunt' to 'in eo quod omnes peccavimus' (that is, from 'in whom all have sinned' to 'inasmuch as we all have sinned'). Translated as 'in quo' ('in whom') in the Vulgate, the verse had been interpreted as giving scriptural basis for the doctrine of original sin, meaning 'in Adam all have sinned,' whereas Erasmus' version meant 'so in all men sin prevailed in so far as all men have sinned.' Because Erasmus explained (at LB VI 586B / CWE 56 141), 'There is nothing in the words here that cannot be accommodated to sin of imitation,' he was thought to have rejected the traditional doctrine that original or inherited sin had a scriptural foundation. Erasmus could not have known that passages he cited from pseudo-Jerome in support of his view were actually written by Pelagius (see CWE 56 155 n22). Readers should be aware that Luther would have read only a small portion of the annotation as it stands in LB because Erasmus several times expanded his explanation of his reading up to the 1531 version on which LB is based. Nevertheless Luther would have seen enough to alarm him. See CWE 56 151–2 nn1–2. Also see xxxvii below.
39 WA *Briefwechsel* 1 90 no 35 / LW 48 39–41 no 13

common enemies. Grane indicates that, 'although later (1518–1519) Luther under the influence of his friends indeed sought to overcome his distant relationship to Erasmus, there is no ground for the assumption that at any period of time he had changed the conception of him as a theologian that he had formed in the winter of 1516–1517.'[40] We shall see that Erasmus, though he rather coldly professed that there were certain good qualities in Luther, also remained generally suspicious and fearful of him.

In subsequent years, Erasmus was charged by conservative Catholic theologians and by others with having inspired Lutheranism. The above episode seems to indicate that he did not. Far from it. But it is true that there were many aspects of Luther's reform program that Erasmus shared, primarily those having to do with placing greater emphasis on the internal, spiritual aspects of Christianity than upon external or ritualistic efforts to achieve holiness. On the other hand, Erasmus strongly rejected Lutheranism on the fundamental question of how salvation occurred, whether by faith alone or by human efforts strongly stimulated and aided and consummated by grace. Erasmus equally emphatically rejected Luther's repudiation of the papacy and the orthodox Christian tradition as the established authority in the church. Yet the possibility of linking Erasmus to some of Luther's positions allowed conservative forces within the church, particularly theologians of the mendicant orders, to attack him. They sought to cast suspicion on the new humanistic theology which he hoped would gradually displace the scholastic-dialectical mode of theologizing. Erasmus favoured his own methodology not just because he was enamoured with it but because he thought it would bring about a more sincere faith, greater piety, and a deeper spirituality. In the sketch of his life written in the third person but thought to be autobiographical, the *Compendium vitae*, Erasmus seems to characterize faithfully the destiny which Luther's coming imposed on his own life: 'The sad business of Luther had brought him a burden of intolerable ill will; he was torn in pieces by both sides, while aiming zealously at what was best for both.'[41]

Before Luther's irruption into his world, Erasmus was in a glowing mood because of his *annus mirabilis*, the year 1516, when he published his *Novum instrumentum*, together with his *Annotationes*, and his edition of the letters of Jerome. He wrote to Wolfgang Capito at the end of February 1517. 'At this moment,' he mused, 'I should almost be willing to grow young again

\* \* \* \* \*

40 Grane 118
41 CWE 4 410:170–3, the final lines of the *Compendium*, on which see James K. McConica's introductory note (CWE 4 400–3)

for a space, for the sole reason that I perceive we may shortly behold the rise of a new kind of golden age.' After speaking of the bright chances of peace between the ruling monarchs and the lustre of the contemporaneous rebirth of the humanities, he turns to the theologians who oppose the humanities and criticize efforts such as his own to restore the true text of the Scriptures and of the writings of Jerome. He sees in this the only cloud on the horizon. 'Not that I would wish to see the kind of theology which today is established in our universities abolished: I want it to be enriched and made more accurate by the incorporation of ancient and genuine texts.' He fears the rebirth of paganism among some of the devotees of ancient literature and also among scholastics who judge everything by ancient philosophy, or of Judaism with the spread of Hebrew studies. 'I could wish that those frigid sophistries could either be quite cut out or at least were not the theologians' only concern, and that Christ pure and simple might be planted deep into the minds of men.'[42]

The references to paganism and Judaism have a further resonance. It was a running theme through Erasmus' scriptural interpretation and his defence of free will that Christianity emerged from a double rejection of the religions of the gentile pagans and of the Jews. The pagans imposed a natural necessitarianism, mediated through their gods, upon their followers. The Jews imposed an elaborate legalism on themselves, negating or at least diluting the internal purity of love of the divine by a myriad of external fleshly rules. Both false religions could re-emerge within Christendom: the one through Aristotelian or Stoic influences towards predestination and cosmic determinism among scholastics, the other out of a deluge of minute behavioural requirements from the strict moralists. There would be overly severe Augustinianism on the one hand and neo-Pelagianism on the other. Little did Erasmus know at this point that a man named Martin Luther would move from the latter extreme to the former, nor did Erasmus know with what forceful resolution Luther would pursue the establishment of the doctrinal counterpart of his conversion.[43]

\* \* \* \* \*

42 Ep 541:11–13, 132–4, 157–9
43 Erasmus would later write in his *Ciceronianus* of the dangers that lay in treating Christian questions in pagan dress: 'Above all we must be on our guard lest an age as yet innocent and unformed be led astray by the outward show of the title "Ciceronian" and turn out not Ciceronian but pagan. This kind of plague is not yet extinct but constantly threatens to break out afresh – under one showy front lurk the old heresies, under another Judaism, under another paganism (CWE 28 447; see also 393–4).

Erasmus' anticipation of a gratifying old age was soon to be shattered. On 31 October of the same year, 1517, Luther posted his ninety-five theses *On the Power and Efficacy of Indulgences*.[44] The action, which was a traditional scholastic invitation to disputation, triggered a predictable but unanticipated reaction. Indulgences were widely questioned and Luther's theses were less challenging than his *Disputation against Scholastic Theology* written but a month earlier. Unfortunately, however, Luther had sent a copy to Archbishop Albert of Mainz, who was to be a beneficiary of the indulgence he had appointed Johann Tetzel to promote. Protests and denunciations followed, leading Pope Leo x to ask the Augustinian order to control Luther. Luther, requesting the right to defend his theses, was allowed to do so at the general chapter of the German Augustinians at Heidelberg on 25 April 1518. Among the doctrines Luther defended at the Heidelberg chapter is that 'the will of man outside the state of grace is enslaved and captive' – phrasing that would provide the title of his reply to Erasmus' *Discussion of Free Will*.[45]

Erasmus remained ignorant of Luther's activities as late as March 1518, when he sent a copy of Luther's *Theses on Indulgences* to Thomas More, seemingly unaware of Luther's name.[46] By 17 October 1518, in a letter to Johann Lang, however, he was well aware of the author of the *Theses* and surmised that they had satisfied everyone except for a few who objected to Luther's denial of purgatory. He considers Prierias' reply 'ill-judged' and cannot understand why Eck would have attacked Luther.[47] Sylvester Prierias, Master of the Sacred Palace, had prepared for Leo x a theological analysis that was critical of Luther, and Johann Maier of Eck, a professor at Ingolstadt, was one of the first to denounce him. On 19 October 1518 Erasmus writes again to Capito and reports that 'someone writes to me that Martin Luther is in danger.'[48] At Leo's order Luther had had his meeting with Cardinal Cajetanus, papal legate to the Diet of Augsburg (12–14 October); the result was a standoff.

Thus in the fall of 1518, almost a year after the ninety-five *Theses* were posted, Erasmus shows at least some awareness of them, a certain sympathy for Luther, and concern over the hostile reactions. It seems probable that Erasmus, when he first became aware of the content of Luther's *Theses*

* * * * *

44  WA 1 233–8
45  WA 1 365–74 / LW 31 58–9
46  Ep 785:39n
47  Ep 872:15–26
48  Ep 877:11–12

*on Indulgences*, was inclined to react favourably. As John Payne has shown, nowhere in his writings was Erasmus anything but dubious about the practice of indulgences, but he accepted them as far as the consensus of the church seemed to support them.[49] At the first moment when Luther appeared to resist the constituted authority of the church, as in his confrontation with Cardinal Cajetanus, Erasmus apparently changed his mind.

And yet he was uncertain. Conservative scholastic theologians attacked Erasmus for taking essentially Lutheran positions. Friends who supported Luther hoped for and encouraged Erasmus' endorsement. On 5 January 1519 Melanchthon wrote: 'Martin Luther, who is a keen supporter of your reputation, desires your good opinion on all points.'[50] In his reply to Melanchthon of 22 April 1519, Erasmus pleaded unfamiliarity with Luther's works and implied criticism of his manner of expression: 'Martin Luther's way of life wins all men's approval here, but opinions vary about his teaching. I myself have not yet read his books. He has made some justified criticisms, but I wish they had been as happily expressed as they were outspoken.'[51]

Writing to John Fisher on 2 April 1519, Erasmus complained that Jacobus Latomus' *Dialogus*, directed against Luther, 'may be supposed by the uninstructed reader to be meant for me.'[52] In fact it was directed against Erasmus and any who followed his *Way of Arriving at a True Theology* (*Ratio ... perveniendi ad veram theologiam*). On 8 April 1519 Wolfgang Capito, aware that Erasmus was seemingly caught between two contending sides of the religious dispute, wrote him:

> 'Do not let Louvain prove an obstacle. We will maintain Germany and Saxony in a proper respect for you, where the prince is a powerful supporter of Luther and so is the flourishing university of Wittenberg, and there are so many persons of distinction who wish equally well to both Erasmus and Luther. There is nothing his enemies wish more than to see you indignant with him. He himself and his party are devoted to you.'[53]

It is a mark of Erasmus' influence and status that without intention or effort on his part he evoked a competition over his favour. It is likely that it was before receiving this letter that Erasmus on 14 April 1519 had written to

* * * * *

49 Payne *Sacraments* 214–16
50 Ep 910:28–9
51 Ep 947:40–3
52 Ep 937:45–6
53 Ep 938:5–11

the elector of Saxony, Frederick the Wise, the supporter and protector of Luther.

This is a remarkable letter, so protective of Luther and indignant towards enemies who attack him with no knowledge of his writings that Erasmus attempted to prevent its publication lest it compromise him with the Catholic side. Again Erasmus sees Luther used as a pretext for attacking the humanities and protests the injustice of these attacks: 'These cunning fellows mix allusions to the ancient tongues and good writing and humane culture, as though Luther trusted to these for his defence, or these were the sources whence heresies were born.' Again he abstains from discussing Luther's positions and praises his reputation: 'I know as little of Luther as I do of any man, so that I cannot be suspected of bias towards a friend. His works it is not for me to defend or criticize, as hitherto I have not read them except in snatches. His life, at least, is highly spoken of by all who know him . . .'[54] Melanchthon and Luther received the text with great pleasure.

*An exchange of letters and its aftermath: spring 1519–summer 1520*
On 28 March 1519 Luther wrote to Erasmus. He had been urged to do so by Capito and others. In the letter he expresses admiration for Erasmus' learning and stylistic skill, and he pleads ignorance and lack of writing ability in addressing Erasmus. He says nothing about his own theology and his distaste for that of Erasmus. He remarks only that 'having heard . . . that my name is known to you through the slight piece I wrote about indulgences, and learning . . . that you have not only seen but approved the stuff I have written, I feel bound to acknowledge, even in a very barbarous letter, that wonderful spirit of yours which has so much enriched me and all of us . . .' Luther professes that he has always wished 'to bury himself in a corner and remain unknown even to the sky and sun that we all share . . . But . . . things have turned out very differently,' he says, 'so that I am compelled, to my great shame, to expose my disgraceful shortcomings and my unhappy ignorance to be discussed and pulled to pieces even by the learned.'[55] The reticent tone is certainly unusual for Luther and demonstrates that he was by no means lacking in the ability to express himself diplomatically.

Erasmus answered two months later. His letter complains that Luther's work was viewed by their mutual enemies, the scholastic theologians at Louvain, as written at least with Erasmus' assistance. As a consequence they took it as a reason to suppress both the humanities, viewing them as

* * * * *

54 Ep 939:57–9 and 69–72
55 Ep 933:22–7 and 39–45

an obstacle to their kind of theology, and Erasmus himself, 'under the impression that I contribute something of importance towards this outburst of zeal.' Erasmus had defended himself by assuring them 'that you were quite unknown to me; that I had not yet read your books and could therefore neither disapprove nor approve anything.' He adds, 'Their attitude to you has softened somewhat. They are afraid of my pen, knowing their own record; and, my word, I would paint them in their true colours, as they deserve, did not Christ's teaching and Christ's example point in quite another direction.' He is offering the example of his own restraint as a suggestion to Luther to moderate his behaviour. He follows this with what might well be interpreted as a thinly veiled criticism of Luther's vehemence of statement:

> I think one gets further by courtesy and moderation than by clamour. That was how Christ brought the world under his sway; that was how Paul did away with the Jewish law, by reducing everything to allegory. It is more expedient to protest against those who misuse the authority of the bishops than against the bishops themselves ... Things which are of such wide acceptance that they cannot be torn out of men's minds all at once should be met with argument, close-reasoned forcible argument, rather than bare assertion.[56]

Erasmus will refer frequently to this warning to Luther as evidence that he was not favouring him in writing this letter to him. The statement is also a clear indication of the mode of reforming action Erasmus favoured in attaining the changes he himself was hoping for in the church. He had, as has been shown, genuine theological differences with Luther, and his fear of the disruptiveness of Luther's violent assertiveness surfaced even as he was very tentatively accepting Luther's proffered hand. 'Everywhere,' he continues, 'we must take pains to do and say nothing out of arrogance or faction; for I think the spirit of Christ would have it so. Meanwhile we must keep our minds above the corruption of anger or hatred, or of ambition; for it is this that lies in wait for us when our religious zeal is in full course.' Then he adds: 'I am not instructing you to do this, only to do what you do always' – a slightly embarrassed softening.[57]

One might call this letter minimally cordial by the standards of that time, and very revealing of the true concerns on Erasmus' mind. Erasmus

* * * * *

56 Ep 980:4–53
57 Ep 980:54–9. Later, when he was accused of supporting Luther through this letter, Erasmus tried to use this rather mild and indirect reproof to show that he had rebuked Luther more severely than he actually had.

undoubtedly discerned a certain element of support in the Lutheran movement for the reforms he was himself hoping to see. So many of his own friends and protégés were joining with it! But he was fearful of its divisiveness and very concerned that its aggressiveness was provoking even stronger attacks on the humanistic studies that were an essential part of the *philosophia Christi* he was formulating and promoting by his own work.[58]

Erasmus' letter to Luther appeared in the *Farrago*, his letter collection of October 1519. During the next several months Erasmus made a number of comments on it. In a letter to Maarten Lips in the fall of 1519 he said:

> Hoogstraten [the inquisitor] is now at Louvain. He has secured a copy of my letter to Luther, and thinks it will serve nicely to show me up as being in favour of Luther, I having published it expressly to prove that Luther and I have nothing in common. And suppose I did favour him, would there be anything monstrous in that?[59]

The letter reveals not only Erasmus' ambivalence towards Luther and the deliberate ambiguity of his writing, but also how he hoped the letter to Luther would be read. In another letter he says:

> I feel no embarrassment at having answered Luther; if he challenged me, I would answer the Grand Turk. I wish well to the good things in him, not the bad; more accurately, I wish well to Christ, not Luther. If I do answer him, it is to correct him on many points at the same time. I corrected him politely, because I know that to be more effective ... In saying this, I should not wish to do Luther any harm. I am neither prosecuting him nor counsel for the defence nor judge ... He is, as even his enemies allow, a man of high character; and he has a warmth of heart which although when exasperated, not without just cause, flared up too far, might yet, if diverted to other ends, prove a capital

\* \* \* \* \*

58 Erasmus made a serious mistake in his letter to Luther, one that caused him severe trouble later, leading him to expose a good friend and supporter to serious difficulties, and giving a former friend who had become one of his worst enemies, Girolamo Aleandro, an opening to pursue his suspicions of Erasmus. Erasmus had needlessly let fall the following lines, too eager, perhaps, to encourage Luther, but devastating for the person named: 'You have people in England who think well of what you write, and they are in high place. There are some here too, the bishop of Liège among them, who favour your views' (Ep 980:41–3).
59 Ep 1040:1–7

instrument in the cause of Christ, who did not quench the smoking flax but revived it.[60]

This would seem to be a fair statement of Erasmus' true view of Luther at this time midway in the crisis that would culminate in the excommunication of Luther in January 1521. Erasmus did not like Luther's abrupt and defiant attitude; he agreed with him on the matter of indulgences but not on how he acted in pressing his judgment. Erasmus recognized that there was a more fundamental difference on the question of salvation, but he preferred to see the church become broad enough to accommodate such diversity of views. The question was whether he would be able to maintain this stance as the confrontation provoked by Luther moved the ecclesiastical authorities towards excommunication and the church towards schism.

This was a hard time for Erasmus. As he had feared, the conservative theologians were aroused by his failure to distinguish his new kind of humanistic theology from the challenge to ecclesiastical authority and the seemingly patent heresy of Luther. He gave a remarkably explicit diagnosis of the situation in his letter to Cardinal Albert of Brandenberg of 19 October 1519.[61] This letter was so outspoken and so greatly misjudged the position necessarily taken by the cardinal that it was never answered.

At first Erasmus disclaimed responsibility for Luther, repeating the position he had taken in his letters of 1519 to Luther and others: 'Of Luther I know as little as I do of anyone; his books I have not yet found time to read, except for dipping into some of them here and there.' Erasmus regrets the way Luther's disputation was received, particularly by those theologians of Louvain who were his old critics: 'They merely traduce him with their crazy clamour before popular audiences and tear him to shreds with the most bitter and venomous denunciations, their mouths full of nothing but the words "heresy" and "heretics."' Linked to these denunciations was the charge that Luther's books were largely drawn from Erasmus.

What, he asks, is the source of the evil that provoked Luther? Much of it must be blamed on the 'tyranny of the mendicant friars.' He does not condemn them all, but there are many who for power and gain 'deliberately ensnare the consciences of men.' He is referring to practices such as the marketing of indulgences, which undermined Christian charity and led to

* * * * *

60 Ep 1041:31–46. The letter is a preface 'to the reader' for an edition of the *Colloquies*.
61 Ep 1033:108–16

over-scrupulous reliance on external acts of formal piety, so that hypocrisy was beginning to replace genuine holiness.

Erasmus had had nothing to do with the cases of either Reuchlin or Luther. But the true objects of the mendicants' campaign against them was 'the new blossoming of the humanities and the ancient tongues' for which Erasmus himself had stood. It was a matter of covering up their sense of inferiority because they lacked these skills and resented the prestige of the practitioners of the new learning. In short, they envied scholars of the humanities such as Erasmus.[62] Erasmus goes even farther in this letter, criticizing the way the charges of heresy against Luther were being handled. But it should be clear that he was not agreeing with Luther's theological doctrines, even though he is sympathetic to his criticism of the abuses arising from indulgences. He did not think of himself as in any way attacking the authority of the papacy but rather as protesting a widespread condition of abuses. In a letter to a Czech nobleman, Jan Šlechta, of 1 November 1519, Erasmus condemns three radical Bohemian sects: 'For if the Roman pontiff is Antichrist because there has now and then been an impious pope, or if the church of Rome is the great harlot because it sometimes has wicked cardinals or bishops or ministers of another kind, then by the same token we should never obey any bishops, any pastors, any kings.'[63] It is not likely that Erasmus would have predicted that within the year Luther would indeed use such language in speaking of the papacy.

During the years 1517–20, and especially 1519–20, Erasmus was irritated and preoccupied by the attacks on him by Louvain theologians, in particular Jacobus Latomus and Edward Lee.[64] Since Luther was even more violently attacked from these and many other quarters, and since Erasmus was linked with Luther in these attacks, he developed a resentment of Luther. He had been able by means of his cordial relations with a number of secular rulers and prominent ecclesiastics to mitigate and hold off the criticisms by the scholastic dialectical theologians. But if the latter succeeded in associating Erasmus with Luther, this would undermine his efforts to defend his own orthodoxy by invoking the respect in which popes and prelates held him. It was fear of this 'guilt by association' that ultimately led Erasmus to launch his own critique of Luther. But he was at first genuinely aroused by the hasty and seemingly unjust rejection of Luther without serious debate of his positions. He was motivated as well by a sympathy for Luther,

\* \* \* \* \*

62 Ep 1033:44–6, 81–4, 133–50, 210–31
63 Ep 1039:138–42
64 Rummel *Catholic Critics* I 63–120

who was under attack by some of the same figures who were criticizing him.

On 15 June 1520 Pope Leo x issued his famous bull *Exsurge Domine*, which set forth forty-one heresies and errors of Luther and called for his works to be burned. The bull was not presented to Luther until 10 October. In the meantime Luther published two tracts that made his total break with Rome apparent to all: *Address to the Christian Nobility of the German Nation* in August and *The Babylonian Captivity of the Church* on 6 October. Erasmus would learn of these only later. Hence he continued to offer limited encouragement to certain supporters of Luther. Shortly before 21 June 1520 he wrote to Melanchthon: 'With us here, the criminal conspiracy against truly Christian scholarship and humane studies knows no rest. New monstrosities arise every day, the latest being Lee, who is as spiteful as he is ignorant ... A big share in all this wickedness belonged to Jacobus Latomus, and still does.'[65] Erasmus sees their attack, then, as against the *studia humanitatis* rather than Luther. Ironically one of the key charges by Lee was that by reformulating Romans 5:12 from 'in quo omnes peccaverunt' to 'quatenus omnes peccaverunt' (from 'in whom all have sinned' to 'inasmuch as all have sinned') Erasmus had undermined the doctrine of original sin. As we have seen, Luther's first notice of Erasmus in October 1516 had made the same charge.[66]

Continuing his letter to Melanchthon, Erasmus tells him that he favours Luther as far as one can, but everyone connects what Luther says with what Erasmus says, and this creates difficulties. He is not surprised that Luther's books were burned in England. Many of his supporters agree with Erasmus that it would have helped if Luther's writings had been more moderately expressed. Things seem to be heading towards civil strife. Offences may come, but he would prefer not to be held responsible for them. 'Remember me to Dr Luther, and to all your friends.'[67]

On 6 July 1520 he wrote to Georgius Spalatinus, a supporter of Luther and a mediator between Luther and Erasmus. He expresses similar fears of a violent outcome of Luther's vehemence and urges that Luther moderate his pen and his mind in such a way that he may be of the greatest benefit to the religion of the gospel. Many of those who oppose Luther do so for worldly reasons. He wishes that 'Luther would take a rest for some time from these controversies ... As it is, he burdens the humanities as well

*  *  *  *  *

65  Ep 1113:4–11
66  See xxvi–xxvii above.
67  Ep 1113:16–33

as himself with unpopularity, which is disastrous for us and does him no good.' Erasmus has become increasingly resentful of Luther specifically because he has endangered the programme of reforms based on the humanities that Erasmus has been striving to introduce into Christianity. His message for Luther: 'The truth need not always be put forward, and it makes a great difference how it is put forward'[68] – a statement that epitomizes the difference between the two. The letter reveals Erasmus' equivocal feelings and makes clear that the situation was becoming more difficult for him. He desired to affirm his orthodoxy in the face of the attacks upon it by the Louvain theologians. At the same time he strove to remain open to Luther because of Luther's close ties to the young German humanists.

Although Erasmus was genuinely defending the new humanist faculties at the universities in Germany and the Netherlands, he was also defending himself and others, presumably including Luther, who were applying the humanist method of textual analysis to the Scriptures.[69] In fact it was Erasmus' own emendation of the New Testament in his 1516 *Novum instrumentum* and especially the *Annotations* which accompanied the edition that aroused suspicion. His letter to Hermannus Buschius of 31 July 1520 charges, convincingly, that there was a concerted effort on the part of the conservative churchmen to hunt systematically through his *Annotations* for new readings that might be made to seem subversive to church doctrine, especially concerning the sacraments. He remarked after an episode he described in detail: 'This is an average specimen of those who rant against the humanities and dismiss everything they have not learnt themselves as "poetry."'[70]

On 1 August 1520 he wrote to Luther in reply to a letter or message now lost. Much of Erasmus' letter is devoted to relating his own problems and quarrels. He reports attacks on Luther and the influence of Dominicans at the French court and of Hoogstraten in the Netherlands. Then he reports that Henry VIII is mild and well disposed towards humane studies, 'but even so he listens every day to men such as I have just described. He asked me what I thought of you.' The king had wished that Luther had written with 'more prudence and moderation,' a wish shared, Erasmus says, by

* * * * *

68 Ep 1119:31–46
69 Actually, it would become clear to Erasmus in replying to Luther's *The Enslaved Will* in his *Hyperaspistes* that, however much Luther derived his theology from a study of the Scriptures, especially the letters of Paul, he adapted the rest of the Scriptures to his theology once that was established.
70 Ep 1126:369–70

those who wish Luther well. Erasmus then delivers a lecture to Luther on the dangers of his procedures: 'It is a serious matter to challenge men who cannot be overthrown without a major upheaval. And I fear upheavals of that kind all the more, because they so often burst out in a different direction from what was intended.'[71] Erasmus was beginning to sense the full consequences of Luther's actions and the alarmed campaign against him. He was not yet aware of the bull *Exsurge Domine*.

*From 'Exsurge Domine' to the Edict of Worms: summer 1520–summer 1521*
Although Leo x had issued *Exsurge Domine* on 15 June 1520, Erasmus' first mention of the bull, before it had actually been brought to the Netherlands by the papal legate Aleandro, was in a letter of 9 September 1520 to the chaplain of the bishop of Utrecht, Gerard Geldenhouwer. 'I am filled with forebodings about that wretched Luther; the conspiracy against him is strong everywhere,' he says early on. And a little later, 'Everyone was waiting for a verdict from the University of Paris; and now, lo and behold, the thing suddenly looks like issuing in a bull and a cloud of smoke. A bull is in print – a terrific affair, but the pope forbade its publication.' What Erasmus fears is that in a violent and organized effort to shut down Luther and his movement, no distinctions will be made, and humanism – especially his own Christian variety of humanism – will come under attack with just as much hysteria and force as will be turned against Luther. 'If only he had followed my advice,' he says, 'and refrained from that offensive and seditious stuff! He would have done more good, and been much less unpopular. One man's undoing would be a small matter; but if they are successful in this campaign, their insolence will be past all bearing. They will not rest until they have overthrown all knowledge of languages and all humane studies.' He also makes the first mention of pressure to get him to attack Luther: 'I am having nothing to do with this miserable business ... There is actually a bishopric waiting for me, if I will attack Luther in print.'[72]

At the same time that he is annoyed with Luther for the great troubles his unyielding demeanour is provoking, Erasmus also feels that Luther is being put down without adequate or equitable procedures. His charges have not been answered; his errors have not been corrected. As he will soon suggest, Erasmus believed that Leo x was pressured into issuing the bull on the basis of hasty conclusions by Eck and Prierias.

\* \* \* \* \*

71  Ep 1127A:64–6 and 68–73
72  Ep 1141:10–37

Erasmus was aware that Leo x had been informed of his letter to Luther of the previous year. In order to forestall further misunderstanding, he wrote to Leo on 13 September 1520, wishing to supply an antidote to some of the distorting voices he believed the pope was hearing. 'I observe that, in order to strengthen their own faction, some attempted to connect the cause of the humanities, Reuchlin's case, and my own with the case of Luther, although they have nothing in common.' He does not know Luther and has read but a few pages. Luther 'seemed to me admirably equipped as an expositor of the mystical Scripture in the ancient manner ... I therefore supported the good qualities in him and not the bad; or rather, through him I supported the glory of Christ.' He was one of the first, Erasmus says, 'to detect the risk that the affair might issue in public strife.' He had advised Froben not to print Luther's works and had urged his friends to warn Luther to promote peace in the church. When he answered Luther's letter, 'I told him in friendly fashion what I wished him to avoid. How I wish he had followed my advice!' Explaining away items that might have disturbed the pontiff, he attempted to put a favourable interpretation on his letter: 'I lent no countenance to Luther, even in the days when one was more or less free to support him. I only objected to the methods by which he was attacked, thinking not of him but of the authority of the theologians.'[73] Judging by Leo's reply of 15 January 1521, he had succeeded.[74]

It was probably inevitable that Erasmus would sound ambiguous and appear ambivalent concerning Luther, but it does not seem that in his own mind he was. From the point of view of the conservative theologians, especially those of Louvain and Cologne, Erasmus was seen as secretly favouring Luther, and they were likely to assume that he only pretended not to do so for tactical reasons, or simply to protect himself until it was clear whether Luther would succeed in overturning Catholic Christianity. Many younger humanists who admired Erasmus were also attracted to Luther. They thought that Erasmus had given sufficient indication that he, too, favoured Luther and that, if he appeared not to, this pretence was designed to deceive his Catholic enemies for self-protection. In other words, both his friends and his enemies thought that Erasmus was dissembling, but for very different reasons.

Erasmus, however, does not seem to have agreed. What he truly thought becomes clear in the three anonymous documents edited by Wallace Ferguson in the *Erasmi opuscula* of 1933 and now translated by Martin

* * * * *

73 Ep 1143:10–29, 72–4
74 Ep 1180 dated 15 January 1521

Lowry in CWE 71. Erasmus aimed to prevent a schism, to soften the harsh intransigence of both parties, and, by some sort of improvised mediation, to lead them to coexistence within the same church. He was objecting to the unwillingness of both the existing Catholic church and the rapidly separating Lutheran church-to-be to accept that there could be any legitimate existence of the other. He had and would continue to have doctrinal differences with Luther, but he strongly felt that these should be settled in the long, slow historical process of accommodation and ultimate concord that characterized the past progress of the church's (indeed of mankind's) history. Erasmus' immediate goal was to head off the drive towards the excommunication and banishment of Luther by questioning the legitimacy of the procedures leading to Leo's bull and those attempting to apply it. His hope was that by slowing down the process towards a final and total rupture the parties could be persuaded to submit the dispute to mediation.

The first document was 'Acts of the University of Louvain against Luther,' which appeared early in November in Cologne.[75] In the fall of 1519 both the University of Cologne and that of Louvain had published condemnations of Luther. After the papal legate Aleandro's arrival with *Exsurge Domine* in late September 1520, Luther's works were publicly burned in Louvain and elsewhere. The corporate body of the university was assembled to hear the legate read the bull. The 'Acts' are the purported minutes of the meeting but written by Erasmus in such as way as to cast doubt on the validity of the supposed endorsement of the bull. The theologians at Louvain proceeded as though the bull was approved when it had not been enacted, the legate Aleandro had not shown his commission, the bull had not been examined by the proper persons, and it had not been approved by all as is required. 'A few books were burned in the market-place, but everyone stood laughing.' Erasmus' enemy Nicolaas Baechem gave a stupid raving speech directed more against Erasmus than Luther.[76]

Then the authenticity of the bull itself is questioned. It was enacted in Rome in a disorderly and questionable manner with important figures opposing it. It was printed before it was proclaimed and differs from what Aleandro brought. Many items in it can be suspected of spuriousness. The style is 'fratalic,' characteristic of the '*fratres*' or 'friars' of the mendicant orders. It is full of solecisms, and no one believes in it except the theologians.[77]

* * * * *

75 *Acta Academiae Lovaniensis contra Lutherum* Ferguson 316–28 / CWE 71 101–5
76 *Acta* Ferguson 319–21 / CWE 71 102
77 *Acta* Ferguson 322–3 / CWE 71 103

'Acts' attempts to sully the reputations of Cajetanus and Aleandro, falsely claiming that the latter is Jewish and, as a relative of Judas, is about to betray the gospel. The statement is an example of Erasmus' anti-Semitism, as charged by Guido Kisch, a charge that Oberman weakens but still affirms.[78] According to 'Acts,' all of these attempts to damn Luther without a proper examination of his positions spring from hatred of the study of languages and good letters, as was evident in the campaign against Reuchlin led by Hoogstraten and taken up by Baechem and Latomus. The mendicant orders followed suit, 'fearing that someone might tell them to fast or work with their hands if the dominion of the Roman pope ... was to be weakened.' There is a conspiracy of many who attack Luther for different reasons. While it is agreed that there are errors in Aquinas, Scotus, Peter Lombard, Augustine, and others, similar errors in Luther are condemned. 'Suppose the matter was taken to the point where the theologians were given a free chance of saying, without reasoned evidence, "This is false, this is heretical, this is offensive." There are no books in which you cannot find something that might attract this sort of charge.'[79]

Erasmus, the anonymous author of 'Acts,' sees that an internal breakdown is occurring in the church which has led to this dangerous mishandling of Luther. He blames it on his two old enemies, the conservative scholastic theologians and the mendicant orders. Their target may well be the new theology he represents, which uses humanistic studies to restore the authentic scriptural texts and revives the early orthodox theologians of antiquity whose mode of theologizing derived from their own rhetorical, classical backgrounds. This new theology seeks not simply a truer knowledge of the Scriptures but the affective generation of charity inspired by reading and preaching from them. Yet the conservative theologians' unintended target may well be the unity of the church and the authority and leadership of the bishops within the church, including that of the Roman bishop. It is noticeable that Erasmus' major supporters within the church were in many instances bishops. His last paragraphs speak directly to this. The pope has been flattered and ill-advised. 'All the writers flatter the pope

* * * * *

78 Heiko A. Oberman *The Roots of Anti-Semitism in the Age of the Renaissance* (Philadelphia 1984) 38–40. Cf Guido Kisch *Erasmus' Stellung zu Juden und Judentum* (Tübingen 1969) and Cornelis Augustijn *Erasme et les Juifs* (Lausanne 1979). On the relationship of Erasmus and Aleandro, see André Godin 'Erasme, Aléandre: une étrange familiarité' in *Actes du colloque international Erasme Tours 1986* (Geneva 1990) 249–74. See also *Acta* 323–4 / CWE 71 103–4.
79 *Acta* Ferguson 324–6 / CWE 71 104–5

with the most disgusting extravagance. The first in the field was Cardinal Cajetan; then came Sylvester Prierias; Thomas Todischus was third, the fourth a Franciscan named Augustinus.' Again the mendicants: three Dominicans and a Franciscan! The Louvain theologians did not publish their nonsense, though Christ did not disdain to teach the humble; they 'think themselves too grand to teach a man of high character and learning [meaning Luther]. If all the bishops go on winking an eye at this sort of conduct, as some are doing at present, they will soon find themselves in a position where the friars have seized absolute control and joined hands with the pope to trample like tyrants on the heads of their bishops.'[80] That is the first danger, and he calls upon the bishops to intervene.

Another, second, danger is greater and harder to overcome. People will not oppose the bull, because they fear to resist the pope. The thing to do is to cast doubt on the pope's involvement and hence on the authenticity of the bull. At least it can be said that he was badly informed. If Aleandro's role is examined, it may well turn out that the wicked Jew forged it. The bull, even if it is authentic, should not be acted on until the pope is better advised. 'Otherwise, there is a danger that this affair will provoke serious disorders throughout the Christian world.' Erasmus was certainly prophetic in this warning, for he had consistently worried that religious peace would be destroyed. He had good reason. 'It's easy enough to remove Luther from the libraries. It's not going to be nearly so easy to remove him from men's hearts, unless those unanswered criticisms of his are met, and unless the pope states the opposing argument with the evidence of Holy Scripture behind him ... Truth will not be crushed, even if Luther is.'[81]

Erasmus' plan to seek a mediation of the conflict was not to be accepted, and it seems not to have been known to more than a handful of intimates. Events, guided by far more powerful persons, would soon take over without his participation to any degree. But as Ferguson suggests, Erasmus did apparently encourage Frederick the Wise, the elector of Saxony, in his protective actions towards Luther. Erasmus knew that after Luther's interview with Cajetanus in the fall of 1518 the elector Frederick had prevented Luther's arrest. On 4 November 1520 Frederick met with the papal legates, Aleandro and Caracciolo, who demanded that Frederick punish Luther severely or arrest him and turn him over to them. On 5 November Frederick met with Erasmus in Cologne and sought his advice. This came in the form known as the 'Axiomata' or 'Brief Notes ... for the Cause

* * * * *

80 *Acta* Ferguson 326–8 / CWE 71 105
81 *Acta* Ferguson 326–8 / CWE 71 105

of Martin Luther,' a list of reasons for caution before the elector decided what to do about Luther.[82] Erasmus' 'Brief Notes' repeated the doubts expressed in his 'Acts' concerning the legitimacy of the bull and warned that since 'certain persons are taking advantage of the pope's good nature,' it would be best to strengthen the pope's position by avoiding hasty decisions and settling the question 'through the sane advice of unbiased and discreet persons.' Erasmus notes that 'the world is thirsting for the gospel truth, and seems to be borne on its way by some supernatural desire,' a desire that 'should perhaps not be resisted by such hateful means.' The next day Frederick told the legates that although he did not favour Luther, he was not sure he had been authoritatively condemned. Erasmus was probably right that by this date suppressing Luther would not have suppressed his movement. In any case, as Ferguson wrote, 'there can be little doubt that Erasmus' advice was of real service to Luther in encouraging Frederick to continue his policy of protection'[83] – a policy reaffirmed in May 1521 after the Edict of Worms when Frederick provided Luther asylum in his castle at Wartburg.

In the third document, known as the *Consilium* or 'Minute Composed by a Person Who Seriously Wishes Provisions to be Made for the Reputation of the Roman Pontiff and the Peace of the Church,'[84] Erasmus argued that only some kind of neutral judgment such as he would propose might reunite the Christian world. A draft of this document had been presented to him by Johannes Faber, a Dominican theologian of Augsburg and an imperial councillor to the previous emperor, Maximilian. Erasmus revised and emended it in his recognizable style and incorporated into it his own previously conceived ideas for a mediation. However, it was issued in the name of Faber and presented at Charles v's court in Cologne this same fall of 1520 to the electors Albert of Brandenberg and Frederick the Wise. It was then printed with the name of no author attached.

The proposal, based on the assumption that Leo x had been misled by his advisors in issuing *Exsurge Domine*, was that the pope should be persuaded to yield his right of investigating matters of faith to a commission of neutral arbitrators to be chosen by the emperor Charles v, King Henry VIII of England, and the king of Hungary. The commission should be composed of 'men of outstanding knowledge, proven virtue, and unstained honour . . .

\* \* \* \* \*

82 *Axiomata Erasmi pro causa Martini Lutheri* Ferguson 336–7 / CWE 71 106–7
83 Ferguson 333
84 *Consilium cuiusdam ex animo cupientis esse consultum et Romani Pontificis dignitati et Christianae religionis tranquillitati* Ferguson 352–61 / CWE 71 108–12

They should read Luther's books through and through with care, hear him in person, and pronounce their decision in his presence. And that decision will be final.'[85]

A number of pronouncements in the 'Minute' suggest that Erasmus was hoping that by avoiding a violent conflict between Luther and the Catholic authorities he might accomplish his own, more moderate reform program. For example, the 'Minute' points out: 'The world seems also to be tired of a theological method which has sunk too far into the niceties of formal logic, and to be athirst for the message of the Gospels. If the doors are not opened to it, the Christian world will break in by force. So even if Luther's ideas are completely rejected, changes should still be brought into this sophistical theology.'[86]

Further clarification of Erasmus' ideas of mediation are to be found in a letter of 9 November 1520 that he wrote to Konrad Peutinger from Cologne, where he and Faber had shown the 'Minute' at Charles v's court. The letter was delivered by Faber and asked Peutinger's assistance for Faber. It discussed the 'Minute' in some detail, stressing the virtue of a via media and the dangers arising from a confrontation of extremes:

> I perceive that things have been handled hitherto in a very different way
> from that which commended itself to men of sense. Even if every word Luther
> wrote were true, he has written in such a way as to prevent the truth from
> doing any good. On the other side, those who have rushed into this business
> headlong have behaved before the public so badly, that even if they had an
> excellent case, they could only do it harm by the clumsiness of their support
> ... In short, these stormy times need some great master of exceptional skill to
> guide the course of the affair, so that it is neither overwhelmed by the billows
> nor driven on to a shallow shore; one who can avoid Scylla ... and not be
> sucked into Charybdis, who can cut down this evil monster in such a way
> that it does not grow afresh hydra-headed.[87]

In his future writings against Luther, Erasmus will use the figure of Scylla and Charybdis many times and strongly urge moderation. Luther replied, as Erasmus' theological critics would also reply, that where there

* * * * *

85 *Consilium* Ferguson 359–60 / CWE 71 111. For the circumstances and plan and
   further proposals of Erasmus see Ferguson 338–48 and CWE 71 xliv–xlvi and
   99–100.
86 *Consilium* Ferguson 359 / CWE 71 111
87 Ep 1156:69–75 and 104–8

was a question of divine truth, no compromise would be acceptable. What was being overlooked was that the principle of accommodation or adaptation was for Erasmus itself a religious principle. It was based on Christ's teachings and actions in the Gospels, where charity and forbearance were inculcated and inspired. It is fully consistent with Erasmus' humanistic and rhetorical theology, so under attack, that he should urge the authorities to give Luther every chance to recognize his errors, if any, and be encouraged to change his soul. So too should the pope wish for this manifestation of Christian piety.

So he argued in his letter to Cardinal Lorenzo Campeggi of 6 December 1520 and elsewhere. For Erasmus truth could be consistent with expediency and sometimes would be destroyed by inexpedient speech, which might be misunderstood or provoke destructive reactions. He was defending to Campeggi and the curia the caution he had urged upon Luther in his letter of the summer of 1519. He warned Compeggi: 'Indeed, while it can never be lawful to go against truth, it may sometimes be expedient to conceal it in the circumstances. And it is always of the first importance how timely, how opportune, and how well judged your production of it is.'[88]

Meanwhile Luther had made it clear enough that no such compromise or policy of moderation as Erasmus had been proposing was any longer possible. On 6 October 1520 he published his *De captivitate Babylonica ecclesiae*,[89] attacking the legitimacy of four of the seven sacraments and radically revising the remaining three. On 10 December he held a public burning of Gratian's *Decretum* and of Leo's bull, and shortly thereafter his *Assertion of All the Articles of Martin Luther Which Were Quite Recently Condemned by a Bull of Leo X*[90] was issued, reasserting all of the heresies and errors with which he had been charged. It was against article thirty-six of the *Assertion* that Erasmus' *Discussion of Free Will* would be addressed. Erasmus' first surviving mention of Luther's *Babylonian Captivity* was in a letter of 25 February 1521 to Nicolaas Everaerts: 'His *De captivitate Babylonica* alienates many people, and he is proposing something more frightful every day

* * * * *

88 Ep 1167:182–5

89 WA 6 497–573 / LW 36 11–126

90 *Assertio omnium articulorum Martini Lutheri per bullam Leonis X novissimam damnatorum* (WA 7 91–151). LW 32 does not contain an English translation of the Latin *Assertio* but translates instead Luther's German version, which does not have the critical language on free will and necessity in article 36 that provoked Erasmus' *Discussion of Free Will*. See *Defense and Explanation of All the Articles* LW 32 7–99. The Latin of article 36 has been translated at 299–309 in this volume.

... Luther destroys himself with his own weapons.'[91] Erasmus first mentions the *Assertion* in a letter to Luigi Marliano of 25 March 1521 in which he tries to refute the charge that Luther has drawn heavily on his books. 'This is a shameless invention,' he says, 'and the very first of his articles [in his *Assertion*] gives the lie to their obvious falsehood. Where do I suggest that whatever we do is sinful?' – a major premise of Luther's denial of free will.[92]

On 3 January 1521 Leo x officially excommunicated Luther. On 26 May 1521, the day after the Diet of Worms was adjourned, the emperor Charles v signed the Edict of Worms placing Luther under the ban of the empire. Erasmus was well aware that the situation had drastically changed.

*Erasmus 'a heretic to both sides': summer 1521–winter 1523*
From the year 1521 on, although Erasmus knew that the possibility of a reconciliation was minuscule, he continued to urge a policy of moderation. He was besieged by letters both from supporters of the papal excommunication and imperial ban on Luther and from supporters of Luther, urging him to make a public stand for one position or the other. Three letters, out of the many he wrote to all sides, may serve to illuminate his position: one to a former friend (now a close collaborator of Luther), one to the Louvain theologians, and one to an old friend at the papal curia.

His letter of 10 May 1521 to his former friend, Justus Jonas, whom he greatly admired but who was becoming a valued collaborator and intimate of Luther, speaks of the moral breakdown and the neglect of scriptural study among the princes of the church: 'The word of God was forced to become the slave of human appetites, and the simple faith of the multitude was distorted to the profit of a few.' The widespread awareness of this commercialization of religion had provided 'such a favourable reception [of Luther] ... as has fallen to the lot of no other mortal, I suppose, for many centuries.' Herein lies the basis for Erasmus' own reform efforts, which were directed against the abuses springing from neglect of Scripture and moral corruption, not, as was true of Luther, against fundamental doctrine and established church authority.

He wonders what led Luther to write with such freedom of invective against the pope, the universities, philosophy, the mendicant orders. Having challenged so many influential people, how could he expect any

\* \* \* \* \*

91  Ep 1186:8–26
92  Ep 1195:72–4; Erasmus is probably referring to the opening of article 36, where Luther does say this, rather than to article 1, as n20 in cwe 8 assumes.

other outcome than what was taking place against him? Whether or not Luther was speaking the truth, his manner had rendered his message unacceptable. Erasmus was accepting the reality of what he had predicted and feared about Luther. What therefore was the point of dealing in paradoxes, and putting some things forward in language that was bound to give even more offence at first sight than when regarded steadily at close quarters? For some things are rendered offensive by a kind of wilful obscurity. What was the point of a savage torrent of invective directed against men whom it was unwise to treat like that if he wished to make them better, and impious if he did it to provoke them and set the whole world by the ears? Erasmus goes on to give a description, which is fundamental to his theology, of the way Christ, Peter, Paul, and Augustine addressed the persons they wished to convert or to reform.[93] This letter to Jonas was intended to inform his humanist friends who had joined Luther why he could no longer support them even to the moderate extent he had before.

A second letter was sent to the theologians of Louvain in June–July 1521. Its aim was to pacify them about his role in the affair of Luther, since some of them had once more begun to attack him in a threatening manner:

> One thing we must avoid, even at this late hour: we must not snap at each
> other till each proves the other's undoing. Civil strife has never been to my
> taste. I have never had a hand in any faction, neither Reuchlin's, nor Luther's;
> the glory of Christ I have always supported to the best of my power. To your
> university I have been no disgrace and no embarrassment. Luther's pamphlets
> I have done more to resist than any mortal man, not that I am unaware that
> much of his advice is sound, but because I see that an honourable silence is
> better than an ill-starred attempt at reform. In all things that truly or falsely
> pass under his name, there is not one letter that belongs to me.

This denial was important because of the widespread tendency either to attribute Luther's writings to Erasmus or to blame him for the rise of Luther. This misunderstanding arose from Erasmus' outspoken criticisms of the moral corruption of the clergy in *The Praise of Folly* and other works, as well as from his repudiation of scholasticism, his attempts to establish a sounder scriptural base for the sacraments, and his dislike of the mendicant orders. Hence it became necessary for him both to promote fairness in the church's response to Luther and at the same time to differentiate

* * * * *

93 Ep 1202:22–31, 41–7, 56–62, 73–140

himself from Luther now that his plea for mediation and conciliation had been brushed aside. Writing to the Louvain theologians, he was attempting to head off further criticism from the group which had been most vocal in questioning his new approach to theology. He stresses his resistance to pressures to join Luther, even though Luther's opponents, especially the monks, had been so vociferous in attacking him that they almost drove him to do so. But none of this has made him abandon his position. Examine everything he has said on Luther, he says, and 'you will find nothing except my dislike of sudden and violent uproar in public places and my preference for settling questions without setting the world by the ears.'[94]

A third letter concerns Erasmus' response to direct requests from the papal curia for him to reinforce his assurances that he was not of Luther's party by employing his enormous talents in criticizing Luther. This demand came from Pope Leo x himself, among others. On 15 January 1521, shortly after he had excommunicated Luther, Leo replied to Erasmus' explanation of what he had really meant in his widely circulated and much discussed letter to Luther:

> It would be well if we might see all other men no less certainly convinced than we are ourselves of your loyalty and good will towards this Holy See and our common faith in God. Never was the time more opportune or the cause more just for setting your erudition and your powers of mind against the impious, nor is anyone better suited than yourself – such is our high opinion of your learning – for this praiseworthy task.[95]

On 18 June 1521 an old friend now an official at the papal curia, Paolo Bombace, reinforced Leo's earlier plea, informing him how well disposed Leo was towards him and how much more he would be if Erasmus would write an attack on Luther:

> If then you have him so well disposed to you while you say nothing in defence of his just and holy cause, what result might you not expect if you were to take up arms and do battle vigorously, as you know so well how to do, in his [that is, the pope's] behalf, or rather in behalf of truth itself, which your supporters of Luther ... are striving to uproot by godless methods and entirely overthrow? This is what most people expected of you.[96]

\* \* \* \* \*

94  Ep 1217:103–29
95  Ep 1180:17–22
96  Ep 1213:42–50

In his reply of 23 September 1521, Erasmus describes the difficulties that stand in the way of his writing, but also suggests that he might undertake such a task within a few years:

> If up to now I have published nothing in opposition to Luther, there are many reasons. These I need not here recount, but the chief reason has been, that I have simply not had the time to read what Luther writes, so busy am I with revisions of my own works. And you see how prolific he is. Nor is he by himself; he has a hundred hands. Nor would it be enough to run through his works once; they would have to be read over and over again. Even that would not suffice. Many people everywhere publish attacks on him, every one of which I should have to look into if I wished to do my job properly ... I am entirely engrossed in revising the New Testament and some other works of mine ... But soon, I hope, I shall be blessed with a little more leisure ... To strengthen the position of the gospel truth I would gladly give even my life. Nor am I ignorant how much I owe to the pope's unheard-of kindness to me personally. If I am granted three or four more years of life, I will either die in the attempt or I will make him agree that I was not wholly ungrateful. His exceptional goodness deserves to be honoured in print by all the learned world.[97]

There is a little ambiguity here as to whether Erasmus had in mind a book honouring Leo x or a response to Luther. But a few lines above he spoke of seeking permission from Aleandro to read Luther and he asks Bombace to get him the pope's permission to do so. Hence he seems to say that, in spite of all the delays and excuses, he intended to write a work that would be directed in some manner against Luther.

Moreover, Erasmus had recently made similar intimations on three occasions: in a letter to William Blount of early summer 1521, in a letter to Pierre Barbier of 13 August 1521, and in a letter to William Warham of 23 August 1521.[98] It seems clear enough that in the summer and fall of 1521 Erasmus had it in mind to write something in connection with the affair of Luther. Despite the pope's excommunication of 3 January 1521, the events at the Diet of Worms, and the imperial Edict of Worms, Erasmus intended to write in such a way as to contribute to a restoration of concord and an ending of the schism. But first he had to carry through the third (and most definitive) edition of the Latin translation and annotations in his

* * * * *

97 Ep 1236:84–92, 124–38
98 Epp 1219:135–7, 1225:330–4, 1228:54–6

New Testament. For this reason, and because he could no longer tolerate the endless attacks from various theologians at Louvain, he set out at the end of October for Basel and arrived there 15 November 1521 to begin a stay of many years.

Within two weeks, on 29 November 1521, he wrote to Willibald Pirckheimer about the loss of civility and of the fair hopes for the humanities that had been gained before Luther:

> I cannot help wondering what god swayed Luther's mind so that, while so many friends tried to deter him from provoking the pope, he has written always with more and more asperity ... Men who write like this and utter these threats should have had troops at their disposal, had they wished to remain unharmed. But see what results they have achieved! They have distorted humane studies with a burden of unpopularity, and every man of good will who is seriously attached to the truths of the Gospel is within range of perilous suspicions. They have opened a great rift which divides the world everywhere, which will last maybe for many years and get steadily worse. In return for a clumsy attempt at liberty, slavery is redoubled, to such a degree that it is forbidden even to maintain the truth.[99]

Still yearning to find concord and a peaceful solution of the new schism, he holds Luther responsible for the hostility he encounters against his own humanistic goals for Christian revival. Erasmus' pessimism was prophetic and his vision of concord the dimmest of hopes. The wars ravaging Italy since 1494 had spread northward and soon would add a religious ingredient to their motivation. On 1 December 1521, Pope Leo x died. On 9 January 1522 Adriaan Floriszoon was elected Pope Adrian vi. The new pope was a fellow Netherlander and had known Erasmus at Louvain. Although there had been friendly contacts, Erasmus was concerned that Adrian, who had been chancellor of the university, might be too close in his thinking to the Louvain theologians who had been hostile to him. It is unlikely that he knew of Adrian's election when he again wrote to Willibald Pirckheimer on 12 February 1522: 'For a long time now I have been waiting to see what will be the upshot of this sorry business over Luther. Unquestionably some spirit is at work in this affair, whether it be of God, I do not know. I, who have never supported Luther, except in so far as one supports a man by urging him towards better things, am a heretic to both sides.'[100]

\* \* \* \* \*

99 Ep 1244:6–21
100 Ep 1259:6–10

The danger on the orthodox side could come from either the pope or the emperor, and Erasmus sought to ensure that each of these powerful figures continued to hold him in cordial admiration. Turning first to the emperor, he dedicated his forthcoming *Paraphrase on Matthew* to him in a preface of 13 January 1522. Charles acknowledged it on 1 April 1522.[101] In early April Erasmus attempted to travel from Basel to the Netherlands to greet Charles before he moved his court to Spain, but he fell ill on the journey and had to return. He quickly sent off two letters to Pedro Ruiz de la Mota and to Luis Núñez Coronel, both influential figures at Charles' court (21 April 1522). To each he disclaimed any support of Luther. To de la Mota he wrote: 'For my own part, neither death nor life shall tear me from the society of the Catholic church,' and he assured Coronel: 'I would sooner meet death ten times over than start or encourage a perilous schism.'[102] He also wrote to Jean Glapion, the emperor's confessor, at greater length, mentioning for the first time, 'a short treatise on how to end this business of Luther.'[103]

Adrian VI did not arrive in Rome until August. Erasmus' first approach to him was through the preface to his edition of the *Commentaries on the Psalms* of Arnobius the Younger. In a world torn with conflicts – antagonisms between princes and perilous differences between sects and schisms – and menaced by the Turks, Adrian offers hope 'that even now the storm-clouds may be dissipated and clear shining and tranquillity return.' In this incantatory introduction Erasmus looks forward to the pope playing on the strings of the Christian word as the Psalmist on his lyre:

> surely Christ's music has words and spells with which we can charm out of hearts the love of things transient and charm into its place the love of heavenly things ... Does not the Christian psalmist command modes whereby he can recall the princes who are endlessly at loggerheads in these most crazy wars to the love of peace? ... But in my view no modes are more powerful than the music of the Psalms; for in this book ... that divine spirit ... enshrined certain musical modes of greatest power, by which we might be changed into a frame of mind worthy of Christ, provided only that there is someone at hand who can wake the strings of this psaltery with proper skill. This is the special duty of bishops and priests, and yet every individual might learn to

\* \* \* \* \*

101 Epp 1255 and 1270
102 Epp 1273:30–1 and 1274:62–4
103 Ep 1275:23–4

play for himself ... Oh that your Holiness might be our new David ... who not only played himself but taught many other singers to do the same.[104]

One can imagine the effect on Adrian of this powerful and inspiring preface. Erasmus bares the secret of his own theology here, for it is the art of the charmer who by the depths of his perceptions of the divine message in the Scriptures leads the souls of his fellow Christians to charity and thus to salvation, as God does through the same Scriptures and Christ taught us by his word and example. It will become clear that this is the theology that he will be opposing to Luther's.

Although it took several months for the exchange to occur, there is no doubt of Adrian's warm response. Erasmus had sent a brief but masterly letter of presentation to the pope with a copy of the Arnobius including the preface. In it he declared: 'Hitherto in religious matters I have shown the spirit proper to an orthodox Christian, and so I shall do to the day of my death. If I can persuade neither side to approve my position, I am confident at least of securing Christ's assent that my conscience is clear.'[105] Adrian's letter of 1 December 1522 reassured Erasmus: 'When you say in your letter that you fear lest some men's enmity and malicious gossip may have made us suspect you of a connection with the party of Luther, we wish to put your mind at rest in this regard.' Then he adds, 'The affection however which we feel for you and the concern we have for your reputation and true glory prompt us to urge you to employ in an attack on these new heresies the literary skill with which a generous providence has endowed you so effectually; for there are many reasons why you ought properly to believe that the task has been reserved by God especially for you.' The pope seeks to persuade Erasmus that he should write and draw off Luther's followers from the punishments of this and the next world that will otherwise await them.[106]

While waiting for Adrian's reply, Erasmus wrote another letter to the pope on 22 December 1522. He repeated what he had said in letters of August and September. 'If your Holiness instructs me, I will make so bold as to give you an outline in a secret letter of my own proposal ... for putting an end to this evil in such a way that it will not easily sprout again ... If there is anything in it worth having, it can be made use of; if there is

* * * * *

104  Ep 1304:371–2, 414–37
105  Ep 1310:38–42
106  Ep 1324:14–16 and 24–9

nothing, it will be known only to us two, and there will be no risk in suppressing it.'[107] Adrian lost no time in replying on 23 January 1523: 'The
greater the speed and secrecy with which you can expound to us your policy in this regard, the greater the service you will render to God and the
more we shall be pleased.'[108]

Erasmus' plan was probably very different from what the pope had in
his mind. Adrian wanted an unmasking of Luther that would reveal his evil
in such a way that his humanist supporters, many of whom were former
or still friends of Erasmus, would turn away from Luther and return to fi-
delity to Rome. Erasmus still hoped that, as in his 'Minute,' some sort of understanding and concord could be negotiated between the two sides.[109] He
could no longer think of an arbitration commission appointed by Charles
v, Henry viii, and the king of Hungary, as Charles had issued the Edict
of Worms and Henry viii had written his *Assertion of the Seven Sacraments*
against Luther.[110] What he now had in mind was a veiled, indirect arbitration by means of three dialogues that he could write as described in his
catalogue of his works in a letter to Johann von Botzheim of 30 January
1523:

> Some time ago I began three dialogues in which I attempted a discussion rather
> than a confrontation[111] on the question of Martin Luther, but under altered
> names: Luther's part will be taken by Thrasymachus, the other side by Eubu-
> lus, and Philalethes will act as arbiter. The first dialogue investigates whether
> this approach would be expedient, even had every word Luther writes been
> true. The second will discuss some of his doctrines. The third will display a
> way of bringing this conflict to a peaceful end in such a way that it cannot

*  *  *  *  *

107 Ep 1329:13–23
108 Ep 1338:43–5
109 See xliv–xlv above.
110 Though he was reluctant because he was faced with French invasions of Spain
and the Netherlands, Charles v was persuaded to sign the Edict of Worms
placing Luther under the ban of the empire on 26 May 1521. Henry viii's
*Assertio septem sacramentorum adversus Martinum Lutherum* (London: R. Pynson,
12 July 1521) was a direct reply to Luther's *De captivitate Babylonica ecclesiae*
(Wittenberg: M. Lotter, c 6 October 1520) which attacked and repudiated all
but three of the seven sacraments and denounced the Roman papacy. Thus
two of the three rulers who in Erasmus' plan were to appoint a board of
impartial arbitrators had committed themselves to either the suppression or
the complete repudiation of Luther and his doctrines.
111 Latin 'collationem verius quam disputationem' (Allen I 34:23–4). Erasmus uses
the word that became part of the title of *De libero arbitrio* διατριβή *sive collatio*.

easily break out again in future. The question will be discussed between the two of them without scurrilities, with no wrangling and no disguise; the bare truth only will be put forward, in a simple and countrified way, with such fairness and such moderation that there will be more danger, I think, from the indignation of the opposite party, who will interpret my mildness as collusion with the enemy, than from Luther himself, if he has any grain of the sense with which many people credit him – and I for one wish him joy of it if he has it, and hope he may acquire it if not.[112]

Unfortunately, if the response to his *Discussion of Free Will* is any measure of the hypothetical response to these dialogues, Erasmus was right about the Catholic reaction and wrong in his hope about Luther.

It seems probable that the dialogues as described embodied the approach Erasmus intended to offer Adrian, but his letter of 22 March 1523 breaks off without revealing his proposal. Much of it consists of an effort to show that he is unfit to undertake a defence of Catholicism against Luther because both sides have turned against him and he no longer has influence:

Time was when hundreds of letters described me as greatest of the great, prince of the world of literature, bright star of Germany, luminary of learning, champion of humane studies, bulwark of a more genuine theology. Now I am never mentioned, or am painted in far different colours ... But your Holiness suggests a remedy for these misfortunes. 'Come to Rome,' you say, 'or write some really savage attack on Luther. Declare war on the whole of Luther's party' ... If I join you, I shall perhaps live or write in greater safety; but that is to think of myself and not of what is at stake. If I write against Luther with some moderation and courtesy, it will look as though I am trifling with him; and if I imitate his own style and challenge Luther's party to a pitched battle, will this do anything but stir up a hornets' nest? ... Thus far, you will say, I hear nothing but complaints; what I am waiting for is a plan. Yet even what I have said hitherto is part of a plan. In any case, for a start, I perceive that many think this trouble should be healed by severity; but I fear the outcome shows that this plan has long been a mistake ... This cancer has gone too far to be curable by the knife or cautery. In former times, I agree, that is how the Wycliffite party was suppressed in England by the royal power; but it was suppressed rather than extinguished ... At any rate, if it has been decided

\* \* \* \* \*

112 Ep 1341A 1338–53. These lines are not from the section of the letter where there are later insertions.

to overwhelm this evil by imprisonment and scourging, by confiscation, exile, excommunication, and death, there will be no need of any plan from me.[113]

Erasmus spoke his mind honestly to the pope. There is evidence that Adrian was not unsympathetic to reform, as is reported in Pirckheimer's letter to Erasmus of 17 February 1523,[114] but, surrounded by men who saw little need for intra-ecclesial reform, and by warring rulers, the pope could do nothing in the little more than a year in which he reigned. Erasmus heard no more from Adrian before the pope's death on 1 September 1523.

*Deepening conflict: spring 1523*

It was by now too late for Erasmus to repair the breach with Luther, and he was becoming more and more worried that his former humanist friends working for the Froben press in Basel would somehow falsely portray him as secretly a supporter of Luther. This anxiety was increased by the arrival of Ulrich von Hutten, the poet and militant supporter of Luther, in Basel in November 1522 and by Hutten's departure to nearby Mulhouse in February 1523. Rumours were circulated there that Erasmus had avoided him in Basel to preserve his good relations with Rome. Erasmus had also become aware of Luther's deeply hostile attitude towards him. On 9 September 1521 Luther had written to Spalatinus:

> Neither Capito's nor Erasmus' opinion moves me in the least. They are only doing what I suspected. Indeed I have been afraid that some day I should have some trouble with one or the other of them. For I saw that Erasmus was far from the knowledge of grace, since in all his writings he is not concerned for the cross but for peace. He thinks that everything should be discussed and handled in a civil manner and with a certain benevolent kindliness. But Behemoth [Satan] pays no attention and nothing improves by this. I remember when [Erasmus] said in his preface to the New Testament, and he must have been thinking of himself, 'The Christian despises glory.' I thought in my heart: Erasmus, I am afraid you deceive yourself. It is a great thing to despise glory. But his way of despising glory was to think lightly of it, not to bear the contempt that others put upon him. Despising glory, however, is nothing, if it is only in words; it is even less than nothing if only in thought. The kingdom of God consists in power, says Paul [1 Cor 4:20] . . . Their writings accomplish nothing because they refrain from chiding, biting, and giving offense. For

\* \* \* \* \*

113 Ep 1352:39–43, 136–8, 161–2, 168–82
114 Ep 1344:70–8

when the popes and bishops are admonished in a civil manner they think it
is flattering and keep on as if they possessed the right to remain uncorrected
and incorrigible, content that they are feared and that no one dares reproach
them.[115]

This was, of course, written while Luther was at the Wartburg, after the
circulation of *The Babylonian Captivity* and the Edict of Worms, and also
after Erasmus' efforts to protect him through the Elector Frederick and the
'Minute.'

What Luther reveals in the letter to Spalatinus goes far in explaining his own actions (and probably something of the success of his reform).
It also reveals how fundamental was the difference of his idea of Christianity from that of Erasmus. Luther's church was the 'church militant,' not
the church of concord. It is probable that Erasmus knew of this letter. But
more certainly he knew of what Luther wrote on 28 May 1522 in a letter without an addressee and intended for broad circulation, which became
known as Doctor Martin Luther's Judgment of Erasmus of Rotterdam (*Iudicium D. Martini Lutheri de Erasmo Roterodamo*). The probable recipient was
Duke George of Saxony, for it begins by speaking of Mosellanus, Erasmus'
admirer and professor of humanities at Leipzig in Duke George's domain.

I knew before that Mosellanus agreed with Erasmus on predestination, for he
is altogether an Erasmian. I, on the contrary, think that Erasmus knows less,
or seems to know less, about predestination than the schools of the sophists
have known. There is no reason why I should fear my own downfall if I do
not change my opinion. Erasmus is not to be feared either in this or in almost
any other really important subject that pertains to Christian doctrine. Truth
is mightier than eloquence, the spirit stronger than genius, faith greater than
learning. As Paul says: 'The foolishness of God is wiser than men' [1 Cor
1:25] ... I shall not challenge Erasmus; if challenged myself once or twice, I
shall not hurry to strike back. I think it unwise, however, for him to array the
power of his eloquence against me, for I am afraid he will not find in Luther
another Lefèvre, he will not be able to glory over me as he glories over him
... But if he casts the die, he will see that Christ fears neither the gates of hell
nor the powers of the air. Poor stammerer that I am, I shall parry the eloquent
Erasmus with all confidence, caring nothing for his authority, reputation, or
good will. I know what is in this man just as I know the plots of Satan; but

\* \* \* \* \*

115 WA *Briefwechsel* 2 387–9 no 429 / LW 48 305–7 no 96

I expect him to reveal more clearly from day to day what grudge he nurses against me.[116]

This letter signalled to Erasmus that Luther had demonized him as a minion of Satan and that he expected Erasmus to attack him.

It would be an essential part of Luther's stance in his reply to Erasmus, *The Enslaved Will*, that Erasmus has the advantage of being a rhetorician but that Luther, the theologian, speaks the truth. On 20 June 1523 he wrote to Oecolampadius in Basel, a former friend of Erasmus and a man whose moves towards Protestantism Erasmus was finding to be increasingly embarrassing:

> May the Lord strengthen you in your task of lecturing on Isaiah, even though this irritates Erasmus, as someone has written to me. Do not be disturbed by his displeasure. What Erasmus thinks, or pretends to think, in his judgment of spiritual matters is abundantly shown in his booklets from the first to the last. Although I myself feel his stings all over, yet since he pretends not to be my open foe, I, too, pretend not to understand his cunning; however, I understand him better than he thinks. He has accomplished what he was called to do: he has introduced among us [the knowledge] of languages, and has called us away from sacrilegious studies. Perhaps he himself will die with Moses in the plains of Moab, for he does not advance the better studies (those which pertain to piety). I greatly wish he would restrain himself from dealing with Holy Scripture and writing his Paraphrases, for he is not up to the task; he takes up the time of [his] readers in vain, and he hinders them in studying Scripture. He has done enough in showing us the evil. He is (in my opinion) unable to show us the good and to lead us into the promised land. But why do I talk so much of Erasmus? Only so that you will not be influenced by his name and authority, but rather be happy when you feel something displeases him in this matter of Scripture. For he is a man who is unable to have, or does not want to have, a right judgment in these matters, as almost the whole world is beginning to perceive of him.[117]

In other words it was time for Erasmus to retire from public life! But this was not going to happen. There would be a lengthy debate between them in Erasmus' *A Discussion of Free Will*, Luther's *The Enslaved Will*, and Erasmus' *Hyperaspistes*, and even after that Erasmus suffered through

* * * * *

116 WA *Briefwechsel* 2 544–5 no 499 / LW 49 7–8 no 122
117 WA *Briefwechsel* 3 96–7 no 626 / LW 49 43–4 no 133

ten more years of battling about Luther. He could not deny how bitterly Luther resented him and how hopeless any effort at reconciliation of the two branches of Christianity had now become. And yet he would persist.

He expresses in detail his new judgments in a letter to Marcus Laurinus. To his deadly enemies among the Dominican inquisitors and the theologians of Louvain there had to be added Luther and his followers. Allen and Estes believe the first part of this letter, up to line 650, to have been drawn from earlier letters. They consider the section examined here to belong to late winter or early spring of 1523, close in time to Erasmus' final letter to Adrian.[118] Erasmus speaks of the rumours coming from both sides intended to provoke him to reveal either that he is secretly Lutheran or that he is financially dependent on Rome:

> If I could have been dragged into this battle by rewards, that would have happened long ago; I was deterred by thoughts of the size of the task on the one hand and my own weakness on the other ... They had put it about that the supreme pontiff had written some sort of an attack on me ... Of course the purpose of this imaginary pope is to provoke me to write or say something unwise ... The other party too tell their own tales ... These men had lately spread a rumour that many of Luther's party were flocking to Basel for the sake of asking my opinion, and even that Luther himself was in hiding here ... Before this division reached its present bitterness I used to enjoy literary friendships with nearly all the scholars in Germany and greatly, to be sure, did I appreciate them. Several of them have now grown cool towards me and some are entirely estranged; there are even those who openly declare themselves my enemies and foretell my destruction. I also enjoyed contacts with many who now take a more savage line against Luther than I could wish.

He speaks of visitors to Basel, including Hutten, uninvited by him and avoided for his own private reasons. But he adds:

> I hate discord as the worst of all evils, not only in accordance with Christ's teaching and example but from some deep-rooted impulse in my nature; and it torments me all the more when I consider how this world of ours is seething with both public and private hate, so that there is scarcely a vestige of true friendship left anywhere ... And it is in this world-wide tempest in human affairs that my unhappy lot is cast, at a time when I should as it were have

* * * * *

118 Allen and CWE Ep 1342 introductory note

> retired long ago to a well-earned leisure ... Both sides, however, have taken
> special care to make this impossible ... Thus it has come about, through no
> fault of my own but as a result of the misguided zeal of certain individuals,
> that in both parties there are certain people ill disposed towards me.

He agrees with both Luther and his scholastic critics that he is unfitted for
combat, but not that he has nothing critically important to say. He believes
that he has answered the scholastic critics sufficiently. He would take on
someone from Luther's side gladly, 'but it must be one with a sense of fairness. I believe I could make even him accept my case, on the basis of points
which he himself will concede me.' He begins here to argue hypothetically
with an imagined Lutheran opponent, and puts forth assumptions that he
believes would be conceded. These hypothetical positions foreshadow in a
striking way some of the major points of his debate to come. It shows that
by the spring of 1523 he was thinking out what he would have to say to
Luther.[119]

First Erasmus will ask 'whether there is any precedent in the Gospels'
for the Lutherans use of 'chicanery and violence to force a man into joining
[their] faction.' In contrast to the Jews, who sought to entrap early Christians
into revealing their dangerous faith, the apostles never used such methods.
He would not have used such methods, but (he implies) Lutherans have,
when they spread the word that he was secretly a member of their sect. They
have kept on doing this from the time the movement seemed admirable to
now even after the publication of *The Babylonian Captivity* and the *Abroga-
tion of Private Masses*, which defend Hussite teachings.[120] Yet their efforts to
entrap him have failed, for he, Erasmus, has made no public utterance on
Luther's opinion, only averring that he is 'entirely opposed to the way the
Lutherans band themselves together.' He will then ask his Lutheran opponent whether this criminal purpose of pretending that Erasmus is a secret
Lutheran and attempting to trick him into exposing himself as such is a noble enterprise. 'He will reply, I suppose, that it is entirely in the spirit of the
apostles.' He will thus have exposed their hypocritical claims about himself. Next Erasmus turns to a more direct attack, exposing the Lutherans'
self-contradictions. If it is 'expedient that Luther's teaching should spread
through the world as widely as possible and prove wholly acceptable alike

* * * * *

119 Ep 1342:716–48, 774–80, 807–10
120 On *De captivitate Babylonica ecclesiae* see xxxvii, xlvi–xlvii and n91, and liv and
    n110 above. *De abroganda privata* is in WA 8 411–76; LW 36 133–230 translates
    the German version (WA 8 482–563).

to high and low,' why are Luther's books not 'free from the two features which do more than anything to reduce their credibility and alienate all men of good will, their arrogant air and their excessive virulence'? This has been and will continue to be a major charge against Luther by Erasmus, one that was to be featured in his *Discussion of Free Will* and *Hyperaspistes*. The crudity of Luther's attack on Henry VIII for writing a work criticizing Luther is an example of the man's arrogance. How, Erasmus asks, can his offer to do what he can for the Holy See and the peace of Christendom be regarded as an attack on Luther? Luther feels free to differ from all the Doctors of the church as well as the decrees of popes and councils but is indignant if anyone differs from him. Luther rejects the historical consensus of the church but is outraged if anyone uses sound reasoning and the testimony of Scripture to disagree with him. 'The Roman pontiff summons us to do no more than put Luther to the test of sound reasoning and the testimony of Scripture.'[121] Here are Erasmus' criteria for sound Christian doctrine, which he holds Luther to have refused: respect for the traditional consensus of Christian learning and debate, sound reasoning, and the testimony of Scripture. All three will be contested in his future debate.

Erasmus proceeds to answer two charges that were being spread against himself. The first was that he was the author of Henry VIII's *Assertion of the Seven Sacraments*.[122] The other was that Erasmus should by now have retired.[123] The first charge he is easily able to answer by the logistical impossibility of his having any influence on Henry's tract other than the general one of his writings. The second charge he rejects: 'But I am not permitted to leave this stage until my heavenly producer has given me my orders ... I measure my capacity according to my voice and physical strength and acting skill.' Why do they wish him to stand aside? Because 'this man ... still values highly and acknowledges the church of Rome.'[124]

Erasmus defends his support of the papacy: 'Wherein the true authority of the Roman pontiff lies is a matter of common knowledge, and I have made it clear in more than one passage of my works.' He adds: '"And who," they say, "is this Roman pontiff? Is he not the one who puts the gospel in the fire, God's enemy who leads astray all Christian people?" If such is the pope of whom they speak, no pope has ever had my approval. And yet,

* * * * *

121 Ep 1342:814–41, 857–63, 870–92, 902–19
122 See n110 above.
123 Luther would make this charge in his letter to Oecolampadius quoted lviii above.
124 Ep 1342:964–80

even were the pope like that, it is not my business to cast him down from his throne. Christ lives to this day, and he has in his hand a scourge with which to drive such characters from the temple.'[125] Erasmus certainly detested individual popes, notably Julius II, who was the subject of his famous exercise in the rhetoric of blame, *Julius Excluded from Heaven.*[126] But his support of Roman primacy was also fundamental to his position in his future debate with Luther. Erasmus' Lutheran interlocutor is made to say: 'This is how Erasmus should speak, "Pope, you are Antichrist; you, bishops, are blind leaders; that Roman see of yours is an abomination in the sight of God."' Erasmus responds: 'The first question I will ask my [Lutheran] judge is, whether he thinks rules of this kind which he lays down for me are fair.' The second question he will ask his judge is whether he thinks acts of this sort 'do any good for Luther's cause. If I were to write like that of good popes, should I not seem offensive? And if I were to rant in this strain against bad ones, the result would be to stir up a hornets' nest to the peril of myself and many others.'[127]

The next charge that he addresses is the one that he would make central to his *Discussion of Free Will.* Thus a full year before his first draft of *A Discussion* was made, Erasmus' approach and thinking concerning this fundamental Christian doctrine, reversed by Luther, is clearly articulated – and not only in its simple affirmation but with the nuances that Erasmus would carefully attach to it. His statement, which follows, also indicates how his *Paraphrases* on the New Testament were for Erasmus an important means for putting forth his humanistic, exegetical theology:

> There still remains one charge against me, the most serious of all. In my paraphrase, where I explain the ninth chapter of Paul the Apostle to the Romans, I allot a very small share to free will, for I was following in the steps of Origen and Jerome. To begin with, since a paraphrase is a kind of commentary, and since I state openly that on most points I follow accepted and ancient interpreters, what sacrilege have I committed if in some places I follow Origen and Jerome, who as authorities on Holy Scripture are, I take it, not to be despised?

* * * * *

125 Ep 1342:986–99
126 Cf *Julius exclusus: Dialogus Julius exclusus e coelis* in Ferguson 38–64 (introduction), 65–124 (text) / CWE 27 156–67 (introductory note), 168–9 (text). See also James K. McConica 'Erasmus and the "Julius": A Humanist Reflects on the Church' in *The Pursuit of Holiness in Late Medieval and Renaissance Religion* ed Charles Trinkaus with Heiko A. Oberman (Leiden 1975) 444–71.
127 Ep 1342:1011–21

And this happened before Luther put out his opinion ... that whatever we do, whether good or bad, is a matter of absolute necessity.[128]

Erasmus held to this view of Romans 9 in his debate with Luther, though he changed it in the 1532 edition of *Paraphrase on Romans* (perhaps to accommodate the Reformers, facilitate peace in the church, or to paraphrase Paul more accurately).[129] In order to explain why he interpreted the passage as he did in 1517 he refers to the dangers latent in the question and expresses what would become a basic motivation for his later writing of *A Discussion of Free Will* and *Hyperaspistes*. He uses the adage of sailing between Scylla and Charybdis, as he often does later, to express the two dangers to the Christian faith that he sought to avoid by his position on free will – a position which attributed a very large amount to grace and a little bit to free will in a person's attainment of righteousness or justification, and consequently salvation:

I could see on one side the peril of Scylla, persuading us to put our trust in good works, which I admit is the greatest threat to religion. On the other side I could see Charybdis, a monster yet more terrible, by whom not a few of them are now held fast, saying, 'Let us do as we please; for whether we torment ourselves or please ourselves, what God has once decided is sure to happen.' I therefore controlled my language so as to allot a very small share to free will, for fear of opening a window for such a mortal form of sloth, which consists in everybody abandoning all efforts towards an improvement of life and doing just anything he takes a fancy to.

He follows this by expressing shock that anyone had 'entirely abolished all the force of free will,' a position he had not encountered when he wrote the *Paraphrase* and 'an opinion which, even though I were certain of its truth, I should be reluctant to spread abroad in so many words.'

* * * * *

128 Ep 1342:1022–31. The translation 'freedom of the will' in CWE 9 has been changed to 'free will' here. As explained in the note on editorial practices (cv below), this change in previously published CWE translations will be made throughout CWE 76 and 77.

129 In his 1517 edition Erasmus included the sentence, 'Or rather, some part of it depends on our own will and effort, although this part is so minor that it seems like nothing at all in comparison with the free kindness of God.' In the 1532 edition Erasmus changed the sentence to read: 'However, it does not follow that God is unjust to anyone, but that he is merciful toward many' (CWE 42 55). See CWE 42 55 and n15. Also see Ep 1268:90–3 and Ep 1342:1032–56.

Referring to the debates among philosophers before the time of Christ and the 'insoluble problems ... about human free will, about contingency of future events,' he adds another topic over which he was to argue forcefully in his debate with Luther: 'I think it the best course not to spend too much anxious time' on these problems, 'since this is an abyss no man can get to the bottom of.' He then adds a sentence which indicates his awareness of the late scholastic, *via moderna* teaching that God will not withhold his grace from those who do the best they can. He will refer sympathetically to this doctrine several times in his debate, and it seems to be a position which he tended to favour, though he was cautious about making too definite a commitment to it. 'I would rather teach the doctrines that encourage us to try for the best in every way we can, while yet at the same time claiming no credit for ourselves, but leaving the judgment of everything to God, having developed perfect confidence in his goodness above all else.'

As a man who is cautious and whose knowledge is insufficient, he pleads with his imaginary Lutheran judges to 'allow him on some occasions to accept the verdict of so many recognized authorities, and in a time of such perilous upheavals silently to vote for the opinion of those whose authority has for so many centuries been followed by the Christian world.'[130] Having laid down the purposes and points for discussion that would arise in his future debate with Luther, without having won the imaginary concessions he boasted he could gain, he ends this long, but surely revealing, letter with cordial greetings to his old Netherlandish friend Marcus Laurinus, then dean of St Donatian's in Bruges.

*Confrontation: summer 1523–summer 1524*
Erasmus' letter to Marcus Laurinus was published in the *Catalogus omnium lucubrationum* by Froben in April 1523 and was read by Ulrich von Hutten, still smarting under the imagined affront by Erasmus during the preceding winter. Enraged by the clearly anti-Lutheran sentiments of the letter, Hutten set to work and wrote his *Expostulatio cum Erasmo Roterodamo* (Strasbourg: Johann Schott, summer 1523). Erasmus felt this was so damaging to his reputation that he had to reply; his *Spongia adversus aspergines Hutteni* (*A Sponge to Wipe Off the Aspersions of Hutten*) was published at Basel by Johann Froben in September 1523. Hutten died at the end of August just before *A Sponge* appeared, and some of the support Erasmus anticipated from it

\* \* \* \* \*

130 Ep 1342:1057–65, 1066–78, 1090–5

was dissipated in sympathy for Hutten and published resentment was expressed by less judicious supporters of Luther. When Erasmus wrote to Johannes Fabri on 21 November 1523, he was aware that Otto Brunfels' *Pro Hutteno defuncto ad ... Spongiam responsio* (*A Response to A Sponge, Defending Hutten after his Death*), published by Johann Schott at Strasbourg early in 1524, was about to appear. Mindful of Luther's letter to Oecolampadius of June 1523,[131] which he describes as saying that Erasmus is 'like Moses and must be buried in the wilderness and that too much weight should not be given to Erasmus in spiritual matters,' he wrote: 'This sort of thing means war.' He reviewed the writings he was engaged on and commented, 'If my strength holds out, I shall add a book on free will.'[132]

Erasmus, though cautious still, has decided upon his course of action. It is notable that three months earlier, when replying to Hutten in *A Sponge*, he speculated that if he should write against Luther, he would treat him very fairly.[133] On the other hand, in his response to Hutten he expressed deep resentment of the way he saw Luther treating him:

> I will argue nothing about the spirit of Luther towards me, nor will I argue about the letters he writes to his friends about me, not exactly friendly ones. Private feelings should not be regarded in such a business, and it does not matter whether Erasmus is in harmony with Luther, but whether the Christian community is in harmony with evangelic teaching. But if I were to concern myself with private grievances, I would be offended by no one more than by Luther, who loads so much ill will on my books and who either disrupts or corrupts almost all my friendships with a bad leaven and brings no little trouble to the humanities, which I have always defended, as well as to the ancient authors whose authority I am attempting to restore.[134]

Erasmus' statement seems to reflect what will continue to be his policy quite accurately. He will try to avoid criticizing Luther personally, except where his behaviour seems to jeopardize his own cause or Christian concord, which Erasmus certainly thought should be Luther's cause. But, as he himself recognizes, there is a strong element of resentment and dislike in his feelings concerning Luther, and he will not always be able to keep

\* \* \* \* \*

131 See lviii above.
132 Ep 1397:10–16
133 *Spongia* ASD IX-1 164:1008–9: 'Et in his tamen promitto summam erga Lutherum aequitatem' ('And yet in these matters I promise I will be very fair to Luther').
134 *Spongia* ASD IX-1 171:118–27

from expressing it in his debate with Luther. Luther's letters make it quite apparent that he suffered from the same hostility in his feelings towards Erasmus but found it simpler to account for it as the presence of something Satanic.

At the very time that Erasmus had first published *A Sponge* he evidently had already decided to write against Luther, for he wrote to Henry VIII on 4 September 1523: 'I have something on the stocks against the new doctrines but would not dare publish it unless I have left Germany first, for fear I prove a casualty before I enter the arena.'[135] But it was not until late November that he reported to Fabri that the work in hand would deal with the subject of free will.[136] Yet his letter to Laurinus in late winter 1523 signals that he was at least contemplating that this was to be the subject.[137] A year later (late February 1524) he sent a first draft to his theologian friend in Basel, Ludwig Baer. Baer responded in a few days, explaining the necessity of consequence and of the consequent, a distinction that will be frequently examined in Erasmus' debate with Luther.[138] At an uncertain date in the spring of 1524 Erasmus sent Henry VIII 'the first draft of a book on free will directed against Luther. The work is not yet finished.'[139]

The news did not take long to spread. In mid-April Luther wrote to Erasmus, warning of the consequences if Erasmus attacked him. He attempts to be polite and forbearing but is actually threatening and scornful. 'When I perceive that the Lord has not yet given you the courage, or even the common sense, to join with me in a free and confident confrontation with those monsters I suffer from, I am not the man to dare to demand from you something beyond your powers and limitations. In fact I have put up with your weakness and respected it, and the measure of the gift of God in you.' He never expected Erasmus with his weakness to 'involve yourself in our camp.' Though his eloquence would be of great service, 'yet as your heart would not be in it, it would be safer to serve within your own gift. The one thing to be afraid of was that you might be persuaded by my enemies to attack my opinions in your published work, and that I should then be obliged to resist you to your face.' Erasmus may think he is modest, but he in fact arouses 'hatred and passion' and 'justified indignation' in his enemies. 'And, to speak freely, since their nature is such that, weak as they

* * * * *

135  Ep 1385:15–17
136  See lxv above.
137  See lxii–lxiv above.
138  Epp 1419 and 1420
139  Ep 1430:15–6

too are, they cannot endure the bitterness and dishonesty which you would like to be taken for caution and modesty, they have some cause at any rate for justified resentment ...' Luther, too, has been 'provoked into writing with some bitterness; yet I have never done so except against the obstinate and the unteachable ... Thus I have restrained my pen hitherto, however much you might prick me, and have written, in letters to my friends which you too have read,[140] that I shall continue to restrain it until you come into the open.'[141]

Erasmus' reply of 8 May 1524 complains of the attacks of Luther's followers, chiefly Hutten and his defenders. To Luther's scornful warning he says:

> No, I do not concede that your passion for the purity of the gospel is more sincere than my own ... What you describe as weakness and ignorance is partly conscience and partly conviction. When I look at certain passages in your work, I am much afraid that Satan is using his wiles to lead you astray; but there are other passages which so delight me that I wish my fears were groundless ... As for me, nothing will tempt me to yield to human weakness and knowingly betray the gospel ... I do not greatly care what you write about me. If I were interested in worldly success, I can think of nothing that would turn out more to my advantage. But I want to present my soul to Christ without spot or stain, and I should like all men to act in the same spirit ... Why should it upset you if someone wants to argue with you in the hope of deepening his understanding? Perhaps Erasmus' opposition will do more for the gospel than all the support you receive from dullards ... I only hope it does not have a tragic ending![142]

Each letter was characteristic of its author and prophetic of the tone in which they engaged in debate. Erasmus will open with a disputation weighing both sides of the question and inviting refutation of his carefully argued stance. Luther will be dismissive of the opponent and bluntly assert his positions with absolute conviction. It can be argued (as Boyle has) that two very contrary rhetorics are in confrontation, but they correspond well to the moral character and deeply considered theologies of each man.[143]

\* \* \* \* \*

140 For example, his letter to Oecolampadius (lviii above).
141 Ep 1443:10–50
142 Ep 1445:1–32
143 *Rhetoric* 12

As Erasmus continued to prepare his disputation, word of the pending confrontation continued to spread. Pope Clement VII wrote on 30 April 1524: 'We have formed great hopes that you ... will take up in God's cause the arms appropriate to your great intellectual gifts and to the piety which you profess. News was in fact reaching us from many quarters that you had it in mind to do so, and that you already planned or had actually started upon a work which would make the light of your learning available for unmasking the errors of many misguided people. This news we were delighted to hear.'[144] Erasmus reported to his friend Willibald Pirckheimer on 21 July of the same year:

> Clement VII has sent me a brief full of compliments with a complimentary present of two hundred florins, which I would not have accepted had he not said expressly that he sent them in return for the dedication of my paraphrase ... The thing [that is, the breach between Lutheran and Catholic churches] spreads more widely every day. Neither side takes any steps towards reconciliation; most of them in fact have no other purpose than to pour oil on the flames ... Literary studies flourish and go forward, to the impotent fury of the theologians. They proclaim that I am a heretic, but no one believes them ... Martin Luther has written to me ... quite a civil letter; but I did not dare send an equally civil answer, for fear of those who distort everything ... Now that rumours have spread about my book on free will, I think it best to publish, so that they cannot suspect it to be worse than it is. For I treat the topic with such moderation that I know Luther himself will not take offence.[145]

Little did he know!

Erasmus' *Discussion of Free Will* was published in early September 1524 by Froben in Basel, Hillen in Antwerp, and Cervicornus (Hirtzhorn) in Cologne with four more printings following shortly.[146] It will be well to summarize Erasmus' state of mind at this point. He was certainly very reluctant to enter into public controversy with Luther. Even though it was clear to him that Luther intended his break away from the Catholic church of Rome to be irreparable and, indeed, correctly thought that it could not be overturned, Erasmus was fearful that a forcible suppression of Lutheranism might be attempted by the secular rulers of Europe and Germany with the support and blessing of the pope and the local bishops. He was eager to

\* \* \* \* \*

144 Ep 1443B:5–10
145 Ep 1466:4–21, 64–7
146 See Walter xiii–xiv.

find and secure some *modus vivendi* between the two religious communities even if no doctrinal and ecclesiastical reunion seemed possible. But Erasmus' desire for reconciliation or coexistence was compromised in a number of ways. He himself was under attack by conservative scholastic theologians at Louvain, Cologne, Paris, and elsewhere. He feared that his own efforts to introduce a new method of theologizing by the use of rhetorical and literary analysis rather than dialectic and Aristotelian metaphysics would be compromised by and confused with Luther's. This had in fact happened. Moreover, many of his own humanist followers and admirers, such as Zwingli in Zürich and Oecolampadius in Basel, had been won over by Luther or were beginning to take the lead in locally separate reform movements. Erasmus was being urged ever more insistently to throw the weight of his great moral and literary prestige against Luther by successive popes (Leo x, Adrian vi, and now Clement vii), by Henry viii, and by many of his friends in the English church.

Erasmus had become increasingly angered by hostile and belittling comments from Luther himself and some of his followers. Though he appreciated that Luther had based his reformation on biblical interpretation and had abandoned his scholastic, *via moderna* formation, he was dubious about a number of Luther's theological positions, especially his denial of free will, his doctrine of salvation by faith alone, his doctrine of *simul iustus et peccator* ('at once righteous and a sinner'), and his absolutizing of divine foreknowledge into absolute necessity. These alone gave him doctrinal reasons for opposing Luther. Although the worst offence was undoubtedly Luther's violent attack upon the universal Christian commonwealth manifested by the Catholic church, Erasmus does not seem to have had much hope of repairing the schism. He had decided to write against Luther for his own doctrinal and theological reasons.

In doing this Erasmus wished to make it clear that he did not stand with Luther theologically, that he was not merely responding to pressures from powerful rulers to get him to write. Most of all he wanted to warn of the religious dangers of Luther's teaching of predestination and absolute divine necessity. He feared these doctrines would make it too easy for the masses of simple Christians, particularly the morally degraded and impious, to find justification for any behaviour, however heinous, and for complete abandonment of piety and a Christian life. His reasons were his own, as he always insisted, and of the most holy kind. He would confess to his own disgust and anger at the taunts of Luther and some Lutherans, but he would not allow these emotions to undermine the serious and dignified demeanour of his writing. It would be a disputation utilizing his own theological mode of textual analysis of the Scriptures. It would also be a comparison of texts which seem to support free will with texts which seem to deny it. Luther, he hopes, will respond in kind, and so mutual clarification and discovery of the divine truth may emerge. Erasmus' underlying fears and suspicions, however, sometimes burst through. He cannot keep utterly calm, and from time to time his good intentions give way to petulant sarcasm.

*Reactions to A Discussion of Free Will: fall 1524*
The publication of *A Discussion* quite predictably prompted a twofold concern in Erasmus. First he wrote to the papal court, sending a copy of *A Discussion* and explaining his motives for the manner of his writing. In a letter of 2 September 1524 he wrote to Gian Matteo Giberti, the papal datary: 'I treat the subject without any personal attacks, so that if they use personalities in reply, it will be all the more evident what spirit drives them on ... I am resolved to go through with anything rather than put my name to this conspiracy ...' He conveys to the pope through Giberti (who was to become a model bishop manifesting Erasmus' vision of reform) the news that he has entered the fray but in a way that he hopes will not cause further bitterness or turmoil.[147]

He also wrote to Cardinal Wolsey on the same date to inform him and the English court that his criticism of Luther has been published: 'I refrained from personal abuse to give them no excuse for resentment. If they reply with the usual calumnies, they will hurt themselves, not me.'[148] On September 4 he wrote similarly to Cuthbert Tunstall, bishop of London, who had forcefully urged him to write against Luther on the topic of free will, to William Warham, archbishop of Canterbury, and to John Fisher, bishop of Rochester, who had already attacked Luther on the same theme.[149] Finally on September 6 he wrote brief letters to Duke George of Saxony and to King Henry VIII reporting that he had written against Luther on free will.[150] Thus he communicated with all of the patrons and dignitaries who had been urging him to take the field. It has been suggested, with good probability, that these letters had been written earlier and held until the work was actually in print.[151] His sensitivity to their expectations is

\* \* \* \* \*

147 Ep 1481:25–9. On Giberti as a reforming bishop see Adriano Prosperi *Tra evangelismo e controriforma, G. M. Giberti ( 1495–1543)* (Rome 1969) 181–288.
148 Ep 1486:5–7
149 Epp 1367, 1487, 1488, and 1489; Fisher had attacked Luther in *Assertionis Lutheranae confutatio* (1523).
150 Epp 1493 and 1495
151 See Ep 1481 introductory note.

apparent, as well as the fear that *A Discussion* would disappoint them in its lack of invective. Whether or not what he had written would satisfy them, at least he had now written.

More difficult and more important was to discover what kind of a reaction there might be in the Protestant camp. To his Catholic sponsors he could simply try to show that his mildness might well be the most effective tactic for exposing the Protestants if they did not respond in a like manner, ready for a civil discussion of the basic religious issues. To the Protestants he would be more self-justifying, stressing the provocative behaviour of some towards him, particularly after the Hutten affair. Writing to Melanchthon on 6 September 1524, he asks, 'Are we driving out our masters, the princes and the bishops, that we may suffer the more pitiless tyranny of pox-ridden Ottos and madmen like Phallicus [meaning Otto Brunfels and Guillaume Farel]?' He further complains even about Capito and Zwingli. Then: 'But away with these complaints. You will wonder why I published my book on free will.' He was caught between the theologians who hated the humanities, the monks, and the Lutheran fanatics, and since Luther had promised he would not attack Erasmus unless Erasmus attacked first, he was forced to write so that it would not be thought that he had a secret agreement with Luther. Yet what he has written is sincere: 'For I myself have treated the subject in a very low key; and yet what I write is never written against my convictions; though I should be quite happy to change them too when anyone convinces me of something better.' Then he throws in: 'But there are some people in your camp who cry to heaven that the gospel is overthrown if anyone resists their own mad conduct. The value of the gospel? not in liberty to sin without penalty, but in keeping us from sin even when no penalty exists.'[152] Erasmus writes in this candid way despite knowing that Melanchthon in his *Eulogy of Erasmus and Luther* had said that he was a moral philosopher like the ancients, not a true theologian.[153]

It may have been Erasmus' intention to make Melanchthon see that he was aggrieved and had remained temperate in the hope that his restraint would moderate any reply by Luther. If this was so, he apparently succeeded, for Melanchthon wrote the very next day to Spalatinus that Erasmus did not seem to be abusive. 'I am desperately eager' he writes, 'that this matter, which is certainly the chief point of the Christian religion, should be diligently investigated, and for that reason I almost rejoice that Erasmus has

* * * * *

152 Ep 1496:70–2, 183–4, 209–12, 220–4
153 Ep 1496 n18

taken the field.'[154] Melanchthon's reply to Erasmus of 30 September 1524 must certainly have encouraged Erasmus in his hope that any response by Luther would not be savage:

> As for your *Diatribe* on free will, it had a very mild reception here. It would be tyranny to forbid anyone inside the church to express an opinion on a religious subject ... Your moderate attitude gave great satisfaction, though you do slip in a barbed remark now and again. But Luther is not so irascible that he can swallow nothing ... It may perhaps be a good thing for everyone to have this problem of free will thoroughly discussed ... I personally am quite clear about Luther's good will towards you, and this gives me hope that he will make a straightforward reply. In return it is your duty, my dear Erasmus, to make sure that this discussion is not embittered by any greater ill will on your side. For one thing, he has Scripture behind him quite clearly.[155]

It is not certain when Erasmus received this letter. He did not reply until 10 December 1524. He had apparently been sufficiently reassured by Melanchthon's mild reaction and good words to write even more openly concerning the difficulties that Luther, in his view, had brought about and concerning his own feelings and judgments about what came to be called the Protestant Reformation. It will be important for a reader of *A Discussion* and *Hyperaspistes* to be aware of these observations on the Reformation, and hence they will be quoted at some length.

Erasmus begins by speaking again of the 'reckless conduct' of Luther's followers. 'But the same is true of both sides. No one has done more harm to the pope than those who are the most ardent champions of the papal cause, and no one has caused greater injury to Luther than those who desperately want to be seen as Lutherans.' He would be wasting his time trying to make Melanchthon leave Luther, but he wishes that Melanchthon had dedicated himself entirely to the humanities where his true talents lay (thus turning back on Melanchthon his judgment in the *Eulogy* that Erasmus was not a true theologian).

He then speaks out against Luther in stronger terms than he had used elsewhere: 'Far be it from me to be upset by the teaching of the gospel, but there is much in Luther's views which I find offensive. I dislike particularly the extraordinary vehemence with which he treats whatever doctrine he decides to defend and that he never stops until he is carried to extremes.'

\* \* \* \* \*

154 See Ep 1496 introductory note.
155 Ep 1500:45–60. On the title *Diatribe* see *A Discussion* n1.

He contrasts Luther's vehemence with the kind of reform that he, Erasmus, wanted: 'My preference was for a temperate frankness so that we might induce even bishops and rulers to share in the endeavour. This was always my aim, nor have I any other aim today.' Luther's followers spurned such methods, thinking 'the gospel has made fine progress if a few monks divest themselves of their cowls ... or if a few priests are on the lookout for a wife or if images have been thrown out of a couple of churches.' By contrast 'I wanted to reform the religious life of the priests without lessening their authority and to aid good men who are now buried beneath the rituals of the monks without giving evil men the opportunity to sin more freely; I also hoped that things to which we had grown accustomed through long familiarity might be gradually corrected in such a way that we could avoid throwing everything into confusion and turmoil and that the liberty of the gospel might be the common possession of all mankind.'

But Erasmus is not simply disturbed about disorder, ignoring the deep theological differences separating the old church from the new ones coming into existence. He is also deeply concerned about the bad effects on the Christian piety of ordinary people who have been exposed to Luther's attacks on the church and its doctrines:

> Is there anything which is less likely to foster Christian piety than for ordinary, uneducated people to hear, and for young people to have it drummed into their ears, that the pope is Antichrist, that bishops and priests are demons, that the constitutions of men are heretical, that confession is a pernicious practice, that works, merit, human effort are heretical ideas, that there is no free will but all is governed by necessity, and that it makes no difference what works a man performs?

Erasmus, of course, had his own criticisms of many of these institutions, practices, doctrines, but not to the extent that he could not see the goodness of the whole of the Christian religion and church. He was very much concerned with what he saw as the morally and religiously debilitating effects of Luther's teachings and policies.

Turning to the question of how Luther will respond to his *Discussion*, he first says, 'I do not greatly care what he thinks of me, especially in a matter like this, where private feelings should not be allowed to count for much.' But a little later he speaks directly of how Luther might respond: 'But as for Luther's intentions, there is much which makes me hesitate; and if I do not dare to trust my own judgment absolutely, I think, nevertheless, that I can plumb a man's mind as well from his writings as from his company. Luther has a fiery and impetuous temperament. In everything he does you can recognize the "anger of Peleus' son [ie Achilles] who knows not how to yield."'

As it will turn out, Erasmus was right in his suspicions about how Luther would respond. Luther was himself and did not hold back; least of all did he pretend to be moderate, and he certainly thought of the cause. But he was also strenuously personal in his treatment of Erasmus.

He ends the letter by speaking of his own motivations. Old age and infirmity have removed any desire for glory in this engagement in the world's troubles. 'My hesitancy and moderation have no other aim than to make myself useful to both parties. I hate dissension and I have constantly and steadily counselled the princes to renounce violence. If I could strangle men's vices without hurting their persons, you would see what a terrible executioner I would be – beginning at home.' In a way he is clinging to his friendship with Melanchthon – across the trenches, as it were – and was to be terribly disappointed later when he suspected Melanchthon of cooperating with Luther in *The Enslaved Will*. He mourns the recent death of William Nesen, another follower and protégé who had deserted to Luther. His inability to preserve his friendship with the German humanists disturbed him deeply and led him to comment: 'Everyone talks of the trustworthiness of the Germans, while the British are spoken of very differently in this respect. But it has been my fate to encounter the truest friends among the British and the opposite among Germans; and I am not generalizing from a few instances.'[156]

Erasmus was not to have Luther's reply to his *Discussion* for another year, for reasons which Luther, himself, explains in a letter of 17 November 1524 to Nicholas Hausmann.[157] He was preparing a book to answer the Protestant dissidents on the Eucharist and had given this project higher priority than a response to Erasmus.

Erasmus continued to be concerned with what his patrons might think of his efforts against Luther. He had sent a copy of *A Discussion* to Duke George of Saxony at the beginning of September 1524 and several months later sent him a letter which reviews the evolution of his own attitude towards Luther and of the changing positions he occupied between the various parties on both sides of the dispute. He had at first (in 1518 after Luther's *Theses on Indulgences* had been circulated) been sympathetic but concerned that Luther's intolerance of any difference would lead to a break. By not entering the fray he was defending himself and the humanities

* * * * *

156 Ep 1523:8–15, 27–56, 69–75, 95–7, 177–82, 202–7, 216–21
157 WA *Briefwechsel* 3 373–4 no 793 / LW 49 88 no 148

against the conservative theologians, who maintained that he knew nothing about theology and whose motives in urging him to refute Luther were not entirely straightforward. He was challenged to prove that he was not for Luther by writing against him. But even if he produced the kind of savage attack that would please his conservative enemies, he would still be the object of their bitter hatred and would at the same time have lost his many humanist friends who were sympathetic to Luther. He would have subjected himself 'unarmed and bereft of the protection of my friends, to those who hate the humanities.' Nor could he have counted on the protection of pope and emperor.

> Surely then, a man like myself, born for other things and ill-equipped for such a fight, had good reason to be afraid ... You see how many distinguished men have risen up to oppose Luther. Yet what have they accomplished? A terrible edict has been issued by the pope and a more fearful one from the emperor, and these have been followed by imprisonments, confiscations, recantations, faggots, and fires. I am not aware that anything has been achieved by this, except that the evil daily spreads more widely. If a pygmy like Erasmus had jumped into the ring, would he have had the least effect on men who take no notice of such mighty giants?

Historically Erasmus was correct both about his own loss of support from both sides and about the ineffectiveness of polemics against Lutheranism to prevent its spread. He was distressed both by Luther's extremism and 'his bitterness, a bitterness which is equalled only by his arrogance.' And he wondered why so many friends admired Luther's cause even though they could give him no satisfactory reasons for doing so. 'There is no reason therefore, why anyone should criticize me for being slow to act. St Hilary hesitated much longer before he lifted his pen against the Arians. It was not collusion, but religious scruple, which kept him silent so long.'

It was a different scruple which held Erasmus back. In revealing this in his letter to Duke George, he sets forth his sense of a moral and religious crisis in Christendom and of the rejection on both sides of any common effort to reach concord by yielding something to the other; both sides would remain obstate and absolute. This was the basis for his hesitation to engage himself in what he foresaw would be a useless endeavour:

> I often feel sad when I think of the extent to which Christian piety had declined. The world had become bewitched by ceremonial, evil monks reigned unchecked, tying the conscience of mankind into inextricable knots. As for theology, think of the subtle sophistries to which it had been reduced. What

dominated the discipline was a reckless passion for definition. I shall say nothing now of bishops and priests and of those who acted like tyrants in the name
of the Roman pontiff. When I reflected on these things the thought came to
me: '... Has it pleased God to use Luther, as once he used the Pharoahs, the
Philistines, the Romans, and men like Nebuchadnezzar?' For Luther's suc-
cesses have hardly come about without God's help ... I came to the conclusion, therefore, that I should leave the outcome of this tragedy to Christ. All I
could do was dissuade everyone I could from joining the sect and encourage
the opposing parties to try to reach an accord which was fair to both sides; in
this way I hoped that peace might gradually be restored.

He had circulated the 'Minute' at the time of the Diet at Worms and cor-
responded with the emperor, popes, Lutheran leaders. He found the latter
'very obstinate and so reluctant to retreat from any of the positions they
had taken that every day they added new bitterness to that which existed
before. And it seemed that the leaders on the other side had made up their
mind to crush dissent with violence.'

He speaks of the fatuousness of attempting a violent repression of
Lutheranism. The church has lived with both sides in many controversies: the differences between Parisian and Italian theologians, between the
Thomists and the Scotists. 'What worries me now is that these common
remedies, that is, recantations, imprisonment, and the stake, will simply
make the evil worse. Two men were burned at Brussels, and it was precisely at that moment that the city began to support Luther ... What is
achieved by punishing one or two people except to provoke anger in a sect
which is far from insignificant in the number of its members? ... I could believe that the pope and the princes might be persuaded to accept a fair set-
tlement, if Luther too could bring himself to make concessions.' He is wishing that the world could return to 1520/1 when he first made this proposal
for arbitration. But he now despairs of the Lutherans ever listening.

Erasmus seems not to recognize that the publication of his *Discussion*
had removed any further possibility that he himself could play a mediatory
role, despite its moderation and the possibility it opened for a two-sided
debate. He does recognize, however, that all he can do is pray that the dove
of Christ 'may descend upon us and bring good out of the reckless deeds of
certain men,' and hope for the best from the influence of his *Discussion*.[158]

* * * * *

158 Ep 1526:86–7, 100–12, 114–15, 128–31, 131–50, 155–9, 173–90, 195–7

*Erasmus caught between Luther and Catholic critics: 1525–7*

It would be a year before Luther was free from controversy over the Eucharist and more than a year before he published his reply to Erasmus' *Discussion, The Enslaved Will* (*De servo arbitrio*) in December 1525. During this time Erasmus had also become involved in disputes with the conservative Catholic theologians of Paris as well as with other critics in Spain and Italy. He had learned that Noël Béda, the syndic of the theology faculty of Paris, had been collecting errors in the *Paraphrases on the New Testament* and wrote to him in April 1525, attempting to head him off by promising to make corrections in his new edition if he were sent the list of errors. These interchanges were to go on for the next seven years, and Erasmus would find himself replying to his Parisian critics almost at the same time as he was writing his response to Luther's *Enslaved Will*.[159] What is notable in Béda's attacks is that Erasmus is identified as a 'theologizing humanist,' along with Lefèvre d'Etaples and Luther. What Erasmus had feared from the time that Luther had appeared on the scene, that his own humanist theology would be confused with Luther's and condemned together with it, as had already happened at Louvain, happened again with the Parisians. In fact Béda's culminating work of 1529 against Erasmus was titled *A Declaration against the Clandestine Lutherans*.[160]

Confusion between humanist theology and Protestant heretical theology was also behind the criticisms of Alberto Pio of Carpi. Erasmus alluded to these criticisms in a letter to Haio Herman of 31 August 1524, just as his *Discussion* was appearing.[161] Erasmus wrote to Pio on 10 October 1525 seeking to convince him to cease his campaign. He says he is no more annoyed if someone declares him to be no philosopher and no theologian than if he were falsely praised as being the greatest. Himself a barbarian, he has written against barbarians – which should be appreciated in Rome. And as a theologian he has no need of philosophy except in dealing with free will – a task he undertook reluctantly and under much pressure, and if it was deficient in learning, it did not lack respect for the faith. But of what use was it for a great man like Alberto Pio to persuade us that Erasmus is a mere beginner? He is far more disturbed at what he hears, that the Prince of Carpi declares in banquets of the cardinals that Erasmus was the

* * * * *

159 Rummel *Catholic Critics* II 29–79 and James K. Farge *Orthodoxy and Reform in Early Reformation France: The Faculty of Theology of Paris* (Leiden 1985) 186–96
160 Rummel *Catholic Critics* II 43–6
161 See Ep 1479 n57.

source of Luther's heresies. Erasmus points out that he urged his German friends to stay away from Luther, since the tumult he aroused would lead to bloodshed. Many of them joined with Luther and became his bitterest enemies.

> On the one side I had the theologians, who, because of their hatred of the humanities, were doing everything possible to push me into a sect which they themselves believed should be condemned out of hand; on the other side I had the Lutherans, who were working in the same direction through wheedling, trickery, threats, and abuse, though their ultimate aim was different from that of the theologians. Yet in spite of this no one has yet been able to move me one finger's breadth from membership in the church of Rome.[162]

According to Myron Gilmore, Pio's *Accurate and Hortatory Response to Erasmus* (published at Paris in 1529) and his *Twenty-three Books against Passages in Various Works of Erasmus* (published posthumously at Paris in 1531) contain the most comprehensive list of all the places in Erasmus' writings thought to be dubious, erroneous, or heretical by his Catholic opponents.[163]

In late December 1525 Luther's *The Enslaved Will* was published by John Lufft at Wittenberg. Highly indignant at Luther's self-assured tone and outraged that his integrity as well as his Christianity should be questioned, Erasmus hastily wrote book 1 of *Hyperaspistes: A Warrior Shielding A Discussion . . . Against The Enslaved Will of Martin Luther* in time to appear at

\* \* \* \* \*

162 Ep 1634:18–42, 43–71
163 Myron P. Gilmore 'Erasmus and Alberto Pio, Prince of Carpi' in *Action and Conviction in Early Modern Europe* ed T.K. Rabb and J.E. Seigel (Princeton 1969) 299–318. See also his '*De Modis Disputandi*: The Apologetic Works of Erasmus' in *Florilegium Historiale, Essays Presented to Wallace Ferguson* ed J.G. Rowe and W.H. Stockdale (Toronto 1971) 63–88 and his 'Italian Reactions to Erasmian Humanism' in *Itinerarium Italicum: The Profile of the Italian Renaissance in the Mirror of Its European Transformation* ed Heiko A. Oberman and T.A. Brady Jr (Leiden 1975) 61–115, where he remarks on Erasmus' encounters with Girolamo Aleandro and Alberto Pio: 'In their attacks on Erasmus and indeed on the whole movement of northern humanism of which he was the chief representative, Girolamo Aleandro and Alberto Pio appear as the first figures of the Counter-Reformation' (83). See also Rummel *Catholic Critics* II 115–23. Pio's works also echoed the point of view expressed by his uncle, Giovanni Pico della Mirandola, in his polemic against Ermolao Barbaro upholding the superiority of scholastic reasoning over humanist rhetoric. See Giovanni Pico's letter to Ermolao Barbaro of June 1485 in CR 9 678–87; English translation by Quirinus Breen in *Christianity and Humanism* (Grand Rapids 1968) 15–25.

the spring book fair at Frankfurt. This book was first published in Basel by Johann Froben on 20 February 1526 and was reprinted by Froben in July.

Meanwhile Luther wrote a letter (no longer extant) to Erasmus 'in which,' as Erasmus points out in book 2 of his *Hyperaspistes*, 'he writes that I myself should give thanks because he has treated me in such a friendly and fair manner, far otherwise than he would have done if the discussion had been with an enemy.'[164] Erasmus answered that Luther's letter would not have moved him to forego his reply to *The Enslaved Will*, especially since in it Luther had called him an opportunistic atheist, a hypocritical Epicurean, and a secret sceptic in matters of Christian faith:

> You imagine, I believe, that Erasmus has no supporters. There are more than you think. But it is not so important what happens to the two of us, especially to me, who will be departing this life before long regardless of whether the entire world should applaud me. What torments me, and any decent person along with me, is that because of that arrogant, insolent, seditious temperament of yours you throw the whole world into deadly hostile camps; you make good men and lovers of the humanities vulnerable to certain raving Pharisees; you arm wicked men and those eager for revolt; in short, you treat the cause of the gospel in such a way as to reduce everything, holy or unholy, to utter confusion, as if you deliberately intended that this storm should never reach a pleasant outcome, which is the goal at which I have always aimed. What you owe to me, how you have repaid me, I will not examine. Whatever it is, it is a private matter. It is the public calamity that torments me and the total and inextricable confusion which derives solely from your uncontrollable personality.[165]

Book 1 of *Hyperaspistes* answered only Luther's attacks on the preface and introduction of *A Discussion*, leaving the main part, his scriptural arguments, for book 2. Erasmus' patrons and friends highly approved of its publication. But as time passed they began to wonder when book 2 would appear. A year later he had heard from both Cuthbert Tunstall and Thomas More in England, urging its early completion. Erasmus replied to More on 30 March 1527 very despondently:

> What should I do in the face of two friends, either of whom could drive me to any course of action, whatever the outcome, simply by wishing me to do so?

\* \* \* \* \*

164 LB X 1486B–C
165 Allen Ep 1688:25–38

Still I would rather that this task were undertaken out of reason rather than feeling. You are persuaded that it would help a great deal if I assailed Luther with all my strength. But I am all but certain that I would do nothing more than stir up the hornets. I didn't expect any more than that when I published my *Discussion*. Cuthbert does a marvellous job of eliminating the power of this faction. If it could be reduced by words, I would cut them down most energetically. But to speak freely just among us, the facts are quite otherwise, and I fear that this hidden fire will soon burst forth into a huge uproar everywhere. That is the direction into which it is propelled by the insolence of the monks and the savagery of the theologians.

He speaks of the difficulties of his life in Basel because of the hostility of the Lutherans. But, though he has been invited to live elsewhere by many powerful rulers, his temperament is such that he would rather be dead than serve in some court. Erasmus points out that he has already dealt with Luther, and that his time is limited:

> If it would have done any good to respond, *A Discussion* and *Hyperaspistes* have already answered any arguments he can bring forward. He has two bastions of defence: that nothing results from the Law except knowledge, or rather recognition, of sin and that through Adam's sin the mass of mankind has been so vitiated that not even the Holy Spirit can do anything with it except evil. If he is dispossessed of these, he will yield. But what weapons can you use to dispossess someone who will not accept anything except Holy Scripture interpreted according to his own rules? ... In this state of health, consider how little time is left to me. Almost half of it is immediately cut away by letters pouring in from all parts of the world, to say nothing of books, some of them sent privately, some of them published. Nor is it easy to imagine the effort expended in this fourth edition of the New Testament, in revising the *Adages*, and also in my translation of Chrysostom and Athanasius, or how much time is wearily wasted in refuting the utterly stupid slanders of Béda and also some others which are being secretly manufactured by the theologians of Paris. And these would have been published if Froben had not been short of time. Some time is spent in revising the *Paraphrases* and Seneca.[166]

In explaining his delay in finishing *Hyperaspistes* book 2 by enumerating the works on which he is engaged, including the controversies with the Paris

* * * * *

166 Allen Ep 1804:2–13, 49–72

theologians, Erasmus reveals in this letter the extent to which he was involved in the fundamental spiritual conflicts of his age. He was of necessity a participant, although he represented neither of the principal sides, because his own prophetic historical insight was so sharp that he was able to rise above both the major factions (and above any of the many minor ones as well) and work for long-term reconciliation – even though he agreed that it was impossible in his own days. This deeply moral and religious and historical wisdom manifests itself in this letter along with Erasmus' sense of helplessness and his view of himself as a scapegoat of the competing forces, each of which found him a convenient target for its frustration in being unable to control or overcome its real enemy.

Then in this critically important letter Erasmus moves to a discussion of the theological issues he must attempt to handle in his promised second book of *Hyperaspistes*. He was speaking his mind to his oldest, most faithful, and most perceptive friend, who was within the decade to be crushed and martyred himself in this giant whirlpool of theological, moral, ecclesiastical, political, diplomatic, military, and personal turmoil. Erasmus goes on to say:

> Now imagine for a moment that I lacked neither the leisure nor the ability. If I handle the subject according to the views of the monks and theologians, who attribute too much to human merit because of the income they get from it, I will certainly be speaking against my conscience and I will knowingly obscure the glory of Christ. If I speak with moderation and attribute something to free will but most to grace, I will offend both sides – and that is what happened to me in *A Discussion*. But if I follow Paul and Augustine, very little is left to free will.[167]

This is the heart of Erasmus' theological discussion of free will, the most fundamental issue of religion and human existence during his age.

He continues, weighing the consequences of Augustine's stance as he faced the extreme challenge of the Pelagians. Now Erasmus, an old

* * * * *

167 Allen Ep 1804:75–82. Much of the second book of *Hyperaspistes*, which Erasmus is projecting here, will be devoted to Augustine and Paul. Erasmus will rely heavily on Augustine to support the minimalist position he chooses to take. He is thus able to cite Augustine as at least recognizing the existence of free will, as over against Luther, and will use him as a foil against Luther, the self-affirmed follower of Augustine. Erasmus will have more difficulty with Paul, arguing that he is being wrongly interpreted, but will find this hard to sustain.

man like Augustine, faces the challenge of the opposite extreme, Luther's Pauline/Augustinian predestinarian challenge to the constituted church:

> For here in the two books which [Augustine] wrote as an old man against Valentinian, he did indeed assert the existence of free will. But he confirmed grace in such a way that I do not perceive what he left over for free will. He confessed that works performed before grace were dead, he attributed it to grace that we come to our senses, that we will to do good, that we do good, that we persevere. He confessed that grace does all these things in us. Where, then, is merit? At this point, hemmed in as he was, he took refuge in saying that God imputes his good works to us as merits and crowns his gifts in us. Isn't this a pretty defence of free will?[168]

Augustine and this argument drawn from him would become central in *Hyperaspistes 2*, upon which Erasmus was clearly now beginning to meditate.

But there is another point that is basic in his speculation: 'I would not find unattractive the opinion which holds that by the powers of nature pure and simple, without particular grace, we are able to establish grace 'fittingly' [*de congruo*], as they say, except that Paul refutes it – although in fact not even the scholastics hold this opinion.' This is the position that he turns to and wishes to endorse time and again in *Hyperaspistes*. He knows that it is the extreme opposite side of the scale from Luther – perhaps the early position that Luther turned away from – and that it is the position of the scholastics of the *via moderna*, deriving from or agreeing with Scotus, to whom Erasmus correctly credits it. But whether it is also the position of the Parisian scholastics who were attacking him is doubtful.[169] As

\* \* \* \* \*

168 Ep 1804:82–91. Cf *De gratia et libero arbitrio* 3.2 and *De correptione et gratia* 1.2. Both works were polemics against Valentinian, a Pelagian.

169 Ep 1804:91–5. References to the 'scholastics' can be confusing because there are conflicting positions and Erasmus rarely names names. He will seem to agree with those of the so-called *via antiqua*, Aquinas and his followers as well as Augustine, but will continually wish, nostalgically, to agree with Scotus (named) or with such followers of the *via moderna* as Ockham, D'Ailly, Biel (all unnamed), or Gerson (named). James Farge in *Orthodoxy and Reform in Early Reformation France; The Faculty of Theology of Paris* (Leiden 1985) throws no light on the theological position of its members. But the Collège de Montaigu where Erasmus attended lectures in the 1490s was known to be Scotist. Erasmus was certainly aware that his statement just above that 'not even the scholastics hold this opinion' is too exclusive. Some of them did, or came very close to doing so.

Myron Gilmore suggests, Erasmus does seem to anticipate the Jesuits of the seventeenth century in their battle with the Jansenists over free will.[170]

Erasmus continues, again defending his delay in embarking on the second book of *Hyperaspistes*:

> Now let us weigh the dangers. There is the fear that once free will has been taken away some people will abandon all effort to do good. This Scylla we see, but there is a greater danger from the side of Charybdis, namely that we will attribute to our own powers what belongs to God's generosity. If this were an argument about something human, we could rightly play such games. But in matters which pertain to piety, it is not safe to indulge in rhetoric. But [you say] the credibility of *Hyperaspistes* must be vindicated. It would have been vindicated long since if her activity had not been blasted by the crosswinds of the Parisian furies. Indeed with one blow I had rebuffed a good many arguments from both sides; but if there had been enough free time, the whole work would have been published. But I thought it better to confront these furies first, not because I intend to engage in perpetual conflict with them or because I have any hope that such numerous sworn enemies might be put down by my writings. But I thought it would be well if the world knew what crows come from that nest where we expected to find a marvellous treasure.

The University of Paris, which should provide treasures of wisdom and piety, sends forth blasts of calumny and rage. Erasmus is thinking out loud (or at least in writing) concerning his plans for dealing with his critics on both sides:

> Tunstall thinks they would be propitiated if I forgot them and fought against Lutherans. But he is very much deceived. I know the ins and out of them, I know their minds. There will be no end of their ravings until either they are suppressed by the authority of the princes, or until the younger generation throws these sexagenarians off the bridge, as they say. Finally, if I utterly scorned my conscience and wrote according to their wishes, what praise would I gain? They will say that I have come to my senses and recanted. Indeed if I have ever been a heretic, then I am willing to go right on being considered one. And though I prefer the previous condition of the

\* \* \* \* \*

170 'Italian Reactions to Erasmian Humanism' (n163 above) 96–8. Also see John C. Olin 'Erasmus and St. Ignatius Loyola' in *Luther, Erasmus and the Reformation* (New York 1969) 114–33.

world, however bad, to the present confusion, still that world had at some
point to be awakened from the lifeless ceremonies in which it had fallen
asleep.[171]

Erasmus turns to Luther and other Protestant attacks on him, returns
again to the Parisian scholastics, and then takes up his Roman critics, Aleandro and Alberto Pio, who also confuse him with Luther. Pio attacks him,
he says, 'indeed with the greatest humanity, and softening everything with
praises ... but meanwhile mixing the business of Luther with mine, violently criticizing my *Paraphrases*, the *Moria*, and good writing.' At last Erasmus affirms: 'Although I am in this situation, nevertheless, reluctantly, I
will do what you wish, whatever the outcome may be. I will finish *Hyperaspistes*, and if it is not safe to publish it, I will send it there promptly by my
own servant if there is some company for the road.'[172] The stage has been
set. Book 2 of *Hyperaspistes* will be finished in the succeeding six months.

III

A DISCUSSION AND HYPERASPISTES:
ERASMUS' 'FABULA CHRISTI'

What has preceded is a story of the process of dialogue and rumination by
which over many years Erasmus arrived at the point of writing his discussion on free will, which for him was a very perilous thing to do. The story
continued as Luther's *The Enslaved Will* appeared in answer to *A Discussion*
and Erasmus reacted angrily in book 1 of his *Hyperaspistes* (1526) and in
book 2 a year later. *Hyperaspistes* was a more carefully pondered work, but
a far more deeply antagonistic one.

Erasmus declared in *A Discussion* that he will act as a disputant, not
a judge, an inquirer, not a dogmatist.[173] He intended the disputation and
comparison to be an object lesson in the value of the kind of theology he
had been espousing and practising as well as a defence against the attacks
of conservative scholastic critics. It was to be the fruit of the careful linguistic and literary analysis manifested in his *Annotations on the New Testament*
and of the theological vision put forward in his *Paraphrases on the New Testament*. He had laid out the elements of his theological method in his *Ratio*

* * * * *

171 Allen Ep 1804:96–110 and 110–20
172 Allen Ep 1804:250–3 and 281–4
173 *A Discussion* 8

... *perveniendi ad veram theologiam* (*Way of Arriving at a True Theology*) and in his letter to Paul Volz, both of 1518.[174]

It has been argued that *A Discussion* was indeed a work of impartial objectivity, as Erasmus professed.[175] Yet there was no question as to the outcome of his surveys of passages in the Old and New Testaments supporting or opposing free will or of the passages cited by Luther in his *Assertion* denying the existence of free will. Although Erasmus arrives at his conclusion by means of metaphorical analysis or by a rhetorical diagnosis of the religious/historical situation which is being addressed by the prophetic voice of Scripture, he nowhere concedes that Luther's proclamation of the fictional character of free will or his assertion that all things happen by absolute necessity might be valid.

At the same time Erasmus relied upon the fundamental practices of the humanistic arts, which would themselves lack verity without the assumption of free will both in the speaker and in the auditor. Freedom of will must have both a divine and a human aspect, and reliance on the humanistic arts would require an emphasis upon the all-embracing importance of the community of the faithful.[176] On the other hand the overwhelming presence of divine grace must be constantly acknowledged, leaving the role of human free will in the dynamics of salvation extremely limited. Such an acknowledgment is in harmony with Erasmus' continuing purpose to find the middle ground of consent that would restore the concord of Lutherans and Catholics. Erasmus' exegesis and theological stance remained in accord with the ideal of conciliation that had been his goal through these years of manoeuvring between the two opposed parties, both of which sought total victory without the compromises which they considered would signal surrender to evil and the enemies of God.

Erasmus finds a unity between his conception of theology as exegetical and his rhetorical vision of a dialogic relationship between God and man that is consistent with his overall purpose of preserving ecclesial concord. At the beginning of the final part of his *Discussion* (Judgments Concerning Free Will and Grace) he claims that, because scriptural passages

\* \* \* \* \*

174 For the textual history and character of the *Annotations* see Bentley 112–93 and Rummel *Annotations* 3–33, 89–121. On the *Paraphrases* see CWE 42 ix–xxxviii. On the *Ratio* see Holborn; Boyle *Language* 59–127; Hoffmann 32–9. For the letter to Paul Volz see Ep 858 and CWE 66 8–23; Chantraine 'Mystère' 99–153.

175 Or, more precisely, a work of scholarly investigation; on the nature and status of the argument see Boyle *Rhetoric* 43–51.

176 See McConica 'Consent' and his *Erasmus* (Oxford 1991) 45–80.

concerning free will are contradictory, or seem to be, and it is agreed that the Holy Spirit cannot contradict itself, it is necessary for the Christian to discover some way to moderate the extremes of contradiction and interpret them in a concordant manner.[177] Different scholars and theologians throughout the history of the church have read the Scriptures differently because they themselves were motivated by different purposes. Those who wished to overcome religious apathy and despair exaggerated free will as an encouragement to the recovery of piety, as Erasmus himself was doing. Those who were outraged by arrogance and self-display weakened free will or attributed everything to absolute necessity, as Luther seemed to Erasmus to have done.[178] Scriptural interpretation then becomes the means to restore the unity of both Scripture and the Christian community. Erasmus hoped he might provide the basis of this unity by resting man's salvation and justification almost entirely on grace and reserving only a small part of the process for human free will. Such was his strategy, which is confirmed by the passage cited from letter 1804 to Thomas More in the spring of 1527.[179]

In keeping with this strategy he follows with a very conciliatory and persuasive reading of what he hopes can be an acceptable position for Luther:

> He [man] should also consider that in this process there is no claim that anyone can make for his own powers, yet he should hope with complete confidence for the reward of eternal life from God, not because he has merited it through his own good deeds, but because God in his goodness has been pleased to promise it to those who trust in him ... Surely this is a godly, pleasing position, which does away with all our arrogance, gives all glory to Christ and places all our trust in him, casts out all our fear of men and demons, makes us distrust our own powers and become strong and courageous in God; we will gladly give it our limitless approval.[180]

* * * * *

177 *A Discussion* 74
178 *A Discussion* 74
179 See lxxxi and n167, lxxxiii–lxxxiv and n171 above. Also see *A Discussion* 79–80. The first impetus arousing man's mind and soul towards piety and the desire for salvation comes entirely from a particular grace. Once aroused, human will can play a part by responding to and working with grace towards the goal. The final part of the process – justification and sanctification – comes entirely from grace. As Manfred Hoffmann has explained in his 'Erasmus on Free Will' *Erasmus of Rotterdam Yearbook* 10 (1990) 101–21, this is Erasmus' formal position in *A Discussion*.
180 *A Discussion* 75

Erasmus, however, cannot rest with this concession, which might, indeed, have seemed completely acceptable to the most fervent Lutheran. He immediately adds:

> But when I hear people maintain that all human merit is so worthless that all human works, even those of godly men, are sins; when they claim that our will does no more than clay in the potter's hands, or attribute everything we do or will to absolute necessity, then I become exceedingly uneasy.[181]

He might have satisfied some of Luther's followers, but, against his deepest hopes, he was aware that this might not include Luther himself. We have seen how much Erasmus hoped from Melanchthon's friendly and mild response and his seeming assurance that his *Discussion* would be found at least tolerable to Luther.[182] It became immediately clear when he first looked at Luther's *The Enslaved Will* in mid-winter 1526 that this was far from being the case. Luther bluntly claimed for himself divinely inspired knowledge such as was denied to Erasmus: 'Although I am unskilled in speech, I am not unskilled in knowledge by the grace of God. For I venture thus with Paul [2 Cor 11:6] to claim knowledge for myself that I confidently deny to you.' He considered himself at fault for having waited so long to reply: 'We ought to have observed the rule of Paul "Be urgent in season and out of season" [2 Tim 4:2] ... There may be, I grant, some who have not yet sensed the Spirit who informs my writings, and who have been bowled over by that *Discussion* of yours; perhaps their hour has yet to come.'[183] Erasmus did not, it seems, anticipate such an abrupt dismissal by Luther. Nevertheless, the debate went on.

The continuing debate will be easier to follow if we bear in mind that each of these polemical works requires another opposed text to be understood. The essential pairings are as follows: Erasmus' *Discussion* with article 36 of Luther's *Assertion*; Luther's *The Enslaved Will* with Erasmus' *Discussion*; Erasmus' *Hyperaspistes* with Luther's *The Enslaved Will*, and reflexively with *Assertion* and *A Discussion* as well (see the tables of divisions and correspondences 311–21 below).

In the first part of *Hyperaspistes 1*, Erasmus rebukes Luther for his highhanded arrogance and reviews their relationship from the first encounter. He is now no longer assuming a stance of judicious moderation but rather

\* \* \* \* \*

181 *A Discussion* 75
182 See lxxii and n155 above.
183 *De servo arbitrio* WA 18 601:15–17, 602:14–18 / LW 33 16–18

one of overt hostility and resentment. He is ironically grateful that Luther chooses to consider him not to be a theologian because this would protect him from attacks by the theologians of the other side.[184]

In the second part of *Hyperaspistes 1*, Erasmus defends his preface to *A Discussion* by elaborating on what he meant by calling himself a 'sceptic,' on the distinction between important questions on which Scripture or the church has pronounced and points which are still unsettled, on which theological issues are critical and which are trivial, and on the false hyperbole of Luther's insulting charge that Erasmus is an atheist. He is prompted in this defence to declare the extent and limits of his Catholic orthodoxy:

> As far as reverence for the church is concerned, I confess that I have always wished that it might be purified of certain practices and that I do not in all respects agree with all the doctrines of the scholastics. But the decrees of the Catholic church, especially those issued by general councils and fully approved by a consensus of Christian people, carry such weight with me that, even if my tiny intellect cannot fully understand the human reasons underlying what is prescribed, I will embrace it as if it were an oracle issued by God, nor will I violate any regulation of the church unless it is absolutely necessary to have a dispensation from the law.

And he defiantly thrusts at Luther his papal loyalty along with his desire for 'correction of the church, in so far as that can be done without serious and violent disturbances.'[185]

Another critical difference with Luther is aired in this part of *Hyperaspistes*: the question of the clarity or the obscurity of Scripture. Erasmus holds that all parts of Scripture are not so transparently clear as to yield the dogmatic certainty that Luther insisted upon but that some parts are obscure and can be interpreted only with varying degrees of probability.[186] This argument leads into a lengthy but critical discussion of whether laymen needed to be made aware of the theological intricacies of scholastic dogmatics. True to his views of piety and the Christian life as requiring knowledge only of the essentials, as he had stressed in his *Enchiridion* and elsewhere,

\* \* \* \* \*

184 *Hyperaspistes 1* 93–117
185 *Hyperaspistes 1* 127
186 See Cornelis Augustijn 'Hyperaspistes 1: La doctrine d'Erasme et de Luther sur la "Claritas Scripturae"' in *Colloquia Erasmiana Turonensia* 2 vols (Paris 1972) II 737–48.

Erasmus attacks a series of propositions Luther insisted any Christian must investigate and affirm, likening Luther to the scholastics in this insistence. Moreover, Erasmus, who had been spoken of by his opponents as ignorant of theology and is frequently still held to be, shows himself as knowledgeable in these passages as Luther, the formally trained scholastic theologian. Erasmus says to him: 'You remove yourself from the ranks and the partisanship of the sophists, but you do so in vain, since all who contend with you cry out that they are dealing with a most crafty sophist; you have not eliminated the sophistical theology but changed it.'[187]

Another theme that is critical to Erasmus' rhetorical theology surfaces a number of times in the course of both books of his *Hyperaspistes*: that one's speech should be moderated in accordance with the character and needs of one's audience. Here in the first part of *Hyperaspistes 1*, citing Paul's 'All things are permitted me but not all things are to my advantage' (1 Cor 6:12), he adds:

> Paul is not dealing with preaching the truth, which he wishes to be preached to all persons whatsoever, at any time or place, in any way, but rather with avoiding giving scandal to the weak. Let us grant what you say, but this opinion by its very nature has a wider application in that the charity which persuaded Paul to abstain from what would otherwise be permissible also persuaded him to dispense the teaching of the gospel according to what is advantageous for mankind.[188]

The third part of book 1 is devoted to a defence of Erasmus' basic position: that Christian doctrine must evolve from and adhere to the historical authority of pope and council, orthodox scriptural interpretation, and the traditions of the community of believers in all regions throughout the history of God's people before and after Christ. This position, set forth in the introduction of his *Discussion*, was attacked by Luther, who rejected any authority of tradition in the second section of his work.[189] Erasmus, on the other hand, claims the authority of tradition in support of his doctrine of free will. He holds that his own ability to discern the truth of Scripture by relying on the holy men who commented on it and applying his methods of scholarship is superior to Luther's reliance on his gift of the spirit within him:

\* \* \* \* \*

187 *Hyperaspistes 1* 163
188 *Hyperaspistes 1* 172
189 *A Discussion* 14–17; *De servo arbitrio* WA 18 639–49 / LW 33 71–84

How the apostles manifested their spirit, I know only from the Acts of the Apostles and the gospel, except that their writings seem to me to breathe a certain fragrance of the Holy Spirit which I do not find in the writings of very many persons. From the same writings I know of the miracles performed by the apostles and I read how their speech was confirmed by God through subsequent signs. By similar tracks I detect the Spirit, holiness, and miracles in other reputable men. There breathes a certain something in their books, though far less than with the apostles, which manifests the Spirit and their holiness. And then I have learned of their lives and miracles in histories, the authority of which is confirmed for me by the consensus of the church, which reveres their memory so devoutly.[190]

Moreover, he connects this question of verifying the truth of tradition with that of the clarity of Scriptures, which Luther had affirmed he understood through his possession of the spirit. The obscurity of Scripture, which Erasmus affirmed and Luther denied, is given by Erasmus as the reason for the historical and exegetical theology he espoused and the need for illumination by his 'grammar of consent.'[191]

In the fourth part of *Hyperaspistes 1*, Erasmus defends his definition of free will, which Luther had attacked as a title rather than a correct definition. His dialectical and rhetorical analysis of the terms and their interrelationships that must be considered in an examination of free will soon turns into a theological discussion. He defends his distinction among laws of nature, works, and faith and examines the distinction between law and grace. He lays out the various historical positions taken on grace and free will and on the kinds or phases of grace. Here he differentiates between the position of Pelagius and that of Scotus (whom he neither rejects nor defends), both of them on the free-will side of the spectrum. Then he differentiates between the position of Augustine (which he finds acceptable, though severely limiting free will) and that of Karlstadt and Luther, who go farthest in restricting the will. Augustine's position is again termed 'more probable,' though Scotus' is not rejected. Erasmus exhibits a certain hesitation about the position he wishes to endorse. Augustine grants the existence of free will but leaves no room for it apart from grace. Scotus and the *via moderna* are attractive but uncertain.[192]

\* \* \* \* \*

190 *Hyperaspistes 1* 199–200; see also 252–3.
191 See n176 above.
192 *Hyperaspistes 1* 261—91

Erasmus' definition is intended to be broad and general so that the specifics and circumstances may be open for disputation: 'At this point we understand free will to be a power of human volition by which man may devote himself to, or turn away from, what leads to eternal salvation.' Against Luther's charge that his definition of free will is inadequate, misleading, and false, he elaborates on the appropriateness of the definition:

> Suppose mankind to be in the condition in which it was created: the definition squares with that ... Suppose mankind to be in the condition of a young person who as a child received the habit of faith through baptism and was cleansed of the sin of the first created man, and has not committed any sin by which grace is lost, although he is nevertheless old enough to know the difference between good and evil: my definition squares with that. For he could apply himself to grace or turn away from grace ... Finally, imagine a person in the condition in which Adam was after he had violated the command of God; here, perhaps, it will seem that my definition does not square with that condition because once he had been given over to sin he can do nothing but be a slave to sin. Where then, is the power of applying oneself or turning away? According to the opinion of some, there remains, I say, some freedom by which he can, without any special grace, solicit justifying grace through his natural powers by means of morally good works.[193]

But however much Erasmus disagrees with Luther's absolute rejection of free will, he himself remains indefinite concerning what option he prefers. The final one mentioned is that of the *via moderna*, and he is attracted by it but is not confident of his grounds for being so. A year and a half later in book 2 of his *Hyperaspistes* he will come closer to endorsing it.[194]

The final section of *Hyperaspistes 1* is a short epilogue in which Erasmus blasts Luther for the reckless charges made against him. He compares Luther's abusive unfairness with his own civility and blames Luther for the disorders that are tearing the Christian community apart, protesting the sincerity of his own faith and his trust in Christ and the Scriptures.[195]

Whereas *Hyperaspistes 1* deals with a number of general considerations in approaching the question of free will, book 2 examines in detail the biblical passages put forth in defence of free will in *A Discussion of Free Will*

* * * * *

193 *Hyperaspistes 1* 287–8
194 See xcvi–xcviii below.
195 *Hyperaspistes 1* 291–7

and Luther's refutation of that defence in *The Enslaved Will*. Luther sticks closely in his work to the order and passages in *A Discussion*. *Hyperaspistes* 2 sets forth Erasmus' original argumentation, Luther's elaborate response, and Erasmus' further theological elaboration in a text nearly three times the length of *Hyperaspistes 1*. The sheer mass of detail may account for the comparative neglect of this book, for the multiple dialogue can be difficult to untangle.[196] But as one scriptural passage after another is woven into the debate, the range and depth of Erasmus' theological vision becomes evident. This introduction cannot mention all of these revelations of Erasmian insight but rather will present only a selection of salient instances.

In dealing with Old Testament passages which command good works for the attainment of salvation, Luther resorts regularly to Paul's statement in Romans 3:20: 'Through the Law comes knowledge of sin.' Basing his argument on this text, Luther sets forth his theology of salvation by faith alone and his rejection of works. Erasmus' reply seeks to undermine Luther's rejection of Old Testament lawgiving by establishing its historical context. Paul's pronouncements on the Law derive from his own context: combatting the refusal of the Jews of his own time to follow Christ. Viewed in their own historical settings, contradictory passages in Scripture may be seen to address different situations and can therefore be reconciled. Acceptable or not to other modes of theologizing, Erasmus' position is illustrative of his own theological methods, in which rhetorical and historical assumptions are applicable to religion, since divinity and mankind participate in a sacred and continuing historical discourse.[197]

In explaining other Old Testament passages, Erasmus employs a series of qualitative distinctions to overcome Luther's practice of opposing irreconcilable extremes to destroy the mediatory positions of Erasmus: salvation is either by grace or by free will (Luther) versus salvation by grace and free will (as Erasmus has it). Here, too, there is an an opposition of dialectical and rhetorical reasoning (1361D–1363E).

\* \* \* \* \*

196 Cornelis Augustijn points out the interacting dialogue in 'Le dialogue Erasme-Luther dans l'Hyperaspistes ɪɪ' in *Actes du colloque international Erasme Tours 1986* (Geneva 1990) 171–83.

197 *A Discussion* 21–39; *De servo arbitrio* WA 18 671–84 / LW 33 117–38; *Hyperaspistes* 2 LB X 1340A–1361D (further references to *Hyperaspistes* 2 in this introduction will give the column numbers of LB X within parentheses in the text). See Boyle *Language* 45–6. Erasmus follows his own norms, derived from church Fathers such as Origen, Chrysostom, and Jerome. Also see Hoffmann and John F. Tinkler 'Erasmus' Conversation with Luther' *Archiv für Reformationsgeschichte* 82 (1991) 59–81, 70–5.

In responding to New Testament passages Erasmus had put forth to support free will, Luther speaks of the hidden and manifest or incarnate wills of God.[198] Erasmus agrees that there is a hidden will of God but cannot agree that 'in all the commandments, all the promises, threats, terrors, frights, expostulations, and blandishments this will should only be adored like a deus ex machina. If Luther had said that some persons, by a special volition of God, are either condemned or drawn to him, it would have been more tolerable' (1379D). For Erasmus the personal, promising, ordained will of God as expressed in Scripture is what he sees and believes in. Whether correctly or not, he attributes to Luther a belief in an absolute and necessitous will of God. Erasmus holds to the related conception of God's two powers: absolute and ordained, but his notion of the two powers is not the traditional thirteenth- and fourteenth-century one that God's absolute power is one which he might have used to create a different universe but did not, thus rendering the creation of this universe a free and contingent act of God's will.[199] As he clearly states in *A Discussion*, he believes that God by his absolute power brings about extraordinary or preternatural events and miracles, a view that was becoming more frequent in the fifteenth and sixteenth centuries.[200]

In replying to Luther Erasmus' purpose is often to interpret statements of Paul, emphasizing divine omnipotence in such a way as to allow some role for free will in the process of justification. Because he has to do this not only for Paul but also for the Old Testament passages quoted by Paul, Erasmus' broader conceptions of Christian religion and theology are expounded and set in contrast to those of Luther. Luther acknowledged in *The Enslaved Will* that he had to thank Erasmus for at least the opportunity provided him to clarify the vital issues of Christianity.[201] Luther provided the same opportunity for Erasmus. Thus in the course of refuting Luther's determinist interpretation of Paul, Erasmus discusses a number of scholastic distinctions. One critical set concerns 'necessity of consequence' and the 'necessity of the consequent.' Another is that between the 'infallible necessity of divine foreknowledge' and 'its inevitable necessity.' Both

\* \* \* \* \*

198 *De servo arbitrio* WA 18 684–8 / LW 33 138–44
199 See Courtenay *Capacity* 96–145.
200 *A Discussion* 50–1
201 *De servo arbitrio* WA 18 786:30–2 / LW 33 294: 'You and you alone have seen the question on which everything hinges, and have aimed at the vital spot; for which I sincerely thank you, since I am only too glad to give as much attention to this subject as time and leisure permit.'

these distinctions were brought into play in debating Luther's insistence that divine foreknowledge made Judas' betrayal of Christ a necessity. Erasmus argued that even though foreknown by God, Judas' betrayal was an act of free will consistent with the contingency of created things, since the alternative possibility existed. Erasmus reinforced this standard scholastic argument by claiming that the freedom of Judas' action was sanctioned by the divine 'covenant' made by God with respect to the ordained works of his will. As such Erasmus' position was more in accord with the theology of the *via moderna*, whereas Luther generally opposed it. Perhaps for this reason Erasmus was more accurate in his understanding of the scholastic arguments used in the debate than Luther (1415E–1482C, especially 1421B–C).[202]

On the other hand, as is generally recognized, Erasmus made use of certain patristic writings and methods. He followed the example of Origen in making use of figures of speech to interpret the meaning of Scripture, and he defends this practice against Luther's criticism of it (1391E–1402E).[203] He also makes extended use of another church Father who was famous for his eloquence, namely, John Chrysostom. He uses selected exegetical homilies of Chrysostom to show how Paul may be interpreted in a pastoral way, revealing him as appealing to 'innate character and a mind capable of grace.' Erasmus translates two long passages from Chrysostom's homily 16 on the Epistle of Paul to the Romans: one on Jacob and Esau and the other on the potter and the clay (1430F–1435B and 1443B–1444A).

*Hyperaspistes* 2 also presents a notable discussion of human nature. Basing his argument on Isaiah 40:6, 'All flesh is grass,' which Luther had used to annihilate free will in his *Assertion* and again in *The Enslaved Will*, Erasmus gives a fuller explanation of his religious anthropology. There is not a dualism of evil flesh and virtuous mind and spirit, but rather a human being can be either wholly good or wholly evil in all these parts or any possible intermediate mixture of the three. The passions especially, usually regarded as evil, can also be shown to support goodness (1457E–1466C).[204]

\* \* \* \* \*

202  See *De servo arbitrio* WA 18 714–22 / LW 33 185–95 and n138 above for Erasmus' exchange with Ludwig Baer on necessity and contingency; see also Courtenay 'Covenant' 94–119 and, for a philosophical consideration of the scholastic discussion of divine foreknowledge and human free will, Linda Trinkaus Zagzebski *The Dilemma of Freedom and Foreknowledge* (New York and Oxford 1991).
203  For Luther's criticism see *De servo arbitrio* WA 18 700–2 / LW 33 161–4.
204  See Luther *De servo arbitrio* WA 18 740–5 / LW 33 222–9 and Augustine *De civitate Dei* 14.6–10.

In a striking short essay on being born and being born again (ie justified), Erasmus notes that even in physical birth there is an effort on the part of the infant, as in many other changes of life, including that of the attainment of grace (1477F–1479B). In his discussion of human nature Erasmus reveals the humanist's and rhetorician's emphasis on activity as a part of mankind's social nature, an activism also manifested in the work of Paul (1482B–1483A).[205]

Religious psychology is also a major feature of Erasmus' critique of Luther's rejection of free will. Earlier he had spoken of the demoralizing effect of being told that one can do nothing towards one's own salvation. This sense of helplessness might well lead to indifference, wild indulgence, or despair. Near the end of Luther's presentation of his case as he concludes *The Enslaved Will*, he speaks of 'the two kingdoms of Christ and Satan':

> The knowledge and confession of these two kingdoms perpetually warring against each other ... would alone be sufficient to confute the dogma of free will, seeing that we are bound to serve in the kingdom of Satan unless we are delivered by the power of God ... I frankly confess that even if it were possible I should not wish to have free will given to me or to have anything left in my own hands by which I might strive toward salvation. For ... I should nevertheless have to labor under perpetual uncertainty and to fight as one beating the air, since even if I lived and worked to eternity, my conscience would never be assured and certain how much it ought to do to satisfy God ... as the experience of all self-justifiers proves, and I myself learned to my bitter cost through so many years.[206]

In reply to this recognition by Luther of a subjective stake in his theology, Erasmus paraphrases Luther and then observes:

> But we are not inquiring here about what he judges to be more advantageous to himself but rather what was the will of God; and it could happen that a person might be confident of his conscience and still not be very safe. But in fact, who can be confident of his conscience when it is uncertain whether he is numbered among those God selected to be saved, even though they do

* * * * *

205 For a consideration of Renaissance activism and its relation to rhetorical theology see Charles Trinkaus 'Themes for a Renaissance Anthropology' in his *The Scope of Renaissance Humanism* (Ann Arbor, Mich 1983) 364–403.

206 *De servo arbitrio* WA 18 782:38–783:1 / LW 33 287–9

not deserve it? For even if he is certain about grace, he is not certain about whether God will take grace away (1516A).

Erasmus anticipates here the well-known anxiety of believers of the Puritan age as to whether they were among the elect and the nervous, never-ending search for proof of their election in the good deeds of their daily lives and in their worldly success.

As Erasmus moves towards his own concluding section he responds to Luther's presentation of his case by listing again the positions he opposes and those he supports on free will. He opposes both Karlstadt's notion that free will can do nothing by itself except evil and Luther's that free will is non-existent and can do neither good nor evil. As to the positions which Erasmus supports, he notes:

> I have often declared that I neither approve nor disapprove of the opinion
> of the scholastics that free will by its own power can merit justifying grace
> at least *de congruo*, but I am more inclined to approve than to disapprove. I
> defended the opinion of Augustine, who teaches that free will does exist in
> mankind but that, because of sin, it is ineffective in obtaining justifying grace
> without the help of grace (1487A–B).

Although Erasmus elaborates and qualifies Augustine's position and some-times seems to consider it definitive, he is also serious in his partial en-dorsement of the scholastic *via moderna*.

He leans sometimes more towards Augustine, sometimes more to-wards the *via moderna*. For example, he replies to Luther's comments on the late scholastic categories of 'congruous' and 'condign' merit, both of which Luther rejected as offering merit of any sort at all. 'Congruous' merit applies to fittingly beneficent actions prior to or without receiving grace; 'condign' merit applies to the truly meritorious cooperation of the sinner with grace received that can lead to justification.[207] Erasmus thinks Luther concedes that man can cooperate with grace:

> Now Luther grants that sometimes the human will cooperates with grace. But
> if it is not absurd that the will should assist, as it were, cooperating grace, why
> should it be absurd for the human will to make itself available, struggling, as
> it were, towards preparatory grace? (1501C–D)

\* \* \* \* \*

207 For the basic *via moderna* theology underlying these terms see Oberman *Har-vest* 146–84 and McGrath *Iustitia Dei* I 189, 70–91, and 109–79. Luther discusses these concepts at *De servo arbitrio* WA 18 769–71 / LW 33 266–70.

The issue is whether particular grace is required to prepare the will to co-operate with grace once it has been granted. Erasmus seems to suggest that the action of the will can precede particular grace and thus attain 'congruous merit.' It seems from what follows that, although he denies that he ever said it, there would be no risk in holding to the notion of 'congruous' merit, 'some work which solicits the kindness of God without any special grace' (1501E). It is beginning to seem, as he approaches his conclusion, that Erasmus will be arguing with Augustine rather than Luther.

Erasmus' selection of Augustine as his model of the position which attributes a little bit to free will in the process of justification but almost everything to grace was partly strategic. He intends to show that Luther's most admired churchman was actually aligned with Erasmus' position. In *Hyperaspistes 1* he had argued that Augustine was not entirely on Luther's side, quoting most often from Augustine's *On Grace and Free Will*, which does indeed affirm that free will exists but considers it totally ineffective without grace from the very beginning of the process of justification.[208] Erasmus regards this and other anti-Pelagian writings of Augustine as weighted towards grace because of his need to combat the dangerous heresy of Pelagianism. Although he quotes Augustine more than any other Father, it becomes clear in *Hyperaspistes 2* that Erasmus admired Origen, Chrysostom, Ambrose, and Jerome more than Augustine. It may well be asked whether his stated inclination towards *meritum de congruo* does not indicate that Erasmus genuinely favoured this late scholastic opinion over Augustine's severe limitation of free will. But even so, Augustine's doctrine would seem to be closer to Erasmus' view than to Luther's.

In his conclusion Erasmus discusses the question of 'fitness' and 'worth' (*congruitas* and *condignitas*) as well as the phases in the process of justification. He shows that Augustine holds that at the outset even a good intention is a gift of grace, so that there is no question of his having approved anything like 'congruous merit' (1523F–1524B). Discussing the human ethics of giving and accepting benefits [*beneficia*], Erasmus quotes Matthew 25:29 to show that grace does not preclude any worthiness in the person to whom it has been given:

> 'To those who have it shall be given and they shall abound; but from those who do not have, even what they have shall be taken way.' For someone is said not to have if he has in such a way that he does not have a benefit, that is, who either ascribes the favour to his own merit or uses it otherwise than he ought.

\* \* \* \* \*

208 *De gratia et libero arbitrio* PL 44 881–912, especially 882

In this case, then, what is called worthiness in someone who receives and uses
something well is what the theologians call congruous merit (1525D–E)

Here he seems to contrive to make 'congruous merit' harmonize with Augustine's views. Whether Erasmus' definition of 'congruous merit' is the
same as that held by the *via moderna* is questionable, but he does reveal his
concern for a redefinition or qualification that might bring opposing positions together.

Erasmus then moves into a brilliant and overwhelming finale, in which
he transcends and synthesizes the many elements in his tradition and becomes the spokesman for his own deeply assimilated humanist theology,
presenting a vision of mankind and salvation which is truly profound and
momentous.[209] His vision is difficult to summarize, and the reader should
savour it in its own fullness. He begins by attempting to allay Augustine's
anxieties that if he accepted the notion of 'preparing' grace man would seem
to be earning justifying grace and grace would seem to have its inception
in free will. Grace, Erasmus suggests, has many kinds and degrees. Grace
is our word for God approaching man beneficently to lure him to salvation.
Augustine has nothing to fear.

> For just as there are various gradations of grace, so too there are various grada-
> tions of goodness or righteousness. Augustine himself invented many names
> for grace, according to the gradations of their effects, distinguishing sufficient
> from proficient, operating from cooperating, and then again operating from
> preparatory. I hardly know whether impelling grace is different from prepara-
> tory grace in the sense that preparatory grace moves the will and sometimes
> impelling does not. Now there can be many gradations of preparatory or im-
> pelling grace, just as God transforms a person in various ways and step by
> step, in the same way as nature forms a person step by step and a physi-
> cian restores a person step by step ... The ways in which God does this are
> innumerable: sometimes by means of a faithful wife, servant, or friend, he
> calls an unfaithful husband, master, or friend; sometimes he gets the same ef-
> fect by sickness, bereavement, or inflicting some other calamity; sometimes he
> does it by the ministry of the word; at other times, by miracles, apparitions, or

* * * * *

209 For an earlier, more diffuse reading of this section of *Hyperaspistes* 2 see
Charles Trinkaus 'Erasmus, Augustine and the Nominalists' *Archiv für Reformationsgeschichte* 67 (1976) 5–32. For a more recent, quite compatible view
see James D. Tracy 'Two Erasmuses, Two Luthers: Erasmus' Strategy in Defense of *De libero arbitrio*' *Archiv für Reformationsgeschichte* 78 (1987) 37–60.

dreams; and often he hunts down a person from ambush, as it were, and saves him through what pleases him most, as, for example uxorious men through their wives, and he snared St Hubert as he was hunting, and he captures avid students through writings; some he draws by the secret whistling of the Spirit (1526E–1527A).

He proceeds to give a series of apt analogies for the gradual reception of grace: approaching light from the darkness of a tunnel, the growth of a foetus into a fully human person, the cure of a disease by a physician. God's grace – not just the grace of a general concursus but specific grace for specific situations and occasions – combines with nature itself and works slowly for the most part, thus eliminating any conflict between nature and grace.

Erasmus is seeking to draw together human will and grace, grace acting on a person and the person willing by assenting, responding to whatever allure is presented. In this convergence of divine and human participation in the conversion of a soul, in this theological delineation of a holy occurrence, Erasmus is also seeking to draw together the Augustinian insistence on divine omnipotence and all-embracing grace and the late scholastic vision of a divine concession of a person's own role in his own salvation. He is seeking to reconcile God and man, and the dividing directions of faith within the Christian community, thinking of his own time and recalling what had happened at many moments in the history of the faith:

> ... so too grace eggs on nature step by step when it is darkling and sickly until it arrives at that gift which makes us blessed, at least so far as this life is concerned. For to be blessed is to be free of sin and endowed with righteousness ... Therefore, what Augustine says is true: a person's good intentions are not aided by grace but given by grace, if he is referring, as I think he is, to the good will by which a person is justified. But just as there is in man a natural inclination to vice which Satan continually exploits to tempt him to sin, so too there is in him a natural desire for virtue, though it is imperfect. The impelling grace of God solicits this desire in thousands of ways to lead it to justification, egging on a person's latent, feeble impulse (1528A–D).

Erasmus would call these impulses and circumstances 'impelling grace':

> Now if you wish to give the name impelling grace to the particular occasions by which a sinner is admonished to repent, I do not have much against it. And yet in these also the will is not entirely inactive ... I am not talking about the assent which gives justification but that which somehow prepares

for it. Now let us grant that such natural movement of our minds, imperfect as they are without grace, spring from our natural power. Does this pose any risk to God's grace? I do not think so (1528E–F).

Erasmus is clearly arguing as much with Augustine as with Luther here. He speaks of the examples of virtue among the pagans and the teachings of the philosophers which seem to accord with dogma, 'works which, I confess, did not merit or give rise to justifying grace but which nevertheless rendered the soul more capable of receiving grace' (1529E). And with this should be included the works of the Old Testament Jews. 'And so just as the law of nature did not justify anyone but rather prepared for justification, so too the law of Moses, although it did not confer perfect justification, nevertheless prepared for it' (1530A). As [pseudo-] Ambrose wrote in *The Calling of All the Gentiles*, 'divine providence was not lacking in any era or to any kind of person' (1529F).[210] The realm of the Christian God, he reminds, is universal and includes all human existence in the divine plan.

Erasmus uses the example of Augustine's own conversion to justify accepting the scholastic doctrine of congruous merit. He lists Augustine's various activities as 'he was wavering about Christ,' relying, of course, on his *Confessions*:

> But if such morally good works, or whatever you want to call them, prepare a person for God's grace or if, as the scholastics say, they earn it by merit *de congruo*, what is absurd about this opinion? And if Augustine, through the power of free will, could listen to the sermons of Ambrose, read holy books, make contributions to the poor, make time for prayers and meditations, converse with pious men and ask them to pray to the Lord for his salvation, what reason is there to hiss so vehemently at the opinion of the scholastics, according to which a person merits justifying grace *de congruo* through morally good works? We are frightened of shadowy words, when in reality there is no absurdity. If someone should say that through such deeds a person can in some sense be prepared for grace, they would put up with it, I think; as it is, even though the same thing is meant by someone who says 'grace is merited *de congruo*,' they are offended (1531C–D).

Erasmus kept insisting that many seemingly serious doctrinal differences can be reconciled if one looks at the living actuality of the situation.

\* \* \* \* \*

210 *De vocatione omnium gentium* 2.25 PL 51 710D–711B

To make clear that he is speaking from the perspective of the *via moderna* (though not as a scholastic) when he seeks to harmonize it with that of Augustine (certainly representative of the *via antiqua*), he offers the following advice to someone seeking faith and a good will:

> 'Read holy books,' I say, 'go to holy sermons, pray frequently, give money to the poor, ask pious men to pray for your salvation, little by little withdraw from vices as much as you can; if you do these things to the best of your ability, God's grace will not be wanting to you' (1531E).

The teaching of the *via moderna* was that 'God will not withhold his grace from one who does the best he can.'[211] Erasmus adds:

> 'Nor does it make much difference whether you say that these works are performed through free will or that they are done with the continual inspiration of particular grace, which advances but does not perfect. But in fact it is more plausible to profess that they are not devoid of the grace of God, who gradually advances the minuscule human power which is inadequate by itself (1531E–F).

Erasmus is dealing with the question of free will within the context of what has been called his 'grammar of consent,'[212] an inseparable part of his humanist theology. The perspective which enables him to harmonize pagan philosophy and the doctrine of the Old Testament law with the preparation of grace, and late medieval scholasticism with Augustinianism, certainly is central to his 'grammar of consent.' It is a historical perspective focused on the resolution of conflict and the peace of the church but also on divine providence and love:

> But if in those stages by which we gradually leave a vicious habit behind and approach justification someone wants to add particular grace, I consider this a

\* \* \* \* \*

211 For a comparison of Erasmus' views with those of late medieval scholastics concerning the initiation of the process of justification, see Oberman *Harvest* 120–45.

212 See n176 above. Erasmus' effort to pull the extremes of Christian doctrine into a middle position that could be tolerated, if not endorsed, is a necessary consequence of what James K. McConica has called Erasmus' 'grammar of consent.' Compatible with this 'grammar of consent' is Erasmus' principle of accommodation: God speaks in differing and appropriate ways to the many kinds and conditions of mankind, and men address their fellow men and even God himself in varying and suitable ways.

pious opinion. But I do not consider it compatible with Christian tranquillity
to whip up melodramatic uproars over these tiny points. Maybe it would have
been better for everyone, according to Paul's saying, to have room to indulge
in his own insights. When he struggles against the Pelagians to protect grace,
Augustine attributed so little to free will as to grant it something in name
more than in fact ... Later theologians tempered both opinions, attributing
somewhat more to free will than he did, and distinguishing congruous merit
from condign merit, acquired faith from infused faith, a perfect will from an
imperfect one (1534C–E).

Here Erasmus projects a vision of world history as the process of salvation
under Christ. It is also a vision of church history, not something new, but
new in its contours.

   Luther, to whom Erasmus returns in his final pronouncements, regarded Augustine's estimate of free will as too high, not too low as the
scholastics did. He did not even allow one the free will to withdraw from
grace: the human will can accomplish nothing, good or evil. Luther so diminished nature to heighten grace that he denied 'that anyone was saved
either under the law of Moses or the law of nature.' Those who were saved
were so by the gift of Christ who is lacking to no one, 'although he bestows
himself differently at various times and to various persons, according to
the disposition of the divine plan' (1534F).

   Erasmus' vision of the Christian faith is more universal than that of all
of his day, including the members of the universal Catholic church to which
he pledged himself. This universality was constructed from the many divergent situations, impulses, and motivations of human life that ran from
the creation of Adam to his own day. Everything had to be judged in its
own terms, but put together they made up the totality of the history of
Christianity and of mankind. Though Erasmus berated Luther for his use
of paradoxes, he himself propounded the colossal paradox that the universality of mankind was constituted from the variety and individuality of all
its parts. These were, to be sure, held together in his mind by God's love of
mankind and the world and the love of every person for God and for himself and his neighbour, though he knew, of course, that in any given case
human love might be distorted and defective or even transformed into its
opposite.

   It is in the name of this catholicity that Erasmus made his closing appeals. This catholicity was too catholic for any of the Christian groups of
his day to accept because they recognized not their brother in the other
but their enemy and God's. Erasmus admonished the Lutherans that their
exaggerations should have been aimed 'at the human folly and malice

into which mankind had cast itself down by means of free will rather than at nature as vitiated by the sin of Adam, so as to avoid agreeing with the Manichaeans' (1535A). Lutherans are tottering on the brink of the Manichaean gutter: in attributing their salvation to grace, they should remember that others by free will may act with grace, and that they themselves can lose their own grace by choosing not to persevere, that furthermore the endowments of nature are the gracious gift of God. He warned the scholastics of the *via moderna* that they were 'not far from the ditch of Pelagianism,' that they should remember 'how accursed it is in the eyes of God for a person to rely on his own powers.' They should give thanks to God for any natural powers they possess. God accepts these powers out of mercy, not justice, and can take them away if they are used wrongly or selfishly. 'They should not deceive themselves because of terms like "freedom," "merit," "worthy," "condign," "congruous," or "debt," since the essence of the whole process is owed to the gratuitous kindness of God' (1535B–C).

Finally, addressing someone who 'thinks Augustine did not do full justice to free will and that recent theologians attribute too much to it,' Erasmus urges such a person to follow the way he has himself propounded:

> Let him proceed safely along the middle way and let him believe that even in those steps by which ... we are prepared for grace we are not without particular grace, so that according to the tiny measure of our progress, for every one of us and in every respect, both free will cooperates with grace and grace with free will ... For through such excessively subtle wars of words we would lose God's grace rather than fully understand by what means grace works in us, especially since God, whose ways are everywhere beyond our full comprehension, reveals his power among his creatures in such various ways (1535D–E).

Making one final effort to reconcile both sides by urging them to adapt to the positions of the other, he emphasizes his way of reading Scripture:

> Furthermore, without too much trouble we will bring into harmony scriptural passages that seem inconsistent with one another if we distinguish the meanings of words – as I have shown – and if we consider that in saving or damning people God acts according to various rationales and that what we read he did in one case or another, according to his administrative plan, he does not automatically do in all cases ... But since Scripture sometimes addresses one group, sometimes the other, it should be interpreted according to the character of those who are being addressed. Otherwise it will seem to contradict

itself in many places, whereas in fact nothing could be more self-consistent than Scripture (1535F–1536A and 1536E).

Erasmus of Rotterdam was a humanist in his theology, a theologian in his humanism.

Within ten years of the publication of *Hyperaspistes* 2 Erasmus had died, within twenty Luther. The year Luther died the religious wars that were to devastate Europe for more than a hundred years began. Erasmus, the man who had sought religious peace, was condemned by both sides and is remembered for his failure to reconcile them. But he also should be remembered for his humanist ideals of concord and civil discourse, a vision he had sought and found in the Gospels.[213] He was remembered for these ideals, at first secretly,[214] and then in later centuries with triumph.

CT

EDITORIAL PRACTICES

The Latin text on which the translation of *De libero arbitrio* is based is that edited by Johannes von Walter; at the foot of each page of the translation, references will indicate the corresponding column in LB IX and page of the Walter edition. The Latin text used by the translator of *Hyperaspistes* book 1 is a transcription of Erasmus' first and second editions (Basel: Johann Froben, February and July 1526) made by Professor Cornelis Augustijn in preparation for his forthcoming edition in the Amsterdam *Opera omnia* of Erasmus. Whenever there seemed to be a difficulty, the translator was also able to consult photocopies of the two early editions, also kindly supplied by Professor Augustijn. *Hyperaspistes* book 2 will be translated

\* \* \* \* \*

213 In evaluating the outcome of the debate between Erasmus and Luther Heiko A. Oberman sees Erasmus as the short-term loser but as the victor in the long run because 'he was ... interested ... in an attitude that with its academic reticence and struggle for objectivity would serve peace in the Church and the world.' But in these writings 'he was more scholastic and medieval than ever before' (*Luther* 216). In fact, however, Erasmus was ambivalent towards the *via moderna* and scholasticism, and primarily he looked for the warm humanity and divine mercifulness of the Greek and Latin Fathers he most admired.
214 See John C. Olin 'Erasmus and St. Ignatius Loyola' in *Luther, Erasmus and the Reformation: A Catholic-Protestant Reappraisal* ed John C. Olin, James D. Smart, and Robert E. McNally SJ (New York 1969) 114–27. For less 'secret' admiration of Erasmus see James K. McConica *English Humanists and Reformation Politics under Henry VIII and Edward VI* (Oxford 1965) 106–99 and Margo Todd *Christian Humanism and the Puritan Social Order* (Cambridge 1987) 22–95.

from Professor Augustijn's transcription of the Froben edition of September 1527. LB X references are given at the foot of the page for *Hyperaspistes* book 1; the translation of *Hyperaspistes* book 2 in CWE 77 will include as well references to Augustijn's ASD edition, if it is then available. The translation of article 36 of Martin Luther's *Assertio* is based on the text of the Weimar edition of Luther's works, volume VII 142–9.

Because Erasmus almost always quotes the Vulgate version of Scripture, biblical references will be identified according to the Vulgate designations and numbering.

In the introduction and editorial commentary, the term 'free will' has been substituted for 'freedom of the will' in quotations from CWE volumes already published. This change has been made, with the agreement of the Editorial Board, so that the terminology used in discussing the debate about free will remains consistent throughout CWE 76 and 77.

In order to assist the reader of these long and complex works, tables of divisions and correspondences have been provided (311–21). Interesting treatments of particular theological and exegetical subjects occur in interaction between Erasmus in *A Discussion*, Luther in his *The Enslaved Will* responding to Erasmus' *Discussion*, and Erasmus responding in turn to Luther in *Hyperaspistes* 1 and 2. Headings have been supplied in the CWE translation for the major parts and particular topics of these works by Erasmus. The corresponding titles for Luther's reply are those furnished by Philip S. Watson in his translation of that work in the series *Luther's Works*, which we have used with the kind permission of Westminster John Knox Press. In the tables, these headings of the three works are arranged in parallel columns showing their inter-relationships. Because Erasmus' arguments against Luther's position on free will were to a large extent supported by his scriptural interpretation, it is possible to examine sequentially Erasmus' interpretation of a particular passage in order to refute Luther, Luther's defence of it, and Erasmus' further efforts to refute Luther's interpretation. Moreover, because these are very long discussions of intricate theological topics, readers who may lack the sixteenth-century scholar's textual and theological endurance might find the tables of divisions and correspondences of assistance.

Indexes to the CWE translations of Erasmus' works in the controversy with Luther will appear in volume 77.

ACKNOWLEDGMENTS
The editor and translators wish to give special thanks to Jerry H. Bentley for his critical reading of the translations and annotations of the works in CWE 76 and the helpful comments he made on them. A number of scholars

contributed in various ways to the annotations: Marjorie O'Rourke Boyle, James M. Estes, Erika Rummel, James D. Tracy, and James Michael Weiss. Professor G.T. Cockburn and Professor A. Woodman of the Classics Department, and Ann Moss, Professor of French, all of the University of Durham, have also contributed neo-Latin expertise and constructive criticism to the translation of *De libero arbitrio*. Special thanks are also due to Alexander Dalzell and Cornelis Augustijn for carefully reading the whole translation and commentary and making many useful queries and suggestions. We are deeply grateful to Professor Augustijn for providing the Latin text of *Hyperaspistes* he has prepared for the Amsterdam *Opera omnia*, together with photocopies of the two early editions on which his text of *Hyperaspistes 1* is based. Finally, Clarence Miller wishes to thank the providers of the Mellon Fund at Saint Louis University for the award of a grant that enabled him to study Emser's German translation of *Hyperaspistes* at Wolfenbüttel.

# A DISCUSSION OF FREE WILL

*De libero arbitrio* διατριβή *sive collatio*

translated by
PETER MACARDLE

annotated by
PETER MACARDLE, CLARENCE H. MILLER, and
CHARLES TRINKAUS

In 1526 Nikolaus Herman of Altdorf, the first translator of *De libero arbitrio*, very modestly wrote that, since he could neither judge nor contribute to the controversy between Luther and Erasmus, he had confined himself to producing the 'closest and best' German version he could manage, in order that the world might reach its own conclusion.[1]

Four and a half centuries later this aim is considerably harder to realize. The Latin of *De libero arbitrio*, basically classical but with patristic and medieval features, is in many respects opaque to us. The treatise stalks scholastic terrain but largely avoids scholastic vocabulary, so that the exact nuances of words are often difficult to determine: I would endorse the judgment of the translators of the *Paraphrases on Romans and Galatians* that Erasmus' theological vocabulary shows variety rather than precision.[2] Then, too, because the problem of free will and justification became one of the theological cruces of the Reformation period, there is the danger of reading back into this early document senses which belong to a later and more systematic stage of the debate. In these circumstances, translation and interpretation unavoidably overlap, and I can only claim to have interpreted as little, as cautiously, and as judiciously as possible.

Erasmus published the first two editions of *De libero arbitrio* in Basel (1524). The translation follows the semi-critical edition of Johannes von Walter,[3] making full use of its textual apparatus and commentary. Walter's text has been closely compared with that of the Leiden edition.[4] I have consulted the English version of Rupp and Marlow[5] and the German translations of Schumacher[6] and Lesowsky[7] at every stage; on occasional problem passages, Mesnard's French version,[8] and indeed Herman himself, were compared. In a very few cases where the Latin wording seemed questionable, I have

\* \* \* \* \*

1 *Eyne vergleychung, odder zusamen haltung der sprüche vom Freyen willen, Erasmi von Roterodam, durch Nikolaum Herman von Altdorff ynss Teutsch gebracht* (no place 1526)
2 CWE 42 xxv–xxviii, especially xxvi–xxvii
3 *De libero arbitrio* διατριβή *sive collatio per Desiderium Erasmum Roterodamum* Quellenschriften zur Geschichte des Protestantismus 8 (Leipzig 1910)
4 LB IX 1215–48
5 *De libero arbitrio* trans and ed E. Gordon Rupp in collaboration with A.N. Marlow in *Luther and Erasmus: Free Will and Salvation* The Library of Christian Classics 17 (London 1969) 33–97
6 *Vom freien Willen* trans Otto Schumacher, 2nd ed (Göttingen 1956)
7 *De libero arbitrio* διατριβή *sive collatio* trans with introduction and notes by Winfried Lesowsky in *Erasmus von Rotterdam Ausgewählte Schriften* ed Werner Welzig, 8 vols (Darmstadt 1967– ) IV (1969) 1–195
8 *Essai sur le libre arbitre* trans Pierre Mesnard (Algiers 1945)

looked at several early printings of *De libero arbitrio*, but until the Amsterdam edition provides us with a proper critical text, such investigation must remain amateurish and its results largely conjectural, so it has been kept to an absolute minimum.

In translating I have tried to reach a plausible twentieth-century English prose as unstilted and as free of unnecessary Latinism as possible, occasionally recasting the original syntactic structures so as to achieve this. The translation attempts to convey something of Erasmus' easy eloquence, though it lags far behind the original in this respect: most significantly it loses the constant play on the meanings and sounds of words which gives the work so much of its rhetorical finesse, but which is nearly always inimitable in English.

Erasmus claimed to have written *De libero arbitrio* in a hurry, and the text bears the marks of haste in the form of occasional lack of clarity and even syntactic incompleteness. Such flaws have been silently corrected or massaged in the translation, though the notes draw attention to one or two problematic passages.

The translation of the countless biblical quotations in the text presented a number of problems. All were newly verified for this translation, making the scriptural references here more comprehensive and more accurate than in most editions so far. The process of verification also confirmed that Erasmus almost invariably quotes from the Vulgate, even where his own translation, the *Novum instrumentum* of 1516 (revised as the *Novum Testamentum* in 1519) comments on the shortcomings of the Vulgate and substitutes radically different readings. Only in one or two instances, recorded in the notes, are *Novum instrumentum* or *Novum Testamentum* readings found in *De libero arbitrio*; it seems that Erasmus wished to conduct this debate on the basis of the received biblical text, presumably so as not to add philological to theological controversy. Yet, on the other hand, hardly a single quotation is exactly as in the Vulgate: the impression is of a writer sometimes quoting familiar material imperfectly from memory, sometimes consciously modifying the traditional wording to achieve greater clarity or elegance. The countless minor deviations from the precise Vulgate text thus produced could not all be recorded in an edition of this kind: some of the more significant are found in the notes. It is, of course, Erasmus' actual wording which is translated, not the exact Vulgate readings, though more often than not this makes little or no difference to the English.

The time is past when biblical passages were as a matter of course rendered in the language of the Authorized (King James) Version, a translation which in any case frequently differs from the Vulgate. Accordingly, versions of the Vulgate here are my own, albeit in the light of the Douay-

Rheims and Knox translations, the original Hebrew and Greek, and modern translations. There are gestures in the direction of the King James version in certain familiar passages where anything else would seem perverse, but in general there is no attempt at an archaic or 'scriptural' style.

PM

# A DISCUSSION OF FREE WILL[1]

## [PREFACE]

### [A temperate debate]

Among the many difficulties encountered in Holy Scripture there is hardly a labyrinth[2] more impenetrable than that of free will: this question has long exercised the minds of philosophers and theologians,[3] ancient and modern, to an amazing degree, but has, I feel, demanded more in labour than it has yielded in results. It was recently revived by Karlstadt and

* * * * *

1 Erasmus' title in the early editions is *De libero arbitrio* διατριβή *sive collatio*. The Greek word, which passed into Latin in the form *diatriba*, is synonymous with the second half of the doublet, *collatio* 'a discussion.' For an analysis of the meaning and rhetorical form of a *diatribē* see Boyle *Rhetoric* 5–9. *Diatriba* was the abbreviated title used by contemporaries and by Erasmus himself. Some have thought that *collatio* might mean 'comparison' because Erasmus compares passages of Scripture for and against free will and compares Luther with the church Fathers who supported it. But *collatio* usually refers to comparisons of similar things, not opposites. Then too, the two elements of the title are alternatives meaning more or less the same thing. One meaning of *collatio* in *Thesaurus linguae latinae* . . . (Leipzig 1900–   ) fits perfectly: 'a communication or conversation or discussion' (B2). Augustine and Cassian have works entitled *Collatio*, which are not comparisons but discussions with another person. Also Ambrosiaster on 2 Tim 2:15 says: 'collatio ergo inter dei servos esse debet non altercatio.' Jerome (Ep 102.2) speaks of 'collatione mutua vel doceremus aliqua vel disceremus.' Augustine (Ep 129.1) says 'collationem quae pacifica et pacata esse debet' and again (*Contra Cresconium* 4.66.83) 'vos non ad contentionem sed ad collationem vocare.' The evidence suggests that a *collatio* is a peaceful discussion, precisely what Erasmus is proposing.

2 *Adagia* II x 51

3 See Augustine *De civitate Dei* 5.1–11, where he argues against pagan philosophers and poets who defended fate or free will as the cause of historical events rather than divine providence.

Eck[4] (though their dispute was relatively moderate); more recently still it was violently stirred up by Martin Luther, who has written an *Assertion* on free will.[5] He has already been answered by more than one writer;[6] nevertheless, since my friends think I should,[7] I too will see if our modest dispute can in its turn succeed in making the truth somewhat clearer. Here I know that some readers will immediately stop up their ears and cry, 'The streams flow upwards! Does Erasmus dare to take on Luther, as a fly might an elephant?'[8] To mollify them (if I may beg for a moment's silence) I will state at present only what is the case: that I have never sworn assent to Luther's words. And so, no one should find it unfitting if I openly disagree with him at some point, merely as one man from another, of course; it is far from a crime to take issue with some teaching of his, and much less so if someone engages in a temperate debate with him with the aim of eliciting the truth. Indeed, I doubt that Luther will take it ill if someone disagrees with him on any point, given that he himself presumes to appeal from the judgments of all the Doctors of the church, and of all the universities, councils, and popes as well. Since he proclaims this freely and openly, I should seem to be guilty of no offence in his friends' eyes if I do the same.

And so that no one interprets this as a fight between two hired gladiators,[9] I will take issue solely with this one teaching of Luther's, with the

\* \* \* \* \*

4 Andreas Bodenstein of Karlstadt (ca 1480–1541), dean of the faculty of theology at Wittenberg, debated with Johann Meier of Eck (1486–1543) at Leipzig in 1519. Karlstadt, an early ally of Luther who later became a more radical reformer, wrote *Epistola adversus ineptam et ridiculam inventionem Johannis Eckii* (Leipzig: V. Schumann 1519). Eck, who was to become a leading Catholic apologist, had replied to an earlier attack by Karlstadt in his *Defensio contra amarulentas D. Andreae Bodenstein Carolstadtini invectiones* (Augsburg: S. Grimm and M. Wirsung 1518). See Eck's *Disputatio Johannis Eckii et Andreae Carolstadtii et Martini Lutheri* (Erfurt: M. Meier 1919) and the edition of it in *Der authentische Text der Leipziger Disputation (1519)* ed Otto Seitz (Berlin 1903). On both Karlstadt and Eck see CEBR; see also *Hyperaspistes* 1 nn97 and 368.

5 *Assertio omnium articulorum Martini Lutheri per bullam Leonis x novissimam damnatorum* (*An Assertion of All the Articles of Martin Luther Which Were Quite Recently Condemned by a Bull of Leo x*) (Wittenberg, December 1520) article 36; WA 7 142–9. See introduction xxxix–xlvii and n90.

6 For replies to Luther see *Hyperaspistes* 1 nn5–11.

7 See Ep 1341A:1362–70, where several such friends are mentioned.

8 *Adagia* I iii 15 and I ix 69; in her prologue (1–4) Boyle *Rhetoric* discusses the elephant metaphor.

9 *Adagia* I iii 76; Erasmus here affirms the purity and single-mindedness of his intentions.

single aim of juxtaposing various scriptural texts and arguments to illuminate the truth, the search for which has always done great credit to scholars. The debate will be carried on without abuse, both because this is more seemly for Christians, and because it is a surer way of discovering the truth, which is often lost in too much angry repartee.

[*Erasmus' aversion to dogmatism and assertion*]
Now for my part I was well aware how poorly suited I was for this wrestling-match – indeed there is hardly a man less practised in the art than I, for I have always had a deep-seated inner revulsion from conflict, and so have always preferred sporting in the spacious plains of the Muses to engaging in swordplay at close quarters.[10] And I take so little pleasure in assertions that I will gladly seek refuge in Scepticism[11] whenever this is allowed by the inviolable authority of Holy Scripture and the church's decrees; to these decrees I willingly submit my judgment in all things, whether I fully understand what the church commands or not.

I prefer, indeed, to have this cast of mind than that which I see characterizes certain others, so that they are uncontrollably attached to an opinion and cannot tolerate anything that disagrees with it, but twist whatever they read in Scripture to support the view they have embraced once for all. Just so boys immoderately in love with a girl imagine they see the object of their love wherever they turn, or, to give a better comparison, when people have come to blows they turn anything that happens to be at hand, be it a cup or a dish, into a weapon. I ask you – what unbiased judgment can there be among people with such an attitude? What results do disputations like this produce, beyond each party going off covered with the other's spit? Yet there will always be many such 'ignorant and restless men,' as the apostle Peter describes them, 'who pervert the Scriptures to their own destruction.'[12]

And so, as far as my own position is concerned, I would say that many and various views on free will have been handed down by the ancient

* * * * *

10 Although reluctant to take on Luther, Erasmus engaged in many controversies; see Rummel *Catholic Critics*.
11 Erasmus refers to the two ancient philosophical schools founded by Pyrrhon of Elis and Antiochus of Ascalon and to Cicero's *Academica*; see Richard H. Popkin *The History of Scepticism from Erasmus to Descartes* (New York 1964) chapters 1 and 2; see also Charles B. Schmitt *Cicero Scepticus: A Study of the Academica in the Renaissance* (The Hague 1972) 59.
12 2 Pet 3:16

writers,[13] and that as yet I have no settled opinion regarding them, beyond a belief that a certain power of free will does exist. I have read Martin Luther's *Assertion*[14] – with an open mind, apart from a slight bias in his favour which I assumed, just as a lawyer will favour a man charged with a crime – and I must frankly admit that, though he deals with the question in all its aspects, using every strategy and showing great élan, he has not succeeded in persuading me.

If anyone should ascribe this to my own slow wits or lack of learning, I will not quarrel with him – as long as we slower mortals are allowed to learn by contending with those more richly endowed with the gift of God; especially given that Luther attributes very little to learning and a great deal to the Spirit, who often instils into the lowly certain things that he has denied to the wise. This is my reply to those who clamour that Luther has more learning in his little finger than Erasmus has in his whole body[15] (a view which I have no intention of refuting here). However prejudiced these people are, they will, I think, grant me this: if in this dispute I concede that Luther is not to be incriminated by judgments already made by doctors, councils, universities, popes, and the emperor, then my case should not be prejudiced by hasty judgments on the part of certain readers. Although I believe that I have grasped Luther's argument, I might be mistaken, and so I will act as disputant, not as judge; as inquirer, not as dogmatist;[16] ready to learn from anyone, if any truer or more reliable arguments can be put forward.

[*The obscurity of Scripture*]
Yet I would be pleased if I could persuade those of average intellect that in discussions of this kind they should not be too persistent in making assertions which may more readily damage Christian harmony than advance true religion. For in Holy Scripture there are some secret places into which God did not intend us to penetrate very far, and if we attempt to do so, the farther in we go the less and less clearly we see. This is presumably in order to make us recognize the unsearchable majesty of divine wisdom,

\* \* \* \* \*

13 Erasmus is thinking primarily about ancient Christian writers.
14 See n5 above.
15 See Erasmus Alber *Iudicium ... de Spongia Erasmi ...* (Hagenau: J. Setzer 1524) in Hutten II 375:13–15. On Alber see *Hyperaspistes* 1 n90 and CEBR.
16 Erasmus' fundamental stance in *A Discussion*; see Boyle *Rhetoric* chapter 2 'Sceptic Debater and Stoic Assertor,' which presents the debate between Erasmus and Luther as a confrontation of these two types of rhetoric (43–66).

and the frailty of the human intellect. It is just as Pomponius Mela tells of a cave near Corycos:[17] Its great natural beauty at first entices and attracts visitors, but then, when they have gone further in, a kind of supernatural dread and the majesty of the divine being that dwells there drive them out again. And so, when we come to such places, I believe that to cry with Paul, 'Oh, the depth of the riches of God's wisdom and knowledge! How incomprehensible are his counsels, and how unsearchable his ways!'[18] and with Isaiah, 'Who has assisted[19] the Spirit of the Lord? Who has been his counsellor?'[20] is more advisable and devout than to define what passes the scope of human thought. Many things are reserved for that time when we no longer 'see through a glass darkly,'[21] but the Lord reveals his face and we behold his glory.

[*A Christian outlook for ordinary persons*]
In my opinion, therefore, as far as free will is concerned, what we have learned from the Scriptures should be sufficient: if we are on the path of righteousness, we should move swiftly on to better deeds, forgetting what lies behind.[22] If we are entangled in sin, we should do our best to struggle out; we should approach the remedy of penance and in all ways seek to obtain God's mercy, without which human will and effort are fruitless; we should impute anything bad to ourselves; anything good we should ascribe entirely to the bounty of God, to which we owe the very fact of our being. Moreover we should believe that everything, happy or sad, that befalls us in this life has been sent by God for our salvation; that no wrong can be done us by a God who is righteous by nature, even if things do in some way seem to happen that we have not deserved; and that no one must despair of forgiveness from a God who is by nature most merciful. To know this, I say, would be enough for a good Christian life, and we would

* * * * *

17 The geographer Pomponius Mela *De chorographia* 1.72.7 tells of a cave which, alluring at first, became more horrific the deeper one penetrated. Luther rejected this analogy to difficult passages of Scripture at *De servo arbitrio* WA 18 607:1 / LW 33 26.
18 Rom 11:33
19 The accepted reading in the Vulgate is *adiuvit* 'assisted' rather than *audivit* 'heard,' which is found in a few manuscripts. Hence *audivit*, which is found in the early editions of *De libero arbitrio* (and perpetuated in later editions), is almost surely a misprint.
20 Isa 40:13
21 1 Cor 13:12
22 Phil 3:13

not have to penetrate with irreverent curiosity into obscure, indeed otiose topics: whether God foreknows anything contingently; whether our will accomplishes anything in matters pertaining to eternal salvation or simply suffers the action of grace; whether we do – or rather suffer – everything, good or evil, by absolute necessity.

There are certain things of which God intended us to be entirely ignorant, such as the day of our death and the time of the Last Judgment. Acts 1[:7]: 'It is not given to you to know the times or the moments which God the Father has placed in his own power'; and Mark 13[:32]: 'But the day or the hour no one knows, neither the angels in heaven, nor the Son, but only the Father.' Certain things he intended us to examine so that we might venerate him in mystical silence; accordingly there are numerous places in the Holy Scriptures whose meaning many have guessed at but whose ambiguity no one has clearly resolved – such as the distinction of persons,[23] the coinherence of divine and human nature in Christ, or the sin that will not be forgiven.[24] Certain other things he intended to be absolutely clear to us: such are the precepts for a good life. Here indeed is the word of God, which need not be sought by scaling the heights of heaven or brought back from far across the sea, but is close at hand, in our mouths and in our hearts.[25] These should be learned by everyone; other things are more properly committed to God. It is more reverent to adore the unknown than to analyse the incomprehensible. How many disputes, or rather squabbles, have been spawned by the distinction of persons, the mode of generation, or the distinction between filiation and procession![26] What confusion the brawling over the conception of the Virgin Mother of God has stirred up in the world![27] What results have these laborious arguments so far brought, I ask, except that,

\* \* \* \* \*

23 That is, in the Trinity
24 That is, blasphemy against the Holy Spirit (Mark 3:29)
25 Deut 30:11–4 and Rom 10:6–8
26 That is, the distinction of persons in the Trinity, the mode of generation of the Son, the distinction between the filiation of the Son from the Father and the procession of the Holy Spirit from the Father and the Son. The question of the procession of the Holy Spirit from both the Father and the Son rather than from the Father alone long divided the Latin and Greek churches. The apparent agreement on the Latin formula *ex patre filioque* at the Council of Florence in 1439 was soon rejected once again by the Greek church.
27 The fierce debate in the later middle ages over the immaculate conception of the Virgin Mary (that is, her freedom from original sin from the first moment of her conception), especially among Dominican and Franciscan theologians

with great cost to unity, we love too little even as we try to know too much?

*[Theological topics unsuitable for public discussion]*
Now, there are certain ideas such that, even if they were true and could be known, still it would not be fitting to expose them to the ears of all and sundry. Perhaps what the sophists[28] are constantly babbling is true – that God, as regards his nature, is no less present in a dung-beetle's lair (to say nothing more indecent, though they are not ashamed to do so) than in heaven;[29] but it would be useless to dispute this in front of the common people. And though the statement that there are three Gods may be true according to the rules of dialectic,[30] if made before the unlearned masses it would cause great scandal. If I were convinced (which is not the case) that confession as we now practise it had not been instituted by Christ, and could not have been instituted by men, and so could not be obligatory for anyone, and that satisfaction for sins could not be demanded either, I would be afraid to publish this opinion, for I see many humans with an amazing

\* \* \* \* \*

28 Erasmus and Luther frequently refer to scholastic theologians as sophists.
29 In his *Sententiae* I dist 37.9 Peter Lombard asks the question whether God, because of his ubiquity, is contaminated by being present in unclean or filthy objects (though he notes that the question is so frivolous as to be unworthy of a response). He answers at length, noting that God is not defiled by filth just as the rays of the sun shine on feces and filth (*feces et sordes*) but are unaffected by them. In commenting on this question of the *Sententiae*, Thomas Aquinas, Scotus, and Gabriel Biel ignore this difficulty, but Denys the Carthusian (1402–71), commenting on the question, presents the objection, offers a possible solution (God is not receptive and hence is unaffected), and presents his own (just as noble things do not ennoble God when he is present in them, so too ignoble things do not touch, defile, change, or affect him). See Dionysius the Carthusian *Opera omnia* 40 vols (Tournai 1896–1913) 20 433, 438, 441. For a survey of scholastic, Renaissance, and Reformation teachings about God's omnipresence see Amos Funkenstein *Theology and the Scientific Imagination from the Middle Ages to the Seventeenth Century* (Princeton 1986) 47–72. On Peter Lombard see *Hyperaspistes* 1 n903.
30 Pierre d'Ailly (1350–1420), a scholastic theologian and later chancellor of the University of Paris, became a cardinal and was an important figure at the Council of Constance (1414–1417). According to DTC 1 651, D'Ailly, in his *Quaestiones super primam, tertium, et quartum Sententiarum* (Venice 1500) I q 5 a 1, explained the Trinity in terminology which was ambiguous, subject to criticism, and untraditional, propounding such propositions as 'Res simplicissima est tres res et quaelibet earum' ('The most unqualified thing is three things and each of them').

propensity for wrongdoing who are to some extent prevented, or at least restrained, by the necessity of confessing their sins.[31]

There are some bodily diseases which it is more harmful to cure than to endure, such as if someone were to bathe in the warm blood of slaughtered children to get rid of leprosy.[32] Just so, there are certain errors which it would be less harmful to overlook than to uproot. Paul knew the distinction between what is lawful and what is expedient:[33] it is lawful to speak the truth; but it is not expedient to do so in front of anyone, at any time, in any way.[34] If I were certain that a synod had reached some misguided decision or definition, it would be lawful for me to proclaim the truth, but not expedient; otherwise the wicked would be given an opportunity to disregard the authority of the Fathers, even in their proper and holy decisions. I would prefer to say that they felt the decision was correct for their own time, but that present needs suggest it should be repealed.

And so, supposing that what Wyclif taught and Luther defended is in some sense true – that whatever we do happens not by free will but by absolute necessity[35] – what could be more useless than to spread this

* * * * *

31 Erasmus had recently published his *Exomologesis sive modus confitendi* (1524). He had been criticized for affirming the view he expresses here; see Rummel *Annotations* 152–6 and Payne *Sacraments* 181–216.

32 Lynn Thorndike *A History of Magic and Experimental Science* 8 vols (New York 1923–58) II 332 reports that Michael Scot (d c 1291) in his *Physiognomia*, which appeared in at least eighteen editions between 1477 and 1660, held that 'bathing in the blood of two-year-old infants mixed with hot water "undoubtedly cures leprosy."' Pliny (*Naturalis historia* 26.1.5) reports that Egyptian kings attempted to cure their leprosy by bathing in human blood. The motif recurs frequently in European medieval literature; the best known example is in *Der arme Heinrich* (c 1192–1200) by Hartmann von Aue (born c 1160). See *Der arme Heinrich* ed Hermann Paul, 14th ed rev Ludwig Wolff, Altdeutsche Texbibliothek 3 (Tübingen 1972) viii–ix. See also *Handwörterbuch des deutschen Aberglaubens* ed Hans Bächtold-Stäubli, 10 vols (Berlin 1927–42) I 728, 1434–42, especially 1447.

33 1 Cor 6:12

34 Erasmus here introduces a key principle of his views on human behaviour, one which he believed was observed by both God and saints. It derives, clearly, from his readings of the Fathers and his own rhetorical commitments: the accommodation of speech to the nature of the audience; see Hoffmann 106–12.

35 John Wyclif (c 1330–87) was an Oxford scholar and reformer, renowned for a translation of the Bible into English once thought to be supervised by him; see Anne Hudson *The Premature Reformation, Wycliffite Texts and Lollard History* (Oxford 1988) 23–4 and 231–47. His doctrine of the absolute necessity of all events (which he expressed in *De dominio divino* 1.13) was condemned by the

paradox abroad? Again, supposing that what Augustine writes somewhere is in some sense true, that God works both good and evil deeds in us, and rewards his good works in us, and punishes his evil works in us;[36] if this were made known to the masses, how wide this would open the door to godlessness in countless mortals, especially given the extent of their dullness, inertia, wickedness, and their incorrigible tendency to all manner of evil? Where is the weak man who will keep up the unremitting and painful struggle against his flesh? Where is the evil man who will strive to correct his life? Who will be able to bring himself to love wholeheartedly the God who has created a hell seething with everlasting tortures where he can punish his own evil deeds in wretched human beings, as though he delighted in their suffering? For thus many will interpret it. Humans are usually dull and carnal by nature, inclined to disbelief, prone to wickedness, given to blasphemy: there is no need to pour oil on the fire.[37]

And so Paul, as a careful steward of the word of God, frequently brings charity to bear and prefers to do what is expedient for his neighbour than what is simply lawful. He has wisdom, which he speaks amongst the perfect: amongst the weak he reckons that he knows nothing except Jesus Christ, and him crucified.[38]

\* \* \* \* \*

Council of Constance; see *Sacrorum conciliorum nova et amplissima collectio* ed Joannes Mansi et al, 54 vols (Paris 1901–27) XXVII 633. Luther propounded the same teaching in article 36 of his *Assertio* (WA 7 146 / 306). Erasmus is merely hypothetically assuming the truth of this doctrine here, and fearing its effects. He denies it strongly in both parts of *Hyperaspistes*.

36 As Erasmus says, this is not a specific reference. Several passages in Augustine approximate it. See, for example, *De gratia et libero arbitrio* 43 PL 4 909: 'His ... testimoniis ... manifestatur, operari deum in cordibus hominum ad inclinandas eorum voluntates quocumque voluerit, sive ad bona pro sua misericordia, sive ad mala pro meritis eorum' ('This testimony makes it clear that God works in the hearts of men to incline their will wherever he wishes, whether to good deeds out of his mercy or to evil one because of what they deserve'). See also *De praedestinatione sanctorum* 16.33 PL 44 984: 'Est ergo in malorum potestate peccare: ut autem peccando hoc vel hoc illa malitia faciant, non est in eorum potestate sed Dei dividentis tenebras et ordinantis eas' ('Malicious persons have it within their power to sin: but whether in that malice of theirs they commit this or that sin is not within their power but rather within that of God, who divides the shadows and orders them'). Erasmus fears the effects of wide knowledge of this teaching but does not necessarily deny its truth.

37 *Adagia* I ii 9

38 1 Cor 2:2–6

Holy Scripture has its own way of speaking, accommodated to our understanding.[39] Sometimes God is angry, sad, indignant; he raves, threatens, hates; at other times he is merciful, repents, changes his mind; not because such changes really take place in the divine nature, but because this manner of speaking is suited to our weakness and stupidity. I believe that the same good sense would befit those who have taken upon themselves the task of dispensing the divine word. Some things are harmful precisely because they are not fitting, like wine for a man with a fever. It might perhaps be permissible to treat such subjects in scholarly discussion, or in the theological schools, though not even there would I consider it expedient unless done with moderation; but to act out such matters before all and sundry like plays in a theatre seems to me not merely pointless but even destructive. I would therefore be happier convincing my readers not to waste their time or talents in labyrinths[40] of this kind than I would be refuting or confirming Luther's teachings. I might deservedly be thought too verbose in these prefatory remarks, if they were not almost more to the point than the disputation itself.

# [INTRODUCTION]

*[Scripture is primary but tradition is also important]*
Now, Luther admits the authority of no writer, however approved he may be, but accepts only the canonical Scriptures – and how gladly I welcome this opportunity of lessening my work! Since there are innumerable authors, among both the Greeks and the Latins, who treat free will either as their principal theme or incidentally, it would have been no mean task to assemble from all of them what each had said for or against free will, and to embark on the long, tedious business of explaining the meanings of their individual statements, or of refuting or confirming their arguments: yet this would have been wasted on Luther and his friends, especially since they contradict not only one another, but also often themselves.[41]

\* \* \* \* \*

39 See n34 above.
40 See n2 above. On the rejection of 'vain curiosity' in theological matters in late scholasticism and Luther, see Heiko A. Oberman 'Contra vanam curiositatem' *Theologische studien* 113 (1974) 33–49.
41 The friends are Karlstadt (see n4 above) and Philippus Melanchthon (that is, Philip Schwarzerd) 1497–1560, humanist professor of Greek and collaborator of Luther at Wittenberg (see CEBR). Luther might seem to Erasmus to have contradicted himself in *Assertio* article 36, by first granting and then denying some reality to free will (WA 7 142:28 and 146:3–6 / 301, 306).

None the less I would remind readers that, if Luther and I seem to be evenly matched on the basis of scriptural testimonies and sound arguments, they should then take into consideration the long list of highly learned men approved by the consensus of very many centuries,[42] all the way up to our own day, most of them commended by their exemplary life as well as by their admirable learning in the Scriptures. Some even gave their testimony in blood to the teaching of Christ which they had defended in their writings. Such are, amongst the Greeks, Origen, Basil, John Chrysostom, Cyril, John Damascene, and Theophylact;[43] and amongst the Latins Tertullian, Cyprian, Arnobius, Hilary, Ambrose, Jerome, and Augustine.[44] I say nothing of those such as Thomas, Scotus, Durandus, Capreolus, Gabriel, Giles, Gregory, or Alexander,[45] whose force and adroitness in argument I feel no one should entirely disdain; not to mention the authority of the many universities, councils, and popes. From the apostles' times to this day, there has not been a single writer who has completely denied the power of free will, excepting only Manichaeus[46] and John Wyclif;[47] for the authority of Lorenzo Valla,[48] who seems virtually to agree with them, carries little weight amongst theologians.

\* \* \* \* \*

42 On the centrality of the theme of consensus in Erasmus see McConica 'Consent.'

43 Origines Adamantius (c 185–255), Basil of Caesarea (c 330–79), John Chrysostom (c 354–407), Cyril of Alexandria (c 380–444), John Damascene (c 675–759), Theophylact of Ochrida (fl 1075)

44 Septimus Tertullianus (fl 190–220), Caecilius Cyprianus (d 258), Arnobius of Sica (c 349–97), Hilary of Poitiers (c 300–67), Ambrose of Milan (c 349–97), Eusebius Hieronymus (c 348–420), Aurelius Augustinus (354–430)

45 Thomas Aquinas (1224–74), John Duns Scotus (c 1265–1308), Durand de Saint Pourçain (c 1270–1332), John Capreolus (c 1380–1444), Gabriel Biel (c 1425–95), Giles of Rome (c 1247–1316) or perhaps Giles of Viterbo (1469–1532), Gregory of Rimini (c 1300–58) although Erasmus may have had other Gregorys in mind, Alexander of Hales (c 1185–1245) or possibly Alexander of Nequam (1157–1217). Erasmus made it clear on many occasions that these scholastics were not his favourite theologians. On this point he could agree with Luther.

46 Mani (216–77), founder of the Manichaean religion and a dualistic determinist. Strictly speaking 'Manichaeus' is not the name of a person but a follower of Mani's religion.

47 See n35 above.

48 Valla (1407–57), an Italian humanist and moralist, was an important influence on Erasmus through his *Adnotationes in Novum Testamentum* (published by Erasmus in Paris: Josse Bade 1505), his *Elegantiae linguae Latinae*, and other works. Erasmus shows little respect for Valla's *De libero arbitrio dialogus* (Strassburg 1482); modern editions by Jacques Chomarat (Paris 1983) and Maria Anfossi (Florence 1934); English translation by Charles Trinkaus in *The Renaissance*

Although the Manichaean dogma has long since been utterly rejected and laughed out of court by universal consensus, yet I would hardly think that it is less conducive to true religion than Wyclif's. For Manichaeus refers good and evil deeds to two natures in man, yet in such a way that our good deeds are owed to God as our creator. And in addition he leaves us grounds for imploring the creator's aid against the powers of darkness, and this helps us to sin less gravely, and to do good more easily.[49] But by referring everything to absolute necessity, what scope does Wyclif leave to our prayers or our endeavours?

And so to return to my actual theme. If the reader sees that my argument proves a match for that of my opponents, then he should consider whether more weight ought to be given to the judgments already made by very many learned and orthodox men, many saints and martyrs, many ancient and modern theologians, many universities, councils, bishops, and popes, or to the private judgment of one individual or another. Not that I would gauge the worth of my opinion by the number of votes or the eminence of the speakers, as in human assemblies. I know it often happens that the more numerous side defeats the better one.[50] I know that what the majority approves is not always the best. I know that in inquiry into the truth there will always be something to add to our predecessors' achievements. I concede that it is right for the authority of Holy Scripture alone to outweigh all the decisions of all mortals. But the debate here is not about Scripture itself. Both sides gladly accept and venerate the same Scripture: the quarrel is over its meaning. And if any weight is given to intelligence and learning in scriptural interpretation, whose minds are sharper and more perceptive than those of the Greeks? Who is more versed in the

\* \* \* \* \*

*Philosophy of Man* ed Ernst Cassirer, Paul Oscar Kristeller, and John Herman Randall (Chicago 1948). Luther praised Valla's book on free will, but in fact Valla's own rhetorical theology was not discordant with that of Erasmus, and in his own terms Valla strongly favoured free will. See Mario Fois *Il pensiero cristiano di Lorenzo Valla nel quadro storico-culturale del suo ambiente* (Rome 1969) 184–8 ('La prescienza divina e la libertà umana') and 188–94 ('La voluntà divina e la libertà umana').

49 See n46 above. Erasmus may be drawing on Augustine's remarks on Manichaeism in *Confessions* 7.2[3]–3[5] CCSL 27 93–5, *De haeresibus* 46.19 CCSL 46 319, or *Contra Fortunatum* 17 CSEL 25 93–5. Also cf Fisher 1523 sig Ee4; 1597 cols 707 bottom–708 top. Passages in John Fisher's *Assertionis Lutheranae confutatio*, first published in Antwerp (Hillenius, [January] 1522) anticipate Erasmus' arguments. On Erasmus and Fisher see Chantraine *Erasme* 461–6.

50 Cf Livy 21.4.1, a commonplace of medieval canonist and political thought.

Scriptures? The Latins, too, lacked neither intelligence nor knowledge of Holy Writ; though their natural ability was less than the Greeks', with the help of the writings the Greeks left they were well able to equal their diligence. And if in this inquiry holiness of life is more regarded than learning, then the quality of those in the party that affirms free will is obvious. But no 'odious comparison,' as the lawyers call it, here[51] – I should not care to compare some of the heralds of this new gospel with those men of old.

[*If Scripture is clear to those who have the Spirit, how do we know who has the Spirit?*]

But now comes the objection, 'What need of an interpreter, when Scripture is perfectly clear?' If it is so clear, why have such distinguished men throughout so many centuries been blind, precisely in a matter of such importance, as Luther and his adherents want us to see it? If there is nothing obscure in Scripture, what need was there for prophecy in the apostles' time?[52] It was a gift of the Spirit, but I suspect that this charism has ceased, just like those of healing and speaking in tongues; and if it has not ceased, the question is to whom has it been handed on? If it has come to anyone and everyone, then every interpretation is uncertain; if to no one (seeing that many obscurities torment scholars even today) then no interpretation is sure. If it has come to the successors of the apostles, my opponents will claim that many men entirely lacking the apostolic spirit have for many centuries now succeeded the apostles. And yet, other things being equal, it is more probable to presume that God has infused his Spirit into those whom he has ordained, just as we believe it is more probable that grace has been given to someone who is baptized than to someone who is not.

But let us grant, as indeed we must, the possibility that the Spirit may reveal to some humble, unlearned individual what he has not revealed to many learned men, seeing that Christ gives thanks to the Father for having

\* \* \* \* \*

51 We have not been able to find a Latin source for the proverb 'comparisons are odious,' but it was common in English from the fourteenth to the seventeenth centuries (and even later); see *The Macmillan Book of Proverbs, Maxims, and Famous Phrases* ed Burton Stevenson (New York 1968) 390–1 and Morris Tilley *A Dictionary of the Proverbs in England in the Sixteenth and Seventeenth Centuries* (Ann Arbor, Mich 1950; repr 1966) c576. There is almost certainly a Latin source.
52 See 1 Cor 13:2.

concealed from the wise and the learned (that is, Scribes, Pharisees and philosophers) what he had revealed to little children (that is, the simple and foolish by the standards of the world).[53] And perhaps Dominic and Francis might have been such fools, had they been allowed to follow their own spirit. Yet if Paul, in his own age, when this gift of the Spirit was flourishing, orders spirits to be tested whether they are of God,[54] what ought we to do in this carnal age?

And so, how shall we test the spirits? By learning? There are scholars on both sides. By behaviour? On both sides there are sinners. On one side there is a whole choir of saints who defend the freedom of the will. My opponents may object that they were only human: yet I am comparing humans with humans here, not with God.[55] 'What help in knowing the Spirit are a great many men?' my opponents ask. 'What help are a very few?' I reply. 'How does a mitre help us to comprehend the Holy Scriptures?' they ask. 'How does a coarse robe help,' I reply, 'or a cowl?'[56] 'What use is an understanding of philosophy in understanding the Scriptures?' they ask. 'What use is ignorance?' I reply. They ask, 'In understanding the Scriptures, what use is an assembled synod, in which it may happen that no one has the Spirit?' I reply, 'What use are small private assemblies, where it is more probable that there is no one who has the Spirit?'

Paul cries, 'Do you seek for proof of Christ who dwells in me?'[57] People did not believe the apostles unless miracles had strengthened belief in their teaching. Nowadays anyone and everyone demands to be believed because he asserts that he has the evangelical spirit. The apostles were at last believed for shaking off vipers, curing the sick, raising the dead, and bestowing the gift of tongues by the laying on of hands; and that belief

\* \* \* \* \*

53 Cf Matt 11:25 and 1 Cor 1:27. The Vulgate translates the Greek word Erasmus has here, νηπίοις, as parvulis 'little ones.' In his Greek New Testament of 1516 Erasmus translated stultis 'foolish' with the note (on Matt 11:25) 'parvulis est νηπίοις, quod et stultum significat et infantem' ('"the little ones" is νηπίοις, which means both "fool" and "child"'). In the second edition (1519) he translated parvulis.

54 1 Cor 12:3; cf 1 John 4:1.

55 Erasmus implies that Luther and his associates are claiming near divine perfection in insisting that they alone are right.

56 Erasmus refers to the coarse robe and monastic cowl Luther wore as an Augustinian friar and was probably still wearing when Erasmus wrote this.

57 2 Cor 13:3. Erasmus quotes this text as a question as it is in the Vulgate, even though he says in his 1516 annotation on the verse (an experimentum quaeritis) that the Vulgate is erroneous in reading the text as a question.

did not come easily, for their teachings were paradoxical. Yet now, though some assert what in the general view are hyper-paradoxes,[58] so far not one of them is to be found who could even cure a lame horse! And miracles apart, I wish that some of them would show the uprightness and simplicity of the apostles' way of life, which would do instead of miracles for us spiritually backward mortals.

I do not intend this as a specific reference to Luther, whom I do not know personally and whose writings produce a mixed impression on me when I read them; I refer to others whom I know better.[59] If, in the event of some disagreement over the meaning of Scripture, we quote the interpretation of the ancient orthodox authorities, they immediately sing out, 'But they were only men.' If asked by what means we can know what the true interpretation of Scripture is, seeing that there are 'only men' on both sides, they reply, 'By a sign from the Spirit.' If you ask why the Spirit should be absent from those men, some of whom have been world-famous for their miracles, rather than from themselves, they reply as though there had been no gospel in the world these thirteen hundred years. If you demand of them a life worthy of the Spirit, they reply that they are justified by faith, not works. If you ask for miracles, they say that miracles have long ceased, and that there is no need of them now that the Scriptures are so clear. And if you then say that Scripture is *not* clear on this point, on which so many eminent men have apparently been blind, the circle is complete.

Now admitting that whoever has the Spirit is certain of the meaning of Scripture, how can I know if the claims he makes for himself are true? What am I to do if many people assert different opinions, every one of them swearing that he has the Spirit? And, since the Spirit does not reveal everything to every single person, even someone who has the Spirit

* * * * *

58 In April 1518, during a disputation before members of his own Augustinian order, Luther portrayed his teaching as paradoxical; see *Heidelberg Disputation* (WA 1 353 / LW 31 39). See also Marjorie O'Rourke Boyle 'Stoic Luther: Paradoxical Sin and Necessity' *Archiv für Reformationsgeschichte* 73 (1982) 69–92 for an explication of both the Stoics' and Luther's use of paradox.

59 In his edition of *De libero arbitrio* 16 n2, Walter claims that when Erasmus says here he does not refer specifically to Luther he contradicts himself because he had earlier mentioned a monk's cowl (see n56 above). But other Lutherans had worn or were wearing monk's cowls, and Erasmus refers here to the persons mentioned at the end of the preceding paragraph. Exactly who they are is not clear, but this paragraph goes on to speak of Luther's followers, if not of Luther himself.

may occasionally be mistaken. So much for those who so readily reject the ancient theologians' interpretation of the Bible and set up their own against us as if it had been spoken by an oracle.[60] And even granting that the Spirit of Christ had allowed his people to err in matters of little importance, on which human salvation does not particularly depend, how credible is it that he should have overlooked his church's error for more than thirteen hundred years,[61] and have found not a single one of all those saintly people worthy of being inspired with what my opponents claim is the most important teaching of the entire gospel?

But to conclude this argument: let others decide what claim they will make for themselves. For myself I claim neither learning nor holiness, nor do I trust in my own spirit. I will simply and diligently expound what is on my mind. If anyone attempts to instruct me, I will not knowingly resist the truth; but if they prefer to hurl insults at me, though I discuss rather than dispute the matter politely and without abuse, will not anyone judge them lacking in the evangelical spirit of which they constantly speak?

Paul proclaims, 'Receive the one who is weak in faith.'[62] Christ 'does not quench the smouldering wick.'[63] And the apostle Peter tells us to be 'always ready to satisfy all those who require you to give an account of the hope that is in you, yet with gentleness and respect.'[64] If my opponents retort that Erasmus is like an old skin, and cannot contain the new wine of the Spirit[65] which they are dispensing to the world, then if they are so sure of themselves they should at least treat us as Christ treated Nicodemus,[66] and the apostles treated Gamaliel.[67] Nicodemus was ignorant yet eager to learn, and so the Lord did not reject him; the disciples showed no aversion to Gamaliel, because he suspended his judgment on them till the outcome of the affair should show in what spirit it was being directed.

\* \* \* \* \*

60 Cf *Adagia* I vii 90.

61 Cf Fisher 1523 sig Ff1v; 1597 col 709 bottom.

62 Rom 14:1

63 Matt 12:20, quoting Isa 42:3; in the notes to his Greek New Testament (1516) Erasmus remarks in a note on Rom 14:1: 'qui nondum perfecte credit, non est rejiciendus, ne linum fumigans extinguatur' ('someone who does not believe perfectly is not to be rejected, lest the smoking wick be snuffed out').

64 1 Pet 3:15–6. In preference to the Vulgate translation 'cum modestia et timore' ('with moderation and awe'), Erasmus here follows the Latin in his translations of the Greek New Testament (1516 and 1519): 'cum mansuetudine et reverentia.'

65 Cf Matt 9:17.

66 John 3:1–21

67 Acts 5:34–9

## [PASSAGES FROM THE OLD TESTAMENT
## SUPPORTING FREE WILL]

I have now completed the first part of this book. If in it I have persuaded my readers of what I undertook, namely that it is preferable not to dispute matters of this kind too pedantically, especially in front of the masses, there will be no need for the argument for which I now gird myself, in the hope that truth may everywhere prevail, shining forth, it may be, from this discussion of the Scriptures like fire from the percussion of flints. First of all, it cannot be denied that there are many passages in Holy Scripture which clearly seem to support the freedom of the human will; and on the other hand, some which seem to deny it completely. Yet it is certain that Scripture cannot contradict itself, since it all proceeds from the same Spirit. And so, we shall first review those which confirm our opinion; then we shall attempt to explain those which seem to oppose it.

*[A brief definition of free will]*
By 'free will' here we understand a power of the human will by which man may be able to direct himself towards, or turn away from, what leads to eternal salvation.[68]

*[Ecclesiasticus 15:14–18: free will in Adam and Eve]*
The passage usually quoted first by the writers who support free will[69] is that found in the book entitled Ecclesiasticus or The Wisdom of Sirach, chapter 15 [:14–18]: 'God created man from the beginning, and left him in the hand of his own counsel. He added his commands and precepts: if you will keep the commandments, and keep acceptable faith forever, they will keep you. He set water and fire before you; stretch out your hand to whatever you

\* \* \* \* \*

68 Erasmus' deliberately general definition of free will, which will be attacked by Luther (*De servo arbitrio* WA 18 661:29–667:14 / LW 33 102–11) and defended at length by Erasmus in *Hyperaspistes* 1 261–91

69 Ecclus 15:14–18; see for example Origen *Commentarius in Epistolam ad Romanos* 1.18 PG 14 866c and *On First Principles* 3.1 trans Butterworth 164. Augustine also quotes it, concluding from it: 'Ecce apertissime videmus expressum librum humanae voluntatis arbitrium' ('See, we find here the free choice of the human will expressed most clearly'); see *De gratia et libero arbitrio* 2.3 PL 44 883. Although Erasmus is aware that Augustine gives almost no leeway for free will, he nevertheless uses this passage from Augustine against Luther in *Hyperaspistes* 2 (LB X 1340A–1361D) as an example of Luther's favourite Father affirming the existence of free will. Cf also Fisher 1523 sig xx2; 1597 col 663 top.

desire. Before man are life and death, good and evil; whatever he pleases shall be given him.' I do not suppose that anyone will plead here against the authority of this work that it was not originally admitted to the Hebrew canon (as Jerome points out),[70] seeing that the church of Christ has unanimously received it into its canon;[71] and I see no reason why the Hebrews should have thought this book ought to be excluded from the canon, given that they accept the Proverbs of Solomon and the Amatory Song.[72] Anyone who reads with reasonable care will easily guess the reasons that influenced them not to admit the last two books of Esdras, the stories of Susanna and of Bel and the dragon in the book of Daniel, the books of Judith and Esther,[73] and certain other passages into the canon, but to classify them among the hagiographa;[74] but nothing of that kind disturbs the reader in this book.

And so this passage declares that Adam, the first of our race, was created in such a way as to have an uncorrupted reason which could distinguish what should be sought and what avoided, but that he was also given a will – it too uncorrupted, yet free – so that he could if he wished turn away from good and direct himself towards evil. The angels were created in the same state before Lucifer defected from his creator along with his companions. In those who fell the will was so utterly corrupted that they cannot return to good; in those who remained loyal their will to good was strengthened so that it cannot henceforth so much as turn towards evil. In man the will was so upright and free that without further grace he could remain in innocence, yet without the help of further grace he could not attain the blessedness of everlasting life which the Lord Jesus promised to his own.[75] Even if all this cannot be proved by clear scriptural testimonies, it has been argued by the orthodox Fathers in a convincing manner.[76]

\* \* \* \* \*

70 In his *Prologus in libris Salomonis* and *Prologus in libro regum* in *Biblia sacra iuxta vulgatam versionem*; see the edition of Robert Weber (Stuttgart 1969) I 365:54–7; II 957:13–21.
71 Protestants generally excluded from the canon books not accepted by the Jews, including Ecclesiasticus. The Council of Trent finally declared them canonical in 1546, ten years after the death of Erasmus.
72 Translating 'Canticum amatorium,' the name Erasmus applies here to the Song of Songs. See *Hyperaspistes 1* 291–3 and n1060.
73 See *Hyperaspistes 1* nn1062–3.
74 This refers to the books which are now called deuterocanonical or apocryphal.
75 Cf Fisher 1523 sig xx3v; 1597 col 665 middle.
76 The issues Erasmus raises here were indeed projected on the situation of Adam in paradise by certain Fathers – for example, by Augustine in *De civitate Dei* books 12–14.

In Eve, however, not only the will seems to have been corrupt, but also the reason or understanding, the very source of all good and evil: for the Serpent seems to have persuaded her that the threats with which the Lord had forbidden them to touch anything from the tree of life were empty. In Adam it is rather the will that seems to have been corrupt, on account of his immoderate love for his wife: he preferred to indulge her wishes rather than God's commands; and yet I believe that reason, which gives birth to the will, was corrupt in him too.[77]

*[Reason, will, and law in postlapsarian mankind]*
Our mental capacity for judgment – it is immaterial whether you prefer to call it νοῦς (mind or understanding) or λόγος (reason) – was darkened, but not extinguished, by sin. The will, with which we choose or reject, was depraved to the extent that it could not mend its ways by its own natural efforts, but lost its freedom and was compelled to serve sin, once it had voluntarily subjected itself to sin. But by the grace of God, its sin has been forgiven and it has been made free. In the Pelagians' view the will can gain eternal life without the help of further grace, yet still owing its salvation to God, who both created free will and restored it. In the orthodox view human effort can, with the constant help of God's grace, continue in goodness, yet never without a proclivity to evil due to the traces of the sin once implanted in it. For just as our first parents' sin has been passed on to their offspring, so a tendency to sin has been transmitted to us all. Yet grace, which destroys sin, lessens this tendency so that it can be overcome, though not extirpated:[78] not that

* * * * *

77 Erasmus subscribes to neither of the scholastic positions which gave primacy to the will or to the intellect. Either may retain its integrity or succumb to corruption. Or both can do either, though the edge may be given to reason which 'gives birth to the will.' He begins here an extended section on the human powers of intellect and will before and after the coming of grace with Christ, and on the powers and limitations of pagans and Jews compared to Christians endowed with faith and charity.
   Duns Scotus treated the question of the nature of Adam's sin in his *Ordinatio* (or *Opus Oxoniense*) II dist 21 q 2 scholium 2; see his *Opera omnia* ed Lucas Wadding, 26 vols (Paris 1891–5) XIII 139–40. Following Augustine, he argued that Adam's first sin was not immoderate love of self but his love of the friendship of his wife. This aberration led to the more serious sin of violating the commandment not to eat the apple. Thus what started as a venial sin became a mortal sin.
78 The darkening of the intellect and the weakness of the will which remains even after original sin has been removed by baptism was technically named

grace would be incapable of this, but because it would not be expedient for us.

Now just as reason has been dulled, but not extinguished, in those who lack grace (I mean particular grace),[79] it is probable that the power of the will has not been absolutely extinguished in them either, but only rendered incapable of doing good. What the eye is to the body the reason is to the mind. It receives its light partly from the native light present (albeit in unequal measure) in everyone, which the Psalmist mentions: 'The light of your countenance is imprinted upon us, O Lord!'[80] and partly from God's commandments and the Holy Scriptures, as our Psalmist says: 'Your word is a lamp for my feet.'[81]

And so it comes about that we have three kinds of law: a law of nature, a law of works, and a law of faith, to use the Pauline terms.[82] The

* * * * *

'concupiscence'; see Thomas Aquinas *De veritate* q 24 a 14 resp. Erasmus refers to it in his *Enchiridion*: 'For even if baptism has removed the stain [of original sin], nevertheless a residue remains in us both as a safeguard of humility and as raw material . . . for virtue' (CWE 66 54). See Payne *Sacraments* 164. The condemnation of Pelagius at the Council of Carthage in 418 charged him with holding that after baptism 'nothing of original sin from Adam' is retained; H. Denzinger and A. Schönmetzer *Enchiridion symbolorum definitionum et declarationum de rebus fidei et morum* 25th ed (Freiburg im Breisgau, Barcelona, and Rome 1991) nos 106–9.

79 *Gratia peculiaris* is grace directed towards a particular individual, not the general or common grace available through Christ's death and resurrection as a general condition to all persons. It is the common grace that Pelagius judged to be sufficient with good works for salvation. Particular grace is imperfect in the sense that it is only the first step towards complete justification, which is effected by justifying grace (also called 'cooperating'). Erasmus also designates particular grace with four other adjectives, according to its varying relations to the person receiving it or to other kinds of grace: 'operating' (*operans*), 'prevenient' (*preveniens*), 'stimulating' (*exstimulans*), and 'impelling' (*pulsans*). Other authors sometimes called particular grace *gratia gratis data* 'grace given gratuitously.'

80 Ps 4:7

81 Ps 118:105. Erasmus suggests that the will possesses some power of choice (if only to choose evil things) derived from reason, which is inherent in the will (whether or not it is informed by Scripture); this power exists even in the absence of a particular grace. This notion is similar to the Stoic conception that seeds of justice are innate to all men, though scriptural enlightenment is not. Thus the biblical golden rule is common to all men by a law of nature.

82 Cf Rom 2:14, 3:27.

law of nature, etched deeply on everyone's mind, among the Scythians as well as the Greeks, declares that it is wrong for someone to do to another what he would not wish to have done to himself.[83] And the philosophers, without the light of faith or the help of Holy Scripture, recognized the eternal power and divinity of God from the created universe, and have left us many precepts on the good life, very close indeed to those of the Gospels; they write at great length exhorting us to do good and abhor vice. In their case it is probable that the will had a certain tendency to moral goodness, but that it was ineffective for eternal salvation without the assistance of grace through faith.

The law of works, however, issues commands and threatens punishment. It increases sin and engenders death, not because it is evil but because it commands things we cannot achieve without grace. The law of faith commands more difficult things than the law of works, and yet, with the addition of abundant grace, it makes things which are intrinsically impossible not merely easy but actually delightful. And so faith heals reason, which has been injured by sin, and charity helps the feeble will forward.[84] The law of works was like this: 'You may eat of every tree in paradise, but of the tree of the knowledge of good and evil you shall not eat. For on the day that you eat of it you will die.'[85] Again, the law of works was handed down by Moses: 'You shall not kill';[86] 'if you kill, you shall be killed';[87] 'You shall

* * * * *

83 See n81 above. By including civilized Greeks and barbaric Scythians, Erasmus again emphasizes the universality of this moral law of nature. Cf Gratian *Concordia discordantium canonum* part 1 dist 1 exordium PL 187 29A. On the barbarism of the Scythians see *Adagia* II iii 35.

84 Erasmus and Luther differed fundamentally in their conceptions of the difference between the status of humankind in relation to God while governed by the Mosaic law and as Christians under the law of faith. Erasmus believed the Old Testament dispensation anticipated that of the Christian faith, particularly in its moral teaching (though not in its ceremonial prescriptions). Luther believed that the Mosaic law was given by God to teach humankind its inherent sinfulness and that it was totally superseded by the coming of Christ. Erasmus is taking pains here to show the difference between what he calls the law of works and the law of faith. As religiously originated 'laws' both differ from the law of nature, which he has just been talking about. He shows here his way of making the distinction between what Luther called Law and gospel.

85 Gen 2:16–17

86 Exod 20:13; Deut 5:17

87 Exod 21:12

not commit adultery';[88] 'if you do, you shall be stoned.'[89] But what does the law of faith say, the law which orders us to love our enemies,[90] to take up our cross each day,[91] to hold our life cheap?[92] 'Do not fear, little flock, yours is the kingdom of heaven';[93] and 'Be comforted, for I have overcome the world';[94] and 'I am with you till the end of the world.'[95] The apostles showed forth this law when they left the presence of the council rejoicing after having been flogged for the sake of Jesus's name.[96] Hence Paul says, 'I can do all things in him who gives me strength.'[97]

This, of course, is what Ecclesiasticus says: 'He added his commands and precepts.'[98] For whom did he add them? Initially (and in person) for those first two among the human race; then for the Jewish people (through Moses and the prophets). The Law shows what God wishes. It lays down punishment if you do not obey, and promises reward if you do. For the rest, God leaves the power of choice to their will, which he created free in them and able to turn in either direction. Hence 'if you will keep the commandments, they will keep you,' and 'stretch out your hand to whatever you desire.'[99] But if the distinction between good and evil, as well as the will of God, had been hidden from man, he could not have been blamed for making the wrong choice. If his will had not been free, he could not have been charged with sin, for sin is no longer sin if it is not voluntary, unless an error or constraint of the will is itself the result of sin: thus a raped woman bears no blame for what she has suffered.

Although the passage which we have quoted from Ecclesiasticus seems particularly applicable to our first parents, in some sense it applies to the whole posterity of Adam: but it would not apply if we lacked the power of free will. For although the freedom of the will has been wounded by sin, it is not dead; and although it has been lamed, so that we are more inclined

\* \* \* \* \*

88 Exod 20:14; Deut 5:18
89 Deut 22:23–4; Lev 20:10; John 8:5
90 Matt 5:44
91 Luke 9:23
92 Matt 10:39 (Luke 14:25, John 12:25)
93 Luke 12:32; cf Matt 5:3.
94 John 16:33
95 Matt 28:20
96 Acts 5:40–1
97 Phil 4:13
98 Ecclus 15:15
99 Ecclus 15:16–17

to evil than to good before we receive grace, it has not been destroyed; it is just that the enormity of our misdeeds and our habit of sinning, which has become second nature, sometimes so cloud our powers of judgment and so smother the freedom of our will that the one seems to be snuffed out and the other dead.

[*Ancient and modern views of free will and grace*]
But as concerns the power of free will in us after sin and before the infusion of grace, the opinions of ancient and modern commentators vary to a remarkable degree, for each is concerned with a different aspect of the question.[100] Those who wished to avoid despair and complacency, and to spur men on to hope and moral endeavour, attributed much to free will. Pelagius taught that once the human will has been freed and cured by the grace of God, there is no further need of grace, but that eternal salvation can be attained by dint of free will;[101] yet humans owe their salvation to God, without whose grace the human will would not be effectively free to do good; and this power of the soul, by which man recognizes good and chooses it, turning away from its opposite, is a gift of

\* \* \* \* \*

100 This view is in keeping with Erasmus' rhetorical approach to theology: interpretations should be made in accord with what will contribute most to saving souls, as he illustrates in this and the succeeding paragraphs. See Hoffmann 156–66.
101 Walter claims that Erasmus makes a blunder here because he first says he will speak of free will before the infusion of grace and then proceeds to speak of what Pelagius thought about free will after it has been cured by grace (26 n1). (Pelagius, who died after 419, was the leader of a heretical movement condemned by the Council of Carthage in 417/18.) In fact, it is clear enough that Erasmus intends to discuss how a sinner (whether before or after baptism) enters upon or returns to a state of justifying grace. For Pelagius such a sinner by freely choosing to do good merits the grace which has become generally available through Christ's redemption; no particular grace is necessary, and the beginning and continuation or reinitiation of the process consists merely in the will's acceptance of grace (though Erasmus adds that grace is necessary and that the will and the healing of the will are gifts). Hence according to the Pelagians, once a sinner's will has the opportunity to be healed by Christ's redemption, it is totally free to merit saving grace and needs no further help from grace in its choices. Erasmus here says how, according to the Pelagians, someone after sin and before grace gets grace. He goes on to report what the Pelagians say about the efficacy of free will after grace. What he fails to mention is that according to the Pelagian view free will without grace merits saving grace.

the creator, who might have created a frog instead of a human being.[102]
Those who follow Scotus' opinions[103] are even more favourable to free

\* \* \* \* \*

102 Apparently an echo of the position of late medieval scholastics who attributed
absolute freedom and power to God (see Oberman *Harvest* 473)
103 It is clear that those who accepted many of Scotus' opinions, such as William
of Ockham, Pierre d'Ailly, and Gabriel Biel, held the view Erasmus describes
here. But modern scholars do not agree about whether Scotus himself held
such views (see McSorley 169 and McGrath 145–54, 163–79).
The subtle doctor speaks of *meritum condignum* in his Oxford commentary on
the *Sententiae* of Peter Lombard, *Ordinatio* [or *Opus Oxoniense*] 1 dist 17 pars 1
q 2 no 149; see his *Opera omnia* (Vatican City 1950–   ) v 210–11: '... Deus,
ab aeterno praevidens hunc actum ex talibus principiis eliciendum, voluit
ipsum esse ordinatum ad praemium ... et voluit ipsum fore meritum qui
tamen secundum se consideratus, absque tali acceptatione divina, secundum
strictam iustitiam dignus tali praemio non fuisset ex intrinseca bonitate sua
quam haberet ex suis principiis: quod patet, quia semper praemium est maius
bonum merito et iustitia stricta non reddit melius pro minus bono. Ideo bene
dicitur quod Deus semper praemiat ultra condignum, universaliter quidem
ultra dignitatem actus qui est meritum – quia quod ille sit condignum meritum, hoc est ultra naturam et bonitatem intrinsecam eius, ex gratuita acceptatione divina; et forte adhuc, ultra illud aliud quod de communi lege esset
actus acceptandus, quandoque Deus praemiat ex liberalitate mera' ('... God,
foreseeing from eternity the eliciting of this act from such principles, willed
that it should be ordained to be rewarded and willed that it be meritorious.
But the act, considered in itself, without any such divine acceptance, according
to strict justice, would not be worthy of such a reward out of its own intrinsic
goodness which it would have from its own principles. This is evident because the reward is always a greater good than the merit of the act, and strict
justice does not render a greater reward for a lesser good. Therefore it is well
said that God always rewards beyond the worth of the act, indeed universally
beyond what is deserved by the meritorious act. This is so because the fact that
the act earns merit which deserves its reward [*meritum condignum*] is beyond
its own nature and intrinsic goodness and comes from God's freely granted
acceptance – and perhaps still further beyond that other act that ought to be
accepted according to ordinary law [that is, human law], since God rewards
out of sheer generosity'). This passage is an explanation of *meritum condignum*.
Scotus' notion of *meritum de congruo* and *quantum in se est* may be gleaned
from his Paris commentary on the *Sententiae, Reportata Parisiensia* 11 dist 28 q 1
scholium 3 no 9; see his *Opera omnia* (Paris 1891–5; see n77 above) xii 140:
'Aliter dicitur quod liberum arbitrium potest considerari dupliciter; vel in se
et absolute, vel ut expositum tentationibus. Primo modo potest vitare pec-
cata committenda. Secundo modo, aut de peccatis commissis bene se habet
quantum potest ex naturalibus, vel male. Si bene, hoc est, displicet sibi quantum tenetur ex naturalibus, ex congruo meretur gratiam gratis datam, et si
bene utitur ipsa, cito dabitur gratia gratum faciens. Si autem male se habet ut

will,[104] for they believe its power to be such that even though man has not received the grace that destroys sin, he can, by his natural powers, perform what they call 'morally good works'[105] which merit sanctifying grace not *ex condigno* but *ex congruo* – such are the terms they use.[106]

At the opposite pole, as they say,[107] are those who assert that all works, however morally good, are no less detestable to God than villainous deeds such as adultery and murder, since they do not proceed out of faith in and love for God. Their view seems too severe, especially given that some philosophers had a certain knowledge of God, and so may well have had

\* \* \* \* \*

complacendo in commissis, cum sibi occurrant, peccat novo peccato ... Igitur quod liberum arbitrium non potest diu stare, quin peccabit novo peccato, vel quin Deus ex liberalitate dabit sibi gratiam, si disponat se quantum in se est' ('In another way it is said that free will can be considered in two ways: either by itself and absolutely or in so far as it is exposed to temptation. In the first way it can avoid committing sins. In the second way it will either behave well concerning sins committed in so far as it can do so by its natural powers or it will behave badly. If it behaves well, that is, if it is displeased with itself in so far as it is required to be by its natural powers, it will merit *ex congruo* gratuitously given grace [that is, prevenient grace]. If it uses that grace well, it will soon be given sanctifying grace. If, however, it behaves badly, as by taking pleasure in the sins it has committed when they occur to it, it commits a new sin ... It follows that free will cannot stand upright for a long time without sinning a new sin unless God out of generosity gives it grace, if it disposes itself as best it can'). For an illuminating study of the history and meaning of these terms see McGrath 109–28.

104 Erasmus exaggerates here in order to place the views of Scotus' followers as far as possible from the next category (those who believe that even 'morally good' acts before grace are evil). In fact Pelagius apparently believed that the good actions of the will before grace actually merit grace not merely *ex congruo* but *ex condigno* (though those terms were not used in Pelagius' time) – which was not the position of Scotus or of the *via moderna*. See McSorley 191–215 and McGrath 76–8, 122–30.

105 'Morally good works' are performed by natural powers; see Oberman *Harvest* 461 (*bonitas moralis* 'moral goodness') and 468 (*ex puris naturalibus* 'out of purely natural capacities'). Cf Fisher 1523 sig Aa3v; 1597 col 683 top and 1523 sig Ee2; 1597 col 704 top.

106 By merit *de congruo* the natural disposition and acts of man can solicit (but not strictly earn) grace because its bestowal is 'fitting'; meritum *de condigno*, on the other hand, is the merit of a good act performed in the state of grace. Such an act meets the standard of God's justice and earns salvation as a reward, but only because God has committed himself to accepting it as fully meritorious. See n103 above, Oberman *Harvest* 471–2, and McGrath 109–19.

107 *Adagia* I x 45

some trust in and love for him too, and not always have acted for vainglorious motives, but out of a love of goodness and virtue, which they teach
should be embraced simply because it is virtuous. (For someone who en-
dangers his life for the good of his country out of vainglorious motives performs a work good in general,[108] but whether 'morally good' is doubtful.)

St Augustine and his followers, considering how harmful to true godliness it is for people to trust in their own abilities, are more inclined to favour
grace, which is constantly stressed by Paul. And so Augustine teaches that
man, in thrall to sin, cannot change his ways so as to amend his life, or do
anything that contributes to salvation, unless he is divinely impelled by the
freely given grace of God to desire what leads to eternal life. Some call this
grace 'prevenient'; Augustine calls it 'operating'; for even faith, the doorway to salvation, is itself a freely given gift of God. The charity added to
faith by an even more generous gift of the Holy Spirit he calls 'cooperating'
grace,[109] for it unceasingly helps those who are making an effort until they
achieve their goal; but although free will and grace cooperate in the same
task, grace is the leader, not merely a partner. Some theologians make a distinction here, however, saying that if you consider an action according to its
nature the more important cause is human will; but if you consider it according to the merit involved, the more important is grace.[110] And yet faith,
the reason that we desire what leads to salvation, and charity, the reason

\* \* \* \* \*

108 Translating *ex genere bonum*; that is, the deed itself is generically good, entirely
apart from the motives of the doer. Cf Fisher 1523 sig Aa3v; 1597 col 683 top.
109 In *De gratia et libero arbitrio* 17.33 PL 44, 901, Augustine distinguished between
operating grace (*gratia operans*), through which man's good will is initially
stimulated, and cooperating grace (*gratia cooperans*) through which God cooperates with man's free will in good acts. See n79 above.
110 In the preceding pages Erasmus has listed many of the questions actually discussed by scholastic theologians from the twelfth to the sixteenth century.
Scotus discusses the primary and secondary causality of a meritorious act in
*Reportata Parisiensia* on Lombard's *Sententiae* II dist 29 q 1 no 7 in *Opera omnia* (Paris 1891–5; see n77 above) XXIII 145, where he concludes: 'Dico igitur
quod illa duo concurrunt, voluntas et gratia, sicut causa superior et inferior, et
hujusmodi causa inferior semper coagit, dum est, quando illa superior, quae
principalis est, agit. Tamen possumus considerare istum actum in se, vel in-
quantum est meritorius: Primo modo est causa principalior voluntas. Secundo
modo dicitur gratia principalius agere, quia est acceptior Deo' ('I say therefore that these two coincide, will and grace, as a superior cause and an inferior one, and in this way the inferior cause, while it exists, always co-acts,
while the superior, which is the principal cause, acts. But we can consider this
act in itself or in so far as it is meritorious. In the first way will is the principal cause. In the second way grace is said to act principally, because it is
more acceptable to God').

that we do not desire it in vain, are distinguished not so much in time as in nature (though they can both increase with time).

And so, since 'grace' means a 'favour freely bestowed,' it is possible to posit three, or indeed even four kinds of grace.[111]

One is the grace naturally present in us, vitiated, as we said, but not destroyed, by sin; some call it a 'natural influence.'[112] Common to all humans, it remains even in those who persevere in sin; for they are free to speak or be silent; to sit or stand up; to help the needy, read the Scriptures, or listen to a sermon, though according to the opinion of some, none of these things leads to eternal life. There is however a considerable body of opinion that, given the immense benevolence of God, man can progress so far by performing such good works as to prepare himself for grace, and to move God to have mercy on him;[113] though there are some who deny that even this can happen without particular grace.[114] Since this natural grace is common to all, it is not called grace, though in reality it is[115] – just as in creating, preserving, and governing the universe God daily performs greater miracles than if he were to cure a leper or exorcize a demoniac, yet they are not called miracles because they are performed for the benefit of all, without distinction, every day.

The second kind is particular grace:[116] through this God in his mercy urges the sinner, still without merit, to repentance, but does not yet infuse the highest grace which destroys sin and makes man acceptable to God.[117] So the sinner, aided by the second kind of grace which we called 'operating'

\* \* \* \* \*

111 The three principal kinds are prevenient, sanctifying, and persevering. Natural grace (or the *concursus generalis* by which God sustains creation, the first kind discussed by Erasmus) can be thought of as a gift or 'grace' but is not strictly a supernatural grace like the others.

112 Latin *influxum naturalem*: a technical term (also named *concursus* or *influxus generalis* or *influentia generalis*) which means 'the cooperation of the first cause – God – with the second cause – creature – indispensable for any action of the second cause irrespective of the presence of grace' (Oberman *Harvest* 48–50, 463). See also n226 below.

113 See n103 above.

114 See n79 above.

115 The *concursus generalis* (what Erasmus here calls 'natural grace') by which God creates and sustains all beings and actions is not a grace in the sense that it does not rise to the level of supernatural gifts, deeds, or rewards, but it is a 'grace' in the general sense of a 'favour' or 'gift.'

116 See n79 above.

117 What is now usually called sanctifying grace; in Erasmus time is was usually called *gratia justificans* ('justifying grace') or *gratia gratum faciens* ('grace that makes pleasing to God').

above, is dissatisfied with himself and, though he has not yet thrown off the attachment to sin, he can give alms, pray, perform pious exercises, listen to sermons, request the prayers of holy men for himself, and perform other works that are morally good, as they say:[118] can behave, as it were, as a candidate for the highest kind of grace. There is, further, the opinion that this second kind of grace which we have just mentioned is, through God's goodness, never lacking to any mortal being, because the divine beneficence supplies everyone with suitable occasions in this life to amend their ways if, as far as they are able, they bring the remainder of their will into harmony with the assistance of the Spirit who invites, but never compels, us to greater goodness.[119] It is even believed that we have the power to choose whether to turn our will towards, or away from, grace, just as it is in our power to open, or close, our eyes to the light that shines on them from without.[120] Since God's great love for humanity does not suffer man to be deceived with false hopes even of the grace known as 'sanctifying grace,' if he strives for it with all his might, it is true that no sinner should be presumptuous, but that none should despair either; and it is also true that no one perishes except through his own fault.

And so there are: natural grace; stimulating grace (admittedly imperfect); the grace that makes the will effective, which we referred to as cooperant grace, which carries on what we have begun; and there is the grace which brings it to completion.[121] These last three are thought to be the same grace, though they have different names from their different effects in us: the first stirring up, the second continuing, the third bringing to completion.

And so those farthest from Pelagius's position attribute a great deal to grace and almost nothing to free will, though they do not deny it altogether. They say that without particular grace man cannot desire good; can neither make a beginning, nor persevere, nor bring to completion without the perpetual help of God's grace from the very beginning. This opinion seems highly probable, for it permits man the opportunity of serious moral endeavour, but not of making any claims for his own powers.[122]

\* \* \* \* \*

118 See n105 above.
119 The doctrine of *facere quod in se est* or *meritum de congruo*: that God will not withhold his grace from those who do their very best. See Oberman *Harvest* 132–3, 468, and 471–2. Cf Fisher 1523 sig Aa2v–Aa3; 1597 col 682 top.
120 Cf Fisher 1523 sig Ff3v; 1597 col 712 bottom.
121 This grace is usually called *gratia perseverans* ('the grace of perseverance'). Cf Fisher 1523 sig Aa3; 1597 col 682 middle.
122 Erasmus indicates in *Hyperaspistes 1* that this is the position of Augustine and Thomas Aquinas. Although he calls it 'highly probable,' he does not definitively endorse it. See *Hyperaspistes 1* nn988–9.

Harder is the opinion of those who assert that free will can do nothing but sin, and that grace alone works good in us, not through or in cooperation with, but in free will, so that our volition does no more in the process than wax does while it is being shaped by the sculptor's hand into whatever shape he, the craftsman, envisages.[123] I feel that these people are so anxious to escape reliance on human works and merits that they 'run away beyond their own house', as the saying goes.[124]

Hardest of all, apparently, is the opinion of those who say that free will is an empty term, that it has not, and never has had, any power, either in the angels or in Adam or in us, before or after the infusion of grace, but that God works evil as well as good deeds in us, and that everything happens out of absolute necessity.[125] And so I will take issue particularly with these last two positions.

I have gone into this at slightly excessive length so as to enable the less expert reader to grasp the rest of the argument – for I write as non-expert for non-experts, and for this reason I first quoted the passage in Ecclesiasticus which seems to offer the clearest description of the origin and power of free will. Now I will review the other scriptural testimonies with more dispatch. Before doing so, I should point out that this passage is different in the Aldine edition than in the version used in the Latin church today. The Greek version does not add 'and they will keep you'; nor does Augustine in his occasional quotations of this text. Also, in my opinion ποιῆται should read ποιῆσαι.[126]

[*Other Old Testament passages supporting free will*]
And so, just as God had offered the choice of life or death in paradise – 'If you obey my commandments you will live; if you do not, you will die. Avoid evil and choose what is good'[127] – in the same way he talks to Cain in Genesis 4[:6–7]: 'Why are you angry, and why has your face fallen? If you do good, will you not receive? And if you do evil, your sin will straight away be at your door. But the desire for it will be within your control, and

\* \* \* \* \*

123 Erasmus holds this to be the position of Karlstadt. See *Hyperaspistes* 1 278–9.
124 *Adagia* I v 3
125 Erasmus identifies this as the opinion of Wyclif and Luther. See *Hyperaspistes* 1 n1002.
126 Ecclus 15:14–18; see n69 above. Walter (32 n3) gives the Greek of the Aldine edition of the Septuagint translation of the Old Testament (Venice 1518), which omits the phrase noted by Erasmus. He also points out in passing that the Aldine edition has a misprint at this point: ποιῆται 'it may or would be done' instead of ποιῆσαι 'to do.'
127 Cf Gen 2:17 and Deut 30:19.

you will master it.' God offers a reward if man will choose what is right and threatens punishment should he prefer to follow the opposite path. And he shows that evil thoughts and desires can be overcome, and do not compel us to sin.

In agreement with these passages are the Lord's words to Moses: 'I have placed before you the way of life and the way of death. Choose what is good, and walk in it.'[128] What could be more clearly expressed? God shows us what is good and what is bad, and shows the two different consequences for each, life and death; the freedom to choose he leaves to man. It would be ridiculous to tell someone to 'choose' if it were not in his power to turn this way or the other, as though someone standing at a crossroads were to be told, 'you see the two roads – take whichever you want,' if only one were open.

Again, in Deuteronomy, chapter 30[:15-19]:

See, this day I have placed before you life and goodness, and on the other hand death and evil, so that you shall love the Lord your God, and walk in his ways, and keep his commandments and his ordinances and his laws, and you may live, and he will multiply you and bless you in the land which you are entering to possess. But if your heart turns away, and you will not hear, and you are deceived by falsehood into worshipping false gods and serving them, I tell you today that you will perish, and you will not live long in the land that you will cross the Jordan to enter and possess. Today I call upon heaven and earth as witnesses that I have placed before you life and death, blessings and curses. And so choose life, so that you and your descendants may live.

Here again we hear the terms 'place before you,' 'choose,' and 'turn away' – terms which would be inappropriate if human will were not free to choose good, but only evil.[129] Otherwise it would be exactly as if someone tied up in such a way that he could only stretch out his arm to the left were to be told, 'There is some excellent wine to your right, and poison to your left. Reach out and take whichever you want.'

Consistent with this are the words of the same Lord in Isaiah [1:19-20]: 'If you are willing and obey me, you will eat the good things of the earth; but if you are not willing and will not obey me, the sword will devour you.' If the human will is in no sense free to do good, or even, as

* * * * *

128 Deut 30:15, 19
129 An allusion to Karlstadt's position

some assert, not free to do either good or evil,[130] what is the meaning of the words 'if you are willing' and 'if you are not willing'? It would have been more suitable to have said, 'if I am willing' or 'if I am unwilling.' And since many similar words are addressed to sinners, I do not see how we can avoid attributing to them a will in some sense free to choose good; unless we prefer to call it a thought or a desire rather than a will, since will is decisive and is the result of judgment. Yet in chapter 21[:12] of the same prophet we read, 'Ask if you will; turn and come back.' What point would there be in urging people to 'turn and come back' if they do not in the least have it in their power to do so? Would it not be exactly like saying to a man in shackles, whom one was not prepared to free, 'Bestir yourself, come and follow me'? And in chapter 45[:20] of the same prophet we find, 'Gather yourselves and come!' and 'Turn to me and you will be saved, all you ends of the earth!'[131] And again in chapter 52[:1-2]: 'Arise, arise, shake off the dust, loose the halter from your neck!' The same in Jeremiah, chapter 15[:19]: 'If you change your ways, I will change you, and if you distinguish the precious from the base, you will be as my mouth.' The use of 'distinguish' indicates the freedom to choose. Zechariah demonstrates more clearly still the exercise of free will, and the grace in store for whoever exercises it: 'Turn back to me, says the Lord of hosts, and I will turn back to you, says the Lord.'[132] In Ezekiel, chapter 18[:21–2] God speaks thus: 'If the sinner does penance for all the sins he has committed, and does what is right, etc' and immediately afterwards 'I will not remember all the wicked deeds he has done'; likewise: 'But if a righteous man turns away from his righteousness, and does what is wrong.'[133] In this chapter the terms 'turn away,' 'do,' 'perform,' constantly recur, in both a good and a bad sense.

And where are those who claim that man does nothing, but is only worked upon by operating grace?[134] 'Cast off all your iniquities,' says the Lord, 'and why do you wish to die, house of Israel? I do not desire the sinner's death; turn back and come to me!'[135] Would the good Lord lament

\* \* \* \* \*

130 Allusions to the view of Karlstadt and then of Luther
131 Isa 45:22
132 Zech 1:3. In Fisher's brief list of commands from Old Testament prophets, this is the only one he has in common with Erasmus (Fisher 1523 sig xx4v; 1597 col 667 top).
133 Ezek 18:24
134 Such as Karlstadt
135 Ezek 18:31–2

the death of his people which he himself brought about in them? If he does not desire our death, we must indeed ascribe it to our own will if we perish; but what can you ascribe to someone who can do nothing, good or bad?[136] It would be futile for the mystic psalmist to sing 'Depart from evil and do good; seek out peace and pursue it'[137] to people who had absolutely no control over their will.

[*Scriptural exhortations are meaningless if we have no power to comply*]
But what point is there in quoting a few passages of this kind when all Holy Scripture is full of exhortations like this: 'Turn back to me with all your heart';[138] 'Let every man turn from his evil way';[139] 'Come back to your senses, you transgressors';[140] 'Let everyone turn from his evil way, and I will repent the ill that I have thought to do them on account of the evil of their endeavours'; and 'If you will not listen to me, to walk in my law.'[141] Nearly the whole of Scripture speaks of nothing but conversion, endeavour, and striving to improve. All this would become meaningless once it was accepted that doing good or evil was a matter of necessity; and so too would all the promises, threats, complaints, reproaches, entreaties, blessings, and curses directed towards those who have amended their ways, or those who have refused to change: 'As soon as a sinner groans at his sin';[142] 'I have seen that this is a stubborn people';[143] 'Oh my people, what have I done to you?';[144] and 'They have rejected my laws';[145] 'Oh, that my

* * * * *

136 Luther's position
137 Ps 33:15
138 Joel 2:12
139 John 3:8
140 Isa 46:8
141 Jer 26:3–4
142 The precise language of this text is not biblical, but it is quoted in the form Erasmus gives (and as if it were biblical) by Peter Lombard *Sententiae* IV dist 17.1 and dist 20.1 (PL 192 880 and 892); by Abelard *In Epistolam Pauli ad Romanos* 2.4.7 (CCCM 11 125:75); by Bernard of Clairvaux *Sententiae* 3.69 and 120 (*Opera omnia* ed Feruccio Gasaldelli (Milan 1984– ) II 418:19–20, 606:9–10) and *Sermones in Cantica Canticorum* 9.4 in *Opera omnia* ed J. Leclercq et al (Rome 1957– ) I 45:23–4; and by several minor writers (CCCM 27B 920:26–7, CCCM 30 247:93–4n, and CCCM 46A 65:734). Editors generally refer to Ezek 18:21, 33:12, 16, 19, and Isa 30:15. It is possible that Erasmus' form of the verse comes from the liturgy, where biblical quotations sometimes differ somewhat from the Vulgate.
143 Exod 32:9
144 Mic 6:3
145 Ezek 20:13

people had listened to me, that Israel had walked in my ways!';[146] 'He who wishes to see good days, let him keep his tongue from evil.'[147] The phrase 'he who wishes to see' speaks of free will.[148]

Since such phrases are frequently encountered, does it not immediately occur to the reader to ask, 'why promise conditionally what is entirely dependent on your will? Why complain of my behaviour, when all my actions, good or bad, are performed by you in me regardless of my will? Why reproach me, when I have no power to preserve the good you have given me, or keep out the evil you put into me? Why entreat me, when everything depends on you, and happens as it pleases you? Why bless me, as though I had done my duty, when whatever happens is your work? Why curse me, when I sinned through necessity?' What is the purpose of such a vast number of commandments if not a single person has it at all in his power to do what is commanded? For there are some who believe that man, albeit justified by the gift of faith and charity, cannot fulfil any of God's commandments, but rather that all good works, because they are done 'in the flesh,' would lead to damnation were not God in his mercy to pardon them on account of the merit of our faith.[149]

Yet the word spoken by God through Moses in Deuteronomy, chapter 30[:11–14], shows that what he commands is not merely within our power, but that it demands little effort. He says: 'The commandment that I lay upon you this day is not beyond you, nor is it far away. It is not in heaven, that you might say, "Which one of us is strong enough to go up to heaven and bring it back to us, that we may hear and fulfil it?" Neither is it beyond the sea, that you should make excuses, and say, "Who among us can cross the sea and bring it back to us, that we may hear what is commanded?" No, the word is very near to you, on your lips and in your heart, that you may do it.'

Yet here he is speaking of the greatest commandment of all: 'that you turn back to the Lord your God with all your heart and with all your soul.' And what is the meaning of 'but if you will listen,' 'if you will keep the

* * * * *

146 Ps 80:14
147 Ps 33:13–14
148 Augustine gives a similar list of scriptural commands in support of free will (*De gratia et libero arbitrio* 2.3 PL 44 883).
149 An allusion to Luther's doctrine of *simul justus et peccator* 'justified and a sinner at the same time.' See his *Assertio* article 36 (WA 7 142:25 / 301): 'In omni opere bono iustus peccat mortaliter' ('When a just man does a good deed, he sins mortally'). The phrase 'on account of the merit of our faith' is a misunderstanding of Luther, who did not believe that we merit anything because of our faith.

commandments,' 'if you will turn back,'[150] if none of this is in our power at all? I will not attempt to quote an extensive selection of such texts, for the books of both testaments are so full of them wherever you look that anyone attempting to search them out would simply be 'looking for water in the sea,' as the saying goes.[151] And so, as I said, a considerable amount of Holy Scripture will obviously become meaningless if you accept the last opinion discussed above, or the previous one.[152]

[God's figurative changes from wrath to mercy imply that our wills can change]
Yet in the Scriptures we do find some texts which seem to attribute a certain contingency, or even mutability, to God;[153] such as what we read in Jeremiah, chapter 18[:8, 10]: 'But if that nation will repent of its evil because I have spoken against it, I too will repent of the evil which I thought to do to it. If it does evil in my sight and will not hear my voice, then I will repent of the good that I said I would do to it.'[154] But of course we know that here Holy Scripture is speaking in human terms, as it often does elsewhere. For God is touched by no mutability; he is said to change from anger to mercy when he deems us worthy of his favour because we are changing our ways for the better; he is said to change from mercy to anger when he punishes and afflicts us for falling into sin once more. Again, in 4 Kings, chapter 20[:1], Hezekiah is told, 'You will die, and not live', but soon, after shedding many tears, he is told by the same prophet, 'I have heard your prayer, and seen your tears, and I have saved you, etc.'[155] Similarly in 2 Kings, chapter 12[:10], David is told by the Lord through Nathan, 'your house shall never have rest from the sword, etc'; but shortly after, having said, 'I have sinned against the Lord,' he hears the gentler sentence, 'and so the Lord has taken away your sin; you will not die.'[156] Since the figurative nature of the language in these and similar verses prevents us

\* \* \* \* \*

150 Deut 30:10
151 *Adagia* I ix 75
152 Those of Luther and Karlstadt
153 Erasmus will argue that these qualities of God's changeableness in Scripture reflect the freedom of human will and variability in man, not in God. He does not relate contingency in the created world to God's absolute power, as some theologians of the *via moderna* do (so that divine decisions could have been other). Erasmus will discuss the related subject of the necessity of consequence and the necessity of the consequent in *Hyperaspistes* 2 LB X 1426D–1428C.
154 Fisher (1523 sig Ee3v; 1597 col 706 bottom) quotes the same text.
155 4 Kings 20:5
156 2 Kings 12:13

from seeing God as mutable, we cannot avoid understanding that we have a will that can turn this way and that; for if it is turned towards evil by necessity, why should it be charged with sin? And if it is turned towards good by necessity, why should God change from anger to mercy, since in that situation we would be no more deserving of favour?

## [PASSAGES FROM THE NEW TESTAMENT SUPPORTING FREE WILL]

[*Gospel exhortations are meaningless if we have no power to comply*]
The quotations so far have come from the Old Testament; this might be cause for objection, had they not been of the kind which the light of the Gospel not only fails to efface, but actually endows with new force. And so let us turn to the books of the New Testament. First we come across that place in the Gospel where Christ, weeping over the destruction of the city of Jerusalem, says: 'Jerusalem, Jerusalem, city that murders the prophets and stones those who are sent to you, how often have I wanted to gather you together, as a hen gathers her chicks under her wings, and you refused!'[157] If everything happens by necessity, could Jerusalem not rightly reply to the Lord's lament, 'Why torment yourself with pointless weeping? If it was your will that we should not listen to the prophets, why did you send them? Why blame us for something that you did voluntarily, and we by necessity? You wanted to gather us together, and yet in us you did not want to: for in us you brought it about that we refused.' Yet in our Lord's words, it is not necessity working in the Jews that is blamed, but their wicked, rebellious will: 'I wanted to gather you together; you refused.'

Again, elsewhere we find, 'If you want to enter into life, keep the commandments.'[158] How on earth could one say 'if you want to' to someone whose will was not free? Or, 'If you want to be perfect, go and sell what you have';[159] or Luke 9[:23], 'If anyone wants to come after me, let him deny himself, and take up his cross, and follow me.'[160] Though the commandment

*  *  *  *  *

157 Matt 23:37. Cf Fisher 1523 sig Dd1; 1597 col 696 bottom. Erasmus wrote *congregare te* instead of the Vulgate *congregare filios tuos* (which matches the Greek here). Such slight variations are not uncommon and not all of them will be pointed out.
158 Matt 19:17
159 Matt 19:21
160 Fisher (1523 sig Ee1v; 1597 col 703 bottom) quotes the same text.

is very difficult, our will is nevertheless mentioned. And shortly afterwards we find, 'Whoever wants to save his life shall lose it.'[161] Are not all Christ's excellent commandments emptied of their meaning if nothing is attributed to human will? 'But I tell you, but I tell you etc';[162] and 'If you love me, keep my commandments.'[163] How greatly John stresses the commandments! How poorly the conjunction 'if' agrees with absolute necessity: 'If you remain in me, and my words remain in you';[164] 'If you want to be perfect.'[165]

Now, when good and bad deeds are mentioned so frequently, as is reward, I fail to see how there can be any room at all for absolute necessity: nature and necessity deserve no reward. And yet in Matthew 5[:12] our Lord Jesus says, 'rejoice and be glad, for your reward is great in heaven.' What is the sense of the parable of the hired labourers in the vineyard?[166] Can they be labourers, if their labour achieves nothing? As agreed, they receive one penny as reward for their labour. Someone will say that it is called a reward because it is in some sense owed by God, who has given his word to man if he will believe in God's promises. But this very act of believing is one in which free will plays some part, turning itself towards, or away from, faith. Why is the servant who increased his master's fortune by his own efforts praised, and why is the lazy good-for-nothing condemned,[167] unless we have some responsibility in such a case? And again, in Matthew, chapter 25, when Christ invites everyone to a share in his eternal kingdom, he refers not to necessity but to people's charitable deeds: 'You gave food and drink'; 'you took in the stranger'; 'you clothed the naked, etc';[168] speaking to the goats on his left he reproaches not necessity, but their voluntary failures to perform good works: 'You saw the hungry, you were given an opportunity to do good, but you gave no food, etc'[169] Are not all the gospel writings in fact full of exhortations?[170] 'Come to me you who are heavy

\* \* \* \* \*

161  Luke 9:24
162  Matt 5:22, 28
163  John 14:15
164  John 15:7
165  Matt 19:21
166  Matt 20:1–16
167  Matt 25:14–30
168  Matt 25:35–6
169  Matt 25:42. Cf Fisher 1523 sig Ee1v; 1597 col 703 bottom.
170  In this paragraph, as in the preceding and the succeeding as well, Erasmus breaks up a series of verses, putting together fragments that have a similar import. This clustered effect was certainly not uncommon in the practice of preachers, who utilized the Scriptures freely for their purposes.

laden'; 'watch, pray'; 'ask, seek, knock'; 'look out, beware.'[171] What is the meaning of the many parables about keeping the word of God, running out to meet the bridegroom, about the thief breaking in by night, the house that must be built on rock?[172] Surely they spur us on to strive, to be eager and diligent, so that we do not neglect God's grace and perish. They will seem meaningless or superfluous if everything is referred to necessity. The same is true of the threats in the Gospels: 'Woe to you, you scribes, woe to you, you hypocrites; woe to you, Chorazin.'[173] The reproaches too become meaningless: 'O you faithless and perverse generation, how long will I be with you? how long must I endure you?'; 'You serpents, you brood of vipers, how will you fly from the damnation of hell?'[174]

'By their fruits,' says the Lord, 'you shall know them.'[175] By 'fruits' he means works, and he calls them ours: but they are not ours if all happens by necessity. On the cross he prays, 'Father, forgive them, for they know not what they do.'[176] How much more just it would have been to pardon them because their will was not free, and they could not have acted otherwise had they wished!

Then, too, John says, 'To those who believed in his name he gave power to become children of God.'[177] How can those who are not yet children of God be given power to become such, if our will has no freedom? When some of the Lord's followers were offended by his words and left him, he said to his closest disciples, 'Do you want to leave me too?'[178] If these followers had not left of their own will but by necessity, why should Christ ask the others if they wanted to?

*[Passages from Paul supporting free will]*
But we will not tax the reader's patience by rehearsing all texts of this kind, since they are both innumerable and such as will easily catch any reader's

* * * * *

171 Matt 11:28; Matt 26:41 (Mark 14:38); Matt 7:7; Mark 8:15 (Luke 12:15)
172 Matt 13:18–25; Matt 25:1–13; Matt 24:42–4 (cf 1 Thess 5:2); Matt 7:24–7 (Luke 6:48–9)
173 Matt 23:13–15; Matt 11:21 (Luke 10:13). Cf Fisher 1523 sig Dd3v; 1597 col 700 bottom.
174 Matt 17:16 (Mark 9:18, Luke 9:41); Matt 23:33
175 Matt 7:20
176 Luke 23:34
177 John 1:12. Cf Fisher 1523 sig Aa2v; 1597 col 681 bottom. Hilary uses the same text against necessity and in favour of free will (*De Trinitate* 1.11 PL 10 33A), as does Augustine (*In Ioannis evangelium tractatus* CXXIV 53.8 CCSL 36 456).
178 John 6:68

attention by themselves. Let us see whether support for free will can be found in Paul, the vigorous champion of grace, who lays unremitting siege to the works of the Law. First of all we come across the passage in the Epistle to the Romans, chapter 2[:4]: 'Do you despise his wealth of goodness and patience and forbearance? Are you not aware that God's goodness leads you to repentance?' How can the accusation of contempt for God's commandment be made if the will is not free? How can God invite us to repentance if he is the cause of impenitence? How can the accused be justly condemned when the judge compels him to crime? And yet Paul had said shortly before, 'We know that God's judgment is according to truth against those who do such things.'[179] There is mention of a deed, and a judgment according to truth: where then is absolute necessity, or a completely passive will? Note where Paul lays the blame for their wickedness: 'In your hardness and impenitence of heart you are storing up wrath for yourself on the day of wrath, when the righteous judgment of God shall be revealed; he will pay everyone according to his deeds.'[180] Here too the 'righteous judgment of God' is mentioned, as are deeds deserving of punishment. Now if God credited only his own good works, which he works through us, to our glory and honour and immortality, his benevolence would be praiseworthy (though even here the Apostle adds the qualification, 'to those persevering in good works,' and 'to those who seek eternal life.')[181] But with what semblance of justice does he visit wrath, indignation, tribulation, and distress on man as an evildoer though man does nothing of his own will, but everything by necessity?

And how can Paul's comparisons with the runners in the stadium, the trophy, and the victor's crown be valid if we can ascribe nothing to our own efforts? [1] Corinthians, chapter 9[:24–5] says: 'Do you not know that in the stadium all the runners compete, but only one receives the prize? Run so as to win it etc.' And shortly afterwards: 'And they run to win a crown that will fade, but we, a crown that never fades.'[182] A crown is given only to those who compete; it is given as a prize, as though they have deserved the honour. Again in 1 Timothy, chapter 6[:12] he says, 'Fight the good fight of faith, take hold of eternal life.' In any contest there is voluntary striving, and there is the danger that if you stop trying you will lose the prize. This is not so if everything happens by absolute necessity.

\* \* \* \* \*

179 Rom 2:2
180 Rom 2:5–6
181 Rom 2:7
182 1 Cor 9:24–5

Again, in 2 Timothy, chapter 2[:5]: 'An athlete receives no prize unless he has competed according to the rules.' And shortly before that: 'Toil away like a good soldier of Christ.'[183] The farmer who gives his labour is also mentioned.[184] The athlete wins his crown, the soldier gets his pay, and the farmer reaps his harvest.[185] Similarly, in chapter 4[:7-8] of the same epistle he says, 'I have fought the good fight, I have run the race to the finish; and now the crown of righteousness awaits me, which the Lord, the just judge, will award me on that day.' I find difficulty in reconciling the terms 'fight,' 'crown,' 'just judge,' 'award,' and 'fighting' with the absolute necessity of all events and a will that does nothing but is merely passive.[186]

James, too, attributes human sins not to necessity and God working in us, but to man's own depraved lusts. 'God,' he says, 'tempts no one; everyone is drawn and lured into temptation by his own lust; then lust conceives sin and brings it to birth.'[187] Paul calls human wrongdoings 'works of the flesh,'[188] not works of God; clearly what James calls 'lust' he calls 'the flesh.' And in Acts Ananias is asked, 'Why has Satan tempted your heart?'[189] In Ephesians, chapter 2[:2], Paul ascribes bad deeds to the 'spirit of the lower air' who 'works in the sons of doubt.'[190] 'Can Christ agree with Belial?'[191] 'Either make the tree good, and its fruit good,' says Christ, 'or else make the tree bad, and its fruit bad too.'[192] Nothing can be better than God: how dare certain people attribute the worst of fruits to him? And although human lust is stimulated by Satan, or by things outside man, or by a sinful tendency within, this stimulation does not compel us to sin if we implore God's help and willingly resist – just as the Spirit of Christ urges us to do good, not by imposing necessity but by offering help. Ecclesiasticus, chapter 15[:21] agrees with James: 'God has commanded no one to be ungodly;

\* \* \* \* \*

183 2 Tim 2:3
184 2 Tim 2:6
185 Cf 1 Cor 9:7.
186 The opinion of Luther and then that of Karlstadt
187 James 1:13–15. Cf Fisher 1523 sig zz1v; 1597 col 674 middle.
188 For example Gal 5:19
189 Acts 5:3. Here Erasmus retains the Vulgate *tentavit* 'tempted,' as he also did in his 1516 *Novum Testamentum*, though in the notes he points out that the Greek means 'filled.' In his 1519 *Novum Testamentum* he translates *implevit* 'filled.'
190 Here Erasmus follows the Vulgate *in filios diffidentiae* 'in the sons of doubt,' though in *Novum Testamentum* he translates the Greek to mean 'sons of disobedience' (1516 and 1519) or 'obstinate sons.'
191 2 Cor 6:15
192 Matt 12:33

he has given no one leave to sin.' And to compel is to do more than to command.

What Paul writes in 2 Timothy 2[:21] is even plainer: 'If anyone will cleanse himself from these things, he will be a vessel of honour.' How can he cleanse himself if he does nothing at all? I know there is a metaphor here, but it is enough for my present purposes that this verse utterly contradicts those who would ascribe everything to absolute necessity. 1 John 3[:3] is in agreement with this: 'Everyone who has this hope in God makes himself holy, just as God is holy.'[193] I will admit that the language is figurative here, if our opponents will allow us to claim the benefit of figurative language in other texts; yet it would be an utterly brazen figure of speech if 'makes himself holy' could be interpreted as 'is made holy by God whether he likes it or not'!

'Let us cast off the works of darkness,'[194] says Paul; and 'sloughing off the old man and all his acts':[195] how can we be ordered to 'throw off' and 'strip off' if we cannot do anything? Then in Romans 7[:18] we read: 'For the will is present in me, but I cannot find how to perform what is good.'[196] Here Paul is apparently saying that it is in man's power to will what is good: but the will to do good is in itself a good work; otherwise the will to evil would not be evil, and it is indisputably evil to wish to kill.

Again, in 1 Corinthians 14[:32] he says, 'The spirit of prophecy is under the prophets' control.' If those moved by the Holy Spirit are moved in such a way that they are free not to speak if they wish, then the human will in itself is under its own control to a much greater degree. For those moved by a fanatical spirit cannot be silent even if they would like to, and often they cannot understand their own utterances.

Paul's admonition to Timothy, 'Do not neglect the grace that is in you'[197] is also relevant here, for it shows that it is in our power to turn away from the grace that we have been given. And again, in another verse, he says, 'and his grace was not bestowed on me in vain.'[198] He means that he

* * * * *

193 The early editions have the error 1 John 5. Erasmus here retains *sanctificat se* 'makes himself holy,' though in the *Novum Testamentum* of 1516 and 1519 he translates the Greek as *purificat* 'purifies.'

194 Rom 13:12

195 Col 3:9

196 Cf Fisher 1525 sig Dd2; 1597 col 698 middle.

197 1 Tim 4:14. Erasmus retains the Vulgate *gratiam* 'grace,' though in the *Novum Testamentum* of 1516 and 1519 he translates the Greek as *donum* 'gift.'

198 1 Cor 15:10

had not fallen short of God's grace: but how could he have avoided falling short of it if he had done nothing? In the first chapter of his second epistle Peter says, 'and you should do your very best to supplement your faith with virtue,' and a little later, 'And so, my brothers, exert yourselves all the more to make your calling and election sure through good works.'[199] He wishes us to add our own efforts to God's grace so that, by stages of virtue, we may arrive at perfection.

But for some time now I have been concerned that someone may think I have overstepped the bounds in piling together these texts, which are found everywhere in the Holy Scriptures: for though Paul writes in 2 Timothy 3[:16], 'All divinely inspired Scripture is useful for teaching and refutation, for correction and instruction etc,' none of these texts would seem to have any point if everything is governed by absolute, ineluctable necessity. What is the sense of the many panegyrics on holy men in Ecclesiasticus 44 and the following chapters[200] if our own efforts deserve nothing? What is the meaning of the constant praises of obedience if to God we are tools for good works as well as bad, just as an axe is to a carpenter?[201]

And yet, we are all such tools if what Wyclif teaches is true – that everything, before and after grace, good, bad, or even indifferent, comes about by absolute necessity; and with this opinion Luther agrees. But to keep anyone from objecting that I have made this up, I will quote his own words from his *Assertion*: 'And so,' he says, 'I must retract this article too. For I misspoke when I said that free will before grace exists in name only; rather I should have simply said "free will is a fiction among real things, a name with no reality." For no one has it within his control to intend anything, good or evil, but rather, as was rightly taught by the article of Wyclif which was condemned at Constance,[202] all things occur by absolute necessity.'[203] This is quoted verbatim from Luther.

I will deliberately pass over many texts in Acts and the Apocalypse so as not to tax the reader's patience. These many verses, not without cause, have influenced learned and holy men not to rule out free will altogether. It is far from true that they have been inspired by the spirit of Satan and have called down damnation on themselves by trusting in their own works.

\* \* \* \* \*

199 2 Pet 1:5, 10
200 Ecclus 44–50
201 Cf Luther *Resolutions of the Heidelberg Theses* 6 WA 1 35 / LW 31 45.
202 See n35 above.
203 *Assertio* article 36 WA 7 146:3–8 / 306

## [PASSAGES FROM SCRIPTURE
## SEEMING TO OPPOSE FREE WILL]

*[The hardening of Pharaoh's heart in Exodus and Romans 9]*
Now it is time to look at the other side of the question and consider certain
scriptural passages that seem to deny free will completely. We come across
a number of these in the Scriptures, but there are two main ones, plainer
than the others, both of which the apostle Paul treats in such a way that at
first sight he seems to attribute nothing at all to our works or to the power
of free will. The first is in Exodus, chapter 9[:12 and 16], and is discussed
by Paul in Romans, chapter 9: 'The Lord hardened Pharaoh's heart, and he
did not listen to them.' And later, 'I have raised you up for the very purpose of showing my strength in you, and so that my name shall be declared
throughout all the earth.' Paul explains it in this manner, comparing a similar verse in Exodus 33[:19]: 'The Lord said to Moses: "I will take pity on
whoever I pity, and I will show mercy to whoever I will show mercy." And
so it depends not on man's will or exertions, but on God's mercy.'[204] The
other verse is in Malachi, chapter 1[:2–3], and is discussed by Paul in Romans, chapter 9[:11–13]: '"Was he not Jacob's brother?" says the Lord. "And
I have loved Jacob, but Esau I have hated."' Paul explains it thus: 'Though
they had not yet been born, or done anything, good or bad, in order that
God's election, based not on works but on his call, might stand firm, she
was told that the older should be servant to the younger, as it is written, "I
have loved Jacob, but Esau I have hated."'[205]

Now it seems absurd that God, who is good as well as just, should
be said to have hardened a man's heart so as to illustrate his own power
through that man's evil; and so Origen resolves the difficulty in *On First
Principles* book 3 thus: whilst admitting that God did send Pharaoh an occasion of hardening his heart, he throws the blame back on to Pharaoh,
who as a result of his own evil was made more obstinate by the very
events which should have led him to repentance. For just as the same rain
brings forth excellent fruit in cultivated ground, but thorns and thistles
in uncultivated ground, and just as wax melts, but mud hardens under
the action of the same sun, so God's lenient toleration of the sinner leads
some to repentance and makes others more persistent in their wrongdoing.[206] And so God has mercy on those who acknowledge his goodness

\* \* \* \* \*

204 Rom 9:15–16
205 Rom 9:11–12
206 Origen *On First Principles* 3.1.10–11 trans Butterworth 172–5

and amend their ways; but the hearts of those who have been given a chance to repent, but disdain his goodness and go on to do worse, are hardened. Origen demonstrates the figure of speech by which the person who has provided the opportunity for something is said to have done it, first from common linguistic usage: a father will commonly say to his son, 'I have ruined you' because he has not immediately punished the boy's faults.[207]

Isaiah uses a similar figure of speech in chapter 63[:17]: 'Lord, why have you made us wander from your ways? Why have you hardened our hearts so that we should no longer fear you?' Jerome interprets this text[208] as Origen does:[209] God hardens the sinner's heart when he does not punish him immediately, and has mercy on him when he urges him to swift repentance by means of affliction. Thus in Hosea, God speaks in his anger: 'I will not punish your daughters for their harlotry';[210] by contrast in Psalm 88[:33] he punishes in his mercy: 'I will punish their iniquities with the rod, and their sins with lashes.' Jeremiah uses the same figure of speech in chapter 20[:7]: 'Lord, you have led me astray, and I have gone astray; you were stronger than I, and you have overcome me.' 'Lead astray' means not to recall immediately from error, and Origen thinks this leads to a more complete healing, just as expert surgeons prefer a wound to scar over rather slowly so that with the wound open, freer suppuration can lead to lasting recuperation.[211] Origen also notes that the Lord says, 'For this very purpose have I raised you up,'[212] not 'for this very purpose have I created you.' For Pharaoh would not have been evil if that was the way he had been created by God, who 'saw everything he had made, and it was very good.'[213] He was created with a will that he could turn in either direction, and by his

\* \* \* \* \*

207 Origen *On First Principles* 3.1.10–11 trans Butterworth 172–5: 'It is not unreasonable to soften down such expressions of speech. For kind masters often say to servants who have been spoiled by their kindness and forbearance, "It was I who made you wicked," or "I am to blame for these serious offences." We must give heed to the character and force of what is said and not misrepresent it through failing to understand the meaning of the expression.' Cf Fisher 1523 sig AA4V; 1597 col 685 top.

208 *Commentarii in Isaiam prophetam* 17 on Isa 63:18, 19 PL 24 619B–C

209 *On First Principles* 3.1.12 trans Butterworth 177–80

210 Hos 4:14

211 *On First Principles* 3.1.13 trans Butterworth 181–2

212 Rom 9:17 on Exod 9:16. For Origen's comment see *Commentaria in epistolam ad Romanos* 7.16 PG 14 col 1146B.

213 Origen *Commentaria in epistolam ad Romanos* 7.16 PG 14 1146B, citing Gen 1:31

own choice he directed it to evil, for he preferred to follow his own will rather than to obey God's commandments.

But God used this evil will of Pharaoh's for his own glory and his people's salvation, and to make it clearer that men who resist God's will strive in vain. Just so a wise king or father uses the cruelty of people he hates in order to punish the wicked:[214] and no violence is done to our will if the outcome of events is in God's hands, or if God in his own hidden wisdom directs men's efforts to another end than the one they had intended. And so, just as evil men's efforts are turned to the advantage of the godly, good men's efforts do not achieve their aims unless aided by God's freely-given support. This, of course, is what Paul adds: 'And so it depends not on man's will or exertions, but on God's mercy.'[215] God's mercy goes before our will, accompanies it in its efforts, and brings about a happy outcome.[216] Yet meanwhile we exercise our will, make progress, reach our goal; but still we attribute what is our own to God, to whom we entirely belong.

The difficult question of how God's foreknowledge does not impose necessity on our will has been explained frequently, but in my opinion by no one more successfully than by Lorenzo Valla.[217] Foreknowledge is not the cause of events, for even we are in the position of foreknowing many events, but they do not happen because we foreknow them; rather we foreknow them because they are going to happen: so an eclipse of the sun does not happen because the astrologers predict it, rather they predict it because it is going to happen.[218]

Admittedly the problem of God's will and predestination is more difficult, for God wills the same things as he foreknows: he must do so in some sense, for even though it is in his power to prevent what he knows is going to happen, he does not do so. And this is what Paul adds: 'Who can resist his will,' if he 'takes pity on whoever he wishes, and hardens the heart of whoever he wishes.'[219] And indeed if there were a king who could

\* \* \* \* \*

214 Origen *Commentaria in epistolam ad Romanos* 7.16 PG 14 1146
215 Rom 9:16
216 Erasmus refers to prevenient, cooperating, and persevering grace.
217 See n48 above.
218 In *De libero arbitrio dialogus* Valla cited Jerome's *In Hieremiam prophetam libri VI* 5.36.5 (CCSL 74 254): 'Non enim ex eo, quod deus scit futurum aliquid, idcirco futurum est, sed quia futurum est, deus nouit quasi praescius futurorum' ('For something does not happen because God knows that it will but rather God knows it because it will happen, since he foreknows what will happen'); see Chomarat's edition (n48 above) page 34 n27.
219 Romans 9:18–19

carry out whatever he wished, and no one could resist him, he would be said to do whatever he wished.[220] Just so God's will, since it is the principal cause of everything that happens, does seem to impose necessity on our will. Paul does not resolve this problem; he simply rebukes anyone who would debate it: 'Man, who are you to answer back to God?'[221] But it is the godless protestor he rebukes, as if a master were to tell a defiant slave, 'What business is it of yours why I order this – just do what I order'; he would give a different reply if a wise and well-meaning slave were to ask him why he wanted something apparently pointless to be done.[222]

God willed Pharaoh's utter ruin, and he was right to will it, and it was good that Pharaoh should be ruined; but he was not compelled by God's will to persist in his godlessness. It is as if a master who knew a slave's bad character were to entrust him with a task which would give him an opportunity to sin, so that he could be caught and punished as an example to the others. The master knows beforehand that the servant is going to act in character and sin; he wants him to come to grief, and in a certain sense he wants him to sin; but this does not excuse the servant: he has sinned through his own wickedness; and even beforehand he deserved that his wickedness should be publicly known and that he should be punished for it. But where would you find any basis for deserving anything where everlasting necessity holds sway and the will has never been free?

As regards what we said about God frequently directing the outcome of events to another end than that which men had intended: though it is true for the most part, it is not invariably the case, and it happens more often in the case of bad acts than of good. By crucifying the Lord the Jews intended to make away with him completely: God turned this evil plan

* * * * *

220 Latin: 'Etenim si esset rex, qui quicquid vellet efficeret, neque quisquam possit obsistere, facere diceretur quicquid vellet.' E Gordon Rupp *Luther and Erasmus: Free Will and Salvation* (Philadelphia 1969) 67 says this sentence is tautological. In order to avoid tautology, Walter (50n4) says 'quicquid vellet' should be taken as the subject of the main clause, which should be translated 'so würde, was auch immer er will, ein Tun genannt werden' ('then whatever he wishes would be called a deed.') But such a construction gives a strained meaning to 'facere.' The question is whether God's irresistible will prevents our will from 'doing' anything so that in effect he is solely responsible for what we do, just as an irresistible king could be said to do the things he wishes others to do because they have no choice in the matter.

221 Rom 9:20

222 Origen *On First Principles* 3.1.22 trans Butterworth 205–6

of theirs to the glory of his Son and the salvation of all the world.[223] But the centurion Cornelius, who sought to win the deity's favour with good works, gained his wish;[224] Paul too ran the race to the finish and won the crown he sought.[225]

I will not here discuss the question of whether God, who is indisputably the first and highest cause of everything that happens, brings about certain events through secondary causes in such a manner that he himself does nothing, or whether he does everything in such a way that the secondary causes merely cooperate with the principal cause, but are not otherwise necessary.[226] It is certainly beyond doubt that God, if he wishes, can reverse the natural effect of all secondary causes: he can cause fire to make things cold and wet, water to make them hard and dry, or the sun to make them dark; he can make rivers harden or rocks melt; he can cause poison to cure and food to kill, just as the fire in the Babylonian furnace refreshed the three young men but burned up the Chaldeans.[227] Whenever God does

* * * * *

223 Cf Acts 2:23, 36.
224 Acts 10
225 2 Tim 4:7–8
226 Even though the *concursus generalis* (see n112 above) was accepted by all, the degree of efficacy attibuted to the primary cause, God, or to secondary causes was much debated and has a bearing on the power of man's will in moral acts. Generally theologians of the *via antiqua* 'the old school' (such as Aquinas or Gregory of Rimini) tended to place more emphasis on God's causality, whereas those of the *via moderna* 'the modern school' (such as Durand de Saint Pourçain and Gabriel Biel) assigned more efficacy to secondary causes. See Oberman *Harvest* 49–50, n110 above, and *Hyperaspistes* 1 153.
227 Dan 3:22–3, 48. Erasmus' point here depends on the distinction between God's *potentia absoluta* 'absolute power' and his *potentia ordinata* 'ordained power.' In agreement with the view of Aquinas quoted in *Hyperaspistes* 1 n521, late medieval scholastics advanced the view that the ordinary course of nature is in accordance with God's 'ordained power,' which God had conceded to nature as well as to men in the governance of their own affairs in keeping with the revealed divine laws of Scripture and the divine covenant. Theologians also attributed a *potentia absoluta* or 'absolute power' to God, which in the thirteenth-century view (including that of Aquinas) was regarded as what God by his absolute power might have done but chose not to do. In the fourteenth and fifteenth centuries it became for some theologians a power to intervene and change or halt the ordinary courses of nature and events, so that by his absolute power God could shield the boys in Nebuchadnezzar's furnace from the effects of the fire or as in Joshua's victory make the sun stand still, but this would be considered extraordinary or miraculous and therefore brought about by God's *potentia absoluta*. See Oakley 77–8. In the concluding section of *Hyperaspistes* 2, Erasmus suggests that Luther, who began

this it is called a miracle. In this way he can deprive the palate of its taste or the eyes of their judgment; he can paralyse the powers of mind, memory, and will and compel them to do whatever he sees fit – as he did to Balaam, who had come intending to curse but could not: he intended one thing, but his tongue spoke another.[228] Rare occurrences admittedly do not make a general principle; and yet in such cases, whatever God wills he wills for reasons that are just, albeit often unknown to us.[229] No one can resist this will: however, God's 'ordained will', or his 'signified will' as the scholastics call it,[230] is frequently resisted – did not Jerusalem resist by refusing to be gathered together, though God wished it to be?[231]

*[Divine foreknowledge and necessity: the case of Pharaoh]*
But someone will object that there is necessity in the outcome of events for two reasons: because God's foreknowledge cannot err, nor can his will be resisted. But not all necessity excludes free will: as, for instance, God the Father necessarily begets the Son, yet does so willingly and freely, because he is not compelled to do so.[232] In the human sphere too we can posit a certain necessity which does not exclude the freedom of our will. God foresaw (and what he foresaw he in a certain sense willed) that Judas would betray our Lord. Therefore, with regard to God's infallible foreknowledge and immutable will, it was necessarily going to come about that Judas would betray the Lord. Yet Judas could have changed his own mind, or could certainly not have conceived the evil intention. What if he had? you will ask. God's foreknowledge would not have been false, nor would his will have

\* \* \* \* \*

as a follower of Ockham but had become a believer in the universal presence and action of God's *potentia absoluta*, also believed human souls were saved only by God's *potentia absoluta* (see LB X 1527F). Courtenay (*Capacity* 77–8, 100–3) regards the late medieval introduction of the distinction into the realm of time as an aberration from the earlier view of figures such as Aquinas.

228 Num 23:4–24:10
229 Because of God's *potentia absoluta*, God does not do things because they are just but they are just by virtue of the fact that God does them, though neither Erasmus nor all followers of the *via moderna* held that view. See n227 above.
230 See n227 above; Oberman *Harvest* 103–4, 476; Oakley 116; on the entire history of the question see Courtenay *Capacity*. (The distinction, however, between the divine powers and the divine wills is not identical in scholastic thought.)
231 Matt 23:37
232 Theologians of the new school generally held that creation and the created universe are contingent but that God's internal actions are not contingent but simultaneously necessary and voluntary. See Oakley 79–81.

been impeded, since he would have foreknown, and willed, that Judas was going to change his mind.[233]

In such cases, those who analyse the matter with scholastic subtlety accept that there is a 'necessity of consequence,' but deny a 'necessity of the consequent': these are their usual terms to explain their opinion.[234] They admit that it necessarily follows that Judas will betray the Lord, if God has willed this to happen from all eternity with his efficacious will; but they say that it does not therefore follow that he will betray him necessarily, since he has conceived the evil plan with his own wicked will.

It is not my intention, however, to pursue such subtle distinctions further here. The verse 'God hardened Pharaoh's heart'[235] can be understood in the same sense as is Paul's 'God has given them over to their own depravity':[236] sin and its punishment are one and the same action. But when God gives people over to their own depravity, he does so because of their previous deserts: like Pharaoh, because he refused to let the Hebrew people go, though urged to do so by a great many signs, or the philosophers, who, though aware of the divinity of God, worshipped wood and stone. But where absolute, perpetual necessity obtains, there can be no question of deserving reward or punishment.

Nor can it be denied that God works concurrently with every human act, since every act has a reality, and has even in a sense a certain goodness

\* \* \* \* \*

233 The same example and argument appear in Valla's *De libero arbitrio dialogus* ed Chomarat 31–3 nos 36–43 / trans Trinkaus in *The Renaissance Philosophy of Man* 162–3 (see n48 above). See also Origen *Commentaria in epistolam ad Romanos* 7.8 PG 14 1126; Jerome *Commentarii in Ezechielem* 1.2 CCSL 75 28:735–41 and *In Hieremiam prophetam libri VI* 5.36.5 CCSL 74 253:1–254:7.

234 Absolute necessity (*necessitas consequentiae* 'necessity of the consequence') springs from God's absolute will; conditional necessity (*necessitas consequentis* 'necessity of the consequent'), from his conditional will. It is absolutely necessary that man be a rational animal, for he was created so. But it is only conditionally necessary that a person make one choice instead of another, for he had the power to make a different choice. In a letter to Erasmus of c February 1524 Ludwig Baer explained the terms in detail (Ep 1420:1–53). The distinction, which was well known to the scholastics but was not well understood by Luther, goes back to Boethius (*The Consolation of Philosophy* 5 prose 6), who gives the following illustration. If I know that a man is sitting, it is necessary that he be sitting, but this necessity (conditional) does not mean that he did not choose to sit or is not free to get up. See McSorley 85 n76, 150–1, 233–5; Oberman *Harvest* 472; McGrath 120–1.

235 Exod 9:12 (cf Exod 7:13)
236 Rom 1:28

– such as an embrace given to an adulteress, or the desire to embrace her.[237] Yet the evil in the act does not does not come from God, but from our will, saving that God, as mentioned before, can in a certain sense be said to effect the wilful malice in us, since he allows it free rein and does not restrain it by his grace.[238] And so he is said to have destroyed someone for having allowed him to come to grief when he could have saved him.

*[Jacob and Esau: the Jews and the gentiles]*

But enough of these matters as far as this quotation is concerned. Now as for the other passage about Jacob and Esau, concerning whom the answer was given in a prophecy before they were born, 'The older will serve the younger,' as is found in Genesis 25[:23], this statement does not actually refer to human salvation, however, for God can will a man to be a slave or a pauper, regardless of the man's wishes, without excluding him from eternal salvation. And then, in the verse from Malachi, chapter 1[:2] which Paul adds, 'I have loved Jacob, but Esau I have hated':[239] if you insist on its literal sense, God does not love in the way we do, nor does he hate anyone, for he is not affected by emotions like these. Besides, as I had begun to say, the prophet here is clearly speaking not of the hatred by which we are eternally damned, but of temporal affliction, as we speak of the 'wrath and fury' of God: the passage reprimands those who wanted to rebuild Edom, which God wished to remain destroyed.

Furthermore, as far as its tropological sense[240] is concerned: God has not loved all the gentiles, or hated all the Jews; he has chosen some from each people; so that, as used by Paul, this quotation serves not so much as a proof of necessity but rather to refute the arrogance of the Jews, who thought that the grace of the gospel belonged exclusively to them because they were the posterity of Abraham, and abhorred the gentiles, refusing to tolerate their admission to a share in that gospel grace. A little later Paul explains this, saying, 'And he has called us not only from amongst the Jews, etc.'[241] But since God, when he hates or loves, does so for just reasons, his hatred and love are no more of an impediment to free will when he

\* \* \* \* \*

237 Cf Fisher 1523 sig Aa3r; 1597 col 682 bottom.
238 See 46–7 above. Cf Origen *On First Principles* 3.1.19 trans Butterworth 197–8 and Fisher 1523 sig Aa3v; 1597 col 683 bottom.
239 Romans 9:13
240 Of the four traditional senses of Scripture (literal, tropological, allegorical, and anagogic), the tropological sense expresses the moral significance of the text.
241 Rom 9:24. In Paul the sentence concludes 'but from the gentiles also.'

shows them to the unborn than they are when he shows them to those already born. He hates those not yet born because he definitely foreknows that they will do things deserving of hate; he hates those already born because they are committing things deserving of hate. The Jews, who were a chosen people, have been rejected; and the gentiles, who were not a people, have been accepted. Why were the Jews lopped off the olive tree?[242] Because they refused to believe. Why were the gentiles grafted on? Because they were obedient to the gospel. Paul himself cites the reason: 'It was for lack of faith that they were lopped off,'[243] he says: just so, because they refused to believe. He both inspires those who have been lopped off with the hope of being grafted on again, if they will abandon their unbelief and believe, and instils into those who have been grafted on the fear of being lopped off if they turn away from God's grace. 'You hold your place by faith,' he says, 'do not be arrogant, but beware!' and shortly afterwards, 'so that you should not congratulate yourselves on your own wisdom.'[244] These quotations clearly show that Paul here is concerned to check gentile and Jewish arrogance alike.

[*The potter and the clay*]
The third quotation is in Isaiah 45[:9]: 'Woe to him who argues with his maker like a vessel made from Samian clay![245] Does the clay ask the potter, "What are you making?" and say, "Your work shows no skill"?' But it is clearer in Jeremiah, chapter 18[:6]: 'House of Israel, can I not deal with you like that potter? Like clay in the potter's hands are you in my hand.' These quotations are more polemical in Paul than in the prophets from whom they are taken. For Paul recounts them as follows: 'Does the potter not have power to make the same lump of clay into one vessel for honourable use, and another for menial use? What if God, wishing to show his anger and make known his power, has very patiently tolerated vessels of anger due for destruction, so as to manifest the riches of his glory for the vessels of mercy which he has prepared for glory? etc.'[246]

Both quotations from the prophets rebuke the people's protests against God because they were being afflicted for their own improvement. The prophet reprimands their godless words just as Paul did the godless

\* \* \* \* \*

242 Rom 11:16–24
243 Rom 11:20
244 Rom 11:20, 25
245 Clay from the island of Samos was of high quality.
246 Rom 9:21–3

objection: 'O man, who are you?'[247] In these matters we must submit ourselves to God exactly as the wet clay obeys the potter's hands. And yet
this does not do away with free will altogether, nor does it exclude the
cooperation of our will with God's will to gain eternal salvation. And indeed in Jeremiah shortly afterwards there follows an exhortation to repentance, which we have already quoted:[248] it would be pointless if everything
happens by necessity.

And indeed, the Second Epistle to Timothy, chapter 2[:20–1] clearly
shows that Paul's words here[249] are not intended to exclude the power of
free will altogether but to quell the impious protests against God on the
part of the Jews, who were excluded from the grace of the gospel on account of their obstinate lack of faith, whereas the gentiles were accepted on
account of their faith. He says: 'In a great house there are not only gold and
silver vessels, but some of wood and clay too, and some are for honourable
use, some for menial use. And so if anyone will cleanse himself from these
things, he will be an honourable vessel, sanctified, and useful to the Lord,
ready for every good work.'

Similes like this are used in the Scriptures in order to teach, but without being consistent in every detail, for if they were, what could be more
stupid than telling a Samian chamber-pot, 'If you clean yourself out you
will be a useful and honourable vessel'![250] It would however be correct to
say this to a rational vessel which could take the advice and conform itself
to the Lord's will. Moreover, assuming man is to God precisely as clay is
to the potter's hands, no one but the potter can be held responsible for the
sort of vessel turned out – especially if he is the kind of potter who has created and mixed the clay as he chooses. In this case a vessel is thrown into
the eternal fire though it has no control over itself and so has been guilty
of nothing!

And so let us interpret the simile to make the point it was employed to
teach, for a slavish attempt to relate all its details to our theme will force us
into many ridiculous statements. The potter here makes a vessel for menial
use, but because it has previously deserved it, as God rejected certain Jews,
but on account of their lack of faith. On the other hand, he has made an
honourable vessel out of the gentiles, on account of their faith. Now, why
do those who harass us with the words of Holy Scripture and demand that

* * * * *

247 In Rom 9:20 the verse concludes 'to answer back to God?'
248 Jer 18:8, 10; see 38 above.
249 That is, Rom 9:21–3
250 Cf Origen *On First Principles* 3.1.21 trans Butterworth 201–4.

the image of the potter and the clay be taken literally not allow us to take the verse 'If anyone will cleanse himself'[251] literally? For if we do, Paul will be found to contradict himself: in the passage quoted earlier[252] he puts everything in God's hands; here he puts everything in man's hands. And yet both passages are correct, though each makes a different point. The first stops the mouth of anyone who would murmur against God; the second is a call to effort and discourages complacency and despair.[253]

[*The workman and the axe*]
The verse in Isaiah, chapter 10[:15] is similar: 'Shall the axe vaunt itself against him who hews with it? Or the saw be exalted over him who wields it? As if a stick were to be lifted up against him who lifts it, or a staff, which is but wood, were to be raised aloft!' These words are directed against a godless king,[254] whose cruelty God had used to punish his people; the king ascribed events which happened with God's permission to his own wisdom and strength, whereas he was but a tool of God's anger. A tool, albeit a living and rational one: if the axe and saw were like this, one could say without absurdity that they too cooperated with the workman. Slaves are their masters' living tools, as Aristotle teaches[255] (as axes, saws, hoes or a plough would be if they could move by themselves, like the tripods and kettles fashioned by Vulcan so as to be able to go into battle on their own).[256] The master gives orders and supplies the necessary materials, and the slave cannot do anything without his master: yet no one says that the slave who follows his master's orders does nothing. Furthermore, the image used is not intended to remove the freedom of the will, but to crush the arrogance of the godless king who ascribed everything he had done not to God but to his own strength and wisdom.

[*Other scriptural examples of divine power and human will*]
It is not difficult, either, to rebut the quotation Origen gives from Ezekiel: 'I will take away their hearts of stone and put hearts of flesh in them.' A

* * * * *

251  2 Tim 2:21
252  That is, Rom 9:21–3
253  Cf Origen *On First Principles* 3.1.24 trans Butterworth 209–10.
254  The king of Assyria, probably Sennacherib, at the time of the invasion of Israel (701 BCE)
255  *Nicomachean Ethics* 8.11.6 1161b4
256  Homer *Iliad* 18.373–7. In Homer they have wheels so as to go by themselves to the gatherings of the gods and return home.

schoolmaster might use the same figure of speech to tell a pupil whose Latin was full of mistakes, 'I will remove your barbarian tongue and put a Roman tongue in you': he none the less requires application on the pupil's part, even if the pupil could not 'change his tongue' without the teacher's help.[257] What is a 'heart of stone'? A heart that is intractable and stubborn in evil. What is a 'heart of flesh'? A heart that is tractable and submissive to God's grace. Those who assert the existence of free will nevertheless admit that a soul stubborn in evil cannot be softened to true penitence without the help of heavenly grace. He who makes you ready to learn also demands your effort so that you do actually become learned.

David prays, 'A pure heart create in me, O God'; and Paul says, 'If anyone will cleanse himself.'[258] Ezekiel says, 'Make for yourselves a new heart and a new spirit'; on the other side David cries, 'and renew an upright spirit deep within me.'[259] David prays, 'Blot out all my offences'; on the other side John says, 'Everyone who has this hope in God makes himself holy, even as he is holy.'[260] David prays, 'Deliver me from blood-guilt, O God'; the prophet cries, 'Loosen the bonds from your neck, captive daughter of Zion!'[261] Paul says, 'Let us cast off the works of darkness'; and Peter says, 'Then, putting away all malice and all deceit and pretence etc.'[262] In Philippians 2[:12] Paul says, 'Work out your salvation with fear and trembling'; yet in 1 Corinthians 12[:6] the same Paul writes, 'But it is the same God who works everything in everyone.'

There are hundreds and hundreds of such quotations in Holy Scripture. If man does nothing, why say, 'Work out'? If man does something, why say, 'God works everything in everyone'? If someone twists one set of these verses to suit his cause, man does nothing; if someone forces the other set to fit his own interpretation, man does everything. But if man does nothing, there is no room for merit; and where there is no room for merit, there is none for punishments or rewards either. If man does everything, there is no room for grace, on which Paul repeatedly and forcefully insists. The Holy Spirit, by whose inspiration the canonical Scriptures were produced, does not contradict himself; and both sides accept and acknowledge

\* \* \* \* \*

257 Cf Origen *On First Principles* 3.1.15 trans Butterworth 186–7, citing Ezek 11:19.
258 Ps 50:12; 2 Tim 2:21
259 Ezek 18:31; Ps 50:12
260 Ps 50:11; 1 John 3:3
261 Ps 50:16; Isa 52:2
262 Rom 13:12; 1 Pet 2:1

the inviolable majesty of Scripture. What is needed is an interpretation that will resolve the problem.

The interpretation of those who do away with free will will be: '"Stretch out your hand to whatever you desire";[263] that is, grace will stretch out your hand to whatever it desires; "Make for yourselves a new heart,"[264] that is, God's grace will make a new heart for you; "Everyone who has this hope in God will make himself holy,"[265] that is, grace will make him holy; and "Let us cast off the works of darkness,"[266] that is, grace will cast them off. Again and again in the Scriptures we hear the refrain "He did justice,"[267] "He worked iniquity";[268] every time we do, we will explain it as "God did justice and worked iniquity in him."'[269] And then if I cite the interpretation of the ancient orthodox Fathers, or even of the councils, they will immediately cry, 'But they were only men!' But in the face of such a violent and twisted interpretation may I not say, 'Luther is only a man'? Of course their side will be victorious if they are allowed to interpret the Scriptures to fit in with their views but we may neither follow the Fathers' interpretations nor put forth our own! Anyway, the quotation 'stretch out your hand to whatever you desire' is too clear to need an interpreter: it means 'grace will stretch out your hand to whatever it desires,' and the interpretation of the most revered Doctors must be a delusion (not to call it – as others have – an inspiration of Satan).[270] Yet these scriptural verses, which seem to be in conflict, are easily reconciled if we join the efforts of our will to the assistance of God's grace.

In the images of the potter and the axe our opponents persistently harass us with a literal interpretation of the text because that suits their purpose; but here they move away from the words of Holy Scripture quite unabashedly, interpreting them with hardly less propriety than if someone said, 'Peter wrote this' and another interpreted it saying, 'It was not Peter who wrote it; someone else wrote it in his house.'

\* \* \* \* \*

263  Ecclus 15:16
264  Ezek 18:31
265  1 John 3:3
266  Rom 13:12
267  For example, Deut 33:21; Ps 105:3
268  For example, Pss 5:7, 27:3
269  This speech is placed in the mouth of Karlstadt and his adherents. See *Hyperaspistes* 1 164 below.
270  Luther had done so in his *Assertio* article 36 (WA 7 145:35–6 / 303).

## [PASSAGES CITED BY LUTHER
## TO DENY THE EXISTENCE OF FREE WILL]

*[Limited application of Genesis 6:3 and 8:21 and Isaiah 40:2]*
Now let us try the strength of the scriptural proofs which Martin Luther
quotes to undermine the power of free will. He cites verses from Genesis
6 and 8. 'My spirit will not remain in man forever, for he is flesh.'[271] In
this verse Scripture does not use 'flesh' simply in the sense of 'a wicked
desire,' as Paul sometimes does, when he orders us to 'mortify the works
of the flesh,'[272] but in the sense of the weakness of our nature with its tendency to sinning, as Paul calls the Corinthians 'fleshly' because they were
not yet ready to receive teaching in the form of solid food, being still (as
it were) babes in Christ.[273] And in *Questions about the Hebrew* Jerome says
that the Hebrew text reads differently from ours, namely, 'My spirit will
not pass judgment on those men eternally, for they are flesh.' These words
speak not of God's severity, but of his clemency: for by 'flesh' he means
men naturally weak, prone to evil, and by 'spirit' he means wrath; and
so he is saying that he will not save these people up for eternal punishment, but in his mercy will exact punishment from them in this life.[274]
And these words do not even apply to the entire human race, but only
to the men of that age, whose heinous vices had utterly corrupted them;
and so he says, 'those men.' And it does not even apply to all the men
of that time, given that Noah is praised as a righteous man, pleasing to
God.[275]

    In the same way it is possible to dismiss his quotations from chapter
8[:21] of the same book, 'For the thought and imagination of man's heart
are inclined to evil from his youth on', and from chapter 6[:5], 'The heart's
every thought is directed towards evil at all times.' Even if the tendency
to evil in most men cannot be overcome without the help of God's grace,
it does not remove the freedom of the will completely,[276] for if no aspect

\* \* \* \* \*

271 Gen 6:3. Luther cites this verse and Gen 8:21 in his *Assertio* article 36 WA 7
    143:19, 34 / 303.
272 Rom 8:13
273 1 Cor 3:1–2
274 Erasmus partly quotes, partly paraphrases Jerome's *Hebraicae questiones in libro
    Geneseos* (on Gen 6:3) CCSL 72 9:30–10:2. Cf Fisher 1523 sig zz3; 1597 col 676
    bottom.
275 Gen 6:8–9. Cf Fisher 1523 sig zz2; 1597 col 675 top.
276 Cf Fisher 1523 sig zz1v; 1597 col 674 top.

of repentance depends on the will, but everything is controlled by God through a kind of necessity, then why are men given time for repentance in this very passage: 'His days will be one hundred and twenty years'?[277] For in *Questions about the Hebrew,* Jerome considers that this verse refers not to the length of human life, but to the interval before the Flood; a time conceded to humans during which to change their ways if they wish, and if not, to be shown to deserve divine condemnation for having disdained God's leniency.[278]

Then, what he quotes from Isaiah,[279] chapter 40[:2], 'From the Lord's hand she has received for all her sins,'[280] is interpreted by Jerome as meaning divine vengeance, not grace given in return for evil deeds.[281] For although Paul says, 'Where sin abounded, grace abounded all the more,'[282] it does not follow from this that before the infusion of sanctifying grace man cannot, with God's help, prepare himself for divine favour by morally good works; as we read of the centurion Cornelius, who had not yet been baptized or inspired by the Holy Spirit: 'Your prayers and your alms have gone up as a memorial before God.'[283] If all works performed before the infusion of the highest grace are evil, does this mean that evil works win us God's favour?[284]

[*All flesh is grass' (Isa 40:6–8) does not mean that all human inclinations and abilities are flesh*]
As for his quotation of Isaiah 40[:6–8] – 'All flesh is grass, and all its glory is as the flower of the grass. The grass is withered and the flower has fallen because the Spirit of the Lord has blown upon it, but the word of the Lord abides for ever'[285] – Luther, I feel, twists this somewhat violently to apply to grace and free will. For here Jerome understands 'spirit' as meaning divine wrath, 'flesh' as man's natural weakness, which is powerless against God, and 'flower' as the vainglory aroused by material good fortune.[286] The

* * * * *

277  Gen 6:3
278  *Hebraicae questiones in libro Geneseos* (on Gen 6:3) CCSL 72 9:9–10:19
279  Luther *Assertio* article 36 WA 7 144:5–6 / 304
280  The full scriptural text has 'received double.'
281  *Commentarii in Esaiam* 11 (on Isa 40:1–2) CCSL 73 454:3–455:57
282  Rom 5:20
283  Acts 10:4
284  Cf Fisher 1523 sig zz4; 1597 cols 677 bottom–678 top.
285  Luther *Assertio* article 36 WA 7 144:15–17 / 304
286  *Commentarii in Esaiam* 11 (on Isa 40:6–8) CCSL 73 457:24–46. Cf Fisher 1523 sig Aa1v; 1597 col 680 top.

Jews gloried in the temple, in circumcision, in sacrifices; the Greeks gloried in their wisdom: but now that the wrath of God has been revealed from heaven by the gospel, all that glory has withered.[287]

Yet not every human inclination is 'flesh': there is 'soul' and there is 'spirit,' by which we strive towards goodness. This part of the psyche is called reason or the ruling principle[288] – or was there not a single one of the pagan philosophers who strove for goodness, though they taught that we should a thousand times more readily go to our death than commit an evil action, even if we knew that it would be unknown to men and pardoned by God?[289] Corrupt reason, it is true, often has poor judgment. 'You do not know,' said the Lord, 'to what spirit you belong': the disciples were mistakenly seeking vengeance, referring to the time long before when fire had come down from heaven in answer to Elijah's prayers and burned up the captains with their companies of fifty men.[290] In Romans 8[:16] Paul states that even in good people the human spirit is distinct from the spirit of God: 'for that spirit [of God] witnesses to our spirit[291] that we are children of God.' And so, if anyone maintains that the highest powers of human nature are nothing but flesh, that is, evil inclinations, I will gladly agree – if he can demonstrate his assertion with proofs from Holy Scripture![292]

'What is born of the flesh is flesh, and what is born of the spirit is spirit.'[293] John further teaches that those who believe in the gospel are born of God and become children of God and even gods;[294] and Paul distinguishes the fleshly man, who does not understand the things that are of

\* \* \* \* \*

287 See, for example, Rom 2:17–23; 1 Cor 1:22–5; Rom 1:18–22.
288 Cicero defines the Stoic concept expressed by the Greek word used by Erasmus here (ἡγεμονικόν) as follows: 'that part of anything which must and ought to have the supremacy in a thing of that sort'; see *De natura deorum* 2.11.29 trans H. Rackham (Cambridge, Mass, and London 1956) 151. See also *Hyperaspistes* 2 LB X 1460A–1161A.
289 See, for example, Plato *Apology* 17 (30B) and *Crito* 16 (54B).
290 Luke 9:54–5; cf 4 Kings 1:8–15
291 Erasmus here follows the Vulgate, though in his *Novum Testamentum* of 1516 and 1519 he translated the Greek to mean 'together with our spirit.'
292 Luther accused Erasmus of intending here to scoff at Melanchthon (*De servo arbitrio* WA 18 740:32–5 / LW 33 222). In *Hyperaspistes* 2 LB X 1458E–F Erasmus does not admit that he intended to attack Melanchthon, but says that it would have been permissible for him to do so. He also wishes that such a talented scholar as Melanchthon had not become involved in Luther's tragedy.
293 John 3:6
294 John 1:12, 10:34–6 (cf Ps 81:6); 1 John 5:1. Cf Fisher 1523 sig Aa2v; 1597 col 681 bottom.

God, from the spiritual man, who can judge all things, and elsewhere he calls him a new creation in Christ.[295] If the whole man, even though reborn through faith, is still nothing but flesh,[296] where is the 'spirit born of the spirit'? Where is the 'child of God'? Where is the 'new creation'? I would like instruction on these points; until then I will take full advantage of the authority of the ancients, who teach that there are certain seeds of goodness planted in men's minds,[297] with the help of which they can to some extent see and strive after the good, though there are also baser tendencies which tug them in the opposite direction. Furthermore, choice means the ability of the will to turn in either direction; and although the will is perhaps more inclined to evil than to good, on account of the tendency to sin left in us, yet no one is compelled to sin unless he actually wills it.

*[Jeremiah 10:23 and Proverbs 16:1–6 and 16:21: divine providence does not preclude free will]*

Then again, his quotation from Jeremiah,[298] chapter 10[:23]: 'Lord, I know that a man's path is not his own; and that it is not for him to walk and direct his steps' applies to the happy or sad outcome of events rather than to the power of free will.[299] For it is often precisely when people take the greatest care to avoid any misfortune that the greatest disasters befall them. But those who suffer misfortune are not deprived of their free will simply because they did not foresee the misfortune; nor are those who inflict it deprived of free will simply because they smite their enemies with a different motive from that of God working through them (doubtless in order to punish). If you twist this ever so violently to apply to free

\* \* \* \* \*

295 1 Cor 2:14–15; 2 Cor 5:17 and Gal 6:15

296 Erasmus alludes here to Luther's doctrine of 'justified and sinful at the same time.' Luther denies he ever said what Erasmus attributes to him here (*De servo arbitrio* WA 18 744:30–745:10 / LW 33 228–9), but he had done so in his lectures on the Epistle to the Romans of 1515–16 (WA 56 268:26–272:21). See also *Assertio* article 36 WA 7 142:25 / 301.

297 See n81 above. Erasmus is alluding to a central idea of the Stoics, which he encountered in the Fathers, especially Jerome, whose *Commentarii in Esaiam* he has just been citing. A comprehensive exposition of Stoic ideas in the works of the Fathers may be found in Marcia Colish *The Stoic Tradition from Antiquity to the Early Middle Ages* 2 vols, Studies in the History of Christian Thought 34–5 (Leiden 1985) II 48–91.

298 Luther *Assertio* article 36 WA 7 144:27–8 / 304

299 In defending his interpretation in *Hyperaspistes* 2 LB X 1466C–1467D Erasmus appeals to Jerome *In Hieremiam libri* VI 2.95–6 (on Jer 10:22–3) CCSL 109:6–110:9. Cf Fisher 1523 sigs Aa2r–Aa2v; 1597 col 681 middle.

will,[300] well, no one denies that without God's grace none of us can steer a straight course in life. Every day we pray, 'Lord God, guide my steps in your sight';[301] yet we continue to do the best we can ourselves. We pray, 'Lord, incline my heart to your testimonies':[302] but the one who asks for help does not give up trying.

Then there is Proverbs 16[:1]: 'It is for man to prepare his heart, but the government of the tongue is from the Lord.' This too applies to the outcome of events, to things that may or may not happen, without the loss of eternal salvation. But how can it be for man to prepare his heart, when Luther asserts that everything comes about by necessity?[303] And then, in the same chapter, Solomon says, 'Reveal your works to the Lord, and your plans will be directed.'[304] Here we have 'your works' and 'your plans,' neither of which could be mentioned if God works everything, good as well as bad, in us. 'The beginning of a good life is mercy and truth, etc';[305] and much else is found in Proverbs supporting those who believe in free will.

As for his quotation from the same chapter,[306] 'The Lord has made everything for his own end; even the wicked man for the day of disaster,'[307] God has not created any nature evil in itself; and yet he controls everything in his ineffable wisdom so as to turn even the bad to our advantage and to his own glory. For not even Lucifer was created evil; God keeps him for eternal punishment because he fell away of his own will, and he uses his evil to train the godly and punish the ungodly.

There is little more force in his quotation from chapter 21[:1]: 'Like streams of water is the king's heart in the hand of the Lord: he will guide it wherever he wishes.'[308] But guiding is not necessarily the same

\* \* \* \* \*

300 In *Hyperaspistes* 2 LB X 1467C–D Erasmus admits that Jerome uses this passage against the Pelagians, who attribute too much to free will. But Jerome does not say that it denies free will.

301 Ps 5:9. In Erasmus' time monks said all the psalms every week, but the verse Erasmus mentions here occurred especially frequently because it was the opening antiphon for the office of the dead ('Dirige, domine meus in conspectu tuo viam meam'). The opening word 'dirige' is the root of 'dirge.'

302 Ps 118:36

303 *Assertio* article 36 WA 7 146:7–8 / 305

304 Prov 16:3

305 Prov 16:5–6

306 *Assertio* article 36 WA 7 144:35–6 / 305

307 Prov 16:4

308 *Assertio* article 36 WA 7 145:12–14 / 305; Erasmus commented on this text at length in his colloquy 'The Godly Feast' CWE 39 184–6.

as compulsion; and anyway, no one denies that God, as I said,[309] can coerce the human mind, can throw out what man had intended and implant a new desire; can even take away his mind altogether. Yet that does not alter the fact that we normally continue to have free will. And if Solomon's opinion here is as Luther interprets it, why should he make this statement specifically of the king's heart, seeing that all hearts are in God's hand? This verse agrees better with what we find in Job 34[:30]: 'He makes a hypocrite king on account of the people's sins' and Isaiah 3[:4]: 'I will give them boys for their rulers, and effeminates shall govern them.' When God, favourably inclined to his people, steers the king's thoughts towards good, he does not impose necessity on his will. On the other hand, he is said to guide towards evil when, offended by his people's sins, he does not restrain a foolish prince's desire for plunder, war, and tyranny, but allows him to be driven on headlong by his passions so as to punish the people through his wrongdoing. Even if it did sometimes happen that God drove a king who had deserved it to evil, there is no necessity to elevate a particular case into a general principle.

From all the Scriptures you could collect a mountain of proofs of the kind Luther cites from Proverbs, but it would swell your forces rather than ensure your victory. Arguments of this sort are the rhetoricians' habitual weapon: they are mostly of the sort that with the right kind of interpretation can be pressed into service for, or against, free will.

*[John 15:5 – 'Without me you can do nothing' – is not to be taken literally]*
Luther sees Christ's words in John's Gospel 15[:5], 'Without me you can achieve nothing,' as an 'Achillean' spear that no one can avoid;[310] but in my view it can be parried in several ways. First, in common usage we say that a man 'achieves nothing' if he does not reach his goal; and yet someone who makes an effort often gets somewhere. In this sense it is absolutely true that we can 'do nothing' without Christ, for in that verse he is speaking of the fruit of the gospel, granted only to those who remain on the vine which is Christ Jesus. Using this figure of speech Paul says, 'And so he who plants and he who waters count for nothing, but God, who gives the increase.'[311] By the word 'nothing' he means things of small importance, useless in themselves. Similarly in 1 Corinthians 13[:2, 3]: 'If I have not charity,

* * * * *

309 On 48–51 above
310 *Adagia* I vii 51; see *Assertio* article 36 WA 7 142:31–2 / 301 and *De servo arbitrio* WA 18 748:10–19 / LW 33 234. Luther often uses Achilles as a symbol of invincibility (for example *De servo arbitrio* 688:33 / LW 33 145).
311 1 Cor 3:7

I am nothing'; and shortly after that, 'It profits me nothing.'[312] Again, in Romans, chapter 4[:17], he says: 'God calls things that do not exist as though they did.' Again, drawing on Hosea, he calls a disdained and rejected people 'not a people.'[313] Using a similar figure the psalm says, 'I am a worm and not a man.'[314] If this were not so and anyone really pressed the word 'nothing,' then it would be impossible even to sin without Christ (assuming that 'Christ' here means 'Christ's grace'); or will they take refuge in the long-discredited view that sin has no reality? And this is true in a certain sense, given that we neither live nor move nor have our being without Christ.[315] But anyway, our opponents do sometimes admit that free will has the power to sin without grace: Luther did so at the beginning of his *Assertion*.[316]

## [ADDITIONAL PASSAGES THAT SEEM TO OPPOSE FREE WILL]

*[Other Gospel passages that only seem to undermine free will]*
Also relevant to this are John the Baptist's words, 'Man can receive nothing unless it is given to him from heaven.'[317] But it does not follow from this that we neither possess nor exercise free will. The heating effect of fire comes from heaven; our natural tendency to seek what is beneficial and avoid what is harmful comes from heaven; that after falling into sin the will is impelled to strive to become better comes from heaven; that by tears, acts of charity, and prayers we achieve the grace that makes us acceptable to God comes from heaven; yet all the while our will is not inactive, even though it could not achieve what it is striving for without the help of grace. But since our contribution is very small, we ascribe it all to God, as a sailor who has brought his ship safely into port in a fierce storm does not say, 'I saved the ship,' but 'God saved it,' though his own skill and hard work were by no means ineffectual.[318]

In the same way a farmer bringing a rich harvest from his fields into his barn does not say, 'I gave such a good harvest,' but 'God gave it'; yet at

\* \* \* \* \*

312 Cf Fisher 1523 sigs yy2–yy2v; 1597 col 669 bottom.
313 Rom 9:24–6 (cf Hos 1:9)
314 Ps 21:7
315 Cf Acts 17:28.
316 *Assertio* article 36 WA 7 142:28 / 301
317 John 3:27
318 Cf Origen *On First Principles* 3.1.19 trans Butterworth 199

the same time who would claim that the farmer had done nothing to make the crops thrive?[319] People commonly say, 'God gave you lovely children' (though their father was not uninvolved in the begetting of them) and 'God brought me back to health' (though the doctor was of considerable assistance); just so we say, 'The king conquered his enemies,' though his generals and troops accomplished the task. Nothing grows without rain from heaven; and yet good ground brings forth fruit, but bad ground bears no good fruit. But since human effort accomplishes nothing without the help of God's favour, all is attributed to God's goodness. 'Unless the Lord builds the house, they labour in vain that build it. Unless the Lord watches over the city, the watchman stands guard in vain';[320] yet all the while neither the care the builders take in building the city nor the vigilance with which the watchmen guard it comes to an end.

Then, 'For it is not you who speak, but the Spirit of your Father who speaks in you'[321] seems at first sight to deny free will, but what it in fact removes from us is the anxiety of working out what we are to say in the service of Christ; for if this were not so, preachers who prepared their sermons with care would be sinning. Nor is it a gift we should all expect, even if the Spirit did inspire the unlettered disciples with what they should say, as he imparted the gift of tongues. And even if he did impart this gift to them, when they were speaking their will conformed itself to the Spirit's inspiration, and worked together with what worked upon it. And this is precisely what free will is meant to do, unless we are to believe that God spoke through the apostles' mouths as he spoke to Balaam through the mouth of his ass.[322]

There is, however, more force in John 6[:44]: 'No one can come to me unless my Father draws him.' The word 'draw' seems to imply necessity and rule out the freedom of the will. But this is not a violent drawing; it makes one want what one may still refuse, just as you show a child an apple and it runs up to you, or you show a sheep a green willow branch and it follows you.[323] Just so God knocks on the door of our soul[324] with his grace

* * * * *

319 Cf Origen *On First Principles* 3.1.19 trans Butterworth 198
320 Ps 126:1; cf Origen *On First Principles* 3.1.19 trans Butterworth 197–8 and Fisher 1523 sig Bb1v; 1597 col 686 middle.
321 Matt 10:20
322 Num 22:21–35
323 Augustine *In Ioannis evangelium tractatus* CXXIV 26.5 CCSL 36 262. Cf Fisher 1523 sigs Dd4–Dd4v; 1597 col 701 bottom.
324 Cf Rev 3:20: 'Behold, I stand at the doorway and knock, and if anyone hears my voice and opens the door for me, I will go in to him.' Bede interprets

and we willingly welcome him. The quotation from John, chapter 14[:6], 'No one comes to the Father except through me,' should be understood in the same way. As the Father glorifies the Son, and the Son the Father, so the Father draws us to the Son, and the Son to the Father. But we are drawn in such a manner that soon we are running willingly: thus we find in the Song of Songs [1:3]: 'Draw me after you; we will run, etc.'

[*Pauline passages that do not preclude free will if they are correctly interpreted*]
From the Pauline Epistles too a number of quotations might be collected which seem to undermine any power of free will. One of these is 2 Corinthians 3[:5]: 'Not that we are sufficient to think anything by ourselves as if from ourselves; all our sufficiency is from God.' But here free will can be defended in two ways. First, certain orthodox Fathers posit three stages of human activity: first comes thought; then follows the wish to carry it out; the third is actually performing it.[325] And in the first and last stages they deny that there is any room for the working of free will. For the soul is impelled by grace alone to imagine the good, and by grace alone is brought to carry out what it has imagined. But in the second phase, wishing to carry it out, grace and human will work together, grace, however, being the principal, and our will the secondary, cause. But since the whole process is attributed to him who has brought everything to completion, man has no claim to any credit for himself as the result of a good work, given that his very ability to consent to and cooperate with God's grace is itself a gift of God. Second, the preposition 'from' denotes an ultimate source, and for that reason Paul writes precisely, 'by ourselves as if from ourselves,' ἀφ' ἑαυτῶν ὡς ἐξ ἑαυτῶν, that is, 'from our very selves.' Even someone who conceded that man can effectively wish the good by his natural capacities

* * * * *

the passage as follows: 'Ostium quidem cordis tui exhortationis dextera pulso, quam si libenter receperis, me inhabitatore et cohaerede dignus habeberis' ('I knock indeed on the door of your heart with the right hand of exhortation, and if you receive it willingly you will be considered worthy of me as a dweller and co-heir'); see *Explanatio Apocalypsis* 1.3 PL 93 142, and see also Alcuin *Commentariorum in Apocalypsin libri quinque* 3.3 PL 100 1114–15.

325 Bernard of Clairvaux (not technically a church Father but sometimes cited by Erasmus as if he were) makes this triple division in his *De gratia et libero arbitrio* 14.49; see *Treatises III: On Grace and Free Choice* . . . trans Daniel O'Donovan, The Works of Bernard of Clairvaux 7, Cistercian Fathers Series 19 (Kalamazoo, Mich 1977) 105, 108–9. H.A. Wolfson *The Philosophy of the Church Fathers* 3rd ed (Cambridge, Mass 1970) 464–7 reports a similar distinction in John Damascene.

could say this, inasmuch as man does not even have these capacities from himself.[326]

Who would deny that all good proceeds from God as from a source? Paul, too, frequently drives this home so as to remove our arrogance and self-reliance – which he does elsewhere too: 'What do you possess that you did not receive? And if you received it, why do you glory in it as though you had not received it?'[327] Note the word 'glory,' which Paul crushes with these words. If the servant who gave his master the profit he had made by moneylending[328] had claimed the praise for having applied his efforts so well, he would have been asked the same thing: 'What do you possess that you did not receive?'; and yet he is praised by his master for having been so enterprising. James [1:17] sings the same refrain: 'Every good gift and every perfect endowment comes down from above.' So does Paul, in Ephesians 1[:11]: 'who works everything according to the designs of his will.' These verses too aim to prevent us from claiming anything for ourselves and to make us attribute everything to the grace of God, who called us when we had turned away from him, purified us through faith, and enabled our will to be the co-worker[329] with his grace, even though grace alone is more than sufficient for everything and has no need of any assistance from human will.

Moreover, Philippians, chapter 2[:13], 'For God works both the will and the deed in us,[330] in accordance with good will,' does not exclude free will; for if you refer 'in accordance with good will' to man, as Ambrose interprets it, it means that man's good will works together with the action of grace.[331] And shortly before Paul writes, 'Work out your own salvation

* * * * *

326 Walter (70 n2) attributes this position specifically to Scotus (as Erasmus does not). Scotus argues, however, that though acts of love (both natural and meritorious) are of the same species, they attain merit through an act of acceptance by the divine will; see Scotus' *God and Creatures: The Quodlibetal Questions* trans Felix Alluntis and Allen B. Wolter (Princeton 1975) 397–8. It is hard to say whether 'effectively' (*efficaciter*) includes the idea of merit or means merely 'fully, successfully.' See also n103 on Scotus above.

327 1 Cor 4:7

328 Matt 25:15–23

329 The Greek is συνεργός (1 Cor 3:9; cf 2 Cor 6:1).

330 Phil 2:13 has 'in you' (*in vobis*), not 'in us' (*in nobis*); the change was probably a misprint (a turned 'u'). Both LB and Walter have *nobis*.

331 See pseudo-Ambrose *In Epistolam ad Philippenses* (on 2:13) PL 17 412A: 'Deum bonos conatus adiuvare testatur, omnem enim gratiam semper reportat ad Deum: ut nostrum sit velle, perficere vero Dei' ('It [the verse] attests that God aids good efforts, for it refers all grace always to God, so that the will is ours

with fear and trembling,'[332] from which it can be deduced that God works in us, and that our will and our anxious concern strive along with God.[333] In case anyone thinks that this interpretation should be rejected, it is preceded, as we said, by the words 'work out your own salvation,' and ἐργάζεσθε more properly means 'work out' than the word ἐνεργεῖν 'to accomplish' which he applies to God, ὁ ἐνεργῶν 'the one who accomplishes'; for properly speaking God ἐνεργεῖ 'accomplishes' by impelling and urging onward. But even if ἐργάζεσθαι and ἐνεργεῖν have the same force, this passage definitely teaches that both man and God 'work.'

But what does man 'work' if our will is to God as clay to the potter? 'For it is not you who speak, but the Spirit of your Father who speaks in you';[334] this was said to the apostles, and yet in Acts [4:8] we read that Peter spoke: 'Then Peter, filled with the Holy Spirit, said to them.' How could these two contradictory statements, 'It is not you who speak, but the Spirit' and 'Peter spoke, filled with the Holy Spirit,' be reconciled unless the Spirit speaks in the apostles in such a way that at the same time they speak in obedience to the Spirit? And yet it is true that they do not speak, not because they are inactive, but because they are not principally responsible for what they say. In the same way we read of Stephen, 'And they could not withstand his wisdom, and the Spirit that was speaking';[335] yet it is he who is speaking to the Sanhedrin. Similarly Paul says, 'But now it is not I who live; it is Christ who lives in me';[336] yet, also according to Paul, 'the just man lives by faith.'[337] How can he live, and yet not live? Because he ascribes the fact that he lives to the Spirit of God. Just so in 1 Corinthians, chapter 15[:10]: 'Not I, but the grace of God which is with me.' If Paul had not done anything, why did he previously say that he had? 'But I have worked harder than all of them,' he says.[338] If what he had said was true, why does he correct it here as though he had been mistaken in saying it? The point of the correction, surely, was not that we should think he had done

* * * * *

but the deed is God's'). The *Glossa ordinaria*, however, interprets the verse contrary to Erasmus, taking 'in accordance with good will' (*pro bona voluntate*) as referring to God's will, not man's (PL 114 604).

332 Phil 2:12
333 Augustine *De gratia et libero arbitrio* 9.21 PL 44 894. Cf Fisher 1523 sig Ee2v; 1597 col 705 top.
334 Matt 10:20
335 Acts 6:10
336 Gal 2:20
337 Rom 1:17 (cf Hab 2:4)
338 1 Cor 15:10

nothing, but so that he should not seem to ascribe to his own powers what he had achieved with the help of God's grace. And so it is the impression of insolence which this correction seeks to rule out, not the possibility of cooperation.

For God does not want man to attribute anything to himself, even if there were something which by rights he could: 'When you have done everything commanded you, say, "We are unprofitable servants; we have done only what we ought to have done."'[339] Has he not done a splendid thing, he who has kept all God's commandments? I wonder whether any such person is to be found at all. Yet those who have done this are ordered to say, 'We are unprofitable servants.' What they have done is not denied, but they are instructed to avoid dangerous pride. Man says one thing, and God says another. Man says, 'I am a servant, and an unprofitable one.' But the Lord? 'Well done, good and faithful servant,' and 'I will no longer call you servants, but friends.'[340] He calls the same people brothers instead of servants: those who call themselves 'unprofitable servants' God calls his children; and those very people who now proclaim that they are unprofitable servants are told by the Lord, 'Come, you blessed of my Father'[341] and hear their good deeds enumerated, which they themselves did not know they had done.

[*Gospel parables do not deny free will if they are interpreted according to their context*]

Now, I think that it is an excellent key to the understanding of the Scriptures if we look carefully at the drift of each passage. Once we have noted this, it will be easy to extract from parables and examples the details relevant for their lesson. In the parable of the steward about to be removed from his position who forges alterations to the accounts of his master's debtors, how many details there are which have nothing to do with the sense of the parable! The only lesson to draw from it is that before death forestalls him, everyone should make his very best effort to lavish the gifts he has received from God on his neighbours who need help.[342] The same applies to the parable we have just mentioned: 'Which one of you who has a servant ploughing or herding oxen will say to him immediately after he

\* \* \* \* \*

339 Luke 17:10
340 Matt 25:21–3 (Luke 19:17); John 15:15
341 Matt 25:34
342 Luke 16:1–9. Gregory the Great interprets the parable in this way; see *Moralia in Iob* 18.18.28 PL 76 52. Gregory's interpretation is quoted by Thomas Aquinas in his *Catena aurea*; see *Opera omnia* 25 vols (New York 1948–9) XII 149.

returns from the field, "Come and sit down at table" and not rather, "Make me something to eat, and get yourself ready and serve me while I eat and drink, and afterwards you may eat and drink"? Will he be grateful to the servant for doing what he was ordered? I think not.'[343] The point of this parable is that people should obey the Lord's commands unreservedly, and do their duty energetically, but should claim no praise for themselves for having done it. In any case, the Lord himself departs from this parable: he acted as a servant and granted his disciples the honour of reclining at table; he thanks his servant when he says, 'Well done, good servant' and 'Come, you blessed ones.'[344] Therefore he does not add, 'And so when you have done everything, the Lord will judge you unworthy of any thanks, and look on you as unprofitable servants,' but rather, 'You should say, "We are un-profitable servants."'[345] So it is that Paul, who worked harder than them all, calls himself the 'least of the apostles', and 'not fit to be called an apostle.'[346]

The same applies to Matthew, chapter 10[:29]: 'Are not two sparrows sold for a penny? And yet not one of them falls to the ground without your Father.' Above all else we must pay attention to the Lord's purpose here.[347] He did not wish to teach what is called the 'Diomedean' necessity[348] of all events: the point of his illustration is to remove the disciples' fear of men, for they should understand that they are in God's care, and cannot be harmed by men without his permission, and that he will not permit it unless it is for their good and the good of the gospel. Contrariwise, in 1 Corinthians 9[:9] Paul asks, 'Do you suppose that God cares about oxen?' It also seems that the next verse in Matthew's Gospel uses hyperbole: 'Every hair on your head is numbered.'[349] So many hairs fall to the ground every day – are they all to be accounted for? What then was the point of the hyperbole? Surely the advice that follows: 'Therefore do not be afraid.'[350] And so, just as these figures of speech remove our fear of men and strengthen our trust in God, without whose providence nothing at all can happen, so too the figures of speech considered earlier serve the purpose not of remov-ing free will, but of discouraging us from arrogance, which is hateful to the

* * * * *

343 Cf Luke 17:7–9.
344 Luke 19:17; Matt 25:34
345 Luke 17:10
346 1 Cor 15:9–10
347 Cf Fisher 1523 sigs cc1–cc1v; 1597 col 691 middle.
348 *Adagia* I ix 4. Erasmus says it applies to 'those who do something under strong compulsion and not of their own free will' (cwe 32 181).
349 Matt 10:30
350 Matt 10:31

Lord. It is safer to put everything in the Lord's hands. He is generous: he will not only let us have what is ours, but what is his he will command to be ours also.

How can the prodigal son[351] be said to have 'squandered his share of the property' if he had no control over any share? What he had, he had received from his father; and we confess that all natural gifts are gifts of God. He had his share even when it was in his father's control; indeed it was more secure thus. So what does his demanding his share and leaving his father stand for? Surely it means claiming gifts of nature as your own, and employing them to satisfy not the commandments of God but the demands of the flesh. And what does the famine mean? An affliction by which God arouses the sinner's mind to self-recognition and self-hate, and affects him with a longing for the father he has left. And the son talking to himself, pondering the possibility of confessing his sin and going home?[352] The human will working together with the stimulating grace known, as we said, as 'prevenient' grace. And the father running out to meet his son? God's grace which assists our will so that we can carry out what we intend. Even if this interpretation were my own invention, it would certainly be more plausible than that of those who interpret 'stretch out your hand to whatever you desire'[353] as 'grace stretches your hand out to whatever it desires' in order to prove that the human will does nothing:[354] but since it has been handed down by the orthodox Fathers,[355] I see no reason to despise it. The poor widow putting two mites, that is, everything she possesses, into the temple treasury makes the same point.[356]

[*The very fact of God's help implies some action by the human will*]
Now, what merit can anyone claim for himself, since he owes whatever man can do with his natural understanding and his free will to him from

\* \* \* \* \*

351 Luke 15:11–32. Erasmus gives a similar (highly traditional) interpretation of the parable in *Paraphrasis in Evangelium Lucae* LB VII 7 406C–410F.
352 Cf Fisher 1523 sig yy3; 1597 col 670 middle and 1523 sig yy4; 1597 col 672 top.
353 Ecclus 15:17
354 See *Hyperaspistes* 1 164.
355 See Jerome Ep 21.4–39 CSEL 54 117–30.
356 According to Thomas Aquinas' *Catena aurea* (*Opera omnia* 25 vols [New York 1948–9] XI 413) and the *Glossa ordinaria* (PL 114 226), Jerome says that the coins offered by the widow stand for the human will, operating human thoughts, words, and deeds, but a search of the genuine and spurious works of Jerome in the CETEDOC database do not reveal the words attributed to Jerome by *Catena* and *Glossa*.

whom he received those very abilities? And yet the very facts that we do not turn ourselves away from God's grace and that we summon our natural powers to unreserved obedience are credited to us as merits by God. This is certainly enough to establish that, while it would be untrue to say that man does nothing, yet he must ascribe the sum total of all his actions to God as their source; for from him comes man's ability to combine his efforts with God's grace. Accordingly Paul says, 'By the grace of God I am what I am,' acknowledging God as author; but when he says, 'His grace was not bestowed on me in vain,' we recognize how human will strives alongside divine assistance. His meaning is the same when he says, 'Not I, but the grace of God which is with me';[357] for in Greek it reads ἡ σὺν ἐμοὶ 'which is with me.'[358] And the Hebrew preacher of wisdom wishes divine Wisdom to stand by him, to be with him and work with him.[359] She stands by him like a directress and helper, as an architect stands by his assistant, telling him what to do, showing him the method of doing it, checking him if he begins to do anything amiss, helping him if he there is something he cannot accomplish. The architect, without whose help nothing could have been achieved, takes the credit for the work, yet no one says that the assistant or pupil has done nothing. As the architect to his pupil, so is grace to our will. Accordingly, Paul says in Romans, chapter 8[:26], 'Likewise the Spirit assists our weakness.' 'Weak' is never used to describe someone who can do nothing, but rather someone whose strength is not sufficient to complete what he attempts; and someone who does everything by himself is not said to 'assist.' The whole of Scripture proclaims assistance, aid, succour, help; but how can you be said to 'assist' a person unless he is doing something himself? The potter does not 'assist' the clay to become a pot, nor does the workman 'assist' the axe to make a bench!

And so to those who conclude: 'There is nothing that man can do without the help of God's grace; therefore there are no human good works' we will oppose a conclusion which I believe is more probable: There is nothing that man cannot do with the help of God's grace; therefore all human works can be good. Therefore, as many references as there are in the Scriptures to God's help, just as many proofs are there of the existence of free will;

* * * * *

357 1 Cor 15:10
358 Here Erasmus follows the Latin translation in his *Novum Testamentum* of 1516 and 1519 (*gratia Dei, quae mihi adest*) rather than the Vulgate (*gratia Dei mecum* 'the grace of God with me').
359 Wisd 9:10

and they are innumerable. And so, if the issue is decided on the number of scriptural proofs, the victory is mine.

## [JUDGMENTS CONCERNING FREE WILL AND GRACE]

*[Motives for overstressing grace or free will]*
Up to this point we have collected scriptural passages which establish the existence of free will and, on the other hand, passages which seem to deny it utterly. But since the Holy Spirit, the author who produced them, cannot contradict himself, we are forced, whether we like it or not, to seek a more moderate opinion.

Now, the reason that different scholars have reached different opinions working from the same Scripture is that they directed their attention to different things, and interpreted what they read in the light of their individual aims. Some reflected on the great extent of human religious apathy and on the great evil of despairing of salvation; in the attempt to remedy these ills, they fell unawares into another evil and exaggerated the role of free will. Others, however, considered how destructive it is of true godliness for man to rely on his own strength and merits, and how intolerable is the arrogance of certain parties who display their own good deeds, and even weigh and measure them out for sale to others, like oil and soap. In their valiant efforts to avoid this evil, they have either taken half of free will away, to the extent that it plays no part at all in a good work, or they have destroyed it altogether by propounding the absolute necessity of all events.[360] Presumably they felt that it was highly conducive to the unreserved obedience proper to a Christian attitude that man should depend utterly on the will of God; that he should place all his hope and trust in God's promises, and, acknowledging how wretched he is in himself, should admire and love God's immense mercy, which freely lavishes so much on us. He should submit himself entirely to God's will, whether that will is to preserve or to destroy him; he should claim no praise for himself for his own good deeds, but ascribe all the glory to God's grace, bearing in mind that man is nothing but a living instrument of the Holy Spirit, who has cleansed and consecrated man to himself through his freely given benevolence, and guides and governs him in his unsearchable wis-

\* \* \* \* \*

360 That is, it wills only evil works, not good ones (as Karlstadt taught) or it wills nothing at all because everything happens by absolute necessity (as Luther taught)

dom. He should also consider that in this process there is no claim that anyone can make for his own powers, yet he should hope with complete confidence for the reward of eternal life from God, not because he has merited it through his own good deeds, but because God in his goodness has been pleased to promise it to those who trust in him. It is man's duty constantly to pray God to bestow his Spirit on us and increase it within us; to give him thanks if anything good has been done because of us; and in all things everywhere to worship his power, admire his wisdom, and love his goodness.

This formulation seems entirely praiseworthy to me, for it is consistent with Scripture and accords with the belief of those who, through baptism, have died to the world once and for all, and have been buried with Christ, so that after this mortification of their flesh they should henceforth live and be guided by the Spirit of Jesus, onto whose body they have been grafted by faith.[361] Surely this is a godly, pleasing position, which does away with all our arrogance, gives all glory to Christ and places all our trust in him, casts out all our fear of men and demons, makes us distrust our own powers and become strong and courageous in God; we will gladly give it our limitless approval.[362] But when I hear people maintain that all human merit is so worthless that all human works, even those of godly men, are sins; when they claim that our will does no more than clay in the potter's hands, or attribute everything we do or will to absolute necessity, then I become exceedingly uneasy.

[*To assert necessity to the exclusion of free will makes God cruel and unjust*]
First, how can you constantly read that holy people, full of good works, 'did justice,'[363] 'walked righteously in the sight of God,'[364] 'turned neither to the left nor to the right,'[365] if everything that even the godliest do is a sin, and such a sin that without the intervention of God's mercy someone for whom Christ died would be cast into hell? How can you constantly read of a 'reward' where there is absolutely no merit? How can the obedience of those

* * * * *

361 Rom 6:4–10, 11:17–18; Gal 6:14; Col 2:20
362 The Latin here (*usque ad hyperbolas*) translates a Greek idiom, εἰς ὑπερβολὰς 'even to excess,' as in Plato *Letters* 326D. Cf *Adagia* IV iii 61. Erasmus plays on the fact that he usually finds Luther's hyperboles quite unacceptable. See 19 and n58 above and *Hyperaspistes* 1 108 and n74, 124 and n157, 186–8.
363 2 Kings 8:15; 1 Macc 14:35; Ps 105:3 (cf Deut 33:21)
364 3 Kings 2:4, 3:6, 8:23 and 25; Isa 38:3; 2 Chron 6:14
365 Deut 5:32; Josh 1:7; 4 Kings 22:2; Prov 4:27

who complied with God's commandments conceivably be praised, and the disdobedience of those who did not be condemned? Why is judgment constantly mentioned in the Scriptures if merits are not weighed at all? Why are we made to appear before the judgment-seat if we have done nothing through our own will, but everything has been done in us by absolute necessity?

There is the further objection: what need is there of the many admonitions, commands, threats, exhortations, and remonstrances in the Scriptures if we do nothing, but God works everything in us, the deed as well as the will,[366] in accordance with his immutable will? God requires us to pray without ceasing, to stay vigilant, to struggle, to contend for the prize of eternal life. Why does he want to be constantly asked for something which he has already decided whether or not to give, seeing that his decisions cannot be changed, since he himself is unchangeable? Why does he tell us to labour to obtain what he has decided to bestow on us as a free gift? We suffer affliction, rejection, ridicule, torture, and death; thus God's grace fights, wins, and triumphs in us. A martyr undergoes such torments, yet no merit is credited to him for doing so – indeed he is said to have sinned in having exposed his body to suffering in the hope of heavenly life. But why did the all-merciful God wish to work in the martyrs in this way? A man would seem cruel if he had decided to make a friend a free gift of something, but would not give it to him until he had been tortured to the point of despair.

But when we come to this obscure aspect of the divine purpose, perhaps we will be told to worship what we are not permitted to understand, so that the human mind should say, 'He is the Lord, he can do whatever he wills, and since he is entirely good by nature whatever he wills must be entirely good.' It is also quite praiseworthy to say that God crowns his own gifts in us and wills his own good deeds to be our reward, and that in his freely given generosity he sees fit to credit what he has worked in us to those who believe in him as though it were a debt that he owed them, so that they may attain immortality. But I can see no consistency in those who exaggerate God's mercy in good men in such a way as to make him seem almost cruel towards others. Believers' ears will readily accept the benevolence of a God who credits his good deeds to us; but it is difficult to explain how it can be just, let alone merciful, for him to condemn others, in whom he has not seen fit to work good deeds, to eternal torment, although they

* * * * *

366 Cf Phil 2:13.

themselves can do nothing good; for either they have no free will, or, if they have, it has the power to do nothing except sin.

If a certain king were to give a huge reward to the man who had done nothing in a war, while the rest, who had acted bravely, received nothing beyond their normal pay, he could perhaps reply to the soldiers' murmurings, 'What injustice do you suffer if it is my pleasure to be gratuitously generous to this man?' But how could he possibly seem just and merciful if he equipped one general for war with an ample supply of siege-engines, troops, funds, and all kinds of supplies, then heaped him with honours for military success, but sent another to war unarmed, without any supplies, then executed him for failure? Would the dying general not be entitled to say to the king, 'Why punish me for a fault for which you are to blame? Had you equipped me in the same way, I would have been victorious too.'

Again, if a master were to free a slave who did not deserve it, he might perhaps have an answer to the murmuring of the other slaves: 'You are no worse off if I am kinder to this man. You have your due.' But anyone would deem a master cruel and unjust if he were to flog a slave for being too short, or having too long a nose, or for some other physical imperfection.[367] Would the slave not be justified in complaining to the master as he beat him, 'Why am I being punished for what I cannot help?' And he would be the more justified in saying this if it were in the master's power to change the slave's bodily defects, as it is in God's power to change our will; or if the master had given the slave the very defect which offended him – had cut off his nose, or hideously scarred his face, just as God, in the opinion of some, works even all bad acts in us. Again, regarding God's commands, if a master were to issue many orders to a slave shackled in a treadmill, 'Go there, do this, run, run back,' threatening dire consequences if he disobeyed, but without unshackling him the while, and then prepared a rod for him because he had not obeyed, would the slave not seem correct in calling his master insane, or cruel, flogging him for having failed to do what was not in his power?

[*Faith must not be exalted to the exclusion of free will: free will cooperates with grace*]
We listen with equanimity, however, to our opponents' boundlessly exalting faith in, and love of, God, for we are of the opinion that the corruption of Christian life everywhere by so many sins has no other cause than the

*  *  *  *  *

367 Cf John Chrysostom *Commentarius in Matthaeum* 60.2 PG 58 575–6, which is quoted by Fisher 1523 sigs xx2–xx2v; 1597 col 663 middle-bottom.

coldness and drowsiness of our faith, which gives us a merest verbal belief in God: a faith on the the lips only, whereas according to Paul 'man is justified by believing from the heart.'[368] Nor will I particularly take issue with those who refer all things to faith as their ultimate source, even though I believe that faith is born from and nurtured by charity, and charity in turn born from and nurtured by faith. Charity certainly feeds faith, just as the light in a lantern is fed by oil, for we more readily trust the person we ardently love: and there is no dearth of people who contend that faith is the beginning, rather than the completion, of salvation. But our argument does not concern these matters.[369]

Yet here we should beware of being so absorbed in enlarging on the praises of faith that we subvert the freedom of the will; and once it has been denied I do not see how the problem of the justice and mercy of God can be resolved. When the ancient authors found they could not extricate themselves from these difficulties, some were forced to posit two Gods: one of the Old Testament who they argued was only just, not good; and one of the New Testament who they argued was only good, not just. Tertullian adequately refuted their wicked fabrication.[370] Manichaeus, as we said, dreamed up the notion of two natures in man, one which could not avoid sinning and one which could not avoid doing good.[371] Pelagius, concerned for God's justice, attributed too much to free will.[372] There is little difference between him and those who attribute so much to human will as to say that through our natural powers, by morally good works, it can merit the supreme grace by which we are justified.[373] They seem to me to have wanted to urge man to moral effort by holding out a good hope of obtaining salvation, just as Cornelius, because of his prayers and almsgiving, deserved to be taught by Peter,[374] and the eunuch by Philip,[375] and Saint Augustine, who assiduously

* * * * *

368 Rom 10:10
369 Tangentially and briefly Erasmus expresses his reservations about Luther's doctrine of salvation *ex fide sola* 'by faith alone.'
370 *Adversus Marcionem* 1.2–8 PL 2 248–55
371 See n46 above.
372 See n101 above.
373 Neither Pelagius nor theologians like Biel believed quite what Erasmus says here: that justifying grace (sanctifying, cooperating grace) could be merited in any fashion. Pelagius held that once justifying grace had been given (not merited), free will was sufficient on its own. Biel held only that prevenient grace (not justifying grace) could be merited *ex congruo*.
374 Acts 10:1–43. Cf Fisher 1523 sig Ff3; 1597 col 712 bottom.
375 Acts 8:26–38

sought Christ in Paul's letters,[376] deserved to find him. Here we can placate those who believe that man cannot do any good deed which he does not owe to God by saying that the whole work is no less due to God, without whom we could achieve nothing; that the contribution of free will is very small indeed; and that our very ability to direct our mind to the things that pertain to salvation, or to cooperate with grace, is itself a gift of God.[377] As a result of the controversy with Pelagius, Augustine reached a less favourable view of free will than he had previously held.[378] In the opposite way Luther, who previously attributed something to free will, has been carried so far by the heat of his defence as to remove it altogether.[379] Yet I believe that among the Greeks Lycurgus is blamed for having had the vines cut down because he hated drunkenness, whereas by bringing the sources of water closer he could have prevented drunkenness without abolishing wine-drinking.[380]

In my opinion free will could have been established in such a way as to avoid that trust in our own merits and the other harmful consequences which Luther avoids, as well as those which we mentioned above, yet so as not to destroy the benefits which Luther admires. This I believe is achieved by the opinion of those who ascribe entirely to grace the impetus by which the mind is first aroused, and only in the succeeding process attribute something to human will in that it does not resist the grace of God. Since there are three parts to everything – beginning, continuation, and completion – they ascribe the first and last to grace and allow that free will has an effect

* * * * *

376 Augustine *Confessions* 7.21[27] CCSL 27 110.1–6
377 The position Erasmus states here is somewhat ambiguous, depending on whether the gift of God is the grace by which the will accepts prevenient grace (as Augustine taught) or whether it is merely the *concursus generalis* or 'general influence' on all our thoughts and actions by virtue of the creation itself (as some followers of Scotus held); see n103 above. See McSorley 72–5.
378 For an account of Augustine's confrontation with Pelagius see Peter Brown *Augustine of Hippo* (London 1967) 340–75.
379 Erasmus claims that the change in Luther's view of free will in his *Assertio* arose as his response to the papal bull *Exsurge Domine* of 15 June 1520. Erasmus is undoubtedly right that the extremity of his position was provoked by the papal condemnation, but he was also aware of how far Luther had already moved in this direction as part of his theological evolution from 1516 to 1520.
380 According to Suetonius *Lives of the Caesars* 8 *Domitian* 7.2, Domitian, not Lycurgus, ordered the vines cut down, but Suetonius' anecdote says nothing about water. Athenaeus *Deipnosophistae* 10.445e mentions that Lycurgus lopped off the drinkers of Dionysus and cast horns and drinking cups out of doors. But Erasmus seems to be drawing on some other source we have been unable to find.

only in the continuation, in so far as in a single, indivisible act there are two causes, divine grace and human will, working together. However, grace is the principal cause and will the secondary cause, unable to do anything without the principal cause, whereas the principal cause is sufficient in itself.[381] Just so the power inherent in fire burns, yet the principal cause is God acting at the same time through the fire, a cause which would be sufficient in itself, and without which fire would have no effect if that cause were to withdraw itself.[382]

On this moderate view man must ascribe his salvation entirely to the grace of God; for what free will accomplishes in this is very insignificant indeed, and what it can accomplish is itself due to divine grace, which first created free will, then freed and healed it. And this will appease (if they can be appeased) those who believe that there is no good in man which he does not owe to God. Owe it he does, but in a different way and for a different reason, as an inheritance falling to children in equal shares is not called benevolence, since it comes to them all in the ordinary course of law. (It is called liberality if one or other of them has been given something over and above his legal due.) Yet children are indebted to their parents even on account of an inheritance.

[*Illustrations of the cooperation of grace and free will*]
We will also try to illustrate what we are saying metaphorically. A human eye, however healthy, sees nothing in the dark, and a blind one sees nothing even in the light. Just so the will, however free, can do nothing if grace withdraws itself from it; and even if it is light a man with healthy eyes can close them so as not to see, and turn them away so as no longer to see what he had been able to see.[383] A man whose eyes have been blinded by some disorder is even more indebted, first to the creator, then to the doctor. However healthy the eye was before sin, it is injured by sin. And so what can the man who sees claim for himself? He can, however, impute something to himself if he deliberately closes his eyes or turns them away.

Here is another illustration. A child who cannot yet walk has fallen, however hard he tried: his father sets him back on his feet and shows him

\* \* \* \* \*

381 See n110 above.
382 See *Hyperaspistes* 1 193 and n521. The view expressed in this paragraph is that of Augustine (*De civitate Dei* 5.10) and Thomas Aquinas (*Summa theologiae* I–II q 109 a 6).
383 See 32 and n120 above.

an apple some distance away.[384] The boy very much wants to run towards it, but because his limbs are so helpless he would soon have fallen again if the father did not put out his hand to support him and did not guide his steps. So, with his father guiding him, he reaches the apple, which his father gladly gives him as a reward for having run. The child could not have stood up unless his father had supported him; he would not have seen the apple unless his father had shown it to him; he would not have been able to walk unless his father had constantly aided his tottering steps; he could not have reached the apple unless his father had placed it in his hands. What claim can the child make for himself in this? And still he has done something, yet he has no reason to glory in his own powers, for he is completely in his father's debt.

Let us suppose for the moment that this is true of God. What does the child do in this process? He leans as best he can on the one who picks him up and adjusts his stumbling steps to his guidance as well as he is able. The father could have dragged him against his wishes, and the child's mind could have resisted by refusing the apple. The father could have given him the apple without making him run, but he preferred to give it to him in this way, because it was better for the boy. I will readily allow that in gaining eternal life somewhat less can be ascribed to our own efforts than to the efforts of the boy running along guided by his father's hand.

Although we see that this attributes very little indeed to free will, even that seems too much to some, for they claim that grace alone works in us, and that in all things our will is entirely passive, like an instrument of the Spirit of God, so that a good act cannot be called ours at all save in so far as divine generosity freely imputes it to us: for grace works in us not so much through, as in free will, just as the potter works in clay, not through it. Why, then, speak of a crown and a reward? God, they say, crowns his own gifts in us, desires his own good deeds to be our reward, and is pleased to count what he has done as fitting us for the heavenly kingdom. I do not see how, on these grounds, they can posit the existence of a free will which achieves nothing. The explanation would be easier if they were to say that it is worked upon by grace in such a way that it acts even as it is acted on; just as our body, according to the natural philosophers, is set in motion by the soul, and cannot move at all without the soul, yet is not only moved itself, but moves other things, and sharing as it were in the activity, is called to

\* \* \* \* \*

384 See 66 and n323 above.

share in the glory. For if God works in us as the potter works in clay, what credit, or what blame, can be imputed to us?

It is distasteful to bring the soul of Jesus Christ, which was itself unquestionably the instrument of the Spirit of God, into this inquiry. Yet if the weakness of the flesh prevents man from having merit, well, Christ himself was terrified of death, but wished that his Father's will, not his own, should be done.[385] Yet those who deprive all the other saints of any merit based on good works say that Christ's will is the source of merits.

*[Absolute necessity makes God unjust]*

Moreover, those who say that there is no such thing as free will, but that everything happens by absolute necessity, are saying that God works not only good deeds in everyone, but bad ones too.[386] It seems to follow from this that, just as man cannot on any account be called the author of good works, he cannot in any sense be called the author of bad ones either. Although this view seems openly to attribute cruelty and injustice to God, a most abhorrent charge to Christian ears (for he would not be God if any vice or imperfection were found in him), they have a counter-argument to support even such an implausible case: 'He is God, and what he does cannot but be entirely good and glorious. Even things which are bad in themselves are good if you consider what is fitting for the universe, and they show forth the glory of God. No creature has any right to judge the creator's plan; it must submit itself absolutely to him in all things, to the extent that if it pleases God to damn this or that man, he must not complain but must willingly accept whatever is God's pleasure, being convinced once and for all that he directs all things in the best possible manner, and cannot direct them in any way but the best. Otherwise, who could tolerate a man if he were to ask God, "Why did you not make me an angel?" Would God not be justified in replying, "You impudent man! If I had made you a frog what cause for complaint would you have?" And if a frog were to remonstrate with God, "Why did you not make me a peacock with colourful, eye-catching plumage?" would God not be right to say, "You ungrateful beast!

\* \* \* \* \*

385 Matt 26:39. See Erasmus' *De taedio Iesu* LB V 1263–94. This brief treatise is a report of a friendly debate between John Colet, who held that Christ's suffering sprang from grief over the defection of his apostles and the Jews, and Erasmus, who held that it was caused by his human fear of suffering and death.
386 Though Erasmus mentions only 'those who say,' he is clearly thinking of Luther in his *Assertio* article 36 WA 7 146:7–8 / 306.

I could have made you a mushroom, or an onion; as it stands you can jump, drink, and croak." And again, if a basilisk or a viper were to ask, "Why did you make me an animal loathsome and deadly to all, instead of a sheep?" what would God reply? He might perhaps say, "So it pleased me, and so it accorded with the beauty and order of the universe. You have suffered no injustice, no more than have flies, gnats, and other insects, every one of which I fashioned so as to be very wonderful to those who behold them. The spider is no less beautiful and wondrous an animal for being different from the elephant; indeed there are more wonders in a spider than in an elephant. Are you not satisfied with being a perfect animal of your kind? And you were not given poison to kill, but as a weapon to protect yourself and your offspring, just as oxen were given horns, lions claws, wolves teeth, and horses hooves. Every single animal has its use: the horse carries burdens, the ox draws the plough, the ass and the dog are helpful working beasts, the sheep serves to feed and clothe humans, and you have your medicinal uses." '[387]

But let us stop reasoning with these creatures devoid of reason.[388] The disputation we undertook was on the subject of man, made in the image and likeness of God,[389] and for whose sake God created everything. And yet when we see that some men are born with well-formed bodies and splendid characters which seem innately inclined to goodness, but that by contrast some are born with monstrous bodies, some suffering from appalling diseases, some with wits so dull as to be scarcely different from brute beasts, some even more brutish than the beasts themselves, some with characters so prone to evildoing that they seem to be drawn to it by the power of fate, and some utterly demented and possessed by demons, how ever shall we solve the problem of the justice and mercy of God? Shall we say with Paul, 'Oh the depth etc'?[390] I think this is better than passing judgment with sinful presumption on God's counsels, which are unfathomable to man.

Still it is far more difficult to explain why in some people God crowns his own good deeds with eternal glory, and in others punishes his own

* * * * *

387 This paragraph setting forth the divine necessity of all creatures in their predetermined modes of existence may echo a passage in Valla's *De libero arbitrio dialogus* ed Chomarat 42–3 nos 79–82 / trans Trinkaus in *The Renaissance Philosophy of Man* 173–4 (see n48 above).

388 There is a suggestion that the animals are not the only ones devoid of reason but also the opponents to whom Erasmus here returns.

389 Gen 1:26

390 Rom 11:33

wrongdoings with everlasting torment. In order to explain this paradox Luther's adherents need many auxiliary paradoxes to hold the line against the opposite side. They vastly exaggerate original sin, by which they claim that even the highest powers of human nature have been corrupted, so that of himself man can only be ignorant of God, and hate him, and even when justified by grace through faith can perform no action which is not a sin. They maintain that the tendency to sinning left in us from our first parents' sin is itself a sin, and an invincible one, so that there is not one of God's commandments which man, albeit justified by faith, can fulfil; and that all God's commandments have the sole purpose of magnifying God's grace, which bestows salvation without regard to merits.[391]

Yet it seems to me that all the while they are diminishing God's mercy in one place in order to increase it in another, as though someone were to serve a miserable lunch to his guests in order to appear all the more splendid at dinner, or were to imitate the painters, who give the illusion of light in a picture by shading the adjacent areas. For a start they make God almost cruel, venting his wrath on the whole of mankind for someone else's sin; especially since the people who committed it amended their ways and were punished most severely for the rest of their lives. Then when they say that those who have been justified by faith do nothing but sin, so that by loving and trusting God we become worthy of his hatred, are they not making God's grace extremely miserly? Grace justifies man by faith in such a way that he is still nothing but sin! Moreover, in saying that God burdens man with so many commandments which have no other purpose than to cause him to hate God more, and so be more utterly condemned, are they not making him even more merciless than Dionysius, the tyrant of Sicily, who deliberately promulgated many laws which he suspected most people would break if no one were to enforce them? At first he turned a blind eye, but soon, when he saw that nearly everyone had offended in some respect, he began to prosecute them, and so brought everyone under his domination; yet his laws were of a kind that could easily have been kept had anyone so desired.[392]

\* \* \* \* \*

391 Erasmus here protests against Luther's exaggerated view of original sin and the consequent doctrine of 'justified and sinner at the same time' (*simul justus et peccator*).
392 The legal trickery used by Dionysius I of Syracuse (c 430–367 BCE) to bilk his people of money and property is recounted in Pseudo-Aristotle *Oeconomica* 2.2.20 1349a–1350a, though this particular ruse is not mentioned there. See also *The Education of a Christian Prince* CWE 27 265 and Thomas More *Utopia*

[*Luther and Karlstadt overreact to abuses of free will*]

I will not now discuss the reasons for which they teach that all God's commandments are impossible for us, for that is not what we undertook to do. I wanted only to show in passing that, by trying too hard to extend the role of grace in the process of salvation, they obscure it in other areas. I do not see how certain of their propositions can be consistent: they destroy free will and say that man is already guided by the Spirit of Christ, whose nature cannot abide the company of sin; and yet the very same people say that man, even after receiving grace, does nothing except sin! Luther seems to delight in hyperboles of this kind in order to drive out the hyperboles of others, as one cracks a tough knot in wood with the proverbial tough wedge.[393] In some quarters audacity had reached enormous proportions: people were selling not only their own merits, but those of all the saints as well. And what manner of works? Singing hymns, muttering psalms, eating fish, fasting, wearing habits, and bearing titles. Luther drove out this nail with another,[394] to the extent of saying that the merits of the saints were non-existent;[395] that all good men's deeds had been sins,[396] which would have drawn eternal damnation down on them unless faith and God's mercy had come to their aid.

In the same way, one side was making a juicy profit from confession and satisfaction, in which they had wonderfully entangled human consciences, and from purgatory, about which they had handed down a number of paradoxes. The opposing faction corrects this error by calling confession an invention of Satan (the most moderate of them say only that it need not be required), that there is no need of any satisfaction for sins, since Christ has paid the price of the sins of all mankind, and finally that purgatory does not exist.

One side says that every little prior's regulations are binding on pain of eternal damnation, and unhesitatingly guarantee salvation to

* * * * *

ed Edward Surtz and J.H. Hexter, vol 4 of The Yale Edition of the Complete Works of St. Thomas More (New Haven and London: 1965) 92:8 and n.

393 *Adagia* I ii 5

394 *Adagia* I ii 4

395 Erasmus refers to Luther's thesis 58 in his *Ninety-five Theses* of 15 October 1521 (WA 1 236 / LW 31 30), elaborated in *Explanations of the Ninety-five Theses* (WA 1 605–14 / LW 31 212–28). Luther does not say that the merits of the saints are non-existent but that they do not constitute a treasury of merits which might be dispensed or even sold as indulgences.

396 See Luther *Assertio* article 31 (WA 7 136:21): 'In omni opere bono iustus peccat' ('in every good deed the righteous man sins').

those who obey them; the opposing side counters this hyperbole by calling all papal, conciliar, and episcopal constitutions heretical and anti-Christian. Thus one side exalts the pontiff's power most hyperbolically; the other side speaks of the pope in a manner I dare not repeat. One side says that monastic and priestly vows bind men in perpetuity under pain of damnation; the other side says such vows are sacrilegious and should not be taken, or, if already taken, not kept. The clash of such hyperboles produces the thunder and lightning which are now battering the world. If both sides continue to defend their overstatements so savagely, I foresee a battle between them such as there was between Achilles and Hector, who, being equally fierce, could only be parted by death.[397]

There is a proverb that you should straighten a bent stick by bending it in the opposite direction;[398] but though that may be advisable in correcting behaviour, I am not sure that it is tolerable in doctrinal matters. I admit there is a certain role for overstatement when encouraging or discouraging. For instance, to boost a fearful person's confidence you might well say, 'Don't be afraid, God will say and do all things in you'; to check someone's sinful insolence you might helpfully say that man was nothing but sin; or to counter those who put their own teachings on a par with the canonical Scriptures you might usefully say that man was nothing but deceit. But when propounding principles in an inquiry into the truth, I do not think that paradoxical formulas like these, not far removed from riddles, should be used: here I favour restraint.

Pelagius seemed to attribute too much to free will; Duns Scotus attributed an ample amount; at first Luther merely mutilated free will by cutting off its right arm, but soon, not content with this, he cut its throat and made away with it altogether. I favour the opinion of those who attribute something to free will, but most to grace. For you must not

\* \* \* \* \*

397 Cf Horace *Satires* 1.7.11–3. These two paragraphs summarize some of the basic issues that were at stake in the Reformation. Erasmus contrasts the exaggeration and abuses of the Catholic clergy with the reformers' extreme rejection of the institutional bases of Catholicism: sacramental confession, the authority of the priesthood, and the power of the papacy.

398 Not in Erasmus' *Adagia*. Cf Aristotle *Nicomachean Ethics* 2.9 1009b5: 'We must drag ourselves away to the opposite extreme, for we shall get into the intermediate state by drawing well away from error, as people do in straightening sticks that are bent.' Aristotle is apparently drawing upon the figure in Plato *Protagoras* 325D.

give so wide a berth to the Scylla of arrogance that you are driven towards the Charybdis of despair or indolence.[399] In treating a dislocated limb you must set it in its proper position, not twist it in the opposite direction. You must not fight the enemy in front of you so incautiously that you are wounded from behind. This moderate view will recognize the existence of some good work, admittedly imperfect, but on account of which man can claim nothing for himself; and of a certain degree of merit, but such that its completion will be due to God. There is such a vast amount of weakness, vice, and villainy in human life that if anyone is prepared to examine himself he will soon hang his head in shame; but we do not assert that man, though justified, is nothing but sin, especially since Christ calls him 'born again'[400] and Paul calls him a 'new creation.'[401]

*[Why we must attribute something to free will]*
Why, you may ask, attribute anything at all to free will? To allow the ungodly, who have deliberately fallen short of the grace of God,[402] to be deservedly condemned; to clear God of the false accusation of cruelty and injustice; to free us from despair, protect us from complacency, and spur us on to moral endeavour. For these reasons nearly everyone admits the existence of free will; but, lest we claim anything for ourselves, they assert that it can achieve nothing without the perpetual grace of God. 'What good is free will,' someone may ask, 'if it can achieve nothing?' What good is the whole man, I reply, if God works in him as the potter works with clay, and as he could have worked with stone? And now, it may be, this subject has been adequately proven to be such that it is not conducive to godliness to examine it in more detail than necessary, especially in front of the unlearned. I believe it has been shown that this doctrine is supported by more, and plainer, scriptural testimonies than the opposite doctrine. It seems clear that in many places Holy Scripture is obscured by figures of speech, or seems at first sight to contradict itself, so that whether we like it or not we must depart from its literal

\* \* \* \* \*

399 Scylla was a sea monster on the Italian side of the straits of Messina; Charybdis, a whirlpool on the Sicilian side (Homer *Odyssey* 12.73–110). See *Adagia* I v 4; Otto no 382.
400 John 3:5–8
401 2 Cor 5:17
402 Heb 12:15

meaning and guide our judgment by interpretation. Finally, it seems obvious how many disagreeable, not to say absurd, consequences follow once free will is denied; and it appears that if we accept the opinion which I have expounded, it does not invalidate Luther's godly, Christian assertions that we must love God above all else, that we must remove our trust from our own merits, deeds, and powers and put it all in God and his promises. If all this is so, I should like the reader to consider whether he thinks it right to condemn the opinion of so many Doctors of the church, approved by the consensus of so many ages and nations, and to accept a number of paradoxes which are causing the present uproar in Christendom.[403]

If these paradoxes are true, then I will frankly admit that I am too dull to follow them. I certainly do not knowingly oppose the truth; I wholeheartedly support true evangelical freedom, and I detest anything contrary to the gospel. I do not play the part of a judge here, but of a disputant, as I have said; and yet I can truly affirm that in disputing I have acted with the same scrupulousness once demanded of those sworn to judge capital cases. Nor, though an old man, will I be either ashamed or reluctant to learn from a young one, if there is anyone who can teach me more evident doctrines with evangelical mildness.

I know I shall hear the objection, 'Erasmus should come to know Christ and bid farewell to human learning. No one understands these matters unless he has the spirit of God.'[404] Well, if I still have no understanding of Christ, I have clearly been far off the mark till now! And yet I would be glad to learn what spirit all the Christian doctors and people (for it is likely that the people agreed with the bishops' teaching) have had these last thirteen hundred years, since they too lacked that understanding.

\* \* \* \* \*

403 See McConica 'Consent.'
404 Erasmus has in mind such accusations as Luther made in a letter to Conradus Pellicanus dated 1 October 1523: 'Moeror est mihi et timor in laudibus mei, gaudium vero in maledictis et blasphemiis; si haec sunt Erasmo mirabilia, nihil miror. Discat Christum et valefaciat humanae prudentiae; Dominus illuminet eum, et alium faciat virum ex Erasmo ... Erasmum, si patitur, saluta meo nomine' ('I grieve and fear when I am praised, but I joy when I am maligned and cursed. If this surprises Erasmus, I am not at all surprised. He should learn to know Christ and say farewell to human wisdom. May the Lord illuminate him and make a new man out of Erasmus ... Give my regards to Erasmus, if he will permit it') (WA Briefwechsel 3 160:32–161:2 no 661; not included in LW 49).

I have discussed the issue.[405] Let others pass judgment.

End of A Discourse or Discussion on Free Will, by Desiderius Erasmus of Rotterdam

* * * * *

405 Latin *Contuli* (printed in capital letters), referring back to the words of his title διατριβή *sive collatio* 'discourse or discussion.' The importance of the title and this conclusion is that Erasmus presents and discusses opposing arguments; this does not mean that one side is not favoured, but the issue is treated as if it were a question open to debate; see also n1 above. At the end of *De servo arbitrio* (WA 18 787:11–12), Luther specifically rejected Erasmus' stance, also in capital letters: 'Non contuli, sed asserui et assero' ('I have not discussed the issue but rather I have asserted and do assert').

# A WARRIOR SHIELDING
# A DISCUSSION OF FREE WILL AGAINST
# THE ENSLAVED WILL BY MARTIN LUTHER
# BOOK ONE

*Hyperaspistes liber unus*

translated by

CLARENCE H. MILLER

annotated by

CLARENCE H. MILLER and CHARLES TRINKAUS

The Latin text here translated was a typescript generously provided by Cornelis Augustijn, who prepared it for the Amsterdam *Opera omnia*. He also provided photocopies of the two early editions (both Froben 1526) on which the text is based. The text has been compared with that in the 1703 Leiden edition, the readings of which are occasionally given and discussed in the commentary. The German translation by Hieronymus Emser has also been carefully read and is referred to in the commentary when it throws any interesting light on the text. The modern German translation by Oskar Johannes Mehl with a commentary by Siegfried Wollgast (Leipzig 1986) and that by Winfried Lesowsky in Erasmus' *Ausgewählte Schriften* ed Werner Welzig, 8 vols (Darmstadt 1967– ) IV (1969) have also been consulted. I have not felt bound to translate a Latin word always with the same English word, except that I have tried to be rigidly consistent in translating technical terms. Erasmus himself noted that he wrote the first part of *Hyperaspistes* very hastily, and it occasionally contains flaws or inconsistencies; the commentary notes such difficulties and tries to resolve them. Otherwise the work is written with Erasmus' usual vigour and lucidity, which a translator may at least hope sometimes to approximate.

CHM

ERASMUS OF ROTTERDAM TO THE READER, GREETINGS

*The Enslaved Will* has been published, by Martin Luther according to the title-page, but actually produced by the labours of many[1] over a long period of time (for the printing of the book began a year ago, as was reported by some who said they had seen some pages of it)[2] and it was worked out with great care, as is obvious from the book itself. It was given to me quite late, and then by chance, for it was kept hidden so that they could stage their triumph at least for a few months;[3] it was concealed not only by Luther's partisans but also by those inimical to both him and me, to me because of true learning [*bonae litterae*] and to him because of condemned doctrine. The length of time that could be given to rereading *A Discussion*, to reading through Luther's book, which is as lengthy as it is garrulous, and to writing my response was no longer than ten days.[4] And when the book was given to me I was worn out and quite busy finishing works which were being prepared for the coming fair.[5] If anyone does not believe this, there are those at Basel who will testify to it.

But nevertheless, since I perceived how haughtily certain persons even then began to exult in the aura of this book, I thought it best to publish some part of a response, however hastily put together, for the upcoming Frankfurt fair, so that they might be more moderate in celebrating their triumph before they have won the victory.[6] And so I have answered the part which takes issue with the preface of my *Discussion*; the rest I will provide in a more carefully thought out form when I have the leisure to do so.[7] In

* * * * *

1 See the passage from Bonifacius Amerbach's letter to Łaski quoted in the introductory note to Allen Ep 1667 (20 February 1526), which is this prefatory letter; see also Chantraine *Erasme* 63 n13.

2 Erasmus' informants were wrong. Luther wrote *De servo arbitrio* in September and November 1525; it was printed in the following December. The preface of *Hyperaspistes 1* is dated 20 February 1526; the colophon at the end of the printed book is dated July 1526. See WA 18 581–5.

3 That is, so that Luther's book could appear in the spring book fair at Frankfurt without any reply from Erasmus

4 Elsewhere Erasmus said 'scarcely twelve days' (Allen Ep 1667 introductory note; Chantraine *Erasme* 68).

5 The Frankfurt fair was the principal forum for displaying and selling new books.

6 *Adagia* i vii 55

7 Actually in *Hyperaspistes 1* Erasmus goes beyond Luther's answer to the preface of *A Discussion*, answering about a third of Luther's attack (up to *De servo arbitrio* WA 18 666:13 / LW 33 110; *A Discussion* 33). He replied to the remaining two thirds of *De servo arbitrio* in *Hyperaspistes 2*.

the margins I have added the numbers of some of the sections in Luther's disputation so that, if you have numbered his sections, you can more easily compare them with my refutation.[8] Farewell, and be assured that my argumentation will result in victory.

Basel, 20 February 1526

* * * * *

8 We have not reproduced these numbers. For the divisions and correspondences of *A Discussion*, *The Enslaved Will*, and *Hyperaspistes 1* see 311–21 below.

Erasmus
Charcoal drawing by Albrecht Dürer (1520)
Louvre, Paris

# HYPERASPISTES:[1] A WARRIOR SHIELDING A DISCUSSION OF FREE WILL AGAINST THE ENSLAVED WILL BY MARTIN LUTHER BOOK ONE

## [CIRCUMSTANCES OF COMPOSITION AND MOTIVATIONS FOR WRITING]

*[Erasmus' temperate discussion vs Luther's inconsistent insults]*
Hoping for good auspices and a favourable outcome, let us get right down to the matter at hand, following, in fact, the Attic rule, without any proem

\* \* \* \* \*

1 Erasmus did not coin this Greek word (as some have thought); though it is rare among classical writers, it is common in the Septuagint Greek translation of the Old Testament, where it appears at least twenty times, sixteen of them in the Psalms (for example, Ps 113:17–19). In a few places the Vulgate renders it as *scutum* 'shield' or *refugium* 'refuge' but it usually translates it as 'protector.' In the Bible the word is usually applied to God as the defender of the psalmist or of God's people, so that the word could have connotations of a divine mission of defence. But Jerome applies it to a writer defending another person; see his *Prologus in Pentateuch* in *Biblia sacra iuxta vulgatam versionem* 2 vols ed Robert Weber et al 1 (Stuttgart 1975) 3:27. The compound combines ὑπέρ 'hovering above or defending' and ἀσπιστής 'warrior bearing a shield.' But ἀσπίς can mean 'viper' or 'asp' as well as 'shield.' Hence in April 1526 Melanchthon called Erasmus as the author of *Hyperaspistes* an 'asp'; see *Philippi Melanchthonis opera quae supersunt omnia* ed Karl G. Bretschneider and Heinrich E. Bindseil, 28 vols, CR 1–28 (Halle/Saale and Braunschweig 1834–60) 1 793. In January 1526, even before the book had appeared, Luther also referred to Erasmus as a 'viper,' repeating the same insult three more times in his correspondence of March, April, and May 1526 (WA *Briefwechsel* 4 19:17 no 973, 42:28 no 989, 62:8 no 1002, 70:15 no 1007; see also ASD IX-1 482:79–80). On 8 October 1527, when the second book of *Hyperaspistes* appeared, Luther wrote to Michael Stifel: 'Erasmus viperinus duas Hyperaspistes vel Hyperaspides potius in me peperit, vere vipereas et supervipereas' ('That viperine Erasmus has given birth to two *Hyperaspistes* or rather *Hyperaspides* [superasps] against me, and they are truly viperous and superviperous'); see WA *Briefwechsel* 4 263:3–5 no 1156. In an edition of the

or passion.[2] If you, Martin Luther, could also have brought yourself to do the same, you would certainly have wasted less of your spare time, of which you complain you have so little, and you would have added less to my commitments, of which I have more than enough. As it is, since you chose to follow the emotions of certain persons rather than your own judgment, how much there is in your book that is completely off target,[3] how much that is superfluous, how many commonplaces dwelled on at length, how many insults, how much that is manifestly inane, how many ruses, how many sly digs, how much that is shamelessly twisted and distorted, and how many tragical conclusions drawn from the distortions, and how much undeserved vociferation inspired by the conclusions! Because you were pleased to spend good time badly in such matters, I too am forced to use up some of my allotted lifespan[4] in refuting them.

My initial reaction is amazement. My *Discussion* contains nothing beyond a moderate discussion of the subject. Near where you are Hieronymus Emser[5] barks at you; from a distance Johann Cochlaeus[6] scolds you. From

\* \* \* \* \*

Latin and a German translation of *De libero arbitrio* and *Hyperaspistes*, Winfried Lesowsky makes the ingenious but somewhat tenuous suggestion that Erasmus, in his confidence of victory (see the conclusion of his dedicatory letter), intended to play on Ps 90:13: 'Super aspidem et basiliscum ambulabis et conculcabis leonem et draconem' ('You will walk over the asp and the basilisk and you will tread under foot the lion and the dragon'), even though the Septuagint has ἔφ' ἀσπίδα not ὑπέρ ἀσπίδα; see *Erasmus von Rotterdam Ausgewählte Schriften* ed Werner Welzig, 8 vols (Darmstadt 1967–   ) IV (1969) 201 n6.

2 Cf Pseudo-Aristotle *Rhetorica ad Alexandrum* 1437b: 'If there is no prejudice against ourselves or our speech or our subject, we shall set forth our proposition immediately.'

3 *Adagia* II iv 57

4 Literally, 'water.' Erasmus compares the timespan of his life to the water dripping from a water-clock. Cf Seneca *Epistulae morales* 24.20 trans Richard M. Gummere, 3 vols, Loeb Classical Library (London and Cambridge, Mass 1917–25) I 179: 'It is not the last drop that empties the water-clock, but all that which previously has flowed out; similarly, the final hour when we cease to exist does not of itself bring death; it merely of itself completes the death-process.'

5 Emser (1479–1527) was a humanist opponent of Luther, against whom he wrote pamphlets, letters, and epigrams. He translated *Hyperaspistes* into German (Leipzig 1526). See CEBR.

6 Johannes Cochlaeus (Dobnek) of Wendelstein (d 1552) was an energetic opponent of Luther. See CEBR. He wrote *De gratia sacramentorum adversus assertionem Martini Lutheri* (Wittenberg 1523), to which Luther replied in *Adversus armatum virum Cokleum* (1523; WA 11 295–306).

England, apart from Ross[7] and others, Bishop John of Rochester[8] harrasses you in full-sized volumes; from France Josse Clichtove[9] assails Luther in his *Antilutherus*; from Italy Christophe de Longueil[10] takes aim at you in an elaborate oration. Finally, here too you have chieftains of your fraternity who make continual trouble for you: Huldrych Zwingli[11] has published a book, not at all toothless they say, in which he assails your doctrine concerning the Eucharist (on which point you partly agree with the church);[12] Capito[13] and Johann Oecolampadius[14] have done the same, and they did it not with insults but with manifold and acute stratagems.[15] Since all of this is so, I cannot imagine, I say, what you had in mind in making no reply to the others and responding to my *Discussion*, especially since (apart from the restraint of my book) it takes up the matter with such flimsy arguments that, according to you, it hurts the very cause it defends. But I do not object to the fact that you responded, nor do I inquire why you began printing the

\* \* \* \* \*

7 Guilielmus Rosseus was the pseudonym adopted by Thomas More in his *Responsio ad Lutherum* (1523), a virulent response to Luther's virulent attack on Henry VIII's *Assertio septem sacramentorum*. See *Responsio ad Lutherum* ed John Headley trans Sister Scholastica Mandeville in vol 5 of The Yale Edition of the Complete Works of St. Thomas More (New Haven and London 1969) 832–7

8 John Fisher (1469–1535), patron of Erasmus who had a high reputation for learning and holiness, wrote *Assertionis Lutheranae confutatio* (Antwerp 1523) against Luther. See CEBR.

9 A Parisian theologian (d 1543) who attacked both Luther and Erasmus in his *Antilutherus* (1524). See CEBR.

10 Christophe de Longueil (1488–1522), a Norman who spent most of his life in Rome, was an extreme Ciceronian who composed *Oratio ad Lutheranos quosdam iam damnatos* in 1520 (Ep 1597). See CEBR.

11 A Swiss reformer (1484–1531) who, unlike Luther, denied the physical presence of Christ in the Eucharist. He circulated an open letter to the Lutheran preacher Matthew Alber (published in March 1525) in which he argued for his view of the Eucharist. He reaffirmed his view at length in *De vera et falsa religione* (Zürich 1525).

12 Luther accepted the orthodox doctrine of the physical presence of Christ in the Eucharist, but he disagreed with the church by asserting that the bread remained after consecration; Luther's view goes under the name 'consubstantiation.'

13 Wolfgang Faber Capito (d 1541), a Strasbourg reformer who took Zwingli's side against Luther concerning the Eucharist. See CEBR.

14 Johann Hussgen (1482–1531), a leading reformer at Basel, agreed with Zwingli's teaching about the Eucharist and criticized Luther's view in *De genuina verborum Dei: 'hoc est corpus meum' etc. expositione* (Basel 1525). See CEBR.

15 Zwingli argued mostly from Scripture and logic; Oecolampadius, from patristic evidence.

work a year ago but only just now have completed it.[16] Rather I am amazed
that in your response you did not imitate my courtesy, which you actually
ought to have surpassed if you want us to place any credit in that attitude
and spirit which you claim for yourself. But in this matter you followed the
wishes of the 'brothers,' among whom I know there are very many whose
behaviour is far removed from the evangelical message from which they
boast they have taken their title.[17] You have been too subservient to their
passions, Luther, not without serious harm to the cause you are supporting.

It is no secret to me whose favour you curried[18] by writing in such
a way against Cochlaeus[19] and against the king of England.[20] Indeed he
was a person in whom you could recognize two stock characters of comedy: the thoroughly stupid and vainglorious Thraso and the utterly fawning
Gnatho.[21] Certainly he was not the sort of person whose advice you should
have taken to write so much as a letter about such a difficult and dangerous business. Instead you should have considered the role you have undertaken to play, namely that of a person who professes to bring back into the
light the gospel, which had been buried under mounds of earth for more
than fifteen hundred years, one who abrogated all the authority of popes,
bishops, councils, and universities, and promised the whole world a certain
and true road to salvation hitherto unknown on earth. It was utterly incon-
gruous for someone who had undertaken such an arduous task, like Atlas[22]
supporting the heavens on his shoulders (for now I will deal with you as
if everything that you claim for yourself were true), for such a person to
amuse himself as if he were dealing with a joking matter, to direct his bons
mots, his mocks and moues, his witticisms at anyone he pleases, and at the

\* \* \* \* \*

16 This is ironical: Erasmus believed the work had been completely printed a year
   earlier but was published only now. See prefatory letter n2 above.
17 'Brothers' refers not to Catholic friars, but to certain Swiss and South-German
   reformers such as Bucer and Zwingli, who disagreed with Luther on such
   important points as the real presence in the Eucharist. In 1530 Erasmus published two works against German reformers: the title of one is *Epistola contra pseudevangelicos*; the other commonly goes under the title *Epistola ad fratres
   Inferioris Germaniae*. See ASD IX-1 327, 322–4.
18 Erasmus reveals towards the end of this paragraph that he believed this person to be "Wilheylus," that is, Wilhelm Nesen. See n23 below.
19 See n6 above.
20 Luther replied to Henry VIII's *Assertio septem sacramentorum* (1521) in his *Contra Henricum regem Angliae* (1522). See n7 above.
21 Characters in Terence's comedy *Eunuchus*
22 Mythological Greek titan who holds up the sky on his shoulders; *Adagia* I i 67

nod of some Wilheyl[23] to sharpen or moderate his style against anyone at
all, much less a king. This same person incited someone else to write a dialogue against Lee[24] and he provided him with all sorts of lies, just as he
did you. Believe me, the person who urged you to write this book of yours
provided no better for you.

Many learned men, many princes of the church, many monarchs all
over the world begged me – some demanded and even threatened – insisting that I use all the eloquence at my command to thunder and fulminate
against you, implying that if I did not I would seem to desert the church
and favour your fraternity. But I excused myself, not because I approved
of your teachings, which (as you correctly write) I did not understand, but
partly lest I unwittingly do injury to a cause which in the beginning almost
the whole world applauded, partly because I knew that the task was beyond my powers. Thus I was afraid that I would perform like an unskilled
physician and make the disease worse by an inept attempt to cure it. Finally, I sometimes thought to myself: what if it has pleased God to provide
for the utterly corrupt morals of these times such a savage physician, who
is to cure by cutting and cauterizing the wound he could not heal by po-
tions and poultices? I saw learned men flocking to approve your doctrines;
I perceived that the world seemed almost destined to favour them; I noticed that the more violently the movement was opposed by theologians
and princes, the more widely it spread and the stronger it grew. Hence I
reasoned that the matter was not happening without divine guidance, and
so I decided to be a spectator at this tragedy,[25] thinking as follows, in accordance with the opinion of Gamaliel: if God is promoting this, I have no
power to resist it; but if what is happening springs from some other source,

\* \* \* \* \*

23 Wilhelm Nesen (1493–1524) or someone like him. Nesen was a protégé and
   friend of Erasmus, who was very disappointed when Nesen went over to
   Luther's camp in 1523. Luther dedicated his *Adversus armatum virum Cokleum*
   (1523; see n6 above) to Nesen. Nesen died in a boating accident on 6 July 1524,
   before *A Discussion* was published. See CEBR.
24 Edward Lee (1482–1544) had attacked Erasmus' *Annotationes in Novum Testamentum*. Lee thought himself satirized in *Dialogus bilinguium ac trilinguium*
   (Paris 1519; translated in CWE 7 329–47), a fierce attack on the conservative theologians of Louvain. The *Dialogus* may well have been written mostly by Wilhelm Nesen, though it was published under the name of his brother Konrad.
   See CEBR.
25 Erasmus echoes a phrase in Luther's letter to him written about April in
   1524 (Allen Ep 1443:68), urging him not to assail the Lutheran movement but
   rather to be 'spectator ... tantum tragoediae nostrae' ('merely a spectator at
   our tragedy').

it will be scattered of its own accord.[26] In the Acts of the Apostles we read: 'None of the others dared to join them.'[27] Out of a similar scruple I kept apart from your movement.

But when I could no longer make excuses to the princes, when I was being overwhelmed by ill will and quite misplaced suspicion, I wrote *A Discussion*, but I did it in such a temperate style that you could not wish for a more courteous disputation, and to some of the Pharisees I seemed not to contend but to collude with you,[28] because I refrained from attacking you with tooth and nail.[29] Certainly I thought that I had clearly avoided giving you any pretext[30] for outrageous insults. I deliberately overlooked some of the more offensive passages in your *Assertion* because they could not be treated without injury to you. When it came to making comparisons of character, I decline to take up that invidious topic, preferring to avoid offence even at the cost of failing to promote my cause. At one place I explicitly ward off any suspicion from you by writing: 'I do not intend this as a specific reference to Luther, whom I do not know personally, etc.'[31] But see how consistent are the judgments of your faction! Philippus Melanchthon wrote to me here that my *Discussion* was received quite equitably at Wittenberg, and he added that he thought it would be quite unfair if everyone in the church was not allowed to express his own opinion.[32] But in your response you temper your style with such skill that you may perhaps have written against others more vociferously but never against anyone with more enmity and bitterness – a claim that I will grant to be completely groundless unless I soon make it quite clear to everyone. I call my disputation a discourse and a discussion; what could be more dispassionate than this title? I myself make no pronouncement, since I am engaged in arguing about a point which it is not right to consider undecided or to call into doubt by disputing about it. In my conflict with you I dispense with the authority of the emperor, popes, councils, universities, and ancient, orthodox Fathers, all of which I could bring to bear against you, even if I should get the worst

\* \* \* \* \*

26 Acts 5:38–9
27 Acts 5:13
28 See Rummel *Catholic Critics* II 9–10, which, however, gives no specific evidence of criticism of *A Discussion* as secretly sympathetic to Luther.
29 Cf *Adagia* I iv 23.
30 Literally, 'giving you a handle' (*Adagia* I iv 4)
31 *A Discussion* 19
32 See Ep 1500:45–7; cf introduction lxxii. Melanchthon (1497–1560), whose German name was Schwarzerd, was a professor of Greek at Wittenberg and a close collaborator of Luther. See CEBR.

of the argument. I join in battle with you according to your own rules, however unfair, and I do not arraign you as you arraign me, for such a charge is in itself contentious and contemptuous. I do not restrict myself to your arguments so as not to appear to quarrel with you specifically, indeed not with you at all but rather what you assert. I do not see how you could wish to be treated more courteously. Do you go so far as to allow no one even to open his mouth in opposition to your opinions? But still you are always challenging everyone to engage you in hand-to-hand combat. What about Peter's admonition: 'Always prepared to satisfy anyone who asks you for the grounds of the hope that is in you, but with restraint and respect.'[33] And Paul wants a bishop to be apt in teaching, not quarrelsome.[34] But if I argued with too little skill, you should have remembered that saying of Paul: 'I owe a debt to the wise and to the foolish.'[35] Those who were once your sworn adherents dare to draw their swords against you and do not refrain from insults, and yet you cannot tolerate Erasmus even when he argues in a very restrained manner? I clung tenaciously to my restraint even though I knew it would bring ill will down upon me. You could and should have imitated my restraint; it would have brought praise to you and advantage to your cause. You say your patience was overwhelmed by the exultation of some who assigned the triumph to me and boasted that you were defeated.[36] What triumphs are you talking about? Here *A Discussion* was greeted with such silence that I almost forgot I had written it.

I always wished to stand alone; I hate nothing worse than sworn adherents and factious partisans. But when your book suddenly rushed out, as if from ambush, good lord, how your supporters exulted, scattering boasts by the handful – 'Erasmus has enough to keep him busy'; 'He has an affliction worse than kidney-stones' – and other extraordinarily evangelical comments. But neither the bitterness of your pen nor the impudence of their claims has driven me to pay more attention to emotion than to reason in this defence. In speech feelings sometimes outrun reason, but in writing we should not give in to emotion; we should look not to what seems emotionally right at the time but rather to what could be thought right for all time. But, to tell the truth, I had to struggle very little with my emotions. I have been so well trained by numerous epistles and defamatory books that I have grown inured to such abuse.

\* \* \* \* \*

33 1 Pet 3:15
34 1 Tim 3:2–3
35 Rom 1:14
36 *De servo arbitrio* WA 18 600:8–12 / LW 33 15

Do you really want to know how much anxiety your barbs have caused me? I only wish that five years ago, when you were singing my praises, you had aimed your pen at me with far more hostility than you have now.[37] But since in this so very unfriendly response you want to appear to be a friend, and (heavens spare us!) a fair-minded one at that, I want you and your adherents to know that I am not so stupid as to be taken in by such tricks or so faint-hearted as to be disturbed by your insults. It would have been simpler if you had openly raged against me in your accustomed way. For you ordinarily put on the lion's skin and conduct your business with a club.[38] Now you have patched the lion's skin with a fox's pelt[39] and smeared me with poisoned honey.[40] And to keep up this fiction, which was almost a year and a half in the making, you found it necessary to join forces with a word-smith[41] to concoct the style and add the rhetorical facade, since, after all, you were writing against a rhetorician. I know the force of your style, which is like a torrent rushing down a mountain with a great roar and sweeping rocks and tree trunks with it. The language of this wordsmith flows more gently but carries more poison with it. I am not unaware who he is.[42] He is one of that number who have soaked up whatever eloquence they have from my lucubrations – a fact even you admit when you have a mind to be fair or to remember accurately. It is nothing new for me to find my own feathers in my wounds.[43] And one substitute rhetorician was not enough: when you are hard pressed by the sheer force of the battle, you send out your Patroclus to fight with us, clad not only in your armour but also in his own (that is the power of his language).[44] For he is so deficient in speaking

* * * * *

37 Luther praised Erasmus lavishly in a letter dated 28 March 1519 (Ep 933). Erasmus means that he would have been spared the trouble caused him by those who thought he supported Luther.

38 *Adagia* I iii 66. The adage alludes to Hercules, who wore a lion's skin and carried a club when he went to the underworld to drag out Cerberus; the saying applies to those who take upon themselves tasks that are beyond their powers.

39 *Adagia* I ix 19

40 *Adagia* II x 9

41 Latin *logodaedalus*, someone skilled in tricking out a speech. Cf Plato *Phaedrus* 266E and Cicero *Orator* 12.39.

42 Here Erasmus refers to some unidentified rhetorician-helper who has learned all his eloquence from Erasmus and is later said not to have read good authors.

43 The feathers are on arrows he provided his enemies. Cf *Adagia* I vi 52.

44 This second rhetorician-helper seems to be Melanchthon, who was a close friend of Luther and who was skilled not only in rhetoric but also in theological argument (the armour of Luther). In Homer's *Iliad* Patroclus was the

that he loads me down with eloquence rather than arguments.[45] And do not think that I am imagining some fine distinction of style: there is only one person who could do what has been done here. Besides, I am personally aware of his talent for style from other sources. For the former rhetorician[46] is eloquent without having read good authors or learned grammar. And if you allow the inept decorations to be attributed to this substitute rather than yourself, I have nothing against it. After all, there are some things mixed in with your book that are so witless and ignorant that I would never have believed they came from you – I will point them out in the places where they occur.

But sometimes the conditions of my battle are less fair than those of gladiators. In the arena one is matched against one, a net-fighter against a mirmillo,[47] but I am one against many, or if against only one, that one is nevertheless a Geryon.[48] Isaac recognized two men in one;[49] I perceive different voices and various hands in one book. I am fighting against a whole phalanx, armed not only with languages, learning, and insults, but also with tricks, cunning, and devious counsels. Now I will show you the counsel of your wordsmiths, who thought to themselves as follows: 'We should not rage against Erasmus with uncontrolled insults, for that would only free him from the burden of suspicion laid upon him by the princes and the weight of ill will imposed on him by theologians and monks. But he is eager for glory; hence we will always hammer at the point that he knows nothing, and we will everywhere spit on him as a person of no account and overwhelm him with scorn and disgust. That will really burn him up, but in order to do this credibly, we will mix in some praise, we will pretend to be his friends, we will put on a show of pity for him rather than hatred; we will attribute to him intelligence and supreme eloquence, so that when

*****

friend of Achilles, who sent him to fight the Trojans in his own armour. Erasmus supposes Melanchthon helped Luther write *De servo arbitrio*. Melanchthon denied and deplored the accusation (Ep 377 in CR 1 793–4). See W. Maurer 'Melanchthons Anteil am Streit zwischen Luther und Erasmus' *Archiv für Reformationsgeschichte* 49 (1958) 98–115.
45 'Deficient in speaking' is ironical as applied to Melanchthon, who, like Patroclus, turns out to be unable to wield Luther's argumentative weapons and relies on mere eloquence.
46 That is, the unidentified rhetorician who was mentioned first
47 A gladiator equipped with a helmet having a fish-crest, regularly matched against a net-fighter
48 A monster with three bodies, slain by Hercules
49 Gen 27:22

the reader sees our candour on these points, he will think we would also attribute other qualities to him if he deserved them. Then by every possible means we will increase and intensify his burden of suspicion and ill will, fashioning our speech as if he agreed with us but pretends not to, partly out of fear, partly out of his love of riches; we will consider the sophists, compared with him, to be far preferable;[50] and then we will act out the play so as to curry favour in both theatres, both that of the "brothers,"[51] who have hated him for some time now, and that of the sophists and pharisees, who have long since been hostile to him because of good learning. Finally we will mix in a good dose of abuse and insults, so that, if we cannot wear out the frail and timid old man with our loquacity or overthrow him with our arguments, we will at least wear him down with verbal abuse.'

Such advice, so straightforward and evangelical, would be immediately detected in your book by a reader of any intelligence, but to your adherents it seemed very clever. In this design who does not see the embrace of the scorpion about to infix his sting? Who does not perceive the poisoned cup smeared with honey?[52] 'Worshipful Erasmus, my dear Erasmus, most beloved Erasmus, most excellent Erasmus, endowed with the highest intelligence, with the greatest gifts, with supreme eloquence, to whom good learning owes so much, etc.'[53] Here indeed is the embrace, here is the honey. But this same praiseworthy Erasmus presently writes so wickedly that not even the impious sophists can put up with him;[54] he blasphemes against God; and worse yet, he doesn't believe anything at all, but inwardly he is a secret Epicurus[55] or an atheist Lucian,[56] saying in his heart, 'There is no God,[57] or if there is, he does not care about the affairs of mortals.'[58]

\* \* \* \* \*

50 'Sophists' was Erasmus' and Luther's satiric nickname for the scholastic theologians. Luther called Erasmus worse than these sophists in *De servo arbitrio* WA 18 601:2 and 613:3–8 / LW 33 16 and 34.

51 That is, the German Protestants (see n17 above)

52 *Adagia* II x 9

53 A mocking paraphrase of Luther; see *De servo arbitrio* WA 18 786:21–5 / LW 33 294.

54 *De servo arbitrio* WA 18 613:5–7 / LW 33 34

55 An Athenian philosopher (342–271 BCE) and moralist who upheld atomism, denied the immortality of the soul and divine providence, but did not deny the existence of the gods

56 A rhetorician and philosopher of Samasota (b c 120 CE), author of satiric dialogues, some of which were translated by Erasmus

57 Cf Ps 13:1 and 52:1: 'The fool says in his heart, "There is no God."'

58 *De servo arbitrio* WA 18 605:27–30 / LW 33 24. The second alternative was the doctrine of Epicurus.

This is the sting, this is the deadly poison, this is the toad's venom. If this book is not everywhere awash with such witticisms, then I am as lying as a Cretan.[59] If, on the other hand, such accusations and many others are everywhere hurled, hammered at, and harped on, show me (I beg you) anyone against whom you have written more venomously. And this very inconsistency of your speech reveals the insincerity of your heart. How can it be consistent for you to say that I am most dear to you, a brother most dear and worshipful, most excellent and what not, and then pronounce the same person to be wicked, blasphemous against God, and finally an atheist? Do you think people are such blockheads that they do not understand by what spirit you are being led when you write such things, blowing hot and cold from the same mouth, offering honey and poison in the same goblet, presenting bread with one hand, hurling stones with the other?[60] In such a book what was the point of wasting so many words about my supreme eloquence and your supreme lack of it? In a disputation about free will what is the use of eloquence? For my part, I do not boast of such eloquence; I do not acknowledge it or pursue it. Certainly, if I do have it, I did not demonstrate it in *A Discussion*, and there was plenty of occasion to do so if I had wanted to. As for your lack of eloquence, when (I ask you) did I ever complain about that? Or when did I ever find eloquence wanting in you? Your eloquence is not inconsiderable; would that it were matched by a sober and sincere attitude! Then again, how far from evangelical frankness it is to beg indulgence so often for your lack of eloquence and then to secretly bring to your cause a person of extraordinary eloquence, as is clearly manifest from the flow of his language. Now what sort of an accolade do you bestow on me when you attribute to me supreme eloquence joined with supreme ignorance of the subject matter?[61] Or what generosity is it for you to grant intelligence to a sixty-year-old[62] and then proclaim he has a talent from which we may hope for good fruit? If I am now so intelligent, how long will it be before I am wise? But this is simply the window dressing of your wordsmith, who feigningly attributes eloquence to me so that

\* \* \* \* \*

59 Cf Tit 1:12 and the saying: 'Epimenides the Cretan said, "All Cretans are liars."' Cf *Adagia* I ii 29.
60 *Adagia* I viii 29–30; cf Lucretius 1.936–50.
61 *De servo arbitrio* WA 18 601:10–17 / LW 33 16–17
62 Luther had not mentioned Erasmus' age but had said: 'for you are no longer young' (*De servo arbitrio* WA 18 610:6 / LW 33 29). The preface to *Hyperaspistes 1* is dated 20 February 1526. On October 28 of that year Erasmus would be sixty years old; see Harry Vredeveld 'The Ages of Erasmus and the Year of his Birth' *Renaissance Quarterly* 46 (1993) 754–809.

he may be believed when he deprives me of knowledge, and mendaciously praises my intelligence so that the charge of dissimulation against me will be more likely to stick. And what you attribute to me in the beginning you take away from me in the course of the disputation, where you make Erasmus so stupid that he cannot see what is clearer than daylight. Time after time you accuse this most eloquent writer of being ignorant of rhetoric: he does not understand the essential point at issue; he often says what is irrelevant or what completely undermines his case; he gives a bad definition, a worse division,[63] and the worst arguments; in short, he does nothing which is not against the precepts of rhetoric. And unless I am mistaken, the person who makes these charges sent a letter here which attributes to me a well-nigh Ciceronian eloquence – which so delighted me when I read it that I could hardly keep from laughing.[64] And you taunt me by claiming that in *A Discussion* I oppose your teaching with all the eloquence at my command, whereas I devoted hardly ten days[65] to that piece of night-work; indeed I was all the while not thinking at all about linguistic ornaments, to which in my other works also I generally do not devote any fussy concern. Such inconsistencies demonstrate sufficiently that you are not saying what you think. And so, once eloquence has been taken away, all that is left is the intelligence which you initially attribute to me. But in the course of the disputation, my *Discussion* is dumbfounded and blind, she snores and dreams, she neither remembers nor understands what others say or even what she herself utters.[66] So much for Erasmus' intelligence! This is the way authors vacillate, Luther, when they do not derive their language from the truth but instead cleverly make up everything they say.

You are no more consistent when, in the prefatory remarks at the beginning of your work, you say the authority of Erasmus is not to be scorned, and then in the course of the work you do nothing but make Erasmus a joke and a plaything, holding him up as a laughing-stock to the whole world. If in fact you are lured out to fight by the authority of the

* * * * *

63 The third part of the Ciceronian pattern for an oration was a division of the arguments to be pursued in the rest of the speech; see Quintilian *Institutio oratoria* 4.5.1 and 5.10.63.

64 In a letter of 1524 Luther praised Erasmus' eloquence (Ep 1443:15–19). But perhaps by 'the person who makes these charges' Erasmus refers to the wordsmith, Melanchthon, who is ghost-writing for Luther here and who had praised Erasmus' eloquence highly (see n88 below).

65 See prefatory letter n4 above.

66 See, for example, *De servo arbitrio* WA 18 669:20–3, 671:7–9, 674:6–18, 706:23–8, 726:22–4 / LW 33 114, 116, 121–2, 171–2.

person who disagrees with you, why not fight hand to hand with Bishop
John of Rochester?[67] He is tried and true, a man of learning, dignity, and
a holiness not often to be encountered; and he challenges you time after
time and you do not come forth to struggle with him. Then again how consistent is this: at the end of the disputation you thank me because my *Discussion* offered you an occasion of confirming your teaching;[68] if you really
meant this, why were you so outrageous to her throughout the whole book,
since she disputed without any insults? These are the arguments which show
your unfailing consistency! As for your claiming knowledge together with
Paul,[69] would that you could truly do so and at the same time would ex-
hibit that evangelical spirit with which the writings of Paul are redolent,
whereas yours are clamorous with a quite different spirit. But in the end
is it any affront to me to have you disparage my knowledge, since you
have long since belittled the knowledge of every council and all bishops
and popes and the Doctors of the church, whether ancient or modern, and
finally of all the universities? Was anyone ever wise if he departed a hair's
breadth,[70] as they say, from your teachings? However wise anyone may
have been before, once he begins to contradict you, he undergoes a metamorphosis: instead of being Lynceus[71] he becomes blind as a bat,[72] he is
changed from a man to a moron.[73] It would have been more just for you
to reproach the ignorance of those who boast very haughtily about their
expert knowledge of Scripture but who proclaim that you know nothing at
all, describing those paradoxes of yours (that is the word I have used for
them till now)[74] by quite different names. I have always frankly confessed
to my ignorance and for that reason I have always excused myself from
contending with you. Hence to taunt me for my ignorance is exactly as if
a blind beggar bewailing his lack of sight were to be reproached because he
sees nothing in full daylight. As for me, I do my best every day to besiege
the ears of Jesus with my laments: 'Have mercy on me, O Lord; grant that
I may see the light.' And to someone who cries out thus, you say 'Be quiet,

* * * * *

67 See n8 above.
68 *De servo arbitrio* WA 18 786:26–34 / LW 33 294
69 1 Cor 2:7; *De servo arbitrio* WA 18 601:16–17 / LW 33 16–17
70 Literally, 'a fingernail's breadth'; *Adagia* I v 6
71 An argonaut famed for his sharp eyesight; *Adagia* II i 54
72 Literally, 'mole'; *Adagia* I iii 55
73 Literally, 'mushroom'; *Adagia* IV i 38
74 As early as 1521 Erasmus objected to Luther's paradoxes (Ep 1195:91); see also
   ASD IX-1 187:521n. Erasmus also called Luther's exaggerations 'paradoxes' in
   *A Discussion* 86. See Marjorie O'Rourke Boyle 'Stoic Luther: Paradoxical Sin
   and Necessity' *Archiv für Reformationsgeschichte* 73 (1982) 69–72.

LB X 1254C

you purblind beggar!'[75] In *A Discussion* itself do I not often profess my ignorance?[76]

Indeed I wish that four years ago[77] you had persuaded the world that I know nothing about theology; you would have done me a most welcome service. For all the eloquence you attribute to me, I was not able to persuade them of what I was trying most of all to make them believe. And I am grievously afraid that even now you will not persuade those whom I wish you could. For in your commentary explicating the Epistle to the Galatians, I am cried up as 'the top man in theology and a victor over ill will' – that is what you say in the preface.[78] Again, on the very first page of the commentary itself, I am immediately 'most theological.' Also in the course of the work I am frequently singled out for honour: in one place Erasmus is correct, 'as always.' In another place I render the Greek 'more accurately.' In another I am 'the most excellent Erasmus.' In another you are very happy to agree with your friend Erasmus.[79] Once more in the appendix which was added by Commodus Britannus,[80] you take second place but I am awarded the highest praise in the restoration of the gospel.[81] I will not set out here the hundreds of letters by your adherents in which I am cried up as the prince of theologians. But the minute I dared to open my mouth against your teaching, I immediately became entirely ignorant of theology. What if the man who wrote that my *Discussion* was received there quite equitably[82] had the leading role in this play-acting? If your judgment is so vacillating, who will have any confidence in it? I wish, however, that they could have the greatest confidence in it, especially in this case. I ask you, what will men of judgment say when they see the inconstancy of your mind as they compare this book with those other writings of yours? You call me a Proteus;[83] this goes beyond

\* \* \* \* \*

75  In the Gospels a blind man cried out to Jesus while the crowd tried to silence him; see Matt 20:29–34 (Mark 10:46–52, Luke 18:35–43).

76  *A Discussion* 8

77  Erasmus may be referring to a letter dated 28 May 1522 from Luther to a Leipzig friend which foreshadowed his future strategy in *De servo arbitrio* (WA Briefwechsel 2 544–5 no 499; see Chantraine *Erasme* 34–5); or he may be referring to a letter from Luther to Oecolampadius (WA Briefwechsel 3 96–7 no 626). Both letters are in LW 49 (nos 122 and 133).

78  *In epistolam Pauli ad Galatas commentarius* (1519) WA 2 449:21–2

79  *In epistolam Pauli ad Galatas commentarius* WA 2 452, 460, 476, 482, 502, 508

80  CEBR suggests that the name Commodus Britannus was a pseudonym for Philippus Melanchthon of Bretten.

81  *In epistolam Pauli ad Galatos commentarius* WA 2 618

82  Erasmus means Melanchthon (see n32 above); cf Ep 1500:45–6.

83  Monstrous shape-shifter, proverbial for inconsistency (*Adagia* II ii 74); see *De servo arbitrio* WA 18 602:1 and 648:17 / LW 33 17 and 82.

any Proteus. Under what pretext will you excuse writings quite inconsistent with one another? You will say, I imagine, that then you were deceived by the spirit of the flesh but that now you are led by the spirit of Christ. There you surely have a fine assumption which lets you justify anything whatever – that is, if we believe you. But at that time many had a high opinion of your spirit, whereas now their opinion has changed and grows worse day by day. Sift through all my writings and if you find anything like this you may call me a Proteus. At that time you were luring me with flattery to join your league,[84] but now that you are vexed by *A Discussion* you try to make Erasmus as blind as a bat.[85] But just as I was not taken in by those high-sounding praises, so too now I am not even the least bit disturbed by this vituperation of yours. I knew that those praises were not truly meant, just as this vituperation was dictated by hatred and anger. But at that time, when I was vaunted as supreme in theology,[86] I became not so much as an iota the more learned; so too now, when I am proclaimed by a similar hyperbole to know nothing at all, I am not rendered a bit more ignorant. Would you like to have an indication of how much I was pleased by those encomiums of yours? I admonished you in a letter to abstain from such commendations in the future.[87] Do you want to know how dissatisfied with myself I am now that you have rejected me? I am all the more eager that you should convince people that what you are trying to persuade them about me is true; even at the cost of such a disgrace I am willing to buy peace and quiet.

Now let us see how the other judgments of your party harmonize with yours. There is in print a letter of Melanchthon in which he attributes a great deal to you, but me he does not hesitate to rank higher than all the ancients.[88] So too a member of your school, a certain Erasmus Alber, taught by God,[89] makes me equal or even superior to St Jerome.[90] If all the an-

\* \* \* \* \*

84 Cf Ep 933 from Luther and Ep 938 from Capito.
85 See n72 above.
86 See n79 above.
87 Ep 1127A:77–81 (dated 1 August 1520)
88 *De Luthero et Erasmo elogion* of 1522 (CR 20 700); Erasmus reports that he read it (Ep 1496:162–4).
89 The Greek word used here (θεοδίδακτος) is taken from 1 Thess 4:9: 'For you have been taught by God to love one another.' It has ironical overtones in Erasmus' context of disagreements and factiousness.
90 Alber (c 1500–53) was a partisan of Karlstadt (see n97 below). He attacked Erasmus in *Iudicium de Spongia Erasmi* (Strasbourg: J. Schott 1523), which is mentioned by Erasmus (Ep 1466:29 and n9; cf Ep 1477:55–7 and n12 and 1477B:28 and n5); In his *Iudicium* Alber paid Erasmus a very backhanded compliment:

cient Fathers, if Jerome himself knew nothing about theology, if they and the church were totally blind, I am sorry for them, and I can put up with my blindness more easily, since I share it with such extraordinary men. But just as I am not even the least bit affected by the praises of your adherents, so too your judgment about me is almost a source of delight. If I had supported your teachings everywhere in my written works, my heavens, how great a theologian would I have been! But since I am aware of my limitations, I preferred like Paul to be prudently wise, since 'knowledge puffs up, charity edifies.'[91] And now I am even overwhelmed with joy that I do not have enough knowledge to earn the name of heresiarch, as it was earned by Arius,[92] who was very well versed in the Scriptures. Therefore, Luther, I beg you to bring all your strength to bear in order to persuade everyone that I know nothing about theology. It will help not only me but also you. For there are those who spread quite false rumours throughout the world and who have convinced quite a few people that whatever Luther writes he has sucked from the breasts of Erasmus, and even in published books they call me your master and you my pupil,[93] at one and the same time

* * * * *

'Erasmum itaque similem, imo superiorem facio Hieronymo caeterisque huius farinae, qui philosophorum persuasionibus in speciem quidem verisimillimis, sed vere perfidis et impiis infecti sunt verius quam adiuti' ('I consider Erasmus to be the equal, nay the superior, of Jerome and others of that sort, who are infected rather than aided by philosophic arguments that have every appearance of being true but are actually wicked and impious'); see Hutten II 374:27–30.

St Jerome (c 340–420) was an ascetic, biblical critic, and translator of the Vulgate version of the Bible, celebrated for his learned commentaries on the Scriptures, especially the prophetic books. Erasmus published the *editio princeps* of his *Opera* (Basel: Froben 1516). See Epp 326 and 396, prefatory letters to his edition.

91 1 Cor 8:1

92 An Alexandrian priest (c 250–336) notorious for his unorthodox denial that the divinity of Christ was of the same substance as the Father. He was condemned at the Council of Antioch (324). At the First Council of Nicaea in the following year, the creed that was formulated adopted the term *homoousios* 'having the same substance' in rejection of Arius' error that the Son is not of the same substance as the Father, which it also subjected to condemnation and anathema. Arius had a reputation for learning and asceticism, as Erasmus remarks in his *Epistola ad fratres Inferioris Germaniae* (ASD IX-1 336:185–6).

93 Such charges had been made against Erasmus as early as 1519; see Cornelis Augustijn *Erasmus: His Life, Works, and Influence* trans J. C. Grayson (Toronto 1991) 123. Erasmus thought that Aleandro (a papal agent at the Diet of Worms and a former friend) had spread such rumours (Ep 1218:8–24). See CEBR under

quite falsely burdening me with praises and quite contemptuously belittling
your knowledge. Vindicate the glory of your self-proclaimed knowledge
against such babblers, and at the same time you will earn my gratitude for
your efforts. Nevertheless, in the proper place in this debate I will make it
clear how little you have displayed of that marvellous and much vaunted
knowledge.

Up to this point I have been dealing only with that wordsmith of
yours, whom you hired to fill in your outline with garish colours and to
whom you turned over the management of your language so as to handle a rhetorician with rhetorical skill. But he wasted much of his skill in
deprecating your lack of eloquence, in extolling your knowledge and my
eloquence, in belittling my knowledge and crying up your spirit. As for
your style, I have never complained about so much a single word. We
have already heard a great deal about your knowledge and have not found
it wanting. My ignorance I have always freely admitted. As for that spirit
you claim for yourself, I wish you had given evidence of it in your writings
as constantly and as emphatically as you assert you have it. However that
may be, if your wordsmith in his bitterness had been content to insult my
folly, my silliness, my utterly blatant ignorance, I would have overlooked
it. But if I were to overlook the charge of wickedness levelled against me,
the accusation of blaspheming God brought against me more than once,
and finally that Lucianic word atheist,[94] I would be worthy of being truly
thought to be what you proclaim I am. But still I will refute these accusations in such a way as not to turn the insult back on you. I will not even load
you down with the condemnations of popes or theologians, whom you now
are almost ready to flatter as a sly trick to stir up hatred against me, even
though what you have written against them has not yet passed out of circulation. But I will take these things up in the proper places. Now I wish to
touch point by point on your mixture of insults and flattery. But before I do
so, I will point out the folly of your wordsmith in comparing my *Discussion*
with Melanchthon's book *Theological Commonplaces*.[95] Melanchthon fights for

* * * * *

'Aleandro.' So, too, Diego López Zúñiga (Stunica) wrote in a letter of 4 May
1522 that Erasmus' works showed him agreeing with Luther, 'for it was Erasmus and Erasmus alone who armed and equipped and trained Luther with
these blasphemous notions of his, turning him against the true religion' (the
Vergara-Zúñiga Correspondence Ep 4:9–11 in CWE 8 345)

94 See n56 above. Luther frequently compared Erasmus to Lucian (see *De servo
arbitrio* WA 18 605:28, 609:21, 663:33 / LW 33 25, 29, 106).

95 *Loci communes rerum theologicarum* (Wittenberg 1521), a compendium of theological fundamentals; see *Melanchthons Werke in Auswahl* ed Robert Stupperich,

you; I, against you. And so all you are doing is comparing fire with water.[96] Among judicious men what weight will this judgment of yours have, since you praise your supporter and put down your antagonist? Actually, though, skilled rhetoricians generally exalt the abilities and intelligence of their adversaries so as to make the glory of victory over them all the more illustrious. Let Melanchthon go over to the other side and take up arms against you: immediately you will find him a stinking rogue and he will undergo a metamorphosis no more lenient than that suffered by Karlstadt,[97] who was swiftly changed from the ointment-box of the Holy Spirit to an instrument of the devil the minute he departed a hair's breadth[98] from your precepts. For the moment I take nothing away from the praises of Philippus;[99] that is not the point. I will only say in passing that some time ago I read, not without care,[100] the *Commonplaces* of Melanchthon, and if he had satisfied me on all points I would have refrained from writing *A Discussion*.

Indulging in irony, you assign to me a twofold victory: on the one hand, by my moderation I restrained your spirit and impulsiveness; on the other, my arguments, which you call scum, were trivial and long since ground down underfoot, so that I argued for free will in such a way as to say nothing new and yet to attribute to it more than the sophists[101] have

* * * * *

8 vols (Gutersloh 1951–75) II part 1 3–163. Luther compares Erasmus's book unfavourably with Melanchthon's at *De servo arbitrio* WA 18 601:4–11 / LW 33 16. Erasmus first mentions having read *Loci communes* in Ep 1496:37–51 (dated 6 September 1524).

96 Cf *Adagia* IV iii 94.

97 Andreas Bodenstein von Karlstadt (c 1430–1530), a 'radical' reformer, a Thomist by education, dean of the theology faculty at Wittenberg. He initiated a Protestant communion service at the Castle Church of All Souls at Christmas 1521, omitting references to the Eucharist as a sacrifice, declining to elevate the host, and distributing the sacrament to the laity under both species (bread and wine). Luther rebuked him in a series of sermons in 1522 (WA 10 part 3 1–64), in *Ein brieff an die Christen zu Strassburg widder den schwermer geist* in 1524 (WA 15 391–7), and in a major polemic of 1525, *Wider die himmlischen Propheten, von den Bildern und Sacrament* (WA 18 62–214). In it he termed Karlstadt the worst enemy of his reform. In a letter of 1524 he also called him one of Satan's minions (WA Briefwechsel 3 505:8–99 no 807).

98 Literally, 'a fingernail's breadth' (*Adagia* I v 6)

99 That is, Melanchthon

100 LB has *non diligenter* 'not carefully, cursorily.' Though it was characteristic of Erasmus to say that he merely glanced at such a book, there is no evidence that he did not read this book with care.

101 See n50 above. *De servo arbitrio* WA 18 600:19–601:11 / LW 33 16

so far assigned to it. As for this last point, in the appropriate place I will make it quite clear how brazen it was of you to assert it. As for your insult about scum, I will set it down to your temperament and your want of eloquence. For I would prefer to be called scum rather than poison; scum can be washed off, but not so poison. But what reader can keep from laughing out loud when you write that my moderation rendered you less energetic and combative, since in fact that courage of yours, for all my vain attempts to restrain it, has shattered the whole world with strife and destruction.[102] When a horse gallops like this, should we spur him on?[103] We have the fruit of your spirit: it has come down to bloody slaughter, and we fear yet worse disasters unless God favours us and averts them. You say that such conflict is inherent in the word. I think it makes some difference how God's word is preached, supposing for the moment that it is God's word you are teaching. You do not acknowledge these rebels, I imagine, but they acknowledge you, and it is already clear that many who boast that they are evangelical have been the cruelest instigators of revolution.[104] If their attempt had succeeded perhaps there would be some who would have supported what they repudiate now that it has failed. To be sure, through your savage booklet against the peasants[105] you deflected suspicion away from yourself, but even so you could not keep people from believing that you provided the occasion for these uprisings by your pamphlets, especially the ones written in German, against those who are oiled and shaved,[106] against monks and bishops, in favour of evangelical freedom, against human tyranny. I still do not have so low an opinion of you, Luther, as to think you intended your designs to come to this, but nevertheless, long ago when you began this whole story, I conjectured from the violence of your pen that this is how it would end; and that is why in my first letter to you[107] I advised you to be upright in dealing with this business and take care not to write anything in an uncontrolled or divisive fashion. It seemed you had undertaken

* * * * *

102 The Peasants' War (1524–5). For a chronicle and judgment of the events in Erasmus' own experience, see Epp 1584–6, 1597–8, 1601, 1603, 1606, 1633, 1653, and Allen Epp 1686, 1717.
103 *Adagia* I ii 47
104 For example, Thomas Müntzer. See Spitz *Reformation* 105.
105 Luther's pamphlet of 1525, *Wider die räuberischen und mörderischen Rotten der Bauern* (WA 18 357–61), vehemently siding with the princes and patricians against the rebellious peasants
106 A contemptuous way of referring to the anointing of ordination and clerical tonsure
107 Ep 980

the task of purifying the morals of the church, which everyone agreed had
fallen so low that both the disease and the cure seemed unendurable.[108] It
had often been tried before, in vain, and the world was victorious.[109] You
seemed to be the right person for the task; the applause of the whole world
and the approval of the princes gave promise of a favourable outcome. I
saw that it would do no good at all for you to direct your violence not only
against popes and bishops (for many interpret your fierceness against them
as springing from a courageous heart devoted to the gospel) but also against
anyone who so much as mutters anything against you. For I was never concerned about what you might write against me, and I almost hoped that
you would challenge me with your pen, though even so I would not reply,
so little was my moderation inspired by any fear of you. As for the fact
that you were prepared to rage against anyone who did not entirely disapprove of the drama you had undertaken but objected to your staging of it,
I testified to that many years ago in quite a few published letters.[110] Why
did you pretend it is not so? But you did not want me to be disburdened
of ill will: that was the careful and clever plan of your adherents. But I was
not the only one who wanted restraint in your writing; even your sworn
adherents wanted it. For they are learning from the event how many thousands of people are being alienated from the gospel (if indeed what you
are teaching is the gospel) by the savageness of your pen or (if you prefer)
by your less-than-evangelical witticisms. Indeed when you made sport of
someone or other, people thought you jovial, or when you mocked the pope
and the king of England[111] they thought you brave and intrepid. But when
you treated Karlstadt with equal restraint,[112] it was amazing how much you
displeased your co-workers[113] here.[114] And you cannot bear it if I, an out-

* * * * *

108 Cf Livy 1 preface 9.
109 A deliberate reversal of 1 John 5:4–5, where the phrase *vincit mundum* is repeated three times
110 See, for example, Epp 980:51–8, 1083:56–8, 1119:39–41, 1128:98–9. The two 1526
Basel editions and LB read 'Quod si' at the beginning of this sentence, but if
we read simply 'Quod' instead, the sentence makes better sense: 'As for the
fact that you were prepared ...'
111 See n20 above.
112 Ironical, since Luther had published several harsh polemics against Karlstadt.
See *A Discussion* n4 and n97 above.
113 The Greek word (συνεργοîς) Erasmus uses here is used twelve times by St
Paul, always referring favourably to those who worked with him to spread
the gospel. Of course, Erasmus uses it ironically here.
114 That is, in Switzerland, where Zwingli defended the sacramentarian position
of Karlstadt that Christ is not physically present in the Eucharist

sider who does not belong to your fellowship, want you to be restrained? But perhaps it would be more appropriate to treat these matters elsewhere.

I had to laugh, I confess, when you said you were not deterred from replying by any fear of me.[115] Oh what a brave man! What's that I hear? Such a great lion as you should be afraid of a fly like Erasmus, who is even weaker than a fly? Do I have any armed battalions? Do I have a party of supporters? Do I move in the courts of princes, so as to stir them up against you? No one avoids courts more than I. And if I do have any contact with them, up to this point I have always done all I could, in speech and in writing, to repress their fierceness; whether or not I was right to do so is for others to judge. I cannot be an executioner; I have always hated factions. Up to now I wanted to stand alone, as long as I am not separated from the Catholic church. There was no reason for you to be afraid since you, together with your guard of sworn adherents, had to deal with a single person, and unarmed at that. But, you say, 'you are armed with eloquence.'[116] If I have any, I certainly didn't use it against you, and I dispensed not only with that weaponry but also with the authority of the princes of the church, which by itself could be thought to be weapon enough for me. What was the point of absolving yourself of any fear of a single, unarmed person, since you have so courageously scorned both popes and emperors and battalions of theologians? But on these points you simply wanted to play the rhetorician.

How, then, can there be any validity in the notion that my *Discussion* has undone many of those who have not drunk in the Spirit from your writings, since it depends on such silly arguments that instead of undoing anyone it elicits laughter and pity from you and your followers? Is it so easy for people to fall away from the gospel? But here, now, is another troubling point: I am always slippery, sailing between Scylla and Charybdis.[117] And here, to be sure, mention is made of Proteus[118] and Ulysses.[119] I am surprised you left out polyps[120] and chameleons,[121] Vertumnuses and

* * * * *

115 *De servo arbitrio* WA 18 601:29–32 / LW 33 17

116 In the introductory section of *De servo arbitrio*, Luther harps on Erasmus' eloquence as his only weapon (WA 18 600–2 / LW 33 15–19).

117 *De servo arbitrio* WA 18 601:33–4 / LW 33 17. See *A Discussion* n399.

118 See n83 above.

119 The Roman name for Odysseus, the crafty and versatile hero of Homer's *Odyssey*

120 Proverbial for stupidity and clinging, but also for changeableness so as to flatter various persons (*Adagia* II iii 91)

121 Proverbially changeable (*Adagia* III iv 1)

Empousas.[122] Your courage, Luther, has brought us to an era when we are prohibited not only from speaking badly about Christ but even from speaking well of him. But for that matter, the role of someone who is not an expert is to assert nothing rashly and to depend more on the judgment of others. Certainly in *A Discussion* I do not play the role of Proteus; rather, having candidly set out the opinions of various persons, I point out the ones with which I disagree the most, and after presenting the arguments I openly proclaim which opinion I follow. As for seeming, as you say, to sail between Scylla and Charybdis, I have nothing to answer unless you declare which church you call Scylla and which Charybdis. From the Catholic church I have never departed. I have never had the least inclination to enlist in your church – so little, in fact, that, though I have been very unlucky in many other ways, in one respect I consider myself lucky indeed, namely that I have steadfastly kept my distance from your league. I know that in the church which you call papistical there are many with whom I am not pleased, but I see such persons also in your church. But it is easier to put up with evils to which you are accustomed.[123] Therefore I will put up with this church until I see a better one, and it will have to put up with me until I become better. And surely a person does not sail infelicitously if he holds a middle course between two evils.

## [RESPONSE TO LUTHER'S REVIEW OF THE PREFACE TO A DISCUSSION]

[*Erasmus' alleged 'scepticism'*]
Now I turn to those points you excerpted from my preface and with marvellous dexterity twisted them so as to slander me, opening up for us the storehouse of remarks about Sceptics. Here you immediately make a melodramatic uproar because I mentioned the Sceptics,[124] as if I thought that nothing at all should be asserted. And you do not cease slandering me until you have made me into an atheist, although you began by saying that you did not want to make any judgment about my mind. How well these

* * * * *

122 Both were proverbially changeable (*Adagia* II ii 74). For Luther's references to Ulysses, Proteus, and Vertumnus as figures of change see *De servo arbitrio* WA 18 602:1, 648:17, 701:1 / LW 33 17, 82, 163.

123 *Adagia* III ix 91

124 *De servo arbitrio* WA 18 603:3–7, 22–3 / LW 33 19, 20. See *A Discussion* 7 and n11.

things dovetail! With the best intentions you say, on the one hand, 'I do not wish now to make any judgment about your mind' and then you follow up with 'in your heart you carry around a Lucianic atheist.'[125] And here you leave it up to me whether I want to appear to be a ridiculous orator or a wicked and insane writer.[126] This is that restraint of yours with which you imitate my *Discussion!* But let me show you how you have slandered me twice over: first I myself explicitly exclude from Scepticism whatever is set forth in Sacred Scripture or whatever has been handed down to us by the authority of the church. There is no need for me to repeat my own words, since you yourself recite them.[127] And so that whole speech in which you so superciliously despise a Sceptical attitude in matters pertaining to the Christian religion and prefer 'those who assert even more stubbornly than the Stoics'[128] is entirely beside the point, an extraordinary performance for such a remarkably wise orator as yourself; so you were not too far wrong when you reproached yourself in these words: 'But I am the biggest fool of all for wasting words and time talking about something clearer than daylight.'[129] And still you cannot stop without adding, with no less waste of time: 'What Christian can tolerate the idea that assertions should be scorned? This would be no more or less than to deny all religion and morality once and for all or else to assert that religion or morality or any dogma does not exist at all. Why, then, do you also assert: "I take no pleasure in assertions" and that you prefer this temperament to any other?'[130] This is how such a very wise man as you argues against an ignorant person, as if your conflict with me did not concern the case itself but rather who takes precedence in ignorance. What follows is no less absurd: 'But what will you say about those words of yours where you are referring not merely to the case of free will but generally to religious teachings altogether and you say that if it were permitted by the inviolable authority of Holy Scripture and the decrees of the church you would take refuge in Scepticism, to such a degree are you displeased by assertions? What Christian would speak this way?'[131] This is what you wrote. I think it is suffi-

\* \* \* \* \*

125 *De servo arbitrio* WA 18 604:8 / LW 33 21, 605:27–30 / LW 33 24. On Lucian see n56 above.
126 *De servo arbitrio* 603:19–21 / LW 33 20
127 *De servo arbitrio* WA 18 603:5–7 / LW 33 19
128 *De servo arbitrio* WA 18 603:22–3 / LW 33 20
129 *De servo arbitrio* WA 18 603:22–604:1 / LW 33 20–1
130 *De servo arbitrio* WA 18 604:2–5 / LW 33 21
131 *De servo arbitrio* WA 18 604:15–22 / LW 33 22

ciently clear from my writings how much I attribute to Sacred Scripture
and how unwavering I am in the articles of faith. On these points I am so
far from desiring or having a Sceptical outlook that I would not hesitate to
face death to uphold them. But I am talking about controverted teachings,
about which the church itself was once sceptical and reflected for a long
time before defining them, such as the procession of the Holy Spirit from
both the other persons, the approval of the word *homoousios* ['of the same
substance'], the transubstantiation of the bread into the body of the Lord,
purgatory, not repeating baptism, baptizing infants, the conception of the
Virgin Mother, and perhaps free will.[132] I am talking about these questions
and others like them; if the church had not defined them and I were asked
what I thought about them, I would reply that it was not clear to me but
was known to God. But now that the church has defined them also, I have
no use for human arguments but rather follow the decision of the church
and cease to be a Sceptic. I will repeat my own words, which you pervert
in a sufficiently rhetorical fashion: 'For I have always had a deep-seated inner revulsion from conflict.' Do you hear me, Luther? I am not dealing with
Scripture but with conflicts, that is, controverted questions. And right after
that I say, 'and so I have always preferred sporting in the spacious plains
of the Muses to engaging in swordplay at close quarters. And I take so little
pleasure in assertions that I will gladly seek refuge in Scepticism whenever

* * * * *

132  The formulation of these doctrines was, indeed, extremely contentious in the
     history of the church. The procession of the Holy Spirit from the other two
     persons of the Trinity was a major cause of dissension between the Greek and
     Latin churches; the insertion of the term *filioque* 'and from the Son' into the
     Nicene-Constantinopolitan Creed was finally approved at the Council of Flo-
     rence (1438) but was subsequently rejected by the Greeks once again. The term
     *homoousios* 'of the same substance,' denoting the consubstantiality of the Son
     with the Father, was defined at the First Council of Nicaea (325) after a bitter
     struggle with the Arians. The term 'transubstantiation,' the change of the sub-
     stance of the Eucharistic bread and wine into the body and blood of Christ
     while accidents or external appearances remain, was employed at the Fourth
     Lateran Council at Rome (1215), the Second Council of Lyon (1274), and more
     amply defined at the Council of Florence (1439). Purgatory was defined at the
     First and Second Councils of Lyon (1245, 1274) and at the Council of Florence
     (1439). The phrase 'one baptism for the forgiveness of sins' was included in
     the creed formulated by the Council of Nicaea. Infant baptism was defined
     at the Council of Carthage (418) in repudiation of the practice of delaying
     the sacrament until adulthood. Mary's freedom of original sin from the mo-
     ment of her conception was declared consonant with the Catholic faith at the
     Council of Basel (1439) but was not formally defined until 1864.

LB X 1258D

this is allowed by the inviolable authority of Holy Scripture, etc.'[133] Certainly it is a wicked attitude not to dare to define what has not yet been defined by the church and in a controverted matter to put aside all doubt once the church has delivered her judgment! What Christian could put up with such an attitude?

Then I compare this attitude of mine not with those who assert the Apostle's Creed or the decisions of councils or the decrees of councils but with those who stubbornly assert all things. For this is what follows: 'And I myself prefer to have this cast of mind than that which I see characterizes certain others, so that they are uncontrollably attached to an opinion and cannot tolerate anything that disagrees with it, but twist whatever they read in Scripture to support their view once they have embraced it, etc.'[134] Since this is quite clear, what is the point of the stock arguments you drag in against those who think nothing is to be asserted about Holy Scripture or matters of the faith? My mind shrinks from rash definitions, not from assertions. Whatever has been handed down as part of our faith is not to be sifted and searched so as to call it into question; rather it is to be professed. And all these things I say in the role of an unlearned man, which I take upon myself with your full approval. Nor do I condemn in an unqualified way those who engage in moderate disputation, seeking to investigate some point which is not expressed in Sacred Scripture or defined by the church, but rather those who indulge in fierce and destructive strife about such matters. These are my words: 'Yet I would be pleased if I could persuade those of average intellect that in discussions of this kind they should not be too persistent in making assertions which may more readily damage Christian harmony than advance true religion.'[135] I do not condemn moderate investigation but rather obstinate strife to the detriment of religion and harmony. You can hear, Luther, that I do not exclude everyone from such questions but only those of average intelligence. Much less do I want to have them handled in the presence of the ignorant mob. But then you bear down upon me with a dilemma: 'If you are speaking about frivolous questions, what has that to do with us, since we are discussing necessary matters? If you are speaking about free will, what you say here is irrelevant and there is no need for you to play the master teacher.'[136] Pay attention now to what I reply to your defective syllogism. There are some questions

* * * * *

133 *A Discussion* 7
134 *A Discussion* 7
135 *A Discussion* 8
136 Erasmus summarizes *De servo arbitrio* WA 18 604:7–33 / LW 33 21–2.

about which restrained investigation is not condemned, such as the age of Methuselah[137] or how old Solomon was when he became a father,[138] but fretful and contentious investigation of them is condemned. Then again, there are many subjects discussed by the scholastic theologians concerning which the church has not yet made a clear pronouncement; these are the ones subject to that attitude of Scepticism. But you insist that we are concerned with free will. If I place that among frivolous questions, 'my language is correct' but my thought is impious. If I place it among necessary questions, my thought is pious but 'my language is impious.'[139] And so I am caught here between a rock and a hard place.[140] But the way out of this is quite easy. I judge the question whether there is such a thing as free will to be so far from superfluous that I think it is heretical to have any doubt about it, since all true believers have handed it down with an overwhelming consensus and the church has clearly defined it as something not be be disputed but to be believed.[141] There has to be some end to disputing. It is you who are forcing us to take up the matter all over again by calling into doubt, indeed by dislodging and demolishing, what has been fully approved, fixed, and immovable for so many centuries. Otherwise not a doubt would ever have entered my mind about the existence of free will.

Nevertheless, though it has been laid down that mankind has free will, many issues have been raised about this question, which (so far as I can judge) could be left alone with no detriment to our salvation, about which orthodox teachers, both ancient and modern, are not in complete agreement, and concerning which the church still suspends her judgment. For it is still disputed among the scholastics[142] whether this proposition, 'God knows some things contingently,' is in any sense true. There is no

\* \* \* \* \*

137 A symbol of longevity; he died at the age of 969 years (Gen 5:27).
138 When Solomon became a father is debatable, since he had 700 wives and 300 concubines (1 Kings 11:3). On 'vain curiosity' see *A Discussion* n40.
139 *De servo arbitrio* WA 18 604:11–14 / LW 33 21
140 Literally, 'between the shrine and the stone' (*Adagia* I i 15 CWE 31 64–5)
141 For example, at the Council of Carthage (canon 5) and at the Council of Orange (canon 13); see H. Denzinger and A. Schönmetzer *Enchiridion symbolorum definitionum et declarationem de rebus fidei et morum* 25th ed (Freiburg im Breisgau, Barcelona, and Rome 1991) nos 108, 180.
142 That is, university-trained theologians. By training Luther was a scholastic theologian, though he sought to break away from them. Erasmus studied scholastic theology at the University of Paris (1495–6), where he became familiar with the kinds of questions he now proceeds to list as examples of what should not be discussed before common people.

lack of those who believe that all contingent things are known by God contingently, though they profess that God's foreknowledge cannot be erroneous. Or again: whether God does all things out of necessity. Likewise nothing can be more certain than that there are three persons, differing among themselves in properties though having the same essence. But concerning this matter many questions were investigated long ago by Augustine[143] and even more by recent theologians:[144] how person differs from person; and why the leading forth of the Holy Spirit from the Father is called procession, not generation; and whether the divine essence generates or is generated; and whether the divine essence is identical with each person of the Trinity in the same way as the divine essence is identical with the divine essence itself; and whether the Father's power of generating is something absolute in itself or is relative to something else; and whether the power of generating can be shared with the Son by the Father. Likewise, if it be granted that God generates God, does he generate himself as God or another God?[145] Innumerable points like these are treated concerning the most straightforward and clearest article of the Catholic faith, and in the universities it is not wrong to dispute about them, as long as it is done with moderation. Thus, concerning predestination, which is related to free will, they ask: whether it is possible for the predestined elect to be damned or the reprobate to be saved; likewise whether, apart from the divine will, there is any other cause of predestination or reprobation. I have no objection to handling these matters in the universities, as long as it is done with moderation, but I think prudence dictates that those of average

* * * * *

143 St Augustine (354–430), a pagan rhetorician, and then a Neoplatonic philosopher before his conversion to Christianity. He became the bishop of Hippo and the most influential theologian among the Latin church Fathers during the Middle Ages and the Reformation. Both Luther and Erasmus were admirers of Augustine but for different doctrines and different writings. Here Erasmus is referring to Augustine's major writing on the Trinity, *De Trinitate* in fifteen books, completed in 419.

144 Erasmus referred to such unsettled questions in *A Discussion* 9–13. The innumerable commentaries on the *Sententiae* of Peter Lombard, which were a standard requirement for completing a theological degree at medieval religious schools and universities, exemplify the range of questions to which Erasmus refers here; on Peter Lombard see n903 below. Erasmus was probably also aware of the trinitarian controversy over the procession of the Holy Spirit debated at the Council of Florence in 1438–9 by representatives of the Latin Catholic and the Greek Orthodox churches.

145 See Thomas Aquinas *Scriptum super libros Sententiarum Magistri Petri Lombardi* I dist 4 q 1 a3.

intelligence should abstain from such questions, where it can be dangerous to make a mistake, and that they not be discussed in front of ordinary
people. And therefore I do not condemn those who teach the people that
free will exists, striving together with the assistance of grace, but rather
those who discuss before the ignorant mob difficulties which would hardly
be suitable in the universities. Thus it would be pious for a priest to teach
the people the existence of the Father and the Son and the Holy Spirit. But
to discuss those difficulties of the scholastics about notions, about reality
and relations, before a mixed crowd, you should consider how much good
it would do. When in *A Discussion* I put forward some examples of this sort,
you throw in the phrase 'not without a suspicion of sarcasm.'[146] What cause
of suspicion is it if I do not want the sort of arguments presented by the
Scotists[147] and Ockhamists[148] to be presented before the unlearned and do
not want even the learned to go into them more deeply than they should?
Or what sarcasm are you talking about? Are you implying that I scoff at
the article concerning the three persons and one and the same essence? For
is there anything you would hesitate to throw up to me, since you are not
ashamed to call Erasmus time after time a Lucian and an Epicurus?[149] The
unforgivable sin[150] will be spoken of later. And so some questions are completely useless, such (I would think) as those about instants and priorities
and whether these are possible propositions: God the Father hates God the
Son and whether the soul of Christ can deceive or be deceived.[151] Again

\* \* \* \* \*

146 *De servo arbitrio* WA 18 607:25–608:1 / LW 33 27
147 Scholastics, notably Franciscans and especially at Oxford and Paris, who fol-
    lowed or developed the thought of John Duns Scotus. Scotus (c 1266–1308),
    known as 'the subtle doctor,' was a Franciscan scholastic who emphasized will
    both in the divine and human natures, and especially in his ethical writings.
    See *Duns Scotus on the Will and Morality* ed and trans Allan B. Wolters (Wash-
    ington, DC 1986) and *A Discussion* n103.
148 Scholastic followers of the thought of William of Ockham (d c 1349), an En-
    glish Franciscan theologian. Ockhamists flourished, especially at Oxford and
    Paris, in the fourteenth and fifteenth centuries. For Ockham's position on the
    subject of Erasmus' debate with Luther, see William of Ockham *Predestination,
    God's Foreknowledge and Future Contingents* trans Marilyn Adams and Norman
    Kretzman (Indianapolis 1983).
149 See nn56 and 55 above.
150 Blasphemy against the Holy Spirit (Mark 3:29–30)
151 Erasmus mocks such questions in his *Praise of Folly*; see *Moriae encomium* ASD
    IV-3 146:400–148:407 / CWE 27 126–7 and elsewhere. They were commonplaces
    of debate among the scholastics of the *via moderna* (mostly but not entirely Ock-
    hamists). Such questions were sometimes not as ridiculous as they appeared

some questions are useful but it is not worthwhile to fight about them so fiercely as to break asunder the harmony of Christendom, but rather it is better to let everyone fully enjoy his own opinion.[152] Then too some dogmas are more necessary but we should go into them only so far as Holy Scripture lights our footsteps. A point of this sort is the doctrine of one God and three persons. But even here there are two ways of going wrong: either by examining it more deeply than is proper or by discussing it before those for whom such matters are not suitable. That this is what I meant will be perfectly clear to anyone who reads my *Discussion* attentively.

Therefore I ask you time and time again, Luther, what is the relevance of all your insults and slanders, all your taunts and outcries and curses, claiming that I want the freedom of the Sceptics in dealing with Holy Scripture; that 'I do not care whether I fully understand or not' what is prescribed by Scripture and the church; that 'the gist of what I say is that it makes no difference what anyone anywhere believes so long as world peace is maintained'; and that, 'out of fear for life, fame, property, or reputation it is permissible to imitate the person whose motto is "They say it, I say it; they deny it, I deny it" and to consider Christian doctrines as in no higher category than the opinions of philosophers';[153] and that the whole thrust of my writing shows that 'in my heart I foster a Lucian or some other pig from the herd of Epicurus,[154] someone who does not believe in God himself and hence secretly laughs at those who believe in God and profess that belief.'[155] And elsewhere you say that my breath has the foul, drunken odour of Epicurus and that I reek of nothing so much as the atheist Lucian.[156] And then, not satisfied with such gross insults, you even add a rhetorical figure, saying, 'You know what I refrain from saying here.'[157] Here you have ready at hand those hyperboles of yours without which you never write anything. To the sophists (for that is your name for the theologians) you everywhere ascribe the worst sort of ungodliness

\* \* \* \* \*

but were raised as part of the dialectic of God's absolute and ordained powers.
152 Cf Rom 14:5.
153 *De servo arbitrio* WA 18 605:17–18 / LW 33 23; cf Terence *Eunuchus* 2.2.21.
154 Horace *Epistles* 1.4.16
155 *De servo arbitrio* WA 18 605:4–30 / LW 33 23
156 *De servo arbitrio* WA 18 609:21–2 / LW 33 29. See nn55 and 56 above.
157 *De servo arbitrio* WA 18 605:23–4 / LW 33 24. In the fourth sentence after this one Erasmus identifies the figure as hyperbole: that is, Luther claims to be holding back some accusation when there could be none worse than those he has already made.

and you claim that I write so wickedly that even these wicked men would tear me limb from limb if you did not hold them back out of the goodness of your heart.[158] It is as if you were to say that a basilisk cannot be tolerated by other venomous creatures.[159] Then after you have so often made me into an atheist Lucian, saying in my heart 'There is no God,'[160] when you have made me into a pig from the herd of Epicurus, as if I believed there is no God or, if there is, that he takes no care of mortals, when (I say) you have taunted me with such insults that none more atrocious could ever be imagined, then you add the hyperbole that I know 'what you refrain from saying here.' This would be the place to rage against you, if I wanted to imitate the impudence of your pen. There was no need at all for such shameless fabrications. I could have revealed from the writings of others what monster you hide in your heart and what spirit your writings breathe out at us. For if you claim the right to throw whatever darts you please at me, whether drawn from the accusations of your postboys or the letters of the 'brothers,' or from your own divining mind, how much greater a right do I have to do the same from the pronouncements of the emperor and of popes, from the books published against you by eminent men? I beseech you, Luther, by that spirit of yours of which you boast so often, do you write these things because you believe them or do you make them up to bring hatred down upon me? If you think I am as you describe me, you have conceived a very false opinion of me; if on the other hand you are making them up, as I believe you are, you can easily imagine what kind of opinion I conceive of you. But if your faithful 'brothers' in Christ have reported such things to you, they lied through their teeth. Do you think that I care nothing about the doctrines of the church simply because I refuse to support your condemned assertions? Do my many writings testify that I do not believe in God at all? What need was there to sweat to produce such works, since it was permissible for me to handle secular subjects? Or who ever heard from me a wicked statement about God? But I know that you think something quite different from what you write, nor is it hard for anyone to perceive what spirit has inspired you to write so odiously. And do not think that those spurious adjurations will make anyone believe you: 'Fear the Spirit of God who searches the loins and the

* * * * *

158 *De servo arbitrio* WA 18 610:8–10 / LW 33 29
159 Pliny *Naturalis historia* 8.33.78 and 29.19.66; Lucan 9.72–6
160 Pss 13:1, 52:1

heart[161] and is not deceived by well arranged words.'[162] If I wished to turn this technique back against you, even you can see, I think, how much material would be provided not so much by the art of rhetoric as by the facts themselves.

But I am determined to keep my promise: I will ward off malicious charges aimed at me, I will not make countercharges, though the charges are so shameless that I would not need any defence if I did so. Therefore, to the matter at hand. If you are so displeased by the Sceptics, if you are so pleased by those who assert, why do you dare to tear to ribbons what all orthodox believers have asserted, what the voice of the church has very clearly prescribed? Which is more wicked: not to dispute about Christian dogmas beyond what is sufficient or to undermine them, throw them out, trample upon them, and decorate them with your kind of verbal decorations? Here once again you will foist upon me your image of me, saying 'as if you revered Scripture and the church.'[163] What remains except for you to claim for yourself the spirit of prophecy, or even a certain divinity, so as to pronounce what everyone is hiding in his heart? And nevertheless, you repeat time and time again that 'you do not intend to make any judgment about my mind.' Only God is called knower of hearts.[164] Examine your own heart and do not judge others. Do you see here, Luther, the reply you deserve? I do not revere Sacred Scripture, and you do revere it? And here, to be sure, there was room for scoffing: 'But here you will wish it to be understood that you were not talking about professing Christ and his doctrines. I am rightly reminded of that, and as a favour to you I waive my right [and my custom][165] and will refrain from making any judgment about your character, keeping that in reserve for another time or other persons.'[166] What is the aroma, the spirit, the flavour of these words? What else but the spirit of evangelical sincerity? I beseech you, you can judge my character if you wish, but if you should judge it, what would you gain by it except shamelessness? What is the right you say you waive in my favour?

\* \* \* \* \*

161 Cf Ps 7:10 and Rev 2:23.
162 *De servo arbitrio* WA 18 605:25–6 / LW 33 24
163 *De servo arbitrio* WA 18 604:20–1 / LW 33 22
164 3 Kings 8:39
165 Luther's text has 'meo iuri et mori cedo.' In quoting it Erasmus inadvertently omitted 'et mori,' ('and my custom') which he intended to include because he takes it up a few lines later.
166 *De servo arbitrio* WA 18 604:6–8 / LW 33 21

Is it a licence to hurl any insult you wish at any person you wish? Or what custom of yours do you relinquish for my sake? Have you not kept to your old custom throughout the whole book, except that you outdo yourself in insults and abuse? Or what time, what other backbiters are you threatening me with? Are you purified in the eyes of the Catholic church if you can skewer me with the false accusation of impiety? With such stratagems as these, I imagine, the apostles coaxed the world to the gospel.

I want you and all of yours to know this: first, as far as the Scriptures are concerned, it is possible that in interpreting them I should make a mistake out of ignorance, which (as you say) Jerome was always doing. But I do not place more hope or find more consolation anywhere than in Holy Scripture, from which I believe I have derived so much light that I may hope for eternal salvation by the mercy of God without any of your contentious dogmas. And so I have no less reverence for Scripture than those who honour it most devoutly. Then, as far as reverence for the church is concerned, I confess that I have always wished that it might be purified of certain practices and that I do not in all respects agree with all the doctrines of the scholastics. But the decrees of the Catholic church, especially those issued by general councils and fully approved by a consensus of Christian people, carry such weight with me that, even if my tiny intellect cannot fully understand the human reasons underlying what is prescribed, I will embrace it as if it were an oracle issued by God, nor will I violate any regulation of the church unless it is absolutely necessary to have a dispensation from the law. And I would be enormously displeased with myself and would suffer mental torment if the leaders of the church had directed at me the judgment they have pronounced against you. As for how your case stands with God, look to that for yourself. This is the attitude I have had and will continue to have. Follow your bent and make whatever interpretation you wish, call me a dyed-in-the-wool papist. You will not be able to impugn my attitude in any way, except that together with all good men I have desired the correction of the church, in so far as that can be done without serious and violent disturbances.

Aren't you ashamed to charge me so often with wishing for the freedom of the Sceptics, as if by repeating and affirming what is false you could make it true? In Sacred Scripture, whenever the sense is quite clear, I want nothing to do with Scepticism, no more than I do concerning the decrees of the Catholic church. But on other points, about which asserters struggle and fight to the death, I readily take refuge in the opinion of the Sceptics, that is, I will consider them at length and refrain from any rash judgment. For a Sceptic is not someone who doesn't care to know what is true or false – the name itself is derived from considering[167] – but rather someone who does not reach a final decision easily or fight to the death for his own opinion, but rather accepts as probable what someone else accepts as certain. You can see that in interpreting Sacred Scripture the ancient orthodox Fathers were often Sceptics such as this, investigating, but for the meantime suspending their judgment, leaving the decision to others. And in reaching a final decision on many points the church was Sceptical, suspending judgment for many centuries. But who could have such a perverse outlook that he would prefer knowing nothing for sure to having certain knowledge about everything? Since, however, many matters are obscure, it is more modest and also more tranquil to adopt the stance of the Sceptic than to play the role of the contentious asserter. But in the end is there anything you cannot distort into slander?

How lovingly, in fact, you interpret the words I wrote: 'whether I fully understand or not,'[168] that is, 'you do not care whether you fully understand or not.' And you gravely add: 'But let any Christian be anathema if he is not certain and does not fully understand what is prescribed for him. For how can he believe what he does not fully understand?'[169] Is it true, most eminent sir, that to understand fully is the same as to know for certain? Does it not rather mean to perceive something difficult to understand by means of the power of the intellect and arguments on the level of nature? You were not unaware of what I meant – you are not that ignorant of the Latin language – you were swept away in that direction out of an eagerness to slander me. And even if your Latin was deficient, the context of the passage indicates what I mean. For what does it mean to submit human understanding to the judgment of the church if not to believe what the church prescribes? I do not fully understand how the Father differs from the Son, how the Holy Spirit proceeds from both, though he is the son of neither one; and still I am more certain about this than about what I touch with my fingers. And see how wickedly you turn everything into slander! The same opinion in my *Discussion* which you misrepresent and rail at so insultingly is the very one you give in the formulation which you use to correct mine:[170] 'wherever,' you say, 'our weak-

\* \* \* \* \*

167 'Sceptic' is derived from the Greek word σκέπτομαι meaning 'to consider, look carefully at.'
168 *A Discussion* 7
169 *De servo arbitrio* WA 18 605:5–8 / LW 33 23
170 *De servo arbitrio* WA 18 604:30 / LW 33 22

ness makes it allowable, etc.' What you call the weakness of the flesh, I call not fully understanding. For the truth itself is not the reason we do not fully understand but rather weakness of intellect, as I profess mine to be weak.

[*The obscurity of Scripture*]
At this point, furthermore, you bring three[171] charges against me: first, that I wrote that there is some obscurity in Sacred Scripture; then that I deprived you of the right to abrogate the decisions of the early Fathers, and finally that I do not want all discussions spread about indiscriminately. To respond to the second point first, let whoever gave you that right deprive you of it. When a later prophet arises, the former prophet is commanded to be silent.[172] What, then, is the consequence of that? Is it right for just anyone to abrogate the judgments of the ancient Fathers which have been fully confirmed by the public decision of the church? Finally, why are you so outraged by the prophets who arise after you? Why don't you give place to them according to Paul's precept?[173] And then, as for what you say about the clarity of Scripture, would that it were absolutely true! But those who laboured mightily to explain it for many centuries in the past were of quite another opinion. The time will come to speak of this matter later. And as you enter into this area you immediately display your skill, saying that I make a distinction among Christian dogmas, making some necessarily to be known, some less so.[174] I ask you, who ever said that Christian dogmas were not necessarily to be known? I am talking about kinds of questions, not Christian dogmas. Also in the passage I am dealing not with professors of theology but with the common people. For nowadays even tanners argue about free will over their cups.

\* \* \* \* \*

171 In the two Basel editions of 1526 the reading is *quadruplicem.* LB X 1262F corrects to *triplicem* on the basis of the context.
172 1 Cor 14:30. Luther had cited 1 Cor 14:29 ('Let two or three prophets speak, and let the others judge') to refute Erasmus' submission to the church, since that would deprive everyone of the liberty Paul attributes to the 'others' (*De servo arbitrio* WA 18 604:34–605:1 / LW 33 22–3). Erasmus replies that the liberty Luther derives from 1 Cor 14:29–30 would allow anyone to overthrow patristic decisions that have been approved by the church and would require that Luther yield to those who arose after him and disagree with him, such as Karlstadt and Zwingli.
173 Erasmus refers to Karlstadt and his adherents, against whom Luther wrote *Wider die himmlischen Propheten* (1525); see *A Discussion* n4 and n97 above.
174 *De servo arbitrio* WA 18 605:20–3, 606:1–3 / LW 33 23–4

Now where you confess that the obscurity is only in the signs, not in the things signified,[175] it makes little difference in eliminating obscurity whether you confess that the things are not understood because the words are not known or that the obscurity of the things is the reason that the words are not understood. But if knowledge of grammar alone removes all obscurity from Sacred Scripture, how did it happen that St Jerome, who knew all the languages, was so often at a loss and had to labour mightily to explain the prophets?[176] Not to mention some others, among whom we find even Augustine,[177] in whom you place some stock. Why is it that you yourself, who cannot use ignorance of languages as an excuse, are sometimes at a loss in explicating the psalms, testifying that you are following something you have dreamed up in your own mind, without condemning the opinions of others?[178] But if the truth is openly known, the opinions of those who diverge from the truth should have been rejected. Certainly that is what befits someone who has such a hatred for Sceptics and professes to be an asserter. Finally, why do your 'brothers' disagree so much with one another? They all have the same Scripture, they all claim the same spirit. And yet Karlstadt disagrees with you violently. So do Zwingli and Oecolampadius and Capito,[179] who approve of Karlstadt's opinion though not of his reasons for it. Then again Zwingli and Balthazar[180] are miles apart on many points. To say nothing of images, which are rejected by others[181] but defended by you,[182] not to mention the

* * * * *

175 *De servo arbitrio* WA 18 606:22–4 / LW 33 25
176 For Jerome see n90 above. Erasmus regarded Jerome's knowledge of Hebrew, Greek, and Latin as the model for scripture scholars. Jerome's exegetical masterpiece is *Opus prophetale* (CCSL 72–6A) on Isaiah, Jeremiah, Ezekiel, Daniel, and the minor prophets.
177 See n143 above.
178 See Luther's *Operationes in psalmos* WA 5 508:6–15.
179 See *A Discussion* n4 and nn97, 11, 14, and 13 above.
180 Balthasar Hubmaier (1481–1528) was theology professor at Ingolstadt and cathedral preacher at Regensburg. In 1525 he allied with the Anabaptists, who acknowledged him as their leader, and also with the revolutionary peasants at Waldshut, where he served as parish priest. Hubmaier had visited Erasmus in 1522 (Allen Ep 1292 introductory note).
181 Erasmus reports the abolition of images in Zürich under Zwingli (Epp 1496:88–9, 1522:71 and 1539:88, 101) and remarks that the inhabitants of Waldshut under Hubmaier even pitched them through the windows of private dwellings (Ep 1522:70–2).
182 Luther had defended images against their rejection by radical reformers at Wittenberg in a series of sermons of 1522 (WA 10 part 3 1–64), and again in

rebaptism rejected by your followers but preached by others,[183] and passing over in silence the fact that secular studies are condemned by others[184] but defended by you.[185] Since you are all treating the subject matter of Scripture, if there is no obscurity in it, why is there so much disagreement among you? On this point there is no reason for you to rail at the wretched sophists: Augustine teaches that obscurity sometimes arises from unknown or ambiguous words, sometimes from the nature of the subject matter, at times from allegories and figures of speech, at times from passages which contradict one another, at least according to what the language seems to say.[186] And he gives the reason why God wished such obscurity to find a place in the Sacred Books.[187] In the passage about the sin against the Holy Spirit never being forgiven you deny that there is any obscurity. Augustine confesses that 'he always avoided the burden of undertaking this most difficult question,' and yet when he did take great pains to deal with it, he had no confidence in himself and suspended his judgment.[188] In short, whether he satisfied himself I do not know, but he did not satisfy me. The words, as you say, are very clear: 'unforgivable sin.'[189] But tell me what is that blasphemy against the Father or the Son which allows of forgiveness, what is that against the Holy Spirit which does not? Does contempt for the Father and the Son have nothing to do with the Holy Spirit? And then what is that future age in which some sins will seem to be pardoned?[190] See how much obscurity there is in the very clearest words! How Augustine twists and turns to extricate himself from these

\* \* \* \* \*

*Wider die himmlischen Propheten, von den Bildern und Sacrament* of 1525 WA 18 62–214.

183 The Anabaptists, whom Erasmus first mentions in Ep 1369:4. The phrase *a tuis reiecto* 'rejected by your followers' is found only in LB X 1263D, not in the two 1526 Basel editions; the parallelism with the other pairs makes it seem a likely emendation.

184 The spiritualists, notably Karlstadt. See *A Discussion* n4 and n97 above.

185 In 1524 Luther wrote *An die Ratherren aller Stadte deutsches Lands: Dass si Christliche Schulen aufrichten und halten sollen* (WA 15 27–53), a refutation of the spiritualists' argument that the priesthood of all believers and the direct communication of the Spirit rendered education unnecessary or even sinful.

186 *De doctrina christiana* 2.6.7, 2.9.15 CCSL 32 35–6, 41

187 *De doctrina christiana* 4.8.22 CCSL 32 131:4–8

188 *Sermones* 71.5.8 and 71.24.38 PL 38 449 and 466–7

189 Mark 3:29–39. Erasmus paraphrases *De servo arbitrio* WA 18 608:5–7 / LW 33 27–8: 'Scripture simply professes the trinity of God and the humanity of Christ and the unforgivable sin. There is no obscurity or ambiguity here.'

190 Matt 12:32

straits, and yet he does not extricate himself, not in my opinion nor in his either.

Furthermore, where you challenge me and all the sophists to bring forward even one obscure or recondite passage from the Sacred Books which you cannot show is quite clear,[191] I only wish you could make good on your promise! We will bring to you heaps of difficulties and we will forgive you for calling us blinder than a bat,[192] provided you clearly explicate the places where we are at a loss. But if you impose on us the law that we believe that whatever your interpretation is, that is what Scripture means, your associates will not put up with such a law and they stoutly cry out against you, affirming that you interpret Scripture wrongly about the Eucharist.[193] Hence it is not right that we should grant you more authority than is granted by the principal associates of your confession. Now we are dealing here with the difficulty of questions which arise from the mystical Scriptures,[194] such as when we inquire what it is that distinguishes person from person in the Holy Trinity, a thing or a relation; and whether the Holy Spirit, since he proceeds from each, proceeds from one principle or two, and numberless other questions. Likewise when we read that the wicked are consigned to the fires of hell after this life,[195] the question is asked whether the wicked are delivered to their punishment right after their souls are torn from their bodies or whether they are reserved so as to begin suffering their pains on the last day, or again whether that fire is material, and if it is, how a corporeal thing can have an effect upon an incorporeal soul.[196] Now you stand alone in never getting off the subject, and so it is amazing that you bring in here scriptural texts and arguments about the stone rolled away from the tomb,[197] the gospel preached to every creature,[198] as if the apostles preached about such difficulties. But if the name of the gospel and the name of Christ include all such questions as

* * * * *

191 *De servo arbitrio* WA 18 607:5–9 / LW 33 27
192 See n72 above.
193 Zwingli and Oecolampadius; see nn11 and 14 above.
194 That is, passages in Scripture which need to be interpreted as revealing mysteries such as those concerning the Trinity
195 Matt 13:41–2
196 These questions are discussed, for example, by Peter Lombard *Sententiae* IV dist 44.7 PL 192 947 and by Thomas Aquinas in his *Summa theologiae* I q 40 a 2 and his commentary on the *Sententiae* I dist 2 q 1 a 5, I dist 11 q 1 a 2, IV dist 44 q 3 a 2.
197 *De servo arbitrio* WA 18 606:24–8 / LW 33 26; cf Matt 28:2.
198 *De servo arbitrio* WA 18 607:5 / LW 33 27; cf Mark 16:15.

these, how did it happen that after the gospel was preached such blindness remained in the church of God that there was no one after the apostles except Jan Hus[199] and Wyclif[200] who did not get stuck in places all through the Scriptures? Unless perhaps you mean that no questions should be asked that go beyond what is directly expressed in Scripture. But it is not likely that either you or your followers think so. For up to this point you agree with the church in pronouncing that the true body and blood are in the Eucharist, that is substantially.[201] But the word 'substance' is not in Sacred Scripture. Then again your adherents contend more stoutly that the body and blood are there only as efficacious signs. Sacred Scripture doesn't say that expressly either.[202] Everyone, you say, knows that 'the Son of God became man, that God is three and one, that Christ suffered for us and will reign forever.'[203] By the same token you could bring forward the twelve articles of the creed. I confess that these things should be preached to the laity repeatedly. But what has that got to do with the difficulties posed by the questions which arise from these articles? For it was these we were saying should not be disputed about before a mixed crowd. And so you see, I imagine, how far off target[204] are those texts you cite: 'Preach the gospel to every creature,'[205] and 'Their sound has gone forth to all the earth,'[206]

and 'Whatever is written is written for our instruction,'[207] and 'All writing inspired by God is useful for teaching, etc.'[208] Who ever denied these points? To be sure, they had to do with the turbot,[209] to make use of your witticism.

Moreover, you reject my Corycian cave,[210] which declares that we should examine Sacred Scripture up to a certain point but that it is wrong

*  *  *  *  *

199 A Czech religious reformer (c 1369–1415), author of theological treatises, biblical commentaries, and devotional literature. He was condemned at the Council of Constance and burned there 6 July 1415.
200 See *A Discussion* n35.
201 See n12 above.
202 Karlstadt, Zwingli, and Oecolampadius; see *A Discussion* n4 and nn97, 11, and 14 above.
203 *De servo arbitrio* WA 18 606:24–9 / LW 33 25–6
204 *Adagia* II iv 57
205 Mark 16:15; *De servo arbitrio* WA 18 607:5 / LW 33 27
206 Ps 18:4; *De servo arbitrio* WA 18 607:5–6 / LW 33 27
207 Rom 15:5; *De servo arbitrio* WA 18 607:6 / LW 33 27
208 2 Tim 3:16; *De servo arbitrio* WA 18 607:7 / LW 33 27
209 Juvenal *Satires* 4.119–21: a blind sycophant at the court of Domitian praises a turbot while gesturing in another direction.
210 See *A Discussion* 8–9 and n17 above.

to go deeper than what is enough for us, lest as we scrutinize majesty we should be overcome by its glory, but you teach that all the most recondite mysteries are available and openly known to all. Indeed you assert this stoutly enough, but the world itself and the very facts of the case cry out against you, and finally even your own writings and your dissenting adherents refute what you assert. I will not spend much time examining that distinction of yours whereby you separate God from Scripture as the creator is separated from the creature.[211] I do not know why, when you are about to propose it, you should profess that you intend to indulge in rhetoric or dialectic; it would have been more appropriate if you had said sophistry. For the sophists are accustomed to escape by means of distinctions, and whenever it suits you, you do the same no less frequently and no less brazenly than they do. Scripture depicts God for us and speaks about the mysteries of the divine nature. Accordingly since the subject is beyond our comprehension, so too the language used about it should also be in some manner beyond our comprehension. And I do not refer the pronoun *eius* to Scripture, as you divine, but to God. 'And so you apply it inappropriately to Scripture,' you say, 'whereas in that passage Paul is speaking of God, as is Isaiah.'[212] But the image and the thing expressed do correspond with one another.[213] And before Paul came to those words, he was dealing with a very difficult scriptural question about Jacob (who was beloved) and Esau (who was hated) and about the potter and the clay he shapes. Hence for me to deal with these places was not as inappropriate as you wish to make it out.[214] But the testimony you bring forward has no bearing on my meaning, as you yourself were aware, since you write as follows: 'If you are speaking of the questions debated by the sophists concerning these points, what

\* \* \* \* \*

211  *De servo arbitrio* WA 18 606:10–12 / LW 33 25
212  At *A Discussion* 9 Erasmus quoted Rom 11:33: 'Quam incomprehensibilia sunt iudicia eius et impervestigabiles viae eius!' ('How incomprehensible are his counsels and how unsearchable are his ways!'). In *De servo arbitrio* (WA 18 607:18–21 / LW 33 27), which Erasmus paraphrases here, Luther claimed Erasmus appeared to apply the pronoun *eius* (which can mean either 'of him' or 'of it') to Scripture, not to God, to whom it obviously applies in Paul's sentence. Here Erasmus sets the record straight. Cf Isa 40:13–14.
213  Erasmus seems to mean that the image of unsearchable ways corresponds not only to God's mysteries but also to what he is expressing, the difficulty of Scripture.
214  Erasmus' discussion of Jacob and Esau and of the potter and the clay in *A Discussion* 53–6 evoked a sustained refutation by Luther at *De servo arbitrio* WA 18 722:30–734:15 / LW 33 195–206. Erasmus responds in *Hyperaspistes* 2 at LB X 1428D–1442A.

has Scripture, which is completely innocent of such matters, done to you, etc.'[215] Therefore you knew that I was not talking about Scripture, but about the questions arising from it. And so what was the point of pouring forth such a flood of useless words? In fact, however, not all questions are sophistical; some are useful and necessary, as long as they are judicious and are not pursued beyond the proper limits. Yet even among these there are some questions not to be taken up by just anybody and not in the presence of just anybody. Then again, that distinction between internal and external obscurity[216] amounts to nothing except to get you off the hook and wear us out with your loquacity. Nor did I say that some places in Scripture offer difficulties in order to deter anyone from reading it,[217] but rather to encourage readers to study it acutely and to discourage the inexperienced from making snap judgments. But perhaps these matters will come up elsewhere.

[*Erasmus' formulation of a Christian outlook for ordinary persons*]
Now we come to my formulation of a Christian outlook, which you pronounce to be quite pagan and Jewish,[218] though I formulated it, as I said, not for people like you but for simple, uneducated people who are no more than Christians. But it is useful to quote the formulation here, so that the reader can see more clearly what we are dealing with. 'In my opinion,' I say, 'as far as free will is concerned, what we have learned from the Scriptures should be sufficient: if we are on the path of righteousness, we should move swiftly on to better deeds, forgetting what lies behind. If we are entangled in sin, we should do our best to struggle out; we should approach the remedy of penance and in all ways seek to obtain God's mercy, without which human will and effort are fruitless; we should impute anything bad to ourselves; anything good we should ascribe entirely to the bounty of God, to which we owe the very fact of our being. Moreover we should believe that everything that befalls us in this life, whether happy or sad, has been sent by God for our salvation and that no wrong can be done us by a God who is by nature just, even if some things do seem to happen that we have not deserved; and that no one must despair of forgiveness from a God who is by nature most merciful. To hold to these principles would be enough for a good Christian life, and we would not have to penetrate with irreverent curiosity into obscure, not to say superfluous,

\* \* \* \* \*

215 *De servo arbitrio* WA 18 608:3–5 / LW 33 28
216 *De servo arbitrio* WA 18 609:4–14 / LW 33 28
217 As Luther had accused him at *De servo arbitrio* WA 18 606:19–21 / LW 33 25
218 *A Discussion* 9–10; *De servo arbitrio* WA 18 609:15–21 / LW 33 29

LB X 1265A

topics: whether God foreknows anything contingently, etc.'[219] First of all, as I have often said, this formula is presented for simple, uneducated Christians, for whom it is enough to try as hard as they can to make progress and to commend themselves entirely to the will of God; you will not require from them, I imagine, that they should torment themselves with questions which even the theologians have not satisfactorily explained concerning future contingencies, concerning the foreknowledge and predestination of God. And you pretend that I have put off the role of Sceptic and made affirmations because I twice add 'in my opinion.'[220] But you often allow yourself to indulge in such things, and so as not to expend too much energy on this point, I close my eyes to many of them. For I have never dissuaded anyone from telling the people too, when the occasion arises, that the will is free but ineffectual without the grace of God. But what you are now teaching the people – that there is no free will, that everything happens by sheer necessity – such things are not only false but also dangerous to preach to the unlearned multitude;[221] nor does it seem to me to be advisable even for those who support free will to handle the other difficulties of this question in front of ordinary people. There are many very pure Christian virgins who have consecrated themselves completely to the will of God but who nevertheless do not understand how God foreknows, and whether he foreknows anything he does not will, and how he wills and does not will the same things, and how he foreknows contingent events which depend on the human will. Our body does not understand how the soul exerts its energy within it; it is sufficient that it makes itself amenable to the mind. So too it is not necessary for the soul to know the ways in which grace operates in it; it is sufficient that it makes itself obedient to grace. But you think that nothing is religious if you take away from the Christian religion such questions as whether our will does anything together with operating grace,[222] whether God foreknows anything contingently. But these things will come up in the proper places.

For I am not now arguing the matter but refuting the slanders with which your book everywhere abounds. One of these shows little sense of shame; how much sense it makes I do not know. You condemn my formula

* * * * *

219 *A Discussion* 9–10
220 *A Discussion* 9; *De servo arbitrio* WA 18 610:13–19 / LW 33 30
221 Cf *De servo arbitrio* WA 18 614–20, 634–8, 720–2 / LW 33 36–44, 64–70, 192–5.
222 *Gratia operans* 'working grace' is an Augustinian term for the grace which works on the soul before the influx of *gratia co-operans* 'co-working grace' with which the human will cooperates. See *A Discussion* 30 and n109 above.

as pagan or Jewish because 'it contains not even one iota about Christ,' as if I were teaching that there is a Christian godliness without Christ 'as long as we try as hard as we can to worship God, who is by nature most merciful,' although the words 'as long as we worship, etc.' you made up on your own, so as to have at least some pretext for your slander.[223] Here I once more appeal to your conscience, Luther: aren't you ashamed to smear your wretched paper with such trash? You twist my words to make it seem that I was setting down a formulation of all of Christianity intended for everyone. In fact, I was setting down what was enough to protect simple people from the contentious and almost inexplicable difficulties which are discussed concerning the subject of free will. Tell me now, when God is mentioned as the God of Christians, is Christ not present there? Yes, unless you do not consider Christ to be God. And when a Christian is mentioned, isn't Christ also understood to be there too? Whose books inculcate the name of Jesus Christ more than mine do? And after such an obvious slander made up out of whole cloth, you indulge in melodrama such as this: 'What am I to say here, Erasmus? You utterly reek of Lucian and your breath has the foul, drunken odour of Epicurus.'[224] You never lack for something to say, but I think the judicious reader will not find it difficult to know what I think of you at this point. And see how inconsistent you are, O man of adamant, who considers Erasmus to be a Proteus.[225] That is what usually happens when someone says what he does not believe. I admonish the Christian to subject himself completely to the will of God and 'I utterly reek of Lucian and my breath has the foul, drunken odour of Epicurus.' Are these the words of someone who denies there is any God? Can this be said to reek of Lucian, who is called an atheist because in his books he made fun of all the pagan gods, so much so that he might have been worthy of the word 'pious' if he had recognized the true God? Can this be equated with breathing out the foul, drunken odour of Epicurus? How can anyone commit himself completely to a God who he does not believe exists, or if he does, has no concern about human affairs? Again, if someone believes that everything, whether happy or sad, has been sent by a gracious God for our salvation, does he think that the affairs of mankind are of no concern to God? Time after time, Luther, see how you are swept away by your impetuous temperament, yielding to it in a way incompatible with the image you chose to project. And even so, as if you had deployed irrefutable

* * * * *

223 *De servo arbitrio* WA 18 609:16–21 / LW 33 29
224 *De servo arbitrio* WA 18 609:21–2 / LW 33 29
225 See n83 above.

arguments to win the victory you sought, you devote several sections to celebrating a glorious, lengthy, and magnificent triumph.[226]

I am not at all surprised, Luther, that when I say, 'We should do our best to struggle out; we should approach the remedy of penance and in all ways seek to obtain God's mercy, without which human will is fruitless, etc.'[227] my words seem to you to be spoken 'without Christ, without the Spirit,' that they seem 'colder even than ice,'[228] since they disagree with your dogmas, and whatever diverges from them is clearly (in your opinion) wicked. And yet these same words seem to you to be spoken not from the heart but wrenched from me by a fear of popes and tyrants so as not to seem completely atheistic.[229] Tell me, you knower of hearts,[230] is there any place in all my writings where I speak about free will any differently than I do here, that is, as the church has defined and the orthodox have believed? Or has anyone ever heard me approve your opinion about free will? How can you have the gall, then, to pretend that now at last these words were wrenched from me by a fear of princes? I would have preferred not to be pitted against you in the gladiatorial arena, either because I foresaw that I would accomplish nothing but to meet you in your own element,[231] or because I would have preferred to have time for other pursuits. Hence if you say that I came out into the arena against my own convictions, you are quite right. But if you think that in my secret heart of hearts I agree with you, either you are totally off course[232] or you have shamelessly fabricated this, as you have so much else. I entered the fray reluctantly and unwillingly, but once in the midst of the fray I defended nothing but what I have always thought and still think today, as I bore witness in my *Discussion*. And some time ago you were already angry with me – as is shown from your letters printed by your followers[233] – because I disagreed with you in the matter

* * * * *

226 *De servo arbitrio* WA 18 611:1–620:37 / LW 33 30–44
227 *A Discussion* 9
228 *De servo arbitrio* WA 18 611:5 / LW 33 31
229 *De servo arbitrio* WA 18 611:5–7 / LW 33 31
230 3 Kings 8:39
231 Literally, 'to call the horse to the plain,' that is, to the place which he likes best and where he functions best (*Adagia* I viii 82)
232 *Adagia* I i 48
233 See Luther's letters to Spalatinus of 15 May 1522 (WA *Briefwechsel* 2 527 no 490), to a friend in Leipzig of 28 May 1522 (WA *Briefwechsel* 2 544–5 no 499), to Oecolampadius of 20 June 1523 (WA *Briefwechsel* 3 96–7 no 626), and to Pellicanus of 1 October 1523 (WA *Briefwechsel* 3 661 no 160–1). See also Chantraine *Erasme* 33–6.

of free will. Where then is this new fear of tyrants[234] which has forced out words contrary to my true belief? You can be sure of this, Luther, I do not entirely agree with any dogma of yours (I mean those that have been condemned) except that what you write about the corrupt morals of the church is truer than I would wish. So far is it from the truth that I disagree with you only on this single point.

Therefore, from now on omit those flattering forms of address, 'my dear Erasmus, my dear Erasmus' and with such soft strokes pet the heads of your sworn adherents. And at this point it is amazing how melodramatic language flows out of you, replete with salty wit and smelling of the barnyard,[235] as if I had forbidden everyone to investigate what our will can do, what God's grace does in us. In fact I simply do not require oversubtle disputations on these points from all Christians, nor do I wish to have them aired in front of ordinary people. And in my *Discussion* you read rebukes aimed at those who go rushing into such matters with irreligious inquisitiveness – which implies that there is a certain godly inquisitiveness which can investigate them without strife and not beyond what is judicious. You insist that no one can be considered a Christian if he does not know that part of us which is called free will, and whether it is only in our will or also in our intellect, and 'whether it is merely passive to the grace which acts on it, etc.'[236] The preceding questions and ones like them simple Christians can simply take on faith, even if they are not scrutinized with scholastic subtlety. Therefore, since you missed the point[237] of what I was saying, the harsh words you heap up in this place such as 'irreligious,' 'wicked,' 'superfluous,' are futile.[238] And then, what need is there for simple Christians to dispute about contingencies and the will as merely passive, since the magisterium of the church regards as settled that the will does do something but that what it does is ineffectual unless grace constantly lends its aid? Christian people have held this doctrine for fifteen hundred years, nor is it right to dispute about it, except in a restrained way and so as to better establish what the church has handed down.[239]

\* \* \* \* \*

234 *De servo arbitrio* WA 18 611:6-7 / LW 33 31
235 Horace *Satires* 1.7.28–9
236 *De servo arbitrio* WA 18 610:1–2, 611:13–14 / LW 33 29, 32
237 Cf *Adagia* I x 30.
238 Luther borrowed these words from a sentence in *A Discussion* (10) and repeatedly threw them back at Erasmus; see for example *De servo arbitrio* WA 18 609:24, 611:12, 614:1 / LW 33 29, 32, 35. See also 155 and n325 below for further response to these charges of Luther.
239 See n141 above.

For the rest, the fact that in our encounter I profess to be examining, not judging – this was a courtesy I extended to you and yours by disarming myself of the authority of councils, popes, and universities. For what was the point of my making pronouncements concerning a matter about which the Catholic church has long since pronounced? Moreover, since my entire *Discussion* is designed to make the point that what the church has defined is true, namely that there is in mankind a power of free choice which operates along with the grace that operates[240] in us but in such a way that it cannot achieve salvation without grace, what point is there in throwing up to me the words in which I assert that our will does do something in matters which pertain to our salvation but that it is ineffectual without the mercy of God? But at this point I contradict myself, you say, since I said before that it shows an excess of curiosity to dispute about such matters.[241] It is not only excessively curious but also wicked to call into question, as you do, what the church has accepted with such an overwhelming consensus. And I add many other questions which are associated with this point; about them you wisely keep silent. But in my formulation I do not delimit what our will can do, what mercy does and 'how we are to understand "being active" and "being passive,"' no doubt with the deliberate intention, as you say, of keeping others in the dark.[242] It is a major crime if I do not explain such things in a formulation designed for simple people, but I do explain it well enough, I think, in the disputation itself and perhaps better than you can bear. But the fact that you are so disparaging, derogatory, and utterly contemptuous towards my *Discussion* argues that it is not as contemptible as you make out. If it did not bear down on you, your pen would not have produced such outrageous insults to its author.

['*Sailing between Scylla and Charybdis': Erasmus' alleged neutrality*]
Then too, see how inappropriate it was for you to say that I decided to adhere to neither side and to come off safely by sailing between Scylla and Charybdis so that, finding myself overwhelmed and confounded by

* * * * *

240 See *A Discussion* n109.
241 *De servo arbitrio* WA 18 611:12–16 / LW 33 32. Erasmus had said it is excessively inquisitive to dispute about whether the will was active or merely passive under grace in matters pertaining to salvation (*A Discussion* 9–10). But Erasmus also says that the human will must exert itself though it is ineffectual without grace (*A Discussion* 9). Hence Luther accuses him of disputing about whether the will is active or passive. LB X 1267E adds a clause here, *cum ipse disputem* 'when in fact I do dispute them' to make the alleged contradiction clearer.
242 *De servo arbitrio* WA 18 611:19–20 / LW 33 33

the waves in the midst of the sea, I assert everything I deny and deny what
I assert.[243] Has anyone who does not use his pen in favour of the church
gone over to your Charybdis? Or has anyone who would rather do something besides doing battle with you left the church? I have always professed to be quite apart from your league; I am at peace with the Catholic
church, to whose judgment I have submitted my writings, to detect any
human error in them, for I know that they are very far from any malice or impiety. I have never opposed what I know to be the truth in order to curry favour with anyone; I have never supported anyone's tyranny
by my writings. It is not my place to wield the rod of judgment over the
lives of popes and bishops. And if anything is accomplished by admonitions, in that matter I think I have been freer than is fitting for that role.
Am I separated from the church simply because there is little agreement
between me and two or three theologians whom you call sophists?[244] Although I have declared all this so many years ago, in so many letters and
writings, whether private or published by the printers, to you I am sailing
'between Scylla and Charybdis' – you seem to be marvellously fond of this
elegant expression, you hurl it at me so often – and do not adhere to either
side.

     If you had persuaded us that you are the man sent to this world by
God to renew the church by the sword of the gospel, who was guided
by the Spirit of God, who stood alone in finding nothing obscure in Sacred Scripture, of our own accord we would have crawled thither, just
to kiss your feet. But however often you claim you are such a person, you have not yet persuaded me. Very many things prevented me
from believing it, but among the principal reasons were the bitterness
of your pen, your unbridled urge to hurl insults, the utterly scurrilous
bons mots, the saucy moues and mocks which you employ against all
who dare to open their mouths against your dogmas. For here we are
not only forced to do without that Spirit of Christ which you so stoutly
claim for yourself but we also perceive a quite different spirit, a Lucianic or Aristophanic or (if you prefer) an Archilochian spirit.[245] You deny

* * * * *

243 *De servo arbitrio* WA 18 611:21–4 / LW 33 33. On Scylla and Charybdis see *A
     Discussion* n399 and *Adagia* I v 4.
244 Erasmus quarrelled, for example, with Jacobus Latomus, Nicolaas Baechem,
     and Noël Béda. See Rummel *Catholic Critics* I 4, 6 and II 2.
245 For Lucian see n56 above. Aristophanes (c 450–c 385 BCE) was an Athenian
     writer of comedies. Archilochus (c 700–650 BCE) wrote elegies, hymns, and
     lampoons. All three were often scurrilous but also created comical, bombastic

that the human soul can carry two riders, for by turns one displaces the other,[246] but whoever reads your writings seems to perceive both spirits riding the same soul at the same time. For when you recommend that we should place our trust in God, when you diminish the power of mankind, when you extol the majesty and authority of Holy Scripture, when you play down all things human by comparison with it, you say many things in such a way that they seem to be derived from the spirit of the gospel. But when you begin to play-act for your Wilheyls[247] and your claque, you are so impudent in your insults and your pantomimed mockery, so tricky and so unrestrained in your abuse when you are hemmed in by arguments, that no one, even if he bent over backwards to be fair to you, could find any excuses for your spirit. In order to inflict more serious wounds you craftily throw in cunning slurs and indirect figures of speech, that is, you smear your sword with poison.[248] That is what you do here, leaving out nothing that might be said against the most deplorable person, making me into a Lucianic atheist, a pig from the herd of Epicurus,[249] a person so wicked as to be intolerable even to the most wicked sophists, an enemy to all of Christianity because I do not wish any disputation before the common people about whether there is any certain truth about future contingencies. Nevertheless, you still keep back certain things in your heart, you depart from your usual manner and 'trim your sails,'[250] and if I were not Erasmus 'you would take out after me in your usual fashion,'[251] as if you were demanding to be thanked for such merciful restraint.

Though all this is clear about you, you require us to believe that you do nothing of your own free will but rather under the guidance of the spirit of Christ, and you are indignant if we do not immediately abandon the teaching embraced and held by the Catholic church for so many centuries in the past and swear allegiance to you. I never had any inclination to join your conspiracy. But still, if I were growing weary of this church, as I wavered in

* * * * *

characters whom Erasmus claims Luther resembles.

246 *De servo arbitrio* WA 18 635:7–22 / LW 33 65–6; cf Ps 72:22. On Luther's image of God and Satan as riders of the human soul, see McSorley 335–40; see also Marjorie O'Rourke Boyle, 'Luther's Rider-gods: From the Steppe to the Tower' *Journal of Religious History* 13 (1985) 260–82.

247 See n23 above.

248 Cf *Adagia* I viii 57.

249 See nn56, 55, and 154 above.

250 *De servo arbitrio* WA 18 610:22 / LW 33 30; see *Adagia* v i 32.

251 *De servo arbitrio* WA 18 603:9 / LW 33 19

perplexity, tell me, I beg you in the name of the gospel, where would you have me go? To that disintegrated congregation of yours, that totally dissected sect? Karlstadt has raged against you, and you in turn against him. And the dispute was not simply a tempest in a teapot[252] but concerned a very serious matter. Zwingli and Oecolampadius have opposed your opinion in many volumes. And some of the leaders of your congregation agree with them, among whom is Capito. Then too what an all-out battle was fought by Balthazar and Zwingli![253] I am not even sure that there in that tiny little town[254] you agree among yourselves very well. Here your disciples openly taught that the humanities are the bane of godliness, and no languages are to be learned except a bit of Greek and Hebrew, that Latin should be entirely ignored.[255] There were those who would eliminate baptism and those who would repeat it; and there was no lack of those who persecute them for it.[256] In some places images of the saints suffered a dire fate; you came to their rescue.[257] When your book about reforming education was published, they said the spirit had left you and that you were beginning to write in a human spirit opposed to the gospel, and they maintained you did it to

\* \* \* \* \*

252 Literally, 'concerning goat's wool,' that is, whether a goat's hair can be considered to be wool (*Adagia* I iii 53)

253 For Karlstadt see *A Discussion* n4 and n97 above; for Zwingli, Oecolampadius, Capito, and Balthazar, nn11, 14, 13, and 180 above.

254 That is, Wittenberg

255 On 10 December 1524 Erasmus wrote to Melanchthon from Basel that in Strasbourg, and not only there, some taught that no subjects or languages should be learned except Hebrew (Ep 1523:162–3). See also ASD IX-1 307:683–4n and 390:385–392:392 and Martin Bucer's *Epistola apologetica* (1530), where he defends the reformers against the charge that only Hebrew should be studied, in *Martini Buceri opera Latina* ed Cornelis Augustijn, Pierre Fraenkel, and Marc Lienhard, Studies in Medieval and Reformation Thought 30 (Leiden 1982) 175:16–176:20. In a letter to Beatus Rhenanus written in August 1525, Bucer defends himself against the charge that he favoured neglecting Latin in favour of Greek and Hebrew; see *Correspondance de Martin Bucer* II [1524–6] ed Jean Rott, Studies in Medieval and Reformation Thought 43 (Leiden 1989) 31:1–32:21 no 100.

256 Erasmus' letter to the Town Council of Basel of January 1525 (Ep 1539) on religious abuses makes no mention of Anabaptism, but he was aware of the suppression of Anabaptists at Waldshut through a letter to him from Johann von Botzheim of 25 January 1525 (Ep 1540:16–23). For a general account of the Anabaptists and the persecution of them, see Spitz *Reformation* 166–74 and Harold Bender *The Anabaptists and Religious Liberty in the Sixteenth Century* (Philadelphia 1970).

257 See nn181–2 above.

please Melanchthon.[258] A tribe of prophets has risen up there with whom you have engaged in most bitter conflict.[259] Finally, just as every day new dogmas appear among you, so at the same time new quarrels arise. And you demand that no one should disagree with you, although you disagree so much among yourselves about matters of the greatest importance!

Imagine, then, that what you repeat so shamelessly over and over is true, that I am floundering wretchedly between Scylla and Charybdis. What shore, what port would you have me go to? If I had enlisted in your league and then returned to the old church you could charge me with disloyalty and inconstancy; others would say I had come to my senses. If the Christian world had approved of your teaching, I might seem stubborn or wicked if I were the only one who did not join in. If you agreed among yourselves on your dogmas, you could accuse me of pride for not paying attention to teachings propounded by learned men with such an overwhelming consensus. As it is, since I have always adhered to the Catholic church and kept away from your fellowship, since your doctrine has been condemned by the princes of the church and the monarchs of the world, to say nothing of the censure by the universities, since you quarrel so much among yourselves, each of you claiming all the while to have the Spirit of Christ and a completely certain knowledge of Holy Scripture, how can you still imagine that I am sailing between Scylla and Charybdis and be outraged that an old man like me who knows nothing of theology should prefer to follow the authoritative consensus of the church rather than to join you, who dissent no less from the church than you dissent from each other? It seems proper to hammer away at this point at some length because you had the effrontery to croak on about Scylla and Charybdis and my mind floating doubtfully between them.[260]

As for me, Luther, I have enough faith in Holy Scripture and the decisions of the church to hope for my salvation from the mercy of God, even without any help from your faith. In the future, therefore, do not claim what belongs to God, do not make pronouncements about a person's spirit,

* * * * *

258  See nn184–5 above. On Melanchthon see n32 above.
259  The Zwickau prophets, Nicholas Storch, Thomas Drechsel, and Marcus Thomas Stübner, who claimed possession by the Spirit in visions and dreams and who preached a radical biblicism, denying infant baptism and proclaiming an imminent millenium. For Luther's dealing with them see his Ep 472 WA *Briefwechsel* 2 493:17–20; see also WA *Tischreden* 2 307:9–14, 3 13:26–16:11.
260  *De servo arbitrio* WA 18 611:21–4; on Scylla and Charybdis see *A Discussion* n399.

but rather examine your own spirit carefully lest it should turn out you have a rider[261] different from the one you proclaim you have. As for me, I have not dared to make any pronouncements about your spirit, though I could have done so on the authority of others. I only said I found it suspicious, and I hoped my suspicions were wrong, and I still hope so today. I had these suspicions from the very beginning, when you determined to dance your part in this pantomime, to the loud applause of the whole world. I constantly professed this attitude long before you turned the point of your pen against me, and I am glad that I did, because if I now make any judgments about your mind, you cannot pretend they do not proceed from my judgment but rather from sorrow and hatred. In some place or other you promise to make me ashamed that I published *The Sponge*.[262] I, on the other hand, would not dare to promise to make you ashamed of anything, such is your pertinacity, but I will make everyone understand how crafty you are in twisting, distorting, misrepresenting, exaggerating whatever you wish, although the world has long since recognized this. There are those who have repeatedly mentioned your inconstancy in published books, and you cleverly pretend not to notice. You croak at me, 'They say it, I say it; they deny it, I deny it'[263] and here you say I assert what I deny and deny what I assert,[264] even though, in spite of your great skill in capturing Proteus,[265] you have not yet been able to bring forward so much as one passage in which I am inconsistent, unless perhaps you think 'They say it, I say it; they deny it, I deny it' applies to those who say what the church affirms and deny what the church rejects, so that it seems the saying should be reversed and turned back against you as 'They say it, I deny it; they deny it, I say it,' so eager are you to dissent from whatever the church

* * * * *

261 See n246 above.

262 Erasmus' *Spongia adversus adspergines Hutteni* (Basel: Froben 1523) trans Randolph J. Klawiter in *The Polemics of Erasmus of Rotterdam and Ulrich Hutten* (Notre Dame, Ind 1977). In this work Erasmus responded to the *Expostulatio* of Hutten (also translated by Klawiter), an attack occasioned by Erasmus' dissociation of himself from Luther's cause (Ep 1342) and by Hutten's subsequent failure to obtain a personal interview with him concerning Luther (ASD IX-1 117–210; Ep 1378). For the epistolary exchange between Luther and Erasmus on the *Spongia* see Ep 1445:41–69 by Erasmus and Ep 1443:25–32, where Luther says he wishes Erasmus had never written *The Sponge*. In *De servo arbitrio* WA 18 615:9–10 / LW 33 37 Luther said he would make Erasmus ashamed of having written *A Discussion*, not *The Sponge*.

263 See n153 above.

264 *De servo arbitrio* WA 18 611:16 / LW 33 33

265 See n83 above.

accepts. I do not assert what I deny, denying what I assert, but you are so clever that whenever it suits you you distort what is rightly said, turning white to black and light to darkness. This too is part of your craftiness: right afterwards you admonish me to fear the Spirit of Christ, saying that 'God is not mocked.'[266] Am I in danger of offending the Spirit of God if I am afraid to dissent from the church of Christ? Indeed the very reason I do not dare to entrust myself to you is that I am afraid to offend the Spirit of God. And afterwards you offer us apologies for that wonderful lack of eloquence of yours, although when it comes to abuse and slander you have a such a great abundance of bitter language that you can exhaust any amount of leisure or patience, and you are so crafty, moreover, that nothing can be said so carefully that you cannot turn it into dreadful melodrama.

[*Theological topics that are unsuitable for public discussion, such as God's foreknowledge or contingency and necessity*]
First of all, when in my preface I remark in passing that it would be better if the difficulties that arise in the area of free will were not disputed by or in the presence of unlearned people[267] – which is now happening in books translated into the vernacular, so that everywhere you can hear soldiers[268] saying, 'What difference does it make? There is no free will; God does everything in us, both good and bad; let him do his work; he knows what he is doing and no one can resist his will' – you interpret this as if I did not want anyone anywhere to speak about free will. With similar craftiness, when I am listing many questions, you bear down on one or two taken from the place where I am going from reasonable to over-subtle questions and after you have distorted everything, you have ready at hand your tragical apparatus of 'over-subtle, futile, superfluous, irreligious'[269] so as to deprive the reader of his sight by throwing such dust in his eyes. I come out as a mediator to separate you,[270] saying first we should not dispute about these matters and that they are above the capacity of

* * * * *

266 Cf Gal 6:7; *De servo arbitrio* WA 18 613:14 / LW 33 34.
267 *A Discussion* 12–13
268 To Erasmus soldiers were typically brutal and ignorant. See, for example, 'Military Affairs' and 'The Soldier and the Carthusian' in Erasmus' *Colloquies* CWE 39 53–63, 328–43.
269 *De servo arbitrio* WA 18 611:12–13, 614:1 / LW 33 29, 35
270 *De servo arbitrio* WA 18 605:21–3 / LW 33 23. Luther means that Erasmus intended to break off the quarrel between Luther and the church by his alleged mediation.

the human intellect,[271] and then I do what I disapprove of. First of all, I do not settle your quarrel, since I profess only to act as a disputant.[272] I attested to this out of courtesy towards you and to disavow to the church a malicious error.[273] Then too, the church is not quarrelling with you; indeed, she quarrels with your dogma, which she has long since laid low. I dispute about it, but soberly and only when forced to do so. If I undertook such a difficult task on my own initiative, I could be charged with rashness; but since I undertook it reluctantly and only when I had run out of excuses, I should not be charged with rashness but praised for obedience. Finally, I do not dispute to overcome you, for I knew I would get nowhere at that, but rather to make it abundantly clear to everyone that I do not agree with you and to deprive some of your adherents of the fabrication they were proclaiming and had gotten many to believe, namely that I agree with you. This suspicion, which is both mortally dangerous and utterly false, you also are trying to nourish, but without success, unless you consider Erasmus to be a blockhead.[274]

Again, I contradict myself because in my formulation I require that we strive with all our might and I assert that our efforts are ineffectual without the mercy of God. You argue thus: anyone who mentions struggle and might thinks that our will does something; anyone who confesses that it is ineffectual without the mercy of God teaches that it is completely passive.[275] Oh the inconsistency of it! What's that you say? Whoever has confessed that man's powers are not sufficient to gain salvation without the mercy of God professes that our will does nothing but is only passive? The premise is denied by none of the orthodox teachers, whether ancient or modern, but they nevertheless teach that the will does act in some way together with the action of grace. Why should it seem absurd that one and the same will, according to different viewpoints, should both act and be acted upon? Why don't you charge Holy Scripture with such inconsistency, since you often read there about the mercy of God, to whom we owe everything, and often

* * * * *

271 *A Discussion* 8–9
272 *A Discussion* 8
273 That is, disbelief in free will. Erasmus is willing to discuss the question with Luther as if it were debatable, but at the same time he holds to the church's position that free will exists.
274 That is, Erasmus would have to be a blockhead to imagine that Luther could have any success in persuading others that Erasmus agreed with him. Cf *Adagia* I iv 89.
275 *De servo arbitrio* WA 18 611:14–18 / LW 33 32–3

read on the other hand, 'Keep it up, keep awake, work'?[276] You read in Paul, 'I have worked harder than the others,'[277] and again, 'Fight the good fight,'[278] and 'I have finished the race.'[279] But you read in the same Paul, 'By the grace of God I am what I am.'[280] Why don't you charge him with inconsistency, as you do me because of two words, 'struggle' and 'mercy'? But I do not define how acting and being passive are to be understood.[281] This indeed was to be explained in the formulation, as if it were not sufficient to do so in the disputation, where it was appropriate. Finally, would a Christian be wicked if he had only learned that whatever good is in us should be completely ascribed to God's goodness unless he can measure with his thumb[282] just how much is owed to his mercy, how much to our powers? But you take up this question a little later, promising to perform marvels.[283] At that place, therefore, I will tell you how far your performance fails to match your promises.

Having so happily accomplished these feats, you celebrate a triumph and expatiate on a rhetorical commonplace just for the fun of it, so that in arguing with a rhetorician you can rhetoricize a bit, for that is what you say,[284] without, however, a bit of rhetoric. And it is marvellous how you bear down on me with comparisons drawn from writing a poem, farming, waging war, and building a tower,[285] drawing on Quintilian's *Art of Rhetoric*[286] and Horace's *Art of Poetry*.[287] And here, for heaven's sake, you cite Virgil's *Georgics*[288] and a saying of Sallust,[289] as if there were any similarity between

* * * * *

276  2 Tim 4:2, 5
277  1 Cor 15:10
278  1 Tim 6:12
279  2 Tim 4:7
280  1 Cor 15:10
281  Luther says this as an accusation against Erasmus at *De servo arbitrio* WA 18 611:19 / LW 33 33. Erasmus repeats it ironically here.
282  Cf *Adagia* IV v 86.
283  *De servo arbitrio* WA 18 614:1–25 / LW 33 35–6
284  *De servo arbitrio* WA 18 606:10–11 / LW 33 25
285  *De servo arbitrio* WA 18 611:25–612:11 / LW 33 33–4. Luther's point in these analogies is that one should take account of one's abilities and resources before undertaking any enterprise. He claims Erasmus has undertaken a task far beyond his abilities.
286  Quintilian *Institutio oratoria* 3.6.80–1; *De servo arbitrio* WA 18 614:34–7 / LW 33 36
287  Lines 21–2, 39–40; *De servo arbitrio* WA 18 611:28 / LW 33 33
288  1.50–3; *De servo arbitrio* WA 18 612:1 / LW 33 33
289  *De conspiratione Catalinae* 1.6; *De servo arbitrio* WA 18 612:6–7 / LW 33 33

a farmer tilling a field with human energy and God working in us. As for the example of the tower which you take from the Gospel,[290] either it does you no good or it does you harm: what[391] can he reckon up if he has nothing to spend?[292] With equal felicity you afterwards draw a comparison from the art of rhetoric concerning the orator himself and his precepts.[293] Good lord! Wasn't that wordsmith[294] of yours ashamed to stuff such nonsense into a disputation concerning what you profess to be the cardinal point[295] of all Christian doctrine? Does someone who teaches a simple Christian, 'Do not torment yourself with questions that are beyond your meagre capacity, but rather follow God's precepts and struggle to avoid what is forbidden, and do what is commanded but do it in such a way that you do not trust in your own strength or claim anything for yourself because of your good deeds but rather attribute them to the goodness of God, to whom you owe not only what you have done well but also the very fact that you can do anything by your natural powers and that you exist at all' – is such a person teaching laziness or is he saying to the budding orator, 'Don't bother about the rules, just write'?[296] You handle me with such stupid jokes, claiming knowledge for yourself like Paul,[297] hardly leaving even common sense for me. Your comparisons would have been a little less inept if you had compared the Christian to a farmer,[298] the method of cultivation to the commandments, favourable skies to divine grace. It is not silly to say to a farmer, 'Work hard according to the rules of agriculture but be aware that everything you do will be in vain if the skies are not favourable, for it is the skies that fructify, not the field, but favourable skies are not within your control, nor do you always know what is favourable, for sometimes what you think is unpropitious is really favourable.' This is like what I set down for the simple Christian. The same should be thought concerning someone who is going to

* * * * *

290 Luke 14:28; *De servo arbitrio* WA 18 612:10–11 / LW 33 34
391 To make the sense clearer LB X 1271A adds *enim* here: 'for what ...'
292 In the Gospel the man who wants to build a tower is supposed to reckon up his resources before he begins. But since according to Luther Erasmus has no intellectual resources at all, he can hardly have reckoned them up to see whether he is capable of discussing free will.
293 *De servo arbitrio* WA 18 614:37–615:2 / LW 33 36
294 See nn41–2 above.
295 Literally, 'hinge' (Latin *cardo*); see *Adagia* I i 19 and *De servo arbitrio* WA 18 614:3 / LW 33 36.
296 Erasmus' paraphrase of *De servo arbitrio* WA 18 614:34–7 / LW 33 36
297 2 Cor 11:6
298 Cf 1 Cor 3:6–9.

speak about Christian doctrine: 'Keep busy studying Holy Scripture, keep thinking about what you are going to say, but first invoke the Spirit of him without whose help human speech is sterile. Nor is it up to you to prescribe to him how he should guide the instrument of your tongue. He knows what works best.' You would have the speaker weigh everything on a delicate scale:[299] I will provide so much, God so much; I will speak so, God will affect mens' minds so. I suppose you would require a martyr, with the instruments of torture and death ready and waiting, to weigh what he can do by his own power and what is done by the mercy of God, and at the same time consider how free will is active or passive, how the mercy of God works. How much more Christian it would be for you to admonish him not to trust in his own strength but to give himself up completely to the mercy of God, only taking care himself not to turn away from grace by taking care to protect his flesh. But let us take leave of these most foolish comparisons of your wordsmith. Whoever teaches that God's mercy effects in us the beginning, growth, and fulfilment but that at the same time our will strives together with it is a godly teacher. Whoever raises the question whether only grace acts, making our will not active but passive, is not a godly disputant. How many holy men do you think there have been who have never investigated how God necessarily foreknows the things that depend on free will, and whether God himself has an immutable will and therefore does everything by necessity, just as we do everything by a sort of necessity because no one can resist his omnipotent will, and why he drew back Peter but did not draw back Judas, and innumerable other such questions. For I am not talking only about the question whether grace does everything in us and the will nothing, but about all those questions which the schools of philosophy bring to bear on it. Also, as I have to repeat often to counter your rude insistence, I am not talking about sober investigations by learned men but about strife and wrangling in front of ordinary people.

Since this is so, consider how out of place it was for you to speak as follows: 'Whoever does not think this confesses that he is not a Christian; whoever disparages or contemns it, let him know he is the greatest enemy of Christians. For if I do not know what, to what extent, and how much I am able to do and actually do towards God, it will be equally uncertain and unknown to me what, to what extent, and how much God is able to do and actually does in me, since God effects everything in everyone. But if I do not know the works and the power of God, I do not know God himself.

\* \* \* \* \*

299 Cf *Adagia* II v 82.

LB X 1271C

If I do not know God, I cannot worship, thank, or serve God, since I do not know how much to ascribe to myself, how much to God.'[300] This is your step-by-step syllogism[301] where, though in our eyes you do a superb job of playing the sophist, you yourself actually imagine that you are a marvellous theologian. It is not necessary for a Christian to weigh in such a delicate balance[302] what he himself can do, what God can do, how much he himself does, how much God does, as long as he knows that whatever good he does he should attribute to the bounty of God. God's power is not known, but rather believed, nor is he completely unknown to someone who, because of the weakness of the human intellect, does not fully understand how 'he effects everything in everyone.'[303] So too we do not fully understand with our intellect how he created the world, and yet we believe that he did. And many godly persons believe that Christ was God and man and yet do not know how and to what extent and by what means the divine nature combined a human nature with itself; they could give no answer if you asked them whether Christ could be said to be a man when his dead body was lying in the tomb.[304] A person does not give thanks to God badly if he ascribes nothing to himself and attributes the sum and substance of a good work to grace, even if he does not measure with his thumb[305] how much he ought to attribute to himself, how much to God. Augustine thanked God and worshipped God and yet he was sometimes ignorant of that 'what, how much, and to what extent' of yours.[306] St Bernard worshipped and thanked God and yet he gets stuck on these questions.[307] Thomas thanked God, I think, and so did Scotus,[308] though they disagreed with each other. Today also

\* \* \* \* \*

300 *De servo arbitrio* WA 18 614:7–15 / LW 33 35
301 Erasmus compares such linked syllogisms (technically called 'sorites') to the steps of a ladder.
302 *Adagia* II v 82
303 1 Cor 12:6
304 Erasmus gives a list of similar questions in *The Praise of Folly* CWE 27 127.
305 *Adagia* IV v 86
306 See n143 above.
307 Bernard of Clairvaux (1090–1153), abbot, Doctor of the church, and illustrious exponent of monastic theology. He investigated the problems of grace and free will in *De gratia et libero arbitrio*; see *Opera omnia* ed J. Leclercq, 8 vols (Rome 1957–  ) III 165–203. An English translation of Bernard's treatise can be found in *Treatises III: On Grace and Free Choice* ... trans Daniel O'Donovan with an introduction by Bernard McGinn, The Works of Bernard of Clairvaux 7, Cistercian Fathers Series 19 (Kalamazoo, Mich 1977).
308 St Thomas Aquinas (c 1225–74), Dominican friar and Doctor of the church, whose *Summa theologiae* is generally regarded as the ultimate synthesis of

many thank God who are content with the definition of the Fathers without weighing on a delicate scale[309] 'what, to what extent, and how much.'
Is someone not a Christian, is he unable to worship God or serve him or
give him thanks, if he believes with his whole heart the article about the
resurrection of the flesh but does not dispute about or fully understand the
many points disputed by the theologians about that subject? Is a person
completely ignorant of God if he hopes for eternal life with full confidence
but has never sorted through the innumerable difficulties treated by the
theologians about seeing God 'face to face, as he is'?[310] The most holy Virgin herself asked the angel only how she would give birth without contact
with a man, and as soon as she heard 'The Holy Spirit will come upon you
and the power of the Most High will overshadow you'[311] made no more inquiries and professed herself to be a handmaiden subject to the workmanship of heaven, and it may well be that she either did not know or did not
inquire about many things theologians dispute about concerning the ways
in which that workmanship of the Holy Spirit was executed in the tender
body of the Virgin. You understand how many examples I could heap up
here to show that that step-by-step argument of yours is absurd and ungodly. How many thousands of Christians there are who sincerely love and
worship God, who, if you asked them what grace is, whether it is a created
or an uncreated thing, and whether the grace by which God draws us is
the same as the grace by which we love him in return, would answer, 'God
knows'? Would you pronounce that such people are absolutely ignorant of
God because they do not know 'what, how much, and to what extent' he
works in them? For this is what those steps of yours will make of them. Is
someone ungodly and unworthy of being called a Christian if he is content to hold what has been handed down, that the true body and blood of
Christ is in the Eucharist, but does not inquire about and fully understand
how a solid body can exist without dimensions, how a human body can be
without distinct members (that is, not having a foot in one place, a head in
another, a chest in another, but complete in every place), and likewise how

\* \* \* \* \*

scholasticism in its reconciliation of Aristotelian philosophy with Christian
doctrine. He discusses free will in *Summa theologiae* I q 59 a 3, I–II q 6 a 1,
*De veritate* q 24, and other places. In *Hyperaspistes* Erasmus usually summarizes many texts of Thomas without citing specific passages. On Scotus see *A
Discussion* n103.
309 *Adagia* II v 82
310 1 Cor 13:12; 1 John 3:2
311 Luke 1:34–5

a solid body can sit in heaven at the right hand of the Father and the same body be eaten by people in so many places? Indeed I think that even you, if I am not mistaken, will not deny that thousands of hundreds of thousands will reign with Christ[312] even though while they were alive they never inquired carefully whether a person's will is merely passive in every way, or whether it is at the same time active in some way; and if it acts, how there can be more than one cause of a single deed, and which cause is primary, which secondary (God or a person's will), and then how both can be primary and secondary if you distinguish substantial being from meritorious being.[313] For you want such points as these, and many others besides, to be thoroughly examined in front of everyone and insist that unless this is done Christianity and the articles of the church are being neglected. If I had said such things, you would have cried out 'ungodly sophist!' As it is, since they seem to contribute to slandering me, you want to make it seem that it is both learned and godly to say them.

That other step-by-step syllogism that comes earlier also smells of sophistry: 'For if they do not know what and how much they are able to do, then they do not know what they do. But if they do not know what they do,[314] they cannot repent if they commit a sin, and impenitence is the unforgivable sin.'[315] Steps such as these do not climb up to the truth but drop down to madness. Does a person not know what he can do if he has been taught that he can do nothing without God's grace, but that with it there is nothing he cannot do?[316] But imagine a simple Christian who does not know how to weigh out, as if on a scale,[317] how much power free will has, how much power comes from the action of grace; does such a person not know what he is doing when he sins against God's precepts, and is he never able to repent? You foist off such super-sophistry on us simple souls, boasting at the same time to the whole world that you have such knowledge in theology that I doubt any of the apostles ever claimed as much. Certainly

* * * * *

312 Rev 20:4
313 See *A Discussion* n110 above.
314 Cf Luke 23:34.
315 *De servo arbitrio* WA 18 613:21–3 / LW 33 34–5. See n150 above. Augustine ends up opining that the unforgivable sin is final impenitence (*Sermones* 71.11.20 and 71.21.35 PL 38 455 and 464). In the sentence preceding this quotation (613:18–21), Luther also accused Erasmus of committing the unforgivable sin by enjoining Christians not to be inquisitive about what they can and cannot do.
316 Cf Phil 4:13.
317 *Adagia* II v 82

no one after the apostles claimed that there was no mystery in Scripture that was not clear to him. Once more you hammer away at the notion that I assert the same thing you assert because in my formulation I teach that 'all the good we do should be attributed to God,' for from this it follows that 'the mercy of God alone does everything and that our will does nothing but rather is passive; otherwise everything would not be attributed to God.'[318] You will never cease deafening your miserable readers with these assertions that are obviously and shamefully groundless, since in my *Discussion* I so distinctly and so clearly explain that there is no contradiction in saying that the sum and substance of a good deed should be attributed to God and asserting also that the human will does something, however tiny its share may be.

Then, after you have played the fool for so long that even I am ashamed of you, you cap it off with an exclamation giving yourself a hand, acting and applauding yourself at the same time. 'But this, you say, is the way a mind not consistent with itself is forced to speak, since it is uncertain and unskilled in religious matters.'[319] What is there left for you to do except usurp the name of God himself, now that you have pronounced so emphatically about the mind of someone else?[320] You hammer away so often at my inconsistency, even though you have not yet been able to show a single passage that proves I am inconsistent, and even if you had done so, you would have proved no more than that what happened to Augustine and Jerome also happened to Erasmus. For never to make a mistake, never not to know, never to regret having said something is peculiar to such a Gnostic and Stoic knower as you. But now tell me this: how are you consistent when you claim I am utterly ignorant of the truth and yet you charge me with the unforgivable sin? But no one who sins through ignorance is held accountable for his offence, for even Paul blasphemed against the gospel, and yet because 'he did it out of ignorance, he received mercy.'[321] Therefore my ignorance exonerates me from this charge, but you, who are ignorant of nothing, have good reason to be afraid that you will have this charge levelled against you, since you stoutly rescind the decisions of the church and assert anything and everything. Again, how can you reconcile the fact that I know nothing with the notion that, though I agree with you, I defend divergent

* * * * *

318 *De servo arbitrio* WA 18 614:22–4 / LW 33 35
319 *De servo arbitrio* WA 18 614:25–6 / LW 33 35–6
320 See 126 and n164 above.
321 1 Tim 1:13. Erasmus here deliberately indulges in sophistry, as does Folly when she makes the same argument (*The Praise of Folly* CWE 27 149).

positions to curry the favour of princes? You want to make me out to be a scoundrel who knowingly impugns the truth out of fear of princes, and at the same time you want to make me utterly ignorant of the truth. This is the way you, O man of the utmost consistency, mix fire with water[322] and, since you are always in the grip of an uncontrollable urge to slander, you follow now one impulse, now another, and so make statements which are inconsistent with one another. How often you excuse my attitude, how often you accuse it! Now you praise my good and peace-loving attitude; then I write against my conscience to curry the favour of tyrants and in my heart of hearts I act like Lucian or Epicurus.[323] But how do such things square with the Spirit of Christ, which you claim for yourself, though the world protests you do not have it?

[*Does God know things contingently?*]
Having felicitously achieved these feats, you go on to propose another example: 'whether God knows anything contingently'[324] and other points which are related to this question. And Luther wants them to be discussed before any and all Christians and to be handled in the presence of a mixed crowd. Here again you hammer away with those harsh words 'irreligious, oversubtle, futile.'[325] But my words were these: 'I would like to persuade persons of average intelligence not to dispute so stubbornly about such questions.'[326] I do not dissuade learned men with well-adapted and well-exercised minds from sober and religious investigation, but not beyond what is sufficient for us. Do such things as this seem to you so utterly intolerable? But how often does Hilary, when he undertakes to discuss the mysteries of the Holy Trinity, ward off the charge of being irreligious because he dares to treat in human words something which is beyond the powers of the human mind?[327] And Augustine makes similar prefatory remarks in

* * * * *

322  *Adagia* IV iii 94
323  See nn56 and 55 above.
324  *De servo arbitrio* WA 18 614–30 / LW 33 36–8
325  *De servo arbitrio* WA 18 614:28–9 / LW 33 36. See n238 above. Throughout this section (*De servo arbitrio* WA 18 614–30, LW 33 36–58) Luther uses this mocking refrain.
326  *A Discussion* 8
327  St Hilary (c 315–c 367), bishop of Poitiers and Latin church Father, wrote the first extensive treatise on the Trinity in Latin, *De Trinitate*; Erasmus edited his *Opera* (Basel: Johann Froben 1523). See Ep 1334, the preface to this edition. For his excusing himself for undertaking something beyond the power of man's mind see *De Trinitate* 2.5 CCSL 62A 41:1–42:36.

his book on the same subject.[328] Now bring together for me the fine points from the philosophers brought to bear on this question by those who enjoy the subtlety of Scotus[329] and seriously insist that these points should be discussed in front of a mixed crowd just as the Scotists discuss them! And here once again, drawing on your rhetoric, of which you profess to be ignorant as a pretext for making my *Discussion* seem more contemptible, you set out to heighten the hyperbole and thicken the plot by a comparison with the sophists. Though you have the very lowest opinion of them – as is clear from your books – still you begin almost to praise them to make me seem hateful. And you do this so lavishly and so craftily as to make me think that, just as you managed to please the princes in your pamphlet against the peasants[330] (which was not unjust but was excessively savage), so too by raging against me you might regain and reconcile to yourself the minds of the theologians, whom you nevertheless dignify in the meantime with no better name than sophists. Indeed I now seem to recognize some of the weapons you have taken from the books of Lee,[331] Latomus,[332] and Zúñiga[333] to hurl them at me. 'The sophists,' you say, 'since

\* \* \* \* \*

328  *De Trinitate* 1.1–3 CCSL 50 27–34. After this sentence LB X 1274A adds: 'Athanasius disputaturus adversos Arianos.' St Athanasius (c 296–373), bishop of Alexandria and Greek church Father, was renowned for his treatises against Arianism, some of which Erasmus published in *Lucubrationes aliquot* (Basel: Johann Froben 1527) together with works by St John Chrysostom (Allen Epp 1790, 1800).

329  Scotus was surnamed 'the subtle doctor.' See *A Discussion* n103.

330  See n105 above.

331  Edward Lee (c 1482–1544), English theologian, later archbishop of York, attacked Erasmus' 1516 and 1519 editions of the New Testament on philological grounds in *Annotationum libri duo* (Paris: Giles Gourmont 1520). Erasmus responded in *Apologia qua respondet invectivis Lei* (Antwerp: Michaël Hillen 1520; ed in Ferguson 236–303) and in *Responsio ad annotationes Lei* (Basel: Johann Froben 1520; LB IX 123–284), as well as in letters. See Rummel *Catholic Critics* I 95–120.

332  Jacobus Latomus (Jacques Masson; 1475–1544), canon at Cambrai, composed a traditionalist dialogue against Erasmus' trilingual reform of theology at Louvain: *De trium linguarum et studii theologici ratione* (Antwerp: Michaël Hillen 1519). Erasmus responded in *Apologia refellens suspiciones quorundum dictitantium dialogum D. Iacobi Latomi de tribus linguis ... conscriptum fuisse adversus ipsum* (Antwerp: J. Theobald 1519). See Rummel *Catholic Critics* I 63–93.

333  Diego López Zúñiga (d 1531), theologian at the University of Alcalá and an editor of the Complutensian Polyglot Bible, criticized Erasmus' editions of the New Testament in a series of publications. For them and Erasmus' replies, see Rummel *Catholic Critics* I 145–77, 247–50.

they know no rhetoric, employ their dialectic far better on this point: when they take up free will, they determine all the questions about it – whether it exists, what it is, what it does, how it is related, etc.'[334] Is it fair, Luther, for you to demand that I bring together in one discussion whatever questions the sophists ask concerning predestination, the will, the foreknowledge of God, good works, human merits, and that in a book which I undertook reluctantly and on which I spent hardly eight whole days (indeed that seemed like too much time) and which I wrote mostly, as I said, to show that my ideas are not the same as yours? If I had tried to do this, how you would have spit upon Erasmus for playing the sophist! And what would I have accomplished with those sophistic subtleties, even if I were quite expert in them, since you don't give a damn about them.'[335]

And yet it was just as shameful for you to write that in my *Discussion* I treated nothing more than whether free will exists as for you to hurl many other charges against me which are not based on fact but on whatever advances your case, as I have partly shown and will later show more clearly. Reread my *Discussion* and have the brazen impudence to dare to deny that I there define free will, that I distinguish kinds of grace, summarize various opinions, and then show to which opinions I mostly intend to take exception and go on to show to what extent I wish to handle this matter, and that afterwards in my book I explain in what part of the mind free will mostly resides and what it can do before grace and what it can do together with grace acting in us and how it stands towards God and towards the praise of good works and many other points. Go on now and throw it up to me that I brought nothing to the discussion except that one point, whether free will exists. Indeed, I deserved to be criticized instead for leaping the bounds of the proposed disputation and running all the way back to Adam before the Fall and to God himself, touching somewhat on his necessary will and action. In this passage, in fact, either I am deceived or you are hardly consistent. For this is what you say: 'Therefore in this book I will keep after you and all the sophists until you determine the powers and the deeds of free will.'[336] But a little before that you said that all the questions about free will had been determined by the sophists. Why do you demand that they do something they have fully accomplished? Why do you deny that I have done something that my *Discussion* itself manifestly shows that I have done even more fully than you prescribe? And here your spirit begins to

* * * * *

334 *De servo arbitrio* WA 18 615:6–8 / LW 33 37
335 Literally, 'care a hair about them' (*Adagia* I viii 4)
336 *De servo arbitrio* WA 18 615:9–10 / LW 33 37

warm up and you promise you will make me sorry I ever published the
*Discussion.*[337] This is something you should perform, not boast of so often,
lest it become, as the Greek say, an encomium before the victory.[338] For in
this whole first part of your book, what else have you done, I ask you, except triumph, lord it over the defeated, show your battle-trophies, and sing
paeans before you have even come up to our battleline?

And then, after this egregious promise, as if you were getting down
to the matter at hand, you teach us that the foreknowledge of God and the
will of God are no less unchangeable than God himself, that nothing whatever happens without his knowledge or consent, and that his foreknowledge cannot be deceived nor his will thwarted (as happens to us), and that
his will does not cease after the deed is done (as our will to build a house
ceases when the house is built, though the work remains).[339] Are these the
recondite mysteries you are teaching? Is there anyone who has read six
pages of theology who does not know these things or is there anyone insane enough to deny them? But meanwhile you do not distinguish the signified will from the efficacious will: the latter is completely immutable but
the former is somehow mutable, since often what he commands is not done
and what he forbids is done.[340] Nor do you distinguish God's acts of willing as applied to things outside himself and to God's natural will or as applied to his internal actions.[341] You also do not distinguish God's absolute
from his conditional will[342] nor his will from his acts of willing. God did
will to create the world: has he not yet ceased to will to create the world?
He did will his Son to assume a human body; has he not yet ceased to will
it?[343]

\* \* \* \* \*

337  *De servo arbitrio* WA 18 615:10–11 / LW 33 37
338  *Adagia* I vii 55
339  *De servo arbitrio* WA 18 615:12–616:12 / LW 33 37–8
340  The signified will is the law God reveals for his creation, and sometimes this
     law is not carried out, so that it is not entirely fixed or unchanging (Oberman
     *Harvest* 476). The efficacious will absolutely and immutably effects what it
     wills.
341  Actions such as God's knowledge of himself and the interaction of the three
     persons of the Trinity are interior (*ad intra*); actions such as creation and in-
     carnation are exterior (*ad extra*). See DTC I 399–400. The translation follows '&
     ad voluntatem' (Froben February 1526 and LB X 1275B) rather than 'ad volun-
     tatem' (Froben July 1526).
342  See *A Discussion* n234.
343  These rhetorical questions (the answer to both is yes) depend on a distinction
     between God's will in general and his individual acts of will. God willed to
     create the world, but once it was created he no longer wills to create it, since to

How cleverly, indeed, you define for us what is contingent: 'what happens to us contingently and as if by chance and without deliberation.'[344] Here for the first time I learn something abstruse: to be contingent is to happen contingently, as if you were to say that an artful work is one made with art. Then what is 'as if by chance'? Is it something which is not chance but as if it were chance? Then you add, 'without our knowing about it ahead of time.' But the word 'contingent' means something quite different to Aristotle, who distinguishes the contingent from fortune and chance. For he opposes the contingent to what is necessary; he attributes fortune to living things and chance to inanimate objects.[345] Therefore we do things contingently not only when we do them by chance and without deliberation but

\* \* \* \* \*

create is to bring from non-being into being and after creation the world has being, not non-being. So too with the incarnation: the Son cannot *become* flesh once he *is* flesh. William Courtenay points out a similar distinction between God's power and his specific acts by which he exercises it: 'Lombard introduced a similar example with regard to God's knowledge of creation. Lombard's response is Abelardian. What is known and affirmed remains the same across time: only the tense form changes ... Later in distinction forty-four Lombard applied the same solution to God's will and power, again drawing directly on Abelard. Before the Incarnation God was able (*potuit*) to be incarnate, able to die and rise again; now he is not able (*non potest*). But that does not mean that God's power is limited by time because he was once able to do what he is now not able to do. "Just as he always knows what he at some time knew, and always wills what he at some time willed ... so he is always able to do what he at some time was able to do, nor is any of his power diminished' (*Capacity* 53–4). See John Duns Scotus *God and Creatures: The Quodlibetal Questions* trans Felix Alluntis and A. B. Wolter (Princeton 1975) Question Twelve: 'Is the Relation of a Creature to God as Creator the Same as the Relation to God as Conserver?' (270–83): 'The divine volition remains the same in regard to anything that is able to be willed' (273); 'The relation of a creature to God as creator and conserver can be said to be the same' (272), citing Augustine *Super Genesim* 4.12.2 PL 34 304: 'For the power of the creator, omnipotent and supporting all, is the cause by which every creature subsists. If such power should cease to rule what has been created, all would cease to be and nature would vanish.' Erasmus' statement is in answer to Luther's too obvious declaration just above 'that his will does not cease after the deed is done.'

344 *De servo arbitrio* WA 18 616:10–11 / LW 33 38
345 See *Physics* 2.6 197b20–2 and *On Interpretation* 9 18b9. Augustine, Boethius, and the scholastics understood contingency according to Aristotle: the contingent is something that might or might not happen according to free choice. Luther, on the other hand, identified contingency with chance or fortune. See McSorley 233–5.

also when we knowingly and willingly do something which we could have chosen not to do – just as I am now writing these things not without deliberation and not out of necessity but by the choice of the will which could have chosen not to write if it had wanted to. Therefore what you show us here is no more than that you aspire to sophistical cleverness, but not very felicitously. The sophists are also tormented by this question: when God knows something inherently contingent – that is, something that depends on human choice, as, for example, when someone sits down who could have stood up if he wished – they ask whether God foreknows in some manner contingently, not because his foreknowledge can be deceived but because the object of his foreknowledge is contingent.[346] But I wonder why you plucked this passage out of the middle of the *Discussion*[347] and thought it should be handled here instead of in its proper place, under necessity of the consequent and of consequence.[348] You claim that you want to handle the matter crudely, but you envelop it with such confusing language that you seem not only not to understand what I wrote but also not to understand your own speech. But because I am pressed for time and because this subject cannot be concluded briefly, it is better to save it for more careful treatment in the proper place.[349]

I must hasten to the remaining points. You want to prove you are very learned in whatever way you can, and so, just as before you taught me from Horace and Quintilian[350] that I should have treated whether it exists, what it is, what sort of thing it is, etc, so now you teach me from the poets that all things happen by sheer necessity, which they call fate. It has such force that it also involves the immortal gods themselves and even Jupiter, the highest of them, in inevitable necessity. And now at last the poets are wise men, more perspicacious even than the philosophers. So praiseworthy is anyone who thinks as you do. Thereupon Virgil is brought in on this point,[351] an unshakeable witness to the truth, who teaches that all the

\* \* \* \* \*

346 On the question of contingency in both *De libero arbitrio* and *De servo arbitrio* see W.L. Craig *The Problem of Divine Foreknowledge from Aristotle to Suarez* (Leiden 1988) 105–7, 141–2, 163–5.

347 *A Discussion* 52

348 See *A Discussion* n234 above and the exchange in February 1524 between Erasmus and Ludwig Baer, his theology teacher at Paris, on this distinction (Epp 1419 and 1420).

349 Erasmus takes up this topic in *Hyperaspistes* 2 LB X 1426D–1428C.

350 See 148 and nn287 and 286 above.

351 At *De servo arbitrio* WA 18 617:23–618:18 LW 33 41 Luther cites *Aeneid* 10.467, 6.146, 6.882, 2.291, also attributing Manilius *Astronomica* 4.14 to Virgil.

endeavours of mankind frequently turn out differently than they expected, if Fate or the three Fates[352] will it. But here we are not arguing about outcomes but whether our will does anything in matters that concern eternal salvation. I believe you threw in this section deliberately to refresh your readers and give them some pleasure, since the rest is so tasteless that it had long since turned their stomach. But what does this have to do with the turbot?[353] You set out to prove that it is godly and holy for anyone, in any forum whatever, to argue both sides of such questions as these, which never reach a final solution, and now you leave off what you began and assert that all things occur by sheer necessity. If this is established and absolutely true, what is the point of tormenting oneself with disputations? On the other hand, if what the church has decided is true and indubitable, it is not safe for the ignorant multitude to hear the reasons, protestations, and oaths for the other side. But this is what I was urging, that simple people be content to accept the Catholic opinion, believing and holding what they have received, that is, the very thing you have undertaken to impugn. You demand that this subject matter, which can be handled soberly among the learned, be called up for public debate, before a mixed audience in this theatre of mortals, as if it were a doubtful point. In Italy almost every year preachers bring up once more the question of the resurrection of the dead, which can be soberly debated in the universities, as no one would deny. But this matter contributed so much to piety that the bishop of Rome forbade it to be aired before the people.[354]

But I will touch lightly on the defects of the remaining points. You teach us quite devoutly that God's will is omnipotent, that God's foreknowledge is absolutely certain, and that if anyone doubts this he does not

* * * * *

352 In Latin the 'Parcae,' the three goddesses who spin, measure, and cut the thread of life
353 See n209 above.
354 Erasmus possibly alludes to the controversy about Pietro Pomponazzi's *De immortalitate animae* (Bologna: Justianus Leonardus Ruberiensis 1516), which denied the immortality of the soul and by implication the resurrection of the body. In December 1513 at the Fifth Council of the Lateran, Leo x proclaimed a bull condemning those who denied the individual immortality of the soul, and in 1518 he issued a papal brief condemning Pomponazzi's mortalism; see Ludwig Pastor *History of the Popes* trans Frederick I. Antrobus et al, 40 vols (St Louis 1923–53) v 155–8, viii 389. See also M. L. Pine, *Pietro Pomponazzi, Radical Philosopher of the Renaissance* (Padua 1986) 59–60, 127 and John W. O'Malley *Praise and Blame in Renaissance Rome: Rhetoric, Doctrine and Reform in the Sacred Orators of the Papal Court, c. 1450–1521* (Durham, NC 1979) 152–5.

know God at all and cannot firmly trust in his promises because he can be deceived and can lie.[355] I grant that such statements are in accord with piety, and I say as much not infrequently in my own writings. But what do they have to do with me, since my point is that they should not be debated, particularly in front of simple people? But if you believe it is certain and indubitable that God knows everything with necessity and nothing contingently, even if we were to agree with your arguments, it would still be quite fitting that we should argue about it to keep us from thinking God is ignorant or deceptive. For just as you think we must argue about free will because it is ungodly not to know that our will is merely passive and that only grace is active, by the same token we will be compelled to call this into question. And yet the theologians who dispute about whether God knows anything contingently, steadfastly affirm what you affirm, that God's foreknowledge cannot be deceived, that God cannot lie, that we should trust most firmly in God's promises, and they do not think that because something happens contingently the certainty of divine foreknowledge is placed at risk, as is elegantly explained by Lorenzo Valla.[356] But they define the contingent somewhat more correctly than you do.[357]

[*Other unsuitable topics*]
As if what you said here amounted to anything, in the next section you hurl the lightning-bolt of your foul abuse at me, saying I teach that God is ignorant, that the faith should be scorned so that we will let go of the promises of God, and many other things 'that even Epicurus would hardly prescribe.' Not content with that, I condemn, I trample Christians under my feet and the whole content of Christianity too – indeed, what not? – because I advise those of moderate intelligence not to engage in contentious disputations on such subjects but to hold to what the church has handed down. And from this you draw the conclusion, logician that you are, that 'my book is so ungodly, blasphemous, and sacrilegious that anything like

\* \* \* \* \*

355 *De servo arbitrio* WA 18 618:19–619:15 / LW 33 42
356 See *A Discussion* n48. See also Valla's *De libero arbitrio dialogus* ed Chomarat 36–8 nos 57–62 trans Trinkaus in *The Renaissance Philosophy of Man* 167–8. Like Luther, Valla denied that man's actions are contingent, but by doing so he did not affirm that they are necessary; and he held that God's infallible foreknowledge and absolute necessity do not eliminate man's free will; see McSorley 327–8 and Trinkaus *Image and Likeness* 165–8.
357 *De servo arbitrio* WA 18 616:7–12 / LW 33 38. On Luther's failure to understand contingency in Aristotelian terms, see McSorley 233–4, 256, 259, 315.

it is nowhere to be found.'[358] If you are ashamed of such accusations I do not know; certainly you would be if you had any sense of shame. But in the next section you soften your fiercely abusive language: 'Such frightful things as this,' you say,[359] 'a man is bound to babble if he has undertaken to support a  bad cause and plays a part that is foreign to him against his conscience.'[360] What you call a bad cause, I, together with the church, call the very best cause; and though I undertook it with feelings of reluctance, still I did so with a completely clear conscience, whether the choice was felicitous or not. And not the favour or the fear of any prince, not even your savagery, could then or could ever bring enough pressure to make me knowingly impugn what is true or defend what I know to be false in matters which concern godliness. Thus when you hammer away again and again at the notion that I yielded to favour or fear against my conscience, you make it clear again and again that you are either miserably deceived or are making up the most malicious lies. As for your admonishing me how risky it is to teach about godliness and begging God's mercy for me,[361] I am not the least bit offended, and to keep from seeming ungrateful I will return the favour by admonishing you in the same phrasing and begging God's mercy for you. But as for your professing that, though I have raised some questions truly sophistical and superfluous, still those who 'defile gold' are more acceptable than I, 'who throw out the gold together with the dung,' see how completely I disagree with you.[362] For I think that those who dispute about frivolous questions are more acceptable than those who by their disputations call back into debate matters about which the church has long since decreed that there should be no disagreement, having condemned what is false and approved what is true. You remove yourself from the ranks and the partisanship of the sophists,[363] but you do so in vain, since all who contend with you cry out that they are dealing with a most crafty sophist; you have not eliminated the sophistical theology but changed it.

\* \* \* \* \*

358 *De servo arbitrio* WA 18 620:10–12 / LW 33 43
359 The two Basel editions of 1526 both have the error *inquit* 'he says,' which is corrected to *inquis* 'you say' in LB X 1276E.
360 *De servo arbitrio* WA 18 620:15–17 / LW 33 43–4; *Adagia* I i 91
361 *De servo arbitrio* WA 18 620:20–3 / LW 33 44
362 *De servo arbitrio* WA 18 620:23–37 / LW 33 44; on defiling gold cf Lam 4:1, to which Luther refers.
363 *De servo arbitrio* WA 18 621:9–11 / LW 33 45

'You ought to have spoken against me,' you say, 'unless you want to waste your paper and your time,'[364] as if in that book I were opposing you alone. I am opposing those who take away free will like you, but do not do so in the same manner. And even if I had been writing particularly against you, was it improper to blend in anything that did not pertain to you? In that book some points pertain to Karlstadt, some to Melanchthon, some to Scotus. In one passage I admonish the reader not to think I am speaking against you, 'whom I do not know,' but rather against others I do know.[365] In this book which you specifically wrote against me by name, there is much that has nothing to do with me, as I have already partly shown and as I will later demonstrate more fully. Where did you get the idea that I wrote the *Discussion* specifically against you? That is not what the title indicates, and the work itself clearly shows otherwise, but you imagine this, or rather you fabricate it, so as to make it seem more just for you to rage against me. That is the reason why in your disputation you take me to task time after time for falsely holding you up to ridicule for interpreting 'stretch out your hand' as meaning 'grace will stretch out' and so on.[366] But in fact Karlstadt[367] said this when he responded to Eck;[368] his words in his first response are as follows: 'For grace moves the hand and stretches it out.' Again in his third response: 'I have sufficiently indicated that grace stretches out the hand of our counsel towards the good.' Again in the same response he interprets 'charity believes everything, hopes everything, etc.'[369] as meaning 'grace makes us patient, believers and doers.'[370] Go on now and complain

* * * * *

364 *De servo arbitrio* WA 18 621:8–9, 11 / LW 33 45. Erasmus combines parts of two sentences to make Luther say this.

365 *A Discussion* 19

366 *De servo arbitrio* WA 18 700:12–701:30 / LW 33 161–4; *A Discussion* 58

367 See *A Discussion* n4 and n97 above.

368 Johann Maier of Eck (1486–1543), theology professor at Ingolstadt and vigorous defender of Catholicism against the Protestant reformers, was also regarded somewhat apprehensively by Erasmus. In his *Obelisci* (February 1518) Eck wrote against Luther's theses on indulgences. He was a major participant in the famous Leipzig debate (27 June to 16 July 1919), reporting his version of it in *Defensio contra amarulentas D. Andreae Bodenstein Carolstatini invectiones* (Augsburg: S. Grimm and M. Wirsung 1518) and *Disputatio Iohannis Eccii et Andreae Carolstadii et Martini Lutheri* (Erfurt: M. Maler 1519). See CEBR at 'Eck' and Seitz *Leipziger Disputation*.

369 1 Cor 13:7

370 Karlstadt's account of the Leipzig debate and his continuation of it can be found in his *Epistola adversus ineptam et ridiculam inventionem Joannis Echii* (Leipzig: V. Schumann 1519) and his *Confutatio* (Wittenberg: M. Lotter 1520).

that you are falsely held up to ridicule! Francis Lambert is sufficiently impudent to make the same accusation against me and to call me a deceiver
in the commentary which he wrote on Hosea, as if I were making up such
lies against the 'brothers.'[371] I had written that some things are true which
nevertheless ought not to be drummed into the ears of the people or ought
not to be set forth in indiscriminate language – as, for example, when certain sophists talk such nonsense as this: 'God is everywhere'; and if that is
granted they conclude 'therefore he is there,' and they name a place which
I out of modesty did not dare to name, and said instead the lair of a bee-
tle[372] (you suspect I mean a privy,[373] though that has nothing to do with it).
At this point you agree with me and you confess that it was right for me
to admonish people to speak about theological subjects conscientiously and
soberly and that it is not enough just to tell the truth if you do not also tell it
circumspectly and in pure language.[374] And nevertheless here again I teach

* * * * *

For these responses quoted by Erasmus, see Seitz *Leipziger Disputation* 16 and
21–2. Actually the first response to Eck was on the first day of the debate. The
third response was on the next day and was to Eck's second and third points:
*Ad secundum* and *Ad tertiam*. Erasmus conflates the second and third.

371 François Lambert of Avignon (c 1487–1530), a former Franciscan Observant,
oversaw the reformation in Hesse and sought to make it a model evangelical territory. Erasmus is referring to his *In ... Oseam ... commentarii* (Strasbourg: Johann Herwagen, March 1525). Fols 98v–135v of this book contain
a *Digressio ... de arbitrio hominis in solo Christo vere libero, in se autem multis
nominibus maxime seruo*, which is directed especially against Erasmus' *Discussion*. There (fol 125r) Lambert accuses Erasmus of lying: 'Instant adhuc lib-
ertatis huius mendacissimae assertores, imponentes nobis quod sic perperam
enarremus scripturas: "Facite vobis cor nouum, id est: gratia faciat vobis cor
nouum. Ad quod velis extende manum, id est: gratia extendat manum tuam
ad quod ipsa velit" ... Quis, obsecro, vt de reliquis sileam, me ita enarrasse
audiuit aut legit? Quis eiusmodi impostoribus de nobis obloquentibus credet,
vbi tam aperto mendacio talia de nobis scribere non verentur?' ('Defenders
of this most illusory freedom still attack us, falsely claiming that we interpret Scripture wrongly in this way: "Make yourselves a new heart; that is, let
grace make a new heart for you. Stretch out your hand to whatever you want;
that is, let grace extend your hand to whatever it wants" ... To say nothing
of other examples, who, I beg you, ever heard me making such interpretations? Who will believe such liars when they defame us, since they are not
afraid to write such patent falsehoods about us?') We owe this quotation to
the kindness of Cornelis Augustijn.
372 *A Discussion* 11 and n29. Cf *Adagia* III vii 1 LB II 867F, where beetles are said
to roll balls of dung into their lair.
373 *De servo arbitrio* WA 18 621:16–18 / LW 33 45
374 *De servo arbitrio* WA 18 622:15–623:17 / LW 33 47

Epicureanism, 'I have descended to the level of contemning and affronting God and Holy Scripture,' I have lapsed into blasphemy and sacrilege. For everywhere such blandishments flow abundantly from your charity.

But to turn to your dilemma. 'If you are talking,' you say, 'about what is contained in Holy Scripture, all of that is clear and salutary and there are no circumstances in which it should not be brought before the public. But if you are talking about something else, that has nothing to do with us.'[375] I will not recall here that the Jews did not allow certain books of Scripture, including Genesis, to be read by anyone who was not more than thirty years old, but that point will be discussed elsewhere.[376] As for that 'nothing to do with us,' pay attention. If a physician who was urging a sick man with a fever not to eat foods that generate heat should distinguish various kinds of fever, indicating what should be avoided or sought for in each case, would the sick man say 'what have these to do with me? tell me about my fever'? Would not the physician reply, 'These cases do pertain to you, to keep you from thinking it is safe for you to eat any kind of food whenever you please.' Just so you, Luther, teach that whatever questions arise out of Holy Scripture ought to be handled in the presence of any person whatsoever. To avoid that I distinguish kinds of questions. First it is not pious to treat those points 'that God wishes should remain unknown to us,' such as the last day.[377] Then there are 'points he wants to be extremely well known to us'; these, I urge, should even be committed to memory.[378] There are some points which it is right to examine up to a  certain point, but not beyond what is sufficient. What goes beyond that should be reserved for that 'time when we will see God face to face, for now we perceive him in a puzzling mirror.'[379] In this class I place questions concerning free will and points related to it and likewise questions concerning the distinction of persons or the difference between generation and procession.[380] In the final category I reckon certain points which, though they are true, can still not be spoken of before just any audience without endangering piety and concord and which should be set forth prudently. And here I place many points which you publish in the German language for uneducated people,

\* \* \* \* \*

375 *De servo arbitrio* WA 18 621:5–6 / LW 33 45
376 In his *Commentarium in Hezechielem* CCSL 75 3–4, Jerome says that the beginning and end of Ezekiel, together with the beginning of Genesis and the Song of Songs, were traditionally considered so difficult by the Jews that no one under the age of thirty was allowed to read them.
377 Matt 24:36 and Mark 13:32; *A Discussion* 10
378 *A Discussion* 10
379 1 Cor 13:12; *A Discussion* 8–9
380 That is, questions concerning the Trinity

such as the liberty of the gospel,[381] which, if treated in judicious sermons on the right occasion, are not fruitless; but if they are treated in such sermons as yours, you see what fruit they produce. I would place in the same class your doctrine on the necessity of all things,[382] even if it were quite true; as it is, since it is false and impious, it brings with it even graver danger when it is bruited about in public. Go on now and claim that these things have nothing to do with you. But I will take up this matter elsewhere. For now it is sufficient to have pointed it out in passing. And so I am not bringing human guilt into the issue, nor am I condemning Scripture because of the offences of preachers,[383] but rather I am reproaching those who handle Scripture otherwise than they should, among whom I also number you.

But here again you confront me with the horns of a dilemma: if it is right to discuss free will, why do you forbid it? but if it is not, why do you put forth your *Discussion*?[384] I give the same answer I gave before: you forced me to treat these matters by dragging the question out of the universities into drinking parties, and I handle it differently than you do, for I do not treat it as a debatable point but rather I condemn your doctrine and defend the position which it is impious to doubt, pious and devout to hold and defend.[385] Now, even though you were to confess that it makes a difference what words are used to explain the truth of Scripture before the people, and even though I were to grant that what you teach is true, judge for yourself what contribution to piety is made by those who proclaim to the ignorant mob such things as these: there is no free will; our will has no effect but rather God works in us both our good deeds and our bad ones. I know some who draw on Thomas[386] and others and

* * * * *

381 In 1520 Luther wrote *Tractatus de libertate christiana* (WA 7 49–73) and in the same year translated it into German (WA 7 20–38).

382 *De servo arbitrio* WA 18 617:19 / LW 33 39–40: 'Adeo stat et permanet invicta sententia: Omnia necessitate fieri' ('Thus the proposition stands, and remains invincible, that all things happen by necessity'). Cf *Assertio* article 36 (WA 7 146:8 / 306).

383 Discussing the foolish questions and discussions of the scholastics, Luther had said their faults are irrelevant to the question and that 'you ought not to blame Christian doctrine because the wicked handle it badly' (*De servo arbitrio* WA 18 620:35–6 / LW 33 44).

384 *De servo arbitrio* WA 18 622:10–11 / LW 33 46

385 In *De libero arbitrio* and *Hyperaspistes* Erasmus frequently professed to be discussing, not asserting, but here he declares his own position.

386 See n308 above. *Summa Theologiae* II–II q 154 on lust (including fornication, adultery, incest, seduction, rape, bestiality, and sodomy) might provide enough basic material for a fairly lurid sermon.

even on Juvenal[387] to portray before an indiscriminate crowd all sorts of obscene passions. Such people are not reproached for teaching falsehoods but rather for presenting truths that are fruitless because they are inopportune. That certainly applies to your adherents, for I did not write about you exclusively. What I say about three gods[388] applies to these same people: although Pierre d'Ailly and theologians who agree with him think that this axiom is in some sense true,[389] nevertheless it would cause great offence if it were discussed before the people. Among the learned it would cause no offence because they know that the word 'god' does not always refer to the divine essence but is sometimes taken to mean 'person,' as when we say 'God begets God' and 'Jesus is the son of God.' The learned take it to mean no more than that there are three persons, to each of whom the word 'God' is applicable. D'Ailly does not absolutely deny that it is possible to speak of three 'omnipotents' and three 'eternals.' And if he did deny it, it would still follow from what he has conceded, namely that it is possible to speak of three Gods (though not in an unqualified way). For just as according to logic it is not absurd to speak of three wise men with one and the same wisdom, three good men with the same goodness, three omnipotent persons with the same omnipotence, three beings with the same essence, three persons willing in the same will, so too I think it is not impious to say that there are three Gods with the same deity. For to be God pertains to his substance no less than to be wise. But D'Ailly does not assert such things, and neither do I. I have brought it up for this reason: to show that it is possible that certain things may be in some sense true which nevertheless it would be inexpedient to proclaim before an unlearned audience. Then too those who know Hebrew tell us that in Genesis 'God made heaven and earth' is in the plural number, for they think that in this way it is made clear that the same nature and operation is in the three persons.[390] I wanted

* * * * *

387 Roman satirist (c 60–140 CE) whose description of vices in Roman society was especially scurrilous.

388 *A Discussion* 11; *De servo arbitrio* WA 18 623:25–7 / LW 33 48

389 See *A Discussion* n30.

390 The Hebrew *elohim* is plural. For the use of this passage to show that the author of Genesis knew of the Trinity, see Magister Bandinus' commentary (1518) on Peter Lombard's *Sententiae* (I dist 2 PL 192 973D–974A): 'Item cum scriptum sit: *In principio creavit Deus caelum et terram* ... sciendum est quod Hebraica veritate habet *eloym*, ubi Deus scribitur, quod est plurale hujus singularis *el*, et interpretur *dii* vel *judices*. Quod ergo *eloym*, non *el* dixit Moyses, personarum pluralitatem indicavit' ('Likewise when it is written "In the beginning God created heaven and earth," we should know that in Hebrew it reads *eloym*,

to mention these peripheral matters because you proclaim in an unqualified way that this axiom is false and completely foreign to Holy Scripture.

Now to turn to the article on confession and satisfaction,[391] which I brought forward only as an example, neither affirming nor denying what is said about it, since I am dealing with a different matter. And lest you should ever be anything but abusive against Erasmus, who handled your teaching quite courteously and did not injure you in any way, you throw it up to me that out of fear of the pope's tyranny I would not dare to condemn confession.[392] I am not so afraid of the pope that if it were clear to me that confession should be condemned, I would not dare to express my opinion among learned men and to speak softly about it in the ears of friends who are disturbed about it, and finally to devote my energies to have it done away with, without any uproar, by the authority of the princes. But as it is, I myself observe it, and I preach nothing different from what I practise, not simply because the bishop of Rome has prescribed it but much more because the Christian people have accepted it. For just as I do not approve of all regulations, so too I am very far from the opinion of those who think that all human regulations and customs are to be rejected and replaced by others, which are perhaps harder to bear than those about which the common people now complain. In fact, even among the very persons who maintain confession, I see that the more prudent do not dare to pronounce whether it was instituted by Christ, or gathered from Holy Scripture, or derived from a general regulation of the church. And is it treading on eggshells[393] not

* * * * *

which is the plural of the singular *el*, and means "gods" or "judges." Therefore, that Moses said *eloym*, not *el*, indicated the plurality of the persons'). Petrus Comestor (c 1100–1180) had made the same point long before (*Historia libri Genesis* PL 198 1055B). The idea was commonplace because it appeared in Paulus de Santa Maria's *Additio* 1 to Nicholas of Lyra's widely known commentary *Biblia 1498* 1 sig c1 (on Gen 1:1). It was also frequently argued that Genesis 1.26 ('Let *us* make man to *our* own image') indicates that man was especially honoured in creation by the entire Trinity; see Alcher of Clairvaux PL 40 805–6 and Peter Lombard *Sententiae* 1 dist 2.4 PL 192 526–7.

391 Erasmus refers to Luther's article on confession in the *Assertio* WA 7 112–22. Erasmus mentioned confession in *A Discussion* 11–12. Luther replied in *De servo arbitrio* WA 18 623:28–624:27 / LW 33 48–50. Erasmus had just published a brief treatise on confession, *Exomologesis sive modus confitendi* (Basel: Froben 1524).

392 *De servo arbitrio* WA 18 623:28–624:3 / LW 33 48

393 Literally, 'walking on the tips of the grain.' Cf Virgil *Aeneid* 7.809 (of Camilla's nimbleness) and Homer *Iliad* 20.226–9. The expression was proverbial and was used by St Jerome; see Otto no 165. Here it means avoiding trouble through prudence.

to make any pronouncement on those points about which the church has not yet pronounced with a clear voice? Here I am not accusing either you or your adherents, but rather I profess what sort of attitude I myself have. Therefore, Luther, if your hatred of Erasmus has not completely blinded you, see how groundless that virulent language of yours really is: 'And so,' you say, 'setting God and conscience aside for the moment – for what is it to Erasmus what God wants in such matters or what is fitting for his conscience – you launch an assault against a straw man and accuse the common people, etc.'[394] If you should ever pour forth such insults against some outrageous misdeed, one already demonstrated as factual, it might be called vehemence. As it is, since you never cease to rattle on in this fashion and never stop even when there is no justification for such insults and you have not proven what you assume, there is no one, Luther, who does not perceive that this uncontrolled abusiveness bespeaks a mental disorder in you which I would rather contemn than imitate.

After this you attack my opinion, having great fun as you ridicule and deride my analogy, a figure of speech 'with which I wish to display my abundant eloquence, an orator well-supplied indeed but understanding none of the things I say.'[395] I am so accustomed to such insults that I would almost take pleasure in them if it were not that I fear this savage attitude of yours will enmesh the world in the worst sort of disasters. For what Erasmus loses is of no importance whatever, as long as the gospel reigns. This was my opinion: just as there are some diseases which do less harm if they are endured than if they are cured, so too some practices have crept in among the people of Christ which it is better to tolerate than to make the evil worse by trying to eradicate it.[396] On this point I did not provide you with any examples, because it is not safe to do so and is not relevant to the issue. But I want you to consider just this single case. If we imagine that the princes treated their peasants very tyrannically (and it is not clear to me that they did), which was more advantageous to the peasants: to bear with their very unjust lords or to experience the effects of a rebellion in which so many thousands perished and the injury was so far from being removed that the yoke was doubled and rendered even more grievous?[397] These words do not so much accuse your adherents as they excuse me, for it has often been thrown up to me that I have not aimed my pen sharply

* * * * *

394 *De servo arbitrio* WA 18 624:3–6 / LW 33 48
395 *De servo arbitrio* WA 18 625:1–6 / LW 33 50
396 *A Discussion* 12; *De servo arbitrio* WA 18 627:3–23 / LW 33 53
397 See n102 above.

LB X 1279C

enough at popes and bishops.[398] And yet they apply to you also, since you take them upon yourself.[399] For even if that cause of yours is as important as you make it out to be, nevertheless that misplaced abusiveness of yours, which spares no mortal at all, has as its result that you not only accomplish nothing but also you double and exacerbate the tyranny you strive to eliminate and you advance those whom you wish to suppress. There is some methodical way of eradicating an evil which has stretched out its roots wide and deep. Magnify your cause now as much as you wish; the better it is, the more you are to blame, since you play the physician so badly. Nor is anyone at odds with the word of God, as you thunder out so often, but with your interpretations. Look now and see whether the apostles introduced the teachings of the gospel into the world with such methods as these, which you use to restore it, as you say. Did they ever slander the innocent? Did they ever rant and rave against anyone with such scurrilous language? Did they turn up their noses at anyone? Did they take up the cause of the gospel with trickery, slander, and threats? Did they ever use such impudent language? Here I could mention many other things, which I hold back; perhaps your insight can divine what I mean. If you know that these uprisings have a divine origin, I do not know it, and I will neither originate nor support them. But still I do not cease to pray to Christ that, whatever their source and however they have progressed, the omnipotent artificer may turn them to his own glory and the welfare of the church.

[*The imperative of expedience*]
You are mightily offended by this opinion of mine: 'It is permissible to speak the truth, but it is not expedient to do so to all persons whatsoever, at any time whatsoever, in any way whatsoever.'[400] And it is quite out of place for me to cite Paul's saying 'All things are permitted to me but not all things

* * * * *

398 Erasmus does not accuse those who were stirred up to rebellion by Luther's harsh criticism of the clergy; but the result of the rebellion justifies Erasmus in refraining from violent criticism of the hierarchy.

399 At *De servo arbitrio* WA 18 626:8–627:2 / LW 33 52–3 Luther insisted that tumults such as the Peasants' War are a salutary and necessary effect of spreading the word of God.

400 *A Discussion* 12. In an extended passage Erasmus debates with Luther on preaching the word of God in different ways according to the capacities and sensitivities of one's audience or readership. While they both argue from scriptural authority, the issue of decorum (suiting speech to the subject and the audience) was also central to traditional rhetorical theory; see *Rhetorica ad Herennium* 3.11; Quintilian *Institutio oratoria* 2.13, 9.1; and Hoffman 176–84.

are expedient,'[401] because in that place Paul is not dealing with preaching the truth, which he wishes to be preached to all persons whatsoever, at any time or place, in any way, but rather with avoiding giving scandal to the weak. Let us grant what you say, but this opinion by its very nature has a wider application in that the charity which persuaded Paul to abstain from what would otherwise be permissible also persuaded him to dispense the teaching of the gospel according to what is advantageous for mankind. And now see how much less applicable are the texts you bring up:[402] 'Preach the word, urge it in season, out of season'; and 'Only let the word of God be proclaimed';[403] again, 'The word of God is not bound';[404] and 'Go, preach the gospel to all creatures.'[405] For these words 'in season, out of season' are spoken as a figure of speech, not indicating that the word is to be preached where it is not appropriate but rather commending to us the urgency of preaching the gospel, although you ought to have added what is added in that passage: 'argue, entreat with all gentleness and instruction,'[406] for even your own adherents require gentleness in you. But when he writes to the Philippians he does not praise those who preach the gospel disingenuously, but rather he rejoices that their disingenuous effort nevertheless results in the advancement of the gospel.[407] Moreover Paul, though bound, rejoices that 'the word of God is not bound,' but rather is spread more widely every day.[408] I ask you, did Paul teach everyone the same things you are teaching? When I caution that instruction should be tempered according to what is advantageous for the listeners, do I bind the word of God? For that is what you accuse me of and at the same time you assume that whatever you teach is the word of God, so that all that remains is for you to become Christ, preaching the gospel anew. But just as it is not clear to us by what spirit you are led, so too we are not yet persuaded that whatever you teach is the word of God. I do not know of what mettle others are made, but I firmly profess that I am of the number of those who would rather die ten times over than even once hinder the course of the word of God. But we were

\* \* \* \* \*

401  1 Cor 6:12
402  Luther introduces a series of biblical texts to prove that the truth cannot be modulated (*De servo arbitrio* WA 18 628:18–629:4 / LW 33 55–60).
403  2 Tim 4:2 and Phil 1:18. Luther refers to these texts only by an indirect paraphrase (*De servo arbitrio* WA 18 628:27–9 / LW 33 56).
404  2 Tim 2:9
405  Mark 16:15
406  2 Tim 4:2
407  See Phil 1:15–18.
408  2 Tim 2:9

not talking about that, but about the questions which are now shaking the world.

And yet the apostles were at first commanded to preach the kingdom of God, hiding the fact that Jesus is the Anointed One.[409] And in the beginning of his preaching Peter called Jesus a man, keeping silent about his divine nature.[410] And Paul acted no differently among the Athenians.[411] He has milk with which he nourishes the weak, he has solid food which he feeds to the strong,[412] and he has wisdom which he does not make known to just anyone, or on every street corner, but rather delivers secretly to those advanced in perfection.[413] This place you do not cite correctly, saying 'wisdom concealed in mystery,'[414] whereas the Greek has 'in secret he speaks wisdom which is hidden.' Indeed, even the apostles themselves, at Christ's command, shake off the dust from their feet, spurning those who reject the preaching of the gospel,[415] and in Acts they command the gentiles to abstain from what has been offered to idols, from what has been strangled, from blood and whoredom,[416] and they do not immediately teach that the Law is to be entirely abrogated. Finally, it is the rudiments of the philosophy of Christ that are handed down to the catechumens until they become advanced enough for what is more hidden Heb 6[:1]: 'Wherefore let us stop speaking about the rudiments of Christianity and go on to what is more advanced, etc.' But even these rudiments the church is not in the habit of casually entrusting to those who ask for initiation, unless their sponsors have pledged that there is no secret malice. And they are called mysteries; that is, the sacraments are so called. Is the reason they are called mysteries, that is, secrets, that they are to be disseminated to any person whatsoever? Do you imagine that the early Christians publicly set forth the mystery of the Eucharist to the Jews and gentiles, who would have ridiculed it? Indeed our Lord himself responded differently to the Pharisees when they were maliciously trying to trip him up than he did to the Sadducees when out of ignorance they proposed a foolish question.[417] His, too, is the saying

* * * * *

409 That is, the Messiah; see Matt 16:15–17, 20.
410 Acts 2:22
411 Acts 17:22–31
412 1 Cor 3:2; Heb 5:12
413 1 Cor 2:6–7
414 *De servo arbitrio* WA 18 778:32 / LW 33 281
415 Matt 10:14
416 Acts 15:20, 29
417 Contrast, for example, Christ's brusque reply to the Pharisees (Matt 22:15–22) and his more patient instruction of the Sadducees (Matt 22:23–33).

'Do not give to the dogs what is holy and do not cast your pearls before swine.'[418] He taught the apostles to go into a village or a town to see if there were any worthy persons there and to go right ahead and proclaim the gospel to them; if there were not, they were to shake off the dust and go elsewhere.[419] Then again our Lord, who said through Ecclesiastes, 'There is a time for speaking and a time to remain silent,'[420] gave no answer at all to the inquiries of Herod,[421] responded very little to Pilate,[422] but on the mountain taught his disciples very fully about the secrets of the evangelical philosophy.[423] Nor did Paul treat the Athenians the same way as he did the Jews: he introduced the gospel to them by means of ideas they knew and accepted; the disbelieving Jews he assailed with the assistance of the Mosaic law. In the presence of Festus and Agrippa how moderately and courteously he spoke[424] – that is, how differently from you. He changed the way he spoke from time to time, promoting the good of his listeners.

You rightly attack Karlstadt's opinion about the Eucharist;[425] but if we suppose it is true, would you not say that he put it out at the wrong time, first of all because in the present state of affairs everything is rubbed raw, and then because he did not hand it over to be aired by the learned but rather exposed it publicly in the German language like a prostitute, to the serious harm of Christian concord. In your *Images*[426] you teach what should be impressed on the dying, reproaching those who burden them with unseasonable talk; and now you say it makes no difference what is said to whom, at what time and in what way. But the wise Jew disagrees with you,

\* \* \* \* \*

418 Matt 7:6
419 Matt 10:11–14
420 Eccles 3:7
421 Luke 23:9
422 Mark 15:2–5
423 Matt 5–7
424 Acts 26
425 On Karlstadt see *A Discussion* n4 and n97 above. In a series of German tracts published in Basel in October and November 1524, Karlstadt denied the real presence, denied even that the bread and the wine are sacramental signs; in fact Karlstadt claimed that when Christ said, 'This is my body,' he was not referring to the bread but was pointing to his own body.
426 Luther's *Tessaradecas consolatoria pro laborantibus et oneratis* of 1520 (WA 6 104–34) was so termed by Erasmus because it contained fourteen *spectra* or pictures modelled on altar screens depicting the fourteen holy helpers, saints (including St Erasmus) who were revered in Germany as protectors against disease. Erasmus mentions this consolation on illness approvingly in Epp 1332:62–8, 1341A:12–13, and Allen Ep 1672:66–8.

saying that 'unseasonable talk is like music in the time of mourning.'[427]
'Paul,' you say, 'said before the whole world "God hardens whomever he
wishes, etc."'[428] But Paul never writes what you foist off on the world, that
free will is nothing but an empty name, that our striving is irrelevant but
rather 'everything happens by sheer necessity,' that 'God performs in us
both good and evil deeds.'[429] These are the things I do not wish to be disseminated. They are enough to make it clear that not even the gospel is to
be preached to all persons whatsoever, at any time, at any place, in any
way, but rather is to be dispensed according to what is advantageous for
the listeners. So much the less is it fitting that this should happen when the
questions are drawn from Holy Scripture or sometimes from human philosophy, such as, when we discuss the Eucharist, how the body can exist
without any dimensions and how the same body can be in different places.
But if you contend that it makes no difference how the gospel is preached,
why do you yourself not rant and rave against the emperor with savagery
like that with which you assail the pope and bishops? For the emperor is
a greater obstacle to your gospel than the pope. Here, to be sure, you are
forced to apply that saying of Paul, 'All things are permitted to me, but
not all are expedient,'[430] which will be spoken by you quite appropriately,
however inappropriately I cited it.[431]

Since these things are self-evident, it is clear as clear could be what
a spate of words you have wasted, how irrelevant is the testimony you cite
from Holy Scripture, how inopportune are those smokescreens you send
up: 'Paul says "The word of God is not bound," and shall Erasmus bind it?'
and 'The Lord says "Go forth to the whole world," Erasmus says "Go to
one place but not to another"'; again '"Preach the gospel to all creatures,"
Erasmus says, "to some but not to others."'[432] Finally, as if all this were
not insipid enough, you add a new witticism, harping away at some Greek
words: respect for persons, respect for places, respect for customs, respect

* * * * *

427 Ecclus 22:6
428 Rom 9:18; *De servo arbitrio* WA 18 631:8–11 / LW 33 59
429 *Assertio* article 36 WA 7 146:6–8 / 306; *De servo arbitrio* WA 18 630:20–4 / LW 33
58, 699:13–17 / LW 33 160; cf *A Discussion* 12–13. Luther's view in this matter was widely disseminated because of a German version of *Assertio*, which
differs in critical respects from the Latin. For an English translation of the
German version of article 36 see LW 32 92–4.
430 1 Cor 6:12
431 *De servo arbitrio* WA 18 628:18–29 / LW 33 55–6, citing *A Discussion* 13
432 *De servo arbitrio* WA 18 628:32–6 / LW 33 56, citing 2 Tim 2:9 and Mark
16:15

for hearts.[433] To these, if they are yours, I am surprised you did not add respect for wine. For either someone else added these stupidities to your book, or you were not sober when you wrote them. Marvellously appropriate is the citation you provide us here: 'God is no respecter of persons,'[434] that is, God admits all kinds of mortals from all nations to the grace of the gospel by means of faith; therefore it makes no difference what you discuss before whom or how you do it. Not content with this, you add a final flourish,[435] saying 'You see once more how rashly you seize upon the word of God, just as if you set your own thoughts and counsels far and away above him.'[436] If such things had been said by someone suffering from a fever, could they have been any more insane? I revere the word of God with my whole heart, but I do not believe that whatever you assert is the word of God. And if you do not treat the word of God with more good faith than you treat what I say, it is clear how much should be attributed to your gospel. If I handle Holy Scripture with less learning, at least I do so cautiously and with reverence, following in the footsteps of the orthodox and fearing to depart from the decisions of the church. You rush in violently and, turning everything upside down, you contend that Scripture means what you want it to mean and what fits your teachings. In brief, you conduct yourself as if you wanted victory for yourself, not the gospel, and as if you demanded to be the lord, not the steward, of Holy Scripture.

You demand that I appoint the proper occasion for teaching the truth.[437] It is shameless of you to demand this from Erasmus, who knows nothing at all and is ignorant of persons, times, methods, and certainly knows nothing of the hearts of men – all of which are known only to

* * * * *

433 *De servo arbitrio* WA 18 628:37 / LW 33 56. The two Froben editions of 1526 and LB X 1281F have the error *chreolepsias* for Luther's transliterated Greek word *chaerolepsias*, which should be *kairolepsias* (from *kairos* 'the right time for action'). Erasmus apparently took *chaerolepsias* as *kerolepsias* 'respect for hearts,' since he concludes a paraphrase of the series at the beginning of the next paragraph with *corda hominum* (we are grateful to Prof Alec Dalzell for pointing this out to us). Emser (sig o2v), taking *Chreo* as if it were from Greek *kreas* 'flesh,' translated: 'Chreolepsias / Das man (die weyl Chreos fleisch heyst) zu teusch nennen möcht fleisch leppich' ('Chreolepsias, which, since "Chreos" means "flesh," could be translated into German as "flesh-foolish"').

434 Rom 2:11

435 Translating *epiphonema*. Quintilian 8.5.11: 'Est enim epiphonema rei narratae vel probatae summa acclamatio' ('For an epiphonema is an exclamatory summary of what has been related or proved').

436 *De servo arbitrio* WA 18 629:3–4 / LW 33 56

437 *De servo arbitrio* WA 18 629:5–7 / LW 33 56

Luther.[438] And in this triumph you present us with the spectacle of the dancing camel,[439] frolicking and altering a verse of Virgil: 'Sooner will time be cut off and the world come to an end.'[440]

Did you ever see such clumsy jests in my *Discussion*? And then you claim that I set down my formulation 'so as not to offend the pope or anger the emperor, etc.'[441] But in fact even these provisos which you imagine to be absurd are not as absurd as you want to make them seem. For what sin is it for a preacher of the truth to temper his speech in such a way that he exasperates persons in power as little as he can but rather entices them instead of challenging them and, if the case is hopeless, at least does not uselessly provoke them? And yet I already did partly supply what you required, not on my own but out of Holy Scripture: it is a sin to throw to the dogs what is holy or to cast pearls before swine,[442] and shake off the dust, spurning those who scorn you.[443] There you have the persons. When there is no hope of success but the only result is to create an uproar, the matter should be put off until a better occasion arises. There you have the time. But as for the method of teaching, it is drawn from all the circumstances and cannot be entirely prescribed because it arises and varies with the case at hand, but rather what is appropriate for each case is left to the prudence of the steward. Paul preferred to stitch together pieces of leather instead of being maintained by the generosity of the Corinthians, which he could have rightfully asked for, and he did not take around with him one of the sisters as his wife but rather he bore all things lest he give the least offence to the gospel.[444] In pursuit of the gospel the apostles left behind the wives they had married, nor did they marry, though it was not

* * * * *

438 Ironical, since the hearts of men are known only to God; see 126 and nn164 and 433 above.
439 *Adagia* II vii 66
440 *Aeneid* 1.374; *De servo arbitrio* WA 18 629:6–7 / LW 33 46
441 *De servo arbitrio* WA 18 629:10–13 / LW 33 56–7
442 Matt 7:6
443 Matt 10:14
444 1 Cor 9:1–18. Latin: *sororem mulierem*. *Sororem* 'one of the sisters' is equivalent to a Christian woman. In his *Annotations on the New Testament* on 1 Cor 5:9 Erasmus reports Valla's opinion that *sororem mulierem* means a Christian woman as a wife. He also notes that, though Ambrose and Jerome read simply *mulieres* 'women' instead of *sororem mulierem*, γυναῖκα regularly means 'wife,' and that, according to Eusebius, Clement of Alexandria took this text to mean that Paul had a wife (LB VI 706C–D). Nevertheless, in his *Paraphrases* he wrote *Christianas matrones* 'Christian matrons,' apparently following Ambrose and Jerome (LB VII 888D).

forbidden to anyone; now those who boast that they would die a thousand times over for the gospel do what alienates very many people from the gospel. If a good physician is one who hands out any drugs whatsoever to any patient whatsoever, then a good theologian is one who disseminates any part whatsoever of God's word, paying no attention either to person or the time. 'All Scripture inspired by God is useful for teaching, for refuting, for correcting, for instructing.'[445] Does it make no difference to you what you present from Holy Scripture, before whom, or how you do it? Will you teach the same things to a catechumen as to someone who is to become a bishop? Will you treat the same places when you deal with a pagan philosopher as with a Jew? Will you present the same mysteries to someone who mocks them as to someone eager to learn? Will you not choose what to draw from Holy Scripture before holy virgins and before pimps and public whores? Will you think it makes no difference whether you admonish a prince or bishop courteously in private or cry out against them seditiously before a public audience? Will you not reproach someone who has a fragile temperament, prone to despair, differently from someone who is constitutionally bold, fierce, and contemptuous? And at this point my *Paraclesis* is brought out against me because there I wish no one to be precluded from reading the sacred books.[446] I make the same point even more thoroughly in the addendum prefixed to the *Paraphrase on Matthew*,[447] but I prescribe what sort of person I want to read the holy books, and I indicate how they ought to be read. Simply because I allow everyone to read the holy books, does that mean there should be debates pro and con on any difficult questions whatever, before any audience, and in any manner whatsoever? And added to this section is a virulent final twist: you say, 'You perniciously promote their insanity, Erasmus, by this advice of yours.'[448]

* * * * *

445  2 Tim 3:16; *De servo arbitrio* WA 18 607:7 / LW 33 27, 655:28–9 / LW 33 94
446  In *Paraclesis*, Erasmus' preface to his Greek and Latin New Testament (1516), he summoned all by its 'trumpet blast' to the pious study of Scripture. Laymen were especially encouraged to do so. See Holborn 139–49; there is an English translation in *Desiderius Erasmus: Christian Humanism and the Reformation, Selected Writings* ed and trans John C. Olin (New York 1965) 92–106.
447  This letter addressed to the pious reader repeated the theme that laymen should read Scripture and urged that translation of it into the vernacular be made for them. It was composed to fill the opening sheets of *Paraphrasis in evangelium Matthaei* (Basel: Froben 1522) and is printed unpaginated preceding the same in LB VII.
448  *De servo arbitrio* WA 18 629:25 / LW 33 57; 'their' refers to 'the pope and his adherents' earlier in the sentence (629:23).

Taxing the discourtesy of some persons, I advised that if something was perhaps laid down wrongly in councils, it should be corrected, but in such a way as to spare as much as possible the authority of popes and councils,[449] for it is not expedient that they should be held up to public scorn. If courtesy has the same effect as uproar, should we not prefer what is more peaceful? If you prefer seditious abuse, I am very far from agreeing with you. Indeed the writing and life of the apostles are at odds with your opinion. What purpose was served by this insult except that you can never get enough of casting aspersions: 'This, of course, is what the pope wanted you to say, and he would rather hear it than the gospel; he is a wretched ingrate if he does not honour you back with a cardinal's hat and the income that goes with it.'[450] Aren't you ashamed, Luther, of this patent inanity? Do I have any income from the pope? Indeed, when Adrian offered it, I refused. As for the cardinal's hat, did anyone ever give it to me or did I ever seek it?[451] In fact I most strenuously[452] turned down dignities far below that.[453] But what can you do? These fables are bruited about among the trustworthy brethren, whom it is a crime not to trust. So little do you care what you say against anyone. But I can hardly tell whether you used 'back' instead of 'in turn,' lest your claim to lack of eloquence appear to be a total pretence.[454] But at the same time you do not stop charging that against my conscience I support what should not be supported to curry favour with the popes[455] and out of hope for rewards – than which nothing could be more false, which I think you also know, however much you pretend not to.

* * * * *

449 *A Discussion* 12; *De servo arbitrio* WA 18 630:1–3 / LW 33 57
450 *De servo arbitrio* WA 18 630:3–6 / LW 33 57
451 In January 1522 Adriaan Floriszoon of Utrecht (1459–1523) was elected pope as Adrian VI. In 1522 he encouraged Erasmus to write against Luther and invited him to come to Rome, where he would find well-stocked libraries and the company of pious and learned men. He also promised he would be well recompensed for this journey and 'most pious labour' (Epp 1324:117–33, 1338:59–64). Later, in 1535, Erasmus was offered a cardinal's hat by Paul III (Allen Ep 3007:5n), but he refused it (Allen Ep 3052:31–5).
452 Literally 'with hands and feet' (*Adagia* I iii 15 and III ix 68)
453 In 1520 Erasmus was promised a bishopric if he would write against Luther, an incentive he evidently ignored (Ep 1141:36–7 and n12).
454 Erasmus twits Luther for the solecism *rursus* 'back' for *vicissim* 'in turn' at *De servo arbitrio* WA 18 630:4 / LW 33 57 (Watson's translation ignores the error).
455 Emser (sig P1r) has 'Bischoffen,' which the Latin *pontificum* can mean, but here the preceding sentences make it clear that the specific meaning 'popes' is intended.

Now since you hammer away so often on the point that human regulations cannot be observed together with the gospel,[456] I utterly disagree
with you, since I see that some human regulations are necessary, some are
useful, although it is not pleasant that we have an inordinate number of
them, among which some could quite rightly be removed.[457] And here, if
I wanted to, I could assail you for inconsistency, since somewhere or other
you declare that ceremonies are necessary for the weak.[458] For it is certain
that human regulations deal mostly with ceremonies. But at the moment
we are here concerned with something else, nor do I have any inclination
to digress from the argument lest we should expend too much effort in
these quarrels. Finally, you close this section also with a dilemma: 'If you
mean this about the word of God, your meaning is impious; if you mean it
about other matters, the lengthy discussion of your advice does not matter
to us.'[459] I have already shown that it does matter to whom you are teaching the Holy Scriptures; then I made it clear that I was talking not only
about Holy Scripture, but rather about questions inherent in it, which in
the final analysis also contain an admixture of human philosophy. Is this
the word of God, that all things happen by sheer necessity and that our
efforts do not matter at all? For the moment I will imagine that this paradox of yours is in some sense true, though if you should ask others about
it, they will say it is heretical.[460] Nor do I want silence maintained about
it simply because it is difficult, as you say I do, but rather because it en-
courages persons who are weak and prone to wrongdoing to sin even more
licentiously. You derive your paradox from Holy Scripture, but the church
also takes its opinion from Holy Scripture, so that the issue depends not on
the words of Scripture but on its interpretation. But you offend precisely in
that you continually foist off on us your interpretation as the word of God.
And so my meaning about Holy Scripture is not impious; in interpreting
Scripture I prefer to follow the judgment of the many orthodox teachers
and of the church rather than that of you alone or of your few sworn fol-

* * * * *

456 *De servo arbitrio* WA 18 630:6–10 / LW 33 57–8
457 LB X 1283D softens this statement by adding *meo quidem animo* 'certainly in my
    opinion.'
458 In *Deutsche Messe und ordnung Gottis diensts* (WA 19 73:14–15 / LW 53 62) Luther
    says 'Aber umb der willen mus man solche ordnung haben die noch Christen
    sollen werden oder sterker werden' ('But we must have such regulations for
    the sake of those who still have to become Christians or grow stronger').
459 *De servo arbitrio* WA 18 630:16–18 / LW 33 58
460 Wyclif's thesis that everything happens by absolute necessity was condemned
    by the Council of Constance (1414–17). Luther specifically aligned himself
    with it in his *Assertio* article 36 (WA 7 146:6–8 / 306). See n429 above.

lowers, and my discussion nevertheless does pertain to you because you din such a dogma into the ears of the unlearned, a dogma which, even if it were incontrovertibly true, could not be disseminated to just any audience whatsoever without danger.

See, once more I am faced with a horned syllogism: 'If these paradoxes,' you say, 'are the inventions of men, why are you upset, against whom are you speaking? etc. If however you believe those paradoxes are the word of God, where is your sense of shame? etc.'[461] Listen to my response: to me they seem to be the fabrications of heretics who twist Holy Scripture to their own meaning. And nevertheless at this point I imagine that they are a human opinion drawn from Holy Scripture, perhaps wrongly understood, an opinion which, once it has been conceived, I would allow to be soberly discussed among the learned, but would not want it bruited about before a mixed crowd. And so away with this 'word of God, word of God.' I am not waging war against the word of God but against your assertion; nor is the word of God inconsistent with itself but rather human interpretations collide with one another. If you are influenced by the judgment of the church, what you assert is human fabrication, what you fight against is the word of God. If you are not, even so you should deploy very clear arguments to prove what you assert before you command us to go over to your position, which is at odds with so many luminaries of the church and even with the public judgment of the church. Now, when you run riot, scoffing and jumping for joy, before you have even come to grips with my *Discussion*, what are you doing but celebrating a triumph before any victory?[462] Rhetoricians keep such gestures for a point that has already been proved, whether they prefer to triumph after each part of the case or are content with only one triumph in the peroration. But it is even more indecorous for you not only to leap, jump, and frisk, but to show off trophies never captured and to carry around a picture of a prostrate enemy whom you have not yet attacked. How absurdly you indulge in your figure of irony, though you will not allow me to do such things, that is, to use this most commonplace of figures: 'To be sure, your creator will learn from his creature what it is useful or useless to preach, and up to now that foolish and ignorant God did not know what ought to be taught until you as his master prescribed for him the way to grow wise and to give commands, as if he himself did not know, etc.'[463] To be sure, these stupidities seem witty to you as if you had proved incontrovertibly that your teaching about free

* * * * *

461 *De servo arbitrio* WA 18 630:29–631:2 / LW 33 59, referring to *A Discussion* 12–13
462 *Adagia* I vii 55
463 *De servo arbitrio* WA 18 631:3–6 / LW 33 59

LB X 1283F

will is the word of God and as if the steward of the divine word ought not to pay attention to what he says to whom, at what time, and in what manner, as he brings forth from the twofold storehouse of Holy Scripture what will contribute to the salvation of his listeners.[464] Tell me, I beg you, have you never seen a preacher who displeased you because what he said was not very timely? During Lent isn't it right to propound to the people ideas that promote penance and the amendment of life and to set forth happier ideas during the Easter season? I imagine that when you are to speak before the people, you also give some thought to what should be said, what should be left unsaid, and how you should treat what you have taken in hand. And someone who advises such things puts himself, a creature, before his creator, and prescribes for God the way to grow wise and to give commands, and he 'imagines that the living God is nothing more than some empty-headed and ignorant wrangler bawling out on some speaker's platform,'[465] and other things so foolish that I can hardly believe that they proceeded from your mind.

This advice of mine has as a consequence what you infer from it: 'Here, my dear Erasmus, you manifestly reveal how sincere you were previously when you encouraged us to venerate the majesty of God's judgments.'[466] Who, Luther, was the incorrigible slanderer who mixed such things in with your book? If a person advises that sacred doctrine should be tempered to promote the welfare of the listeners, does that mean that he is feigning when he teaches that mysteries in Sacred Scripture which surpass the measure of the human intellect ought to be approached with reverence? Is he a blasphemer against God – for that is what you adduce in the next section[467] – if he does not want anyone to penetrate into the sanctum sanctorum of these questions any more deeply than is beneficial to the welfare and harmony of Christ's flock, if he wants the steward of the divine word to be sober and circumspect so as to know what is proper for whom? There is no one, then, who does not see how much tragic eloquence you spew forth, making yourself all the more ridiculous the more you rant and rave, violently and uncontrollably, beyond the limits of the case. Does a person teach that God is not to be feared if he teaches that no one can achieve salvation apart from the mercy of God, if he believes that God draws some persons and, by his secret and inscrutable counsel, leaves others to their own inclinations?

* * * * *

464 Cf Matt 13:52 and Luke 12:42; 'twofold' refers to the Old and New Testaments.
465 *De servo arbitrio* WA 18 631:23–4 / LW 33 60
466 *De servo arbitrio* WA 18 631:26–8 / LW 33 60
467 *De servo arbitrio* WA 18 632:10 / LW 33 61

Does anyone who does not agree with your assertions and interpretations weigh Holy Scripture according to the understanding of most wicked men? And if a person, either out of the ignorance you abundantly attribute to me or because of weakness of mind, does not dare to commit himself to your faith, which has already been condemned by the public judgment of the church, and prefers to follow the opinion of so many outstanding men and to accept the decision of the church rather than your teaching and that of Wyclif,[468] is such a person declaring his impious disdain of God? Such are the conclusions you, as a man of logic, draw from my words and with marvellous sedulity you box with these shadows,[469] or with something emptier than shadows, if such there be. Since these things, then, are totally off the point and are manifestly false besides, they should have been left unspoken by someone who claims for himself not only the highest erudition but also the Spirit of God; far less fitting was it to speak them repeatedly, to hurl them, to hammer away at them. Even if they were true and relevant, still (as I said) they should have been triumphantly chanted after the victory had been gained.[470]

Thereupon you answer my questions as if I had taught that people can amend their lives without the Spirit or as if the Spirit does not operate in the minds of men by means of a person who circumspectly deals out the language of the gospel – unless perhaps you mean that only God's election is sufficient and the office of teacher is not necessary.[471] What is the reason, then, that in Ezekiel the Lord picks such a quarrel with bad pastors?[472] To the second question you reply as if I teach that anyone can love God even if God has not drawn him on. In Isaiah why are silent pastors rebuked?[473] Because they were silent when they should have brought forth the word of God. By the same token reproach should be aimed at those who either preach something other than the word of God or preach it in some other way than they should. And here once more you make Erasmus into a blasphemer, though you yourself abound in all manner of blasphemies. Acknowledge your words – and I tell you, Luther, they are truly yours. This is what they say. When I had portrayed the wicked murmuring against the goodness and justice of God, you say this: 'No man will believe

\* \* \* \* \*

468 See *A Discussion* n35 and nn429 and 460 above.
469 *Adagia* IV vi 48
470 *Adagia* I vii 55
471 *De servo arbitrio* WA 18 632:3–8 / LW 33 60–1
472 Ezek 34:1–10
473 Isa 56:10–11

or can believe, but the elect will believe; the rest, who do not believe, will perish in their anger, blaspheming as you do here.'[474] What blasphemy of mine do you see here? Is it because I recite what the wicked will say? And lest anyone should suspect that I speak these things in my own person, I add: 'For thus many will interpret it. For the minds of mortals are mostly dull and carnal, inclined to disbelief, prone to wickedness, disposed to blasphemy, so that there is no need to pour oil on the fire.'[475] Thus is it in my *Discussion*. Don't these words make it sufficiently clear whose murmurs I am reciting? Am I a blasphemer precisely because I do not want any occasion to be given to those who are disposed to blasphemy? Such things, to be sure, are poured forth by that spirit who masters and rules you.

[*The human will is not completely passive but cooperates with grace*]
But I must hurry on to what is left. Things go well! Finally, having had your fill, I imagine, of insults, you give us a little breather, for you turn now to teaching – and would that that were the only thing you ever did! You adduce, then, two reasons why your teaching should be proclaimed to everyone: one is so that a person who is cast down and despairs of himself will not hope for salvation from anywhere but God, and he is near to God's mercy if he understands that he himself by his own power cannot even do the least bit to achieve salvation; the other is so that by this teaching there may be some scope for faith, which would not be unless God should seem to be unjust though he is just, and should seem to be cruel though he is merciful, and unless he should seem to destroy even though he is bringing to life.[476] I could object that these ideas also are not spoken in the right place, except that according to your teaching it does not matter where anything is spoken. Since they are treated in my discussion, it would have been more timely for you to speak of them when you take issue with my arguments. But nevertheless, since you are taking up a serious point, I am not unwilling both to listen and to respond. But you must provide us with very compelling and weighty reasons if you want to persuade us that the position held already for centuries by the people of Christ together with their teachers and still held by the church to this day is a pernicious teaching, wicked, heretical, and blasphemous, but that your teaching is a principal

\* \* \* \* \*

474  *De servo arbitrio* WA 18 632:8–10 / LW 33 61, replying to *A Discussion* 13: 'Who will be able to bring himself to love God wholeheartedly?' Luther misreported this as 'Who will believe he is loved by God?'
475  *A Discussion* 13; *Adagia* I ii 9
476  *De servo arbitrio* WA 18 632:27–633:23 / LW 33 61–3

article of the Christian faith, without which no one can be saved. Do not say, then, that out of an abundant supply of reasons you have brought forth two.[477] For the first reason you use to silence us, saying it is enough that God wishes these things to be proclaimed and it is not man's place to inquire why he wishes it,[478] has no validity against us because it assumes as obvious what is actually controversial, namely that your teaching is the word of God. Hence do not ply us with this response in the future unless you have first shown your assumption to be completely certain, whereas in fact it is not only doubtful but also condemned by the universities and the leading men of the church.

Let us examine, then, your Achillean[479] and invincible reasons. Certainly to me neither seems impious in and of itself. For who would not confess that it is pious for a person not to have faith in himself and to depend totally on the mercy of God? And it is a pious teaching that we are not to judge God's actions but rather we should firmly believe that God is always entirely just even though at times he seems unjust to human understanding, and that he is entirely merciful even though at times he seems cruel. All such teachings, I say, are pious and holy, but nevertheless they are very far from proving the necessity of your teaching to the degree you imagine they do. For you say somewhere that it would be preferable for the whole world to sink into chaos than that this teaching should be rejected.[480] On the contrary, the benefits you seek from your reasons flow rather from the view which the church has followed up till now as pious, so that there is no need for such a new and seditious teaching, not to mention for the moment the avoiding of the dangers which your teaching carries with it and, on the other hand, the gaining of the benefits which our opinion brings with it. As for the first reason, I demonstrate in *A Discussion* that there follows from the opinion I defend the same advantage from dejection as follows from yours.[481] For why should anyone have faith in himself if he knows that he can neither begin nor complete anything without the help of God's grace, to whom I profess that the sum and substance of all things rightly done ought to be attributed? Nor is there any difference between you and me except that I make our will cooperate with the grace of God and you make it completely passive. You add this: 'As long as a person is persuaded that

\* \* \* \* \*

477 *De servo arbitrio* WA 18 632:26–7 / LW 33 61
478 *De servo arbitrio* WA 18 632:22–3 / LW 33 61
479 *Adagia* I vii 41: as invincible as Achilles, the hero of Homer's *Iliad*
480 *De servo arbitrio* WA 18 625:13–17 / LW 33 50
481 *A Discussion* 9–10

he can do the least bit towards his salvation, he continues to have faith in himself and does not utterly despair of himself, and therefore he does not humble himself before God, etc' and 'secretly he remains proud and hostile to God's grace.'[482] You say these things boldly but you likewise say them with no proof whatever and in contradiction to Scripture, and there is nothing whatever original about them except hyperbole. You say: 'Whoever does not hesitate to depend on the will of God, he despairs of himself completely, he chooses nothing, but rather waits for the action of God. He is near to the grace which will save him.'[483] We say the same except that we do not quite understand what is meant by that phrase 'he chooses nothing,' unless perhaps you mean that he has no faith in God if he chooses a way of life which he judges to be more fitting or even safer. As for your immense exaggeration of his despair in himself and his total devaluation of himself, they are your hyperboles. Otherwise the conclusion of your statement matches our teaching no less than yours. It reads thus: 'This, I say, is the only way for the pious to humble themselves, recognizing, invoking, and accepting the promise of grace.'[484] How will a person rise up against God if he knows that he has in himself no hope of salvation without the singular grace of God, if he is persuaded that all human powers are of no avail for salvation without the aid of grace, especially since he is not unaware that everything he can do by his natural powers is the free gift of God? If a person wishes to cross the ocean, is he confident that he can achieve this without a ship and wind? And yet he is not idle while he is sailing. For professing free will does not tend to make a person attribute less to the mercy of God but rather keeps him from not responding to operating grace[485] and gives him reason to blame himself if he perishes. I exalt God's mercy so much, I diminish human power so much, that in the matter of salvation no one can claim anything for himself, since the very fact of his existence and whatever he can do by his natural endowments is the gift of God. You exalt grace and demean mankind so much that you open another pit which we had closed over by attributing just a little bit to free will, namely that it accommodates itself to grace or turns away from grace.

The second reason is not indeed wicked but has no force against me. I teach the very same thing that you do: a person should have no faith in his own powers and make himself completely available to operating

* * * * *

482  *De servo arbitrio* WA 18 632:33–633:5 / LW 33 62
483  *De servo arbitrio* WA 18 632:36–633:1 / LW 33 62
484  *De servo arbitrio* WA 18 633:5–6 / LW 33 62
485  See *A Discussion* n109.

grace,[486] and he should believe that God is just even if to human understanding he seems unjust, merciful even if he seems cruel. Even this, however, is not always true. For in Isaiah God challenges the Israelites to come
and accuse him if they can,[487] and in Ezekiel 18[:25–9] he argues with the
people on their level as it were, showing their injustice and vindicating his
justice. And God does not always hide his mercy towards us so as to give
scope to faith, but rather by many arguments he demonstrates it to us. Nor
does he hide his truth so that we may gain more merit by believing him
truthful, but rather he has made it clear that he is truthful by so many oracular pronouncements of the prophets, by so many figures[488] and miracles,
and finally by fulfilling his promises through his Son and the apostles. Indeed our Lord himself, though he dissembled about his divine nature for
a while, nevertheless did not hide the truth but made it clear in every possible way so that unbelievers would have no pretext for their guilt. And
so when you add hyperbolically, 'If we could by any means comprehend
how God is merciful and just when he displays so much anger and injustice, there would be no need for faith,'[489] no one will grant you that. Instead
God in his goodness nourishes our faith in such a way that from some arguments which we comprehend from sense and reason we may also believe
what cannot be understood. Thus much on these matters is sufficient at this
point.

I thought I had escaped, but lo and behold, another horned dilemma
has been prepared for me: 'If we believe,' you say, 'that the paradoxes
are true, since they are of the greatest importance, you could find no better way to stir up people's curiosity and make them investigate them than
by teaching that they are not to be divulged. But if you believe they are
not true, teach that they should be concealed, not because they do no good
but because they are false.'[490] Listen a minute to this: if I thought your
paradox were true, I would never have set my *Discussion* up against it.
And if you are so offended by the courtesy with which I imagined for
the sake of argument that it is true in some sense and was content to call
it a paradox, avail yourself of the words and judgments of others who

* * * * *

486  See *A Discussion* n109.

487  Isa 5:3

488  That is, persons and things in the Old Testament which foreshadow persons
     and things in the New Testament. The fulfilment of the foreshadowing demon-
     strates God's truth.

489  *De servo arbitrio* WA 18 633:19–21 / LW 33 63

490  *De servo arbitrio* WA 18 634:3–13 / LW 33 63; Erasmus partly paraphrases Luther.

assail your paradoxes. For they are ready at hand. In them you will find not the Sceptical ambiguities which you execrate but the pure Stoic assertions in which you delight. But let it not be to my discredit that I dealt with bitter matters affably and in softened language so that matters which are already sufficiently exacerbated should not be thrown into further confusion and so that the truth might shine out more clearly. It is absurd for you to bid me to be the first one to remain silent since you had already publicized this enigma, in which it is dangerous to din into the ears of the people the side that you support. But this is what burns you up: I dared to touch on that cherished opinion of yours differently than you wanted me to. In your eagerness to support it you prematurely begin to prove to us the necessary occurrence of everything, assuming what you have not yet proved as if it were yours by right, namely that we do not do anything but that God alone works our good and evil deeds in us.[491] And yet you go right on to make two gods who sit on our wills by turns and make them go wherever they want.[492] And thus you distinguish between the necessity of coercion and that of immutability as if we had confused them. When you say that a person taken captive by sin cannot by his own power turn his will to good unless he is blown upon by the breath of grace, we also profess this, especially if you mean turning effectively. But I disagree with you when you say that a person in whom grace works cannot turn away from grace, just as someone in sunlight could not close his eyes. Otherwise why are those 'who were once enlightened,' having tasted the heavenly gift and 'made partakers of the Holy Spirit,' reproached by Paul for 'backsliding to evil ways'?[493] Nor does your simile prove that our wills do absolutely nothing. For it is true that a mule is directed by its rider, but still when it obeys him it does something together with him. Sometimes it struggles against the reins, kicks, resists, at times even throws off its rider – not that God can be thrown off but that he is offended by our disobedience and leaves us to our own desires. Thus that passage from the Psalms, 'I have become like a mule

* * * * *

491 Luther's discussion of necessity and free will begins at *De servo arbitrio* WA 18 634:14 / LW 33 64 and continues to 639:12 / LW 33 71.
492 Luther speaks of the human will as like a mule ridden either by God or by the devil, unable to choose between them, and completely controlled by one rider or the other; *De servo arbitrio* WA 18 635:17–22 / LW 33 65–6. For the antecedents of the image and a critique of its implications, see McSorley 335–40 and Marjorie O'Rourke Boyle 'Luther's Rider-gods: From the Steppe to the Tower' *Journal of Religious History* 13 (1985) 260–82.
493 Heb 6:4–6

before you, and I am always with you,'[494] has been read also by those who are not pleased by that necessity of all occurrences.[495] They have also read that Christ sat upon an ass,[496] but from that they argue no more than that grace guides and directs and they warn us not to fight against grace.[497] But, as I mentioned, what you have said prematurely I will treat with more care in the proper place. For you make these points triumphantly indeed, but prematurely, without having proved the point on which you base them.

Elated now with success, you dare to promise something even greater, the finest point of victory, to hoist me with my own petard[498] and to clearly convict me of unskilfully denying what I skilfully try to prove. And if you do not do this promptly, you take an oath that you will be willing to revoke everything that you write against me in this book and on the other hand to confirm whatever my *Discussion* has asserted or sought to prove against you.[499] Well now, Luther, we accept the condition, but see to it that you do not go back on your oath. We are poised, waiting for this overwhelming argumentation. 'You confess,' you say, 'that free will without grace is ineffective in gaining salvation.' I acknowledge it. 'Therefore when grace is taken away it does nothing good.' Nothing. 'Therefore it is not free but captive.' I confess it. Here you grant me that the force of free will, which I have diminished, even if I should make it angelic, would still be proved by you to be non-existent because it effects nothing by itself. And in passing you mix in the idea that free will without grace can no more correctly be called free than if you were to call fire cold or earth hot,[500] what the scholastics call

\* \* \* \* \*

494 Ps 72:23
495 According to Nicholas of Lyra's widely known biblical commentary, the first part of the verse means that the understanding of God is as far above us as our knowledge is above that of beasts; 'I am always with you' indicates that when we realize our wickedness and ignorance we rely completely on God (*Biblia 1498* III sig D7v). The scholastic theologians interpreted the image of animal and rider from Ps 72:23 as applying to grace riding the will, which is free to cooperate or not cooperate with grace; see McSorley 337 and nn246 and 492 above.
496 Matt 21:1–6
497 According to St Bernard (*Sermo in Dominica Palmarum* PL 184 877) the ass, when untied and brought to Jesus, stands for those who are converted to Jesus and go on to perform virtuous deeds in order to obtain salvation.
498 Literally, 'to slay me with my own sword' (*Adagia* I i 51)
499 *De servo arbitrio* WA 18 635:23–8 / LW 33 66
500 Earth, not as soil but as one of the four elements constitutive of all matter, is cold and dry (fire is hot and dry; air, hot and moist; water, cold and moist).

a contradictory modifier.[501] Listen now to the case against you. First of all, you remove grace from free will, but when I say free will does something good, I join it with grace, and while it obeys grace it is acted upon and it acts felicitously. When it resists it deserves to be deserted by grace, and when it is deserted it does nothing but evil, which at this point you also admit. It follows that it is something which does something, nor is there any contradictory modifier. For just as we distinguish freeborn men from slaves when they are captured together in war, not because they still have their power but because they are born free and, if they could escape from the hands of their conquerors, would revert to their natural liberty, so too mankind was created so as to have free will; the tyrant Satan took it away as a captive, grace restored and augments it. Nor do I reject the sophists' distinction concerning mankind's natural condition,[502] whereby it is fit to be seized by the Spirit, as long as you add this: 'whereby it is fit to act together with the Spirit who acts.' If this condition is not, as you say, in beasts but only in men and angels, let us give thanks to God who in this matter set us apart from the beasts and made us equal to the angels.[503] You see that there is no contradictory modifier here. But I could have thrown up to you the inscriptions on tombs: 'Here lies Hannibal,' when Hannibal is not there. This was enough to excuse the misuse of a word.[504]

Now see how you bear down upon me: it effects nothing without grace; therefore it does nothing at all with grace. Is this the trap you have set to catch me?[505] In Latin does *inefficax* [ineffective] apply to something that does nothing at all? Do *facere* [act] and *efficere* [effect] mean the same

* * * * *

501 *De servo arbitrio* WA 18 635:27–636:13 / LW 33 66–7. The Latin phrase is *oppositum in adiecto*. According to Peter of Spain, contraries are a kind of opposite (*oppositum*) which are mutually exclusive and as far as possible from each other. They can be by turns in one and the same thing, unless one of them is in that thing by nature, as heat is in fire. Hence the opposite of heat, that is, cold, cannot be attributed adjectivally to fire. See *Tractatus Called Afterwards Summule Logicales* ed L.M. De Rijk (Assen 1972) 39; English translation in *The Cambridge Translations of Medieval Philosophical Texts. Volume One: Logic and the Philosophy of Language* ed Norman Kretzmann and Eleonore Stump (New York 1988) 99. For an example, see Thomas Aquinas *Summa theologiae* I q 29 a 1 obj 2.
502 See Peter Lombard *Sententiarum libri quatuor* II dist 28.7 PL 192 718 and Thomas Aquinas *Summa theologiae* I–II q 110 a 4.
503 *De servo arbitrio* WA 18 636:16–22 / LW 33 67
504 Just as Hannibal is not in the tomb completely, body and soul, but still he is there because his body is there, so too the will can be called free in some real sense, even though not in an unqualified way.
505 Erasmus paraphrases *De servo arbitrio* WA 18 636:23–9 / LW 33 68

thing? We call a drug effective not because it acts upon the body in some fashion but because it carries out what was intended for it; on the other hand, we call it ineffective not because it does nothing in the body but because it is unequal to the task of expelling the disease. You commonly hear people complaining that, though they did everything, they still could not effect what they wanted. Likewise this is not a new meaning of the word but one observed from the earliest times until now. 'What,' you say, 'is an ineffective force but no force at all?'[506] Just as you here teach us to speak Latin, in the course of disputing you deny, with sufficient superciliousness, that in Latin a person who undertakes a useless activity can be said to be doing nothing, because that suits your purpose. What then is the meaning of that clever reply of Cato that it is better to be at leisure than to do nothing?[507] What does Seneca mean when he writes that the greatest part of life is spent while we are doing nothing?[508] Is there no power in a boy pulling a large boat which he cannot move without the help of someone stronger? There is definitely some power there, though ineffective, acting together with the pulling of the strong person, though by itself it cannot effect what it wishes. Here, to be sure, you would be victorious if I would grant you that free will without grace cannot be said to be free will, if I would grant that free will cannot be taken as a natural faculty capable of receiving divine grace, and finally if I would grant that 'ineffective' means no more than doing nothing at all. This is that overwhelming victory of yours! It seems to me more like a victory by entreaty, just as if you said to the enemy, 'I will hoist you with your own petard,[509] provided you throw away your shield and do not strike with the point of your sword.' It is quite obvious, Luther, how far you are from keeping your promise. What remains but for you to recant[510] everything and stop making trouble for my *Discussion* in contravention of your oath? If you had me in your grip as I have you here, who could endure your triumphs? But there will be time to triumph elsewhere. Now let us hurry on to what is left.

\* \* \* \* \*

506 *De servo arbitrio* WA 18 636:10 / LW 33 67
507 Not Cato but Pliny the Younger *Epistles* 1.9.8: 'Satius est otiosum esse quam nihil agere,' which is Erasmus' Latin also. But see Cicero *De officiis* 3.1.1, where the saying is attributed by 'Cato' to Publius Scipio Africanus: 'Numquam se minus otiosum esse, quam cum otiosus' ('He was never less leisurely than when at leisure').
508 Seneca *Epistulae morales* 1.1
509 See n498 above.
510 Literally, 'sing a palinode' (*Adagia* I ix 59)

As for your contention that free choice can be attributed only to God because only he effects whatever he wishes,[511] I confess that this is in some sense true; and yet we do not hesitate to attribute immortality to angels because only God may be said to be immortal, nor are we afraid to call a person good or wise because only God may be called good or wise. For I have no inclination to split hairs with you about whether free choice is inconsistent with being directed by necessity. Since God's will is no more changeable than God himself, no one does everything more completely out of necessity than God, who, if he can be other than he is, can also will otherwise than he does. Again, if you measure all human actions by his will, you make them all equally necessary, including those which you now want to be considered contingent.[512] And then, if whatever effects nothing by its own power cannot be called free choice, we will not even speak of choice at all because we say that a person who freely does what he wishes acts according to his own choice, nor is the modifier any less contradictory when you say 'ineffective free choice' than when you say 'captive choice.' Where there is slavery and captivity there is no choice. What if we cannot even properly speak of 'will' if it chooses nothing, seeks nothing, does nothing? But for all I care you can give this faculty another name.[513] Nor does it concern me what you scrape together about stoning us if we use the term 'free choice,'[514] though we attribute to it only the tiniest bit of power. Anyone who does a good job of teaching the people that there is free choice but that it is ineffective without God's grace does not deserve to be stoned. But this is your temperament: you say nothing without melodramatic hyperbole, as in your words about the fire of hell or about an angelic or even divine power.[515] You prefer above all to seem uniquely learned by means of paradoxes and hyperboles, although no technique tends more to sedition than they do.

And yet I do not see what need there was for those insipid comparisons with the beggar who may be called most rich because the king could enrich him, or with a weak little man, or an intestinal worm if you like, who may be called the lord of heaven and earth if God wishes to grant that to

* * * * *

511 *De servo arbitrio* WA 18 636:27–30 / LW 33 68
512 Luther admitted free choice and contingency in actions not concerned with salvation.
513 As Luther had asserted should have been done, to prevent people from imagining they have any meaningful free choice (*De servo arbitrio* WA 18 637:3–7 / LW 33 68)
514 *De servo arbitrio* WA 18 637:10–14 / LW 33 69
515 *De servo arbitrio* WA 18 636:7–15 / LW 33 67

him.[516] This is the way you talk, lest you should stop being melodramatic. We are speaking of a natural faculty, which, though it may be overcome by force, still retains the name of a quality. And then if you are so deeply offended by the name 'free choice' because it effects nothing on its own, take away at one and the same time the words 'choice' and 'will,' since there is no choice where you can do nothing of your own choosing, nor is there any will if it can effect nothing on its own, as you argue. Even more insipid is your allegation about the titles of princes who foolishly claim for themselves titles to countries which are held by someone else.[517] If this comparison has any validity, it is valid against you.[518] In this chapter you are completely frigid, Luther, even though you imagine, by a most hyperbolic hyperbole, that you have brought in the force of hell fire.[519] Here is a comparison that would be more to the point: this person has a very happy temperament if he were free of fever. As for what you say about fire, which you will not allow to be called fire if it does not burn, your assertion does not make it true, unless perhaps it was not fire which refreshed the three young men in the furnace at Babylon[520] and unless the opinion is groundless that is held by those who think the first cause operates principally in all natural phenomena and deny that there is any miracle if fire does not burn[521] or if the sun does not shine, except that such occurrences are unusual.[522] Finally you become more courteous and allow us to use the phrase 'free choice' in inferior matters which do not pertain to salvation, such as possessions.[523] But in your *Assertion* you teach that free choice is so non-existent that we cannot pick up a straw from the ground without absolute

* * * * *

516 *De servo arbitrio* WA 18 637:25–638:1 / LW 33 69–70
517 *De servo arbitrio* WA 18 637:20–5 / LW 33 69
518 That is, a ruler's title to another country may be valid, factual, existent, even though a usurper possess the country
519 *De servo arbitrio* WA 18 636:14–16 / LW 33 67
520 Dan 3:19–28
521 Thomas Aquinas (*Summa theologiae* I q 105 a 5) refutes this position: 'Dicendum quod Deum operari in quolibet operanti; aliqui sic intellexerunt quod nulla virtus creata aliquid operaretur in rebus, sed solus Deus immediate omnia operaretur; puta quod ignis non calefaceret sed Deus in igne, et similiter de omnibus aliis. Hoc autem est impossibile ... ('We should say that God acts in everything that acts; some have understood this to mean that no created power effects anything, but that God alone effects all things without intermediaries – for example, that fire does not warm but God in the fire, and similarly in all other things. But this is impossible ...') In *De potentia* 3.7 he attributes this position to Islamic theologians.
522 See *A Discussion* n227 and DTC II part 2 2024–6.
523 *De servo arbitrio* WA 18 638:4–9 / LW 33 70

necessity,[524] and now you also confirm that the choice which we have in lower matters is governed by the beck and call of God. Indeed with the same thoughtlessness you grant that something can be called free even if it depends on the beck and call of another. If free choice is a completely empty name and if all things are accomplished by absolute necessity, why do you here subject the immutable will of God to human choice?[525] But more about this elsewhere.

[*A summary of why not all topics are suitable for all audiences*]
Finally, after taking long detours, you sum up your argument: 'If your preface,' you say, 'is speaking about the word of God, it is completely impious. If you are talking about the words of men, it is completely futile.'[526] I have replied to this so as to show that your dilemma is defective because some statements are not strictly the words of men nor those of God but rather interpretations of God's word which may sometimes rightly be doubted, or questions dug out of God's word which may be mishandled in many ways: either they are scrutinized more deeply than is necessary; or the nature of the question is such that it tends to promote discord more than piety (like the question whether, when free will shares in a good work, grace or free will is the primary or secondary cause, leading to the pronouncement that with regard to substantial being free will is the principal cause, but as regards meritorious being, grace is the principal cause);[527] or something accepted by the consensus of the church is called into question; or the subject and the manner of the argument are inappropriate. For I do not condemn the temperate investigation of such questions among the learned, but I exclude the public from such disputes, just as it is not appropriate to discuss

\* \* \* \* \*

524 Luther does not make precisely this assertion, but he does completely deny the existence of free will: 'Male enim dixi, quod liberum arbitrium ante gratiam sit res de solo titulo, sed simpliciter debui dicere "liberum arbitrium est figmentum in rebus seu titulus sine re." Quia nulli est in manu sua quippiam cogitare mali aut boni, sed omnia (ut Vigliphi articulus Constantiae damnatus recte docet) de necessitate absoluta eveniunt' ('For I misspoke when I said that free will before grace exists in name only; rather I should have simply said "free will is a fiction among real things, a name with no reality." For no one has it within his control to intend anything, good or evil, but rather, as was rightly taught by the article of Wyclif which was condemned at Constance, all things occur by absolute necessity'). See *Assertio* article 36 (WA 7 146:4–8 / 306).
525 That is, by freeing human choice from divine necessity in the inferior matters of earthly life
526 *De servo arbitrio* WA 18 638:15–17 / LW 33 70
527 See *A Discussion* n110 above.

before the people what Thomas has to say about simple fornication, ask-
ing whether it is a capital sin and giving arguments on both sides.[528] That
this is so is made clear in the passage with which I conclude this discussion:
'Just so it might be permissible to treat such subjects in scholarly discussion or in the theological schools, though not even there would I consider it
expedient unless done with moderation. But to act out such matters before
all and sundry like plays in a theatre seems to me not merely pointless but
also destructive. I would therefore be happier convincing my readers not
to waste their time or talents in labyrinths of this kind than I would be refuting or confirming Luther's teachings.'[529] Do you hear, Luther, 'theatre
open to an indiscriminate multitude,' do you hear 'not to waste their time,'
and you are not sure what I mean? For the moment I do not accuse you
of bringing back into question something defined by the church. And if it
were quite true that I was speaking of the word of God, I answered that
this also could be mishandled if it was dispensed improperly. But in fact
we are not dealing with the word of God but rather with your interpretations and assertions. On this point you cannot justly blame me for anything
except being more polite towards you than the subject required.

Since these things are so evident they cannot be denied, you certainly
do understand how futile it was for you to spew out so many words, so
many dilemmas and jests, so much impiety and blasphemy. But I do not
call your teachings play-acting, as you falsely charge,[530] but I say that those
who treat such questions with arguments pro and con before an ignorant
mob are like actors who perform a play not suited to everyone before an
indiscriminate audience. Nor are you so ignorant of the Latin language that
you did not understand what I meant, but rather, as Midas turned whatever he touched into gold,[531] so you were determined to turn whatever you
could get your hands on into slander. I was already hoping that your mind
was now at least satiated with insults. But there is no limit to it: whatever
I say is foolish and ignorant, because I mention that Holy Scripture, together with its figures of speech, has a language peculiar to itself.[532] And
you, who always say everything aptly and knowledgeably, interpret my
words as if I were trying to demonstrate the obscurity of Scripture from
figures of speech, whereas my point was quite different, namely that, just

* * * * *

528 Thomas Aquinas *Summa theologiae* II–II q 154 a 2. See CWE 40 693:4 and n112.
529 *A Discussion* 14. The passage concludes Erasmus' preface, not the whole book.
530 *De servo arbitrio* WA 18 638:20 / LW 33 70
531 See, for example, Ovid *Metamorphoses* 11.100–45.
532 *A Discussion* 14

as the divine wisdom tempers its speech according to our feelings and our capacity to understand, so too the dispenser of Holy Scripture accommodates his language to the benefit of his audience. If you protest that this is a rhetorical fabrication, listen to my words, which are as follows: 'not because such changes really take place in the divine nature, but because this manner of speaking is suited to our weakness and stupidity. I believe that the same good sense would befit those who have taken upon themselves the task of dispensing the divine word. Some things are harmful precisely because they are not fitting.'[533] Since this language in my *Discussion* is quite clear, see how fittingly, how adroitly you slander me about the obscurity of Scripture. But in fact, who ever conceded to you that figures of speech in Holy Scripture are not at all obscure as long as grammar is available,[534] since everywhere in *Genesis* we are tormented by figures and the most erudite men sweat so much over the allegories of the prophets?

You make a terrible fuss about this also: I wrote that it is better when dealing with the uneducated mob to be like Paul in not knowing anything 'except Jesus Christ, and him crucified,' and you make fun of me for believing that Paul taught the Corinthians nothing more than these syllables, 'Christ was crucified.'[535] If anyone else said this, Luther, we would rightly call him a quibbler. But your wit here is just as inappropriate as in another place your assertion is impudent, where you contend that Christ crucified embraces all abstract points, all questions, all your teachings and that all Christians are perfect so that it is not proper to conceal any mystery from them but that the Jews are children from whom we should hide the mysteries.[536] If nothing should be concealed from Christians because they are perfect, why does Paul say that he has a 'wisdom that he speaks secretly among the perfect' which he thinks the Corinthians are not worthy to hear because 'they are still carnal'?[537] Why did he not share with all Christians what he heard when he was rapt into the third heaven?[538] Why did he nourish the Galatians with milk, putting off solid food till later?[539] And here you once again forget what you taught before, that the word of God should be

\* \* \* \* \*

533 *A Discussion* 14
534 *De servo arbitrio* WA 18 639:11–12 / LW 33 71
535 *A Discussion* 13; *De servo arbitrio* WA 18 638:24–639:6 / LW 33 70–1; 1 Cor 2:2
536 *De servo arbitrio* WA 18 639:1–4 / LW 33 71
537 1 Cor 2:6, 3:1
538 2 Cor 12:4
539 Not Galatians but 1 Cor 3:2 or Heb 5:12–4

preached to all creatures;[540] now you confess that the Jews are not capable of receiving this wisdom and that it should be preached only among Christians. In the one case you contradict yourself; in the other you boldly declare what no one will believe, namely that whoever teaches Jesus crucified teaches at the same time whatever is discussed concerning free will, foreknowledge, future contingencies, the necessity of all occurrences. Likewise everyone will cry out against you on the third point, when you say that all Christians are perfect.

## [ERASMUS' RESPONSE TO LUTHER'S REVIEW OF THE INTRODUCTION TO A DISCUSSION]

[*The centrality of Scripture in the debate must also include its interpreters*]
Afterwards, in the very vestibule of the disputation, using language as copious as it is vehement, you handle what I desired you to teach me, arguments which would make us believe with certainty that you and your few adherents teach the truth, while so many Doctors of the church, so many universities, councils, and popes[541] etc were blind, even though both sides have Scripture in common.[542] This is the knot I wish you could really untie.[543] For I have often enough tried to get your adherents to do it, but I have not yet found anyone who could. I frankly admit it, this worry really torments my mind, and if (as you say) you want to 'win over your most beloved brother,'[544] the first thing you should do is to remove this obstacle. I will put up with the blows and fisticuffs of your insults provided you furnish what I want. It would take too long to repeat here what I said on this point; whoever wants to can reread the passage in *A Discussion*.[545] As for now, note how you do not perform the task you undertook with such dust and heat. You immediately charge that I said in my preface that in this discussion I would not make use of the assistance of orthodox teachers or councils but only of the authority of Holy Scripture so as to avoid labouring to no avail among those who accept nothing except Holy

* * * * *

540 *De servo arbitrio* WA 18 628:25–6 / LW 33 56
541 Emser (sig 51v) translates 'so vil Bebst und Bischoff' ('so many popes and bishops'), declining to choose between the two possible meanings of 'pontifices.'
542 *De servo arbitrio* WA 18 639:13–640:14 / LW 33 71–2
543 *Adagia* 1 i 6
544 *De servo arbitrio* WA 18 602:21–2 / LW 33 18
545 *A Discussion* 15–17

Scripture.[546] I frankly confess this is true. Nor do I make use of these authorities except occasionally in explaining a passage in Scripture, for you would immediately have rejected my interpretation even before you had heard all of it. Moreover, I do not deny that I do not judge those writers to be entirely useless in deciding an issue. For even though I attribute primary authority to Holy Scripture, I am not scornful if such great men can contribute something to the understanding of the holy books, even if I am not unaware that as men they sometimes fall into error. I do not see why you would think you should say this, unless perhaps you also consider it impious and blasphemous to attribute something to the Fathers, to whom the Catholic church has granted so much authority over the centuries, whose testimony even you do not hesitate to cite whenever it suits your purpose. But you are wrong to appropriate that entire comparison to yourself, since I make an exception of you by name lest I should seem to be directing at you everything I say against 'certain persons better known to me.'[547] It goes without saying that in number, dignity, authority, and even in duration of time you people are inferior to them. I attributed learning, insight, spirit, holiness to them in such a way as not to detract from you, and I avoided making any odious comparisons[548] about morals or way of life in order not to offend anyone. Hence it is irrelevant for you here to mention your way of life,[549] since I never said so much as a word touching your way of life. For I am not so shameless as to attack the life of a person I do not know, nor so discourteous that, when the argument is about doctrine, I should bring forth any baseness of life or pull skeletons out of any closets, even if I knew anything reprehensible. So too in another place you disavow any suspicion of greed or vainglory,[550] defending yourself when no one is accusing you. For in such matters I will allow you to plead your case with God, before whom you stand or fall. But if the splendid reputation, the holiness, dignity, authority of those whom I set over against you has sometimes affected your outlook so that you felt as I now do and you completely despaired of being able to overthrow such a thoroughly reinforced authority,[551] you should be so much the more equitable towards me, who know less and therefore dare less. And I beg you to show me by what methods

* * * * *

546 *De servo arbitrio* WA 18 639:13–640:1 / LW 33 71; *A Discussion* 14
547 *A Discussion* 19
548 See *A Discussion* 17 and n51.
549 *De servo arbitrio* WA 641:3–20 / LW 33 72–3
550 *De servo arbitrio* WA 18 625:19–29 / LW 33 51
551 *De servo arbitrio* WA 18 641:3–12 / LW 33 72–3

you banished this uneasiness from your own mind and gained so much self-confidence. Indeed you call God as your witness, swearing that your conscience is clean.[552] But what I was after was for you to tell how we could be sure that what your adherents claim for themselves is true, especially when we see those who struggle equally to claim the Spirit for themselves disagree so violently among themselves about so many things. An easy believer is light-headed, and you would rightly find us lacking in manly constancy if we rashly defected from the universal Catholic church unless the matter was proved to us with ironclad arguments. Otherwise you would have to fear that you have disciples who are not very firm, since they so readily departed from the ancient Fathers and went over to your opinion.

For I am not disturbed by such insults as these: 'You are nothing but a voice'[553] and 'But if I were to ask you what a manifestation of the Spirit is, what miracles are, what holiness is, to these three questions, so far as I know you from your writings and books, you would seem too inexperienced and ignorant to be able to make them clear by so much as a single syllable.'[554] If you, O most learned of all, would only teach us what we want to know! But you remind me, Luther, of some schoolmasters who are fond of flogging:[555] though they have undertaken to instruct their tender-aged students, they spend a good part of their time beating, scolding, and insulting their charges. You are so omniscient it seems that you are not permitted to use the most ordinary words, to call a spade a spade and tell it like it is.[556] And I think you would define Spirit, holiness, miracles so cleverly that you would make it clear there is no Spirit, no holiness, no miracles in the church. How the apostles manifested their spirit, I know only from the Acts of the Apostles and the gospel, except that their writings seem to me to breathe a certain fragrance of the Holy Spirit which I do not find in the writings of very many persons. From the same writings I know of the miracles performed by the apostles and I read how their speech was confirmed by God through subsequent signs. By similar tracks I detect the Spirit, holiness, and miracles in other reputable men. There breathes a certain something in their books,

* * * * *

552 *De servo arbitrio* WA 18 641:7–9 / LW 33 73
553 *De servo arbitrio* WA 18 641:2 / LW 33 73. Luther was apparently referring to a German saying, 'Voice and a to-do is what is left, otherwise nothing, said the wolf to the nightingale'; see WA 18 793 (addition to the note on 641:2) and *Deutsches Sprichwörter-Lexikon* ed Karl F.W. Wander, 5 vols (Leipzig 1867–80) IV 861 no 12.
554 *De servo arbitrio* WA 18 641:20–4 / LW 33 73
555 Cf Horace *Epistles* 2.1.70.
556 Literally, 'to call figs figs and a hoe a hoe' (*Adagia* II iii 5)

though far less than with the apostles, which manifests the Spirit and their holiness. And then I have learned of their lives and miracles in histories, the authority of which is confirmed for me by the consensus of the church, which reveres their memory so devoutly.

Against such arguments not much weight can be given to that proverb which is bruited about in the universities: 'Many pass for saints on earth whose souls are in hell.'[557] Though you picked up this saying from the streetcorner,[558] nevertheless you upbraided me a little before because 'I employ many expressions commonly used and accepted in ordinary speech which are remarkably inappropriate if they are called to the judgment bar of conscience.'[559] But my point there was that, since we have not been given the gift of discerning spirits[560] and therefore cannot be sure about your conscience, we should be shown some reason why we can safely believe in your teaching, rejecting the doctrine handed down by so many learned and famous men and accepted by the whole Christian world with such an overwhelming consensus. You try many ways to avoid this knot. First you claim that none of the ancients ever performed any miracles in the name of free will but rather in the name of Jesus Christ.[561] But a little earlier you taught us that this name Jesus Christ also embraces these doctrines which you now teach.[562] From this it follows that whoever performed a miracle in the name of Jesus believing that free will works together with his grace performed a miracle in the name of free will. And I do not teach that 'free will is not of the Spirit but is something human';[563] rather I think that among the perfect the apostles taught that free will works in us together with the grace of God, especially since this is the opinion which very learned men affirm from their writings. You open another crack to get away.[564] You say that however spiritual they were, as human beings they sometimes perceived things according to the flesh.[565] I do not deny it, but what you object

* * * * *

557 *De servo arbitrio* WA 18 641:28–9 / LW 33 73. A German version of this proverb may be found in *Deutscher Sprichwörter-Lexikon* (n553 above) II 465 no 54.
558 Latin *trivium* regularly meant 'crossroad, public street'; in the Middle Ages it also referred to grammar, logic, and rhetoric, the first stages of university study.
559 *De servo arbitrio* WA 18 641:26–8 / LW 33 73
560 Cf 1 Cor 12:10.
561 *De servo arbitrio* WA 18 641:30–642:6 / LW 33 73–4
562 *De servo arbitrio* WA 18 639:1–3 / LW 33 71
563 *De servo arbitrio* WA 18 642:9–12 / LW 33 74
564 *Adagia* III ii 75
565 *De servo arbitrio* WA 18 642:6–8 / LW 33 74

against them you have in common with them, and so we come back to the comparison: should the Spirit be attributed to you or to them? I do not demand miracles from you, but I argue that, other things being equal, we should place more faith in those who are famous for their miracles than in those who come recommended by no miracles. Likewise it is not right for you in turn to demand miracles of us.[566] For we are not the authors of this new teaching, but rather we follow the authority of those who are famous for their holiness and miracles. Likewise it is as immodest of you to demand that we confirm free will with miracles as it would be for someone to demand that theologians should prove the truth of the gospel with miracles. For it is enough that it has been proved once and for all by miracles and the consent of the whole world.

But whereas you say in jest that proof is required from those who affirm, not from those who deny, and bring up again that proverb from the schools of the sophists and lawyers, 'The negative side proves nothing,'[567] I reply first of all that that sophistical rule has no place in the decisions of the church, unless perhaps someone who denies that Christ was born of the Virgin Mary or that his mother was a perpetual virgin is not required to offer any proof. Moreover, you not only deny an accepted teaching but also assert your own. It is just as if someone should come to another person's farm and drive away by force the person whose family has owned it for many generations, denying that it belongs to him and asserting that it belongs to himself. Would he not be required to offer some proof? Indeed the law will favour an owner by the right of possession even if there is a defect in his proof of ownership.[568] If fifty years of possession invalidates any claim and establishes the right of ownership,[569] we have held this teaching more than a thousand years. And so you are to be rejected even if all you do is deny our teaching; as it is you assert your new teaching in such a way as to drive

\* \* \* \* \*

566 *De servo arbitrio* WA 18 642:17–19 / LW 33 74
567 *De servo arbitrio* WA 642:20–3 / LW 33 74. The logical treatises of Peter of Spain and William of Ockham do not seem to contain such a maxim. Perhaps it means that the prosecution has to prove that the defendant is guilty but the defendant is required only to refute the prosecution, not to prove he is innocent.
568 On the right of possession (*praescriptio longi temporis*) see Berger 645.
569 Constantine established the *praescriptio quadraginta annorum* by which anyone who held another's property for forty years could not be sued for its restitution, no matter what the origin of his possession might have been (Berger 645). Erasmus may have written 'quinquagenta' instead of 'quadraginta' by a slip of the pen.

us out of such an ancient possession. And since I see you are so conversant with matters rhetorical, I imagine you know that in counterpleas, since the accusation of an alleged crime has been turned back by the defendant against the plaintiff,[570] both sides are equally required to provide proof, as in that controversy between a blind man and his stepmother: 'you killed my father' – 'not I but you.'[571] Here each one becomes both defendant and plaintiff, and the judge expects proofs from each of them. Likewise you say 'my teaching is pious; yours is heretical.' In the same words we direct the charge back to you. You see how foolish you were to be so taken by that proverb 'The negative side proves nothing.'

Finally, you talk as if none of the ancients had ever proved free will, even though that matter is treated in a great many books even today, and not by one person merely. Granted, they differ, but they agree on the point that free will is something which, when grace works with it, contributes something to salvation. But you will not accept human proofs without miracles and the authority of Holy Scripture. I have already spoken about miracles; and these writers also confirm their opinion by the testimony of Holy Scripture, but you reject their interpretation. But by the same token we can reject yours in the absence of miracles. Accordingly, falling back on insults and jests which are not suited to the role you are undertaking or to such a serious discussion, you challenge our Baal[572] to let us create by means of free will just one frog or kill just one louse: you have the impudence first of all to identify Baal with the God of our church, who is adored by so many thousands of saints that supported and support free will, and then to claim the true God for your flock. But at the same time you contribute nothing to solving the difficulty.

No more to the point is what you throw together in the next section. For you demand that we show you what good deed the saints have

* * * * *

570 On counterpleas (*anticategoria*) see Quintilian *Institutio oratoria* 2.10.5, 7.2.9, 12.1.2 and Julius Victor *Ars rhetorica* 3.2 in *Rhetores Latini Minores* ed Karl Halm (Leipzig 1863) 377. By a counterplea the defendant turns the charge back on the plaintiff.

571 We have not been able to discover the suit and countersuit between a blind man and his stepmother. Julius Victor 3.2 (see preceding note) tells a similar story: a brave man who had a stepmother won as a prize the right to marry a captive woman. He died with signs of poisoning. The captive and the stepmother accused each other of poisoning him.

572 *De servo arbitrio* WA 18 642:36–643:10 / LW 33 75; 3 Kings 18:17–30. In his *Assertio* article 36 (WA 7 146:13–15 / 306–7) Luther had similarly compared the adherents of free will to the prophets of Baal and had taunted them like Elijah.

done by the power of free will. And here you imagine that we will all be 'more silent than frogs or fish.'[573] Anyone could readily ask in turn what good deed grace has done in us? If you name one, he will say it was done by free will. But if you prefer a more appropriate response, no one is so ignorant or tongue-tied that he would not immediately respond, 'We are not dealing with asserting or denying free will by means of miracles, for instead of a miracle we have the authority of Scripture together with the definition of the church.' What then are we dealing with? We are dealing with this: would a stable mind depart from the opinion handed down by so many men famous for holiness and miracles, depart from the decision of the church, and commit our souls to the faith of someone like you who has sprung up just now with a few followers, although the leading men of your flock do not agree either with you or among themselves – indeed though you do not even agree with yourself, since in this same *Assertion* you say one thing in the beginning and something else later on, recanting[574] what you said before.[575] For where you argue in passing that free will is not of the Spirit but is a human invention, arguing from my initial concession that this question was bruited about by the philosophers before Christ,[576] I think you see how feeble your reasoning is. Plato and the poets teach that the world was created,[577] and for that reason is it wrong for Christians to assert that the world was created, refuting those who teach that the world had no beginning? Plato teaches that souls survive the death of the body,[578] and is that a reason we should not assert the same? The philosophers taught that God is mind, all powerful and all good, present everywhere, though no place can hold him.[579] Do not Christians piously assert these same things? In his *Treatise on Household Affairs*,

* * * * *

573  *De servo arbitrio* WA 644:17–645:7 / LW 33 77–8. Luther referred to the Seriphian frogs described in Pliny's *Naturalis historia* 8.83.227, which were proverbial for silent persons (*Adagia* I v 31). Fish were also proverbial for silence (*Adagia* I v 29).

574  See n510 above.

575  In the beginning of chapter 36 of the *Assertio* (WA 7 142:22–3 / 301), Luther quotes the article to be defended ('After sin free will exists in name only ...') but later in the chapter he says: 'For I misspoke when I said that free will before grace exists in name only; rather I should have simply said "free will is a fiction among real things, a name with no reality"' (WA 7 146:4–6 / 306).

576  *De servo arbitrio* WA 18 646:4–8 / LW 33 80

577  Plato *Timaeus* 29A; Ovid *Metamorphoses* 1.5–88

578  For example, *Apology* 40C

579  For example, Cicero *De natura deorum* 1.2.4

Aristotle teaches that between husband and wife there should be a mutual love and a lasting friendship closer than any other human relationship,[580] and is that a reason to think Paul was wrong to command, 'Husbands, love your wives, etc'?[581] And there are innumerable other points we have in common with pagan philosophers, but that fact does not diminish the authority of our teachings but rather confirms that by the light of nature they saw some of the things handed on to us by Holy Scripture. But we do not believe the philosophers unless they agree with Scripture.[582] True enough. And we assert free will from Scripture – wrongly understood, you will say. Therefore the argument is about interpretation. A little earlier you proved the necessity of all occurrences from Virgil,[583] and you think free will should not be asserted simply because it has been treated by the philosophers?

As for the rest, the more copiously you pursue it, the more words you waste, since it has nothing to do with what I proposed. You demand that we describe to you the form and power of free will, what it is, what it can do, what it does.[584] But you already confessed earlier that all this has been set forth by the sophists, what it is, what it avails, what it does, how it is related, etc.[585] Your rhetoric, namely, demanded that in order to cast aspersions on me you should praise the sophists; though you are always calling them impious and blasphemous, you there deny that they blaspheme the way I do.[586] If they are blasphemous, impious, enemies of Christianity, blind when they teach what they have in common with me, how can you exonerate them from the blasphemy you charge against me? In agreement with the church, we described to you the nature, power, and action of free will, but the description which suits the Catholic church does not suit you and your adherents. We prove it from Holy Scripture, but our interpretation does not suit you. You prove necessity from Virgil and Holy Scripture, but your interpretation does not suit the church. How, then, will you prove your teaching to us? You stipulate that we should not ask for or accept anything

* * * * *

580  Pseudo-Aristotle *Oeconomia* 1343b
581  Eph 5:25
582  Cf Erasmus *Enchiridion* CWE 66 47.
583  See n351 above.
584  *De servo arbitrio* WA 18 644:20–645:7 / LW 33 77
585  *De servo arbitrio* WA 18 615:5–7 / LW 33 36–7; these questions are discussed by Peter Lombard in *Sententiarum libri quatuor* II dist 24–6 (PL 192 701–14). Elaborations and refinements on them were produced by the many commentators on the *Sententiae*.
586  *De servo arbitrio* WA 18 613:5–7 / LW 33 34

but Holy Scripture, but you do it in such a way as to require that we permit you to be its sole interpreter, renouncing all others. Thus the victory will be yours if we allow you to be not the steward but the lord of Holy Scripture. And then, as for your insulting here the holy and orthodox men praised by me, that is hardly something unusual for you to do. It is tiresome to respond to such loquacity when everything is beside the point. When will you begin to get down to brass tacks?[587] Put an end to my discussion and indicate whom we ought to believe, you or such an august assembly. You cannot tolerate my speech because I am nothing but a voice,[588] and we are supposed to tolerate such an endless Archytean clatter,[589] grating on our ears with so much that is superfluous, abusive, and insulting?

At this point my writings are once more brought up against me. I advised that we should ignore the mere inventions of men and go to the springs of Holy Scripture, and now I contradict myself and do not practise what I preached. How so? Because 'I write *Discussions*, I celebrate the decisions of popes,'[590] I boast of the authority of men.'[591] In *A Discussion* I do not employ the authority of either popes or councils or orthodox teachers to support free will, and even if I had done so, that would have been somewhat more tolerable than your citing of Melanchthon's pamphlet[592] as if it had the same authority as canonical Scripture. But I introduce this comparison for one purpose only, to get you to show us why we should believe you rather than them. So too you yourself see how shameless and baseless is the accusation you add, that I leave nothing untried in my attempt to divert you from the simplicity of Christian piety.[593] In *A Discussion* I do not defend my teaching but that of the church, but I do so without the assistance of the church, and I defend it from Holy Scripture, not as a fabrication of men but as the determination of Holy Scripture. And you are so little ashamed of this patent nonsense that you always add impudence to impudence. For this is the way you go from false premises

\* \* \* \* \*

587 Literally, 'talk about three she-goats' (Martial 6.19)
588 See n553 above.
589 Archytas of Tarentum (fl c 400–365) was a Pythagorean philosopher who excelled in mechanics. He invented a brass rattle that became proverbial for a chatterbox (*Adagia* II vii 44).
590 Emser (sig T3v) translates Luther's *decreta pontificum* as 'die satzungen der Bischoffen' ('the decisions of bishops'), a possible meaning of *pontificum*. But *decreta* suggests Gratian's *Decretum* and the papal decretals of canon law.
591 *De servo arbitrio* WA 18 648:3–10 / LW 33 82
592 See nn32 and 95 above.
593 *De servo arbitrio* WA 18 648:10–13 / LW 33 82

to a totally false conclusion: 'From that,' you say, 'we can easily understand that you were not sincere in giving us that advice or serious in anything you wrote, but you were confident that with the empty bubbles[594]
of your words you could lead the world wherever you wanted. And nevertheless you do not lead it anywhere, since you utter absolutely nothing but sheer contradictions, always and everywhere.'[595] This is truly what
you said, Luther. Before, you decided to excuse my outlook but now you
make this pronouncement about it: I was not sincere in what I wrote even
when I wrote correctly according to your judgment. What could be more
shameless than for me to want to lead the world with my writings, since
I always wanted to stand alone and I never allowed the tiniest faction to
be attached to me – something which you do in the most ambitious way.
Nor do I regret this attitude; I prefer, indeed I prefer to be a sheep in the
flock than a leader of a herd of pigs or goats. Now, though 'I utter nothing but sheer contradictions world without end[596] and everywhere,' nevertheless you have not yet been able to bring forward one place where I
am not consistent. You should not have laid this charge against Erasmus
before you yourself had responded to those writers who have published
books accusing you of many contradictions excerpted from your writings.
You add: 'as was quite rightly said by the person who called you a perfect
Proteus or Vertumnus.'[597] Did I not know that you would borrow something from scurrilous books to hurl against me? And nevertheless the person, as I conjecture, who you said had spoken quite rightly, seems to your
Philip to have been out of his mind when he wrote those things, as he
also testified in a letter of his.[598] And if that person spoke quite rightly,

* * * * *

594 Latin *bullis*, which could mean either 'bubbles' or 'papal bulls'
595 *De servo arbitrio* WA 18 648:13–17 / LW 33 82
596 Erasmus here mocks Luther's phrase *per omnia* 'always' by expanding it into
the liturgical phrase *per omnia secula seculorum*. Emser translates Luther's *per
omnia* as 'durch aus' (sig T4) but he then puts the Latin *per omnia secula seculorum* right after it because he knows his audience will recognize the liturgical
phrase, which was sung at the end of many prayers at mass.
597 In 1524 Otto Brunfels published a scurrilous addendum to Hutten's *Expostulatio* attacking Erasmus: *Pro Vlricho Hutteno defuncto, ad Erasmi Roter. Spongiam
Responsio*. In it he called Erasmus more changeable than Vertumnus; see the
edition of Brunfels' tract in Hutten II 327:17. On Proteus and Vertumnus see
nn83 and 122 above.
598 In a letter of 23 August 1523 to Joachim Camerarius, Melanchthon says that
someone who wrote against Erasmus was out of his mind: 'Hodie certo ac-
cepi eum quem dixere nuper cum adesses mortuum, superesse. Quid dicam?
quo me vertam? nostro periculo furit. Quanta nos invidia onerat apud omnes

you spoke quite wrongly when you made me into a supreme theologian.[599] But it is no wonder that instead of a supreme theologian I have become a Vertumnus, since I was once called in your writings an extraordinary ram caught in a thorn-bush[600] and now I have become a pig from the herd of Epicurus.[601]

After that you absurdly repeat for us that we are on the affirmative side, you on the negative; I have already spoken about that before. And you call us utterly insane because we require you to grant the doctrine of free will for no other reason than that it has been asserted by many great and ancient men.[602] Could anything more shameless be imagined, since I profess during the course of the struggle in A Discussion that I will yield if I do not cite testimony from Scripture to prove what I assert.[603] And here once more you have the impudence to scoff at orthodox Greek writers whom you deprive of all authority by a marvellous assumption, that the saints have sometimes erred because they are human, and you point out the danger of believing that, because Peter was a saint, he was right when he admonished the Lord not to suffer.[604] Such a method of arguing we have from one who says nothing that is not clever, nothing that is not apt. It is brilliant, to be sure, to compare Peter when he was still a Jew with Peter inspired by the Holy Spirit. And how could anyone think Peter was right to say, 'Let this

* * * * *

bonos? et provocat Erasmum, in nos ut videtur vehementius saeviturum quam in illum purphóon [transliterated Greek]' ('Today I learned for sure that the person who they said was dead when you were here is still alive. What can I say? Where can I turn? His craziness is a danger to us. How he heaps upon us the ill will of good men! And he challenges Erasmus, who will, it seems, rage against us more violently than he did against that fire-eater [perhaps Hutten]'). See Philippi Melanchthonis opera quae supersunt omnia ed Karl G. Bretschneider and Heinrich E. Bindseil, 28 vols, CR 1–28 (Halle/Saale and Braunschweig 1834–60) 1 647 no 254. The opponent of Erasmus whom Melanchthon deplores was probably Otho Brunfels (see the preceding note). In a letter of 26 March 1524 Erasmus wrote that Luther and Melanchthon are forced to write against such stupid and insane (insanos) writers as Brunfels. See Epp 1405 (introductory note) and 1432:59–61.

599 See 109 above.

600 Gen 22:13. Luther applied this simile to Erasmus in his reply to the theologians of Louvain and Cologne, Responsio Lutheriana ad condemnationem doctrinalem (WA 6 184).

601 See n154 above.

602 De servo arbitrio WA 18 648:20–8 / LW 33 83

603 A Discussion 14

604 De servo arbitrio WA 18 648:28–649:3 / LW 33 83

not happen to you, Lord,' since he was immediately rebuked by the Lord: 'Get behind me, etc'[605]

And as if it were not enough to set forth these clever sayings once, you add in the next section that those who cite the opinion of ancient saints 'are like those who, for the sake of a joke, babble that not everything in the gospel is true, alleging that question from John, "Are we not right to say that you are a Samaritan and have a demon?"[606] or again, "He deserves to die." '[607] What are you about, Luther, or what do you mean by these truly blasphemous comparisons of yours? A person who cites something from the books of those whose memory has been sacrosanct to the church for so many centuries, whose writings are read publicly in church,[608] does no better than buffoons who cite the sayings of wicked Jews from the gospel? But how often do you also cite the testimony of Augustine or Gregory?[609] How does your comparison apply any less to you than to us? Did they speak in the Spirit when they say what makes for you but according to the flesh when they say what counts against you? Therefore do not insist that on the issue of free will you have the advantage of having Augustine so often on your side – as you boast, though I will soon show that this is quite false – lest we turn your comparison back against you. Or if you deprive them of all authority, stop making use of their testimony. If they said many things devoutly, many things excellently, although they sometimes made mistakes, allow us to make use of what they said well, as you claim the right to do also. But you command us to choose what is better in their books, passing over what they said according to the flesh.[610] We chose what is better; you likewise chose what is better. But we say that what is better is what agrees with the teachings of the church; you say it is what makes for your teachings. Who can settle the dispute here about which side chooses better? But this is the question posed by my comparison, to which as yet you have given no response, nor is it likely that you ever will. It seems that up to now you have not ranted and raved enough against the most approved Doctors of the church unless you accuse St Jerome of impiety, sacrilege,

* * * * *

605 Matt 16:22–3
606 John 8:48
607 Matt 26:66; Mark 14:64; *De servo arbitrio* WA 18 649:4–7 / LW 33 84
608 This refers not to the mass, which contained no readings from the Fathers, but to the divine office, in which matins had patristic selections.
609 On Augustine see n143 above. St Gregory the Great (c 540–604) was pope and one of the four major Latin Fathers of the church.
610 *De servo arbitrio* WA 18 649:9–16 / LW 33 84

and blasphemy because he wrote, 'Virginity fills up heaven; marriage, the earth.'[611] Clearly impious, sacrilegious, and blasphemous, as you have perverted it! 'As if,' you say, 'patriarchs, apostles, and Christian spouses were entitled to earth, not heaven, or as if pagan vestal virgins without Christ were entitled to heaven.'[612] How shamelessly you distort it! Was Jerome talking there about virginity which is celibate without Christ? Was he so crazy that he would promise heaven to such persons? Again, does he exclude the patriarchs from heaven because they had wives? What, then, is he saying? He sets holy virginity above holy marriage because marriage was instituted so that the human race might grow and be propagated, according to the command 'Increase and multiply and fill the earth.'[613] Virginity, however, although it does not increase the number of people on earth, nevertheless, by teaching and by the greatest purity of life draws people to heaven and begets them, as it were, for heaven. Hence the Lord calls blessed those who make themselves eunuchs because of the kingdom of God.[614] Of this number were the apostles: just as we read that some of them had wives,[615] we also do not read that after undertaking the business of the gospel they made use of their wives.[616] In your disputation how irreverently you take Jerome to task for this reason: he wrote that some testimonies from Scripture offer support as Paul cites them, but not in their own context.[617] Here it is not enough to call him a dim-sighted, silly trifler without finally execrating his mouth as sacrilegious. Even if Jerome should have made a mistake, we can courteously find an excuse for him, or if there is no room for an excuse, the decent thing to do is to correct the error modestly. That, I suppose, is the service you would want to be furnished to you if something similar should happen. For you knew that Jerome had the highest opinion of Paul, nor did he make that charge against him because he misused scriptural testimony but because there was nothing so recondite in Scripture that he could not accommodate it to proving the gospel. You

\* \* \* \* \*

611 Ep 22.19 CSEL 54 168; see n90 above.
612 *De servo arbitrio* WA 18 649:17–21 / LW 33 84
613 Gen 1:28
614 Matt 19:11–12
615 The Gospels record that Christ cured Peter's mother-in-law; Matt 8:14–15 (Mark 1:30–1, Luke 4:38–9).
616 Erasmus' phrasing is careful: 'we do not read that they made' is quite different from 'we read that they did not make.'
617 *De servo arbitrio* WA 18 722:31–723:15, 724:15–20 / LW 33 196, 198. Folly cited the same passage in *The Praise of Folly* (CWE 27 145), where the Latin *pugnat* means 'fight for, support,' as it also seems to here (ASD IV-3 183 999–1004nn).

rant and rave thus against Jerome, but you do not allow anyone to disagree with you, however courteously.

Now whereas I said it is not credible that God for so many centuries should have overlooked such a harmful error in his church without revealing to some of his saints the point which you contend is the keystone of the teachings in the gospel,[618] you play the sophist and refute this by saying that no error whatever was overlooked in any of the saints or in the church, since 'no one is a saint unless he is moved by the Spirit of God' – and the Spirit cannot be in error – and since 'Christ remains with his church till the end of time.'[619] But the whole drift of your reasoning is to make us understand that it is unknown who the saints are and what the church is. You even go so far as to try to persuade us that God guides the affairs of mortals in such a way that the church of the saints seems to be where it is not, and, on the other hand, is where it does not seem to be, and likewise that those who are wicked are always considered to be saints, and that those who are saints are considered to be wicked.[620] But when you declaim all this so copiously, you do nothing but confound and entirely subvert all judgments made by the church, and you claim authority for all heretical conventicles. You deny that 'if God allowed the most learned men to err over a long series of centuries, it immediately follows that the church erred,'[621] – I mean that church which you say is hidden and cannot be shown. How, then, are you sure that Wyclif[622] was a holy man and the Arians were heretics? Is Wyclif holy precisely because he was condemned by the church which you call papistical? By the same token you will say that Arius[623] was holy because he was condemned by the same church. At this point if you appeal to Scripture, did the Arians have any lack of Scripture? No, they did not, you will say, but they interpreted it wrongly. But how can we be sure of that except that the church rejected their interpretation and approved that of the other side? The same could be said of Pelagius,[624] whom you also hold to be a wicked heretic, not so much, I imagine, because he was condemned by

* * * * *

618  *A Discussion* 20
619  *De servo arbitrio* WA 18 649:26–650:1 / LW 33 85
620  Luther's argument in favour of an invisible and inerrant church (*De servo arbitrio* WA 18 649:26–652:22 / LW 33 85–9)
621  *De servo arbitrio* WA 18 650:9–11 / LW 33 85
622  See *A Discussion* n35.
623  See n92 above.
624  A lay ascetic (360?–420?) who argued that the will is free to do either good or evil and that grace is conferred in proportion to merits as a mere facilitator of what the will itself could perform. He was attacked by Augustine, Orosius, Jerome, and others, and he was condemned at the Council of Carthage (418).

the Roman church as because he disagrees with your teaching. But let us grant it is possible that a general council is so corrupt that either there is no one moved by the Spirit of God, or if there is, he is not listened to, and that a conciliar decree is issued from the opinion of evil men, still it is more probable that the Spirit of God is there than in private conventicles, where the spirit of Satan is quite likely to be detected. If the church of God cannot be shown but there is a need for some certain judgments, I think it is safer to follow public authority rather than the opinion of someone or other who scorns everyone and boasts of his own conscience and spirit. If it is enough to say 'I have the Spirit,' then we will have to believe many people urging various opinions upon us, and if the opinions disagree with one another they cannot be true. But in fact I did not discuss whether we must believe whatever the saints have taught or whether whatever the church has defined is undoubtedly true, but rather I wanted to show that, other things being equal, the greater probability lies on the side of what is approved by such men and confirmed by the public authority of the church rather than with what someone or other brought up on his own. But even you do not dare to say that 'from the beginning of the world the condition of the church on earth has been such that those who were not the people of God were said to be so and, on the other hand, some others who were both saints and the people of God were not said to be so,' but rather you set forth the proposition in this way: 'Who knows?'[625] If you confess that you don't know, what are you about in your *Assertion*, which rejects the authority of all councils and orthodox teachers and rescinds just about all the decrees of the church?[626] If we were sure that the Spirit of God is in your church, we would rightly reject this church, since it conflicts with yours. As it is, since you confess that you are not certain where the saints are, where the true church is which does not err, either we will waver in uncertainty or we will follow what is nearer to the truth. But whereas you challenge me to bring forward from the reign of the pope even one bishop who fulfils his duty or one council in which anything was decreed which contributed to the Christian religion rather than to profane trifles about palliums,[627] dignities, and revenues,[628] as for the first point, just as I confess that there are few bishops who truly play the role of bishops, so too it is possible to bring

\* \* \* \* \*

625 *De servo arbitrio* WA 18 650:27–30 / LW 33 86
626 In his *Assertio omnium articulorum M. Lutheri* (WA 7 91–151) Luther explicitly rejects the authority of the church on many points.
627 A pallium is a short woolen cape worn over the chasuble, granted by the pope as a symbol of the jurisdiction of metropolitan bishops.
628 *De servo arbitrio* WA 18 650:35–7 / LW 33 86

forward some in whom you will not find anything lacking in the duties of
a pious prelate, among whom I number John, the bishop of Rochester.[629]
But you will immediately reject him because he wrote against you (and so
your rejection has no weight). Nor is there any reason for you to cry out
here that I write to gain his favour: I neither receive nor desire any income
from him, and on many points he disagrees with my opinions, nor does
he have such a high regard for my studies. Finally, nothing could be less
comparable than the comparison you propose: God permitted Cicero to err
in the case of free will; therefore it is not unlikely if someone should say
that God permitted the most learned and holy men of the church to err like
Cicero.[630] At the moment we are not investigating what God revealed to
pagan philosophers or orators but rather what eluded men who have tasted
the Spirit of God and devoted themselves most diligently to Holy Scripture
for many years. Did they not achieve anything precisely because their opinions vary or because they dispute without rendering any opinion? So too
you people disagree in your teachings. And here you say, 'Who knows?'
But do Christians fail to believe most firmly in the resurrection of the body
simply because the greatest philosophers vacillate and argue about it? You
add that God conceals his saints like a splendid pearl which is not to be cast
before swine 'lest a wicked man should see the glory of God.'[631] And nevertheless the Gospel says, 'by their fruits you shall know them.'[632] If a good
tree as well as a bad one is known by its fruit, we can make some judgments
about the pious and the wicked even in this world, though the most certain
judgments are those of God. And this would be the place for a discussion
comparing fruits, if I had not decided not to stir up such a hornets' nest.[633]

At this point, Luther, I seem to be dealing with the rhetorician,[634]
whose modesty I wish you had imitated in all of your writings; you would

\* \* \* \* \*

629 John Fisher, author of *A Confutation of Luther's Assertion*. See n8 above.
630 *De servo arbitrio* WA 18 651:7–12 / LW 33 87. Cicero wrote on free will, fate, and
    divine foresight in his *De natura deorum* (especially book 3), in the fragmen-
    tary *De fato*, and in *De divinatione*. Both Luther and Erasmus were certainly
    familiar with Augustine's extended polemic against Cicero on this subject in
    *De civitate Dei*. Luther's argument here, however, is not so much that Cicero
    erred about free will as that free will did not get Cicero or pagan philosophers
    grace and salvation.
631 *De servo arbitrio* WA 18 651:26–8 / LW 33 88; Matt 7.6
632 Matt 7:16–20 (Luke 6:43–4); *Adagia* I ix 39
633 Literally 'to move Camarina.' The citizens of Camarina drained a pestilential
    swamp despite warnings, thus exposing their city to invasion by 'moving' it
    (*Adagia* I i 64).
634 See nn41 and 42 above.

have alienated far fewer from yourself or, if we give you any credence, from the gospel. Your insults know no bounds, and you do not approve of anything at all in a person who opposes your opinion. This rhetorician, though he engages in sufficient buffoonery by dallying with my *Discussion* – 'What are you about, my little Discussion?' and 'Lady Discussion,'[635] – still he is more moderate than you are, unless he strove to preserve the decorum of the role he is playing. But in fact his arguments about saints and the church do not have much validity against me because I am not using their authority but rather Holy Scripture to refute your opinion. But if we posit an equal balance in the things by which you wish to be judged and the opinion of men is wavering in the balance, I ask you whether the authority of the ancient Fathers and the church should have any weight. This was the drift of my discussion, to which you should have directed your arguments. You confess that the church I allege does exist, you confess that the saints I bring up do exist, but you distinguish the rule of charity, which can be deceived, from the rule of faith, which cannot[636] – a distinction aimed at preventing us from believing anyone is a saint unless God declares him to be so. Charity believes that all who are baptized are saints, but faith does not. Although this is the case, nevertheless, because 'charity, which hopes for all things'[637] and which is also confirmed by many arguments, believes that the orthodox Fathers were saints, it should have enough weight, when the scale is evenly balanced, to incline us towards those who have been commended for so many centuries by the public favour of the whole world than towards those who are commended for no other reason than that they are baptized. And so if you insist that their authority has no value in confirming an opinion, then neither does yours or anyone else's. I have already answered about choosing the better parts[638] as well as about the testimony of Scripture, since each side chooses and interprets. Likewise I am unaffected by that old song of yours about some who fail to exercise judgment and devour everything indiscriminately, or by a perversion of judgment spit out what is better.[639] Though there may be some such, still charity is not so wrongly suspicious as to conceive such an opinion

* * * * *

635 At *De servo arbitrio* WA 18 669:20 / LW 33 114 Luther begins to personify *A Discussion* as a woman (the Latin and Greek designations in the title of *De libero arbitrio* are feminine). See *De servo arbitrio* WA 18 678:13, 744:32 / LW 33 128, 228.
636 *De servo arbitrio* WA 18 651:31–652:11 / LW 33 88
637 1 Cor 13:7
638 *De servo arbitrio* WA 652:11–17 / LW 33 89
639 *De servo arbitrio* WA 652:17–21 / LW 33 89

about the leaders of the church unless what they prescribe is manifestly wicked.

But finally you approach the heart of the matter. 'If the church is concealed' you say, 'if the saints are hidden, what and whom shall we believe? And as you argue very pointedly, who will give us certainty? Where will we discover the Spirit? If you consider learning, there are erudite teachers on both sides. If you look for morals, there are sinners on both sides. If you look to Scripture, both sides embrace it.' But if we make Scripture the judge, the interpretation of it is uncertain in many places, and both sides pull Scripture towards their meaning. Hence it follows that here we play the Sceptics, 'unless you take the best line of all when you express your doubt in such a way as to aver that you are seeking to learn the truth, inclining in the meantime towards the side that supports free will, until the truth shines forth.'[640] Imagine, if you like, that I have no feeling for talent or phrasing: do you really think, Luther, that it is unclear to me who wrote this? One voice is as different from the other as a parrot's from a quail's.[641] Could you ever bear to say 'as you very pointedly argue,' since for you I always speak ignorantly and stupidly. Could you say such a thing as 'unless you take the best line of all,' since up to now you have so shamelessly ranted and raved against Erasmus as a Sceptic and worse than a Sceptic, namely a thoroughgoing Lucian and Epicurus?[642] Again, could you say 'there is something in what you say but not the whole truth,'[643] since you always bawl out that I have nothing to say and utter nothing but verbal bubbles and bombast? But however this may be, it doesn't much matter.

[*Not all of Scripture is fully clear*]
Finally, when you are ready to untie the knot,[644] you do what you regularly and wrongly blame the sophists for doing: you introduce a twofold clarity of Holy Scripture and likewise a twofold judgment to test spirits. The first is the one by which everyone 'enlightened by a special gift of God judges and discriminates all teachings with full certainty.' Paul is speaking about such a person in 1 Cor 2[:15]: "The spiritual man judges all things and is judged by no one."' And you call this 'the interior clarity of Holy Scripture.' 'This,' you say, 'is perhaps what was meant by those who replied to you

*  *  *  *  *

640 *De servo arbitrio* WA 18 652:23–34 / LW 33 89
641 Cf Martial 10.3.7.
642 See nn56 and 55 above.
643 *De servo arbitrio* WA 18 652:34–5 / LW 33 89–90
644 *Adagia* I i 6

that all things were to be decided by the judgment of the Spirit.'[645] Indeed I know someone[646] who I did not believe had this Spirit, which he claimed for himself, since I had learned by most certain evidence that he was a consummate liar, brim-full of vainglory, an insatiable backbiter; but then he did not understand this matter as you interpret it. For when I agreed with him so far as to allow that some person or other might be certain because of his own spirit, I went on to ask how that would give me any certainty, since I do not have the gift of distinguishing the spirits[647] of others and I said that in this way, as you also confess, his certitude did not remove my doubt. He brought the argument back to Scripture, but when I objected that the interpretations are various, he had no answer but 'Spirit, Spirit.' Hence if you can solve the difficulty you have taken in hand, you will be performing no mean task. And so you confess that this judgment does no good for others but only for the person provided with this spirit. Otherwise we would have to have faith in all the fanatics who boast more contentiously about having the Spirit than those who truly have this special gift.

And so you display also the other clarity of Scripture, namely that which is external, and also the external revelation of the spirit by which we promote the salvation of others also by judging quite certainly about spiritual things and the teachings of everyone.[648] Come on, then, I am waiting for this certainty with bated breath. You add that 'this judgment is mainly the concern of leaders and heralds of the word,'[649] which I take to mean either bishops or theologians; if they should agree among themselves in explaining Holy Scripture, we would have something certain to follow. As it is, our heralds teach something different than you do, and your adherents disagree among themselves and even go so far as to cry out boldly against you. Where, then, even in the church, is this certain judgment by which we prove or disprove teachings drawn from Holy Scripture, a rule which is completely certain, 'a spiritual light brighter than the sun?'[650] But you yourself perceive and confess that you will get nowhere unless you prove what you assume, even though it is debatable, and you promise you

* * * * *

645 *De servo arbitrio* WA 18 653:13–20 / LW 33 90. In *A Discussion* (19) Erasmus had spoken of the *indicio* 'sign' of the Spirit, but Luther misread the word as *iudicio* 'judgment.'
646 Erasmus' reference is unclear. Was it Hutten or someone else?
647 Cf 1 Cor 12:10.
648 *De servo arbitrio* WA 18 653:22–4 / LW 33 90–1
649 *De servo arbitrio* WA 18 653:24–5 / LW 33 91
650 *De servo arbitrio* WA 18 653:30 / LW 33 91

will do it. Come on, we will follow you if you perform what you promise; certainly we want to. In Deuteronomy 17[:8–13] Moses speaks of referring judgment to the priests if there is any difficulty about which the judges disagree and which they cannot resolve, etc. 'How,' you say, 'how can they give a judgment about a controverted matter according to the Law unless the Law is externally quite clear?'[651] I reply in two ways. First, if the Law had been externally quite clear to anyone who has common sense, why did the judges themselves not unravel the knot, since it is probable that they were not ignorant of the Law? They are said to have differed in their opinions not because they did not know the Law, but because the case was difficult, and therefore it was referred to the priests as more skilled in the Law. Secondly, I reply that in that place Moses did not mean difficulties which arise concerning the question of free will or the like but rather concerning more material affairs, of which he gives some examples there, such as a case of blood against blood, lawsuit against lawsuit, leprosy or not leprosy. Then, too, when you try to confirm your argument by adducing secular laws, by which suits cannot be settled unless they are quite clear, you work against yourself. For just as I do not deny that many disputes are settled by the laws, it is also obvious that there are many obscurities in the laws of princes. Otherwise what point would there be in devoting so much effort over many years to learning the law if it were so obvious that it would be completely clear to anyone at all who knows the language and is not lacking in common sense? Therefore those who wrote so many volumes in an attempt to iron out the difficulties of the law were wasting their energy. Judges and senates are foolish to wear themselves out for years sometimes to understand just one case. The poet was wrong when he said, 'who unties the knots[652] of justice and solves the riddles of the law.'[653] Nor is this conclusion of yours valid: if there is so much lucidity in secular laws, how much more should there be in writings which pertain to eternal salvation?[654] First of all, the matters treated in Holy Scripture are more obscure. Next, it was not impious either for other orthodox Fathers or for Augustine, to whom (not without cause) you attribute so much, to say that God deliberately left some obscurity in Holy Scripture to stir up in us a greater desire to scrutinize it.[655]

* * * * *

651 *De servo arbitrio* WA 18 654:4–5 / LW 33 91
652 *Adagia* I i 6
653 Juvenal 8.50
654 *De servo arbitrio* WA 654:13–17 / LW 33 91–2
655 *De doctrina christiana* 2.6.7–8 / CCSL 32 35–6

From Psalm 18[:9] you bring up the verse: 'the command of the Lord
is clear, enlightening the eyes.'[656] But he says the command is clear, not
all of Scripture; and even if all of Scripture were clear to David and others inspired by a prophetic spirit, it is not immediately clear to all who
know grammar and have common sense, as you so often affirm. Again,
from Psalm 118[:130] you bring in the verse: 'The disclosure of your speech
illuminates and gives understanding to children.' I will accept this testimony if you mean such children as David was and those upon whom the
Spirit of God rests; but if you apply it to whoever knows the language, that
is quite another matter. Then too, in what you cite from Isaiah, chapter 8
[verse 20], 'Go rather to the Law and the testimony, etc,' the prophet is not
saying there is no obscurity in the sacred books, but rather he is threatening that darkness will come upon those who consult soothsayers and ven-
triloquists. For he adds in the same place, 'Shall the common people not
ask God' for vision, etc? Christ lay hidden in the Law, but the words of
the Law were not clear to everyone who knew Hebrew; rather they asked
the Scribes who were well versed in the Law for advice from the Law, as
when Herod consulted them about where the boy Jesus would be born.[657]
Again, the second chapter of Malachi [verse 7] commands the people to
ask for the Law from the mouth of a priest. 'A very fine messenger indeed,' you say, 'who will announce what is both ambiguous to him and
unclear to the people.'[658] Why then do you people not follow the advice
of Malachi and ask for the Law from the mouths of priests and bishops?
Moreover, what need was there to learn the Law from the mouth of a priest,
since anyone of the people who knew the language and had common sense
could easily understand a Law that was perfectly clear. Therefore someone who orders that the Law be sought from the mouth of a priest indicates that the Law is not clear to just anyone, but rather he points out
the fitting interpreter of the Law. Again, Psalm 118[:105], 'Your word is
a lamp to my feet and a light on my paths,' does not deal with intricate
questions, but rather with the rules of a good life which shine forth and
show what we ought to seek and what we ought to avoid. And even if
you twist it violently so as to extend it to the whole Law, what applies to
David does not apply to just anyone skilled in grammar. So much for Old
Testament passages, but of texts such as these you could have brought up
hundreds.

\* \* \* \* \*

656 *De servo arbitrio* WA 18 654:21–2 / LW 33 92
657 Matt 2:3–4
658 *De servo arbitrio* WA 18 654:28–30 / LW 33 92

You go on to the New Testament. 'In the second chapter of Romans,[659] Paul says that the gospel was promised in Holy Scripture. What sort of witness is it,' you say, 'if it is obscure?'[660] If nothing is obscure in the predictions of the prophets and in the figures of the Law, why are they called shadows?[661] And why do we speak of the light of the gospel, if not because what is wrapped and covered up by figures in the Law is brought out into the open by the gospel? Is nothing there predicted about Christ which is not perfectly clear to all, provided they know Hebrew? Indeed, even the disciples of the Lord, after hearing so many sermons, after seeing so many miracles, after so many signs and tokens which the prophets foretold concerning Christ, did not understand Scripture until Christ opened up the meaning so that they understood Scripture. Now in Paul's letter to the Corinthians, when he discusses the brightness of Moses and Christ, he makes the brightness of the gospel so pre-eminent that he says 'the brightness of that part – he is speaking of the Law – was not even glorified.'[662]

What if God deliberately wanted prophecies about Christ not to be clear to just anyone at all, just as on earth he also did not want anyone to preach before his death that he was the Messiah,[663] because that was expedient in carrying out the program of saving mankind? But when the apostles announced that the predictions of the prophets had been fulfilled, both the Law was clearer through a comparison with the events, and it also turned out that the Law contributed to belief in the gospel and the gospel threw light on the enigmas of the Law. Surely this is what Peter meant when he compared the speech of the prophets to a torch 'shining in a dark place,'[664] nor did he take everything else to be dark, since Paul attributes even to the pagan philosophers enough light for them to know God and his sempiternal divinity.[665] All truth is light. And many truths promulgated by them agree with the teachings of Christians. John was a burning lamp[666] because he preached the word of God. For the same reason Paul called the Thessalonians lights of the world[667] because they knew the word of life. But that

*  *  *  *  *

659 The correct reference is Romans 1:2.
660 *De servo arbitrio* WA 18 654:39–40 / LW 33 92–3
661 Heb 10:1
662 2 Cor 3:7–11
663 Matt 16:20
664 2 Pet 1:19
665 Rom 1:19–20
666 John 5:35
667 Phil 2:1; *Thessalonices* in the two Basel editions of 1526 and LB X 1301B is a slip of the pen for *Philippenses*.

was not reason enough for any of them who knew grammar to understand whatever is difficult in Holy Scripture. Christ was 'the light of the world,'[668] but nevertheless the divine nature was hidden in him, nor do we immediately grasp whatever is in Christ. You could have thrown together hundreds of such testimonies, even from indexes, where light is mentioned.[669]

What follows is even more banal: 'What are the apostles doing when they support their preaching by Scripture? Do they do it to add darkness to darkness so as to make what is obscure to us even more obscure, or to prove what is better known by what is less known?'[670] At this point when will you stop throwing prophets, baptists, and apostles at us? No one doubts their Spirit, and their authority is sacrosanct. Because they had the Spirit teaching them from within, they explained what is obscure in the writings of the prophets. We were talking about your spirit and that of your followers, who profess that there is nothing in Holy Scripture which is obscure to you as long as you know grammar, and we demanded that you establish the credibility of this certainty, which you still fail to do, try as you may. In John, you say, Christ commands the Jews to search the places in Scripture which speak of him;[671] if they are obscure, he is throwing them into doubt. Indeed, if there is no obscurity in them, what is the meaning of that word 'search'? For we do not search for the sun, which is open to all eyes, but we search to find something that is hidden. And nevertheless, when the Lord added 'for those places speak of me,'[672] he added a good deal of light, pointing out the aim of the prophecy. Just so in Acts, when Paul had taught and admonished them, they compared the scriptural passages with what had been carried out and what had been propounded to them;[673] and there was much they would not have understood if the apostle had

\* \* \* \* \*

668 John 8:12, 9:5
669 At *De servo arbitrio* WA 18 654:40–655:10 / LW 33 93 Luther cited the scriptural passages on light which Erasmus has just discussed. The first concordance of the Bible was completed in 1230. Fuller concordances were printed in 1470, 1475, 1485, and 1496; see *The Catholic Encyclopedia* 15 vols (New York 1907–12) IV 195.
670 *De servo arbitrio* WA 18 655:11–13 / LW 33 93. The Latin *notius per ignotius* is Luther's variation of *ignotum per ignotius*. Though this must have been a well-known saying, we have been able to find it only in Chaucer's *Canon's Yeoman's Tale* VIII (G) 1457 (where Chaucer's source is a Latin translation of an arabic book on alchemy) and in a nineteenth-century book.
671 John 5:39; *De servo arbitrio* WA 18 655:13–15 / LW 33 93
672 John 5:39
673 Acts 17:11; cf *De servo arbitrio* WA 18 655:15–18 / LW 33 93.

not supplied this additional light. Therefore I am not making the passages
obscure, but rather God himself wanted there to be some obscurity in them,
but in such a way that there would be enough light for the eternal salvation
of everyone if he used his eyes and grace was there to help. No one denies
that there is truth as clear as crystal in Holy Scripture, but sometimes it is
wrapped and covered up by figures and enigmas so that it needs scrutiny
and an interpreter, either because God wanted in this way to arouse us
from dullness and also to set us to work, as Augustine says,[674] or because
truth is more pleasant and affects us more deeply when it has been dug
out and shines forth to us through the cover of darkness than if it had
been exposed for anyone at all to see,[675] or because he did not want that
treasure of wisdom to be prostituted to anyone no matter who. And so you
accomplish nothing at all by bringing up one place or another where there
is no obscurity.

'God created heaven and earth.'[676] You propose this place as not at
all obscure, for in the words there is no figure of speech or ambiguity.[677]
But yet you see how here too the interpreters have sweated over what is
meant here by heaven, what by earth, or whether he created individual
things in series or all things together with one nod.[678] And when all this
is explained, there remains the cloud of allegory, as Jerome calls it.[679] You
will say: 'A knowledge of such difficulties is not necessary to salvation.' The
same thing was meant by the Corycian cave which upset you so much:[680]
when we search in Holy Scripture more deeply than is necessary or than
we are capable of understanding, then the vision of our minds encounters
the darkness in which the majesty of the eternal wisdom is concealed, to
be worshipped rather than investigated. When you yourself teach the same

* * * * *

674 See n655 above.
675 A commonplace argument in medieval and Renaissance defences of poetry.
   See, for example, Erasmus *Ratio verae theologiae* (LB V 117B / Holborn 259:33–
   260:5); Augustine *De doctrina christiana* 2.6.7–8.
676 Gen 1:1
677 *De servo arbitrio* WA 18 655:18–21 / LW 33 93
678 *Adagia* IV ix 39
679 Jerome Ep 74.6 CSEL 55 28. On Jerome see n90, above. That allegory clouds or
   veils the truth was a hermeneutical commonplace deriving from the Alexandrian school of literary criticism. Its principal exponent among patristic ex-
   egetes was the pioneering theologian Origen of Alexandria (c 185–254). Jerome
   accepted his tripartite division of scriptural senses into the historical, tropological, and spiritual (Ep 12 PL 22 1005) and employed allegory to elucidate
   Scripture.
680 See *A Discussion* n17.

thing in different words, distinguishing the light of glory from the light of grace,[681] what was impious when I taught it becomes pious when you teach it. 'The word was made flesh.'[682] What could be clearer? But it is so to us, to whom the mystery has been explained. If the same words were read by Demosthenes,[683] come to life once more, he would not understand them, and certainly we all know and profess that the Son of God took on a human nature. And yet many points are handled concerning these words: how only the Son took on a human nature; and how the divine nature, by means of a human soul, combined with itself a mortal body into the same hypostatic union; and how that holy little body was fashioned by the Holy Spirit from a little drop of the purest blood, as big (they say) as a tiny spider; and whether the soul of Christ, immediately after it was created and infused into the body, was granted the beatific vision; and whether God could have imparted to him more grace than he did.[684] These questions and countless others like them exist about those words, 'the word was made flesh.'

You say the same thing about the articles of the faith: since there is no one who does not understand them, we have drunk them in from Holy Scripture that is most clear; otherwise how could we believe or teach them with certainty? You add: 'What are those who preach about Holy Scripture doing still today, interpreting and expounding it?' If it were obscure, 'who could make us certain that their exposition is certain? Another new exposition? And who will expound that? And so there will be a regression to infinity.'[685] This is what you say, Luther, in a very declamatory strain.[686] But if, as you teach, nothing is needed for Holy Scripture except grammar, what need is there to hear a preacher expound and interpret it? It would

\* \* \* \* \*

681 *De servo arbitrio* WA 18 785:20–38 / LW 33 292
682 John 1:14
683 Athenian orator and statesman (384–322 BCE)
684 For example, Thomas Aquinas *Summa theologiae* III q 3 aa 4–8, q 2 a 3, q 31 a 5, q 34 a 4, q 7 a 12. The hypostatic union in Christ means that he has two natures, divine and human, neither of which has a separate being of its own but both of which are united into one being or substance (*hypostasis*). Erasmus defended the hypostatic union in Epp 730:5–12, 731:10–16, 732:41–4, 734:1– 30 against a misreading of what he had said in his *Apologia ad Fabrum* LB IX 34E–36A.
685 *De servo arbitrio* WA 18 654:20–5 / LW 33 93
686 In classical times and during the Renaissance, declamations were oratorical exercises defending either side of fictitious and improbable cases, with little or no regard for real issues. See Quintilian *Institutio oratoria* 3.8.55–9, 7.9.4–8 and Heinrich Lausberg *Handbuch der literarischen Rhetorik: Die Grundlegung der Literaturwissenschaft* 2 vols (Munich 1973) I 547–8.

be enough to read out a prophet or the gospel to the common people who do not have the sacred books without explaining anything at all, unless there might perhaps be some underlying difficulty about the words. But if you press the point about what the heralds of the gospel are doing, I will say this: often from the same words, which you would like us to think are most clear, they elicit various opinions, as if from the same flint one person would strike fire, another water.[687] Nor is there any reason for you to shout back that this happens among the papists and the carnal sophists; it happens among the heralds of your communion, who claim the Spirit for themselves no less immovably than you do. If Holy Scripture is perfectly clear in all respects, where does this darkness among you come from, whence arise such fights to the death about the meaning of Holy Scripture? You prove from the mysteries of Scripture that the body of the Lord is in the Eucharist physically;[688] from the same Scripture Zwingli, Oecolampadius, and Capito[689] teach that it is only signified. This is the main point of this disputation, that you make us certain that you alone teach what is most true and most certain on issues about which up till now the orthodox Fathers have been deluded, the leaders of the church have been deluded. If you will not allow us to consider their judgment certain in any respect, certainly you will allow us simple and unlearned folk to give as much weight to the judgment of such men as to yours or Wyclif's.[690] But if you claim the right to rescind the decisions of the church in so far as you find it convenient to do so, you will permit the church also to give tit for tat[691] by rescinding and condemning yours. And if you think it is right for the whole assembly of the church, together with so many orthodox Fathers, to yield to you, a newly arisen prophet, you also ought to yield to the others who arise after you.[692] Consider all this as said for the sake of argument.

But I will follow the course of your speech. 'If Scripture,' you say, 'is obscure or ambiguous, what need was there for God to deliver it to us? Do we not have enough obscurity and ambiguity without having our

\* \* \* \* \*

687 Cf *Adagia* IV iii 94.
688 Although Luther had rejected transubstantiation in *De captivitate Babylonica ecclesiae praeludium* of 1520 (WA 6 502:1–526:33), he defended the real presence of Christ in the Eucharist in many polemics, principally in *Wider die himmlischen Propheten, von dem Bildern und Sacrament* of 1525 (WA 18 62–214). His doctrine, called consubstantiation, holds that both Christ and the bread are truly present. See nn97 and 12 above.
689 See nn11, 14, and 13 above.
690 See *A Discussion* n35.
691 Latin *par pari referens* 'repaying like to like'; see *Adagia* I i 35 and Otto no 1337.
692 See n172 above.

obscurity and ambiguity and darkness increased from heaven?'[693] You say this as if I said that all Scripture is obscure and ambiguous, though I confess that it contains a treasure of eternal and most certain truth, but in some places the treasure is concealed and not open to just anybody, no matter who.[694] The sun is not dark if it does not appear when it is covered by clouds or if a dim-sighted person gropes about in full daylight. But actually all this I am saying to you is beside the point; I was dealing with intricate questions which arise from Holy Scripture as it is interpreted first in one way and then in another. Here was the place you should have brought forth that most certain light of yours by which you convict the whole church of blindness. For, as to that quibble of yours that this light is always concealed in that church which is hidden and not thought to be the church, even if I granted you this (which you cannot prove), it is more probable that the holiest and also most learned men belonged to that hidden church than that you and your few adherents do.

You still do not perform what you promised, but rather you go on: 'All divinely inspired Scripture,' you say, 'is useful for teaching, rebuking, and censuring.'[695] And here you indulge in marvellous rhetorical flourishes, or rather someone else under your name,[696] for you are not able to set forth ten words without insults. 'No, Paul, it is completely useless; rather, such things as you attribute to Scripture we must seek from the Fathers accepted over the course of the centuries and from the see of Rome. Hence you must revoke your opinion when you wrote to Titus that a bishop should be powerful in exhorting and reproving objecters by sound doctrine, etc. How will he be powerful,' you say, 'when you leave to him an obscure Scripture, that is, arms made of tow and thin blades of grass instead of a sword?'[697] I have no doubt that you imagine this is quite cleverly said, though it does not untie the knot I proposed and is false besides. Leave out the Tituses and Timothys here, one of whom was conversant with Holy Scripture from his childhood, and both of whom had Paul for a teacher, and besides that a spirit not subject to any doubt. Is it so that no bishop today can use divinely inspired Scripture to teach or rebuke[698] if he is at a loss in certain places? Does a physician have no advice to give a patient if he has doubts about

* * * * *

693 *De servo arbitrio* WA 18 655:25–7 / LW 33 94
694 Cf *A Discussion* 8–9.
695 *De servo arbitrio* WA 18 655:28–9 / LW 33 94; cf 2 Tim 3:16.
696 See nn41 and 42 above.
697 *De servo arbitrio* WA 18 655:29–35 / LW 33 94; cf Titus 1:9.
698 The two Basel editions of 1526 read *increpandum* 'rebuke,' where LB X 1303B has *interpretandum* 'explain.'

some passage in the medical books? Is no one powerful in sound doctrine unless he can truly claim that there is no place in the mysteries of Scripture where he is at a loss? I hardly know whether the apostles would have dared to profess so much as this. How did it happen that for thirteen hundred years the Doctors of the church have been shutting the mouths of heretics, as so many of them arose, one after the other, against the truth of Scripture? Did they fight with arms made of tow, and instead of the sword of the word, which you brandish, did they have flimsy blades of grass? And yet those men, who had such strength with the help of Scripture, confess that in Holy Scripture some things are obscure, some things are beyond human understanding. And how did it happen that the church suspended judgment for so long concerning the procession of the Spirit from both[699] if the light of Scripture is so bright that a knowledge of grammar is enough to understand it? Why should it be so monstrous if, when some ambiguity or other arises in Scripture, we ignorant souls should prefer to consult the see of Rome rather than that of Wittenberg, which is full of disagreements at that?[700] And who would believe the church of Rome if it should make pronouncements without Scripture? Nor does it interpret Scripture without the help of a council made up of learned men. You interpret at your own whim, with the help of your spirit, which is unknown to us (not to say that we *do* know it).

There is no reason why Christ should be forced to recant his saying, 'I will give you speech and wisdom which all your adversaries will not be able to resist.'[701] Why do you throw up the apostles to me when we are dealing with your spirit? Christ provided his apostles with what he promised them. He did not promise it to you or to just anybody, and if he also provided it for you, prove to us with irrefutable arguments that he gave to you alone what he denied to that numberless multitude. This is what we are dealing with, this is the knot which must be untied, and in the meantime you waste our time with prolix declamations[702] and do not provide what you promise. As for me, I do not compare you with Christ or the apostles,

* * * * *

699 A reference to the debate over the *filioque* clause in the Nicene Creed – whether the Holy Spirit proceeds from the Father only (the Greek position) or from both the Father and the Son (the Latin, *filioque*, position). The dispute was settled (briefly) in favour of the Latin side at the Council of Florence in 1439.
700 The word is, of course, ironical as applied to Wittenberg, which was never a bishopric.
701 Luke 21:15; *De servo arbitrio* WA 18 655:35–656:2 / LW 33 94
702 See n686 above.

but rather I compare a person whose spirit is unknown with so many orthodox teachers, with the leading men of the church; though we admit we are
not certain about their spirit, nevertheless, according to your own rule,[703]
charity has had a good opinion about them for so many centuries past, even
though faith approves of nothing except what has been commended to us
by God. And yet you demand that we reject their authority, that we hold
to your teachings as if they were articles of the faith. At least grant us, for
their teachings as well as yours, the same right to suspend judgment about
either. I do not say these things as my sincere opinions, but rather in order
to confute you.

Finally your speech diverges from the apostles and Christ. Why, you
say, 'do you prescribe a formulation of Christianity[704] if Scripture is obscure to you?'[705] On my behalf I reply: I do not prescribe a formulation
of Christianity in *A Discussion*; I only show how far the inquiry of ordinary people should go. Nor do I wish to attribute anything more to my
formulation than other orthodox writers wished to attribute to their writings, to whom we owe a good deal that contributes to piety. If you also
profess this, since they confess that they find not a few places in Scripture
obscure, either recant what you have often confessed, that they discoursed
about many things correctly, or grant us the right to teach some things as
best we can, even though we do not deny that we find some obscurity in
the sacred books. But if you abrogate all faith in these writers, why do you
demand that we have faith in your writings, since you confess that you are
at a loss in some places and since you sometimes bring forth varying interpretations – which you would hardly do if there were no obscurity or
ambiguity. The same thing also happens to your followers: Bugenhagen[706]
and Oecolampadius[707] speak about some places with doubts and hesitation,
as in the end even Philippus[708] does, for whom there is no end to your
praises. Everything which you thundered with such vehemence and lav-
ishness against those who think there is anything obscure in Scripture re-
coils on the heads of your followers and even on your own. Finally, you

* * * * *

703 *De servo arbitrio* WA 18 651:31–652:11 / LW 33 88
704 *A Discussion* 9–10
705 *De servo arbitrio* WA 18 656:3–4 / LW 33 94
706 Johann Bugenhagen (1485–1558), known in Latin as Pomeranus, was city pas-
    tor at Wittenberg and, next to Melanchthon, the most influential member of
    Luther's circle there. See CEBR.
707 See n14 above.
708 That is, Melanchthon. See n32 above.

yourself confess that obscurity occurs in the mysteries of Scripture because of ignorance about words,[709] and you will add, I think, because of corruptions in the manuscripts, figures of speech, and places which conflict with one another. Once you admit this, all the disadvantages return which you attributed to obscurity. For it does not matter where the obscurity comes from as long as some is there. Such obscurity you certainly cannot deny. But if you eliminate all faith in those who are at a loss anywhere, you yourself are at a loss and so are your adherents, in whom you wish us to have wholehearted faith. They are not only at a loss, but they also disagree so much among themselves that they boldly reject and condemn your teaching as well, with no other aid except Scripture. Now bring out all the copiousness and power[710] of the eloquence you pretend not to have, and say against yourself and your adherents what you have said against us. As for the argument you add – if you deny that Scripture is clear, you profess that the saints I bring up are even less clear[711] – you might have said it against me with some appearance of probability if I had used them to assail your teaching; as it is I use Holy Scripture to engage you. And I do not bring up how numerous and gifted they were except to force you to bring forth a manifest argument by which we may know that we can safely believe in you and piously diverge from them. Although you have accepted this position, still, after so many blows and fisticuffs, after so much spitting, you teach nothing to the point. You grant that I do not mean all of Scripture, but only those places from which such question arise. If you grant this, what is the point of speaking so many words as if I had said all of it is obscure But what applies to me, as you say, is that I confess that some things are obscure; you want no part of Scripture to be obscure.[712] I hear 'I want,' a word of command, but I preferred the voice of a teacher. What you affirm, I wish; what you say you know, I desire to learn; nor is it enough for me that you firmly assert this – I demand the certitude which you profess to have. Teach us the external clarity of Scripture, seeing that you take it away from the church herself and the luminaries of the church and claim it for yourself, throwing the world into the most tumultuous uproar.

Nor is your assumption true that the church drew upon obscure places in Scripture in her pronouncement about free will, although I confess that

* * * * *

709 *De servo arbitrio* WA 18 606:22–4 / LW 33 25
710 The original is a Greek word (δείνωσιν) transliterated into the Latin alphabet (*dinosim*).
711 *De servo arbitrio* WA 18 656:7–9 / LW 33 94
712 *De servo arbitrio* WA 18 656:12–16 / LW 33 94

the abyss of this question is unsearchable and therefore should not be penetrated more deeply than is sufficient; but I am persuaded that the ancient Fathers and the church asserted what they asserted on the basis of passages in Scripture that are quite clear in themselves. Even so the authority of the church did not put forward a judgment on this matter immediately but rather turned her eyes for a while on the light of Scripture and finally, having perceived the manifest truth, made a pronouncement. For it often happens that when someone comes out of the dark, he does not see anything even in full sunlight unless he has focused his eyes for a while, and some things we do not see immediately through the darkness, but as we focus our eyes what was doubtful before gradually begins to be clear to us, and the same thing happens when things are far away from us. But out of courtesy I pretended that the interpretations on both sides were ambiguous so that on a level playing field you might show something that would incline towards your side those of us who were vacillating in the middle. With similar restraint I called it a discussion, not an assertion, and I conclude that I follow the probable opinion, not because I have any doubts about the received opinion but because it is dangerous to put yours forth before crowds, either because in this way the people learn to disbelieve the decrees of the church (and it could turn out that they will finally begin to doubt even the most certain articles of faith), or else because it is not safe to debate for and against received articles before uneducated people, or else because this question has such profound depths that the unlearned should be kept away from them, since it is enough for them to hold to the teachings handed down by the church.

I also do not agree with you when you make all the articles of faith equal. For some are so evident that it would be wrong to argue about them, such as these: that Christ was born of a virgin, that he suffered under Pontius Pilate.[713] Some are such that only after long investigation were they finally approved by public authority. Concerning some there is not sufficient agreement even now. Some had doubts about the perpetual virginity of Mary[714] until their mouths were shut by arguments from Scripture rightly

* * * * *

713 Articles of the Apostles Creed, affirmed by both the Catholic and the Lutheran interlocutors in Erasmus' colloquy 'An Examination Concerning the Faith' (CWE 39 419–47)
714 The teaching that Mary was a virgin not only in conception but also in parturition and thereafter (as affirmed, for example, by Thomas Aquinas in *Summa theologiae* III q 28 aa 1–3), although never directly defined, was accepted by the Council of Chalcedon (451) and the Lateran synod of 649.

interpreted. Some ancient Fathers had doubts about whether the bishop of Rome is the universal pastor of the church, and it was permissible to do so until the church made a decision.[715] And there is still controversy in the schools about whether the authority of the bishop of Rome is greater than that of a general council.[716] Accordingly, if you want your teaching to be believed with faith equal to that we have in the Apostle's Creed, bring forth testimony from Scripture which is equally clear, show that your teaching came down to us directly from the time of the apostles together with the gospel. Therefore, just as I believe those things most firmly, so too I had no doubts about the dogma of free will after the Catholic church had pronounced on it. Why then, you say, are you arguing as if you would follow something more correct if anyone could show it? Why did you prefer the title *A Discussion* rather than *A Confutation*? Why do you not exhort everyone to reject my teaching and hold firmly to what the church has handed down?[717] I had no lack of words I could have applied to my discussion and to your teaching (and they are not new to you), but I was disposed to try to see whether I could either heal you by this courtesy or invite you to respond more gently. Then, since I saw that human affairs were more than sufficiently inflamed, I did not want to have the fierceness of my pen pour oil, as it were, on the fire.[718] Finally, I would not have argued at all if you had not promulgated this fable of yours so that now in weavers' shops and cobblers' stalls it is argued everywhere that there is no free will but rather that everything is done by sheer necessity. And as if you hadn't done enough already, they say that this disputation of yours is being translated into German by Jonas[719] so that you can stir up weavers and farmers against

* * * * *

715 Erasmus had detailed the ancient controversy about Matt 16:18 in his *Annotationes in Novum Testamentum* (LB VI 88C–F) and had remarked in *Ratio verae theologiae* (LB V 86C / Holborn 198.5–8) that the verse extended Peter's pastoral province to the entire church, according to 'some.' The qualification 'some' drew the charge of Lutheranism from Diego López Zúñiga, to which Erasmus replied in *Apologia adversus libellum Stunicae cui titulum fecit, Blasphemiae et impietates Erasmi* (Basel: Froben 1522), where he asserted that the papal primacy was divinely instituted (LB IX 388A). The decree to which he refers is that of the Council of Florence (1439). See Rummel *Catholic Critics* I 145–77, II 126–7.

716 The conciliarist doctrine that a general council constitutes the supreme authority in the church; Erasmus also refers to it in Ep 1596:40–1.

717 These words, which Erasmus puts in Luther's mouth, were suggested by *De servo arbitrio* WA 18 658:1–2 / LW 33 97 and 660:1–5 / LW 33 100.

718 *Adagia* I ii 9

719 Justus Jonas (1493–1555) was provost at the Castle Church of All Saints and

me, and once they have been stirred up I cannot placate them because I do not know the language.[720]

When you have been driven hither and thither by all the arguments, you finally escape by making common sense the arbiter[721] of those who fight about the clarity of Scripture. For, as you say, even those who have been vanquished by the most clear testimony of Scripture offer resistance, but common sense shows that they have nothing they can rightly say in reply.[722] Thus when the Sadducees were confuted, they were indeed silent, but they did not relinquish their error.[723] It would be foolish to suggest what replies the Sadducees might have made: they could have said, first, that the souls of the dead cannot rightly be called human beings; secondly, that, while it is not absurd to speak of the God of Abraham, Isaac, and Jacob, who worshipped him while they were alive, just as in the ordinary way of speaking fathers are still called fathers even when they have survived their children,[724] yet at that point they were dealing with the resurrection of the body, which cannot be proved from these words. You will say, 'Why, then, were they silent?' Because there was divine power in the words of Christ which attracted the minds of believers and overthrew the consciences of the wicked. But this is beside the point. And so if you also wish to shut our mouths so that we do not dare to open them, bring forth similar testimony from Scripture, show us the Spirit speaking in you, so that if we attempt to resist you the common sense of everyone will condemn us and approve of you. But even today plenty of people who seem to have common sense

* * * * *

professor of canon law at Wittenberg. He translated Luther's *De servo arbitrio* into German under the title *Das der freie wille nichts sey, Antwort D. Martini Luther an Erasmum Roterdamum* (Wittenberg: Hans Lufft 1526).

720 In fact *De libero arbitrio* was translated into German by Nicolaus Herman of Altdorf (no place 1526), and so was *Hyperaspistes 1*, by Jerome Emser (Leipzig: Melcher Lotter 1526). Emser (sig AA1) makes Erasmus' meaning more explicit: 'dieweyl mir das hochteusch gezünge vnbekant' ('because the high-German tongue is unknown to me'); Erasmus knew only Dutch or low-German (*Plattdeutch*).

721 Latin *arbitrum*, with wordplay on *liberum arbitrium* 'free choice'

722 Erasmus summarizes *De servo arbitrio* WA 18 656:35–40 / LW 33 95.

723 Matt 22:31–3; *De servo arbitrio* WA 18 656:1–657:4 / LW 33 95–6

724 To Jesus' first reply about marriage in heaven, that it is spirits which survive in the afterlife, the Sadducees could have replied that a spirit is not properly a human being. To Jesus' second argument, that the God of Abraham must be a god of the living, they could have replied that 'God of Abraham' is a common figure of speech, meaning the God whom Abraham once worshipped, just as men who survive their children are still called 'father.'

cry out against you. And who would deny that those orthodox Fathers and the whole Christian people had common sense? It is more likely that you and your adherents lack common sense: you, because you rant and rave with such uncontrollable abuse against those who contradict your teachings even for the sake of discussion; your adherents, because with unrestrained factionalism in support of you they approve of whatever you have taught: *ipse dixit.*[725] If you appeal to the Spirit, once more I demand a manifest sign. The rest of what you bring up, I pass over, since it has no force against me.

Nor is it my place to judge Jan Hus.[726] He had his judges among men – would that he has found God to be a more merciful judge. I will only say this: I thought less badly of the man before I sampled the book he wrote against the Roman pontiff.[727] What does such laborious abuse have in common with the Spirit of Christ? And in our discussion it does not matter what sort of pope condemned Hus; he is unknown to me, and popes have their own judge before whom they stand or fall. They are my judges; I am not theirs. Now where you say some people feign simplicity so that they can have a better excuse to resist the truth they know, saying 'I am a man, I can err, I want to learn' and then adding 'It does not satisfy me, he is doing violence to Scripture, etc,'[728] whether you are saying this about me or about others, I for one certainly exclude myself from the number of those who knowingly and willingly reject known truth, especially concerning the articles of the faith. As for you, see to it that you find a way to excuse what you are doing. But I do not yet hear anything that cuts the knot[729] so as to give us clear proof of your spirit. But you seem to me to fight like that dog sent by the king of Albania[730] as a gift to Alexander: when the dog fought with an elephant, he skilfully ran around in circles barking on one side and then the other, until he wore the beast out, making it dizzy from turning around so often, and in this way brought it down.[731] You do not deny that very many men distinguished for ability, learning, and rank, and some also

* * * * *

725 That is, 'he himself has spoken' (*Adagia* II v 87); Erasmus gives the saying in Greek.

726 *De servo arbitrio* WA 18 657:21–8 / LW 33 96–7; on Hus see n199 above.

727 Asserting that Christ is the only head of the church, Hus challenged the primacy of the bishop of Rome as orginating merely in Constantine's sanction. See his *Tractatus de ecclesia* ed S. Harrison Thompson (Boulder, Col 1956) 4.9.12–13, 15.

728 *De servo arbitrio* WA 18 657:35–658:4 / LW 33 98

729 *Adagia* I i 6

730 That is, Caucasian Albania, near the western Caspian Sea

731 Pliny *Naturalis historia* 8.149

for their miracles and martyrdom, reject your teachings; you confess that they were saints, or rather you grant it and we accept it.[732] In other respects my case is as good as yours. At this juncture it remains for you to bring forward a most manifest argument to show why we ought to take sides with people such as you rather than with men such as they – not to go over the whole comparison once again. You excuse them by saying that perhaps they came to their senses before they died,[733] but that otherwise they must be damned. It is hardly likely that those who firmly held the same opinion in so many volumes should change their opinion on their deathbed. But when he was about to die Bernard said 'I have wasted my time because I have lived wastefully.'[734] But is this a recantation?[735] What saint didn't say such things? This is the voice of modesty, not of recantation. You have not yet been able to make a convincing case for the clarity of Scripture, and I will soon touch on this point somewhat. And if you had made a case, it is more probable that you are blind than that they were. If you bring up their spirit, a charitable judgment inclines towards them, though I grant we cannot be certain. If you call for choosing what is preferable, it is reasonable to think that they, together with the church, chose what is preferable. If you rely on common sense, the opinion of common sense comes down on their side. If you respond that it is not surprising that such spiritual men sometimes perceived according to the flesh, the identical words of your response can be turned back against you. If you respond that the world is the kingdom of Satan, and therefore it is not surprising that so many great men through-out the long course of centuries were so blinded that they did not see the light of Scripture, all of this, with much more probability, will be turned back against you. For you too are carrying the flesh around with you, and you dwell in the world you share with them, in which Satan reigns. And in getting out of this tight spot you are not helped by your lengthy addi-tions about those blinded for the glory of free will, those who hearing do not hear and understanding do not understand,[736] for this applies more to you than to the luminaries of the church. Nor is it appropriate to this topic for you to compare yourself to Christ, your disciples to the apostles, the

\* \* \* \* \*

732 *De servo arbitrio* WA 18 641:30–1 / LW 33 73–4, 651:31–652:1 / LW 33 88
733 *De servo arbitrio* WA 18 650:4–9 / LW 33 85
734 St Bernard of Clairvaux *Sermones super Cantica canticorum* 20.1 (*Opera omnia* ed J. Leclerq et al, 8 vols [Rome 1957–   ] I 114:17). On St Bernard see n307 above.
735 See n510 above.
736 *De servo arbitrio* WA 18 658:17–23 / LW 33 98; cf Matt 13:13.

Doctors and leading men of the church to the Jews, and for you to call your
doctrine light and the decision of the Fathers and the church darkness.[737]
If you wish to press us with comparisons, you will have to look for others; those we do not accept. It is much more stupid for you to bring up
the Arians and the philosophers.[738] The church has judged the Arians, and
you approve of her judgment. But the same church condemned your teachings. And yet here I do not burden you with the authority of the church.
We have nothing in common with the Jews, since we recognize Christ as
our saviour. Even the most learned philosophers erred, as if I had written
that learned men endowed with great intelligence could not be blind. You
hang your argument from one tiny thread. Gather together a heap of likely
conjectures and from that show us that we should believe you rather than
them.

But how sophistical you are when you deny that what I said is true,
namely that Scripture is sometimes not understood because of the weakness of the human intellect. 'Nothing,' you say, 'is more suited to grasp the
words of God than the weakness of the intellect; because of the weak and
to the weak Christ both came and sent the word of God.'[739] If you mean by
weak what I mean, ignorant and feeble (like the Galatians[740] and like many
whom we see) and unsuited for the study of the humanities, why do we
not seek for a knowledge of Scripture from such persons rather than from
learned theologians or from you, who claim to have such great knowledge?
But if you call weak those who are unassuming and obedient to the Holy
Spirit, I agree with you. But it is amazing how lacking this weakness is in
your writings! Just as if you had won the victory in every battle, you hasten to the final goal of the disputation, but before I allow that, I will say
a few words about the obscurity of Scripture, though I think enough has
been said before about that matter. For unless you show us that Scripture
is clearer than the sun as long as skill in grammar is available, you confess
that you cannot untie the knot of proving what your spirit is. Here if I sing
you the old song about how much all the ancient Fathers constantly complain about the difficulties of Scripture, how they sweat in order to explain
Genesis, how much darkness Jerome saw in the beginning and conclusion
of Ezekiel,[741] how often Augustine was at a loss, you will respond that it is

\* \* \* \* \*

737 *De servo arbitrio* WA 18 658:27–659:4 / LW 33 98
738 *De servo arbitrio* WA 18 659:11–14 / LW 33 99; on the Arians see n92 above.
739 *De servo arbitrio* WA 18 659:28–30 / LW 33 99–100; cf Mark 2:17, Luke 5:32.
740 Gal 4:9
741 See n376 above.

no wonder that dim-sighted men even in sunlight collided with something. And if I propose to you from the psalm 'Deep calls to deep,' which Augustine and Jerome interpret as meaning the darkness of the mysteries of Scripture,[742] or likewise 'Day utters a word to day and night shows knowledge to night,' which they explain similarly,[743] or the passage from Ezekiel about the torrent whose waters swell up and cannot be crossed;[744] likewise in Psalm 17 'and darkness beneath his feet' is cited as referring to the profundity of Scripture,[745] and again the verse 'he placed the darkness as his hiding place' is interpreted by Jerome as meaning that Christ's birth, which you want to be perfectly clear, is obscure to us,[746] and the verse 'dark water in the clouds of the air' is interpreted as referring to the obscurity of Scripture,[747] and if I should propose other testimony like this, you will reject the exposition of the ancient Fathers and present me with a new interpretation, twisting Scripture to the advantage of your cause.

But I wish you would disentangle this puzzle: if linguistic skill and common sense are enough for a clear understanding of Scripture, why was there any need in Paul's time for prophets among those who spoke in tongues? Paul distinguishes the gift of tongues from that of prophecy, and he places the gift of prophecy on a much higher level than the gift of tongues.[748] This clearly argues that there are hidden things in Scripture

\* \* \* \* \*

742 Ps 41:8; Augustine *Enarrationes in psalmos* CCSL 38 470; Jerome *Commentarii in prophetas minores, In Ionam* 2.6.200–3 CCSL 76 399; and *In Michaeam* 1.3.31 CCSL 76A 636; Pseudo-Jerome, *Breviarium in Psalmos* on Ps 41:8 PL 26 951

743 Ps 18:3. See Augustine *Enarrationes in psalmos* CCSL 38 102 and 108 and Jerome *Commentarioli in psalmos* CCSL 72 196.

744 Ezek 47:5; Jerome interpreted the passage as referring to unsurmountable thoughts but did not associate it specifically with scriptural obscurity; see *Commentarii in Hezechielem* CCSL 75 711.

745 Ps 17:10; on the interpretation to mean the darkness of Scripture, see Jerome *Commentarioli in psalmos* CCSL 72 195 and *Tractatus sive homiliae in psalmos* on Pss 66:3, 91:3 and 103:6 CCSL 78 35, 134–5, and 183.

746 Ps 17:12; in *Commentarioli in psalmos* CCSL 72 195, Jerome actually remarks that some interpret it as concerning the day of Christ's passion. But Pseudo-Jerome *Breviarium in Psalmos* PL 26 866 interprets the verse as meaning that Christ's incarnation or birth is obscure.

747 In *Enarrationes in psalmos* on Ps 17:12 CCSL 38 96, Augustine says: 'In prophetis enim atque in omnibus diuini uerbi praedicatoribus obscura doctrina est' ('For in the prophets and in all the preachers of the divine word there is obscure doctrine'). *Glossa ordinaria* PL 118 868 also interprets this phrase as referring to the obscurity of the prophets.

748 1 Cor 14:1–6

which are not clear to just anybody who knows languages. If what you say is true, that whoever has the Spirit of God perceives no obscurity in the sacred volumes, why is the person who prophesied earlier commanded to be silent when another prophet arises to whom something has been revealed?[749] Many persons had the gift of prophecy, and yet what was clear to one was obscure to others, for this reason: the Spirit does not bestow everything on everyone, but distributes gifts to individuals according to his own will. And so you are marvellously fortunate, since you profess that there is nothing in Holy Scripture which is not perfectly clear to you. And after the prophecies have been heard, Paul wants a judgment about what has been said: 'Of the prophets,' he says, 'let two or three speak, let the rest be silent.'[750] Then, too, among the gifts of the Spirit he reckons the distinguishing of spirits.[751] These facts argue that Scripture is not as manifest and obvious to just anybody as you want to make it seem. Again, he says, 'We see now in a puzzling mirror, but then face to face.'[752] You hear 'puzzling,' and you proclaim to me clarity of the very clearest. We see by faith and the light of faith is in Holy Scripture. And he says there: 'We know partially and we prophesy partially,' and a little further on 'Now I know partially, but then I shall know as I am known.'[753] By prophecy Paul means the interpretation of the mysteries of Scripture; why would he profess that it is imperfect if there is nothing which is not perfectly clear? And if Paul here acknowledges imperfection, where are those who now boast of omniscience? I wish that they would at least clarify for us 'as I am known.' Is there anyone who knows or will know God in the same way as he is known by God? I think it is peculiar to God himself to know himself perfectly. The eunuch read Isaiah, and he was undoubtedly fluent in the language, and yet he did not understand the hidden meaning.[754] Now I imagine that you number the epistles of Paul among the writings of Scripture. But here is Peter's pronouncement upon them: 'Our most beloved brother Paul wrote to you according to the wisdom given to him, as he does in all his epistles, speaking in them about some points which are difficult to understand etc.'[755] You will reply, 'They were difficult for the ignorant.' But you don't

\* \* \* \* \*

749  1 Cor 14:30
750  1 Cor 14:29
751  1 Cor 12:10
752  1 Cor 13:12
753  1 Cor 13:9 and 12
754  Acts 8:27–31
755  2 Pet 3:15–16

demand anything more than skill in grammar. If you say they lacked the
Spirit, the inquiry comes full circle, since this is what you promised us, that
you would prove to us you have the Spirit. But it is easy to wiggle out
of this if you will only prove what you assume; you will say that out of
stubborn malice we oppose the known truth, as the Pharisees did. Who can
catch someone who has gotten ready so many bolt-holes for his escape?

[*Who has the Spirit that understands Scripture?*]
Well now, I come to those to whom you attribute the Spirit, which, as you
write, they have drunk in from your books.[756] Where do the quite significant disagreements in their writings come from? If they are all moved by
the same Spirit and are dealing with the same Scripture, there cannot be
such perspicuous clarity that linguistic skill and common sense are sufficient. But you will say that Zwingli and Oecolampadius[757] lost the Spirit
after they started writing against you. Does not Philippus Melanchthon
sometimes speak hesitantly and suspend judgment in his brief commentaries?[758] But you say it is wrong to do this in dealing with Holy Scripture, where the clear truth is to be boldly asserted. When Oecolampadius
had not yet disagreed with you, he did not deny that there was any obscurity in Isaiah, but he thought it sufficient if he could keep the pious and
persistent reader from falling into despair, and in his preface he was so
far from professing that there is nothing he has not explained that he confesses that his attempt would have been futile if he had not been aided by
the Hebrew commentaries, at the same time speaking of Jerome with somewhat more reverence than you do[759] when you make such a man out to be

* * * * *

756 *De servo arbitrio* WA 18 601:24 / LW 33 17
757 See nn11 and 14 above.
758 In his *Commentarius in Genesin* of 1523, Melanchthon says he has not yet made
    up his mind what it means that man is God's image; he also says that there
    are many things in Scripture that are uncertain, so that it is better to linger
    over things that contribute to faith and charity rather than questions which
    are over-curious rather than useful; see *Philippi Melanchthonis opera quae super-
    sunt omnia* ed Karl G. Bretschneider and Heinrich E. Bindseil, 28 vols, CR 1–28
    (Halle/Salle and Braunschweig 1834–60) 13 771 and 782–3. On Melanchthon
    see n32 above.
759 In the preface of his *In Iesaiam prophetam ... commentariorum ... libri sex* (Basel:
    Andreas Cratander 1525), Oecolampadius says what Erasmus attributes to him
    here (sigs b4v–b5), and he repeats it in a second preface to the city council
    of Basel. For a modern edition of this second preface see *Brief und Aktem zum
    Leben Oekolampads* ed Ernst Staehelin, 2 vols, Quellen und Forschungen zur Re-
    formationsgeschichte 10 and 19 (Leipzig 1927 and 1934) I 348 no 241. Erasmus

a sacrilegious blasphemer in this book of yours, so perfect as it is in all respects. Is not Bugenhagen, whom you praise so much, a Sceptic in some places in his commentary on the Psalms, walking on eggshells, as you say, with hesitant steps?[760]

But perhaps you will find a way to evade what others have said; I will press you with what you yourself have said, since you consider it an affront and blasphemy against Holy Scripture if someone attributes any obscurity to it.[761] Note how this paradox agrees with your preface to the Psalms. There you say as follows: 'I am teaching the Psalter etc, but I teach it in such a way that I would not want anyone to presume to get from me what none of the most learned and holiest men has yet been able to furnish, that is, an understanding and explanation of the proper meaning of the Psalter in all respects. It is enough to understand some of its meaning and that only partially. The Spirit keeps many things to himself, so that he may always have students; many things he displays only so as to lure us on, he hands down many things to move our feelings. And, as St Augustine has excellently said, "no one ever spoke so as to be understood by everyone on every point."[762] Even more so the Holy Spirit himself is the only one who understands all his own words. Hence I must frankly confess that I do not know whether or not I have a proper understanding of the Psalms etc.'[763] Again, somewhat further on: 'What, then, remains but that we help each other, forgiving those who make mistakes because we ourselves have erred or will err?'[764] Again, in that place: 'I know that it would bespeak a most shameless recklessness if anyone should dare to profess that he understands any one book of Scripture in all respects. Indeed who would dare to presume

\* \* \* \* \*

had apparently seen this second preface before it was published, and he asked Oecolampadius not to refer to him in the preface as 'our Erasmus'–a request with which Oecolampadius complied; see Ep 1538:11–15 and n1.

760 Bugenhagen's *In librum psalmorum interpretatio* (Basel: Adam Petri 1524) was published with a foreword by Luther (WA 15 8). In this commentary Bugenhagen says, for example, that the Hebrew title of Psalm 4 has been interpreted in so many ways that its meaning is uncertain; hence he has recourse to the Greek (sig B6v–7). He notes that Ps 7:11 is ambiguous (sig d3v). He also finds Ps 17:8–17 so obscure that he presents various opinions before giving his own (sig H6v).

761 Cf *De servo arbitrio* WA 18 607:16–17 / LW 33 27.

762 *De Trinitate* 1.3.5 CCSL 50 32:14–15

763 Erasmus quotes Luther's *Operationes in psalmos* of 1519–21 (WA 5 22:24–34 / Luther *Operationes* 13:1–12). He congratulated Luther on it in Ep 980:59–61 (30 May 1519).

764 WA 5 23:5–6 / Luther *Operationes* 14:6–7

that he understands one psalm entirely?'[765] There is an enormous difference between your language here, Luther, and the paradox about the wonderful clarity of Scripture which you teach in this book with such earnest perseverance, asserting that unless this point is granted everything will be transformed into darkness and there will be no certainty in human affairs. Who would believe that it is the same man who wrote these things when he was about to comment on the Psalms and who now challenges all comers to bring forth even one place which is obscure to you?

But what good does it do now to pick out places from your commentary where you profess that you have been abandoned by the interpreters, who disagree with each other, and are following what your own mind has dreamed up, or again, where you confess you do not understand at all how a verse hangs together with the preceding verse and call your opinion mere folly.[766] Thus on Psalm 17 you say, 'The doctrine of the church is beyond the grasp of human understanding,'[767] and now skill in grammar is enough! On Psalm 19 you speak as follows: 'I have expounded this psalm as an example of the faith of some king or other, nor is it certain that I have reached the right meaning,'[768] and then you put off onto your reader what judgment to make about your interpretation.[769] Once more, on Psalm 20 you confess you are uncertain 'whether to understand it as concerning Christ or rather some king,'[770] and you accuse me of a theology of Scepticism because I would not dare to make pronouncements on the intricate difficulties of scholastic questions![771] Where was that Stoic asserter then? Where was that know-it-all? You say to me, no one but a Lucian or an Epicurus speaks so hesitantly,[772] and you forgive yourself for speaking the same way in a profoundly religious work. At the end of this book you say, 'I do not want anyone to have the right to judge, but I urge everyone to assent'[773] and on the psalm you pass the judgment on to your reader. You make me into a Proteus,[774] but in doing such things

* * * * *

765 WA 5 23:9–12 / Luther *Operationes* 14:6–7
766 *Operationes in psalmos* WA 5 508:6–15
767 *Operationes in psalmos* WA 5 531:31–2
768 *Operationes in psalmos* WA 5 580:20–1
769 *Operationes in psalmos* WA 5 580:30
770 *Operationes in psalmos* WA 5 583:11–13
771 *De servo arbitrio* WA 18 613:1–24 / LW 33 34–5
772 *De servo arbitrio* WA 18 609:15–23 / LW 33 29; on Lucian and Epicurus see nn56 and 55 above.
773 *De servo arbitrio* WA 18 787:12–13 / LW 33 295
774 See n83 above.

how are you consistent with yourself? Did you not have the Spirit at that time? I imagine you will say 'I did not.' But if you had only persevered in such modesty! There you call the ancient, orthodox writers consummately orthodox, holy, and learned; here you laugh at me for attributing holiness to them, while you charge them with blindness, ignorance, even blasphemy and sacrilege. And you can find no other excuse that would enable them to be saved except that they meant something different from what they wrote or repented of their error before they died.[775] And since you require internal clarity from all Christians in such a way that without it you give them no hope of salvation, what can we think but that they all perished because concerning such a necessary article of the faith they were, I will not say ignorant, but recalcitrant, overthrowing necessity and professing free will. You call me blasphemous so often because I have doubts about your teaching and argue about it, and do you imagine it is not clear what such a judgment would lead you to pronounce about them?

And here again is a new paradox: if someone has the Spirit, nothing is obscure to him; if he does not, he understands not even a single iota.[776] There is nothing in between. Therefore if someone professes that he is in doubt about some places in Scripture, either he has the Spirit and is lying about a non-existent obscurity or he does not have it and does not understand a single iota. Tertullian, an outstanding Doctor of the church, later slipped over into the teachings of Montanus[777] and left the communion of the church.[778] When he lost the Spirit, did he not understand a single iota? But you take 'he did not understand' to mean 'he did not feel, he was not affected.' But we were dealing with the certainty of doctrine, not with a person's unknown feelings, about which you confess that no one can pronounce with certainty except God alone. For since, according to Paul, some only pretend to have the Spirit, and an angel of Satan 'transforms him-

\* \* \* \* \*

775 *De servo arbitrio* WA 18 644:5–15 / LW 33 76–7, 650:4–9 / LW 33 85
776 *De servo arbitrio* WA 18 609:5–12 / LW 33 28
777 The founder of an elite and ecstatic movement originating in Phrygia in 156, he believed himself to be the charismatic vessel of a new effusion of the Holy Spirit whose oracles supplemented Scripture.
778 Tertullian (c 160–c 230) was a Roman jurist who converted to Christianity and was for a time an orthodox church Father. Later, as an instructor of catechumens, he broke with the church, joining forces with the heretical Montanists, but as the leader of his own sect known as Tertullianists. He was a brilliant but difficult rhetorician, author of thirty-one extant treatises – apological, polemical, and ascetical. For Erasmus' opinion of him, see Ep 1232:4–32.

self into an angel of light,'[779] even someone who believes he is moved by
a good spirit can be deceived. But if you attribute a total understanding
of the Holy Scripture to the Holy Spirit, why do you make an exception
only for ignorance of grammar? In a matter of such importance will the
Spirit allow grammar to stand in the way of man's salvation? Since he did
not hesitate to impart such riches of eternal wisdom, will he hesitate to impart grammar and common sense? Whoever attributes even the tiniest bit
to free will blasphemes against God; and are you pious when you grant
such importance to grammar that it alone darkens the supremely bright
light of Scripture? Those who complain that there is darkness in Scripture
hardly deny that it is perfectly clear to the Spirit who is the author of Scripture, but rather they impute this darkness to the weakness of human nature. Though you profess this most openly in the preface which I just cited,
here you most boldly deny it, affirming that nothing is more capable of understanding Holy Scripture than human weakness.[780] But, to press you to
deal with the matter at hand, show us by what arguments we can be sure
that you have the Spirit as your master and are not deceived in explaining
Scripture, even though all the Doctors of the church were deluded about it.
You confess that some obscurity arises from ignorance of languages.[781] On
this point, then, since many disagree with each other and each one of them
claims to have skill in languages, how will I be certain who is blind about
language and who is not? For on this, as you say, depends the certitude of
interpretation.

You do not entirely deny that some obscurity arises from figures of
speech, and even though you teach that they should not be rashly allowed
in exegesis, nevertheless, whether you like it or not, they occur frequently
in the prophets, in parables, in enigmas. I too do not like far-fetched figures
of speech, especially when they undermine the historical sense; but if you
exclude figurative speech from Holy Scripture, we lose a good deal both
of the pleasure and the utility in the secrets of Scripture. Moreover, if you
confess that obscurity comes from ignorance of grammar, you will at the
same time also confess that darkness arises from translations and from corrupt copies.[782] Oecolampadius also complains about this in Isaiah.[783] Therefore, when one person says there is a figure of speech and another denies

* * * * *

779  2 Cor 11:14
780  *De servo arbitrio* WA 18 659:27–30 / LW 33 99–100
781  *De servo arbitrio* WA 18 606:22–4 / LW 33 25
782  On Erasmus' method of biblical criticism, see Bentley chapter 4.
783  See n759 above.

it, or if they both agree there is a figure of speech but disagree in interpreting the figure, how can I be certain which one of them has hit the mark?[784] By comparing passages? Both sides have passages to compare; I am still stuck in my doubts. Similarly, when I hear several interpreters disagreeing with one another while each contends that his copy is free of corrupt readings, what can clear away all ambiguity for me? Now who will dare to affirm that obscurity does not frequently arise from places which conflict with one another? Or if someone does affirm it, who will believe him? What is simpler than the story of the gospel? And yet how many talented men have sweated to harmonize inconsistencies in it? Augustine tried with all his might and did not accomplish what he wished.[785] Do us this service at least, so that we may not lack faith in you. Many fail to grasp what is taught in Sacred Scripture because they are dull-witted, many because they are lazy, many because their minds are devoted to human desires; for the contentious twist Scripture to fit their own teachings, while the opposite is what should be done. Finally, the Spirit does not reveal everything to everyone. So many are the ways, then, in which we will have doubts about the interpreter. And all the abuse which you heaped up against those who think there is some obscurity in Scripture, all the insults you hurled at them, this will be thrown back at you, since you cannot avoid confessing that in some fashion there is obscurity in Holy Scripture. But for you there is no obscurity. Let us stipulate that what you say is true, but how will you make this clear to us? For this is what you undertook to prove, confessing that you have no reply to my question unless you did prove it quite clearly. But after you tried everything and were not able to do it, like Proteus bound tightly in chains,[786] you return to your native form and heap hatred upon me because I make Scripture obscure, just as if I denied there is any light at all in it. I said there is darkness in many places, but the Spirit wills that they should be clarified sufficiently to provide for our salvation, for he keeps some things hidden away for future ages. If you infer from this that nothing can be certainly proved from Scripture, tell me this: how did the orthodox Fathers instruct the people of Christ for so many centuries, how did they drive heretics out of the church? By means of Scripture that is ambiguous and not understood? Finally, you cast the blame on Satan: it is his work that Scripture is clear to so few; if he would

* * * * *

784 *Adagia* i x 30
785 *De consensu evangelistarum* PL 34 1223–4
786 Only when he was tightly held could Proteus be forced to assume his true shape (Homer *Odyssey* 4.354–569). See n83 above.

take a rest, a single word of God heard only once would convert the whole world.[787]

At this point, although you have run completely aground,[788] you nevertheless act as if you had done very well, threatening to trap me with my own snares,[789] and you wield against me a syllogism with a horn on each side, so twisted that there is no escape. 'From your own words,' you say, 'you will be justified, and from your own words you will be condemned.[790] You say Scripture is not clear on this point.' But if that is not true, why do you suspend your judgment in *A Discussion*? If it is true, what are those orthodox people doing, the ones whose intelligence, learning, sanctity, miracles, martyrdom, dignity, antiquity, and numbers you boast about, who used doubtful Scripture to assert free will?[791] Where shall I turn, hemmed in as I am by horns blocking me on both sides? In fact, I will cut off one horn of your syllogism; then I will deal with the other. My *Discussion* does not say that Scripture is obscure on this matter. Her words are as follows: 'But the debate here is not about Scripture; the quarrel is over its meaning. In interpreting it etc.'[792] Do you hear? I say 'quarrel,' not 'obscurity.' Were the scriptural passages used to vanquish Arius[793] obscure because he opposed them? And if I had granted that on this question Scripture was obscure – which I do not – I would have granted it for the sake of argument, as many things are conceded to opponents in the universities. If you choose to seize upon this concession, you will still have to admit that the interpretation on both sides is doubtful. You will say: if Scripture is clear in the parts used by the ancient Fathers to assert free will, why did you like the title 'discussion,' why do you profess to be an inquirer, not an asserter, why did you say in the conclusion 'I have discussed the issue; let others pass judgment.'[794] I reply: when they are disputing in the universities, one disputant proving what is in Scripture and the other refuting him with other scriptural passages and arguments from reason, why do they refer the decision to the senior professors or to the one who is presiding, as they say? For it could be that the ancient Fathers correctly asserted free will from

* * * * *

787 *De servo arbitrio* WA 18 649:32–4 / LW 33 100
788 *Adagia* IV iii 70
789 *Adagia* I i 53; cf Ps 9:10.
790 Matt 12.37
791 Cf *De servo arbitrio* WA 18 659:34–660:11 / LW 33 100.
792 *A Discussion* 16
793 See n92 above.
794 *A Discussion* 89

perfectly clear passages in Holy Scripture but that I have defended it with insufficient skill against the battleline of your arguments. And once before I already gave you the reason for my procedure: to find out whether you could dispute without insults and, since the whole matter has been rubbed raw, not to throw oil on the fire,[795] as they say. And this courtesy of mine you throw back in my face time and again, whereas instead you ought to have approved of it and imitated it. And if you take such pleasure in assertion, why do you need to find it in me, since the church long ago handed down her judgment on the matter and recently confirmed it?[796] And so, you say, 'They considered Scripture to be clear.'[797] I grant it, in so far as it was enough to dispel any doubt about free will. And what then? Why then, you say, do you make Scripture obscure on this point? My *Discussion* does not do so; rather you pretend that it does, as I said just now. If you contend that there is no obscurity whatever in Holy Scripture, do not take up the matter with me but with all the orthodox Fathers, of whom there is none who does not preach the same thing as I do. But whenever my *Discussion* mentions obscurity in this matter, she is either speaking in your person or conceding for the sake of argument something she could refuse to grant. For example, she says this: 'If you then say Scripture is *not* clear on this point, on which so many eminent men have been blind etc.'[798] Do you think I am speaking for myself when I say 'on which so many eminent men have been blind'? Such words are attributed to you, and I seize on them to use against you because you want your interpretation to be taken as if it came from an oracle. Here is a similar example: 'If it is so clear, why have such distinguished men throughout so many centuries been blind, precisely on a matter of such importance?'[799] These words do not convict the ancient Fathers of blindness; rather they urge you either to confess that they speak the truth or to stop demanding that we consider your interpretation to be an oracle from on high. Again, when I say 'If [this gift of the spirit has come] to no one (seeing that many obscurities torment scholars even today), then no interpretation is certain,'[800] what is the thrust of this argument but to

\* \* \* \* \*

795 See *A Discussion* n37.
796 Erasmus probably refers to the condemnation of Wyclif's teachings at the Council of Constance (4 May 1415) and of Luther's in the bull *Exsurge Domine* (15 June 1520).
797 *De servo arbitrio* WA 18 660:14–15 / LW 33 100
798 *A Discussion* 19
799 *A Discussion* 17
800 *A Discussion* 17

get you to let others reject your interpretation by the same right you claim to reject the interpretations of everyone else?

And then behold how fiercely but irrelevantly you say this: finally 'what a frivolous and foolhardy outlook it takes to shed your blood for something uncertain and obscure! This is done not by Christian martyrs but by demons.'[801] Don't you see that this horn has been cut off? But where was your mind when you wrote, 'This is done not by Christian martyrs but by demons?' Do demons have blood to shed? Then who ever said that these holiest of men shed their blood for free will? You will say: they shed it for Holy Scripture, which you claim is obscure. Once more you talk as if I had said that all of it is obscure or as if, though it might be obscure to me and you, it would also be obscure to those who defined the doctrine of free will. Cyprian[802] shed his blood. Let us grant that he shed it for Scripture. Does it follow that nothing in all of Scripture was ever obscure to Cyprian? Imagine that Augustine had been slain when the Donatists tried to ambush him.[803] He would have been reckoned among the martyrs. Would you think this canonization absurd if he had found something unclear? On this frivolous foundation rests what you say at the end of the section: 'That is nothing but making them perfect dullards in what they knew and total fools in what they asserted.'[804]

I have broken up that horned syllogism, but alas, here comes another. 'If you think they judged correctly,' you say, 'why do you not imitate them? If you do not think so, why do you boast with such abundant bombast etc?'[805] I think that those who asserted free will, as the church does, judged correctly. Why, then, you say, do you not assert instead of arguing? Is someone in doubt because he argues? I do not argue because I am in doubt but rather to refute you for attacking our assertion. Equally irrelevant is what you then stuff in: 'Now you should also place before your eyes and ponder

* * * * *

801 *De servo arbitrio* WA 18 660:15–16 / LW 33 100–1

802 St Cyprian (c 200–58), bishop of Carthage, was martyred during the Valerian persecution. Erasmus edited his *Opera* (Basel: Froben 1520), to which Ep 1000 is the preface.

803 Augustine, as bishop of Hippo, was the chief polemicist against the Donatists, a rigorous heretical sect in North Africa which claimed that the holiness of the church resided in it alone and held that the sanctity of the ministers was necessary for the validity of the sacraments. The Donatists made several attempts on Augustine's life; for one which he foiled see *Enchiridion ad Laurentium de fide et spe et caritate* 5.17 CCSL 46 57:32–8.

804 *De servo arbitrio* WA 18 660:30–1 / LW 33 101

805 *De servo arbitrio* WA 18 660:24–5 / LW 33 101

in your mind whether you judge that we should place more weight on the judgment of so many learned men, so many orthodox teachers, so many saintly Fathers, so many martyrs, so many ancient and modern theologians, so many universities and councils, so many bishops and popes who thought that Scripture is clear and confirmed that view in their writings and with their blood, or rather on the private judgment of you alone, who deny that Scripture is clear but who perhaps never shed a tear or breathed a sigh for the teachings of Christ.'[806] I will pass over the judgments you make in your usual manner about what tears I shed or what sighs I breathe out. What is your point here, Luther? That the scriptural passages on which the ancient Fathers based their assertion of free will were clear to them? How, then, do you have the nerve to say they blasphemed when they defined doctrine on the basis of clear Scripture? And time and time again you sing me the old lying tune that I make out that Scripture is obscure on this point. I say the interpretations vary, and I called into question which interpretation we should follow, that of the ancient Fathers, which has been approved for so many centuries, or yours, which has sprung up so recently. In that place I certainly do my best to show that the Doctors of the church did not err in asserting free will but rather that you are blind about it. This is what I say: 'If you then say that Scripture is *not* clear on this point, about which so many eminent men have been blind, we have come full circle.'[807] You see that I am not speaking for myself when I say 'about which so many eminent men have been blind.' These are your words, not mine. And if what you say is true, either Scripture was obscure to them or they wickedly resisted the Holy Spirit. Nor is there any danger in saying that on this subject Scripture was sometimes obscure to them but that their assertion was none the less correct and certain, seeing that in councils what is obscure to some is revealed to others by the Spirit, so that through discussion by various individuals obscurity disappears as each brings forward his own revelation. But if you push us to include all of Scripture, then I confess that some things in it are obscure to me and the likes of me. You will immediately object that more weight should be given to the judgment of such a large crowd of eminent men than to the private judgment of me alone. What are you saying? Is it the private judgment of me alone when in fact none of the most praiseworthy men, whom you list for the sake of irony, has not professed the same? For which of them, in explaining the mysteries in these

\* \* \* \* \*

806 *De servo arbitrio* WA 18 660:17–24 / LW 33 101; here Erasmus quotes Luther's
    ironic paraphrase of *A Discussion* 16.
807 *A Discussion* 19

volumes, does not complain about the obscurity of Scripture? Not because they blame Scripture, as you falsely charge, but because they deplore the dullness of the human mind, not because they despair but because they implore grace from him who alone closes and opens to whomever he wishes, when he wishes, and as much as he wishes. Since you confess the same thing in your commentaries,[808] why do you call it the private judgment of me alone and make me out to be an enemy of those who are on my side? You make out that Scripture was obscure to them because you boldly reject their interpretations. If you had not done so, there would be no quarrel.

It is amusing that you turn against me the very comparison I made between you and the ancient Fathers. I do not require anyone to reject the opinion of all of them on a matter of such great importance and to believe me alone – which is what you do, and not on this dogma alone, entreating and even demanding assent as rightfully due to you, threatening to trample in the mire of the streets whoever resists you as you preach the word of God. Therefore fairness requires that you give us firm arguments showing us why your judgment alone should carry more weight with us than that of so many great men (not to repeat all their qualities so often). If your belief is certain, you say, what is the meaning of the words 'discussion' and 'discourse'? Why 'do you suspend judgment and argue on both sides, sometimes for, sometimes against?'[809] If that is proof of a divided mind, let all the scholastics be summoned to court. Thomas asks whether the Eucharist is a sacrament of the church, and he gives arguments on both sides.[810] Does that mean he has doubts on the matter he is arguing about? Jerome did the same thing when he wrote against the Luciferians;[811] Augustine also, when he wrote against the Manichaeans.[812] And should we immediately

\* \* \* \* \*

808 See nn763–770 above.

809 Cf *De servo arbitrio* WA 18 600:1–2 / LW 33 100

810 *Summa theologiae* III q 73 a 1

811 *Dialogus contra Luciferianos* PL 23 163–92. Luciferus, bishop of Cagliari in Sardinia (d c 370), was a strict interpreter of the Council of Nicaea concerning the Trinity; he also did not wish to receive back bishops who had gone over to the Arians but repented and wanted to be accepted back into the orthodox church. Since Jerome's work is a dialogue between Luciferianus and Orthodoxus, he naturally presents the arguments of his opponents.

812 *De libero arbitrio* CCSL 29 211–321, *De moribus ecclesiae catholica et de moribus Manichaeorum* PL 32 1309–78, *De genesi contra Manichaeos* PL 34 173–220 and nine other anti-Manichaean works in that volume, *Contra Secundinum Manichaeum* PL 42 577–602. The Manichaeans were the followers of Mani (c 216–76), a prophet of the radical cosmic dualism of light and dark, spirit and matter, good and evil. Although Erasmus' context suggests they were Christian

think they had doubts on the point they were arguing about? How in the world could I refute your arguments if I did not recount them? Do you not see that such discussions occurred frequently among the ancients, to see if perhaps they could settle the matter without any uproar? The civility of my title contrasts with that irritable temperament of yours; it contrasts with some who are more than sufficiently inclined to rebellion. And whenever the philosophers fought so bitterly among themselves, each sect defending its own view – for they called these conflicts 'discussions' – did they all suspend their judgment? Rather did not each want his own opinion to be victorious? You see that you accuse me of nothing more heinous than that I preferred to argue rather than to accuse. And here, according to you, I am trying to overthrow you with a flood, as it were, of oratory, but it turned out differently: I am overwhelmed by the waves, while your ark rides aloft in safety.[813] Nay rather your dinghy has run aground in the Syrtes,[814] and you do not set forth what you promised, though you left no stone unturned.[815]

And still, just as if you were victorious in battle, you prepare a triumph.[816] 'With a horned syllogism,' you say, 'I have got you.' Either you are wrong when you say that they were endowed with an admirable knowledge of Scripture, and also blessed in their lives and in their martyrdom, or you are wrong when you say that Scripture is not clear.[817] Hurray, hurrah! Whether it is false that there is any darkness in Scripture has already been discussed. But you are incontrovertibly wrong when you say I declared that the ancient Fathers asserted free will on the basis of obscure scriptural passages. Rather I pretend that it is not clear to me, as if I were ignorant in the matter, whether those men, so numerous and so great, interpreted Scripture correctly or whether you with your few adherents do so, and on the basis

* * * * *

heretics (Augustine was for a time attracted to them – see *Confessions* 3, 6, and 7), this merely reflects the apologetic tradition. Manichaeanism was rather a universal religion combining elements of Christian Gnosticism, Buddhism, and Zoroastrianism. It was condemned by a Roman synod in 444. Naturally Augustine had to present Manichaean ideas and arguments in order to refute them, but he usually allows them very little say before crushing them completely.

813 Cf Gen 7:17–18; *De servo arbitrio* WA 18 660:25–7 / LW 33 101.
814 Sandbanks in the gulf of Sidra on the Mediterranean coast of Africa; cf *Adagia* IV iii 70.
815 *Adagia* I iv 30
816 Cf *Adagia* I vii 55.
817 *De servo arbitrio* WA 18 661:1–4 / LW 33 101

of this supposition I require from you firm proofs showing why we should abandon them and get on your bandwagon.[818] In the schools you have often seen, if I am not mistaken, that for the sake of argument something not true is conceded to an opponent. If someone in an argument should imagine that he is Tarquin[819] and you are Apollo, would you bear down on the man as if the concessions were serious?[820] You add a shameless hyperbole, namely that in the entire course of the pamphlet *A Discussion* I do nothing but argue that Scripture is not clear.[821] What good can it do to waste time in refuting manifest nonsense?

Not satisfied with all this, you add an even more shameless fabrication: you deny that I am serious when I attribute knowledge of Scripture to very holy men; 'I do it only to present a false face[822] to the ignorant mob, intending really to make trouble for Luther and to use empty words to overwhelm his position with hatred and contempt.'[823] If I had in mind to do what you imagine, I would not have tempered my style so much, I would not have been so circumspect in avoiding any appearance of tooth and claw[824] in *A Discussion*, I would not have taken such care to handle a vexing subject without being vexatious. If I had published *A Discussion* to curry favour with princes, the best way to please them would have been to rant and rave against you with the full force of my eloquence. As it is, I have written so unvexatiously that my restraint has rendered me suspect to some people; and yet it was not unclear to me how affectionately you had thought and written about me for some time now.[825] But I am resolved in matters of faith not to give any weight to private feelings. Do you take it as contemptuous of you that I compare you with so many luminaries of the church, with general councils, with all the universities? What then will you say about those who have made you the object of far different comparisons in their published books? And you are silent about them and complain about my courtesy. Writing in Latin 'I put on a false face before the ignorant multitude.' You see to it that this disputation of yours is translated

* * * * *

818 Literally 'vote for you with their feet' (*Adagia* II vii 12)
819 An Etruscan tyrant (Livy 1.49–60)
820 In declamations or mock debates students sometimes spoke as if they were historical characters; see n686 above.
821 *De servo arbitrio* WA 18 661:5 / LW 33 101
822 *Adagia* I v 52
823 *De servo arbitrio* WA 18 661:5–8 / LW 33 101
824 Cf *Adagia* I iv 23.
825 As early as August 1523 Erasmus was aware that Luther had a low opinion of him; see Epp 1384:60–4, 1397:9–12, 1408:14–15, 1443:37–42 and 50–2, 1522:43–7.

into German[826] so that you can expose Erasmus to ridicule among farmers, sailors, and cobblers, to whom he cannot speak,[827] and do you think learned men do not see what you are doing? Insurrection is what you have in mind; you see that that is what has so often resulted up to now from your German pamphlets.[828] That is what the apostles did, indeed! I debated with you, subject to the judgment of the community of learned men; you transfer your case to the ignorant mob and you make false charges against me among workmen, tanners, and farmers, who favour you and do not know me. They understand you when you make false charges; they do not understand me when I reply. What a pretty victory you are out to get!

What you add next, I do not fully understand. For this is what you write: 'As for me, I say that neither is true but both are false. First, that Scripture is perfectly clear; then that they, in so far as they assert free will, were most ignorant of Holy Scripture; then that they asserted it with neither their lives nor their deaths but only with their pens – and that while their wits were wandering.'[829] Up to now you have contended that Scripture is perfectly clear, and now you say that is false. And then, you have always asserted that the ancient Fathers proved free will from scriptural passages wrongly understood, and now you say that this is also false. To these two statements you add a third, apparently also false, which up to now you have insisted was very true. But let us not indulge in verbal chicanery: what you wrote is clear for all to see, but what you mean I can guess well enough – though if I had blurted out such a mistake, there would have been no end to your misrepresenting and berating me. But here is a fine way for you to excuse the ancient orthodox Fathers: they thought and lived and died quite differently than they wrote concerning free will. You say that only their pens sputtered out this blasphemy, but 'their wits were wandering.' This is how we excuse those who commit a sin out of madness.[830] And you

\* \* \* \* \*

826  See 228–9 and n719 above.
827  In fact, *Hyperaspistes 1* was translated into German in 1526 (see n5 above).
828  See 114 and nn102, 105 above.
829  *De servo arbitrio* WA 18 661:8–12 / LW 33 101–2. Luther had understood 'I say' (from the preceding sentence) before the clauses beginning with 'First,' but it is also possible to refer the two clauses back to 'both,' thus interpreting the sentence to mean the opposite of what Luther intended. Erasmus uses the ambiguity to twit Luther, though he is quite aware of what Luther really meant. On 'wits were wandering' see *Adagia* III vi 47.
830  St Thomas Aquinas teaches that *stultitia* is not sinful if it results from a congenital indisposition (*Summa theologiae* II–II q 46 a 2). Cf *The Praise of Folly* CWE 27 109.

can find no other excuse for the church, which approved of their opinion, or for the universities but that, when they assert free will, their mind is not at home but is wandering[831] among the Sogdians.[832] How likely is it that writers who assert free will in books clearly devoted to that subject, who often inserted into their commentaries what they taught about it, and who fought against those who disagreed with them about it, should make a mistake about it merely through a slip of the pen when they were out of their minds? If St. Augustine thoughtlessly asserted free will, why did he not at least come to his senses in the books of his *Retractions*? And there he asserts what he asserted before,[833] and the authority of his judgment is all the weightier because he rebukes himself for some places in which he attributed more than he should have to free will. Someone who criticizes his own work and cuts away what is superfluous gives strong confirmation to what he leaves untouched. Are their deaths and their lives inconsistent with their pens because they had no confidence in their own merits but ascribed their salvation completely to the mercy of God? Those of us who assert free will do the same. What a convenient crack you have found here, one through which you can slip away[834] whenever you are confronted with the authority of the ancient Fathers: they didn't mean this, but rather they brought such things forth with a wandering pen and a meandering mind. And all the time you do not see that this device of yours can be turned back against you, not only by us but also by your followers.

And so, Luther, since you cannot escape from the snare of my question and have poured forth clouds of smoke[835] before our eyes, playing the part not so much of Proteus as of Cacus,[836] I once again place before your eyes the gist and the upshot of the whole business. In my *Discussion* I say that I do not wish to fight with you using the authority of the ancient orthodox Fathers or the previous judgment of the church, which condemned your teaching long ago, not because I think their opinion has no weight but because these weapons would get me nowhere with you. But rather, if it should happen that we seemed equal in testimonies out of Scripture and judgment hung in the balance, wavering in either direction, I asked whether

* * * * *

831 Again, cf *Adagia* III vi 47.
832 A remote and wild people who lived in what is now Turkey
833 *Retractationum libri duo* 1.9.1–7 CCSL 57 23–9
834 *Adagia* III ii 75
835 *Adagia* IV viii 83
836 On Proteus see n83 above. Cacus was a monster who breathed fire and smoke when he was slain by Hercules (Virgil *Aeneid* 8.252–61).

it seemed right in this state of affairs that the authority of the ancients, together with the decision of the church, should certainly have a tiny bit of influence to make us more inclined towards their judgment rather than yours.
And I do not speak this way because my opinion truly wavers, but I made
this supposition so that you would approve of my fairness and could not
complain that the victory was wrung from you by unfair rules. Place, then,
free choice in the middle, held in good faith by the Catholic church for
more than thirteen hundred years. Place yourself on one side assailing it
with the assistance of Scripture and me on the other side defending it with
the same assistance. Add spectators who, like me, think all our evidence is
equal, although you demand to be at one and the same time both contestant
and umpire and superintendant of the games. Who will award the prize[837]
either to you or to me, and by whose choice shall free choice be preserved
or else destroyed?

Whenever opposite judgments in trials are balanced on either side, circumstances are usually taken into account, and at that point opinions are
not counted but evaluated. The defendant is given the benefit of the doubt;
some allowance is made for the age, dignity, and authority of the other side.
Likewise I suggested that when opinions waver the circumstances on either
side ought to have some weight. On the right-hand side we have placed
you together with Manichaeus, Jan Hus, and Wyclif,[838] all of whom have
been struck by the thunderbolt of the church;[839] as for the judgments of
God, they are unknown to us. Add, if you like Lorenzo Valla, though he
does not positively defend your opinion, but gives up, overcome by the difficulty of the question. And I don't know whether you set much store by
Lorenzo, first because he is a rhetorician, and then because he treats the
question of foreknowledge not out of Holy Scripture but by human reasoning and secular examples.[840] Now when you say Augustine is completely

* * * * *

837 The rare Latin (and Greek) word used here (*brabeum*) shows that Erasmus is
alluding to 1 Cor 9:24.
838 On these three figures see nn812 and 199 above and *A Discussion* n35.
839 That is, excommunication; see *The Praise of Folly* CWE 27 139.
840 On Valla see *A Discussion* n48. In fact, Valla based his position about free will
on Paul's Epistle to the Romans. Concerning Valla's discussion of free will
Ernst Cassirer says: 'For the first time since antiquity, the problem of freedom is taken before an entirely secular forum, before the bench of "natural reason"'; see his *Individuum und Kosmos in der Philosophie der Renaissance*
(Hamburg 1927) trans Mario Domandi (Oxford 1963) 78. But both Erasmus
and Cassirer exaggerate and perhaps misconstrue.

on your side,[841] I cannot get over my amazement: in the books of his *Retractions* he excuses himself for some things in those three books which he began in Rome and finished in Carthage after his ordination,[842] because in them he seemed to attribute more than enough to free will and to take too little account of grace, but he still persevered in the opinion that free will is something.[843] What more need I say? If Augustine thought like you, why did he write a book in his old age against those who rushed to opposite errors, some denying free will entirely because they heard so much attributed to grace, others attributing too little to grace because they heard free will asserted? We find this in the first chapter. The second chapter begins as follows: 'So he has revealed to us through Holy Scripture that man's will has free choice.'[844] You hear free will being asserted not from the dreams of the philosophers but by the authority of Holy Scripture. And in another place he recants[845] something he wrote following Origen, if I am not mistaken, to the effect that we can will good deeds but cannot accomplish them without the assistance of grace; but he does not renounce free will.[846] Now, as for what he says somewhere about God performing both good and bad deeds in us, in the proper place I will show how that is so.[847] Now we are dealing with another matter.

\* \* \* \* \*

841 *De servo arbitrio* WA 18 640:8–9 / LW 33 72
842 Of the three books of Augustine's *De libero arbitrio*, the first was written in Rome (388) and the last two in Hippo (391); see Peter Brown *Augustine of Hippo* (London 1967) 74 Chronological Table B.
843 *Retractationum libri duo* 1.9.1–6 CCSL 57 23–9
844 *De gratia et libero arbitrio* 1.1 and 2.2 PL 44 881–2
845 See n510 above.
846 In *De diversis questionibus ad Simplicianum* 1.1.11 CCSL 44 15:188–92 Augustine had quoted Paul (Rom 7:18): 'Velle enim adiacet mihi, perficere autem bonum, non' ('For to wish for the good lies in my power but not to perform it'), arguing that it did not deny free will but rather affirmed it; he drew similar conclusions from the same text in *In Iohannis evangelium tractatus* 41.12 CCSL 36 364:22. In his later anti-Pelagian works, however, he emphasized another text of Paul (Phil 2.13): 'Deus est enim qui operatur in vobis et velle et perficere' ('For it is God who works in you the will and the performance'), arguing that grace is necessary from the very beginning of our good deeds (*De gratia Christi et de originali peccato* 5.6 CSEL 42 129:16–26; see also *Contra duas epistulas Pelagianorum* 2.9.21 CSEL 60 483:10–18).
847 See *A Discussion* 13 and n36, and Augustine *De gratia et libero arbitrio* 43 (first sentence) PL 44 909; in *Hyperaspistes* 2 LB X 1475D–1481A Erasmus takes up the question of how free will and grace work together.

And so we will allow Lorenzo, Jan Hus, and Wyclif to stand on your side; but the first was in grave danger because of his opinion,[848] the other two were condemned by the judgment of the church, and one of them was also burned at the Council of Constance.[849] Here do not immediately shout back at me that this was done by the judgment of Satan, not of the church; now I am only reporting what happened. Let your friends also stand with you, though their vote has less weight, either because they have sworn to uphold your teachings or because they do not constantly adhere to the same wisdom either among themselves or with you. And you know that a witness from one's own household is rejected,[850] and you are not unaware that nothing impairs the credibility of witnesses more severely than inconsistent testimony. This is your chorus.[851] On the opposite side stand those famous luminaries of the house of God, among whom are so many men outstanding for their intelligence and well versed in the philosophy of God, first the Greeks, who always had the highest authority in treating Holy Scripture, then the Latins,[852] who emulated the Greeks – and among them many recommended by very holy lives, some also illustrious because they gave witness with their blood, men whose memory to this very day has always been sacrosanct to the whole people of Christ – so many bishops, so many popes whose opinion has been accepted and approved down through many centuries and confirmed finally by the public decision of the church. In agreement with these add the judgment of all the universities, add the repeated assessment by theologians and by the church, add finally a precept strengthened by the long time it has endured. Do we not then need most manifest evidence for you to convince us that such a venerable chorus of Fathers together with the leaders of the church were utterly blind to Holy Scripture,

* * * * *

848 For Lorenzo Valla's brush with the Neapolitan Inquisition see Giovanni di Napoli *Lorenzo Valla: Filosofia e religione nell'umanesimo italiano* (Rome 1971) 279–312.

849 For Hus' heresy and trial see Gordon Leff *Heresy in the Later Middle Ages* (Manchester 1967) 606–707.

850 See Berger 726; see also *Digesta Justiniani* 22.5.6 and 9, *Codex Justinianus* 4.20.3, and *Institutiones Justiniani* 2.10.8–9 in *Corpus iuris civilis* ed Paul Krueger, Theodor Mommsen, et al, 3 vols (Berlin 1954–9) I 17 and 328, II 158.

851 Erasmus may well be thinking of the choir of a church, where the two sets of choir stalls face one another.

852 That the Greeks were superior to the Latins in exegesis is a characteristic judgment of Erasmus, expressed most famously in his assertion that he benefited more from one page of Origen than from ten pages of Augustine (Ep 844:272–4).

that they were driven by the spirit of Satan, or (to put it quite mildly) were out of their minds to have given their verdict for a dogma which is heretical, impious, blasphemous, against the clearest evidence of Scripture, and most dangerous to the human race? Do we not need such evidence for us to abandon our fathers, by whose teaching, laws, and authority we have been nourished and guided up to now, to spurn our mother whose milk has nourished us, to desert such a large confraternity of Christian people with whom we have associated for so many years, and with the highest risk to our property, lives, and souls to assent to your covenant, in which, apart from a few persons and even those in disagreement with each other, we see nothing but fierce assertions? You seem willing to yield to them in dignity, authority, antiquity, intelligence, and learning.[853] You call their miracles into question,[854] but they have been approved for a long time now by the public and unshaken opinion of the Christian people, whereas there is not even a suspicion or a rumour of such a thing about you. As for your quibble that none of them worked miracles by means of free will,[855] I have already answered that.[856] Then again, you call into question the holiness of their lives;[857] but opinion is on their side. Nor do I wish to press that side of it. We are moved by their authority, we are moved by the steadfastness with which you and yours make your assertions – for I had pretended it was so – but we do not dare to withdraw from our church and to commit our salvation to your faith. What sign do you show us that we should believe you rather than them? Now even if we should grant that you have the spirit you so boldly claim, that you alone find all of Scripture perfectly clear, though this may be true, it is true for you; for us, as you yourself confess, it does no good.[858] And so you promised that the external clarity of Holy Scripture would persuade everyone that your interpretation is the truest of all and that the opinion of all others, however numerous and great, however holy and learned, is false, blind, and deadly, and that whoever follows it is hurrying straight to hell. No one in his right mind believed the Donatists[859] when with their mighty assertions they tried to show that everyone in the other churches had lost the grace of baptism and that it remained uncorrupted

* * * * *

853 *De servo arbitrio* WA 18 640:2–14 / LW 33 72, 641:19–20 / LW 33 73
854 *De servo arbitrio* WA 18 642:12–16 / LW 33 74
855 *De servo arbitrio* WA 18 641:31–642:3 / LW 33 74
856 See 199–201 above.
857 *De servo arbitrio* WA 18 632:6–13 / LW 33 74
858 *De servo arbitrio* WA 18 653:20–1 / LW 33 90
859 See n803 above.

only in their own church. And you want us to go right ahead and believe that for so many centuries the gospel has been shrouded by Satan, that it is now unveiled by you, and that there is no pure interpretation of Scripture anywhere but in Wittenberg. In a matter so hard to believe and so dangerous that it cannot be enough to deal in assertions and commonplace arguments you must bring forth manifest, firm, indeed Achillean arguments.[860] And now that the testimony of Scripture has been brought forward on both sides, will you call upon common sense to settle the controversy?[861] Both the Spirit and common sense and the clarity of Holy Scripture are claimed by both sides. As the case now stands, your prolix discourse about the obscurity or the light of Scripture has little or nothing to do with the matter. Grant that Scripture is perfectly clear: what will we unlearned people do when we see both sides contending with equal assertiveness that they have the Spirit who reveals mysteries and that they find Scripture absolutely clear? Grant that it is obscure in some places: what will we do when each side accuses the other of blindness? However these things may be, we are certainly left wavering in doubt, and in the meantime you neither acquit your faith by fulfilling your promise nor set us free by removing our doubt.

Perhaps you will go back to those suppositions you began to lay out for us earlier: I know that my conscience is clear, I know that I am moved by the Spirit of God, I neither have nor desire money, I am not looking for glory – and what pleasure could I hope for in the midst of such great labours and dangers?[862] Such statements, Luther, we accept from you in such a way as to hope they are true, but they do not persuade us and they do not provide that full conviction[863] about external clarity, but instead you try to force people rather than draw them on. It may be that you are such a man as you proclaim yourself to be, but we would be more ready to believe it if there were less arrogance in your writings, less bitterness, less trickery and craftiness. If I saw as much of these in the writings of the apostles, I doubt if I would have faith in them. For I imagine the Manichaeans and Donatists said such things: I do not desire money or glory or the other advantages of this world. For some spirits are impostors according to Paul,[864]

\* \* \* \* \*

860  See n479 above.
861  *De servo arbitrio* WA 656:35–40 / LW 33 95
862  *De servo arbitrio* WA 625:19–29 / LW 33 51
863  Erasmus borrows a Greek word ($\pi\lambda\eta\rho o\phi o\rho\iota\alpha\nu$) from Paul (Col 2:2; 1 Thess 1:5; Hebr 6:11 and 10:22).
864  2 Cor 11:13; at 1 Tim 4:1 Paul applies to spirits the Greek word which Erasmus transliterates here (*plani*). The Vulgate translates *erroris spiritibus*.

and the spirit of Satan 'transforms himself into an angel of light,'[865] and it is not safe to believe just any spirit.[866] As far as fame is concerned, you could not hope for more, and you have gained it in a brief period of time: you reign far and wide in the minds of men; you are armed with very many partisans; you have a theatre ringing with wonderful applause; to the nobles you are more to be feared than loved; you have your bodyguard; you have your spies and couriers, you have people to collaborate in your writings, you have translators to turn them into German. What is left but a crown? Even an incorrupt mind could be corrupted by so fortunate a turn of events. I do not care how much money you have, but in other matters also I think you are a little better off than you would have been if you had not stirred up this hornets' nest.[867] Certainly I know many people for whom this gospel of yours has brought forth both revenue and a wife and many other benefits, although they were out of luck before.

Now if you want to hear the reward of my flattery (for such you consider it to be), I have lost half of the little fortune I had so as not to go into the arena against you, I have gained much suspicion and ill will, but I am not a penny[868] the richer; and the fact that I have more than once refused a fortune joined with dignity argues that I have an attitude which scorns such things.[869] But I do not allow myself to judge your attitude; it has its own judge who alone knows the secrets of the heart.[870] This is what we demand: that you make us certain concerning your teaching – which you had taken upon yourself to do. If you can't do it, allow us little sheep and simple souls to follow the voice of the church.[871] You will say that those who drank in the Spirit from your writings are satisfied.[872] I only wish that you could impart a good spirit by laying on your hands, for I have grave doubts about the spirit which is drunk in from your writings. Here I am not reporting my own experience, but am only saying what is public knowledge: very many persons imitate the violence and superciliousness of your pen. Formerly Jonas seemed to me to have a gentle and sound

* * * * *

865  2 Cor 11:14
866  Cf 1 John 4:1.
867  See n633 above.
868  Literally, 'one quarter of an as'; *Adagia* I viii 9
869  See Epp 1408:11–13, 1477:26–9, 1477B:64–7, 1510:23–5, and nn451 and 453 above; Erasmus is denying charges that he attacked Luther for reasons of material gain.
870  See n164 above.
871  Cf John 10:3–5.
872  *De servo arbitrio* WA 18 601:24–5 / LW 33 17

temperament.[873] I began to read attentively the book he wrote against Johannes Fabri,[874] desiring to see what arguments he would use to win his case, but there he was so raucously insulting that I was driven by disgust to put the book down – there were no bounds or end to it. The same thing happened to me with your *Abolition of the Mass*[875] and some other little works of yours. At this point, naturally, you distinguish faith from charity; you say that faith is fierce, charity puts up with everything.[876] But we see the fierceness; we do not perceive that charity which puts up with everything. At the same time you do not consider how much harm you do your cause by directing the licentiousness of your pen first at one person, then at another, egged on by frivolous persons. And unless my guess is completely wrong, you were driven to this last burst of ranting by some of your adherents who were offended by nothing more than this: when asked for my opinion, I disagreed with Karlstadt about the Eucharist.[877] They wanted you to take vengeance for this vexation of theirs, even though on this point I agree with you.[878] If you had overwhelmed *A Discussion* with untrammelled reasoning and strong arguments, you would not have offended me in the least. Perhaps you would have drawn me over to your opinion – which I would not find so abhorrent if we were dealing merely with a doctrine of the schools, and not of the church also – and you would have gained less hostility and more credibility in the minds of others. As for me, I challenged you to a struggle of arguments, not of insults, and you see how large a part of your volume you devote to insults. But enough of such things.

\* \* \* \* \*

873 See n719 above.
874 Fabri (1478–1541) became a doctor of civil and canon law at the University of Freiberg in 1510 or 1511. In 1517 he became vicar-general of Constance and in 1521 he was appointed suffragan bishop of Constance. His first book against Luther (1522) was fairly conciliatory. Luther scorned it and asked Jonas to reply to it. Jonas' response, *Adversus Iohannem Fabrum . . . pro coniugio sacerdotali . . . defensio* (Wittenberg 1523) was vicious and insulting. See CEBR.
875 Luther's *De abroganda missa privata Lutheri sententia* of 1521 (WA 8 411–76 / LW 36 133–230) was mentioned disparagingly by Erasmus in Ep 1342:829–31.
876 *De servo arbitrio* WA 18 651:34–652:7 / LW 33 88
877 In a series of German tracts published in Basel in October and November 1524, Karlstadt denied the physical presence of Christ in the Eucharist, thus launching the sacramentarian controversy which was later taken up by Zwingli and Oecolampadius. See *A Discussion* n4 and nn97, 11, and 14 above.
878 Erasmus agreed with Luther against Karlstadt's denial of the real presence, but he does not say he agrees with Luther's doctrine of consubstantiation; see n12 above.

With the following conclusion you end the prolix disputation assailing the preface of my *Discussion*: 'Therefore I conclude this little disputation as follows: up to now nothing has been certainly laid down by Scripture, since it is taken to be obscure, nor can it lay down anything about free will, as you yourself testify; but in the lives of all men since the beginning of the world nothing has been shown in favour of free will, as was said above. Therefore to teach something which is not prescribed by a single word in Scripture nor demonstrated by any deed – this does not pertain to the teachings of Christians but rather to the *True History* of Lucian,[879] except that Lucian in his intentional jokes and playful treatment of playful matters neither deceives nor harms anyone, whereas these friends of ours on a serious matter, one which pertains to eternal salvation, are raving mad and cause the perdition of innumerable souls. In this way I also might have concluded this whole question of free will, since the testimony of my adversaries themselves makes for me and opposes them – and there is no stronger proof than a defendant's own confession and testimony against himself.'[880] Here we have a pretty conclusion of a well-managed disputation! I have already said enough about obscurity. I supposed that there is obscurity in those places where interpretations vary. If you approve of this supposition, you will thereby confess that the scriptural passages you use to destroy free will are also ambiguous and obscure. But if you reject it, we will make use of our right to take back the concession we made. Neither do I prove free will by the lives of orthodox teachers. But when the testimony is equally balanced in number and weight, I want the commendable lives of the witnesses to be taken into account. Thus in a trial, if the arguments on each side are equally balanced and the witnesses disagree, we more readily believe a man who has fought bravely for his country, who has been an incorruptible magistrate, than we do someone whose honesty has no public testimony to recommend it and whose dishonesty is notorious. You will say: what do his brave deeds or his magistracy have to do with the case in which he is giving testimony? This is what they have to do with it: no one can easily suspect that in this case he will either lie or be deceived, since in many other circumstances he has been a manifest model of an upright and prudent man. Now if there is a ruling about the doctrine of free will in Scripture, why do you reject the testimony of the Fathers taken from Holy Scripture? If there is not, why do you assert it without Scripture? If each side rejects

* * * * *

879 A fantastic satirical narrative; on Lucian see n56 above.
880 *De servo arbitrio* WA 18 651:12–24 / LW 33 102

the interpretation of the other, claiming there is no obscurity in Scripture, certainly there is doubtfulness for us unlearned souls, except that the decision of the church does not allow us to vacillate. And in my argument I presuppose vacillation precisely because I said at the outset that I would make no use of ecclesiastical judgments. If you will accept nothing apart from Scripture unless it has been directly revealed by God, why do you accept the perpetual virginity of Mary?[881] It is not expressed in Scripture and it has not been revealed by God through any miracle. If you consider the perpetual consensus of the church to be a miracle, we will confront you with that same consensus in favour of free will. And wasn't it enough for you to say that nothing is to be accepted unless it is expressed in Holy Scripture or revealed by a sign from God without adding your hyperbole about the *True History* of Lucian? Are you saying that whatever the ancient writers set forth about the lives and martyrdom of the saints, whatever church history has to say, and also the exhortations and the practices of the ancient Fathers and the regulations of prelates have no more weight than the *True History* of Lucian? Liturgical readings in which famous Doctors of the church have exercised their eloquence recount the martyrdom of St Andrew, St Lawrence,[882] and others.[883] And all this is nothing more than the ridiculous fables of Lucian? You might have cracked this

\* \* \* \* \*

881 Luther defended the virgin birth forcefully, for example in his *Sermon von dem Sacrament des Leibs und Bluts Christi widder die Schwärmgeister* WA 19 490:1–491:13. The 'perpetual virginity of Mary' is the belief that Mary was an intact virgin before her conception of Jesus and remained so during and after his birth. See DTC IX part 2 2349 and 2369–85.

882 According to legend St Andrew the apostle was crucified at Patra in Greece about the year 70. St Lawrence, a Roman deacon, was put to death by the sword in the year 258, although by legend he is reputed to have been roasted on a gridiron. For their miracles and martyrdom see *The Golden Legend of Jacobus de Voragine* trans Granger Ryan and Helmut Rupperger, 2 vols (London, New York, and Toronto 1941) I 7–16 and II 437–45.

883 Erasmus is thinking here not of readings in the mass but rather in matins of the divine office. See n608 above. Leo the Great tells of the martyrdom of Lawrence in the lessons of matins on his feast day (August 10) in a passage taken from *Tractatus septem et nonaginta* 85:27–70 (CCSL 138A 535–7). Gregory the Great praises Andrew in the lessons of matins on his feast day (November 30) in a passage taken from XL *homiliarum in evangelia libri duo* 2.5.1–2 (PL 76 1093). In the early sixteenth century breviaries varied somewhat from place to place, but the passage from Gregory appeared in the breviary of Utrecht (*Breviarium ... Ecclesiae Traiectensis*, Venice: Johann Herzog 1497, sig o2r–v); and the passage from Leo appears in a seventeenth-century Carmelite breviary (*Breviarium Carmelitarum ...* Antwerp: Marcellus Parys 1672, sigs Bbb9v–Bbb10).

joke more opportunely elsewhere, Luther. And so where is that defendant with his confession now?[884] Indeed he denies it loud and clear, and shows that everything you assume is quite false. Hence it follows that your conclusion is also no more true than those things you assume as if they were confessed.

What was the point of throwing this insult into your mixture: 'These people, on a serious matter, one which pertains to eternal salvation, are raving mad and cause the perdition of innumerable souls.'[885] Don't you understand that this charge of blasphemy falls not only on me or on the theologians and popes of our times, but on all the most approved Doctors of the church almost from the time of the apostles to this very day, on all Christian people, who probably held that opinion, which they had gotten from their teachers? And you add: 'and cause the perdition of innumerable souls.' But a little before, when my *Discussion* charged that you alienated many by your bitterness and paradoxes, you replied that there is no danger: only the wicked who are perishing are offended, the elect are safe.[886] Are you saying those who follow your teaching are safe and those who agree with so many orthodox teachers and the definition of the church are perishing? And where is that scrupulousness now that made you complain about me because I put you in a bad position where you were forced either to yield or to speak against such great men?[887] You put your own self in that position before I ever put you anywhere. For how often did you assail them as ignorant of Scripture, blind, sacrilegious, blasphemous! Here you add 'raving mad,' just as a little before you said they were out of their minds. And you complain about me, as if you were not accustomed to say on your own hook whatever you like against them. If you were proclaiming the truth, even then what pious person could bear the wicked licentiousness of your pen? As it is, since you are proclaiming falsehoods, it is even less endurable. This is your triumph before the victory,[888] Luther. Now you are girding yourself for battle, and the victory is in your hands – that is, if we were willing to accept, before the encounter, the laws which the victors usually lay down for the vanquished.

First of all, you usually reject, with marvellous indignation, whatever might be brought up from the scholastic theologians. Now you reduce

* * * * *

884  See 257 above.
885  *De servo arbitrio* WA 18 661:20–1 / LW 33 102
886  *De servo arbitrio* WA 18 632:5–6 / LW 33 60–1
887  *De servo arbitrio* WA 18 641:17–19 / LW 33 73
888  *Adagia* I vii 55

everything to scholastic reasoning, and for no other reason than to make things dark and difficult for me, since I have little experience in it – this is, as they say, to pull a fish out of water.[889] But you usually accept nothing except what is in Scripture, and using that alone I contended with you. But you changed your mind and you drag us off into the midst of these thorns of sophistry, which, if they were as lacking as they are hateful to you, you would frequently be confused and at a loss. And whenever it is convenient, you reject any assistance from them, but you do so by confronting us with another sophistical argument no less sophistical than the previous one, and you devise new cracks for you to slip through.[890] For here there is such a mass of distinctions that you cannot be taken hold of anywhere. You distinguish the Law from the gospel, but in such a way that each is in the other; the internal clarity of Scripture from the external; God from Scripture; God preached from God not preached; the Spirit of the gospel from the spirit of error; a negative opinion which has nothing to prove from an affirmative one which has a duty to prove. You show us a twofold showing of the Spirit; a twofold rule, one of charity and one of faith; a twofold necessity, one of a deed and one of time, and also one of compulsion and one of immutability; a twofold omnipotence of God, one of nature and one of operation; a twofold respect, to what is above and what is below. Indicative verbs are distinguished from imperatives and subjunctives; writing is set over against life and death,[891] a disputation from a prayer; and finally what seems to be the church but is not is distinguished from what seems not to be the church but is, and those who seem to be saints but are not are distinguished from saints who are thought to be wicked although they are truly saints. I do not list these because I disapprove of all your distinctions, but rather because you claim for yourself in explicating Holy Scripture a privilege you withhold from others and because you ordinarily hiss at the distinctions of others but want your own to be considered oracular. For us you shut up every way out; and for yourself you want all your bolt-holes to be open.

\* \* \* \* \*

889 Literally, 'to pull a gelding into a ditch' (*Adagia* I vi 21). According to Erasmus, the saying derives from an episode in Livy (23.47.6) where a Roman horseman fighting an enemy horseman in single combat is put at a disadvantage by complying with a request that he ride into a sunken road where he cannot manoeuvre.
890 *Adagia* III ii 75
891 Erasmus refers to Luther's distinction between what the Fathers wrote about free will and how they lived and what they believed on their deathbeds.

Now look at the laws which you prescribe, though you are not yet the victor: lay down whatever arms are supplied by the ancient orthodox teachers, the schools of the theologians, the authority of councils and popes, the consensus of the whole Christian people over so many centuries; we accept nothing but Scripture, but in such a way that we alone have authoritative certainty in interpreting it; our interpretation is what was meant by the Holy Spirit; that brought forward by others, however great, however many, arises from the spirit of Satan and from madness; what the orthodox taught, what the authority of the church handed down, what the people of Christ embraced, what the schools defend is the deadly venom of Satan; what I teach is the spirit of life; believe that in Scripture there is no obscurity at all, not even so much as to need a judge; or, though all are blind, I am not blind; for I am conscious that I have the Spirit of Christ, which enables me to judge everyone but no one to judge me; I refuse to be judged, I require compliance;[892] let no one be the least bit moved by the multitude, the magnitude, the breadth and depth, the miracles, the holiness of the church's saints; they all were lost if they meant what they wrote, unless perhaps they came to their senses before the last day of their lives; whoever does not believe my proofs either lacks common sense or commits blasphemy against the Holy Spirit and subverts Christianity. If we accept such laws as these, the victory is indeed yours. Then again, you demand that we not believe the ancient orthodox Fathers because they sometimes disagreed among themselves, whereas the few of you fight very much with each other about the prophets, images, church rules, baptism, the Eucharist; and you want us nevertheless to believe your teachings, especially because every day we expect new ones. And we are called blasphemous because we still cling to the old church and do not dare to join your camp; and you croak at us that text from the gospel: 'Whoever is not with me is against me, and whoever does not gather with me scatters.'[893] I am not making any of this up; I am saying what is certain and well known.

[*Erasmus' definition of free will*]
Now it will be worthwhile to see how insincerely you treat *A Discussion*, leaving nothing undistorted, nothing not falsely blamed, nothing not

* * * * *

892  Cf Luther's concluding words (*De servo arbitrio* WA 18 787:12–13 / LW 33 295): 'Penes nullum volo esse iudicium, sed omnibus suadeo, ut praestent obsequium' ('I refuse anyone the right to judge, but rather I urge everyone to be compliant').

893  Matt 12:30

condemned. You would have been more believable if you had approved of some things, for you would have seemed to condemn the other things out of judgment, not because of a diseased mind. For who is such a bad writer than he never puts in something which should be approved? And so you rail especially at my definition which I propose as the subject of our debate: 'Free choice is a power of the human will by which a person can apply himself to what leads to eternal salvation or turn away from it.'[894] Though I proposed this brief definition only in order to show the scope of the argument and keep it from digressing more than was necessary, you heap up here everything babbled by the boys in the schools of the sophists. You object that I do not unfold the parts of the definition – afraid as I am to be shipwrecked more than once – even though that is usually done by others.[895] It is usually done, but by those who propose to debate about something controversial or less well known; but I undertook a brief little debate on a subject already treated by very many writers, and I did not take it upon myself to teach a class of pupils *ex cathedra* or to write a commentary on a work by a difficult author, so as to need either to defend or to explain individual parts of a definition. I knew that free choice had been defined by various people in various ways; you make short work of it in your definition, 'a name without reality.'[896] It would have caused too long a delay to reject or assert or explain the definitions of others. I decided not to delay very long in this arena, and anyway it was superfluous to describe a well-known and frequently defined phrase. Why define it then? I do not so much define the basic meaning of the phrase as set limits to what I had undertaken to do in this book. Call me a liar if my words do not show this: 'And so by free choice in this place I mean etc.' What does 'this place' mean? Nothing more than that here we will dispute about free will understood to this extent, lest anyone should expect whatever can be or usually is debated concerning free choice. What good would it have done to explain the individual parts of the definition – as teachers do when they lecture to schoolboys on Aristotle[897] – since that would be done in the course of the debate. Writers usually give a summary of what they intend to talk about, pointing out the target, as it were; that is what I do in *A Discussion*.

\* \* \* \* \*

894 *A Discussion* 21
895 *De servo arbitrio* WA 18 661:32–662:2 / LW 33 103
896 *Assertio* article 36 WA 7 146:6 / 306; cf *A Discussion* 45.
897 Cf Aristotle's *Topica* 6.1–14 139a24–155b25; Erasmus alludes to the scholastic method of defining in detail, point by point.

And you thrust upon me another sophistical slander: what is defined is broader than the definition itself, for there is the free will of God, which is the only one that can truly be called free, there is a certain free will in the angels, and you limit it to the will of mankind.[898] I have already responded that I said this at the outset precisely to exclude from this little debate any disputing about the choice of God, the demons, or the angels, especially since your *Assertion* attacks nothing but human choice. But a graver crime is that the phrase which I define conflicts with the definition, that is, the 'what of the name' with that which is the 'what of the thing.' I recognize the language of schoolboys. For whoever hears the phrase 'free will,' you say, takes it as properly meaning 'that which can and does do, in relation to God, whatever it wishes, constricted by no law, no commanding authority.' For if a slave who lives under the command of his lord cannot be said to be free, so much the less can the will of man, which is subject to the commanding authority of God. And so you would rather it were called 'vertible' instead of 'free.'[899] First of all, as for your contending that the honour of this phrase applies properly to God alone, I have already discussed how this is so, and I do not make man's will free in an unqualified way, as is sufficiently clear from the debate. Why then use the phrase? I am not the inventor of the phrase. Hence it would be more appropriate for you to expostulate with all the ancients and the moderns and even with Augustine himself, for, though he attributes very little to free will, nevertheless in the titles of his books and throughout the debate he uses the accepted phrase.[900] But as for your saying that by the judgment of everyone's ears this phrase means nothing but the free power to do, in relation to God, whatever one wishes etc, the truth is far otherwise among Christians. Augustine rightly advises us to make it a fixed rule to speak in sober and appropriate words,[901] but he himself, who gives this advice, very often hammers away at the phrase 'free choice' in his books. You yourself do not refrain from using the accepted phrase – how sober you are in changing either the teaching or the words of the church is known to those who read your writings. And now you croak Augustine's admonitions at me because I used a phrase accepted by everyone.

* * * * *

898 A summary of *De servo arbitrio* WA 18 662:2–12 / LW 33 103
899 *De servo arbitrio* WA 18 662:2–15 / LW 33 103
900 For example, *De libero arbitrio* (written 388–91 CE; see n842 above) and *De gratia et libero arbitrio* (426–7 CE)
901 *De civitate Dei* 10.23 CCSL 47 297; cf *De doctrina christiana* 4.8.22 CCSL 32 131–2.

Then too, you demand dialectic and pagan philosophy, which you usually call the plague of Christianity. But you grant both points: the use of the phrase and the restriction of the definition to the human will.[902] But what are you granting me if you concede what is a public right? Or what are you bestowing upon me if I show the reader within what limits I intend to speak of free will in this book? For that description of mine does nothing more than give the reader notice at the outset: in this book you will not hear about the free choice of God, angels, or demons, or brute beasts if they have any, but about what is attributed to the human will, nor will I discuss what it can do in unimportant matters which do not contribute to eternal happiness but only what it does in those matters which pertain to eternal salvation. If it is a crime to discuss anything unless you go through all its parts and everything connected with them, many writers are guilty of it. If someone does well to show the reader what he should expect and what he should not, what is there, pray tell, for you to forgive me?

But once again there is another false charge against the definition. Peter Lombard and the sophists make the power of free choice twofold: the power to discern, which is a property of the intellect, and the power to select or reject, which is a property of the will;[903] but my definition touches only on the power to select or reject, and so I propose only half of an act of the will. I respond briefly: in this question of freedom the most important point is the will, by which, as Augustine says, a person sins or lives rightly.[904] Though reason is not separate from this will – for we do not properly give the name 'will' to what follows sense perception and emotion rather than the judgment of reason – nevertheless I preferred to propose as the subject of this inquiry the principal and the only thing capable of liberty, especially because, once that is proposed, the thing which naturally precedes it is also understood at the same time, just as a person speaking about the pursuit of virtue includes at the same time the points

\* \* \* \* \*

902 *De servo arbitrio* WA 18 662:21–6 / LW 33 104
903 Peter Lombard was a theologian and bishop of Paris (c 1097–1160) renowned for his compendium of Christian doctrine culled from biblical, patristic, and contemporary texts, his *Sententiae in quatuor libris distinctae* ('*Opinions Divided into Four Books*') on which the major scholastic theologians wrote lengthy commentaries. Here Erasmus refers to book II dist 24.5 and 25.1 PL 192 702, 706. Cf Magister Bandinus' commentary (PL 192 1052D): 'Est autem liberum arbitrium in voluntate et ratione' ('Free will, however, is in the will and in the reason').
904 *Retractationum libri duo* 1.9.95 CCSL 57 26

which distinguish virtue from vice. And in the course of the debate I touch sufficiently on the judgment of reason.[905]

And now, just as if we were sitting in the school of Chrysippus,[906] my little definition is laid bare to the very bone.[907] It is accused of obscurity and the individual sections are picked apart and rigorously examined. There is more than one reason for giving a definition: sometimes so that the nature of the thing being discussed can be known; sometimes a thing very well known is merely touched on by its label, as, for example, a person of our times discussing anatomy does not need to define anatomy in the company of learned physicians – the label is enough. Sometimes a definition, or rather a description, is added to let the reader know what he should expect, what he should not, as, for example, someone who proposed to discuss animals, intending to keep his readers from expecting to hear what is usually said about their nature, generation, parts, diseases,[908] and remedies, might warn them as follows: 'This discussion will treat animals of land and sea, but only those which are harmful because of poison.' And that was the only reason I gave that little description of a subject which is presently bandied about and very familiar to all educated persons. But come on, then, however that may be, I will not beg to escape a severe examination, and I am not as afraid of your judgment, however unfair, as you think I am. I have already replied about the use of the phrase,[909] and I will not tolerate any more objections on that score. According to you these parts are clear: 'power of the human will,' and also 'by which a person can,' and also 'to eternal salvation.' On the other hand these parts are obscure: 'apply himself' and 'turn away,' and also 'to eternal salvation,' and also 'leads.'[910] You interpret 'power of the human will' as 'a power or faculty or ability or aptitude

* * * * *

905  *A Discussion* 22–3
906  A Stoic philosopher (c 280–207 BCE) who was said to have written 700 books and was known for his hair-splitting (Diogenes Laertius 7.7)
907  Literally, 'examined to the quick' (*Adagia* II iv 13)
908  The two Basel editions of 1526 have *moribus* 'habits'; LB 1321C has *morbis* 'diseases,' which seems to be a proper correction, particularly in the light of the next word, *medicinis* 'remedies.'
909  Erasmus means he has already replied to Luther's objection that the phrase 'free will' is broader than Erasmus' definition, since it applies to God and angels as well as men. See 263 above.
910  *De servo arbitrio* WA 662:30–2 / LW 33 104. Erasmus erroneously includes 'to eternal salvation' as both clear and unclear according to Luther, who had said it was clear. Also he would have been more exact if he had written 'what leads,' which is what Luther wrote.

to wish, not wish, select, scorn, approve, resist,[911] and whatever other actions of the will there may be.' You do not see how 'apply himself' and 'turn away' can mean anything but 'wish' or 'not wish,' 'approve' or 'disapprove,' which are actions elicited by the power of the will, and you imagine that power to be some intermediary between the will and the completed action of the will.[912] And here, for heaven's sake, you cite a rule of law, to let us know that you consulted a lawyer[913] when you were writing these things. I know that all the gods brought what they considered to be their principal gifts to this Pandora.[914] But what does this rule of law actually prescribe? That obscure language is to be interpreted against the person who speaks it.[915] But what is prescribed by the rule of charity which you claim for yourself? That everything is to be interpreted in the most favourable sense and that whoever is more steadfast and learned should minister to the weakness of others. See now how far you are from the rule of charity, going beyond even the rule of the law: it was intended to prevent obscurity of language from being an advantage to someone who might have deliberately and intentionally spoken so as to deceive. But you make clear language obscure so as to provide an occasion for slander, as I will soon demonstrate.

But to the matter at hand. Up to this point your interpretation is tolerable: 'what leads to salvation' you interpret to mean 'the words and works which God offers to the human will so that it may apply itself to them or turn away from them.' 'The words of God' you divide into 'the Law and the gospel; the Law requires works and the gospel faith.' For you say you do not see 'anything else that leads to the grace of God or to eternal salvation except the word and work of God, because grace or the Spirit is the very life to which we are led by the word and work of God. But this life or eternal salvation,' you say, 'is something incomprehensible to

* * * * *

911 The two Basel editions of 1526 have the error *reputandi*, which was corrected to *refutandi* in LB X 1321D.
912 *De servo arbitrio* WA 18 662:40–663:7 / LW 33 104–5
913 *De servo arbitrio* WA 18 663:8–10 / LW 33 1050; Erasmus probably alludes to Justus Jonas, who was trained as a lawyer (see n719 above).
914 Pandora (the 'all-gifted') was endowed by the gods with all the gifts of feminine beauty and charm, but also with flattery and deceit. 'Hesiod's Pandora' refers to a work executed by many hands (Tertullian *Adversus Valentinianos* 12.4.23 CCSL 2 764). See Hesiod *Theogony* 585–616 and *Works and Days* 42–105.
915 *De servo arbitrio* WA 18 663:8–10 / LW 33 105. On the legal rules about interpreting obscure terms see Berger 605 and 677; see also *Digesta Justiniani* 50.17.56 and 114 in *Corpus iuris civilis* ed Paul Krueger, Theodor Mommsen, et al, 3 vols (Berlin 1954–9) I 922–3.

the human intellect.' Therefore I am wrong when I attribute to the human will the power to apply itself, since no one's heart can know what these things are unless the Spirit has revealed them. And to Paul's testimony[916] you add an argument from experience: the philosophers, Portius Festus, and Pliny ridiculed the resurrection promised by the gospel.[917] And you add that today there is no lack of those who laugh at this article of the faith as a fable, although in their speech and writings they claim that they believe it.[918] What you say up to this point is not without piety, but it does no damage to my definition. But when you hope that I am not sprinkled with the same leaven,[919] I willingly accept your prayer, and I in turn pray for the same for you, except that that wish of yours is an insult to my faith. Whether my faith is sufficient for salvation, let the Lord look to it, but certainly it is not feigned; I do not write one thing and think another in my heart, and in my daily prayers I beg that Christ in his mercy will increase my faith. But I am surprised that you have anything to do with this wish, since you profess that you are certain you have the Spirit, who bestows all things – how I wish this were entirely true and my suspicion quite groundless! But here you seem to be using a wrestler's trick: you lower yourself in order to throw me down, and you do so with your usual candour.

We have heard a clever interpretation of my definition, indeed one that throws it back at me by a rule of the Law. Now let us hear the terrible additions assembled with the same skill: Erasmus teaches 'that free choice is a power of the will which by itself can will or not will the word and work of God, by which it is led to things which exceed its understanding and its grasp. But if it can will and not will, it can both love and hate, and it can to some degree do the works of the Law and believe the gospel, because, if it can will or not will, it is impossible for it not to be able to perform some of the work by that will, even if someone else prevents it from completing the work. Thus, since death, the cross, and all the evils of the world are numbered among the works of God which lead to salvation, the human will would be able to will both its death and its own perdition. Indeed it can will all things if it can will the word and the work of God.' For what is left except

* * * * *

916 1 Cor 2:9–10
917 For Festus see Acts 24:21 and 26:24–5. Pliny the Younger (c 61–c 112 CE), a Roman lawyer and official, wrote about Christian customs in his letters (Ep 10.96).
918 *De servo arbitrio* WA 18 663:12–34 / LW 33 105–6
919 *De servo arbitrio* WA 18 663:38–9 / LW 33 106; cf 1 Cor 4:6–7.

God himself?[920] What in the world is left? Here I attribute nothing to grace but I clearly attribute a certain divinity to free will. Come hither, all diviners and soothsayers! Listen to a strange portent: out of nothing Erasmus has made a God.[921] Throw Helicon open, O goddesses![922] Here is an open field for Luther to display his tragic eloquence: Erasmus goes far beyond the impious sophists, for whatever they think, they certainly speak more sparingly about free will; he is a Pelagian;[923] indeed, he goes far beyond Pelagius, who did indeed attribute divinity to free will, but to the whole of free will, whereas Erasmus attributes the same to half of it![924] O heavens, O earth, O seas of Neptune![925] Is there more? There is: he goes beyond even the heathen philosophers. How so? For this reason: though it is not yet agreed among the philosophers whether anything can move itself, for me free will not only moves itself and does so by its own power, but it also applies itself to things which are eternal, that is, incomprehensible to itself. What horrors you relate! But is there more yet? There is: up till now Erasmus has surpassed everyone in impiety, and now at last he surpasses himself. How so? For this reason: though he confessed before that free will was ineffective without grace, here he lays it down that the human will has a power whereby it may be able to apply itself to what pertains to eternal salvation.[926] For the moment I overlook that you changed 'can' to 'is effective' and for 'ineffective' you put down 'entirely ineffective,' so as to make the words serve your slander the better, and I take no account of your jeer about my naming grace in jest but leaving it out here when I speak seriously. We come to the highest pitch. What is left but a triumphal chant? He adds this final flourish:[927] don't you see, my dear Erasmus, that you betray yourself – unwittingly, I believe – by this definition as someone who understands nothing whatever about these matters or else writes about them with total thoughtlessness and contempt for them, unaware of what you are saying or affirming.[928]

Now pay attention to my answer, Luther, and I will show how much you betray yourself as a worker of magic tricks, and reveal how much

* * * * *

920 *De servo arbitrio* WA 18 664:1–11 / LW 33 106
921 Erasmus plays on the meaning of 'create': to make out of nothing. God created the world out of nothing, but by Luther's hyperbole Erasmus has created God.
922 Virgil *Aeneid* 7.641; Helicon was a mountain in Boeotia sacred to the Muses.
923 See n624 above.
924 That is, to the part of free will that resides in the will itself, without considering the part that resides in the intellect
925 Terence *Adelphi* 790
926 *De servo arbitrio* WA 18 664:14–665:1 / LW 33 107–8
927 See n435 above.
928 *De servo arbitrio* WA 18 665:1–4 / LW 33 108

smoke and how many horrible but empty and baseless pictures of things you pour forth before our eyes. I have already spoken often about the use of the phrase and you have sung that old song in vain time and time again. I have just now refuted your false charge about cutting free will in half. For how can the charge be other than false, since you find wanting in my definition what you immediately condemn in the definition of the theologians? This is what you say: 'The sophists are also deficient in that they attribute to free will the power to distinguish good from evil.'[929] And so my sin is less than theirs. But from this you conclude that my sin is graver – such is your skill in dialectic. You profess that you wish to speak in plain language[930] but you deliberately introduce darkness even into what is clear. Here, then, is something even more uncultivated: using words taken from the language of ordinary speakers, I call eternal salvation what we enjoy undyingly in the presence of God. Is there any darkness here? For here we live in hope for the time being, we hold the pledge, we look for the promise. And as for what leads to that happiness, I mean everything that arouses our mind to any desire, of any sort, for that happiness, whether it be effective or ineffective. As for 'turn away,' you know that means: it happens when someone neglects grace that is offered, preferring darkness to the light. And then the opposite of this I called 'applying one's self,' that is, 'making oneself available' to grace. But you say, 'You exclude the grace of God.'[931] In fact the very words 'applying' and 'turning away' signify that it is not excluded: no one applies himself unless he has been admonished by a sense of something to be sought after; no one turns away if nothing has been offered. When you examined the syllables of my definition, you should have examined the implied force of these words, and at the same time you should have noticed that I did not say 'is able' but 'may be able,' because I wanted to include something beyond our natural powers. You will say: 'Why did you not expressly include the word "grace" in your definition, since you earlier professed that free will is ineffective without grace?' Rather why didn't you, as a man full of Christian charity which never does anything wrong, why didn't you interpret the definition as implying what I so often inculcated in *A Discussion*? Why was it not enough for you that grace was signified by those two words?[932] But if you press me to say why I did not explicitly name grace here, I will tell you: I had not yet distinguished the word 'grace' into natural grace, preparatory or imperfect grace, and effective grace which

* * * * *

929 *De servo arbitrio* WA 18 666:9–10 / LW 33 110
930 *De servo arbitrio* WA 18 663:11–12 / LW 33 105
931 *De servo arbitrio* WA 18 665:11–13 / LW 33 108–9
932 That is, *applicandi* 'applying' and *auertendi* 'turning away'

abolishes sin. Even now there is insufficient agreement among theologians
about whether or not a person without a special grace can solicit the effective grace of God by means of morally good deeds.[933] My definition is open
to both opinions, since I reject neither one, though I am inclined to the one
which attributes more to grace. But according to you 'I exclude the Holy
Spirit together with all his power as superfluous and not necessary.'[934] How
do you draw that conclusion, my good man?[935] Evidently from one syllable:
'himself.'[936] O mighty syllable! In fact that syllable is meant to do no more
than let you understand that our natural powers are not completely inactive
when we are admonished[937] by grace. And if we accept the opinion of those
who teach that without special grace, by our natural powers – which are
themselves nevertheless gratuitous gifts of God – anyone can strive to such
an extent that the mercy of God will not be lacking to those who do the best
they can,[938] then it would be true here that the will without grace applies itself to what leads to eternal salvation. For just as no one suddenly becomes
most corrupt, so too we are led gradually and step by step to the perfect gift
of God, just as when someone is dwelling in the most impenetrable shadows,
first the darkness thins out and then a doubtful light appears far away until
finally vision becomes clear. For Augustine was fond of this comparison.[939]

Just so I include in what leads to eternal salvation those things that
admonish us from far off and prod the mind, as it were, to a desire of
eternal salvation. 'But no one desires something unless he knows it, and if

* * * * *

933 This issue was especially a matter of contention between the Augustinians
and certain of the late medieval theologians of the *via moderna*; see Oberman
*Harvest* 160–5.

934 *De servo arbitrio* WA 18 665:15–16 / LW 33 109

935 The Greek phrase Erasmus uses here (ὦ βέλτιστε, literally 'O best of men')
is a frequent colloquial formula of address; see, for example, Aristophanes
*Plutus* 1172 and Plato *Republic* 337E.

936 *De servo arbitrio* WA 18 665:13–15 / LW 33 109; in Latin the word is one syllable,
*se*. The Latin phrases for 'apply himself' and 'turn away' are both reflexive (*se
... applicare ... aut ... avertere*).

937 Here the two Basel editions of 1526 and LB 1323E have *monemur*. It might be
thought that *mouemur* 'moved' (which can easily be corrupted by a turned *u*)
would make better sense, but ten sentences earlier Erasmus spoke of grace
as admonishing someone by imparting a sense of something to be sought
after.

938 See *A Discussion* n119.

939 See *De dialectica* 8.14.3–14 ed Jan Pinbog, trans B. Darrell Jackson (Dordrecht
and Boston 1975) 104–5; cf *De peccatorum meritis et remissione* 2.5.5 PL 44 153
and *Hyperaspistes* 2 LB X 1527B–D.

he knows it he already has it.'[940] In fact, if he desires he neither has nor entirely lacks what he hopes for. But God admonishes us in various ways: sometimes by the light of nature, by which we understand that virtue is to be sought for its own sake and vice is to be avoided because of what it is; sometimes by adversity; sometimes by reading or the admonitions of friends; sometimes also by the soft whistling of the Spirit. Before he drank in the Spirit of Christ, Augustine read the epistles of Paul attentively and made some progress, brought nearer to the light of grace, but he was even more inflamed by the discourse of Potitianus.[941] Though we admit the grace of God was not lacking here, certainly it was imperfect, not yet freeing him from sin but preparing him for a richer gift; but if he had turned away from that grace, he would have been the cause of his own destruction. As it was, he made himself available to the call of grace and he gained salvation. And so in what leads to salvation I include not only the words and works of God and his grace but also the natural desire for virtue,[942] which, though it has been overwhelmed, has still not been extinguished in us; I include the love of reading and listening to what stimulates us to a contempt of the world; I include prayers, alms, fasting. But you will say that these things are so far from calling for grace that they are damnable works which stir up the anger of God. But what you assume as axioms is a matter of dispute between us. About Cornelius[943] I will say something in the proper place. For it is not surprising that you make such judgments about works performed without grace, since you claim that no one's deed is good, even if it is accomplished by God in us after we have been justified by grace. For you the mass of corruption[944] has such force that even God cannot perform a work in it that is good, much less perfect. Thus you see that the whole melodrama which you stir up out of my definition, once it is examined closely, is nothing but a huge and gross cloud of empty verbal fumes, the empty mockery of a juggler's tricks.

You go on to make false charges against my distinctions: in recounting the opinions of others about free will, I make Pelagius[945] almost evan-

* * * * *

940 Cf *De servo arbitrio* WA 18 663:25–7 / LW 33 105–6
941 Augustine *Confessions* 7.21, 86–7. Potitianus, a Roman civil servant in Africa, encouraged Augustine to become a Christian.
942 See Oberman *Harvest* 467–8 (*Ex naturae rei debita* and *Ex puris naturalibus*).
943 Acts 10:1–33
944 The phrase is Pauline (Gal 5:9). Cf Augustine *De diversis quaestionibus* IV *ad Simplicianum* 1.2.16 CCSL 44 421.
945 See n624 above.

gelical. I attribute a sort of faith and charity to some philosophers.[946] Concerning Pelagius I report nothing except what Augustine professes about him,[947] nor do I make him evangelical, but rather I number him among those whom the church has condemned for heresy. I do not make up a fourfold distinction of grace – and if I did so for pedagogic reasons there would be no danger in it – but rather I drew this distinction from the books of orthodox writers,[948] who confess that whatever we are and can do is attributable to grace and then posit a prevenient grace which invites, as it were, but is imperfect; there is cooperating grace (for so Augustine calls it)[949] which makes our will effective, once it has been stimulated by the first grace; there is a grace which perfects the whole process of salvation, for Bernard makes this distinction.[950] And yet I confess that these three are the same grace, although they have different names because of their different effects. You do not like this distinction, though there is no lack of piety in it, because it does nothing to confirm your teaching. Concerning the philosophers, I bear witness only to what Paul writes to the Romans;[951] I wouldn't dare to attribute so much to them if I did not have such a great authority for it. You also, at the end of your work, attribute something to the light of nature,[952] for you know that my citation from the psalm, 'the light of your countenance is stamped upon us,'[953] is not something I made up.[954] And just as I frankly confess that it is aptly interpreted as the light of faith, so too I deny what you assert, that it cannot be taken as the light of nature:[955] 'the light is

* * * * *

946 *De servo arbitrio* WA 18 666:30–667:2 / LW 33 111. Erasmus means that Luther accuses him of doing these things.

947 Although several of Pelagius' writings are extant, he was principally known through polemical writings against him, especially by Augustine, such as *De natura et gratia, De spiritu et litera, De gratia Dei, Contra duas epistolas Pelagianorum*, and *De gratia et libero arbitrio*.

948 *A Discussion* 31–2

949 See *A Discussion* n109.

950 See *A Discussion* n325 and n307 above.

951 Rom 1:19–20, 2:14–16

952 *De servo arbitrio* WA 18 785:26–38 / LW 33 292

953 Ps 4:7

954 *A Discussion* 24. Luther had already opposed this traditional application of the verse to the light of nature in *Operationes in Psalmos* WA 5 119 / Luther *Operationes* 203–4. The interpretation of *lumen* here as meaning natural reason was widespread because it had been propounded by Nicholas of Lyra (*Biblia 1498* III sig n7v).

955 *De servo arbitrio* WA 18 667:3–6 / LW 33 111

stamped' because God created man in his own image and likeness,[956] which was obscured but not extinguished by sin.[957] Therefore I do not misapply the psalm to a blinded reason but rather I accommodate it to a darkened reason. If the light of nature is completely extinguished in us, how did the philosophers know God without the grace of God? How did they bring forward so much about virtue, about living rightly, about the immortality of the soul, the beginning and the end of the world, the differing rewards of the pious and the impious, about not repaying an injury, about the pursuit of virtue for its own sake, avoiding vice because of what is is, about educating children, loving one's wife, fulfilling the duties of office conscientiously, loving one's country? And in their biographies we read of many deeds in keeping with their precepts. And so why was it a crime for me to say that they put forth some ideas that agree with the precepts of the gospel? So too, did not the laws of the pagans punish theft, murder, adultery, perjury just as the law of Moses also did? Hence I conclude that the light of reason was not entirely extinguished in them, and I add that it seems not improbable that they had 'a will which was in some way inclined to virtue but not able to achieve eternal salvation without the access of grace through faith.'[958] Concerning the faith and charity which you say I attribute to the philosophers in my *Discussion*, I make no firm assertions, although there is some debate about what faith would be sufficient for unlearned Jews and about whether there is some sort of faith whereby a pagan could be saved.[959]

You call my threefold distinction of the laws of nature, works, and faith mere storybook fiction.[960] First of all, the law of nature is not in doubt. My discussion of the law of works and the law of faith I took from Augus-

* * * * *

956 The underlying image is that of a seal: the light of God's countenance is imprinted on man as the design of a seal is impressed on wax or a coin.

957 For Luther's view of the extinction of the divine image in man after the Fall, see Charles Trinkaus 'Luther's Hexameral Anthropology' *The Scope of Renaissance Humanism* (Ann Arbor 1983) 404–21 (especially 406–7).

958 *A Discussion* 25

959 The most famous examples of saved pagans are Trajan and Ripheus in Dante's *Paradiso* 20.88–129. According to a legend well known in the Middle Ages, Trajan was brought back from hell to life at the prayers of St Gregory; see John the Deacon *Vita Sancti Gregorii* 2.44 PL 75 105 and John of Salisbury *Policraticus* 5.8 trans Cary J. Nederman (Cambridge 1990) 80–1. According to Dante and Thomas Aquinas (*Summa theologiae* III suppl q 71 a 5), Trajan was baptized, did penance, and was finally saved.

960 *De servo arbitrio* WA 18 667:2–4 / LW 33 111

tine: in the book which he entitled *The Letter and the Spirit*, he followed the opinion of Paul in distinguishing the law of works or deeds from the law of faith. He claims the law of deeds is the law of Moses, written on the tablets, prescribing without grace. He claims the law of faith is the New Testament, which prescribes the same things as the law of works but by the addition of grace softens the precepts of faith.[961] And among many other things, he says as follows: 'What the law of works commands with threats, the law of faith accomplishes by means of belief.' And a little later: 'By the law of works God says, "Do what I command." By the law of faith we say to God, "Give what you command."' Then again, somewhat later: 'When the works of charity are written on the tablets, it is the law of works and the letter which kills the transgressor. But when charity is poured forth into the hearts of those who believe, it is the law of faith and the Spirit who gives life to those who love.'[962] This is what he says. To be sure, I do not condemn the opinion of those who claim that the Law consists of precepts, the gospel of promises and consolation, so that each is included in the other – that is, the gospel is also in the Mosaic law and the Law is in the gospel. But Augustine, though he does not seem very far from this opinion, still does not seem to agree with it completely. For in the same work he distinguishes the Old Testament from the New by the kinds of promises in each: the Old promises what is temporal; the gospel, what is eternal. These are the words of Augustine: 'Therefore, just as the law of deeds written on stone tablets and the reward it gets – that promised land which the carnal house of Israel received when it was freed from Egypt – pertain to the Old Testament, so too the law of faith written on the hearts of the faithful and the reward it gets – that species of contemplation which the spiritual house of Israel achieves when it is freed from this world – pertain to the New Testament.'[963] He says something in accord with this when he comments on these words from John's Gospel: but 'the only begotten Son who is in the bosom of the Father has made him known.'[964] Though I imitated Augustine, still I come closer than he does to the opinion which you approve, since among other things I say as follows:[965] 'Moses says, "Do not commit adultery; if you do so, you will be stoned."'[966]

\* \* \* \* \*

961 *De spiritu et littera* 13.22 CSEL 60 175
962 *De spiritu et littera* 17.29 CSEL 60 183
963 *De spiritu et littera* 24.41 CSEL 60 194
964 See Augustine on John 1.18 in *In Iohannis evangelium tractatus* CXXIV 3.19 CCSL 36 28–9.
965 *A Discussion* 25–6
966 Exod 20:14; John 8:4–5

But what does the law of faith say, the law which commands us to love our enemies,[967] to take up our cross every day,[968] to contemn this life?[969] "Do not be afraid, my little flock, for yours is the kingdom of heaven."[970] And also: "Trust me, because I have conquered the world."[971] And also: "I am with you until the end of the world etc." '[972] You see that when I want to show what the law of faith is, I bring forward words of trust and consolation. And my intention here was not to discuss in what ways the old law is distinct from the gospel, but the distinction was brought forward in passing so that I could more easily show the reader how the dimmed light of nature could be brightened by the gift of faith and the corrupted will set right by charity. I think I have made it clear to the reader that thus far I have done nothing reprehensible in *A Discussion* but rather that you distort everything by reporting it wrongly; so much the more do we distrust you when you interpret Holy Scripture because from these distortions we discover your bad faith.

Now behold how much melodrama you stir up out of nothing! These are your words: 'If some Christian should put all this together, he will be forced to suspect that you are ridiculing and making fun of the teachings and the religion of Christians. For I find it very difficult to attribute so much ignorance to someone who has read through all our writings and so diligently committed them to memory.'[973] This is what you say. Why am I accused of such a horrendous crime? Because I said Pelagius was almost evangelical, that is, a heretic. For what else does it mean to be almost evangelical? Pagans are not called almost evangelical, for they are far removed from the gospel; but Arius was almost evangelical, for he confirmed his teachings from the gospel.[974] And then I confess that among the philosophers reason was darkened but not extinguished – for they judge well about many things by the light of nature – and likewise that the will was not completely corrupted, since they manifested certain natural strivings towards virtue, for

* * * * *

967 Matt 5:44
968 Luke 9:23; cf Matt 16:24.
969 Matt 10:39 (Mark 8:35, Luke 9:24)
970 Luke 12:32
971 John 16:33
972 Matt 28:20
973 *De servo arbitrio* WA 18 667:6–10 / LW 33 111
974 See n92 above. The Arians compiled a formidable array of scriptural texts to support their teachings. Jaroslav Pelikan *The Christian Tradition: A History of the Development of Doctrine* I: *The Emergence of the Catholic Tradition (100–600)* (Chicago 1971) shows Arius using John 1:18, Gal 3:19, and Heb 1:1–4 to support his doctrines (197–202).

which you substitute faith and charity. I distinguished three kinds of law: the law of nature, of works, and of faith. No one denies there is a law of nature. The distinction between the other two I drew from Augustine. I said that in the opinions and precepts of the philosophers there are some things which agree with the teachings and precepts of the gospel. The verse in Psalm 4, 'The light is stamped etc,' I apply to the light of nature in such a way as not to deny that it may rightly be interpreted as meaning the faith by which the light of nature is assisted.[975] After these points come those monstrous charges which I just now recited: 'If some Christian etc.' But where can you show us this Christianity of yours? In your church opinions vary; in ours there are no Christians, if we believe you; and then you teach that neither saints nor Christians nor the church can be pointed out. Moreover, since Christian charity does not know how to suspect something is evil, who is this Christian without charity who is so wickedly suspicious that 'he is forced' by what is well said 'to suspect that I am ridiculing and making fun of the teachings and religion of Christians'?[976] I think Christians would suspect this much more readily if I deserted the fellowship of the church and fought to promote your teachings. Here you surely betray how wickedly eager you are to make false charges: up till now I knew nothing, but in everything I say I am thoughtless, addle-pated, and ignorant. Now, in order to get an opportunity for a new slander, you cannot attribute such complete ignorance to me, but rather you give back the knowledge you took away, so that you can brand me with the more serious crime of ridiculing the religion and teaching of Christians. But what are those writings of your camp which I have read through so diligently and retain in my memory?[977] Your own teachings? I have hardly been able to read any of your books all the way through because they are filled with such verbosity and such an insatiable passion for insults. And anyone who is to understand your writings would have to be very learned indeed, since they cannot be understood without your spirit. And I hardly know whether you think there are any Christian teachings besides yours. As for me, I thought you were talking about the pronouncements of the Catholic faith; those I certainly do not ridicule, nor have I ever had any mind to do so, thank God, although I cannot and will not justify how I have lived. So it is that you make up now one thing, now another, no matter what, just as long as I look to you like a suitable target for false accusations. How you ranted and raved in the

\* \* \* \* \*

975 See n954 above.
976 *De servo arbitrio* WA 18 667:7–8 / LW 33 111
977 *De servo arbitrio* WA 18 667:9 / LW 33 111

opening of your book about my sceptical attitude! How often you charged me with not asserting anything in *A Discussion*! And then a little later I am the finest of fellows for the same reason, that I assert nothing and merely debate out of a desire to learn and eagerness to pursue the truth.[978] You are so consistent in your slanders that you can make the same circumstance into a double crime.

And then, as if it were not very slanderous to have charged me with the crime of a wicked and blasphemous mindset, you restrain yourself: 'But for the moment,' you say, 'I will leave that problem alone and will be content to have pointed it out until a more suitable occasion offers itself.'[979] And immediately after that I hear 'my dear Erasmus,' and I am lovingly admonished not to be numbered among those who say 'Who is looking at us?'[980] This is a tune you should be singing rather than I: though you play games with such manifold trickery, you think you deceive us and that your spirit is not detected. You say, 'Do not try me so.'[981] If I try you when I debate with you without any insults, why are you not stirred up against those who harass you and tear you to pieces in large volumes, not debating as I do but calling you and your teachings by their proper names? But if you ignore them because they are outside your church – since Paul did not deign to pass judgment on outsiders[982] – I have always been no less a stranger to your church than they are. Why do you not rage against those who have published books in which they openly rant and rave against your teachings, although up till now they embraced your church?[983] Paul handed over to Satan only those who broke away from the gospel.[984] You cannot bring that charge against me: I always wrote and said and thought the same things. You frequently charge the Roman church with tyranny. If the charge is true, this state of affairs crept in over a long period of time, gradually nourished by wealth and worldly power. But if the outlook that breathes from your writings were to acquire the wealth, authority, and power of the Roman pontiffs, it is clear enough what we should expect. Unless I am mistaken,

* * * * *

978 See the passage cited by Erasmus at n640 above.

979 *De servo arbitrio* WA 18 667:10–11 / LW 33 111

980 Cf Ps 63:5: 'They have strengthened their evil speech; they have told tales in order to lay their snares; they have said, "Who will see them?"' Luther refers to those who sin because they think they are unobserved and will not get caught.

981 *De servo arbitrio* WA 18 667:11–12 / LW 33 111

982 1 Cor 5:12

983 See nn11, 13, 14, and 17 above.

984 1 Cor 5:5

you would send your minions and armed forces here, and you would treat those who disagree with you somewhat less mercifully with the sword than you now do with the pen. And meanwhile, where is that marvellous evangelist who professes that he will defend the gospel against the gates of hell, using only the sword of the Spirit, which is the word of God?[985] You do nothing but stoop to slander, to insults, to threats, and yet you want to appear guileless and undefiled, not led by human emotions but by the Spirit of God. You are right when you teach that God must be believed to be just even if both the light of nature and the light of grace cannot grasp how he is just,[986] but you are not right to make the same claim for yourself.

Furthermore, I commit an even graver sin in distinguishing opinions, since I make one into three,[987] and if a person sees one thing as three he is certainly afflicted either with insanity or drunkenness. Indeed, I recount several opinions, of which the first is that of Pelagius, which I abandon as condemned. Secondly, I give the opinion of those who attribute the least possible to free will but nevertheless do so in such a way as not to take it away entirely; for they say that of itself it can do nothing effectively without the access of grace, whether stimulating grace or operating or cooperating or consummating. And yet in all of these they profess that there is an application or a turning of the human will or a cooperation, since they posit that the human will has some power which acts somewhat while grace acts. This is the opinion of either Augustine[988] or Thomas,[989] who follows the opinion of Augustine in attributing as little as possible to free will. And I call this opinion probable precisely because it leaves to mankind longing and striving. And here you pour out a tremendous flood of words about how what should be imputed is not imputed and how something that can do nothing of itself is said to be able to do something, although in the debate I make the solution of that difficulty as clear as your hand in front of your face, as they say.[990] The third that I recount I assign to Karlstadt, who

\* \* \* \* \*

985 Eph 6:17; Erasmus seems to paraphrase *De servo arbitrio* WA 18 625:26–626:10 / LW 33 51–2.
986 *De servo arbitrio* WA 18 785:21–38 / LW 33 292
987 *De servo arbitrio* WA 18 667:15 / LW 33 112
988 Erasmus synthesizes Augustine's position from many texts, notably *De gratia et libero arbitrio* and *De spiritu et littera* (PL 44 880–912, 199–246).
989 *Summa theologiae* I–II q 111 a 2
990 Latin 'huiusmodi difficultatem palpabiliter, vt aiunt, expediam'; the tag *vt aiunt* 'as they say' suggests that this a proverbial saying, but it does not appear in the usual collections (including Erasmus' *Adagia*). The adverb *palpabiliter* is not classical, but it is found in at least one medieval dictionary: R.A.

does not altogether take away free will – for the moment allow me to use that phrase, although if someone wants to call it beta or delta,[991] it makes no difference to me – but he says that in the performance of a good work it is not at all active but merely passive, so that grace does not work through our will but in our will, which is merely passive. The fourth I assign to you: in the course of your *Assertion* you deny that free will has any place in the nature of things and that our will acts at all when we do good or bad deeds, but that everything is done by sheer necessity.[992] I call this the harshest of all the opinions, and I profess that I must take issue most of all with your opinion and that of Karlstadt.[993] I do not pass over the opinion of Scotus, who thinks that, by morally good works, through the general influence of nature, a person can merit the effective grace of God *de congruo*,[994] because God in his kindness will not allow someone to perish if only he does the best he can[995] – not that he achieves salvation by his own power, but he somehow becomes capable of divine grace.[996] Since the church, so far as I know, has not yet rejected this opinion,[997] I neither defend it nor refute it.

Setting aside, then, the opinions of Pelagius and Scotus, you say[998] that the three remaining opinions differ only verbally. The first, namely Augustine's, grants that choice or will can do evil by its own power and it

* * * * *

Latham *Revised Medieval Latin Word-list from British and Irish Sources* (London 1965). Perhaps the tag is simply an apology for a non-classical word. The classical *palpabilis* is used metaphorically, sometimes with the phrase *ut ita dicam*; see *Thesaurus linguae Latinae* (Leipzig 1900– ) sv *palpabilis* 2.

991 Erasmus probably chose these Greek letters because the first meant 'beet' in Latin and the second also referred to the delta of the Nile.

992 *Assertio* article 36 WA 7 146:4–8 / 306

993 *A Discussion* 33

994 See *A Discussion* n106.

995 See *A Discussion* n119 and 270 above.

996 *A Discussion* 28–9

997 It had in fact been rejected by the so-called Second Council of Orange (529) which approved anti-Pelagian canons culled from Augustine's polemics in canon 18: 'Debetur merces bonis operibus, si fiant; sed gratia, quae non debetur, precedit, ut fiant' ('A reward is owed to good deeds, if they are done; but grace, which is not owed, precedes them so that they may be done'). The document was apparently lost by the tenth century. Thus the issue of man's role in the initiation of justification became in medieval theology once again a disputed question. The document was recovered and published in *Concilia omnia tam generalia quam particularia* (Cologne 1538), two years after Erasmus' death.

998 The two Basel editions of 1526 have *doce*; LB X 1327E has *doceo*. Neither of these make good sense, and *doces* must be what Erasmus intended.

does not make God the sole agent, with the will merely being acted upon, as you do;[999] and to this extent Karlstadt agrees with Augustine and dissents from you. For when Augustine calls grace cooperating, he means at least our will does operate to some extent,[1000] and then when they posit a stimulating but imperfect grace, they do not exclude turning towards it or turning away, whereas you completely exclude both by introducing the absolute necessity of all things. For I have no quarrel with the principle which you assert but rather with the recantation[1001] by which you correct what you originally said – namely that free will has no power except to sin – and approve the teachings of Wyclif.[1002] And those who hold the first opinion make our will vitiated, wounded, and crippled, not extinguished; and so there remains some judgment, though imperfect, some power, though ineffective. You see, then, that this is not the same opinion stated in other terms, as you pretend. But you compare the first opinion, which I say is probable, with my definition, excluding for the moment the opinion of those who think that God's goodness is called upon to confer grace by morally good work without any special grace.[1003] But in fact I formulated the definition so that it leaves room even for that opinion, since it has not yet been condemned. But imagine that the opinion of Scotus is rejected. Let the first opinion be that of Augustine which posits stimulating grace: it does not exclude application and aversion. When he was chastized Pharaoh began to come to his senses; and if he had not turned away from stimulating grace, he would not have fallen into the abyss of

\* \* \* \* \*

999 Augustine *De gratia et libero arbitrio* 17.33 PL 44 901

1000 See *A Discussion* n109.

1001 Latin *palinodia* (*Adagia* I ix 59)

1002 Erasmus seems to mean that he can accept the thesis itself which Luther defends in *Assertio* article 36, but not his extension of it in the course of the defence (WA 7 146:4–8 / 306; see n992 above). But it is hard to see that Erasmus could agree with the thesis itself: 'Liberum arbitrium post peccatum res est de solo titulo, et dum facit, quod in se est, peccat moraliter' ('After sin free will exists in name only and when it does what in it lies it sins mortally'); see WA 7 142:23–4 / 301.

1003 Erasmus attributed this position to Scotus, though it could be argued that it is that of William of Ockham or of Erasmus' near contemporary Gabriel Biel (see Oberman *Harvest* 131–41 for Biel's doctrine of salvation). But Erasmus may not have been entirely wrong in assigning this doctrine to Scotus; he had studied at the Collège de Montaigu in Paris, where he would have become familiar with Scotist teachings. For a clarifying comparison of Scotus and Ockham on merit and salvation, see William J. Courtenay *Schools and Scholars in Fourteenth-century England* (Princeton 1987) 212–14.

evil.[1004] Let us also grant this, according to Bernard: the entire initiation is owing to grace.[1005] Certainly, when our will operates with operating grace, it applies itself to grace, accommodating its natural powers to operating grace, just as when the sun rises we open our eyes, or else it turns away, just as if we should close our eyes when the sun is up.[1006] Show us then, Luther, the drowsiness or the dullness of my judgment. This is what you do: you say that the first opinion, which confesses that free will vitiated by sin cannot will the good without grace, is probable. And the definition attributes to it the power to apply itself to the good or to turn away from the good without grace. 'The definition,' you say, 'affirms what the example of it denies etc,'[1007] as you run on with sufficient impudence and loquacity. Hear now, on the other side, how subtle your slander is: I define free will in general, whether as it was first created, or as it is in those who have been freed by grace, or as it is crippled in those who have not yet been freed from the slavery of sin. What has all this got to do with the first opinion, which is only part of what is included in the definition? The definition also does not exclude special grace, unless we accept the opinion which is closest to Pelagianism,[1008] of which you do not approve, but which I may nevertheless use to assist me in making my argument, nor do I see any danger even in defending it. And then you do not notice that I posit two kinds of willing or two kinds of striving for virtue, effective and ineffective. The ineffective is also in those who are subject to sin, according to some by means of the general influence,[1009] according to others not without grace but imperfect grace, which indeed does not yet abolish sin but nevertheless prepares for effective grace. Nor am I disturbed because you allow no middle position but make either God or Satan the rider;[1010] for what you should have demonstrated you shamelessly bring forward to refute me. You remember what I said about the light.[1011] And that blind man in the gospel first sees nothing, then he sees men who look like walking trees, and then he sees

* * * * *

1004 Exod 9:27, 10:17, 12:31–2, 14:5–28. Erasmus discussed Pharoah's fall in *Hyperaspistes 2* LB X 1395–1402.

1005 Bernard *De gratia et libero arbitrio* 14.46; see *Treatises III: On Grace and Free Choice* ... trans Daniel O'Donovan, The Works of Bernard of Clairvaux 7, Cistercian Father Series 19 (Kalamazoo, Mich 1977) 105–6.

1006 Cf Augustine *De peccatorum meritis et remissione* 2.5.5 PL 44 153.

1007 *De servo arbitrio* WA 18 667:27–668:5 / LW 33 112–13

1008 That is, the opinion of Scotus, which allows for merit *de congruo*

1009 See *A Discussion* n112.

1010 See n246 above.

1011 See 271 above.

everything clearly.[1012] But I will take this up elsewhere; for here I assert nothing.

You see now that what I have said solves the problems you repeat in the next section, hammering away at them, not without wanton insults.[1013] You take one part of what is defined, that is, free will vitiated by sin, and with that you compare one opinion: to apply oneself to the good is good; therefore free will can do good by itself. I grant it, if you are talking about the morally good. Again, I grant it, if you are talking about pious deeds, as long as you join to it preparatory or stimulating grace, as, for example, when from reading the Bible or listening to a preacher we feel our mind moved to love piety and hate wickedness. This opinion I do not exclude, either in the definition or in recounting the opinions; I exclude only the opinions of Pelagius, Karlstadt, and you. Where, then, are the two free wills in conflict with one another?[1014] Does a genus conflict with itself because it includes different species? Will you deny that an ass is an animal because it is distinguished from a man by reason of its specific difference and properties?[1015] Would you make two purses out of one because it contains gold and silver? Here, then, no Proteus has been caught;[1016] rather you yourself are playing Proteus, turning yourself into whatever you wish in your eagerness to slander me, and also making me first one thing and then right away something else, whatever you think suitable for the darts of your slander. I confess that according to one opinion the human will, corrupted by sin, cannot, in so far as it is corrupted, turn to the good without special grace, whether it be effective or stimulating grace. I confess that in those who have been freed by baptism and faith, the human will in and of itself is more prone to evil than to good. And I confess that according to one opinion the human will by its natural powers can turn to efforts, attempts, and works. If anyone claims these are evil and call forth wrath, I will deny it. If anyone claims that they are not good because they are performed without grace, I will grant it, if he will only confess that they are morally good and do call upon the effective grace of God. Therefore I do not contradict myself when I say different things in the context of different opinions. For here I do not yet declare what I think, but I gather together

\* \* \* \* \*

1012 Mark 8:22–5
1013 *De servo arbitrio* WA 18 668:6–669:6 / LW 33 113–14
1014 *De servo arbitrio* WA 18 668:4–5 / LW 33 113
1015 Qualities not essential to a species but always connected with it and with it alone – for example, braying
1016 *De servo arbitrio* WA 18 668:14–15 / LW 33 113; see n83 above.

the subject matter of the ensuing debate for the unlearned reader. So the triumph which you stage here should have been reserved for the concluding part of the debate where I declare which of all the opinions I favour most; at this point I am only girding myself for the battle. But when did I ever shout at you for professing that free will subject to sin cannot turn to what is better without the help of grace?[1017] No, I condemned you instead for teaching that there is no human will either for good or for evil, that it plays no part at all in a good or evil deed, either with or without grace – which you will never read in Augustine. Finally, when you have poured out such a useless spate of verbiage, clearly doing no more than beating the air, as they say,[1018] then, according to your custom, you set up a triumph, as if you had fought valiantly. You are also afraid that no one will believe you when you recount so many absurdities, so many contradictions: 'Read this passage in A Discussion,' you say, 'and you will be amazed.'[1019] Read this passage in A Discussion, I say, and whoever reads it will immediately be amazed to find in the herald of the gospel such a malicious eagerness to slander. It is wearisome to recount the other vainglorious boasts you thunder out in that passage.

Equally intemperate is what you heap up in the next section:[1020] how can it be consistent for free will to do something and still for the sum total to be imputed to grace? Since I explain this at length at the end of the debate,[1021] what need was there to waste time here with empty verbiage? It should not be imputed, because whatever man can do by his natural power is a gratuitous gift of God.[1022] Nor is there any need here for the logician's conception of an absolute act of willing by the human will, with no regard to good or evil, a notion you condemn,[1023] though you would approve of it if it helped your case. Why is it absurd if, for pedagogical reasons, someone should posit an absolute when there is in reality no such absolute?

\* \* \* \* \*

1017 *De servo arbitrio* WA 18 668:17–19 / LW 33 113
1018 1 Cor 9:26; Otto no 28; cf *Adagia* III vi 38.
1019 *De servo arbitrio* WA 18 668:20 / LW 33 113
1020 *De servo arbitrio* WA 18 669:7–36 / LW 33 114–15
1021 See *A Discussion* 77–83
1022 This sentence is hardly clear. Erasmus seems to mean that the action of the will need not be imputed to supernatural grace because the will does make its own contribution; but in another sense all is due to grace because the ability of the will to do anything is a free gift of God. Or the antecedent of 'It' may be the 'something' the will does, which should not be imputed to free will because the will's ability to act comes from God.
1023 *De servo arbitrio* WA 18 669:20–33 / LW 33 114–15

How, then, do the philosophers dispute about prime matter and pure elements[1024] or the mathematicians about forms abstracted from matter? Nor is it as unlikely as you would like to make out if someone attributes to our will a pure act of willing so that it does not consider its object under the aspect of good or evil but only as a being or as something by its own nature intermediate, even if there are some who deny that there is anything intermediate. Your loquacity is everywhere so troublesome that I think that no Bolanus[1025] could have a temperament so felicitous as to put up with your veritable steeplefull of bronze bells,[1026] since everything you say is beside the point and yet you never stop talking. You dispatched the first opinion, that of Thomas or Augustine, and now you attribute the second to Augustine, though it belongs to Karlstadt, who denies that the human will acts at all in a good work, though he admits it does in a bad one. And from this we can guess how dexterously you handle a topic, since you muddle together even the distinct opinions. Among those which I do not reject, I set the opinion of Augustine over against that of Pelagius, from which it is most widely different, and I compare Scotus' opinion with Pelagius' as coming the nearest to it. Reread A Discussion and you will find that it is so.[1027] To the opinion of Augustine, I subjoin that of Karlstadt, which I call more harsh; intoxicated with your endless babbling,[1028] you now attribute this one to Augustine. In the third place I put the opinion of you and Wyclif, which I call the harshest of all. I say that my quarrel will be primarily with the last two, that is, with Karlstadt's and yours. I have put you back on track. Now what remains is for you to demonstrate to us that the last two opinions are the same as the first. When Augustine posits co-operating grace, he confesses that free will also does something in a good

* * * * *

1024 In Aristotelian metaphysics, prime matter is the purely potential principle of being which, when joined with the active principle, form, constitutes an existing material thing (such as those we see around us). On the elements see n500 above.

1025 Horace Satires 1.9.11–12. Erasmus seems to take the the speaker in the satire to mean he wishes he had the patience of Bolanus, who was apparently able to put up with fools gladly. But today cerebrum, which is here translated 'temperament,' is thought to mean 'anger': Horace wishes he had the spirit to shake off the bore as Bolanus might have done.

1026 Literally, 'Dodonean bronze,' applied to those who speak too loud and too long (Adagia 1 i 7)

1027 A Discussion 27–31

1028 Latin multiloquio; cf Prov 10:19 and Matt 6:7.

work; Karlstadt affirms that it does nothing but remains passive; you teach that it does nothing in a good work or a bad one, either before grace or after grace, but that it is a meaningless word, pure and simple. This opinion is in conflict with the first and it goes beyond the second. And here, having fallen off your ass,[1029] as they say, or rather having gone off your rockers,[1030] you do not understand what you are saying and resort to oaths. 'As God is my witness,' you say, 'I intended to say nothing else, and I intended nothing else to be understood, by the words of the last two opinions but what is said in the first opinion. I think that neither Augustine meant anything else nor do I understand anything else from his words than what the first opinion states, so that the three opinions recited by *Discussion* are for me no more than that one opinion of mine.'[1031] If I had said anything so mindless[1032] as you do here, how you would overwhelm me with insults! There would be no end to your scoffing! And still you never cease to indulge in evasions, returning to your old plea about the name, though I have excluded it often enough and replied to it in more than one way. You yourself seem to be aware of your mistake, but still you did not want to erase what you had written. And so you do not end this section as you usually do, with a triumph, but rather you withdraw crestfallen.[1033] 'If I am mistaken here,' you say, 'may I be corrected by anyone who can do so; if these points are obscure and ambiguous, let them be illuminated and firmly established by anyone who can do so.'[1034] Here you admit a corrector and an enlightener, though in your conclusion you refuse all judgment.[1035]

But in the next section you pluck up your spirits. 'But away with these verbal monstrosities! For who can bear such an abuse of language?'[1036] In so many words Echo[1037] plays back your utterance: 'But away with these verbal

* * * * *

1029 Aristophanes *Clouds* 1255; Plato *Laws* 3.701D; *Adagia* I vii 31A

1030 Literally, 'from your mind.' Erasmus plays with the echoing sounds of the Greek phrases ἀπ' ὄνου 'off your ass' and ἀπὸ νοῦ 'out of your mind.'

1031 *De servo arbitrio* WA 18 670:28–33 / LW 33 116

1032 Latin *sine mente*; cf Virgil *Aeneid* 10.640.

1033 Literally, 'like a rooster with drooping wings'; cf *Adagia* II ii 36.

1034 *De servo arbitrio* WA 670:38–671:1 / LW 33 116

1035 *De servo arbitrio* WA 18 787:12 / LW 33 295

1036 *De servo arbitrio* WA 18 671:4–5 / LW 33 116

1037 A nymph who loved Narcissus in vain and grieved until only her voice remained (Ovid *Metamorphoses* 3.356–402); Erasmus composed a colloquy entitled 'Echo,' first printed in the *Colloquia* of June 1526 issued by Froben at Basel and based on the acoustical conceit (ASD I-3, 555–8 / CWE 40 796–801).

monstrosities! For who can bear such an abuse of language?' Concerning the use of an accepted phrase, go quarrel with Hilary[1038] and Ambrose,[1039] with Augustine[1040] and Jerome.[1041] Here you had proposed to say that the three opinions are not at all distinct from each other, and skipping over this, you quibble about the term 'free will,' and you still don't stop asserting what is manifestly false. Is it one and the same thing to say that free will cooperates with grace, and that it is only passive in a good work but acts in a bad one, and that it does nothing in either a good or a bad work but God alone works whatever is done, whether good or evil? You sum up your argument as follows: after sin the human will without grace is free only to do evil; therefore, once freedom is gone, slavery takes its place; that cannot be denied; where there is slavery there is sheer necessity; and where there is necessity free will does nothing; if it does nothing it is purely passive; your grammar cannot call lost health, health.[1042] But in order to defend my definition and to pick apart your tangled arguments at one and the same time, I will sum up the matter in stark propositions:

The will of mankind, like that of the angels, after its creation was free to do good or evil in such a way that it could cling to the grace offered to it without the special help of any new grace, and it could turn away from grace.

After the fall of our first parents, this natural liberty was vitiated, not extinguished. For there remained in them some spark of reason which distinguished virtue from vice and likewise some striving of the will which fled from vice and yearned for virtue in some fashion.

But this striving and this reason are ineffective without a special grace, according to some; according to others it has only enough strength to be able

\* \* \* \* \*

1038 See n327 above. The term *libera voluntas* (or variations on it) occurs, for example, six times in *De Trinitate* 9.50 PL 10 520–1.

1039 St Ambrose (c 340–397), bishop of Milan, Latin Father and Doctor of the church, wrote copious exegetical, moral, and dogmatic works, as well as orations, epistles, and hymns. The term *liberum arbitrium* occurs in *De Jacob et vita beata* (1.3.10, 2.3.11 CSEL 32 10–11, 38), the *editio princeps* of which Erasmus published in the same volume as his own *De pueris instituendis* (Basel: Hieronymus Froben, Johann Herwagen, and Nicolaus Episcopius 1529). It can also be found in *De Cain et Abel* 2.9.28 CSEL 32 part 1 402 and *De fide* 2.11.97 CSEL 78 93.

1040 He used the term (with varying inflections) at least 569 times and wrote whole treatises about it; see n947 above.

1041 Jerome used the term (with varying inflections) at least fifty times; see, for example, *Adversus Jovinianum* 2.3 PL 23 (1883) 299.

1042 Cf *De servo arbitrio* WA 18 670:33–671:3 / LW 33 116

to merit grace *de congruo*, whether preparatory or even justifying grace, by means of morally good works. This opinion, I think, has not been condemned by the church,[1043] though it has also not rejected the one that precedes it, so that on this point it allows everyone to indulge his own judgment.[1044]

Those freed by grace are in the same condition as mankind was when it was first created, in that they can apply themselves to grace when it is offered and can turn away from it, except that, because of Adam's sin and their own, there remains in them a certain darkness of the reason and a certain inclination to sin, which nevertheless does not take away their freedom but rather exercises their piety.

This application and aversion holds good for both kinds of grace, what we have called stimulating grace and justifying grace. For the will applies itself when it makes itself available to grace and at the same time strives with its natural power towards those things to which it is called by grace; it turns itself away when it neglects the whistling of the Spirit and turns to the desires of the flesh. Likewise, it applies itself to justifying grace when, with the little natural power it has, it works with the grace working powerfully upon it; and it turns away when it neglects the gift of God and turns back to the flesh.

My definition, which I made general precisely so as to include all the probabilities, squares with all these opinions, none of which (if I am not mistaken) has been condemned by the church, and it also conforms to every condition of mankind. You accomplish nothing, therefore, when you bear down on this or that opinion and twist the definition in some other direction. Suppose mankind to be in the condition in which it was created: the definition squares with that. Here you bear down on us with the idea that free will was vitiated after the Fall. Suppose mankind to be in the condition of a young person who as a child received the habit of faith[1045] through baptism and was cleansed of the sin of the first created man, and has not committed any sin by which grace is lost, although he is nevertheless old enough to know the difference between good and evil: my definition squares with that. For he could apply himself to grace or turn away from grace. He will

\* \* \* \* \*

1043 See n997 above.
1044 Rom 14:5
1045 In Aristotelian terms a *habitus* is a quality by which a power is well or ill disposed to do something (Thomas Aquinas *Summa theologiae* I–II q 49 a 1. According to Aquinas faith is a habit (*Summa theologiae* II–II q 4 a 5). A child receives 'the habit of faith' when it is baptized.

apply himself if he struggles by his natural powers to go where grace leads him; he will turn away if he scorns God's grace and goes off to the flesh. Finally, imagine a person in the condition in which Adam was after he had violated the command of God; here, perhaps, it will seem that my definition does not square with that condition because once he has been given over to sin he can do nothing but be a slave to sin. Where, then, is the power of applying oneself or turning away? According to the opinion of some, there remains, I say, some freedom by which he can, without any special grace, solicit justifying grace through his natural powers by means of morally good works.[1046] This position you oppose with your paradoxes; but you should prove them first before you use them to refute us. According to the opinion of others, which agrees with the opinion of Augustine, he can apply himself to the grace which stimulates and calls him back, and on the other hand he can spurn it; here you see there is some liberty.[1047] Then again, he can make himself available to justifying grace; he can turn away from it. And perhaps it would not be absurd to posit a certain middle condition between justification and the lack of it, as, for example, when a person struggles to merit grace by his natural powers or else is aroused by the stimulating grace which we call imperfect so that he applies his natural power to that grace and struggles after innocence. He does not seem entirely unjustified, since he is disgusted with his own wickedness and strives after justification; nor does he seem entirely justified, since he has not yet achieved innocence. And in such a middle condition St. Augustine seems to place Cornelius,[1048] in whom both conditions were present but imperfectly,[1049] as if, for example, someone who is hastening to a place of refuge is neither completely safe nor caught in the very midst of danger, but the further he gets away from

\* \* \* \* \*

1046 A clear statement of the position attributed by Erasmus to Scotus
1047 In his early writings on free will, especially *De libero arbitrio* (388–95 CE), Augustine propounded the view (later endorsed by Pelagius) that man can respond to initial grace by his natural powers, as Erasmus says here that he did; but after 396–7 CE Augustine recanted that view. For example in *De spiritu et littera* (412 CE) he says: 'Free will is such a neutral power as can either incline towards faith or turn towards unbelief. Consequently a man cannot be said to have even that will with which he believes in God without having received it, since this rises at the call of God out of the free will which he received naturally when he was created' (chapter 58; see also chapter 52). See also *Retractationum libri duo* 23.2–3 PL 32 321–2), *Liber de predestinatione sanctorum* 3.7 PL 44 964–5, *De dono perseverantiae* 20.52 PL 45 1025–6, and McSorley 72–6.
1048 *Sermones* 269.2 PL 38 1235–6; *Liber de praedestinatione sanctorum* 7 PL 44 969–70; *Epistulae ad Romanos inchoata expositio* 8 CSEL 84 171:10–18
1049 Acts 10

danger, the closer he is to safety. Here you croak away about the sudden rapture of the Spirit, which I do not deny. For the moment I am speaking not about what God sometimes does or what he can do, but rather what he generally does with us.[1050] But I will discuss this in the appropriate place.

Compare with these opinions those three which you conflate into one. You will find only the first one is true. For when Augustine posits operating and cooperating grace,[1051] he clearly confesses that a person is free to apply himself to stimulating grace, if he accommodates his natural power to it. That imperfect effort is aided and fulfilled by cooperating grace, which would not be rightly called cooperating if our will did not operate at all, as Karlstadt claims it does not. What you assert is even less true: that the human will cannot do anything either for good or for ill, but that all things happen by pure and sheer necessity; for I call this opinion yours because you approve of the opinion of Wyclif, which was condemned.[1052] What then is left but a quarrel about the name? Free will properly applies only to God. True, but in the same way we use many other names: wise, good, powerful, immortal. But since freedom has been lost through sin, it is now only an empty name, just as in a sick man lost health is not health. I grant that here there is some misuse of the word, but you ought not to blame it on me. And still it is not absurd to say that the reality behind the name remains in a sinner, just as freeborn men captured in a war retain the designation 'free' because of their native condition and the hope of regaining their original freedom. Moreover, there are vestiges of original freedom which remain in a person even after he has committed a sin; and these vestiges are not nothing simply because they are in themselves insufficient to regain freedom: it is enough that they do something by their own power and accomplish it also with the assistance of grace. You make lost health into death. Some natural strength remains in a sick man, fighting with the disease as best he can and sometimes winning the battle without the help of a physician. So too you represent reason as totally blind after sin; I say it is dimsighted or blear-eyed. For someone whose vision is blurred by rheum is not completely blind, and someone who is struggling against a disease is not completely dead.

Now, if you please, summon that sophist, that agreeable drinking companion, and propose to him that comparison to the stone which falls down

* * * * *

1050 This distinction derives from the late medieval usage of the older distinction between God's absolute and ordained powers.
1051 See *A Discussion* n109.
1052 See *A Discussion* n35.

by its natural force but does not go up except by some violent thrust, and ask him whether he attributes free will to the stone;[1053] perhaps he will not be able to keep from laughing and will reply that whoever asks such questions is a stone.[1054] For a stone, like every heavy body which lacks reason, has only one natural impetus, but free will, as it was created, was able to turn in either direction. You will say: we are talking about a corrupt will. We will grant that if you will only keep in mind during the debate that it was created free and hence the substance behind the name remains, although the reality is partly lost. But after original sin and even more after actual sin, just as freedom is not totally lost, so too it is not reduced to absolute slavery. Sin introduced impaired vision, not blindness; lameness, not destruction; it inflicted a wound, not death; it brought on weakness, not annihilation. For some spark of reason remains, some inclination of the will towards the morally good remains, although it is ineffective. And it is not nothing simply because in itself it is not enough to recover its original liberty. But wounded and weak as it is, it is not strong enough to be able to do it, but nevertheless whatever vestiges of power it has it accommodates to the grace which is raising it up – unless perhaps you say that a boy alone has no power because he cannot move a wagon, though he can do it if he combines his effort with someone stronger.[1055] But keep your comparison of the stone for men of stone, and do not throw at us your ridiculous conclusions: 'no one is everyone and nothing is everything.'[1056] But what if that sophist should be a Scotist? Will he not immediately shut your mouth for you? Unless, perhaps, you call him agreeable because he responds agreeably to your questions. Finally, so far as the phrase is concerned, Thomas would perhaps concede that after sin it is not properly called free will, but he will deny that it is simply nothing or that it does not act at all together with the action of grace.[1057]

This is what I put before the readers at the outset of the debate so that they might be more prepared to understand the rest.[1058] For I professed that I am writing for uneducated readers, and you attack this section without having even read, I think, the rest of *A Discussion*, as if I had already made

* * * * *

1053 *De servo arbitrio* WA 18 665:27–666:3 / LW 33 109; Erasmus himself used Aristotelian dynamics to moralize about sin in his colloquy 'A Problem' of 1533 (ASD I-3, 713–19 / CWE 40 1056–69).
1054 That is, a blockhead (*Adagia* I iv 89)
1055 See 189–90 above.
1056 *De servo arbitrio* WA 18 666:4 / LW 33 109
1057 Aquinas *Summa theologiae* I q 83 a 2
1058 *A Discussion* 22–7

some pronouncement. With the same injustice you pick apart the scriptural evidence which I treat, as if I had made a definitive pronouncement in each case. Indeed I bear witness that I have set out the texts from Holy Scripture, taken from here and there, which seem to contradict one another. And those conclusions which you rail at so mightily are not offered by someone who is defining but rather arguing, not teaching but debating, so that truth may shine forth by the collision of testimonies and interpretations. And for the moment I use the right of debaters, who seek out what is wrong so as to disclose what is right. For a debater frequently does this, not so as to declare what he himself thinks but to snare and trip up his adversary. Furthermore he not infrequently uses assumptions which are false but have been granted by his adversary, and from them he concludes what goes beyond the truth, so that his adversary may better understand that he is defeated and so stop fighting back and become willing to be taught. And then someone who teaches uses far different methods than someone who is disputing. But for a while now lack of time has been pressing me to break off this debate. What remains will be handled more carefully and at leisure.

[*Luther's distortion of some minor points; his malevolence and Erasmus' sincerity*]

Note, I beg you, how much time, paper, and effort I have lost in refuting your quibbles, insults, and slanders. You could have defended your teaching boldly, without injuring anyone and gaining praise for yourself. And that much was deserved by my modest *Discussion*; the duller and sleepier she was – for that is how you interpret my courtesy – the less she deserved the uncontrollable rage of your pen. As it is, while you twist and turn everything into slander and insults, you lose a good part of your leisure, and so do I and the reader. And you are so far from gaining any credit for yourself by revealing your disordered mind here that even what you rightly teach or warn or inculcate will not be credited by many – and I confess that there are very many such things in your writings. For what led you to make false charges about something that never even crossed my mind? You say that I satirize and ridicule the canon of the Jews.[1059] This is one source of slander. Another is that I make some jesting double entendre when I call the Song

\* \* \* \* \*

1059 *De servo arbitrio* WA 18 666:19–21 / LW 33 110. The thirty-nine books of the Old Testament accepted by the Jews, including the Law, the prophets, the historical books, and the wisdom books. Erasmus, as well as many Protestant reformers, would have preferred to exclude some of the deuterocanonical books not accepted by the Jews; they were, however, retained as canonical by the Council of Trent.

LB X 1332D

of Songs the Amatory Song.[1060] A third is that I compare the Proverbs of Solomon and the Song with the two books of Esdras, Judith, and the stories of Susanna and of the dragon Bel.[1061] Here, where I never even dreamed of any offence, you think up three great crimes. I will quote the place from *A Discussion* so that you can better recognize that you have incriminated me without any justification. It goes as follows: 'I do not think anyone would take exception to the authority of this work' – I am speaking of the book entitled Ecclesiasticus – 'because, as Jerome indicates, it was long ago not included in the canon by the Jews, since the church of Christ has accepted it into its canon with great unanimity. Nor do I see any reason why the Jews should have thought this book should be excluded from their canon, since they accept the Proverbs of Solomon and the Amatory Song. As for the fact that they did not accept into the canon the last two books of Esdras, the stories in Daniel about Susanna and the dragon Bel, Judith, Esther, and some other books but rather numbered them among the hagiographa, anyone who reads those books carefully can easily guess their motives. But in this work nothing of that sort strikes the reader.'[1062] Up to this point I have quoted the words of *A Discussion*.

Do I satirize and ridicule the canon of the Jews because I say that it is not clear to me why they excluded Ecclesiasticus from the canon? I had reason to want that work to be considered especially worthy of being in the canon, and still I say nothing else but that it is not clear to me why the Jews did not accept it whereas the church did, at least among the hagiographa. You boldly pronounce that the book of Esther is more worthy than all the others of being excluded from the canon, although it is in the canon of the Jews. Which of us, then, is ridiculing and satirizing the canon: I, who say that I don't see the reason why they did not accept Ecclesiasticus into their canon, or you, who judge the book of Esther quite unworthy of being in the canon, condemning at one and the same time the canon of the Jews and the canon of the church, since on this point it agrees with the canon of the Jews?[1063] So much for the first crime. The second is just as shameless: I call

\* \* \* \* \*

1060 Perhaps Luther insinuated that a title analogous to Ovid's *Ars amatoria* might be thought improper. See *A Discussion* 22.
1061 *De servo arbitrio* WA 18 666:19–24 / LW 33 110
1062 *A Discussion* 22. What Erasmus calls 'hagiographa' are now generally called 'apocrypha' or 'deuterocanonical' books. Only portions of Esther are deuterocanonical. He will take up Ecclesiasticus early in *Hyperaspistes* 2 LB X 1340A.
1063 Esther was considered canonical by both Jews and Christians, but a portion of it preserved only in Greek versions was not accepted by the Jews. Luther had noted that it is held to be canonical by both Jews and Christians, but said he

the Song of Solomon the Amatory Song. Suppose I had no more reason to call it that than that I wanted to or in order to speak a purer Latin, where is the jesting double entendre? Is it not an amatory song? Does 'amatory' always have bad connotations? Now note the reason why I preferred to call it that: since two words are modified by the phrase 'of Solomon,' namely 'Proverbs' and 'Song,' if I had said 'Song of Songs,' the two genitives 'of Solomon' and 'of Songs' would not have fit well together, and I would have seemed to mean that Solomon wrote many other songs. If I had said simply 'Song,' someone might have suspected that I was talking about some song like the ones in the Psalms. And so from the subject matter of the work, I add the qualifier 'amatory.' As for me, I never thought worse of this Song than of Proverbs, of which I have the highest opinion. What, then, was the occasion for slandering me? And if I am not mistaken, you borrowed this barb from the books of Lee,[1064] about which you are beginning to have a better opinion, I think. Now your third crime is manifestly groundless. For I do not compare Proverbs and the Song with the two books of Esdras or the stories of Susanna and of the dragon Bel, but with Ecclesiasticus, which treats subject matter similar to that of Proverbs. And in those which they rejected, I say that the careful reader will find something striking to show why they were not accepted, whereas in Ecclesiasticus there is no sign of such a striking reason. But if there is no striking reason in Ecclesiasticus, much less is there any in Proverbs or the Song.

I would not have expended this energy in refuting these trivial points except to draw you away from this immoderate passion of attacking everything without exception. If it injured only me, the loss would be negligible, certainly, or if it hurt you alone, it would be more tolerable. As it is, it not only hinders the cause you are working for – for you are engaged, as you affirm, in the business of recalling the gospel, which up till now has been buried all over the world – but this seditious wantonness of your pen also brings destruction down on all good things. The people are stirred up against bishops and princes; magistrates are hard pressed to put down mobs eager to revolt; cities which once were joined by very close ties now quarrel among themselves with fierce hatred; now you can hardly find any man

* * * * *

thought it deserved canonicity less than the two books of Esdras, Judith, and the story of Susanna and the dragon; see *De servo arbitrio* WA 18 666:23–4 / LW 33 110.

1064 See n24 above. On Erasmus' controversy with Lee, see Erica Rummel *Catholic Critics* I 95–120. Erasmus probably refers to Lee's *Annotationes in annotationes Erasmi* (Paris: Gourmont 1520).

you can safely trust; all freedom has been taken away. For you have not removed but rather you have aggravated the tyranny (for so you usually call it) of princes, bishops, theologians, and monks. All deeds and words are immediately subject to suspicion, and it is not allowed even to open one's mouth about points which once could be debated pro and con. The slavery which you set out to shake off has been redoubled; the yoke is heavier; the chains are not shaken off but tightened.[1065] Formerly no one made any to-do if someone ate a suitable meal at home for reasons of health. Now, even if you have many good reasons for eating and do not lack a licence from the pope,[1066] still someone who does not fast is called a Lutheran. Formerly, the Roman pontiff easily relaxed the law for those who had become monks or nuns at an age when they were immature and not yet prudent through experience and judgment.[1067] Now he is very reluctant to relax it. Liberal studies, together with languages and good writing, are everywhere disregarded because you have loaded them down with ill will. The outstanding monuments of the ancients are rejected, and in their place the world is filled with quarrelsome and defamatory books which infect the reader with poison and disease. I know some good and learned men who at first were not unwilling to read your lucubrations with a desire to know and judge them. They were finally forced to reject them because they confessed that they were infected by the many grimaces, jests, witticisms, insults and unchristian slanders with which you contaminate your doctrine, not unlike those whose occupation is to stuff capons or pheasants with garlic. And at first these things have a certain titillation and we itch to read them, but when they gradually creep into the mind, they infect the sincerity and gentleness of the heart. And although you see how many evils this ferocity of yours has brought into the world, though you have been warned so often, even by those who wish you well, still you continually get worse and worse, both uselessly drawing into danger those who commit themselves to your faith and alienating those whom you could have attracted to you –

* * * * *

1065 Erasmus is thinking of the repression of the peasants after the Peasants' Revolt (see n105 above).
1066 Erasmus had a papal dispensation to eat meat during Lent; see Epp 1079 n1, 1353:7 and 63–5, 1542 and the colloquy 'A Fish Diet' of 1526 (ASD I-3, 495–536 / CWE 40 675–762).
1067 Erasmus had taken vows as an Augustinian canon regular; see his *Compendium vitae* CWE 4 406–7. He obtained from Pope Julius II a brief (dated 4 January 1506) releasing him from the obligation of residence in his home monastery of Steyn and from the impediment against accepting ecclesiastical benefices because of his illegitimate birth; see Ep 187A.

for now I once more pretend that your doctrine is orthodox – and finally preventing this worldwide uproar, however it arose, from ever bringing forth for us some degree of beneficent tranquillity. You have drawn numberless people away from their bishops, and now they wander around like scattered sheep, having no shepherd,[1068] especially when they see that your church is shaken by so many quarrels and thrown into tumult by internal warfare.

And amidst all this you still have leisure to write such large books, such elaborately abusive books, against a person whose mind is completely unknown to you, at least it is so if you judge it to be only like what you make it out to be. If you had ranted and raved with free and open insults, we could praise your frankness and put it down to your temperament; but as it is you carry on with crafty malice. If you had been content with two or three insults, they might seem to have just slipped out; as it is your whole book swarms everywhere with abuse. You begin with it, you proceed with it, you end with it. If you had glutted yourself with only one kind of insult, calling me a blockhead, an ass, or a mushroom, one after the other, I would have given no answer except that line from the comedy: 'I am a human being and I consider nothing human foreign to me.'[1069] But such things could not satiate your hatred; you had to go on to make me into a Lucian or an Epicurus, disbelieving Holy Scripture to the extent that I think there is not even a God, an enemy of Christianity, finally a blasphemer against God and the Christian religion. Such are the charms scattered throughout your book, which is set over against my *Discussion*, which contains no insults. If some lightweight and lying tattler, of which there is no lack in your confraternity, brought this perverse opinion to you, you ought to consider how such levity fits the character you have taken it upon yourself to play. If you conceived it in your own mind, who would believe that any good man could have such horrible suspicions about someone he doesn't know. But if you made them up out of a desire to injure me, it cannot be obscure to anyone what should be thought of you. But because my writings clearly refute your slanders, since they everywhere preach the majesty of Holy Scripture and the glory of Christ, you deny that I was sincere when I wrote them. A ready and easy solution: if you cannot slander something, it was written as a joke; if anything is open to slander, it was written seriously. And such distinctions as these enable you to incriminate; yet you hiss at sophistical distinctions which were invented in order to teach. I ask

* * * * *

1068 Cf Matt 26:31 and Mark 14:27, quoting Zech 13:7.
1069 Terence *Heautontimorumenos* 77; Otto no 821

you, what is such a mind, such a nature, if indeed it is a nature? Or what kind of spirit, if it is a spirit? And finally what is such a non-evangelical way of teaching the gospel? Has the rebirth of the gospel taken away all secular laws, so that now it is permissible to say and write whatever you like against anyone you please? Is this the complete liberty you are restoring to us? If someone claimed I had no intelligence, judgment, or learning, I could bear it with moderation. If someone accused me of ignorance or thoughtlessness in handling Scripture, I would recognize a human failing. But if someone accuses me of disregarding God and scorning Scripture, he either does this because he is persuaded by the speech of some talebearer and so is most frivolous or, if he makes it up himself, he is an unbearable backbiter. At this point look for yourself to what your conscience tells you.

For myself, as God is my judge, I will not pray to escape his anger if I engage in any conscious deception here; I wish to bear witness to all Christians, heretics, and half-Christians that I have no less faith in Holy Scripture than if I heard Christ himself speaking to me in his own voice, and I have no less doubt about what I read there than I do about what I hear with my ears, see with my eyes, touch with my hands. And just as I believe most firmly that what the Holy Spirit predicted in the types of the Law and the predictions of the prophets was fulfilled by the gospel, so too I believe with equal firmness in the promise of the second coming and the differing rewards of good and evil. And relying on this confidence, I patiently bear labours, injuries, diseases, the afflictions of old age, and the other troubles of this life, hoping that the mercy of Christ will put an end to all evils and bring me to eternal life with him. I am so far from knowingly opposing the gospel that I would rather be slain ten times over than to contravene what I think by opposing one iota of the truth in the gospel. Nor is this an attitude which has recently emerged; from my childhood it was never any different, and today, thanks be to God, it is firmer than it ever was. In what concerns salvation I ask no other assistance than the mercy of God, and after God I have no more hope or consolation in anything except Holy Scripture. And just as I do not deny that it could have happened that somewhere in my writings I did not arrive at the genuine meaning of Scripture, so too I could swear most solemnly that I never curried the favour of anyone or feared anyone so as to knowingly teach what I did not think to be true, or at least probable. Those who have lived in my household may not be witnesses for my holiness – which I desire rather than possess – but they can certainly testify about this attitude of mine and bear witness that I never let slip a single word, seriously or in jest, that savoured of Lucian, Epicurus, or

Porphyry.[1070] It would be inappropriate to testify to this in writing except that Luther, the vindicator of the gospel, wished to mock his friend Erasmus in an elaborate book full of such jests. As it is, if someone prefers to believe a most shameless calumny by someone who does not know me rather than my own testimony, he will do so at his own peril; this declaration of my mind will set me free of responsibility. And I pray that the gospel of Christ will reign in the minds of everyone and that all intellect and human power will yield to it – so far am I from wishing to wage war against the teachings of heaven. At the same time I also pray for you, Luther, that the Lord may renew a good spirit in you, that you may be as effective in restoring the tranquillity of God's church as you have been up till now in disrupting the harmony of the Christian world, so that with the same thoughts we may pray with one voice to him whose teachings we now assert with discordant voices. Here, then, let me end the first, hasty volume. I will soon present another, more carefully worked out, if only Christ deigns to assist me.

\* \* \* \* \*

1070 On Lucian and Epicurus see nn56 and 55 above. Porphyry (c 232–c 305), an adherent and proponent of Neoplatonic philosophy, wrote a treatise (no longer extant) against the Christians in fifteen books, which was publicly burned under the emperor Theodosius II (435).

# AN ASSERTION OF ALL THE ARTICLES OF MARTIN LUTHER WHICH WERE QUITE RECENTLY CONDEMNED BY A BULL OF LEO X, ARTICLE 36

*Assertio omnium articulorum
Martini Lutheri per bullam Leonis x
novissimam damnatorum,
articulus 36*

translated and annotated by
CLARENCE H. MILLER

Leo x's bull *Exsurge Domine* of 15 June 1520 contains forty-one articles listing forty-one theological and ecclesiological errors or heresies of Martin Luther. Although widely circulated, it was not shown officially to Luther until 10 October 1520. Luther had begun to reply to the bull article by article about 1 December 1520. By 29 December 1520 a German version of *Assertio* was said by Luther to have been printed, and the Latin seems to have appeared by the end of December 1520 or the beginning of January 1521. Article 36 contains Luther's rejection of free will and declaration of the necessity of all things. Erasmus, after he had decided in the spring of 1523 that he would write against Luther, concluded that the teaching of Luther with which he most fully disagreed was that contained in article 36, and this became the subject of *A Discussion of Free Will*, published at the beginning of September 1524. The translation which follows is based on the Latin edition in WA 7 142–9.

CHM

# MARTIN LUTHER'S ASSERTION

## THE THIRTY-SIXTH ARTICLE

After sin free will exists in name only and when it does what in it lies[1] it sins mortally.

Unhappy free will! When a just man does a good deed, he sins mortally, as we have seen, and free will boasts that before justification it is something and can do something. Oh, wretched are they who condemn my article, which rests on the first sentence of chapter 4 in Augustine's *Concerning the Spirit and the Letter*: 'Free will without grace can do nothing but sin.' I ask you, what sort of freedom is it that can choose only one alternative, and that the worse one? Does freedom mean to be able to do nothing but sin? But let us say I don't believe Augustine. Let us listen to Scripture. In John 15[:5] Christ says: 'Without me you can do nothing.' What is this 'nothing' which free will does without Christ? It prepares itself for grace, they say, by morally good works. But here Christ calls these nothing; therefore it prepares itself by nothing. A marvellous preparation that is accomplished by nothing!

But he goes on to explain what this 'nothing' is, saying: 'If anyone does not dwell in me, he will be thrown out like a branch and he withers and they gather him up and throw him on the fire and he burns.'[2] I beg you, most holy vicar of Christ, how can you have the meretricious effrontery to dare to contradict your Lord in this way? You say that free will can prepare itself to proceed to grace. On the other hand, Christ says that it is thrown out, so that it is further away from grace. How beautifully your bull harmonizes with the gospel! Let us listen, then, to Christ, who posits five steps in the perdition of the pruned branch, showing that it can not

* * * * *

1 See *A Discussion* n119.
2 John 15:6

AETHERNA IPSE SVAE MENTIS SIMVLACHRA LVTHERVS
EXPRIMIT AT VVLTVS CERA LVCAE OCCIDVOS

M·D·XX·

Luther
Copperplate engraving by Lucas Cranach the Elder (1520)
Kupferstichkabinett, Staatliche Museen zu Berlin, Preussischer Kulturbesitz

only not prepare itself for doing good but necessarily grows worse. The first is that it is thrown out and therefore not brought in; it is given over to the power of Satan, who does not allow it to attempt anything good. For what else can it mean to be thrown out? Secondly, it withers; that is, left to itself, it grows worse every day, and these are the two works of free will: namely, to sin and to persevere and grow worse in sinning, to be thrown out and to wither. For if free will can do anything else, Christ is certainly a liar. There are three punishments after that: they gather it up, that is, for judgment, so that it may be convicted together with the others. Then, when the sentence has been handed down, they throw it into eternal fire, where it finally does nothing but burn, that is, suffers eternal punishment. Therefore, that free will can do nothing does not mean, as they pretend, that it can do nothing meritorious, but that it is thrown out and withers. The pruned branch does not prepare itself for the vine, nor can it do so, but it becomes more removed from the vine and comes closer and closer to perishing: so too free will or a wicked person.

Genesis 6[:5] and 8[:21]: 'The understanding and every thought of the human heart is inclined to evil at all times.' I beg you, if someone says that every thought of the heart is evil, and is so at all times, what good thought does he leave which can prepare for grace? Does evil dispose someone to good? Nor can anyone escape from this authority by saying that a person can sometimes repress his evil thought. For a thought which does this, actively or passively, is good in either case, but it will not be included among those which are said to be all thoughts. If a single good thought can be there, Moses is a liar because he affirms that they are all evil. Moreover, we may represent the Hebrew text as follows: 'Because whatever the human heart desires and thinks is only evil every day'; to 'evil' it adds an exclusive particle which our translation did not render. It also did not render 'desires,' and the translation 'thought' does not fully render 'thinks.' For Moses intended to include not only idle and spontaneous thoughts but also thoughts conceived by the mind and thoughts by which a person deliberately intends to do something, and he also says that they are evil without exception, so that these Pelagians have no way of attributing to free will the power to do something good, if it works hard enough at it.

Again Genesis 6[:3]: 'My spirit does not remain in mankind, because it is flesh.' If mankind is flesh, what progress can it make towards good? Do we not know the works proper to the flesh in Galatians 5[:19–20], which are fornication, impurity, lewdness, anger, envy, murder, etc? These are the things free will does when it does what in it lies; and these are all mortal sins. For Romans 8[:7] says: 'For the prudence of the flesh is death and an enemy to God.' How can death lead to life? How does enmity dispose itself to grace? For if the Spirit is not in mankind, it is dead before God. But a dead person necessarily does the works of death, not of life, and the work of death does not dispose to life. Therefore everything that has been treated in so many books about the preparation of free will for grace is mere fiction.

Isaiah also says in chapter 40[:2]: 'She has received at the Lord's hand double measure for all her sins.' What will they say here? He says grace is not given by the Lord except for sins, that is, for evil deeds, and that he says 'all' here means that before grace she did nothing but sin and that all her works were sins. But if it happens that someone receives grace through fitting works which are not sins, Isaiah told a lie here and the grace of God is cheapened, since he does not give it to those who are completely unworthy, as the Pelagians taught, with whose opinion we differ only verbally, since we also preach that we merit grace, although not *de condigno*,[3] which they would also have granted; for they would not have held the grace of God so cheap as to say it was given to merit that is worthy of receiving it.

Isaiah says the same thing in the same place: 'All flesh is grass and all its glory is like the flower of the grass. The grass is withered and the flower has fallen, because the Spirit of the Lord has blown upon it. But the word of the Lord remains forever.' Explain the grass and the flower. Is it not the flesh, man, or free will and whatever man has? Its flower and glory, is that not the power, wisdom, and justice of free will, which enable it to glory in the fact that it is something and can do something. What is the reaon, then, that when the Spirit blows it is withered and falls and perishes, whereas the word remains? Is the Spirit not grace, by which you said free will is assisted and its preparation fulfilled? Why then does he say here that even the best parts of the flesh are withered and fall? Do you not see that the Spirit and free will are opposed to one another? For when the one blows the other falls and does not remain with the word. And it would not have fallen and perished if it had been fit and prepared for the breath of the Spirit and of the word.

Also Jeremiah in chapter 10 [verse 23] says as follows: 'I know, Lord, that a person's path is not his own and that a man does not have the power to direct his own steps.' What statement could be clearer? If a person's path and his steps are not in his power, how can God's path and God's steps be in his power? A person's path is what they call the natural power of doing what in him lies. See now that this is not in man's choice or free

\* \* \* \* \*

3 On merit *de congruo* and *de condigno* see *A Discussion* n106.

will. What, then, is free will but a thing in name only? How can it prepare itself for the good when it does not even have the power to make its own paths evil? For God does even bad deeds in the wicked, as Proverbs 16[:4] says: 'The Lord made everything for his own sake, even the wicked for the evil day.' And Rom 1[:28]: 'God gave them up to their own depraved perception so that they do what is not fitting.' And in chapter 9 [verse 18]: 'He hardens as he wishes; he has mercy as he wishes.' Just as Exodus 9[:16] says about Pharaoh: 'For this very purpose I aroused you, that I might show my power in you.' For that is why God is terrible in his judgments and his deeds.

Again, Proverbs 16[:1] says this: 'It is man's part to prepare his heart, but it is the Lord's to govern his tongue.' That is, a man usually proposes many things, when in fact his deeds are so little in his control that he does not even have within his power the words for this deed of his but rather is forced by the marvellous providence of God both to speak and to act differently from what he had in mind, as was shown in Balaam (Numbers 24[:5–27]). And Psalm 138[:4]: 'My tongue has no speech.' And even more clearly further on in Proverbs 16[:9]: 'The heart of a man thinks of his own path and the Lord directs his steps.' See, the path of a man does not proceed as he thinks, but as the Lord ordains. For that reason chapter 21[:1] says: 'Like water divided into channels, so the heart of the king is in the hand of the Lord; he will turn it wherever he wishes.'[4] Where, then, is free will? It is completely fictitious.

And if Scripture did not show this, we would have abundant evidence of its truth from all histories, and everyone would see it from his own life. For who is there who always carried out everything he wanted to? Indeed, who is there who has not often had it in mind to do something and then suddenly changed his mind so as to do something else, not knowing how he changed it? Who would dare to deny that even in evil works he has been forced to do something different from what he had in mind? Don't you think the authors of this bull applied the sum total of their power of free will to the task of speaking in their favour and against Luther? And see how this thought and its execution did not lie in their choice! For they did everything against themselves and brought it all down on their own heads, so that I have never read of any persons who disgraced themselves more foully and more abominably, and out of blindness and ignorance they cast themselves quite openly into the shameful depths of error, heresy, and malice

* * * * *

4 There is a long discussion of this text in the colloquy 'The Godly Feast' ASD I-3 242–4 / CWE 39 184–6.

– so little control of himself does a person have, even when he conceives and executes evil deeds. And Paul spoke the truth in Ephesians 1[:11]: 'God works all things in all persons.'[5]

Here, then, that general influence disappears[6] by which, according to their babble, we have it in our power to perform natural operations. The experience of everyone shows that this is not the case. And see how stupid we are: we know that the root of our works, namely our life, which is the source of all our works, is never for a single moment under our control, and do we dare to say that any intention is under our conrol? Could we say anything more absurd than that? Did God, who kept our life under his control, place our motions and works under our control? Far from it. Hence there can be no doubt that the teaching of Satan brought this phrase 'free will' into the church in order to seduce men away from God's path into his own paths. The brothers of Joseph fully intended to kill him, and lo and behold! they had so little choice about that very intention that they even changed it immediately to something entirely different, as he said, 'You intended to do me harm, but God changed it to something good.'[7]

Have you got anything, miserable pope, to snarl against this? Hence it is also necessary to revoke this article. For I misspoke when I said that free will before grace exists in name only; rather I should have simply said 'free will is a fiction among real things, a name with no reality.' For no one has it within his control to intend anything, good or evil, but rather, as was rightly taught by the article of Wyclif which was condemned at Constance, all things occur by absolute necessity. That was what the poet meant when he said, 'All things are settled by a fixed law.'[8] And Christ in Matt 10[:29–30]: 'The leaf of a tree does not fall to the earth apart from the will of your Father who is in heaven, and the hairs of your head are all numbered.'[9] And Isaiah 41[:23] taunts them: 'Do good also or evil, if you can!'

Hence, as Elijah exhorted the prophets of Baal,[10] I egg on these proponents of free will: 'Come on, be men, do what in you lies, at least for once put to the test what you teach, prepare yourselves for grace, and obtain what you want, since you say God does not deny anything if you do what free will can do. It is a dreadful disgrace that you cannot bring forward

* * * * *

5 Luther actually quotes 1 Cor 12:6, a verse which is similar to Eph 1:11.
6 On *concursus generalis* see *A Discussion* n112.
7 Gen 50:20
8 Virgil *Aeneid* 2.324
9 Luther adapts Matt 10:29, substituting 'leaf' for 'sparrow.'
10 3 Kings 18:25–7

a single example of your teaching and you yourselves cannot provide a single work so that your wisdom consists merely in words.' But these efforts of theirs are a pretext for supporting Pelagius. For what does it matter if you deny that grace comes from our works if you nevertheless teach that it is given through our works? The meaning remains equally impious, since grace is believed to be given not gratuitously but because of our works. For the works which the Pelagians taught and performed and because of which they held that grace is given are not different from the ones you teach and perform. They are works of the same free will and of the same bodily members, but you gave them one name and they gave them another: fasting, prayer, almsgiving were the same things, but you said they are fitting for grace and they claimed they are worthy of grace,[11] but everywhere the same Pelagius carried on triumphantly.

These miserable people are deceived by the inconstancy or (as they call it) the contingency of human affairs. They fix their stupid eyes on things in themselves and the actions of things and never lift them up to the sight of God so that they might recognize in God the things above things. For when we look at things here below they seem to be fortuitous and subject to choice but when we look upward all things are necessary, because we all live, act, and suffer everything not as we wish but as he wills. The free will which seems to bear on us and temporal things has no bearing on God, for in him, as James says, there is no variation or shadow of change,[12] but here all things change and vary. And we are so stupid we measure the divine by the temporal, so that we presume to get ahead of God by free will and to wrest grace from him while he is asleep, as it were, whenever we please, as if he were able to change together with us and and as if he willed something that at one time he did not will, and all by the working and willing of our free choice. Oh monstrous madness beyond all madness!

And Paul in Ephesians 2[:3] says: 'We too were by nature sons of wrath like the rest.' If everyone apart from grace is a son of wrath by his very nature, then free will is also a son of wrath by its very nature; if it is so by its very nature, it is much more so by all its works. And how can someone be a son of wrath by his nature except because everything he does is evil, preparing not for grace but for wrath, indeed meriting wrath? Go on now, you Pelagians, and prepare yourselves for grace by your works, since Paul says here that by them no one merits anything except wrath. It would have

* * * * *

11 See *A Discussion* nn103 and 106.
12 James 1:17

been milder if he had said only 'We were sons of wrath,' but by adding 'by nature' he wanted it to be understood that everything we are and do by our nature merits wrath and not at all grace. You could hardly find a briefer, clearer, or more emphatic statement against free will in Scripture.

Why should we go on at length? From what has been said above, it is abundantly clear to us that even the just struggle mightily against their flesh in order to do good and that free will and the prudence of the flesh resist them; the flesh yearns with all its power against the spirit, despising whatever belongs to the Spirit and the law of God. And how could it be possible that by its own nature and without the Spirit it could yearn for the Spirit or prepare itself for the Spirit by doing what in it lies? While it was in a state of grace, its nature was such that it fought fiercely against grace, and apart from grace can its nature be such that it assists the spirit? Could you imagine anything crazier than that? For such an unheard-of monstrosity would be as if someone who could not control an untamed wild animal while it was tied up should be mad enough to boast that before it was tied up or without being tied up it is so tame and gentle that it willingly tames itself or makes an effort to be tame. Stop being so crazy, I beg you, you miserable Pelagians! If free will in a state of grace sins and rages against grace, as we are all forced to recognize and as the Apostle and all the saints complain, certainly it goes against all common sense that it should be upright apart from grace or prepare itself for grace when it is absent, since it hates and persecutes grace when it is present.

It follows necessarily, then, that whatever is taught and done before grace in order to obtain grace is sheer fabrication and hypocrisy, for it is necessary that we should be preceded by the mercy of God even to wish for it, just as Augustine, writing against the epistles of Pelagius, says that God converts the reluctant and unwilling, as he demonstrated in the case of Paul, whom he converted when he was set against grace and at the height of his burning rage to persecute; and Peter did not look back at the Lord, so as to remember the words Jesus had said to him, but rather Jesus looked back at Peter, in the midst and at the very height of the business, and so Peter remembered the words and wept bitterly.

And so we see in the meaning of this article how deceptively Satan works in teaching this error. For since they cannot deny that we must be saved through the grace of God and cannot avoid this truth, impiety takes another path to avoid it, pretending that if our role is not to save ourselves, nevertheless it is our role to be prepared to be saved by the grace of God. What glory, I beg you, is left for God if we can do so much to be saved by his grace? Is such power a small thing if someone who does not have grace has enough power to be able to have grace whenever he wishes? What difference does it make if you do [not][13] say that we are saved without grace, as the Pelagians do, since you place the grace of God within the choice of men? You seem to me worse than Pelagius when you place the necessary grace of God, which he completely denied was necessary, within the power of men. It seems less impious, I say, to deny grace completely than to say it is prepared by our effort and work and to give us, as it were, control over it. And nevertheless the working of this error has prevailed because it is specious and pleasing to nature and free will, so that it is difficult to confute it, especially when dealing with ignorant and crude minds.

We could put up with the frivolity and stupidity of the pope and his minions in the other articles about the papacy, councils, indulgences, and other unnecessary nonsense, but in this article, which is the best of all and the sum and substance of my case, we must deplore and lament that these wretches are so insane. For I believe the heavens will fall down before the pope and his disciples will ever understand a single jot about this mystery of God's grace. The truth of this article cannot coexist with the church of the pope, no more than Belial with Christ or light with darkness. For if the church of the pope had not taught and sold good works or had sincerely taught that we are justified by grace alone, it would not have grown so full of pompous display and, if by some chance it had done so, it would not have remained that way for a single hour. For this theology which condemns whatever the pope approves of and makes martyrs is based on the cross. That is why the best part of the church and almost all of it flourished when the period of the martyrs came to an end. Soon pleasure took the place of the cross, poverty was replaced by opulence, ignominy by glory, until what is now called the church has become more worldly than the world, so to speak, and more fleshly than the flesh itself. And I have no more powerful argument against the reign of the pope than that he reigns without the cross. His whole aim is not to suffer at all but rather to abound and to exult in all things, and he has not been cheated of his desire. He has what he wanted, and the faithful city has become a whore and truly the kingdom of the true Antichrist.

In this section my prolixity was necessitated by the subject itself, which has been repressed and extinguished not only by this bull (which I consider to be not worth the paper it's written on) but also by almost all teachers in the schools for more than thirteen hundred years. For on this point everyone writes against grace, not for it, so that no point needs to be handled as

\* \* \* \* \*

13 The early texts do not have *non*, but the sense clearly requires it.

much as this one, and I have often wished to handle it, leaving aside that trivial papistical nonsense and matters which do not pertain to the church at all except to destroy it; but by length of time and widespread prevalence, the working of Satan has fixed itself so firmly in men's hearts and has used this error to blunt their minds so badly that I do not see anyone who is fit to understand it or even to dispute with me about it. Scripture is abundant on this subject but it has been so ravaged by our Nebuchadnezzar that the very form and knowledge of the letters is gone, and we need some new Esdras who will discover new letters and recover the Bible for us once more, which I hope is now being done as the Hebrew and Greek languages are flourishing all over the world. Amen.

# DIVISIONS AND CORRESPONDENCES IN ERASMUS' DISCUSSION OF FREE WILL, LUTHER'S THE ENSLAVED WILL, AND ERASMUS' HYPERASPISTES

The pages of Erasmus' *Discussion* cited in the tables are those of the translation in this volume; the corresponding Latin text is indicated in the references at the foot of each page to LB IX and to Walter's edition. References for Luther's *The Enslaved Will* include the pages in WA 18 600–787 and the translation in LW 33 15–295; the headings are those of the translator, Philip S. Watson, and are used here by permission of the Westminster John Knox Press. The pages cited for Erasmus' *Hyperaspistes* book 1 are those of the translation in this volume, which gives the location of the Latin text in LB X at the foot of each page. Column references in LB X are given for Erasmus' *Hyperaspistes* book 2.

# TABLE A
## ERASMUS' DISCUSSION OF FREE WILL
## AND LUTHER'S THE ENSLAVED WILL

**Erasmus** *A Discussion of Free Will*

Preface 5–14

    A temperate debate 5
    Erasmus' aversion to dogmatism
    and assertion 7

    The obscurity of Scripture 8
    A Christian outlook for ordinary
    persons 9

    Theological topics unsuitable for
    public discussion 11

Introduction 14–20

    Scripture is primary but tradition
    is also important 14
    If Scripture is clear to those who
    have the Spirit, how do we know
    who has the Spirit? 17

Passages from the Old Testament
supporting free will 21–39
    A brief definition of free will 21

    Ecclesiasticus 15:14–18: free will
    in Adam and Eve 21
    Reason, will, and law in postlap-
    sarian mankind 23
    Ancient and modern views of free
    will and grace 27

**Luther** *The Enslaved Will*

Review of Erasmus' preface 600–39 /
15–71
    Luther's delay in writing 600 / 15
    Christianity involves assertions;
    Christians are not sceptics 603 /
    19
    The clarity of Scripture 606 / 24
    It is vital to know the truth about
    free will and God's foreknowledge
    609 / 29
    Should divine truth be kept
    from common ears and God's
    necessitating will be suppressed?
    Divine necessity and the human
    will 620 / 4

Comments on Erasmus' introduction
639–61 / 71–102
    The evidence of tradition: the true
    church is hidden 639 / 71
    Internal and external clarity of
    Scripture is the test of who has the
    Spirit 652 / 89

Refutation of Erasmus' arguments
supporting free will 661–99 / 102–61
    Erasmus' definition of free will
    661 / 102
    Ecclesiasticus 15:14–18: the fool-
    ishness of reason 671 / 117

    Three views of grace and free will
    – or three statements of one view
    667 / 112

| Erasmus *A Discussion of Free Will* | Luther *The Enslaved Will* |
|---|---|
| Other Old Testament passages supporting free will 33 | Other Old Testament passages and the imperative and indicative moods 676 / 125 |
| Scriptural exhortations are meaningless if we have no power to comply 36 | Erasmus fails to distinguish between Law and gospel 680 / 132 |
| God's figurative changes from wrath to mercy imply that our wills can change 38 | God preached, God hidden; God's will revealed, God's will secret 684 / 138 |
| Passages from the New Testament supporting free will 39–45 | New Testament passages 688–99 / 144–60 |
| Gospel exhortations are meaningless if we have no power to comply 39 | Man must not pry into the secret will of God 688 / 144 |
| Passages from Paul supporting free will 41 | Precepts and rewards in the New Testament: the question of merit 690 / 147 |
| | Erasmus undermines his own case 696 / 156 |
| Passages from Scripture seeming to oppose free will 46–58 | Defence of passages seeming to oppose free will 699–733 / 160–212 |
| | Erasmus' use of tropes in interpreting Scripture 700 / 161 |
| The hardening of Pharaoh's heart in Exodus and chapter 9 of Romans 46 | The hardening of Pharaoh's heart: Exodus 4:21 702 / 164 |
| Divine foreknowledge and necessity: the case of Pharaoh 51 | How God's omnipotence can be said to work evil 709 / 175 |
| | How God's foreknowledge imposes necessity 714 / 184 |
| | Two kinds of necessity: the case of Judas 720 / 192 |
| Jacob and Esau: the Jews and the gentiles 53 | Jacob and Esau 722 / 195 |
| The potter and the clay 54 | The potter and the clay 727 / 203 |
| The workman and the axe 56 | |
| Other scriptural examples of divine power and human will 56 | Erasmus' way of reasoning does not allow God to be God 730 / 206 |

**Erasmus** *A Discussion of Free Will*

Passages cited by Luther to deny the
existence of free will 59–65
>Limited application of Genesis 6:3
>and 8:21 and Isaiah 40:2 59
>All flesh is grass (Isaiah 40:6–8)
>does not mean that all human
>inclinations and abilities are flesh
>60
>Jeremiah 10:23 and Proverbs 16:1–
>6 and 16:21: divine providence
>does not preclude free will 62

>John 15:5 – 'Without me you can
>do nothing' – is not to be taken
>literally 64

Additional passages that seem to
oppose free will 65–74
>Other Gospel passages that only
>seem to undermine free will 65
>Pauline passages that do not
>preclude free will if they are
>correctly interpreted 67
>Gospel parables do not deny
>free will if they are interpreted
>according to their context 70
>The very fact of God's help implies
>some action by the human will 72

Judgments concerning free will and
grace 74–89
>Motives for overstressing grace or
>free will 74
>To assert necessity to the exclusion
>of free will makes God cruel and
>unjust 75
>Faith must not be exalted to the
>exclusion of free will: free will
>cooperates with grace 77
>Illustrations of the cooperation of
>grace and free will 80

**Luther** *The Enslaved Will*

Rebuttal of Erasmus' critique of the
*Assertio* 733–56 / 212–46
>Genesis 6:3 and the biblical
>meaning of 'flesh' 733 / 212
>Other Old Testament passages
>– the universal sinfulness and
>impotence of man under the Law
>736 / 215
>The whole man – body, soul, and
>'spirit' – is 'flesh' 740 / 222

Erasmus persistently evades the
issue 745 / 229
John 15:5 etc: free will is 'nothing'
*coram deo* 748 / 234

Divine grace and human cooperation 753–5 / 241–5

Erasmus' 'middle way' leads
nowhere 755–6 / 245–6

A display of the forces on Luther's
side 756–85 / 246–92
>St Paul: universal sinfulness
>nullifies free will 757 / 247
>Free will may do the works of the
>Law but not fulfil the Law 763 /
>257
>'Congruous' and 'condign' merit
>769 / 266

The righteousness of works and of
faith; and a summary of St Paul's
testimony against free will 771 /
270

**Erasmus** *A Discussion of Free Will*

Absolute necessity makes God unjust: he would punish people who are not responsible for their sins 82

Luther and Karlstadt overreacted against abuses associated with free will 85

Reasons why we must attribute something to free will 87

**Luther** *The Enslaved Will*

St John: free will is of 'the world,' 'the flesh'; grace is of Christ, by faith. The two are opposites 776 / 277

The two kingdoms of Christ and of Satan. The assurance of faith 782 / 287

The mercy and justice of God in the light of nature, grace, and glory 784 / 289

Conclusion: That the case against free will is unanswerable, let Erasmus be willing to admit 786 / 293

# TABLE B
## LUTHER'S THE ENSLAVED WILL
## AND ERASMUS' HYPERASPISTES BOOK 1

| Luther *The Enslaved Will* | Erasmus *Hyperaspistes* book 1 |
|---|---|
| | Prefatory letter 93–4 |
| Foreword 600–2 / 15–19 | Circumstances of composition and motivations for writing 96–117 |
| His delay in responding 600 / 15 | Erasmus' temperate discussion vs Luther's inconsistent insults 96 |
| Review of Erasmus' preface 603–39 / 19–71 | Erasmus' response to Luther's review of the preface to *A Discussion* 117–197 |
| Christianity involves assertions; Christians are not sceptics 602 / 19 | Erasmus' alleged scepticism 117 |
| The clarity of Scripture 606 / 24 | The obscurity of Scripture 129 |
| It is vital to know the truth about free will and God's foreknowledge 609 / 19 | Erasmus' formulation of a Christian outlook for ordinary persons 135 |
| God's foreknowledge, contingency, and necessity 614 / 36 | 'Sailing between Scylla and Charybdis': Erasmus' alleged neutrality 140 |
| Should divine truth be kept from common ears and God's necessitating will be suppressed? 620 / 44 | Theological topics that are unsuitable for public discussion, such as God's foreknowledge or contingency and necessity 146 |
| Should the truth of God's necessitating will be suppressed? 630 / 58 | Does God know things contingently? 155 |
| | Other unsuitable topics 162 |
| | The imperative of expedience 171 |
| Divine necessity and human will 634 / 64 | The human will is not completely passive but cooperates with grace 184 |
| Erasmus makes unnecessary difficulties 638 / 70 | A summary of why not all topics are suitable for all audiences 194 |
| Comments on Erasmus' introduction 639–61 / 71–102 | Erasmus' response to Luther's review of the introduction to *A Discussion* 197–261 |
| The evidence of tradition: the true church is hidden 639 / 71 | The centrality of Scripture in the debate must also include its interpreters 197 |

| **Luther** *The Enslaved Will* | **Erasmus** *Hyperaspistes* **book 1** |
|---|---|
| Internal and external clarity of Scripture is the test of who has the Spirit 651 / 89 | Not all of Scripture is fully clear 214 |
| Erasmus is in a dilemma 659 / 100 | Who has the Spirit that understands Scripture? 235 |
| Refutation of Erasmus' arguments supporting free will 661–99 / 102–61 | Erasmus' definition of free will 261–91 |
|    Erasmus' definition of free will 661 / 102 | |
|    Three views of grace and free will 667 / 112 | Luther's distortion of some minor points; his malevolence and Erasmus' sincerity 291–7 |

# TABLE C
## LUTHER'S THE ENSLAVED WILL
## AND ERASMUS' HYPERASPISTES BOOK 2

| Luther *The Enslaved Will* | Erasmus *Hyperaspistes* book 2 |
|---|---|
| | Introduction and recapitulation of book 1 1337A–1339F |
| Refutation of Erasmus' arguments supporting free will 671–99 / 117–61 | Erasmus' response to Luther's critique of Erasmus' arguments supporting free will 1340A–1391A |
| Old Testament passages 671 / 117 Ecclesiasticus 15:14–18: the foolishness of reason 671 / 117 | Old Testament passages 1340A The interpretation of Ecclesiasticus 15:11–22 1340C The use of conditional assertions 1343E The value of ordinary human speech in theology 1344E Are divine precepts issued to show they cannot be observed? 1346D The meaning of Romans 3:30: 'Through the Law comes knowledge of sin' 1347A God as teacher: the spiritual progression of mankind from Law to grace 1352F Return to interpretation of Ecclesiasticus 15:11–22 1355E |
| Other Old Testament passages and the imperative and indicative moods 676 / 125 | Other Old Testament passages held to support free will 1361E |
| Imperative and indicative moods 676 / 125 | The parting of the ways 1362D Imperative and indicative moods 1363D The position of man in the presence of grace 1365E |
| Erasmus fails to distinguish between Law and gospel 680 / 132 | On the distinction between Law and gospel 1368E |
| God's revealed and God's hidden will 684 / 138 | The secret and revealed wills of God 1374B |

**Luther** *The Enslaved Will*

New Testament passages: man must not pry into the secret will of God 688 / 144

Precepts and rewards in the New Testament: the question of merit 690 / 147

Erasmus' arguments undermine his own case 696 / 156

Defence of arguments against free will 699–733 / 160–212

Erasmus' use of tropes in interpreting Scripture 700 / 161

The hardening of Pharaoh's heart 702 / 164

How God's omnipotence may be said to work evil 709 / 175

How God's foreknowledge imposes necessity 714 / 184

Two kinds of necessity: the case of Judas 720 / 195

Jacob and Esau 722 / 195

The potter and the clay 727 / 203

Erasmus' way of reasoning does not let God be God 730 / 206

Rebuttal of Erasmus' critique of Luther's *Assertio* 733–56 / 212–46

Genesis 6:3 and the biblical meaning of 'flesh' 733 / 212

Other Old Testament passages: the universal sinfulness and impotence of man under the Law 736 / 215

**Erasmus** *Hyperaspistes* **book 2**

New Testament passages 1378B

Necessity and the hidden will of God 1378B

Keeping the precepts, and the question of merit and reward in the Gospels 1381D

Does Erasmus subvert his own position? 1387A

Erasmus' response to Luther's defence of scriptural passages opposing free will 1391A–1450F

The use of figures of speech in Scripture 1391E

Is the hardening of Pharaoh's heart a figure of speech? 1395C

Does God's omnipotence produce evil? 1402C

Paul's explanation why God rejected the Jews and received the gentiles 1411F

Does divine foreknowledge impose necessity? 1414C

Judas and the necessity of immutability 1424C

The meaning of the story of Jacob and Esau: Genesis 24:23, Romans 9:11–13 1428D

The meaning of the potter and the clay 1442A

Does free will violate God's power and freedom? 1446F

Erasmus' response to Luther's defence of his *Assertio* 1451A–1486F

On spirit and flesh: Genesis 6:3 1451A

Other Old Testament passages: Genesis 6:5, Isaiah 40:2, Isaiah 40:6 1454D

**Luther** *The Enslaved Will*

The whole man – body, soul, and 'spirit' – is 'flesh' 740 / 222

How Erasmus persistently evades the issue 745 / 229

John 15:5 etc: free will is nothing *coram deo* 748 / 234
Divine grace and human cooperation 753 / 241
Erasmus' middle way leads nowhere 755 / 245

A display of the forces on Luther's side 756–85 / 246–92
St Paul: universal sinfulness nullifies free will 757 / 247
Free will may do the works of the Law but not fulfil the Law 763 / 257
'Congruous' and 'condign' merit 769 / 266
The righteousness of works and faith; and a summary of St Paul's testimony against free will 771–6 / 270–7
St John: free will is of 'the world,' 'the flesh'; grace is of Christ, by faith. The two are opposites 776 / 287
The two kingdoms of Christ and of Satan. The assurance of faith 782 / 287
The mercy and justice of God in the light of nature, grace, and glory 784 / 289

**Erasmus** *Hyperaspistes* **book 2**

Reason, spirit, and flesh: τὸ ἡγεμόνικον and the virtue of the pagans 1459F
Does divine providence remove free will? 1466C
Jeremiah 10:23 1466C
Proverbs 16:1, 21:1 1468A
John 15:5 and similar passages 1469F
How free will and grace work together 1475D
Luther's diverse charges against free will in his *Assertio* and *The Enslaved Will* 1480E
Luther and St Paul: a contrast 1481E

Erasmus' response to Luther's presentation of his case 1486F–1521B
Is mankind universally sinful and lacking free will? 1486F
Can free will fulfil the Law? 1494F

'Congrous' and 'condign' merit 1500C
The true relation of faith and works; and final assessments of Paul 1502C

The testimony of John the Evangelist: is free will of 'the world' and of 'the flesh'? 1505B

The kingdoms of Christ and of Satan 1512E

God's justice and mercy 1516D

**Luther** *The Enslaved Will*

Luther's conclusion: that the case
against free will is unanswerable let
Erasmus be willing to admit 786–7 /
293–5

**Erasmus** *Hyperaspistes* **book 2**

On Luther's epilogue 1518C

Erasmus' conclusions 1521B–1536F
    The terms of the controversy and
    their history 1521B
    Grace and the process of conver-
    sion 1523F
    Augustine's stance on the human
    will 1528D
    The virtues of the pagans and of
    the Old Testament Jews 1529D
    Augustine and congruous merit
    1531B
    Erasmus' peroration: admonitions
    to all parties 1534D

# WORKS FREQUENTLY CITED

## SHORT-TITLE FORMS
## FOR ERASMUS' WORKS

# WORKS FREQUENTLY CITED

This list provides bibliographical information for publications refered to in short-title form in introductions and notes. For Erasmus' writings see the short-title list following.

Allen      *Opus epistolarum Des. Erasmi Roterodami* ed P.S. Allen, H.M. Allen, and H.W. Garrod (Oxford 1906–58) 11 vols and index

ASD      *Opera omnia Desiderii Erasmi Roterodami* (Amsterdam 1969– )

*Assertio*      *Assertio omnium articulorum M. Lutheri per bullam Leonis X novissimam damnatorum* in WA 7 91–151

Bentley      Jerry H. Bentley *Humanists and Holy Writ* (Princeton 1983)

Berger      Adolf Berger *Encyclopedic Dictionary of Roman Law* Transactions of the American Philological Society n s 43 part 2 (Philadelphia 1953)

*Biblia 1498*      *[Biblia] cum glosa ordinaria et expositione lyre literali et morali: necnon additionibus ac replicis* ... (Basel: Froben 1498) 6 vols

Boyle *Language*      Marjorie O'Rourke Boyle *Erasmus on Language and Method in Theology* (Toronto 1978)

Boyle *Rhetoric*      Marjorie O'Rourke Boyle *Rhetoric and Reform: Erasmus' Civil Dispute with Luther* (Cambridge, Mass 1983)

CCCM      *Corpus christianorum, continuatio medievalis* (Turnhout 1971– )

CCSG      *Corpus christianorum, series Graeca* (Turnhout 1977– )

CCSL      *Corpus christianorum, series Latina* (Turnhout 1953– )

Chantraine *Erasme*      Georges Chantraine *Erasme et Luther: libre et serf arbitre: étude historique et théologique* (Paris and Namur 1981)

Chantraine *'Mystère'*      Georges Chantraine *'Mystère' et 'philosophie du Christ' selon Erasme* (Namur and Gembloux 1971)

CEBR      *Contemporaries of Erasmus: A Biographical Register of the Renaissance and Reformation* ed P.G. Bietenholz and T.B. Deutscher (Toronto 1985–7) 3 vols

Courtenay *Capacity*
William J. Courtenay *Capacity and Volition: A History of the Distinction of Absolute and Ordained Power* (Bergamo 1990)

Courtenay 'Covenant'
William J. Courtenay 'Covenant and Causality in Pierre d'Ailly' *Speculum* 46 (1971): 94–119

CR
*Corpus reformatorum* (Halle an der Salle 1834– ; repr Frankfurt am Main 1963)

CSEL
*Corpus scriptorum ecclesiasticorum Latinorum* (Vienna 1866– )

CWE
*Collected Works of Erasmus* (Toronto 1974– )

De libero arbitrio
Erasmus *De libero arbitrio* διατριβή *sive collatio* ed Johannes von Walter, Quellenschriften zur Geschichte des Protestantismus 8 (Leipzig 1910)

De servo arbitrio
Martin Luther *De servo arbitrio* in WA 18 600–787

DTC
*Dictionnaire de théologie catholique* (Paris 1900–50) 15 vols plus 2 index vols

Emser
*Schirm, vnd schutzbuchlein der Diatriba wider Martini Luthers knechtlichen willen durch Erasmum von Roterdham* (Leipzig: Melcher Lotter 1526)

Ferguson
Wallace Ferguson *Erasmi opuscula: A Supplement to the Opera omnia* (The Hague 1933)

Fisher 1523
St John Fisher *Assertionis Lutheranae confutatio* (Colone: P. Quentel 1523)

Fisher 1597
St John Fisher *Opera omnia* (Würzburg: Fleischmann 1597; repr Farnborough, England 1967)

GCS
*Die griechischen christlichen Schriftsteller der ersten drei Jahrhunderts* (Leipzig 1897)

Grane *Modus loquendi*
Leif Grane *Modus Loquendi Theologicus: Luthers Kampf um die Erneuerung der Theologie (1515–1518)* (Leiden 1975)

Hoffmann
Manfred Hoffmann *Rhetoric and Theology: The Hermeneutics of Erasmus* (Toronto 1994)

Holborn
*Desiderius Erasmus: Ausgewählte Werke* ed Hajo and Annemarie Holborn (Munich 1933; repr Munich 1964)

Hutten
*Ulrichs von Hutten Schriften* ed Eduard Böcking (Leipzig 1859–61; repr Aalen 1963) 5 vols

| | |
|---|---|
| *Hyperaspistes 1* | Erasmus *Hyperaspistes Diatribae adversus Servum arbitrium Martini Lutheri liber primus* LB X 1249–1336 |
| *Hyperaspistes 2* | Erasmus *Hyperaspistes Diatribae adversus Servum arbitrium Martini Lutheri liber secundus* LB X 1337–1536 |
| LB | Erasmus *Opera omnia* ed Jean Leclerc (Leiden 1703–6; repr Hildesheim 1961–2) 10 vols |
| Luther *Operationes* | Martin Luther *Operationes in psalmos 1519–1521* part 1, Psalms 1–10 ed Gerhard Hammer, Manfred Biersack, et al, vol 2 part 2 (Cologne and Vienna 1981) |
| LW | *Luther's Works* ed Jaroslav Pelikan, Helmut T. Lehmann, et al (Philadelphia 1958–   ) 55 vols |
| LW 33 | Luther *The Bondage of the Will* trans Philip S. Watson (Philadelphia 1972) |
| McConica 'Consent' | James K. McConica 'Erasmus and the Grammar of Consent' in *Scrinium* |
| McGrath | Alister E. McGrath *Iustitia Dei: A History of the Christian Doctrine of Justification* (Cambridge 1986) 2 vols |
| McSorley | Harry J. McSorley CSP *Luther: Right or Wrong? An Ecumenical-Theological Study of Luther's Major Work, The Bondage of the Will* (New York and Minneapolis 1969) |
| Oakley | Francis Oakley *Omnipotence, Convenant, and Order* (Ithaca and London 1984) |
| Oberman *Harvest* | Heiko A. Oberman *The Harvest of Medieval Theology* (Cambridge, Mass 1963; repr Grand Rapids 1967 and Durham, NC 1983) |
| Oberman *Luther* | Heiko A. Oberman *Luther: Man between God and the Devil* trans E. Wallisers Schwartzbart (New Haven 1982) from *Luther: Mensch zwischen Gott und Teufel* (Berlin 1992) |
| Origen | *Origen On First Principles* trans G.W. Butterworth (New York: Harper and Row 1966) |
| Otto | August Otto *Die Sprichwörter und sprichwörtlichen Redensarten der Römer* (Leipzig 1890; repr Hildesheim 1968) |
| Payne *Sacraments* | John B. Payne *Erasmus: His Theology of the Sacraments* (Richmond, Va 1970) |

PG        *Patrologiae cursus completus ... series Graeca* ed J.-P. Migne (Paris 1857–1912) 162 vols

PL        *Patrologiae cursus completus ... series Latina* ed J.-P. Migne (Paris 1844–1902) 221 vols

Rummel *Annotations*        Erika Rummel *Erasmus' Annotations on the New Testament: From Philologist to Theologian* (Toronto 1986)

Rummel *Catholic Critics*        Erika Rummel *Erasmus and his Catholic Critics* (Nieuwkoop 1989) 2 vols

*Scrinium*        *Scrinium Erasmianum* ed J. Coppens (Leiden 1969) 2 vols

Seitz *Leipziger Disputation*        Otto Seitz ed *Der authentische Text der Leipziger Disputation (1519)* (Berlin 1903)

Spitz *Reformation*        Lewis W. Spitz *The Protestant Reformation 1517–1559* (New York 1985)

Trinkaus *Image and Likeness*        Charles Trinkaus *In Our Image and Likeness: Humanity and Divinity in Italian Humanist Thought* (London and Chicago 1970; Notre Dame 1995)

WA        *D. Martin Luthers Werke, Kritische Gesamtausgabe* (Weimar 1883– )

WA *Briefwechsel*        *D. Martin Luthers Werke, Briefwechsel* (Weimar 1930– )

WA *Tischreden*        *D. Martin Luthers Werke, Tischreden* (Weimar 1912–21) 6 vols

Walter        Erasmus *De libero arbitrio* διατριβή *sive collatio* ed Johannes von Walter, Quellenschriften zur Geschichte des Protestantismus 8 (Leipzig 1910)

Watson        Philip S. Watson, translator of Luther's *De servo arbitrio* into English (see LW 33 above)

# SHORT-TITLE FORMS FOR ERASMUS' WORKS

Titles following colons are longer versions of the same, or are alternative titles. Items entirely enclosed in square brackets are of doubtful authorship. For abbreviations, see Works Frequently Cited.

Acta: Acta Academiae Lovaniensis contra Lutherum *Opuscula* / CWE 71

Adagia: Adagiorum chiliades 1508, etc (Adagiorum collectanea for the primitive form, when required) LB II / ASD II-1, 4, 5, 6 / CWE 30-6

Admonitio adversus mendacium: Admonitio adversus mendacium et obtrectationem LB X

Annotationes in Novum Testamentum LB VI / CWE 51-60

Antibarbari LB X / ASD I-1 / CWE 23

Apologia ad Caranzam: Apologia ad Sanctium Caranzam, or Apologia de tribus locis, or Responsio ad annotationem Stunicae ... a Sanctio Caranza defensam LB IX

Apologia ad Fabrum: Apologia ad Iacobum Fabrum Stapulensem LB IX / ASD IX-3 / CWE 83

Apologia adversus monachos: Apologia adversus monachos quosdam Hispanos LB IX

Apologia adversus Petrum Sutorem: Apologia adversus debacchationes Petri Sutoris LB IX

Apologia adversus rhapsodias Alberti Pii: Apologia ad viginti et quattuor libros A. Pii LB IX

Apologia contra Latomi dialogum: Apologia contra Iacobi Latomi dialogum de tribus linguis LB IX / CWE 71

Apologia de 'In principio erat sermo' LB IX

Apologia de laude matrimonii: Apologia pro declamatione de laude matrimonii LB IX / CWE 71

Apologia de loco 'Omnes quidem': Apologia de loco 'Omnes quidem resurgemus' LB IX

Apologiae contra Stunicam: Apologiae contra Lopidem Stunicam LB IX / ASD IX-2

Apologia qua respondet invectivis Lei: Apologia qua respondet duabus invectivis Eduardi Lei *Opuscula*

Apophthegmata LB IV

Appendix de scriptis Clithovei LB IX / CWE 83

Appendix respondens ad Sutorem LB IX

Argumenta: Argumenta in omnes epistolas apostolicas nova (with Paraphrases)

Axiomata pro causa Lutheri: Axiomata pro causa Martini Lutheri *Opuscula* / CWE 71

Carmina LB I, IV, V, VIII / ASD I-7 / CWE 85-6

Catalogus lucubrationum LB I

Ciceronianus: Dialogus Ciceronianus LB I / ASD I-2 / CWE 28

Colloquia LB I / ASD I-3 / CWE 39-40

Compendium vitae Allen I / CWE 4

Concionalis interpretatio (in Psalmi)

Conflictus: Conflictus Thaliae et Barbariei LB I

[Consilium: Consilium cuiusdam ex animo cupientis esse consultum] *Opuscula* /
 CWE 71
De bello Turcico: Consultatio de bello Turcico (in Psalmi)
De civilitate: De civilitate morum puerilium LB I / CWE 25
Declamatio de morte LB IV
Declamatiuncula LB IV
Declarationes ad censuras Lutetiae vulgatas: Declarationes ad censuras Lutetiae
 vulgatas sub nomine facultatis theologiae Parisiensis LB IX
De concordia: De sarcienda ecclesiae concordia, or De amabili ecclesiae concordia
 (in Psalmi)
De conscribendis epistolis LB I / ASD I-2 / CWE 25
De constructione: De constructione octo partium orationis, or Syntaxis LB I /
 ASD I-4
De contemptu mundi: Epistola de contemptu mundi LB V / ASD V-1 / CWE 66
De copia: De duplici copia verborum ac rerum LB I / ASD I-6 / CWE 24
De esu carnium: Epistola apologetica ad Christophorum episcopum Basiliensem de
 interdicto esu carnium LB IX / ASD IX-1
De immensa Dei misericordia: Concio de immensa Dei misericordia LB V / CWE 70
De libero arbitrio: De libero arbitrio diatribe LB IX / CWE 76
De praeparatione: De praeparatione ad mortem LB V / ASD V-1 / CWE 70
De pueris instituendis: De pueris statim ac liberaliter instituendis LB I / ASD I-2 /
 CWE 26
De puero Iesu: Concio de puero Iesu LB V / CWE 29
De puritate tabernaculi: De puritate tabernaculi sive ecclesiae christianae (in
 Psalmi)
De ratione studii LB I / ASD I-2 / CWE 24
De recta pronuntiatione: De recta latini graecique sermonis pronuntiatione LB I /
 ASD I-4 / CWE 26
De taedio Iesu: Disputatiuncula de taedio, pavore, tristicia Iesu LB V / CWE 70
Detectio praestigiarum: Detectio praestigiarum cuiusdam libelli germanice
 scripti LB X / ASD IX-1
De vidua christiana LB V / CWE 66
De virtute amplectenda: Oratio de virtute amplectenda LB V / CWE 29
[Dialogus bilinguium ac trilinguium: Chonradi Nastadiensis dialogus bilinguium
 ac trilinguium] *Opuscula* / CWE 7
Dilutio: Dilutio eorum quae Iodocus Clithoveus scripsit adversus declamationem
 suasoriam matrimonii CWE 83
Divinationes ad notata Bedae LB IX

Ecclesiastes: Ecclesiastes sive de ratione concionandi LB V / ASD V-4, 5
Elenchus in N. Bedae censuras LB IX
Enchiridion: Enchiridion militis christiani LB V / CWE 66
Encomium matrimonii (in De conscribendis epistolis)
Encomium medicinae: Declamatio in laudem artis medicae LB I / ASD I-4 / CWE 29
Epistola ad Dorpium LB IX / CWE 3 / CWE 71
Epistola ad fratres Inferioris Germaniae: Responsio ad fratres Germaniae Inferioris
 ad epistolam apologeticam incerto autore proditam LB X / ASD IX-1
Epistola ad graculos: Epistola ad quosdam imprudentissimos graculos LB X

Epistola apologetica de Termino LB X
Epistola consolatoria: Epistola consolatoria virginibus sacris, or Epistola consolatoria in adversis LB V / CWE 69
Epistola contra pseudevangelicos: Epistola contra quosdam qui se falso iactant evangelicos LB X / ASD IX-1
Euripidis Hecuba LB I / ASD I-1
Euripidis Iphigenia in Aulide LB I / ASD I-1
Exomologesis: Exomologesis sive modus confitendi LB V
Explanatio symboli: Explanatio symboli apostolorum sive catechismus LB V / ASD V-1 / CWE 70
Ex Plutarcho versa LB IV / ASD IV-2

Formula: Conficiendarum epistolarum formula (see De conscribendis epistolis)

Hyperaspistes LB X / CWE 76–7

In Nucem Ovidii commentarius LB I / ASD I-1 / CWE 29
In Prudentium: Commentarius in duos hymnos Prudentii LB V / CWE 29
Institutio christiani matrimonii LB V / CWE 69
Institutio principis christiani LB IV / ASD IV-1 / CWE 27

[Julius exclusus: Dialogus Julius exclusus e coelis] *Opuscula* / CWE 27

Lingua LB IV / ASD IV-1A / CWE 29
Liturgia Virginis Matris: Virginis Matris apud Lauretum cultae liturgia LB V / ASD V-1 / CWE 69
Luciani dialogi LB I / ASD I-1

Manifesta mendacia CWE 71
Methodus (see Ratio)
Modus orandi Deum LB V / ASD V-1 / CWE 70
Moria: Moriae encomium LB IV / ASD IV-3 / CWE 27

Novum Testamentum: Novum Testamentum 1519 and later (Novum instrumentum for the first edition, 1516, when required) LB VI

Obsecratio ad Virginem Mariam: Obsecratio sive oratio ad Virginem Mariam in rebus adversis LB V / CWE 69
Oratio de pace: Oratio de pace et discordia LB VIII
Oratio funebris: Oratio funebris in funere Bertae de Heyen LB VIII / CWE 29

Paean Virgini Matri: Paean Virgini Matri dicendus LB V / CWE 69
Panegyricus: Panegyricus ad Philippum Austriae ducem LB IV / ASD IV-1 / CWE 27
Parabolae: Parabolae sive similia LB I / ASD I-5 / CWE 23
Paraclesis LB V, VI
Paraphrasis in Elegantias Vallae: Paraphrasis in Elegantias Laurentii Vallae LB I / ASD I-4
Paraphrasis in Matthaeum, etc (in Paraphrasis in Novum Testamentum)

Paraphrasis in Novum Testamentum LB VII / CWE 42–50
Peregrinatio apostolorum: Peregrinatio apostolorum Petri et Pauli LB VI, VII
Precatio ad Virginis filium Iesum LB V / CWE 69
Precatio dominica LB V / CWE 69
Precationes: Precationes aliquot novae LB V / CWE 69
Precatio pro pace ecclesiae: Precatio ad Dominum Iesum pro pace ecclesiae LB IV,
   V / CWE 69
Psalmi: Psalmi, or Enarrationes sive commentarii in psalmos LB V / ASD V-2, 3 /
   CWE 63–5
Purgatio adversus epistolam Lutheri: Purgatio adversus epistolam non sobriam
   Lutheri LB X / ASD IX-1

Querela pacis LB IV / ASD IV-2 / CWE 27

Ratio: Ratio seu Methodus compendio perveniendi ad veram theologiam (Methodus
   for the shorter version originally published in the Novum instrumentum of
   1516) LB V, VI
Responsio ad annotationes Lei: Liber quo respondet annotationibus Lei LB IX
Responsio ad collationes: Responsio ad collationes cuiusdam iuvenis gerontodidas-
   cali LB IX
Responsio ad disputationem de divortio: Responsio ad disputationem cuiusdam
   Phimostomi de divortio LB IX / CWE 83
Responsio ad epistolam Pii: Responsio ad epistolam paraeneticam Alberti Pii, or
   Responsio ad exhortationem Pii LB IX
Responsio ad notulas Bedaicas LB X
Responsio ad Petri Cursii defensionem: Epistola de apologia Cursii LB X / Allen
   Ep 3032
Responsio adversus febricitantis libellum: Apologia monasticae religionis LB X

Spongia: Spongia adversus aspergines Hutteni LB X / ASD IX-1
Supputatio: Supputatio calumniarum Natalis Bedae LB IX

Tyrannicida: Tyrannicida, declamatio Lucianicae respondens LB I / ASD I-1 /
   CWE 29

Virginis et martyris comparatio LB V / CWE 69
Vita Hieronymi: Vita divi Hieronymi Stridonensis *Opuscula* / CWE 61

This book

was designed by

VAL COOKE

based on the series design by

ALLAN FLEMING

and was printed by

University

of Toronto

Press